Biology
Miller & Levine

Multilingual Glossary

PEARSON

Boston, Massachusetts   Chandler, Arizona   Glenview, Illinois   Upper Saddle River, New Jersey

This Multilingual Glossary contains all highlighted terms from *Miller & Levine Biology*. In addition to English-language definitions, the glossary provides translations of the same terms in these ten languages:

- Arabic
- Brazilian Portuguese
- Chinese (Simplified)
- Chinese (Traditional)
- Haitian Creole
- Hmong
- Korean
- Russian
- Spanish
- Vietnamese

ISBN-13: 978-0-13-368319-0
ISBN-10:   0-13-368519-5

1 2 3 4 5 6 7 8 9 10   12 11 10 09 08

Strategies for Relating to English Language Learners

There are a number of basic strategies teachers can implement to meet the needs of their English Language Learners. These common-sense strategies lay the foundation for a positive learning relationship between you and your ELL students.

Simplify Your Teacher Talk

One of the most important strategies is to modify and simplify your "teacher talk," or the way you speak to your students during instruction. Often, the vocabulary and sentence structure that teachers use are beyond the comprehension of their ELL students. To avoid this problem, speak directly and succinctly, using simple words and sentences with students who are at a beginning-language level. Since ELL students are learning a new language as well as new academic concepts, avoid using slang or idiomatic expressions, which can add to their confusion. Using body language to emphasize important words or rephrasing a sentence or definition will also aid the English Language Learner in understanding new information.

Learn About Your Students' Heritage

You do not need to be able to speak a second language to make your ELL students feel you are interested in them. Learn as much as you can about the cultures and languages represented by the students in your classroom. Not only will you increase your own knowledge, but you will enhance the self-esteem of your students as they become aware of your interest in their heritage. You can also use your knowledge to broaden the horizons of the English-speaking students in your class.

Limited English Proficiency Does Not Mean Limited Thinking Skills

English Language Learners possess higher-order thinking skills. Avoid the trap of thinking that because these students are not proficient in English, they do not have those skills. Encourage hypothesizing, analyzing, inferring, asking questions, and making predictions, as well as other thinking skills. Students need opportunities to observe and use these skills in the classroom.

Give ELL Students Time to Respond

Increase response "wait time" for English Language Learners. These students must process information in two languages and will respond more quickly in a relaxed, risk-free environment. Then, repeat student responses in a natural manner in standard English. Repeating a response correctly will validate each student's response.

Give ELL Students a Sneak Preview

Provide an outline or list of instructions and review these with your ELL students. Give them an opportunity to look ahead in the text or view a model of the assignment. By doing so, you also inform students of your expectations.

Watch for Nonverbal Signals

English Language Learners use a number of nonverbal signals to show lack of understanding. These may include lowering the head, avoiding eye contact, covering the assignment paper, or simply a general look of confusion. Watch for these signs and be prepared to provide individual attention or assign the student to a partner in the classroom for help.

Provide a Risk-Free Learning Environment

Many English Language Learners come from cultures in which they were taught not to question the teacher, critique the information presented, or in general request clarification, simplification, or repetition. Some ELL students do not ask for help because their lack of English language proficiency makes them feel uncomfortable. Often, these students will nod their head in agreement, smile, and appear to understand exactly what you are saying—until their test results prove otherwise. Be prepared to teach students that it is acceptable to ask questions and critique information presented. At the same time, try to provide a risk-free environment that will foster questioning, no matter what the level of your students' language proficiency. Help your students view you as being sensitive to their needs and as someone who will provide guidance in understanding content material.

Allow Students to Use Their Native Language

Let students know that it is acceptable to use their native language in the classroom. One way to allow students to use their native language is student-to-student collaboration. Because many ELL students feel that their native language is not valued, you may want to use your knowledge of the students' language in instruction. This not only helps those students with very limited English proficiency, but it also shows acceptance and appreciation of the students' native language. Encourage students to bring to class an English/native-language dictionary.

For more information on best practices and teaching strategies for English Language Learners, refer to the *Teacher's ELL Handbook* that accompanies *Miller & Levine Biology*. Also look for content-specific strategies in *Miller & Levine Biology Teacher's Edition*.

Miller & Levine

Biology Glossary

A

abiotic factor physical, or nonliving, factor that shapes an ecosystem

abscisic acid plant hormone that inhibits cell division and, therefore, growth

acetylcholine neurotransmitter that produces an impulse in a muscle cell

acid compound that forms hydrogen ions (H^+) in solution; a solution with a pH of less than 7

acid rain rain containing nitric and sulfuric acids

actin thin filament of protein found in muscles

action potential reversal of charges across the cell membrane of a neuron; also called a nerve impulse

activation energy energy that is needed to get a reaction started

active immunity immunity that develops as a result of natural or deliberate exposure to an antigen

adaptation heritable characteristic that increases an organisms ability to survive and reproduce in an environment

adaptive radiation process by which a single species or a small group of species evolves into several different forms that live in different ways

adenosine triphosphate (ATP) compound used by cells to store and release energy

adhesion force of attraction between different kinds of molecules

aerobic process that requires oxygen

age structure number of males and females of each age in a population

aggression threatening behavior that one animal uses to exert dominance over another animal

algal bloom increase in the amount of algae and other producers that results from a large input of a limiting nutrient

allele one of a number of different forms of a gene

allergy overreaction of the immune system to an antigen

alternation of generations life cycle that has two alternating phases—a haploid (N) phase and diploid (2N) phase

alveolus (pl. alveoli): tiny air sacs at the end of a bronchiole in the lungs that provides surface area for gas exchange to occur

amino acid compound with an amino group on one end and a carboxyl group on the other end

amniotic egg egg composed of shell and membranes that creates a protected environment in which the embryo can develop out of water

amylase enzyme in saliva that breaks the chemical bonds in starches

anaerobic process that does not require oxygen

anaphase phase of mitosis in which the chromosomes separate and move to opposite ends of the cell

angiosperm group of seed plants that bear their seeds within a layer of tissue that protects the seed; also called flowering plant

anther flower structure in which pollen grains are produced

antheridium (pl. antheridia) male reproductive structure in some plants that produces sperm

anthropoid primate group made up of monkeys, apes, and humans

antibiotic group of drugs used to block the growth and reproduction of bacterial pathogens

antibody protein that either attacks antigens directly or produces antigen-binding proteins

anticodon group of three bases on a tRNA molecule that are complementary to the three bases of a codon of mRNA

antigen any substance that triggers an immune response

aphotic zone dark layer of the oceans below the photic zone where sunlight does not penetrate

apical dominance phenomenon in which the closer a bud is to the stem's tip, the more its growth is inhibited

apical meristem group of unspecialized cells that divide to produce increased length of stems and roots

apoptosis process of programmed cell death

appendage structure, such as a leg or antenna that extends from the body wall

appendicular skeleton the bones of the arms and legs along with the bones of the pelvis and shoulder area

aquaculture raising of aquatic organisms for human consumption

aquaporin water channel protein in a cell

Archaea domain consisting of unicellular prokaryotes that have cell walls that do not contain peptidoglycan; corresponds to the kingdom Archeabacteria

archegonium (pl. archegonia) structure in plants that produces egg cells

artery large blood vessel that carries blood away from the heart to the tissues of the body

artificial selection selective breeding of plants and animals to promote the occurrence of desirable traits in offspring

asexual reproduction process of reproduction involving a single parent that results in offspring that are genetically identical to the parent

asthma chronic respiratory disease in which air passages narrow, causing wheezing, coughing, and difficulty breathing

atherosclerosis condition in which fatty deposits called plaque build up inside artery walls and eventually cause the arteries to stiffen

atom the basic unit of matter

ATP synthase cluster of proteins that span the cell membrane and allow hydrogen ions (H^+) to pass through it

atrium (pl. atria) upper chamber of the heart that receives blood from the rest of the body

autonomic nervous system part of the peripheral nervous system that regulates activities that are involuntary, or not under conscious control; made up of the sympathetic and parasympathetic subdivisions

autosome chromosome that is not a sex chromosome; also called autosomal chromosome

autotroph organism that is able to capture energy from sunlight or chemicals and use it to produce its own food from inorganic compounds; also called a producer

auxin regulatory substance produced in the tip of a growing plant that stimulates cell elongation and the growth of new roots

axial skeleton skeleton that supports the central axis of the body; consists of the skull, vertebral column, and the rib cage

axon long fiber that carries impulses away from the cell body of a neuron

B

bacillus (pl. bacilli) rod-shaped prokaryote

background extinction extinction caused by slow and steady process of natural selection

Bacteria domain of unicellular prokaryotes that have cell walls containing peptidoglycan; corresponds to the kingdom eubacteria

bacteriophage kind of virus that infects bacteria

bark tissues that are found outside the vascular cambium, including the phloem, cork cambium, and cork

base compound that produces hydroxide ions (OH^-) in solution; solution with a pH of more than 7

base pairing principle that bonds in DNA can form only between adenine and thymine and between guanine and cytosine

behavior manner in which an organism reacts to changes in its internal condition or external environment

behavioral isolation form of reproductive isolation in which two populations develop differences in courtship rituals or other behaviors that prevent them from breeding

benthos organisms that live attached to or near the bottom of lakes, streams, or oceans

bias particular preference or point of view that is personal, rather than scientific

bilateral symmetry body plan in which a single imaginary line can divide the body into left and right sides that are mirror images of each other

binary fission type of asexual reproduction in which an organism replicates its DNA and divides in half, producing two identical daughter cells

binocular vision ability to merge visual images from both eyes, providing depth perception and a three-dimensional view of the world

binomial nomenclature classification system in which each species is assigned a two-part scientific name

biodiversity total of the variety of organisms in the biosphere; also called biological diversity

biogeochemical cycle process in which elements, chemical compounds, and other forms of matter are passed from one organism to another and from one part of the biosphere to another

biogeography study of past and present distribution of organisms

bioinformatics application of mathematics and computer science to store, retrieve, and analyze biological data

biological magnification increasing concentration of a harmful substance in organisms at higher trophic levels in a food chain or food web

biology scientific study of life

biomass total amount of living tissue within a given trophic level

biome a group of ecosystems that share similar climates and typical organisms

biosphere part of Earth in which life exists including land, water, and air or atmosphere

biotechnology process of manipulating organisms, cells, or molecules, to produce specific products

biotic factor any living part of the environment with which an organism might interact

bipedal term used to refer to two-foot locomotion

blade thin, flattened part of a plant leaf

blastocyst stage of early development in mammals that consists of a hollow ball of cells

blastula hollow ball of cells that develops when a zygote undergoes a series of cell divisions

bone marrow soft tissue found in bone cavities

bottleneck effect a change in allele frequency following a dramatic reduction in the size of a population

Bowman's capsule cuplike structure that encases the glomerulus; collects filtrate from the blood

brain stem structure that connects the brain and spinal cord; includes the medulla oblongata and the pons

bronchus (pl. bronchi) one of two large tubes in the chest cavity that leads from the trachea to the lungs

bryophyte group of plants that have specialized reproductive organs but lack vascular tissue; includes mosses and their relatives

bud plant structure containing apical meristem tissue that can produce new stems and leaves

buffer compound that prevents sharp, sudden changes in pH

C

calcitonin hormone produced by the thyroid that reduces blood calcium levels

Calorie measure of heat energy in food; equivalent to 1000 calories

calorie amount of energy needed to raise the temperature of 1 gram of water by 1 degree Celsius

Calvin cycle light-independent reactions of photosynthesis in which energy from ATP and NADPH is used to build high-energy compounds such as sugar

cancer disorder in which some of the body's cells lose the ability to control growth

canopy dense covering formed by the leafy tops of tall rain forest trees

capillary smallest blood vessel; brings nutrients and oxygen to the tissues and absorbs carbon dioxide and waste products

capillary action tendency of water to rise in a thin tube

capsid protein coat surrounding a virus

carbohydrate compound made up of carbon, hydrogen, and oxygen atoms; type of nutrient that is the major source of energy for the body

carnivore organism that obtains energy by eating animals

carpel innermost part of a flower that produces and shelters the female gametophytes

carrying capacity largest number of individuals of a particular species that a particular environment can support

cartilage type of connective tissue that supports the body and is softer and more flexible than bone

Casparian strip waterproof strip that surrounds plant endodermal cells and is involved in the one-way passage of materials into the vascular cylinder in plant roots

catalyst substance that speeds up the rate of a chemical reaction

cell basic unit of all forms of life

cell body largest part of a typical neuron; contains the nucleus and much of the cytoplasm

cell cycle series of events in which a cell grows, prepares for division, and divides to form two daughter cells

cell division process by which a cell divides into two new daughter cells

cell membrane thin, flexible barrier that surrounds all cells; regulates what enters and leaves the cell

cell theory fundamental concept of biology that states that all living things are composed of cells; that cells are the basic units of structure and function in living things; and that new cells are produced from existing cells

cell wall strong, supporting layer around the cell membrane in some cells

cell-mediated immunity immune response that defends the body against viruses, fungi, and abnormal cancer cells inside living cells

cellular respiration process that releases energy by breaking down glucose and other food molecules in the presence of oxygen

central nervous system includes the brain and spinal cord; processes information and creates a response that it delivers to the body

centriole structure in an animal cell that helps to organize cell division

centromere region of a chromosome where the two sister chromatids attach

cephalization concentration of sense organs and nerve cells at the anterior end of an animal

cerebellum part of the brain that coordinates movement and controls balance

cerebral cortex outer layer of the cerebrum of a mammal's brain; center of thinking and other complex behaviors

cerebrum part of the brain responsible for voluntary activities of the body; "thinking" region of the brain

chemical digestion process by which enzymes break down food into small molecules that the body can use

chemical reaction process that changes, or transforms, one set of chemicals into another set of chemicals

chemosynthesis process in which chemical energy is used to produce carbohydrates

chitin complex carbohydrate that makes up the cell walls of fungi; also found in the external skeletons of arthropods

chlorophyll principal pigment of plants and other photosynthetic organisms

chloroplast organelle found in cells of plants and some other organisms that captures the energy from sunlight and converts it into chemical energy

chordate animal that has, for at least one stage of its life, a dorsal, hollow nerve cord, a notochord, a tail that extends beyond the anus, and pharyngeal pouches

chromatid one of two identical "sister" parts of a duplicated chromosome

chromatin substance found in eukaryotic chromosomes that consists of DNA tightly coiled around histones

chromosome threadlike structure within the nucleus that contains genetic information that is passed from one generation to the next

chyme mixture of enzymes and partially-digested food

cilium (pl. cilia) short hairlike projection that produces movement

circadian rhythm behavioral cycles that occur daily

clade evolutionary branch of a cladogram that includes a single ancestor and all its descendants

cladogram diagram depicting patterns of shared characteristics among species

class in classification, a group of closely related orders

classical conditioning type of learning that occurs when an animal makes a mental connection between a stimulus and some kind of reward or punishment

climate average year-to-year conditions of temperature and precipitation in an area over a long period of time

clone member of a population of genetically identical cells produced from a single cell

closed circulatory system type of circulatory system in which blood circulates entirely within blood vessels that extend throughout the body

coccus (pl. cocci) spherical prokaryote

cochlea fluid-filled part of inner ear; contains nerve cells that detect sound

codominance situation in which the phenotypes produced by both alleles are completely expressed

codon group of three nucleotide bases in mRNA that specify a particular amino acid to be incorporated into a protein

coelom body cavity lined with mesoderm

coevolution process by which two species evolve in response to changes in each other over time

cohesion attraction between molecules of the same substance

collenchyma in plants, type of ground tissue that has strong, flexible cell walls; helps support larger plants

commensalism symbiotic relationship in which one organism benefits and the other is neither helped nor harmed

communication passing of information from one organism to another

community assemblage of different populations that live together in a defined area

companion cell in plants, phloem cell that surrounds sieve tube elements

competitive exclusion principle principle that states that no two species can occupy the same niche in the same habitat at the same time

compound substance formed by the chemical combination of two or more elements in definite proportions

cone in the eye, photoreceptor that responds to light of different colors, producing color vision

coniferous term used to refer to trees that produce seed-bearing cones and have thin leaves shaped like needles

conjugation process in which paramecia and some prokaryotes exchange genetic information

connective tissue type of tissue that provides support for the body and connects its parts

consumer organism that relies on other organisms for its energy and food supply; also called a heterotroph

control group group in an experiment that is exposed to the same conditions as the experimental group except for one independent variable

controlled experiment experiment in which only one variable is changed

convergent evolution process by which unrelated organisms independently evolve similarities when adapting to similar environments

cork cambium meristematic tissue that produces the outer covering of stems during secondary growth of a plant

cornea tough transparent layer of the eye through which light enters

corpus luteum name given to a follicle after ovulation because of its yellow color

cortex in plants, region of ground tissue just inside the root through which water and minerals move

corticosteroid steroid hormone produced by the adrenal cortex

cotyledon first leaf or first pair of leaves produced by the embryo of a seed plant

courtship type of behavior in which an animal sends out stimuli in order to attract a member of the opposite sex

covalent bond type of bond between atoms in which the electrons are shared

crossing-over process in which homologous chromosomes exchange portions of their chromatids during meiosis

cyclin one of a family of proteins that regulates the cell cycle in eukaryotic cells

cytokinesis division of the cytoplasm to form two separate daughter cells

cytokinin plant hormone produced in growing roots and in developing fruits and seeds

cytoplasm fluid portion of the cell outside the nucleus

cytoskeleton network of protein filaments in a eukaryotic cell that gives the cell its shape and internal organization and is involved in movement

D

data evidence; information gathered from observations

deciduous term used to refer to a type of tree that sheds its leaves during a particular season each year

decomposer organism that breaks down and obtains energy from dead organic matter

deforestation destruction of forests

demographic transition change in a population from high birth and death rates to low birth and death rates

demography scientific study of human populations

dendrite extension of the cell body of a neuron that carries impulses from the environment or from other neurons toward the cell body

denitrification process by which soil bacteria convert nitrates into nitrogen gas

density-dependent limiting factor limiting factor that depends on population density

density-independent limiting factor limiting factor that affects all populations in similar ways, regardless of the population density

deoxyribonucleic acid (DNA) genetic material that organisms inherit from their parents

dependent variable variable that is observed and that changes in response to the independent variable; also called the responding variable

derived character trait that appears in recent parts of a lineage, but not in its older members

dermis layer of skin found beneath the epidermis

desertification lower land productivity caused by overfarming, overgrazing, seasonal drought, and climate change

detritivore organism that feeds on plant and animal remains and other dead matter

deuterostome group of animals in which the blastopore becomes an anus, and the mouth is formed from the second opening that develops

diaphragm large flat muscle at the bottom of the chest cavity that helps with breathing

dicot angiosperm with two seed leaves in its ovary

differentiation process in which cells become specialized in structure and function

diffusion process by which particles tend to move from an area where they are more concentrated to an area where they are less concentrated

digestive tract tube that begins at the mouth and ends at the anus

diploid term used to refer to a cell that contains two sets of homologous chromosomes

directional selection form of natural selection in which individuals at one end of a distribution curve have higher fitness than individuals in the middle or at the other end of the curve

disruptive selection natural selection in which individuals at the upper and lower ends of the curve have higher fitness than individuals near the middle of the curve

DNA fingerprinting tool used by biologists that analyzes an individual's unique collection of DNA restriction fragments; used to determine whether two samples of genetic material are from the same person

DNA microarray glass slide or silicon chip that carries thousands of different kinds of single-stranded DNA fragments arranged in a grid. A DNA microarray is used to detect and measure the expression of thousands of genes at one time

DNA polymerase principle enzyme involved in DNA replication

domain larger, more inclusive taxonomic category than a kingdom

dopamine neurotransmitter that is associated with the brain's pleasure and reward centers

dormancy period of time during which a plant embryo is alive but not growing

double fertilization process of fertilization in angiosperms in which the first event produces the zygote, and the second, the endosperm within the seed

E

ecological footprint total amount of functioning ecosystem needed both to provide the resources a human population uses and to absorb the wastes that population generates

ecological hot spot small geographic area where significant numbers of habitats and species are in immediate danger of extinction

ecological pyramid illustration of the relative amounts of energy or matter contained within each trophic level in a given food chain or food web

ecological succession series of gradual changes that occur in a community following a disturbance

ecology scientific study of interactions among organisms and between organisms and their environment

ecosystem all the organisms that live in a place, together with their nonliving environment

ecosystem diversity variety of habitats, communities, and ecological processes in the biosphere

ectoderm outermost germ layer; produces sense organs, nerves, and outer layer of skin

ectotherm animal whose body temperature is determined by the temperature of its environment

electron negatively charged particle; located in the space surrounding the nucleus

electron transport chain series of electron carrier proteins that shuttle high-energy electrons during ATP-generating reactions

element pure substance that consists entirely of one type of atom

embryo developing stage of a multicellular organism

embryo sac female gametophyte within the ovule of a flowering plant

emerging disease disease that appears in the population for the first time, or an old disease that suddenly becomes harder to control

emigration movement of individuals out of an area

endocrine gland gland that releases its secretions (hormones) directly into the blood, which transports the secretions to other areas of the body

endoderm innermost germ layer; develops into the linings of the digestive tract and much of the respiratory system

endodermis in plants, layer of ground tissue that completely encloses the vascular cylinder

endoplasmic reticulum internal membrane system found in eukaryotic cells; place where lipid components of the cell membrane are assembled

endoskeleton internal skeleton; structural support system within the body of an animal

endosperm food-rich tissue that nourishes a seedling as it grows

endospore structure produced by prokaryotes in unfavorable conditions; a thick internal wall that encloses the DNA and a portion of the cytoplasm

endosymbiotic theory theory that proposes that eukaryotic cells formed from a symbiotic relationship among several different prokaryotic cells

endotherm animal whose body temperature is regulated, at least in part, using heat generated within its body

enzyme protein catalyst that speeds up the rate of specific biological reactions

epidermis in plants, single layer of cells that makes up dermal tissue; in humans, the outer layer of the skin

epididymis organ in the male reproductive system in which sperm mature and are stored

epinephrine hormone released by the adrenal glands that increases heart rate and blood pressure and prepares the body for intense physical activity; also called adrenaline

epithelial tissue type of tissue that lines the interior and exterior body surfaces

era major division of geologic time; usually divided into two or more periods

esophagus tube connecting the mouth to the stomach

estuary kind of wetland formed where a river meets the ocean

ethylene plant hormone that stimulates fruits to ripen

Eukarya domain consisting of all organisms that have a nucleus; includes protists, plants, fungi, and animals.

eukaryote organism whose cells contain a nucleus

evolution change over time; the process by which modern organisms have descended from ancient organisms

excretion process by which metabolic wastes are eliminated from the body

exocrine gland gland that releases its secretions, through tubelike structures called ducts, directly into an organ or out of the body

exon expressed sequence of DNA; codes for a protein

exoskeleton external skeleton; tough external covering that protects and supports the body of many invertebrates

exponential growth growth pattern in which the individuals in a population reproduce at a constant rate

extinct term used to refer to a species that has died out and has no living members

extracellular digestion type of digestion in which food is broken down outside the cells in a digestive system and then absorbed

F

facilitated diffusion process of diffusion in which molecules pass across the membrane through cell membrane channels

family in classification, group of similar genera

fat lipid; made up of fatty acids and glycerol; type of nutrient that protects body organs, insulates the body, and stores energy

feedback inhibition process in which a stimulus produces a response that opposes the original stimulus; also called negative feedback

fermentation process by which cells release energy in the absence of oxygen

fertilization process in sexual reproduction in which male and female reproductive cells join to form a new cell

fetus a human embryo after eight weeks of development

fever increased body temperature that occurs in response to infection

filtration process of passing a liquid or gas through a filter to remove wastes

fitness how well an organism can survive and reproduce in its environment

flagellum (pl. flagella) structure used by protists for movement; produces movement in a wavelike motion

food chain series of steps in an ecosystem in which organisms transfer energy by eating and being eaten

food vacuole small cavity in the cytoplasm of a protist that temporarily stores food

food web network of complex interactions formed by the feeding relationships among the various organisms in an ecosystem

forensics scientific study of crime scene evidence

fossil preserved remains of ancient organisms

founder effect change in allele frequencies as a result of the migration of a small subgroup of a population

frameshift mutation mutation that shifts the "reading frame" of the genetic message by inserting or deleting a nucleotide

fruit structure in angiosperms that contains one or more matured ovaries

fruiting body reproductive structure of a fungus that grows from the mycelium

G

gamete sex cell

gametophyte gamete-producing plant; multicellular haploid phase of a plant life cycle

ganglion (pl. ganglia) group of interneurons

gastrovascular cavity digestive chamber with a single opening

gastrulation process of cell migration that results in the formation of the three cell layers—the ectoderm, the mesoderm, and the endoderm

gel electrophoresis procedure used to separate and analyze DNA fragments by placing a mixture of DNA fragments at one end of a porous gel and applying an electrical voltage to the gel

gene sequence of DNA that codes for a protein and thus determines a trait; factor that is passed from parent to offspring

gene expression process by which a gene produces its product and the product carries out its function

gene pool all the genes, including all the different alleles for each gene, that are present in a population at any one time

gene therapy process of changing a gene to treat a medical disease or disorder. An absent or faulty gene is replaced by a normal working gene.

genetic code collection of codons of mRNA, each of which directs the incorporation of a particular amino acid into a protein during protein synthesis

genetic diversity sum total of all the different forms of genetic information carried by a particular species, or by all organisms on Earth

genetic drift random change in allele frequency caused by a series of chance occurrences that cause an allele to become more or less common in a population

genetic equilibrium situation in which allele frequencies in a population remain the same

genetic marker alleles that produce detectable phenotypic differences useful in genetic analysis

genetics scientific study of heredity

genome entire set of genetic information that an organism carries in its DNA

genomics study of whole genomes, including genes and their functions

genotype genetic makeup of an organism

genus group of closely related species; the first part of the scientific name in binomial nomenclature

geographic isolation form of reproductive isolation in which two populations are separated by geographic barriers such as rivers, mountains, or bodies of water, leading to the formation of two separate subspecies

geologic time scale timeline used to represent Earth's history

germ theory of disease idea that infectious diseases are caused by microorganisms

germination resumption of growth of the plant embryo following dormancy

giberellin plant hormone that stimulates growth and may cause dramatic increases in size

gill feathery structure specialized for the exchange of gases with water

global warming increase in the average temperatures on Earth

glomerulus small network of capillaries encased in the upper end of the nephron; where filtration of the blood takes place

glycolysis first set of reactions in cellular respiration in which a molecule of glucose is broken into two molecules of pyruvic acid

Golgi apparatus organelle in cells that modifies, sorts, and packages proteins and other materials from the endoplasmic reticulum for storage in the cell or release outside the cell

gradualism the evolution of a species by gradual accumulation of small genetic changes over long periods of time

grafting method of propagation used to reproduce seedless plants and varieties of woody plants that cannot be propagated from cuttings

gravitropism response of a plant to the force of gravity

green revolution development of highly productive crop strains and use of modern agriculture techniques to increase yields of food crops

greenhouse effect process in which certain gases (carbon dioxide, methane, and water vapor) trap sunlight energy in Earth's atmosphere as heat

growth factor one of a group of external regulatory proteins that stimulate the growth and division of cells

guard cell specialized cell in the epidermis of plants that controls the opening and closing of stomata

gullet indentation in one side of a ciliate that allows food to enter the cell

gymnosperm group of seed plants that bear their seeds directly on the scales of cones

H

habitat area where an organism lives, including the biotic and abiotic factors that affect it

habitat fragmentation splitting of ecosystems into pieces

habituation type of learning in which an animal decreases or stops its response to a repetitive stimulus that neither rewards nor harms the animal

hair follicle tubelike pockets of epidermal cells that extend into the dermis; cells at the base of hair follicles produce hair

half life length of time required for half of the radioactive atoms in a sample to decay

haploid term used to refer to a cell that contains only a single set of genes

Hardy-Weinberg principle principle that states that allele frequencies in a population remain constant unless one or more factors cause those frequencies to change

Haversian canal one of a network of tubes running through compact bone that contains blood vessels and nerves

heart hollow muscular organ that pumps blood throughout the body

heartwood in a woody stem, the older xylem near the center of the stem that no longer conducts water

hemoglobin iron-containing protein in red blood cells that binds oxygen and transports it to the body

herbaceous plant type of plant that has smooth and nonwoody stems; includes dandelions, zinnias, petunias, and sunflowers

herbivore organism that obtains energy by eating only plants

herbivory interaction in which one animal (the herbivore) feeds on producers (such as plants)

heterotroph organism that obtains food by consuming other living things; also called a consumer

heterozygous having two different alleles for a particular gene

histamine chemical released by mast cells that increases the flow of blood and fluids to the infected area during an inflammatory response

homeobox gene The homeobox is a DNA sequence of approximately 130 base pairs, found in many homeotic genes that regulate development. Genes containing this sequence are known as homeobox genes, and they code for transcription factors, proteins that bind to DNA, and they also regulate the expression of other genes.

homeostasis relatively constant internal physical and chemical conditions that organisms maintain

homeotic gene a class of regulatory genes that determine the identity of body parts and regions in an animal embryo. Mutations in these genes can transform one body part into another

hominine hominoid lineage that led to humans

hominoid group of anthropoids that includes gibbons, orangutans, gorillas, chimpanzees, and humans

homologous term used to refer to chromosomes in which one set comes from the male parent and one set comes from the female parent

homologous structures structures that are similar in different species of common ancestry

homozygous having two identical alleles for a particular gene

hormone chemical produced in one part of an organism that affects another part of the same organism

Hox gene a group of homeotic genes clustered together that determine the head to tail identity of body parts in animals. All hox genes contain the homeobox DNA sequence.

humoral immunity immunity against antigens in body fluids, such as blood and lymph

humus material formed from decaying leaves and other organic matter

hybrid offspring of crosses between parents with different traits

hybridization breeding technique that involves crossing dissimilar individuals to bring together the best traits of both organisms

hydrogen bond weak attraction between a hydrogen atom and another atom

hydrostatic skeleton skeleton made of fluid-filled body segments that work with muscles to allow the animal to move

hypertonic when comparing two solutions, the solution with the greater concentration of solutes

hypha (pl. hyphae) one of many long, slender filaments that makes up the body of a fungus

hypothalamus structure of the brain that acts as a control center for recognition and analysis of hunger, thirst, fatigue, anger, and body temperature

hypothesis possible explanation for a set of observations or possible answer to a scientific question

hypotonic when comparing two solutions, the solution with the lesser concentration of solutes

I

immigration movement of individuals into an area occupied by an existing population

immune response the body's specific recognition, response, and memory to a pathogen attack

implantation process in which the blastocyst attaches to the wall of the uterus

imprinting type of behavior based on early experience; once imprinting has occurred, the behavior cannot be changed

inbreeding continued breeding of individuals with similar characteristics to maintain the derived characteristics of a kind of organism

incomplete dominance situation in which one allele is not completely dominant over another allele

independent assortment one of Mendel's principles that states that genes for different traits can segregate independently during the formation of gametes

independent variable factor in a controlled experiment that is deliberately changed; also called manipulated variable

index fossil distinctive fossil that is used to compare the relative ages of fossils

infectious disease disease caused by microorganism that disrupts normal body functions

inference a logical interpretation based on prior knowledge and experience

inflammatory response nonspecific defense reaction to tissue damage caused by injury or infection

innate behavior type of behavior in which the behavior appears in fully functional form the first time it is performed even though the animal has had no previous experience with the stimuli to which it responds; also called instinct

insight learning type of behavior in which an animal applies something it has already learned to a new situation, without a period of trial and error; also called reasoning

interferon one of a group of proteins that help cells resist viral infection

interneuron type of neuron that processes information and may relay information to motor neurons

interphase period of the cell cycle between cell divisions

intracellular digestion type of digestion in which food is digested inside specialized cells that pass nutrients to other cells by diffusion

intron sequence of DNA that is not involved in coding for a protein

invertebrate animal that lacks a backbone, or vertebral column

ion atom that has a positive or negative charge

ionic bond chemical bond formed when one or more electrons are transferred from one atom to another

iris colored part of the eye

isotonic when the concentration of two solutions is the same

isotope one of several forms of a single element, which contains the same number of protons but different numbers of neutrons

J

joint place where one bone attaches to another bone

K

karyotype micrograph of the complete diploid set of chromosomes grouped together in pairs, arranged in order of decreasing size

keratin tough fibrous protein found in skin

keystone species single species that is not usually abundant in a community yet exerts strong control on the structure of a community

kidney an organ of excretion that separates wastes and excess water from the blood

kin selection theory that states that helping relatives can improve an individual's evolutionary fitness because related individuals share a large proportion of their genes

kingdom largest and most inclusive group in classification

Koch's postulates set of guidelines developed by Koch that helps identify the microorganism that causes a specific disease

Krebs cycle second stage of cellular respiration in which pyruvic acid is broken down into carbon dioxide in a series of energy-extracting reactions

L

language system of communication that combines sounds, symbols, and gestures according to a set of rules about sequence and meaning, such as grammar and syntax

large intestine organ in the digestive system that removes water from the undigested material that passes through it; also called colon

larva (pl. larvae) immature stage of an organism

larynx structure in the throat that contains the vocal cords

learning changes in behavior as a result of experience

lens structure in the eye that focuses light rays on the retina

lichen symbiotic association between a fungus and a photosynthetic organism

ligament tough connective tissue that holds bones together in a joint

light-dependent reactions set of reactions in photosynthesis that use energy from light to produce ATP and NADPH

light-independent reactions set of reactions in photosynthesis that do not require light; energy from ATP and NADPH is used to build high-energy compounds such as sugar; also called the Calvin cycle

lignin substance in vascular plants that makes cell walls rigid

limiting factor factor that causes population growth to decrease

limiting nutrient single essential nutrient that limits productivity in an ecosystem

lipid macromolecule made mostly from carbon and hydrogen atoms; includes fats, oils, and waxes

lipid bilayer flexible double-layered sheet that makes up the cell membrane and forms a barrier between the cell and its surroundings

logistic growth growth pattern in which a population's growth slows and then stops following a period of exponential growth

loop of Henle section of the nephron tubule that is responsible for conserving water and minimizing the volume of the filtrate

lung respiratory organ; place where gases are exchanged between the blood and inhaled air

lymph fluid that is filtered out of the blood

lysogenic infection type of infection in which a virus embeds its DNA into the DNA of the host cell and is replicated along with the host cell's DNA

lysosome cell organelle that breaks down lipids, carbohydrates, and proteins into small molecules that can used by the rest of the cell

lytic infection type of infection in which a virus enters a cell, makes copies of itself, and causes the cell to burst

M

macroevolution large-scale evolutionary change that takes place over long periods of time

Malpighian tubule structure in most terrestrial arthropods that concentrates the uric acid and adds it to digestive wastes

mammary gland gland in female mammals that produces milk to nourish the young

mass extinction event during which many species become extinct during a relatively short period of time

matrix innermost compartment of the mitochondrion

mechanical digestion physical breakdown of large pieces of food into smaller pieces

meiosis process in which the number of chromosomes per cell is cut in half through the separation of homologous chromosomes in a diploid cell

melanin dark brown pigment in the skin that helps protect the skin by absorbing ultraviolet rays

melanocyte cell in the skin that produces a dark brown pigment called melanin

menstrual cycle regular sequence of events in which an egg develops and is released from the body

menstruation discharge of blood and the unfertilized egg from the body

meristem regions of unspecialized cells responsible for continuing growth throughout a plant's lifetime

mesoderm middle germ layer; develops into muscles, and much of the circulatory, reproductive, and excretory systems

mesophyll specialized ground tissue found in leaves; performs most of a plant's photosynthesis

messenger RNA (mRNA) type of RNA that carries copies of instructions for the assembly of amino acids into proteins from DNA to the rest of the cell

metabolism the combination of chemical reactions through which an organism builds up or breaks down materials

metamorphosis process of changes in shape and form of a larva into an adult

metaphase phase of mitosis in which the chromosomes line up across the center of the cell

microclimate environmental conditions within a small area that differs significantly from the climate of the surrounding area

migration seasonal behavior resulting in the movement from one environment to another

mineral inorganic nutrient the body needs, usually in small amounts

mitochondrion cell organelle that converts the chemical energy stored in food into compounds that are more convenient for the cell to use

mitosis part of eukaryotic cell division during which the cell nucleus divides

mixture material composed of two or more elements or compounds that are physically mixed together but not chemically combined

molecular clock method used by researchers that uses mutation rates in DNA to estimate the length of time that two species have been evolving independently

molecule smallest unit of most compounds that displays all the properties of that compound

molting process of shedding an exoskeleton and growing a new one

monocot angiosperm with one seed leaf in its ovary

monoculture farming strategy of planting a single, highly productive crop year after year

monomer small chemical unit that makes up a polymer

monophyletic group group that consists of a single ancestral species and all its descendants and excludes any organisms that are not descended from that common ancestor

monosaccharide simple sugar molecule

motor neuron type of nerve cell that carries directions from interneurons to either muscle cells or glands

multiple alleles a gene that has more than two alleles

multipotent cell with limited potential to develop into many types of differentiated cells

muscle fiber long slender skeletal muscle cells

muscle tissue type of tissue that makes movements of the body possible

mutagen chemical or physical agents in the environment that interact with DNA and may cause a mutation

mutation change in the genetic material of a cell

mutualism symbiotic relationship in which both species benefit from the relationship

mycelium (pl. mycelia) densely branched network of the hyphae of a fungus

mycorrhiza (pl. mycorrhizae) symbiotic association of plant roots and fungi

myelin sheath insulating membrane surrounding the axon in some neurons

myocardium thick middle muscle layer of the heart

myofibril tightly packed filament bundles found within skeletal muscle fibers

myosin thick filament of protein found in skeletal muscle cells

N

NAD+ (nicotinamide adenine dinucleotide) electron carrier involved in glycolysis

NADP+ (nicotinamide adenine dinucleotide phosphate) carrier molecule that transfers high-energy electrons from chlorophyll to other molecules

natural selection process by which organisms that are most suited to their environment survive and reproduce most successfully; also called survival of the fittest

nephridium (pl. nephridia) excretory structure of an annelid that filters body fluid

nephron blood-filtering structure in the kidneys in which impurities are filtered out, wastes are collected, and purified blood is returned to the circulation

nervous tissue type of tissue that transmits nerve impulses throughout the body

neuromuscular junction the point of contact between a motor neuron and a skeletal muscle cell

neuron nerve cell; specialized for carrying messages throughout the nervous system

neurotransmitter chemical used by a neuron to transmit an impulse across a synapse to another cell

neurulation the first step in the development of the nervous system

niche full range of physical and biological conditions in which an organism lives and the way in which the organism uses those conditions

nitrogen fixation process of converting nitrogen gas into nitrogen compounds that plants can absorb and use

node part on a growing stem where a leaf is attached

nondisjunction error in meiosis in which the homologous chromosomes fail to separate properly

nonrenewable resource resource that cannot be replenished by natural process within a reasonable amount of time

norepinephrine hormone released by the adrenal glands that increases heart rate and blood pressure and prepares the body for intense physical activity

notochord long supporting rod that runs through a chordate's body just below the nerve cord

nucleic acid macromolecules containing hydrogen, oxygen, nitrogen, carbon, and phosphorus

nucleotide subunit of which nucleic acids are composed; made up of a 5-carbon sugar, a phosphate group, and a nitrogenous base

nucleus the center of an atom, which contains the protons and neutrons ; in cells, structure that contains the cell's genetic material in the form of DNA

nutrient chemical substance that an organism needs to sustain life

nymph immature form of an animal that resembles the adult form but lacks functional sexual organs

O

observation process of noticing and describing events or processes in a careful, orderly way

omnivore organism that obtains energy by eating both plants and animals

open circulatory system type of circulatory system in which blood is only partially contained within a system of blood vessels as it travels through the body

operant conditioning type of learning in which an animal learns to behave in a certain way through repeated practice, to receive a reward or avoid punishment

operator short DNA region, adjacent to the promoter of a prokaryotic operon, that binds repressor proteins responsible for controlling the rate of transcription of the operon

operon in prokaryotes, a group of adjacent genes that shares a common operator and promoter and are transcribed into a single mRNA

opposable thumb thumb that enables grasping objects and using tools

order in classification, a group of closely related families

organ group of tissues that work together to perform closely related functions

organ system group of organs that work together to perform a specific function

organelle specialized structure that performs important cellular functions within a eukaryotic cell

osmosis diffusion of water through a selectively permeable membrane

osmotic pressure pressure that must be applied to prevent osmotic movement across a selectively permeable membrane

ossification process of bone formation during which cartilage is replaced by bone

osteoblast bone cell that secretes mineral deposits that replace the cartilage in developing bones

osteoclast bone cell that breaks down bone minerals

osteocyte bone cell that helps maintain the minerals in bone tissue and continue to strengthen the growing bone

ovary in plants, the structure that surrounds and protects seeds; in animals, the primary female reproductive organ; produces eggs

oviparous species in which embryos develop in eggs outside a parent's body

ovoviparous species in which the embryos develop within the mother's body but depend entirely on the yolk sac of their eggs

ovulation the release of a mature egg from the ovary into one of the Fallopian tubes

ovule structure in seed cones in which the female gametophytes develop

ozone layer atmospheric layer in which ozone gas is relatively concentrated; protects life on Earth from harmful ultraviolet rays in sunlight

P

pacemaker small group of cardiac muscle fibers that maintains the heart's pumping rhythm by setting the rate at which the heart contracts; the sinoatrial (SA) node

paleontologist scientist who studies fossils

palisade mesophyll layer of cells under the upper epidermis of a leaf

parasitism symbiotic relationship in which one organism lives on or inside another organism and harms it

parathyroid hormone (PTH) hormone produced by parathyroid gland that increases calcium levels in the blood

parenchyma main type of ground tissue in plants that contains cells with thin cell walls and large central vacuoles

passive immunity temporary immunity that develops as a result of natural or deliberate exposure to an antigen

pathogen disease-causing agent

pedigree chart that shows the presence or absence of a trait according to the relationships within a family across several generations

pepsin enzyme that breaks down proteins into smaller polypeptide fragments

period division of geologic time into which eras are subdivided

peripheral nervous system network of nerves and supporting cells that carries signals into and out of the central nervous system

peristalsis contractions of smooth muscles that provide the force that moves food through the esophagus toward the stomach

permafrost layer of permanently frozen subsoil found in the tundra

petiole thin stalk that connects the blade of a leaf to a stem

pH scale scale with values from 0 to 14, used to measure the concentration of H^+ ions in a solution; a pH of 0 to 7 is acidic, a pH of 7 is neutral, and a pH of 7 to 14 is basic

pharyngeal pouch one of a pair of structures in the throat region of a chordate

pharynx tube at the back of the mouth that serves as a passageway for both air and food; also called the throat

phenotype physical characteristics of an organism

phloem vascular tissue that transports solutions of nutrients and carbohydrates produced by photosynthesis through the plant

photic zone sunlight region near the surface of water

photoperiod a plant response to the relative lengths of light and darkness

photosynthesis process used by plants and other autotrophs to capture light energy and use it to power chemical reactions that convert carbon dioxide and water into oxygen and energy-rich carbohydrates such as sugars and starches

photosystem cluster of chlorophyll and proteins found in thylakoids

phototropism tendency of a plant to grow toward a light source

phylogeny study of evolutionary relationships among organisms

phylum (pl. phyla) in classification, a group of closely related classes

phytoplankton photosynthetic algae found near the surface of the ocean

pigment light-absorbing molecule used by plants to gather the sun's energy

pioneer species first species to populate an area during succession

pistil single carpel or several fused carpels; contains the ovary, style, and stigma

pith parenchyma cells inside the ring of vascular tissue in dicot stems

pituitary gland small gland found near the base of the skull that secretes hormones that directly regulate many body functions and controls the actions of several other endocrine glands

placenta specialized organ in placental mammals through which respiratory gases, nutrients, and wastes are exchanged between the mother and her developing young

plankton microscopic organisms that live in aquatic environments; includes both phytoplankton and zooplankton

plasma straw-colored liquid portion of the blood

plasmid small, circular piece of DNA located in the cytoplasm of many bacteria

plasmodium amoeboid feeding stage in the life cycled of a plasmodial slime mold

plate tectonics geologic processes, such as continental drift, volcanoes, and earthquakes, resulting from plate movement

platelet cell fragment released by bone marrow that helps in blood clotting

pluripotent cells that are capable of developing into most, but not all, of the body's cell types

point mutation gene mutation in which a single base pair in DNA has been changed

pollen grain structure that contains the entire male gametophyte in seed plants

pollen tube structure in a plant that contains two haploid sperm nuclei

pollination transfer of pollen from the male reproductive structure to the female reproductive structure

pollutant harmful material that can enter the biosphere through the land, air, or water

polygenic trait trait controlled by two or more genes

polymer molecules composed of many monomers; makes up macromolecules

polymerase chain reaction (PCR) the technique used by biologists to make many copies of a particular gene

polypeptide long chain of amino acids that makes proteins

polyploidy condition in which an organism has extra sets of chromosomes

population group of individuals of the same species that live in the same area

population density number of individuals per unit area

predation interaction in which one organism (the predator) captures and feeds on another organism (the prey)

prehensile tail long tail that can coil tightly enough around a branch

pressure-flow hypothesis hypothesis that explains the method by which phloem sap is transported through the plant from a sugar "source" to a sugar "sink"

primary growth pattern of growth that takes place at the tips and shoots of a plant

primary producer first producer of energy-rich compounds that are later used by other organisms

primary succession succession that occurs in an area in which no trace of a previous community is present

principle of dominance Mendel's second conclusion, which states that some alleles are dominant and others are recessive

prion protein particles that cause disease

probability likelihood that a particular event will occur

product elements or compounds produced by a chemical reaction

prokaryote unicellular organism that lacks a nucleus

promoter specific region of a gene where RNA polymerase can bind and begin transcription

prophage bacteriophage DNA that is embedded in the bacterial host's DNA

prophase first and longest phase of mitosis in which the genetic material inside the nucleus condenses and the chromosomes become visible

prostaglandin modified fatty acids that are produced by a wide range of cells; generally affect only nearby cells and tissues

protein macromolecule that contains carbon, hydrogen, oxygen, and nitrogen; needed by the body for growth and repair

protostome an animal whose mouth is formed from the blastopore

pseudocoelom body cavity that is only partially lined with mesoderm

pseudopod temporary cytoplasmic projection used by some protists for movement

puberty period of rapid growth and sexual maturation during which the reproductive system becomes fully functional

pulmonary circulation path of circulation between the heart and lungs

punctuated equilibrium pattern of evolution in which long stable periods are interrupted by brief periods of more rapid change

Punnett square diagram that can be used to predict the genotype and phenotype combinations of a genetic cross

pupa stage in complete metamorphosis in which the larva develops into an adult

pupil small opening in the iris that admits light into the eye

R

radial symmetry body plan in which any number of imaginary planes drawn through the center of the body could divide it into equal halves

radiometric dating sample from the amount of a radioactive isotope to the nonradioactive isotope of the same element in a sample

reabsorption process by which water and dissolved substances are taken back into the blood

reactant elements or compounds that enter into a chemical reaction

receptor on or in a cell, a specific protein to whose shape fits that of a specific molecular messenger, such as a hormone

recombinant DNA DNA produced by combining DNA from different sources

red blood cell blood cell containing hemoglobin that carries oxygen

reflex quick, automatic response to a stimulus

reflex arc the sensory receptor, sensory neuron, motor neuron, and affector that are involved in a quick response to a stimulus

relative dating method of determining the age of a fossil by comparing its placement with that of fossils in other rock layers

relative frequency number of times that an allele occurs in a gene pool compared with the number of times other alleles for the same gene occur

releasing hormone hormone produced by the hypothalamus that makes the anterior pituitary secrete hormones

renewable resource resource that can be produced or replaced by healthy ecosystem functions

replication process of copying DNA prior to cell division

reproductive isolation separation of a species or population so that they no longer interbreed and evolve into two separate species

resource any necessity of life, such as water, nutrients, light, food, or space

response specific reaction to a stimulus

resting potential electrical charge across the cell membrane of a resting neuron

restriction enzyme enzyme that cuts DNA at a sequence of nucleotides

retina innermost layer of the eye; contains photoreceptors

retrovirus RNA virus that contains RNA as its genetic information

ribonucleic acid (RNA) single-stranded nucleic acid that contains the sugar ribose

ribosomal RNA (rRNA) type of RNA that combines with proteins to form ribosomes

ribosome cell organelle consisting of RNA and protein found throughout the cytoplasm in a cell; the site of protein synthesis

RNA interference (RNAi) introduction of double-stranded RNA into a cell to inhibit gene expression

RNA polymerase enzyme that links together the growing chain of RNA nucleotides during transcription using a DNA strand as a template

rod photoreceptor in the eyes that is sensitive to light but can't distinguish color

root cap tough covering of the root tip that protects the meristem

root hair small hairs on a root that produce a large surface area through which water and minerals can enter

rumen stomach chamber in cows and related animals in which symbiotic bacteria digest cellulose

S

sapwood in a woody stem, the layer of secondary phloem that surrounds the heartwood; usually active in fluid transport

sarcomere unit of muscle contraction; composed of two z-lines and the filaments between them

scavenger animal that consumes the carcasses of other animals

science organized way of gathering and analyzing evidence about the natural world

sclerenchyma type of ground tissue with extremely thick, rigid cell walls that make ground tissue tough and strong

scrotum external sac that houses the testes

sebaceous gland gland in the skin that secretes sebum (oily secretion)

secondary growth type of growth in dicots in which the stems increase in thickness

secondary succession type of succession that occurs in an area that was only partially destroyed by disturbances

seed plant embryo and a food supply encased in a protective covering

seed coat tough covering that surrounds and protects the plant embryo and keeps the contents of the seed from drying out

segregation separation of alleles during gamete formation

selective breeding method of breeding that allows only those organisms with desired characteristics to produce the next generation

selectively permeable property of biological membranes that allows some substances to pass across it while others cannot; also called semipermeable membrane

semen the combination of sperm and seminal fluid

semicircular canal one of three structures in the inner ear that monitor the position of the body in relation to gravity

seminiferous tubule one of hundreds of tubules in each testis in which sperm develop

sensory neuron type of nerve cell that receives information from sensory receptors and conveys signals to central nervous system

sex chromosome one of two chromosomes that determines an individual's sex

sex-linked gene gene located on a sex chromosome

sexual reproduction type of reproduction in which cells from two parents unite to form the first cell of a new organism

sexually transmitted disease (STD) disease that is spread from person to person by sexual contact

sieve tube element continuous tube through the plant phloem cells, which are arranged end to end

single-gene trait trait controlled by one gene that has two alleles

small intestine digestive organ in which most chemical digestion and absorption of food takes place

smog gray-brown haze formed by a mixture of chemicals

society group of closely related animals of the same species that work together for the benefit of the group

solute substance that is dissolved in a solution

solution type of mixture in which all the components are evenly distributed

solvent dissolving substance in a solution

somatic nervous system part of the peripheral nervous system that carries signals to and from skeletal muscles

speciation formation of a new species

species diversity number of different species that make up a particular area

spirillum (pl. spirilla) spiral or corkscrew-shaped prokaryote

spongy mesophyll layer of loose tissue found beneath the palisade mesophyll in a leaf

sporangium (pl. sporangia) spore capsule in which haploid spores are produced by meiosis

spore in prokaryotes, protists, and fungi, any of a variety of thick-walled life cycle stages capable of surviving unfavorable conditions

sporophyte spore-producing plant; the multicellular diploid phase of a plant life cycle

stabilizing selection form of natural selection in which individuals near the center of a distribution curve have higher fitness than individuals at either end of the curve

stamen male part of a flower; contains the anther and filament

stem cell unspecialized cell that can give rise to one or more types of specialized cells

stigma sticky part at the top of style; specialized to capture pollen

stimulus (pl. stimuli) signal to which an organism responds

stoma (pl. stomata) small opening in the epidermis of a plant that allows carbon dioxide, water, and oxygen to diffuse into and out of the leaf

stomach large muscular sac that continues the mechanical and chemical digestion of food

stroma fluid portion of the chloroplast; outside of the thylakoids

substrate reactant of an enzyme-catalyzed reaction

suspension mixture of water and nondissolved material

sustainable development strategy for using natural resources without depleting them and for providing human needs without causing long-term environmental harm

symbiosis relationship in which two species live close together

synapse point at which a neuron can transfer an impulse to another cell

systematics study of the diversity of life and the evolutionary relationships between organisms

systemic circulation path of circulation between the heart and the rest of the body

T

taiga biome with long cold winters and a few months of warm weather; dominated by coniferous evergreens; also called boreal forest

target cell cell that has a receptor for a particular hormone

taste bud sense organs that detect taste

taxon (pl. taxa) group or level of organization into which organisms are classified

telomere repetitive DNA at the end of a eukaryotic chromosome

telophase phase of mitosis in which the distinct individual chromosomes begin to spread out into a tangle of chromatin

temporal isolation form of reproductive isolation in which two or more species reproduces at different times

tendon tough connective tissue that connects skeletal muscles to bones

territory a specific area occupied and protected by an animal or group of animals

testis (pl. testes) primary male reproductive organ; produces sperm

tetrad structure containing four chromatids that forms during meiosis

tetrapod vertebrate with four limbs

thalamus brain structure that receives messages from the sense organs and relays the information to the proper region of the cerebrum for further processing

theory well-tested explanation that unifies a broad range of observations and hypotheses, and enables scientists to make accurate predications about new situations

thigmotropism response of a plant to touch

threshold minimum level of a stimulus that is required to cause an impulse

thylakoid saclike photosynthetic membranes found in chloroplasts

thyroxine hormone produced by the thyroid gland, which increases the metabolic rate of cells throughout the body

tissue group of similar cells that perform a particular function

tolerance ability of an organism to survive and reproduce under circumstances that differ from their optimal conditions

totipotent cells that are able to develop into any type of cell found in the body (including the cells that make up the extraembryonic membranes and placenta)

trachea tube that connects the pharynx to the larynx; also called the windpipe

tracheid hollow plant cell in xylem with thick cell walls strengthened by lignin

tracheophyte vascular plant

trait specific characteristic of an individual

transcription synthesis of an RNA molecule from a DNA template

transfer RNA (tRNA) type of RNA that carries each amino acid to a ribosome during protein synthesis

transformation process in which one strain of bacteria is changed by a gene or genes from another strain of bacteria

transgenic term used to refer to an organism that contains genes from other organisms

translation process by which the sequence of bases of an mRNA is converted into the sequence of amino acids of a protein

transpiration loss of water from a plant through its leaves

trochophore free-swimming larval stage of an aquatic mollusk

trophic level each step in a food chain or food web

tropism movement of a plant toward or away from stimuli

tumor mass of rapidly dividing cells that can damage surrounding tissue

U

understory layer in a rain forest found underneath the canopy formed by shorter trees and vines

ureter tube that carries urine from a kidney to the urinary bladder

urethra tube through which urine leaves the body

urinary bladder saclike organ in which urine is stored before being excreted

V

vaccination injection of a weakened, or a similar but less dangerous, pathogen to produce immunity

vaccine preparation of weakened or killed pathogens used to produce immunity to a disease

vacuole cell organelle that stores materials such as water, salts, proteins, and carbohydrates

valve flap of connective tissue located between an atrium and a ventricle, or in a vein, that prevents backflow of blood

van der Waals force slight attraction that develops between oppositely charged regions of nearby molecules

vas deferens tube that carries sperm from the epididymis to the urethra

vascular bundle clusters of xylem and phloem tissue in stems

vascular cambium meristem that produces vascular tissues and increases the thickness of stems

vascular cylinder central region of a root that includes the vascular tissues—xylem and phloem

vascular tissue specialized tissue in plants that carries water and nutrients

vector animal that transports a pathogen to a human

vegetative reproduction method of asexual reproduction in plants, which enables a single plant to produce offspring that are genetically identical to itself

vein blood vessel that carries blood from the body back to the heart

ventricle lower chamber of the heart that pumps blood out of heart to the rest of the body

vertebrate animal that has a backbone

vessel element type of xylem cell that forms part of a continuous tube through which water can move

vestigial organs structures that are reduced in size and have little or no function

villus (pl. villi) fingerlike projection in the small intestine that aids in the absorption of nutrient molecules

virus particle made of proteins, nucleic acids, and sometimes lipids that can replicate only by infecting living cells

vitamin organic molecule that helps regulate body processes

viviparous animals that bear live young that are nourished directly by the mother's body as they develop

W

weather day-to-day conditions of the atmosphere, including temperature, precipitation, and other factors

wetland ecosystem in which water either covers the soil or is present at or near the surface for at least part of the year

white blood cell type of blood cell that guards against infection, fights parasites, and attacks bacteria

woody plant type of plant made primarily of cells with thick cell walls that support the plant body; includes trees, shrubs, and vines

X

xylem vascular tissue that carries water upward from the roots to every part of a plant

Z

zoonosis (pl. zoonoses) disease transmitted from animal to human

zooplankton small free-floating animals that form part of plankton

zygote fertilized egg

A

abiotic factor | عامل مضاد للحياة عامل مادي أو غير حي يشكل نظاماً بيئياً

abscisic acid | حمض الأبسيسيك هرمون نباتي يثبط انقسام الخلية، ومن ثم يثبط النمو

acetylcholine | أسيتيل كولين ناقل عصبي يحدث نبضة في الخلية العضلية

acid | حمض مركب يشكل أيونات الهيدروجين (+H) في محلول؛ المحلول الذي يكون فيه جهد أيون الهيدروجين أقل من 7

acid rain | أمطار حمضية أمطار تحتوي على أحماض النيتريك والأحماض الكبريتية

actin | أكتين خيط رقيق من البروتين يوجد في العضلات

action potential | جهد الفعل انعكاس الشحنات خلال الغشاء الخلوي للخلية العصبية؛ كما يطلق عليه أيضاً النبضة العصبية

activation energy | طاقة التنشيط الطاقة المطلوبة لبدء التفاعل

active immunity | مناعة فعالة المناعة التي تنمو كنتيجة للتعرض الطبيعي أو المتعمد لأحد مولدات المضادات

adaptation | تكيف صفة وراثية تزيد من قدرة الكائنات الحية لتبقى وتتكاثر في البيئة

adaptive radiation | إشعاع تكيفي العملية التي يتطور فيها نوع فردي أو مجموعة صغيرة من الأنواع إلى أشكال متنوعة مختلفة تعيش بطرق مختلفة

adenosine triphosphate (ATP) | ثلاثي فوسفات الأدينوسين (ATP) مركب تستخدمه الخلايا لتخزين الطاقة وتحريرها

adhesion | التصاق قوة الجذب بين أنواع الجزيئات المختلفة

aerobic | هوائي العملية التي تتطلب وجود الأكسجين

age structure | هيكل عمري عدد الذكور والإناث في نفس العمر في التعداد السكاني

aggression | عدوان سلوك تهديدي يستخدمه أحد الحيوانات لفرض السيطرة عل حيوان آخر

algal bloom | ريعان طحلبي زيادة في كمية الطحالب و المتكاثرات الأخرى التي تنتج عن إدخال كبير لأحد المغذيات المحدودة

allele | أليل أحد الأشكال المختلفة للجين

allergy | حساسية تفاعل مفرط للجهاز المناعي لأحد مولدات المضادات

alternation of generations | تبادل الأجيال دورة الحياة التي لها طوران متبادلإن – طور فردي (N) وطور ثنائي (2N)

alveolus (pl. alveoli) | حويصلة أكياس هوائية صغيرة في نهاية الشعبية في الرئتين توفر مجالاً سطحياً لحدوث تبادل الغازات

amino acid | حمض أميني مركب بمجموعة أمينية في أحد أطرافه ومجموعة كربوكسيل في الطرف الآخر

amniotic egg | بيضة أمينوسية بيضة تتكون من قشرة وأغشية تخلق بيئة محمية يستطيع الجنين فيها أن ينمو خارج المياه

amylase | أميليز إنزيم يوجد في اللعاب يكسر الرابطة الكيميائية في النشويات

anaerobic | لا هوائي عملية لا تتطلب وجود الأكسجين

anaphase | طور الصعود طور الانقسام الفتيلي التي تنفصل فيها الصبغيات وتتوجه إلى الطرفين المتقابلين للخلية

angiosperm | كاسيات البذور مجموعة من النباتات البذرية التي تحمل بذورها داخل طبقة من النسيج الذي تحمي البذرة؛ ويطلق عليه أيضاً النبات الزهري

anther | مئبر (عضو التذكير) الهيكل الزهري الذي تنتج فيه حبوب اللقاح

asthma | ربو مرض تنفسي مزمن يكون فيها ممر الهواء ضيقاً، مسبباً أزيزاً وكحة وتنفساً صعباً

atherosclerosis | تصلب الشرايين حالة تتراكم فيها رواسب دهنية تسمى لويحة داخل جدران الشرايين وتتسبب في النهاية في تصلب الشرايين

atom | ذرة الوحدة الأساسية للمادة

ATP synthase | سينيز ثلاثي فوسفات الأدينوسين تجمع من البروتينات يمتد فوق غشاء الخلية ويسمح لأيونات الهيدروجين (+H) أن تمر من خلالها

atrium (pl. atria) | أذين الحجرة العلوية للقلب التي تتلقى الدم من باقي الجسم

autonomic nervous system | جهاز عصبي مستقل جزء من الجهاز العصبي المحيطي ينظم الأنشطة اللاإرادية، أو التي ليست تحت سيطرة الوعي؛ يتألف من تقسيمات فرعية ودية ونظير الودية

autosome | صبغي جسدي صبغ غير جنسي؛ يطلق عليه أيضاً اسم الكروموزوم الصبغي الجسدي

autotroph | ذاتي التغذية كائن حي يستطيع التقاط الطاقة من ضوء الشمس أو المواد الكيميائية ويستخدمها لإنتاج غذائه الخاص به من المكونات غير العضوية؛ ويطلق عليه أيضاً اسم المنتج

auxin | أوكسين مادة تنظيمية تنتج في طرف النبات النامي تحفز تطويل الخلية ونمو الجذور الجديدة

axial skeleton | هيكل محوري الهيكل الذي يدعم المحور المركزي للجسم؛ ويتكون من الجمجمة والعمود الفقري والقفص الضلعي

axon | محور عصبي ليفة طويلة تحمل النبضات بعيداً عن جسم الخلية العصبية

B

bacillus (pl. bacilli) | عصوية بدائيات النواة في شكل عصاة

background extinction | انقراض خلفي انقراض يحدث نتيجة لعملية بطيئة وثابتة للانتقاء الطبيعي

Bacteria | بكتريا حقل بدائيات النواة أحادي الخلايا له جدران خلية يحتوي على الببتيدوجليكان؛ ينتمي إلى مملكة الجراثيم الحقيقية

bacteriophage | جراثيم البكتريا نوع من الفيروسات يصيب البكتريا

bark | لحاء الأنسجة الموجودة خارج القلُب الوعائي ويشمل اللحاء، والقلب الفليني، والفلين

antheridium (pl. antheridia) | مئبرية الهيكل الذكري التناسلي في بعض النباتات التي تنتج النطفة

anthropoid | شبيه البشر مجموعة رئيسية تتكون من القرود والبشر

antibiotic | مضاد حيوي مجموعة من العقاقير تستخدم لمنع نمو وتكاثر الكائنات البكتيرية

antibody | جسم مضاد بروتين يهاجم مولدات المضادات مباشرة أو ينتج بروتينات رابطة لمولدات المضادات

anticodon | مضاد التخثر مجموعة من ثلاث قواعد علَى جزيء الحمض الريبي النووي الناقل (tRNA) والمكمل للقواعد الثلاثة لكودون الحمض الريبي النووي الرسول (mRNA)

antigen | مولد المضادات أي مادة تحفز الاستجابة المناعية

aphotic zone | منطقة ظلامية الطبقة المظلمة من المحيطات تحت المنطقة الضوئية والتي لا يخترقها ضوء الشمس

apical dominance | سيادة قمية الظاهرة التي كلما اقترب فيها البرعم من طرف الساق كلما ثبط نموه

apical meristem | نسيج إنشائي قمي مجموعة من الخلايا غير المتخصصة التي تنقسم لتنتج زيادة في طول السيقان والجذور

apoptosis | استماتة عملية موت الخلية المبرمج

appendage | لاحقة بنية، مثل الساق أو قرن الاستشعار تمتد من جدار الجسم

appendicular skeleton | هيكل زائدي عظام اليدين أو الرجلين مع عظام الحوض ومنطقة الكتف

aquaculture | زراعة مائية تربية الكائنات المائية لاستهلاكها من قبل الإنسان

aquaporin | أكوابورين بروتين القناة المائية في الخلية

Archaea | أرشاية حقل يحتوي على أحاديات الخلية، بدائيات النواة التي لها جدار خلية لا يحتوي على الببتيدوجليكان؛ تنتمي إلى مملكة أرشيا بكتريا

archegonium (pl. archegonia) | عدابة بنية في النباتات تنتج خلايا البيض

artery | شريان وعاء دموي كبير يحمل الدم بعيداً عن القلب إلى أنسجة الجسم

artificial selection | انتقاء اصطناعي توليد انتقائي للنباتات والحيوانات لتعزيز ظهور سمات مرغوب فيها في السلالة

asexual reproduction | توالد لا جنسي عملية التوالد التي تتضمن والداً واحداً وينتج عنها سلالة تتطابق جينياً مع الوالد

base | قاعدة مركب ينتج أيونات الهيدروكسيد (-OH) في المحلول؛ المحلول الذي يكون فيه جهد أيون الهيدروجين أكثر من 7

base pairing | ازدواج القواعد مبدأ مؤداه أن الروابط في الحامض النووي الوراثي تستطيع أن تتكون فقط بين الأدينين والثايمين وبين الجوانين والسيتوسين

behavior | سلوك الطريقة التي يتفاعل بها الكائن الحي مع التغيرات في حالته الداخلية أو بيئته الخارجية

behavioral isolation | عزل سلوكي صورة من صور العزل التناسلي ينمو فيه اثنان من السكان نمواً مختلفاً في طقوس تودد أو سلوكيات أخرى تمنعهم من التكاثر

benthos | قاعيات الكائنات الحية التي تعيش مرتبطة بقاع البحيرات أو المجاري المائية أو المحيطات أو قريبة منه

bias | تحيز تفضيل أو وجهة نظر خاصة شخصية وليست علمية

bilateral symmetry | تناظر الجانبين تصميم جسم يمكن فيه لخط تخيلي مفرد أن يقسم الجسم إلى جانبين أيسر وأيمن يكون كل جانب فيه صور مطابقة للآخر

binary fission | انشطار ثنائي نوع من التكاثر غير الجنسي يضاعف فيه الكائن الحي الحامض النووي الوراثي الخاص به وينقسم إلى قسمين، منتجاً خليتين بنتيتين متماثلتين

binocular vision | رؤية بالعينين القدرة على دمج الصور البصرية من كلا العينين، بما يقدم إدراكاً عميقاً ورؤية ثلاثية الأبعاد للعالم

binomial nomenclature | تسمية ثنائية نظام تصنيف يعطى فيه كل نوع اسماً علمياً من جزأين

biodiversity | تنوع بيولوجي مجموع الكائنات الحية المختلفة في الكرة البيولوجية، ويطلق عليه أيضاً اسم تنوع أحيائي

biogeochemical cycle | الدورة الحيوية الجغرافية الكيميائية العملية التي يتم فيها انتقال العناصر والمركبات الكيميائية وأشكال المادة الأخرى من كائن حي إلى كائن حي آخر ومن جزء من الكرة البيولوجية إلى جزء آخر

biogeography | جغرافيا حيوية دراسة التوزيع السابق والحالي للكائنات الحية

bioinformatics | معلوماتية حيوية تطبيق علوم الرياضيات والكمبيوتر لتخزين البيانات الحيوية واسترجاعها وتحليلها

biological magnification | تكبير حيوي التركيز الزائد لمادة ضارة في الكائنات الحية في مستويات غذائية أعلى في سلسلة غذائية أو شبكة غذائية

biology | أحياء الدراسة العلمية للحياة

biomass | كتلة بيولوجية إجمالي كمية النسيج الحي في مستوى غذائي معطى

biome | مجتمع أحيائي مجموعة من النظم البيئية التي تشترك في مناخ مشابه وكائنات حية متطابقة

biosphere | كرة بيولوجية جزء من الأرض تتواجد فيه الحياة ويشمل ذلك الأرض والماء والهواء أو الجو

biotechnology | تكنولوجيا حيوية عملية تداول الكائنات الحية أو الخلايا أو الجزيئات لإحداث نتائج معينة

biotic factor | عامل حيوي أي جزء حي من البيئة قد يتفاعل معه الكائن الحي

bipedal | ذو قدمين مصطلح مستخدم للإشارة إلى التحرك بقدمين

blade | نصل الجزء الرقيق المسطح لورقة النبات

blastocyst | متبرعمة كيسية مرحلة النمو المبكر في الثدييات والتي تتكون من كرة مجوفة من الخلايا

blastula | بلاستولة كرة مجوفة من الخلايا تنمو عندما تُجري الخلية الملقحة سلسلة من الانقسامات الخلوية

bone marrow | نخاع عظمي نسيج رقيق يوجد في تجاويف العظام

bottleneck effect | تأثير عنق الزجاجة تغير في تكرار الأليل يتبع انخفاضاً حاداً في حجم السكان

Bowman's capsule | كبسولة بومان بنية تشبه الكوب تحتوي على الكبيبة؛ تجمع ما ترشح من الدم

brain stem | جذع المخ بنية توصل الدماغ والحبل الشوكي؛ تشمل البصلة والجسر

bronchus (pl. bronchi) | قصبة واحدة من أنبوبتين كبيرتين في تجويف الصدر توصل من القصبة الهوائية إلى الرئتين

bryophyte | نباتات طحلبية مجموعة من النباتات لها أعضاء تناسلية خاصة ولكنها تفتقد إلى النسيج الوعائي؛ وتشمل الأشنات وأقرباءها

bud | برعم بنية نباتية تحتوي على نسيج إنشائي قمي يستطيع إنتاج سيقان وأوراق جديدة

buffer | دارئ مركب يمنع التغيرات الحادة والمفاجئة في جهد أيون الهيدروجين

C

calcitonin | كالسيتونين هرمون تنتجه الدرقية يقلل من مستويات الكالسيوم في الدم

Calorie | سعر حراري مقياس الطاقة الحرارية في الطعام؛ يعادل 1000 سعر حراري

جدار الخلية | cell wall طبقة قوية داعمة حول غشاء الخلية في بعض الخلايا

مناعة متواسطة بالخلايا | cell-mediated immunity الاستجابة المناعية التي تدافع عن الجسم ضد الفيروسات والفطريات والخلايا السرطانية الشاذة داخل الخلايا الحية

تنفس خلوي | cellular respiration العملية التي تطلق الطاقة بتكسير الجلوكوز والجزيئات الغذائية الأخرى في وجود الأكسجين

جهاز عصبي مركزي | central nervous system يشمل الدماغ والحبل الشوكي، يعالج المعلومات ويخلق استجابة توجه للجسم

وكتة | centriole بنية في الخلية الحيوانية تساعد على تنظيم انقسام الخلية

قسيم مركزي | centromere منطقة من الصبغ يتصل فيها الشقين الصبغيين الشقيقين

تدمغ (ترؤس) | cephalization تركيز أعضاء الحس والخلايا العصبية في النهاية الأمامية للحيوان

مخيخ | cerebellum الجزء من الدماغ الذي ينظم الحركة ويتحكم في التوازن

قشرة المخ | cerebral cortex الطبقة الخارجية من المخ من دماغ الثدييات؛ مركز التفكير والسلوكيات المعقدة الأخرى

مخ | cerebrum ذلك الجزء من الدماغ المسئول عن الأنشطة الإرادية للجسم، منطقة «التفكير» في الدماغ

هضم كيميائي | chemical digestion العملية التي يقوم من خلالها الإنزيم بتكسير الطعام إلى جزيئات صغيرة يمكن للجسم استخدامها

تفاعل كيميائي | chemical reaction العملية التي تغير أو تحول مجموعة من المواد الكيميائية إلى مجموعة أخرى من المواد الكيميائية

تخليق كيميائي | chemosynthesis العملية التي تستخدم فيها الطاقة الكيميائية لإنتاج الكربوهيدرات

كيتين | chitin كربوهيدرات معقد يركب جدران الخلية في الفطريات؛ كما يوجد أيضاً في الهياكل الخارجية للمفصليات

كلوروفيل | chlorophyll الصبغ الرئيسي للنباتات والكائنات الحية الأخرى ضوئية التخليق

بلاستيدة خضراء | chloroplast عضي يوجد في خلايا النبات وبعض الكائنات الحية الأخرى التي تلتقط الطاقة من ضوء الشمس وتحولها إلى طاقة كيميائية

حبلية (كورداتا) | chordate حيوان يكون له في مرحلة واحدة من مراحل العمر على الأقل: حبل عصبي ظهري مجوف، وحبل ظهري وذيل يمتد وراء الشرج وأكياس بلعومية

سعر حراري | calorie كمية الطاقة المطلوبة لرفع درجة حرارة 1 جم من الماء بمقدار 1 درجة مئوية

دورة كالفين | Calvin cycle التفاعل الضوئي المستقل للتركيب الضوئي تستخدم فيها الطاقة من ثلاثي فوسفات الأدينوسين وفوسفات ثنائي نيكليوتيد نيكوتين أدينين لبناء مركب ذي طاقة كبيرة مثل السكر

سرطان | cancer اضطراب تفقد فيه بعض خلايا الجسم القدرة على السيطرة على النمو

ظلة | canopy غطاء كثيف يتكون من القمم الورقية لأشجار الغابة الطويلة المطرية

وعاء شعري | capillary أصغر الأوعية الدموية؛ تجلب المغذيات والأكسجين للأنسجة وتمتص ثاني أكسيد الكربون والنواتج المائية

فعل شعري | capillary action ميل المياه إلى الارتفاع في الأنبوب الرفيع

حافظة الفيروس | capsid غطاء البروتين المحيط بالفيروس

كربوهيدرات | carbohydrate مركب يتكون من ذرات الكربون والهيدروجين والأكسجين؛ نوع من المواد المغذية يمثل أكبر مصدر للطاقة للجسم

لاحم | carnivore كائن حي يحصل على الطاقة بتناول كائنات حية أخرى

خباء (كربلة) | carpel أعمق جزء من الزهرة ينتج النابتات المشيجية الأنثوية ويحميها

قدرة الحمل | carrying capacity أكبر عدد من أفراد نوع معين يمكن لبيئة ما أن تتحمله

غضروف | cartilage نوع من الأنسجة الضامة تدعم الجسم، وهي أنعم وأكثر مرونة من العظم

شريط كاسباري | Casparian strip شريط صامد للماء يحيط بالخلايا الأديمية الباطنية للنبات ويشترك في الممر أحادي الاتجاه للمواد إلى الأسطوانة الوعائية في النبات

محفز | catalyst مادة تسرع من معدل التفاعل الكيميائي

خلية | cell الوحدة الرئيسية لجميع صور الحياة

جسم الخلية | cell body أكبر جزء من الخلية العصبية المثالية، ويحتوي على النواة وكثير من الحشوة

دورة الخلية | cell cycle سلسلة من الأحداث تنمو فيها الخلية وتستعد للانقسام وتنقسم لتكون خليتين ابنتين

انقسام الخلية | cell division العملية التي من خلالها تنقسم الخلية إلى خلتين ابنتين جديدتين

غشاء الخلية | cell membrane حاجز رقيق مرن يحيط بجميع الخلايا، وينظم ما يدخل ويخرج من الخلية

نظرية الخلية | cell theory مفهوم رئيسي للأحياء يشير إلى أن جميع الكائنات الحية تتكون من خلايا؛ وتعد هذه الخلايا هي الوحدات الرئيسية لهيكل ووظيفة الكائنات الحية؛ وتنشأ الخلايا الجديدة من خلايا موجودة

collenchyma | نسيج غروي في النباتات، نوع من الأنسجة الأرضية لها جدران خلية قوية ومرنة؛ تساعد في دعم النباتات الأكبر

commensalism | تعايش علاقة معايشة ينتفع فيها كائن حي ولا يساعَد فيها الكائن الآخر ولا يضَر

communication | اتصال مرور المعلومات من كائن حي لآخر

community | مجتمع تجمع سكان مختلفين يعيشون معاً في منطقة محددة

companion cell | خلية رفيقة في النباتات، خلية لحائية تحيط بعناصر الأنبوب المنخلي

competitive exclusion principle | مبدأ الإقصاء التنافسي المبدأ الذي يشير إلى استحالة شغل نوعين اثنين لنفس الموضع في نفس الموطن في ذات الوقت

compound | مركّب مادة تشكلت من التركيب الكيميائي لعنصرين أو أكثر بنسب محددة

cone | مخروط في العين، مستقبلة ضوئية تستجيب لضوء الألوان المختلفة محدثة رؤية اللون

coniferous | صنوبري مصطلح يستخدم للإشارة إلى الأشجار التي تنتج أكواز صنوبر تحمل البذور ولها أوراق رقيقة تشكلت مثل الإبر

conjugation | اقتران عملية تتبادل فيها الكائنات أحادية الخلايا وبعض بدائيات النواة المعلومات الوراثية

connective tissue | نسيج ضام نوع من الأنسجة يقدم الدعم للجسم ويضم أجزاءه

consumer | مستهلك كائن حي يعتمد على الكائنات الحية الأخرى لتزويده بالطاقة والغذاء، ويطلق عليه أيضاً اسم غيري التغذي

control group | مجموعة ضابطة مجموعة في تجربة تتعرض لنفس الظروف مثل المجموعة التجريبية باستثناء متغير مستقل واحد

controlled experiment | تجربة موجهة تجربة يتم فيها تغيير متغير واحد فحسب

convergent evolution | تطور مقارب عملية تتطور فيها كائنات حية لا ترتبط ببعضها البعض تطوراً مستقلاً متشابهاً عندما تتكيف مع بيئات متشابهة

cork cambium | قُلب فليني نسيج مريستيمي ينتج الغطاء الخارجي للسيقان خلال النمو الثانوي للنبات

cornea | قرنية طبقة صلبة شفافة للعين يدخل الضوء من خلالها

corpus luteum | جسم أصفر يعطى الاسم لجريب بعد التبويض نظراً للونه الأصفر

cortex | قشرة في النباتات، منطقة النسيج الأرضي داخل الجذر مباشرة والذي تتحرك من خلاله المياه والمعادن

chromatid | شق صبغي جزء من جزأين متطابقين «شقيقين» لصبغ مزدوج

chromatin | كروماتين مادة توجد في الصبغيات حقيقية النواة وتتكون من الحامض النووي الوراثي ملفوفاً بإحكام حول الهيستونات

chromosome | كروموزوم بنية تشبه الخيط داخل النواة وتحتوي على المعلومات الوراثية التي تمر من جيل إلى الجيل التالي

chyme | كيموس خليط من الإنزيمات والطعام المهضوم هضماً جزئياً

cilium (pl. cilia) | هدب نتوء قصير يشبه الشعر يحدث الحركة

circadian rhythm | إيقاع يومي دورات سلوكية تحدث يومياً

clade | كليد فرع تطوري من الكلادوجرام يشمل سلفاً واحداً وجميع سلالاته

cladogram | كلادوجرام رسم بياني يصف نماذج للصفات المشتركة بين الأنواع

class | صنف في التصنيف، مجموعة من الرتب شديدة الصلة

classical conditioning | اشتراط تقليدي نوع من التعلم يظهر عندما يقوم الحيوان بالربط الذهني بين حافز ما ونوع من أنواع المكافأة أو العقاب

climate | مناخ متوسط أحوال درجات الحرارة والترسب من عام لعام لمنطقة ما خلال فترة زمنية طويلة

clone | نسخة عضو مجموعة سكانية ذات خلايا وراثية متطابقة تنتج من خلية واحدة

closed circulatory system | جهاز الدوران المغلق أحد أنواع جهاز الدوران يدور فيه الدم بالكلية داخل أوعية دموية تمتد في جميع أنحاء الجسم

coccus (pl. cocci) | مكورة بدائية نواة كروية

cochlea | قوقعة جزء من الأذن الداخلية يمتلئ بالسائل، ويحتوي على خلايا عصبية تكتشف الصوت

codominance | سيادة مشتركة الحالة التي يتم فيها التعبير عن الأنماط الظاهرية التي ينتجها كلا الأليلين تعبيراً كاملاً

codon | كودون مجموعة من ثلاث قواعد نيكلوتيد في الحمض الريبي النووي الناقل تحدد حمضاً أمينياً معيناً ليدخل في بروتين

coelom | جوف تجويف جسدي ينتظم مع الأديم المتوسط

coevolution | تطور مشترك العملية التي يتطور فيها نوعان كنتيجة لتغيرات تحدث في كل منهما بمرور الوقت

cohesion | تماسك تجاذب بين جزيئات نفس المادة

corticosteroid | كورتيكوستيرويد هرمون ستيرويد تنتجه قشرة الكظر

cotyledon | فلقة أول ورقة من أول زوجين من الأوراق ينتجه جنين النبات البذري

courtship | مغازلة نوع من السلوك يرسل فيه الحيوان مثيراً ليجذب عضواً من الجنس الآخر

covalent bond | رابط تساهمي نوع من أنواع الروابط بين الذرات يتم فيه المشاركة في الإلكترونات

crossing-over | عبور عملية تقوم فيها الأصباغ المتماثلة بتبادل بروتينات الشق الصبغي الخاص بها خلال الانقسام المنصف

cyclin | سايكلين أحد العائلات البروتينية التي تنظم دوران الخلية في الخلايا حقيقية النواة

cytokinesis | الحركة الخلوية انقسام الحشوة لتكوين خليتين ابنتين منفصلتين

cytokinin | سايتوكاينين هرمون نباتي ينتج في الجذور النامية وفي الفواكه والبذور المتنامية

cytoplasm | سيتوبلازم بروتين الخلية السائل خارج النواة

cytoskeleton | هيكل الخلية شبكة من الخيوط البروتينية في الخلية حقيقية النواة والتي تعطي للخلية شكلها وتنظيمها الداخلي وتشترك في الحركة

D

data | بيانات أدلة، معلومات يتم جمعها من الملاحظات

deciduous | سلبية مصطلح يستخدم للإشارة إلى نوع من الأشجار تسقط أوراقها خلال فصل معين كل عام

decomposer | محلل كائن حي يحلل ويحصل على الطاقة من مادة عضوية ميتة

deforestation | إزالة الغابات تدمير الغابات

demographic transition | تحول ديموغرافي التغير في السكان من معدلات الولادة والوفاة المرتفعة إلى معدلات الولادة والوفاة المنخفضة

demography | ديموغرافيا الدراسة العلمية للسكان البشريين

dendrite | تغصن تمدد جسم خلية الخلية العصبية الذي يحمل النبضات من البيئة الخارجية أو من الخلايا العصبية الأخرى في اتجاه جسم الخلية

denitrification | تحرير النيتروجين العملية التي تقوم فيها بكتريا التربة بتحويل النيترات إلى غاز النيتروجين

density-dependent limiting factor | عامل محدد قائم على الكثافة عامل محدد يعتمد على الكثافة السكانية

density-independent limiting factor | عامل محدد غير قائم على الكثافة عامل محدد يؤثر في جميع السكان بنفس الأساليب، بغض النظر عن الكثافة السكانية

deoxyribonucleic acid (DNA) | الحامض النووي الوراثي (DNA) المادة الوراثية التي ترثها الكائنات الحية من آبائها

dependent variable | متغير تابع المتغير الذي يتم ملاحظته ويتغير استجابة للمتغير المستقل؛ ويطلق عليه أيضاً المتغير المستجيب

derived character | صفة مشتقة سمة تظهر في الأقسام الحديثة من سلالة ما، ولكنها لا توجد في أعضائها الأقدم

dermis | أدمة طبقة من الجلد توجد تحت البشرة

desertification | تصحر إنتاجية منخفضة للأرض نتيجة للزراعة المفرطة والرعي المفرط، والجفاف الموسمي والتغير المناخي

detritivore | مترمم كائن حي يتغذى على بقايا النبات أو الحيوان والمواد الميتة الأخرى

deuterostome | ثنائي الفم مجموعة من الحيوانات يكون فيها فم الجسترولة شرجاً، ويتكون الفم من الفتحة الثانية التي تنشأ

diaphragm | حجاب حاجز عضلة كبيرة مسطحة في أسفل تجويف الصدر تساعد في عملية التنفس

dicot | ثنائي الفلقة كاسيات البذور لها ورقتا بذور في مبيضها

differentiation | تمايز العملية التي تصبح فيها الخلايا مخصصة في البنية والوظيفة

diffusion | انتشار العملية التي تتجه فيها الجزيئات إلى الانتقال من جهة تتركز فيها تركيزاً أكبر إلى جهة تتركز فيها تركيزاً أقل

digestive tract | قناة هضمية أنبوب يبدأ عند الفم وينتهي عند الشرج

diploid | مضاعف مصطلح يستخدم للخلية التي تحتوي على مجموعتين من الصبغيات المتماثلة

directional selection | انتقاء اتجاهي نوع من الانتقاء الطبيعي يكون فيها للأفراد في أحد طرفي منحنى التوزيع لياقة أعلى من الأفراد في منتصف المنحنى أو الطرف الآخر منه

disruptive selection | انتقاء تمزقي عندما يكون للأفراد في الطرفين الأعلى والأدنى من المنحنى لياقة أعلى من الأفراد بالقرب من منتصف المنحنى

DNA fingerprinting | بصمة الحامض النووي الوراثي أداة يستخدمها علماء الأحياء تحلل المجموع الفريد لشظايا تقييد الحامض النووي الوراثي؛ وتستخدم لتحديد ما إذا كانت عينتان من المادة الوراثية هي من نفس الشخص أم لا

DNA microarray | منظومة ميكرونية للحامض النووي الوراثي شريحة زجاجية أو رقاقة سليكون تحمل الآلاف من شظايا الحامض النووي الوراثي أحادية الحبل مختلفة الأنواع منظمة في شبكة. وتستخدم المنظومة الميكرونية للحامض النووي الوراثي لاكتشاف وقياس تعبير الآلاف من الجينات في وقت واحد

DNA polymerase | بوليميريز الحامض النووي الوراثي إنزيم أساسي متضمن في تناسخ الحامض النووي الوراثي

domain | حقل تصنيف أكبر وأكثر شمولاً من المملكة

dopamine | دوبامين ناقل عصبي يرتبط بمركزي المتعة والثواب بالدماغ

dormancy | هجوع فترة زمنية يكون فيها الجنين النباتي حياً ولكن لا ينمو

double fertilization | إخصاب مضاعف عملية إخصاب في كاسيات البذور ينتج فيه الحدث الأول اللاقحة وينتج الثاني السويداء داخل البذور

E

ecological footprint | أثر بيئي إجمالي حجم الاشتغال الذي احتاجه النظام البيئي ليوفر كلاً من الموارد التي يستخدمها السكان البشر، وليمتص الفضلات التي ينتجها السكان

ecological hot spot | بقعة بيئية ساخنة منطقة بيئية صغيرة يكون فيها عدد كبير من المواطن والأنواع على خطر فوري للانقراض

ecological pyramid | هرم بيئي توضيح لكميات الطاقة أو المادة النسبية المحتواة في كل مستوى غذائي في سلسلة غذائية أو شبكة غذائية معينة

ecological succession | تعاقب بيئي سلسلة من التغيرات التدريجية التي تظهر في مجتمع ما بعد اضطراب

ecology | علم البيئة الدراسة العلمية للتفاعلات بين الكائنات الحية بعضها بعضاً وبين الكائنات الحية وبيئتها

ecosystem | نظام بيئي جميع الكائنات الحية التي تعيش في مكان ما جنباً إلى جنب مع بيئتهم غير الحية

ecosystem diversity | تنوع النظام البيئي تنوع المواطن والمجتمعات والعمليات البيئية في الكرة البيولوجية

ectoderm | أديم ظاهر الطبقة الجرثومية الأبعد؛ تنتج أعضاء الحس، والأعصاب وطبقة الجلد الخارجية

ectotherm | متغير الحرارة حيوان تتحدد درجة حرارته بدرجة حرارة بيئته

electron | إلكترون جزيء سلبي الشحن، يقع في الفضاء المحيط بالنواة

electron transport chain | سلسلة النقل الإلكتروني سلسلة من البروتينات الحاملة للإلكترون والتي تنقل الإلكترونات ذات الطاقة الكبيرة مكوكياً خلال تفاعلات توليد ثلاثي فوسفات الأدينوسين

element | عنصر مادة نقية تتكون بالكامل من نوع واحد من الذرات

embryo | جنين مرحلة نامية من كائن حي متعدد الخلايا

embryo sac | كيس جنيني نابت مشيجي أنثوي داخل بويضة نبات زهري

emerging disease | مرض جديد مرض يظهر في السكان للمرة الأولى، أو مرض قديم تصير السيطرة عليه فجأة أمراً أكثر صعوبة

emigration | هجرة تحرك الأفراد خارج منطقة ما

endocrine gland | غدة صماء غدة تخرج إفرازاتها (الهرمونات) إلى مباشرة إلى الدم الذي ينقل الإفرازات للأجزاء الأخرى من الجسم

endoderm | أديم الباطن الطبقة الجرثومية الأعمق؛ تنمو داخل بطانات القناة الهضمية والكثير من الجهاز التنفسي

endodermis | أدمة باطنية في النباتات، طبقة نسيج أرضي تحيط تماماً بالأسطوانة الوعائية

endoplasmic reticulum | شبكة هيولية باطنة جهاز الغشاء الداخلي الموجود في الخلايا حقيقية النواة؛ المكان الذي تتجمع فيه المكونات الشحمية لغشاء الخلية

endoskeleton | هيكل داخلي هيكل داخلي؛ جهاز دعم هيكلي داخل جسم الحيوان

endosperm | سويداء نسيج غني غذائياً يغذي الشتلة أثناء نموها

endospore | بوغ داخلي هيكل تنتجه بدائيات النواة في ظروف غير مفضلة؛ جدار داخلي سميك يحيط بالحامض النووي الوراثي وبروتين الحشوة

endosymbiotic theory | نظرية تكافلية داخلية نظرية تفترض أن الخلايا حقيقية النواة تشكلت من علاقة تكافلية بين العديد من الخلايا المختلفة بدائيات النواة

endotherm | ثابت الحرارة حيوان درجة حرارة منتظمة، جزئياً على الأقل، مستخدماً حرارة تتولد داخل الجسم

enzyme | إنزيم محفز بروتيني يسرع من معدل تفاعلات بيولوجية معينة

F

epidermis | بشرة في النباتات، طبقة مفردة من الخلايا تكون النسيج البشري؛ في الإنسان، الطبقة الخارجية للجلد

epididymis | بربخ عضو في الجهاز التناسلي الذكري تنضج فيه النطفة وتختزن

epinephrine | إبينيفرين هرمون تنتجه الغدد الكظرية تزيد من سرعة القلب وضغط الدم وتهيئ الجسم للنشاط البدني المكثف؛ يطلق عليه أيضاً اسم الأدرينالين

epithelial tissue | نسيج ظهاري نوع من الأنسجة يبطن السطحين الداخلي والخارجي للجسم

era | عصر تقسيم كبير للزمن الجيولوجي؛ عادة ما يقسم إلى فترتين أو أكثر

esophagus | مريء أنبوب يوصل الفم إلى المعدة

estuary | مصب النهر نوع من المستنقعات والأراضي المبتلة الأخرى حيث يلتقي البحر مع المحيط

ethylene | إيثيلين هرمون نباتي يستثير الفواكه لتنضج

Eukarya | حقيقيات النواة حقل يحتوي على جميع الكائنات الحية التي لها نواة؛ وتشمل وحيدات الخلايا، والنباتات والفطريات والحيوانات

eukaryote | حقيقي النواة كائن حي تحتوي خلاياه على نواة

evolution | تطور التغير بمرور الزمن؛ العملية التي تنحدر من خلالها الكائنات الحية الحديثة من كائنات حية قديمة

excretion | إخراج العملية التي من خلالها تخرج الفضلات الأيضية من الجسم

exocrine gland | غدة إفراز خارجي غدة تخرج إفرازاتها من خلال بنيات تشبه الأنبوب تسمى قنوات، إلى العضو مباشرة أو خارج الجسم

exon | إكسون متوالية الحامض النووي الوراثي التي يرمز إليها؛ شفرات للبروتين

exoskeleton | هيكل خارجي هيكل خارجي؛ غطاء خارجي متين يحمي ويدعم جسم الكثير من اللافقاريات

exponential growth | نمو بمعدل متزايد نموذج نمو يتكاثر فيه الأفراد من السكان بمعدل ثابت

extinct | منقرض مصطلح يستخدم للإشارة إلى الأنواع التي انقرضت وليس لها أعضاء حية

extracellular digestion | هضم خارج الخلية نوع من أنواع الهضم يتحلل فيه الطعام خارج الخلايا في الجهاز الهضمي ثم يمتص بعد ذلك

facilitated diffusion | انتشار ميسر عملية انتشار تمر فيه الجزيئات من خلال الغشاء خلال قنوات غشاء الخلية

family | فصيلة في التصنيف، مجموعة من الأجناس المتشابهة

fat | دهن شحم؛ يتكون من الأحماض الدهنية والجليسرول؛ نوع من الغذاء يحمي أعضاء الجسم، ويعزل الجسم ويخزن الطاقة

feedback inhibition | تثبيط ارتجاعي العملية التي يصدر فيها المنبه استجابة عكس المنبه الأصلي؛ ويطلق عليها أيضاً الارتجاع السلبي

fermentation | تخمر العملية التي تحرر فيها الخلايا الطاقة في غياب الأكسجين

fertilization | إخصاب عملية التكاثر الجنسي التي تتصل فيها الخلايا التناسلية الذكرية والأنثوية لتكون خلية جديدة

fetus | جنين اسم يعطى للمضغة البشرية بعد ثمان أسابيع من النمو

fever | حمى زيادة في درجة حرارة الجسم تظهر كأثر لعدوى

filtration | ترشيح عملية تمرير سائل أو غاز من خلال مرشح لإزالة الفضلات

fitness | جدارة كفاءة الكائن الحي في البقاء والتكاثر في بيئته

flagellum (pl. flagella) | سوط بنية تستخدمها وحيدات الخلايا للحركة؛ تحدث تحركاً يشبه الموج

food chain | السلسلة الغذائية سلسلة الخطوات في النظام البيئي التي تنقل فيه الكائنات الحية الطاقة بأن تأكل وتؤكل

food vacuole | فجوة غذائية فجوة صغيرة في السيتوبلازم في وحيدات الخلايا تخزن الغذاء مؤقتاً

food web | الشبكة الغذائية شبكة تفاعلات معقدة تتشكل بعلاقات التغذية بين الكائنات الحية المتنوعة في نظام بيئي

forensics | الطب الشرعي علم دراسة دليل مسرح الجريمة

fossil | حفرية بقايا محفوظة لكائنات حية قديمة

founder effect | أثر المؤسس تغير تكرارات الأليل نتيجة لهجرة مجموعة فرعية صغيرة من السكان

frameshift mutation | طفرة نزوح الإطار طفرة تنزح «إطار قراءة» الرسالة الوراثية بإدراج النيوكليوتيد أو حفه

fruit | ثمرة بنية في كاسيات البذور تحتوي على مبيض واحد ناضج أو أكثر

fruiting body | جسم مثمر الهيكل التناسلي للفطريات الذي ينمو من الغزل الفطري

gamete | مشيج الخلية الجنسية

gametophyte | نابتة مشيجية نبات ينتج المشيج؛ الطور الفردي متعدد الخلايا لدورة حياة النبات

ganglion (pl. ganglia) | عقدة مجموعة من الخلايا العصبية المتوسطة

gastrovascular cavity | تجويف بطني وعائي حجيرة هضمية بفتحة واحدة

gastrulation | تكون المعدة عملية هجرة الخلية التي ينتج عنها تكون طبقات الخلية الثلاثة وهي الأديم الظاهر، والأديم المتوسط والأديم الباطن

gel electrophoresis | هجرة كهربائية هلامية إجراء يستخدم لفصل وتحليل شظايا الحامض النووي الوراثي بوضع مزيج من شظايا الحامض النووي الوراثي على أحد طرفي هلام مسامي وإعطاء فولت كهربي للهلام

gene | جين تتابع الحامض النووي الوراثي والذي يعطي شفرة للبروتين ومن ثم يحدد السمة؛ عامل ينتقل من أحد الأبوين إلى الذرية

gene expression | التعبير عن الجين العملية التي ينتج فيها الجين منتجه ويقوم المنتج بتنفيذ وظيفته

gene pool | مجموع الجينات جميع الجينات، وتشمل جميع الأليلات المختلفة لكل جين، الموجودة في تجمع سكاني في وقت واحد

gene therapy | علاج بالجينات عملية تغيير جين لعلاج مرض أو اضطراب طبي. غياب الجين المعيب أو استبداله بجين طبيعي يعمل

genetic code | الشفرة الوراثية مجموعة كودونات الحمض الريبي النووي الرسول، والتي يقوم كل واحد منها بتوجيه تضمين حامض أميني معين في البروتين خلال تخليق البروتين

genetic diversity | التنوع الجيني جميع الصور المختلفة للمعلومات الوراثية التي يحملها نوع معين، أو تحملها جميع الكائنات الحية على الأرض

genetic drift | انسياق جيني تغير عشوائي في تكرر الأليل نتيجة لسلسلة من التغيرات التي تحدث وتتسبب في أن يصبح الأليل وإلى حد ما أقل شيوعاً في السكان

genetic equilibrium | توازن جيني الموقف الذي تظل فيه تكرارات الأليل نفسها في السكان

genetic marker | واسم جيني الأليلات التي تنتج اختلافات يمكن تتبعها في الأنماط الظاهرية وتكون مفيدة في التحليل الوراثي

genetics | علم الوراثة الدراسة العلمية للوراثة

genome | مورث إجمالي المعلومات الوراثية التي يحملها الكائن الحي في الحامض النووي الوراثي الخاص به

genomics | علم الجينات دراسة جميع المورثات، والتي تشمل الجينات ووظائفها

genotype | نمط جيني التركيب الوراثي في الكائن الحي

genus | جنس مجموعة من الأنواع التي ترتبط ارتباطاً شديداً؛ الجزء الأول من الاسم العلمي في التسمية الثنائية

geographic isolation | عزل جغرافي نوع من العزل التناسلي ينفصل فيه اثنان من السكان بالحدود الجغرافية مثل الأنهار أو الجبال أو الأجسام المائية، مما يؤدي إلى تكون نوعين فرعيين منفصلين

geologic time scale | مقياس زمني جيولوجي خط زمني يستخدم لتمثيل تاريخ الأرض

germ theory of disease | النظرية الجرثومية للمرض فكرة أن الأمراض المعدية تحدث بسبب الميكروبات

germination | إستنبات استئناف نمو جنين النبات بعد الخمول

giberellin | جيبرلين هرمون نباتي يحفز النمو وقد يؤدي إلى زيادات مثيرة في الحجم

gill | خيشوم بنية ريشية مخصصة لتبادل الغازات مع الماء

global warming | إحماء عالمي زيادة متوسط درجات الحرارة على الأرض

glomerulus | كبيبة شبكة صغيرة من الأوعية الشعرية مغطاة في الطرف العلوي من وحدة الكلى، حيث يحدث ترشيح الدم

glycolysis | تحلل السكر المجموعة الأولى من التفاعلات في التنفس الخلوي حيث يتحلل جزيء الجلوكوز إلى جزيئين من حمض البيروفيك

Golgi apparatus | جهاز جولجي عضية في الخلايا تقوم بتعديل وتصنيف وتعبئة البروتينات والمواد الأخرى من الشبكة الهيولية الباطنة لتخزينها في الخلية أو إطلاقها خارج الخلية

gradualism | تدرج تطور الأنواع بالتراكم التدريجي للتغيرات الوراثية الصغيرة خلال فترات زمنية طويلة

grafting | تطعيم طريقة توالد تستخدم لتكاثر النباتات غير البذرية والعديد من النباتات الخشبية التي لا تستطيع التوالد بسبب القطع

gravitropism | انجذاب استجابة النبات لقوة الجاذبية

green revolution | ثورة خضراء نمو سلالات المحاصيل عالية الإنتاج واستخدام التقنيات الزراعية الحديثة لزيادة إنتاجية المحاصيل الزراعية

greenhouse effect | **تأثير الدفيئة** العملية التي تقوم فيها غازات معينة (ثاني أكسيد الكربون، والميثان، وبخار الماء) بحبس الطاقة الشمسية في جو الأرض كحرارة

growth factor | **عامل النمو** أحد مجموعات البروتينات التنظيمية التي تستحث نمو الخلايا وانقسامها

guard cells | **خلايا الحماية** خلايا مخصصة في بشرة النباتات والتي تتحكم في فتح الفوهات وغلقها

gullet | **مريء** انبعاج في أحد جانبي الهدبة يسمح للطعام بدخول الخلية

gymnosperm | **عارية البذور** مجموعة من النباتات البذرية التي تحمل بذورها مباشرة في قشرات الأكواز

H

habitat | **موطن** المنطقة التي يعيش فيها الكائن الحي وتشمل العوامل الحيوية وغير الحيوية التي تؤثر فيه

habitat fragmentation | **تجزؤ الموطن** انقسام النظم البيئية إلى أجزاء

habituation | **ترويض** طريقة تعلم يقوم فيها الحيوان بتقليل أو إيقاف استجابته لمنبهات متكررة لا تكافئ الحيوان ولا تضره

hair follicle | **جريب الشعرة** جيوب تشبه الأنابيب لخلايا البشرة التي تمتد إلى الأدمة؛ خلايا في قاعدة الجريبات الشعرية تنتج الشعر

half life | **العمر النصفي** طول الزمن المطلوب لنصف الذرات المشعة في عينة لتتحلل

haploid | **فردي** مصطلح مستخدم للإشارة إلى الخلية التي تحتوي على مجموعة واحدة فقط من الجينات

Hardy-Weinberg principle | **قاعدة هاردي-واينبرج** قاعدة تنص على أن تكرار الأليل في السكان يظل ثابتاً إلا أن يتسبب عامل أو أكثر في تغيير هذه التكرارات

Haversian canal | **قناة هافرس** إحدى شبكات الأنابيب التي تمر من خلال العظم المكتنز وتحتوي على أوعية دموية وأعصاب

heart | **قلب** عضو عضلي مجوف يضخ الدم في جميع أنحاء الجسم

heartwood | **خشب قلبي** في السيقان الخشبية، نسيج الخشب الأقدم القريب من مركز الساق والذي لم يعد يوصل الماء

hemoglobin | **هيموجلوبين** بروتين يحتوي على الحديد في خلايا الدم الحمراء يضم الأكسجين وينقله إلى الجسم

herbaceous plant | **نبات عشبي** أحد أنواع النباتات التي لها سيقان ناعمة غير خشبية؛ وتشمل هندباء البر والبطونيات وعباد الشمس

herbivore | **آكل العشب** كائن حي يحصل على الطاقة بتناول النباتات فقط

herbivory | **أكل العشب** تفاعل يقوم فيه أحد الحيوانات (آكل العشب) بالتغذي على محاصيل (مثل النباتات)

heterotroph | **غيري التغذية** كائن حي يحصل على الطعام باستهلاك كائنات حية أخرى؛ يطلق عليه أيضاً المستهلك

heterozygous | **متغاير الزيجوت** له أليلين اثنين مختلفين لجين معين

histamine | **هيستامين** مادة كيميائية تطلقها الخلايا البدينة تزيد من تدفق الدم والسوائل للمنطقة المصابة بالعدوى خلال الاستجابة للالتهاب

homeobox gene | **جين الصندوق المتماثل** الصندوق المتماثل هو تتابع الحامض النووي الوراثي لنحو 130 من أزواج القواعد، ويوجد في الكثير من الجينات المتماثلة التي تنظم النمو. وتعرف الجينات التي تحتوي على هذا التتابع باسم جينات الصندوق المتماثل، وتشفر لعوامل النسخ، البروتينات المرتبطة بالحامض النووي الوراثي وتنظم تعبير باقي الجينات

homeostasis | **اتزان** الظروف الفيزيائية والكيميائية الداخلية الثابتة نسبياً التي يحافظ عليها الكائن الحي

homeotic gene | **جين متماثل** صنف من الجينات التنظيمية تحدد هوية أجزاء ومناطق الجسم في الجنين الحيواني. ويمكن أن تؤدي الطفرات في هذه الجينات إلى تحول جزء من الجسم إلى جزء آخر

hominine | **بشري** السلالة الإنسانية التي تؤدي إلى البشر

hominoid | **إنسان** مجموعة من الإنسانيات التي تتضمن قردة الجبون وإنسان الغاب، والغوريلا والشمبانزي والبشر

homologous | **متماثل** مصطلح يستخدم للإشارة إلى الصبغيات التي تأتي مجموعة منها من الذكر وتأتي مجموعة منها من الأنثى

homologous structures | **تراكيب متماثلة** تراكيب تتشابه في أنواع مختلفة ذات أسلاف مشتركة

homozygous | **زيجوت متماثلة الألائل** له أليلان متطابقان لجين معين

hormone | **هرمون** مادة كيميائية في جزء من الكائن الحي يؤثر في جزء آخر لنفس الكائن الحي

Hox gene | **جين هوكس** مجموعة من الجينات المتماثلة المجتمعة سوياً وتحدد هوية أجزاء الجسم في الحيوانات من الرأس إلى الذيل. وتحتوي كل جينات هوكس على تتابع الحامض النووي الوراثي للصندوق المتماثل

humoral immunity | **مناعة خلطية** المناعة ضد مولدات المضادات في سوائل الجسم، مثل الدم والليمف

humus | **دبال** مادة تتكون من الأوراق البالية والمواد العضوية الأخرى

index fossil | حفرية دالة حفرية مميزة تستخدم لمقارنة الأعمار النسبية للحفريات

infectious disease | مرض معد مرض تتسبب فيه الميكروبات ويخل بالوظائف الطبيعية للجسم

inference | استدلال تفسير منطقي قائم على معرفة وتجربة سابقين

inflammatory response | الاستجابة للالتهاب رد فعل دفاعي غير محدد لتلف النسيج نتيجة لإصابة أو عدوى

innate behavior | سلوك فطري نوع من السلوك يظهر فيه السلوك في شكل وظيفي تماماً في أول مرة يحدث فيها حتى وإن كان الحيوان ليس لديه خبرة سابقة بالمثيرات التي يستجيب لها؛ يسمى أيضاً الغريزة

insight learning | تعلم تبصري نوع سلوكي يطبق فيها الحيوان شيئاً قد تعلمه بالفعل على موقف جديد، دون فترة تجربة وخطأ؛ ويسمى أيضاً استخلاص

interferon | إنترفيرون إحدى مجموعات البروتين التي تساعد الخلية على مقاومة العدوى الفيروسية

interneuron | خلية عصبية متوسطة أحد أنواع الخلايا العصبية تعالج المعلومات وقد تنقل المعلومات إلى الخلايا العصبية الحركية

interphase | طور بيني فترة دورة الخلية بين انقسام الخلية

intracellular digestion | هضم داخل الخلايا أحد أنواع الهضم الذي يهضم فيه الطعام داخل خلايا خاصة تمرر المواد المغذية إلى الخلايا الأخرى بالانتشار

intron | إنترون تتابع الحامض النووي الوراثي لا يشترك في تشفير البروتين

invertebrate | لافقاري حيوان يفتقد إلى العمود الفقري، أو سلسلة الظهر

ion | أيون الذرة التي لها شحنة سلبية أو إيجابية

ionic bond | رابطة أيونية رابطة كيميائية تتكون عندما ينتقل إليكترون أو أكثر من ذرة لأخرى

iris | حدقة الجزء الملون للعين

isotonic | مساوي التوتر عند تساوي تركيز محلولين

isotope | نظير أحد الصور المختلفة للعنصر الواحد، والتي تحتوي على نفس عدد البروتونات ولكن مع اختلاف عدد النيترونات

J

joint | مفصل المكان الذي تتصل فيه إحدى العظام بعظام أخرى

---

hybrid | هجين نسل التهجين بين آباء ذوي سمات مختلفة

hybridization | تهجين تقنية تكاثر تتضمن خلط أفراد غير متشابهين ليوجدوا معاً أفضل سمات كلا الكائنين الحيين

hydrogen bond | رابطة هيدروجينية التجاذب الضعيف بين ذرة هيدروجين وذرة أخرى

hydrostatic skeleton | هيكل هيدروستاتيكي هيكل مصنوع من قطع جسدية مملوءة بالسائل وتعمل مع العضلات للسماح للحيوان بأن يتحرك

hypertonic | أكثر أسموزية عند مقارنة محلولين، المحلول ذو التركيز الأكبر للمذابين

hypha (pl. hyphae) | خيط واحدة من الخيوط الكثيرة الطويلة الرفيعة التي تكون جسم الفطر

hypothalamus | تحت المهاد هيكل المخ الذي يعمل كمركز تحكم لإدراك وتحليل الجوع والعطش والتعب والغضب ودرجة حرارة الجسم

hypothesis | فرضية تفسير محتمل لمجموعة من الملاحظات أو إجابة محتملة لسؤال علمي

hypotonic | منخفض الأسموزية عند مقارنة محلولين، المحلول ذو التركيز الأقل للمذابين

I

immigration | هجرة تحرك الأفراد إلى منطقة يشغلها سكان موجودون

immune response | استجابة مناعية الإدراك والاستجابة والتذكر المحددة للجسم لهجوم كائن ممرض

implantation | زرع العملية التي تلتحق فيها الكيسة الأريمية بجدار الرحم

imprinting | سمة نوع من السلوك يقوم على تجربة مبكرة؛ وبمجرد ظهور السمة، لا يمكن للسلوك أن يتغير

inbreeding | استيلاد داخلي التكاثر المستمر بين الأفراد ذوي الصفات المتشابهة للحفاظ على الصفات المشتقة من نوع من أنواع الكائنات الحية

incomplete dominance | سيادة ناقصة الحالة التي لا يسود فيها أحد الأليلات على أليل آخر سيادة كاملة

independent assortment | تصنيف مستقل أحد قوانين مندل التي تنص على قدرة الجينات ذات السمات المختلفة على الانفصال انفصالاً مستقلاً خلال تكون الأمشاج

independent variable | متغير مستقل العامل في تجربة موجهة الذي يُتعمد تغييره؛ ويطلق عليه أيضاً المتغير المعالَج

light-dependent reactions | تفاعلات قائمة على الضوء مجموعة من التفاعلات في البناء الضوئي تستخدم الطاقة من الضوء لإنتاج ثلاثي فوسفات الأدينوسين و ثنائي نيكليوتيد النيكوتين والأدينين المختزل

light-independent reactions | تفاعلات غير القائمة على الضوء مجموعة من التفاعلات في البناء الضوئي لا تتطلب الضوء؛ وتستخدم الطاقة من ثلاثي فوسفات الأدينوسين و ثنائي نيكليوتيد النيكوتين والأدينين المختزل لبناء مركبات عالية الطاقة مثل السكر؛ ويطلق عليها أيضاً اسم دورة كالفين

lignin | لجنين مادة في النباتات الوعائية تجعل جدران الخلية صلبة

limiting factor | عامل محدد عامل يتسبب في نقصان النمو السكاني

limiting nutrient | مغذ محدد مغذ أساسي واحد يقيد الإنتاج في نظام بيئي

lipid | شحم جزيء كبير يتكون في الغالب من ذرات الكربون والهيدروجين؛ ويشمل الدهون والزيوت والشحوم

lipid bilayer | طبقة مزدوجة شحمية ورقة مرنة مزدوجة الطبقة تبني غشاء الخلية وتكون حاجزاً بين الخلية ومحيطها

logistic growth | نمو إمدادي نموذج نمو يبطأ فيه النمو السكاني ثم يتوقف بعد فترة من النمو بمعدل متزايد

loop of Henle | عروة هينل قسم من أنبوب وحدة الكلى الصغير مسئول عن المحافظة على الماء وتقليل حجم الترشيح

lung | رئة عضو التنفس؛ مكان يتم فيه تبادل الغازات بين الدم والهواء المستنشق

lymph | لمف سائل يترشح خارج الدم

lysogenic infection | عدوى مستذيبة نوع من العدوى يطمر فيه الفيروس الحامض النووي الوراثي الخاص به في خلية الحامض النووي الوراثي المضيف ويتضاعف مع الحامض النووي الوراثي لخلية المضيف

lysosome | يحلول عضي خلية يحلل الشحوم والكربوهيدرات والبروتينات إلى جزيئات صغيرة يمكن أن تقوم بقية الخلية باستخدامها

lytic infection | عدوى حالة نوع من العدوى يدخل فيه الفيروس الخلية، ويصنع نسخاً من نفسه، ويتسبب في انفجار الخلية

M

macroevolution | تطور كبير تغير تطوري كبير المقدار يقع على مدار فترات زمنية طويلة

K

karyotype | نمط نووي صورة مجهرية لمجموعة الصبغيات الثنائية الكاملة المتجمعة سوياً في أزواج، مرتبة لتقليل الحجم

keratin | كيراتين بروتين ليفي صلب يوجد في الجلد

keystone species | نوع حجر أساس نوع مفرد لا يكون وفيراً عادة في مجتمع ما، ولكن يمارس سيطرة قوية على بنية المجتمع

kidney | كلى عضو إخراج يفصل الفضلات والماء الزائد من الدم

kin selection | انتقاء من الأقارب نظرية تنص على أن مساعدة الأقرباء يمكن أن تحسن من اللياقة التطورية نظراً لمشاركة الأفراد الأقارب في نسبة كبيرة من جيناتهم

kingdom | مملكة أكبر مجموعات التصنيف وأكثرها شمولاً

Koch's postulates | مسلمات كوتش مجموعة من الإرشادات التي طورها كوتش تساعد على تحديد الميكروب الذي يتسبب في مرض معين

Krebs cycle | دورة كريبس المرحلة الثانية من التنفس الخلوي الذي يتحلل فيه حمض البيروفيك إلى ثاني أكسيد الكربون في سلسلة من تفاعلات استخراج الطاقة

L

language | لغة نظام للتواصل يجمع الأصوات والرموز والإيماءات طبقاً لمجموعة من القواعد تتعلق بالتسلسل والمعنى مثل النحو وبناء الجملة

large intestine | الأمعاء الغليظة عضو في الجهاز الهضمي يزيل الماء من المواد غير المهضومة التي تمر به؛ ويسمى أيضاً القولون

larva (pl. larvae) | يرقة المرحلة غير الناضجة من الكائن الحي

larynx | حنجرة بنية في الحلق تحتوي على الأحبال الصوتية

learning | تعلم تغيرات في السلوك نتيجة للتجربة

lens | عدسة بنية في العين تركز الأشعة الضوئية على الشبكية

lichen | أشنة ارتباط تكافلي بين فطر وكائن حي ضوئي التخليق

ligament | رباط نسيج ضام صلب يمسك العظام مع بعضه البعض في المفصل

Malpighian tubule | أنبوب مالبيغية صغير بنية في معظم المفصليات الأرضية يركز حمض اليوريك ويضيفه إلى الفضلات المهضومة

mammary gland | غدة ثديية غدة في الثدييات الأنثوية تنتج اللبن لتغذية الصغير

mass extinction | انقراض جماعي حدث تنقرض فيه الكثير من الأنواع خلال فترة زمنية قصيرة نسبياً

matrix | مصفوفة الجزء الأعمق للمتقدرة

mechanical digestion | هضم ميكانيكي التحلل الفيزيائي لقطع كبيرة من الطعام إلى قطع صغيرة

meiosis | انقسام منصف العملية التي ينقسم فيها عدد الصبغيات في الخلية إلى النصف من خلال فصل الصبغيات المتماثلة في الخلية ثنائية الصبغ

melanin | ميلانين صبغ بني داكن في الجلد يساعد على حماية الجلد بامتصاص الأشعة فوق البنفسجية

melanocyte | خلية ميلانينية خلية في الجلد تنتج صبغ بني داكن يسمى الميلانين

menstrual cycle | دورة الحيض التتابع المنتظم للأحداث الذي تنمو فيه البويضة وتتحرر من الجسم

menstruation | حيض تخريج الدم والبويضة غير المخصبة من الجسم

meristem | مرستيمة مناطق الخلايا غير المخصصة المسئولة عن النمو المستمر طوال فترة حياة النبات

mesoderm | أديم متوسط الطبقة الجرثومية المتوسطة؛ تنمو في العضلات والكثير من الجهاز الدوري والتناسلي والإخراجي

mesophyll | نسيج أوسط نسيج أرضي متخصص يوجد في الأوراق؛ ويقوم بمعظم البناء الضوئي للنبات

messenger RNA (mRNA) | حمض ريبي نووي رسول نوع من أنواع الحمض النووي الريبوزي يحمل نسخاً من التعليمات لتجمع الأحماض الأمينية في البروتينات من الحامض النووي الوراثي لباقي الخلية

metabolism | أيض مجموع التفاعلات الكيميائية التي يبني من خلالها الكائن الحي المواد أو يحللها

metamorphosis | تحول عملية التغيرات في الصورة والشكل من يرقة إلى البلوغ

metaphase | مرحلة انتقالية طور الانقسام الفتيلي الذي تصطف فيه الصبغيات عبر مركز الخلية

microclimate | مناخ محلي الظروف البيئية في منطقة صغيرة والتي تختلف اختلافاً كبيراً عن مناخ المنطقة المحيطة

migration | ارتحال السلوك الموسمي الذي ينجم عن الانتقال من بيئة لأخرى

---

mineral | معدني مغذيات غير عضوية يحتاجها الجسم، عادة في كميات صغيرة

mitochondrion | متقدرة عضي خلية يحول الطاقة الكيميائية المخزنة في الغذاء إلى مركبات أكثر ملاءمة للخلية أن تستخدمها

mitosis | انقسام فتيلي جزء من انقسام الخلية حقيقية النواة والتي تنقسم فيها نواة الخلية

mixture | مزيج مادة تتكون من عنصرين أو مركبين أو أكثر تختلط فيزيائياً مع بعضها البعض ولكن دون أن تتحد كيميائياً

molecular clock | ساعة جزيئية طريقة يستخدمها الباحثون تستخدم معدلات الطفرة في الحامض النووي الوراثي لتقدير طول المدة التي استغرقها نوعان في التطور تطوراً مستقلاً

molecule | جزيء أصغر وحدة لمعظم المركبات تستعرض جميع خصائص المركب

molting | انسلاخ عملية طرح هيكل خارجي ونمو هيكل جديد

monocot | أحادي الفلقة كاسيات البذور ذات البذرة الواحدة في مبيضها

monoculture | حراثة أحادية إستراتيجية زراعية لزرع محصول واحد ذي إنتاجية كبيرة عاماً بعد عام

monomer | مونومر وحدة كيميائية صغيرة تكون البوليمر

monophyletic group | مجموعة أحادية السلف مجموعة تتكون من نوع سلفي أحادي وجميع سلالاته وتستبعد أي كائنات حية لا تنحدر من السلف المشترك

monosaccharide | أحادي السكاريد جزيء سكر بسيط

motor neuron | خلية عصبية حركية أحد أنواع الخلية العصبية التي تحمل الاتجاهات من الخلية العصبية المتوسطة إلى الخلايا العضلية أو الغدد

multiple alleles | أليلات متعددة جين له أكثر من أليلين

multipotent | متعددة القدرات خلايا ذات قدرة محدودة على التطور إلى أنواع كثيرة من الخلايا المتمايزة

muscle fiber | ليف عضلي خلايا عضلية هيكلية طويلة ورفيعة

muscle tissue | نسيج عضلي أحد أنواع النسيج الذي يجعل حركات الجسم أمراً ممكناً

mutagen | مطفر عوامل كيميائية أو فيزيائية في البيئة تتفاعل مع الحامض النووي الوراثي وقد تحدث طفرة

mutation | طفرة تغير في المادة الوراثية للخلية

mutualism | تنافع علاقة تكافلية ينتفع فيها كلا النوعين من العلاقة

mycelium (pl. mycelia) | غصين الشبكة المتفرعة الكثيفة لخيوط الفطر

mycorrhiza (pl. mycorrhizae) | تعايش فطري
جذري ارتباط تكافلي لجذور النبات والفطريات

myelin sheath | غمد مياليني غشاء عازل يحيط
بالمحور العصبي في بعض الخلايا العصبية

myocardium | عضل القلب طبقة عضلية وسطى
سميكة للقلب

myofibril | ليفة عضلية حزم خيطية متضامة بإحكام
توجد داخل الألياف العضلية الهيكلية

myosin | ميوزين خيط سميك من البروتين يوجد في
الخلايا العضلية الهيكلية

N

NAD⁺ (nicotinamide adenine dinucleotide) |
ثنائي نيكليوتيد النيكوتين والأدينين + إليكترون
حامل متضمن في تحلل السكر

NADP⁺ (nicotinamide adenine dinucleotide
phosphate) | فوسفات ثنائي نيكليوتيد
النيكوتين والأدينين جزيء حامل يحول الإليكترونيات
عالية الطاقة من الكلوروفيل إلى جزيئات أخرى

natural selection | انتقاء طبيعي العملية التي تبقى
فيها الكائنات الحية الأصلح في بيئتها وتحقق أنجح
تكاثر؛ ويطلق عليه أيضاً البقاء للأصلح

nephridium (pl. nephridia) | كلية الصغيرة
هيكل إفرازي للدودة الحلقية يرشح سوائل الجسم

nephron | وحدة الكلى بنية لتنقية الدم في الكلى
يتم فيها تنقية الشوائب، وجمع الفضلات ويعود الدم
المنقى للدوران

nervous tissue | نسيج عصبي نوع من الأنسجة ينقل
نبضات العصب في جميع أنحاء الجسم

neuromuscular junction | موصل عصبي عضلي
نقطة الاتصال بين الخلية العصبية الحركية وخلية
عضلية هيكلية

neuron | الخلية العصبية الخلية العصبية؛ مخصصة
لنقل الرسائل في جميع أنحاء الجهاز العصبي

neurotransmitter | ناقل عصبي مادة كيميائية
تستخدمها الخلية العصبية لنقل النبضة من خلال نقطة
الاشتباك العصبي إلى خلية أخرى

neurulation | تكون العصبية الخطوة الأولى في نمو
الجهاز العصبي

niche | موضع إجمالي الظروف الفيزيائية والكيميائية
التي يعيش فيها الكائن الحي والطريقة التي يستخدم بها
الكائن الحي تلك الظروف

nitrogen fixation | تثبيت النيتروجين عملية تحويل
غاز النيتروجين إلى مركبات النيتروجين التي يمكن
للنباتات أن تمتصها وتستخدمها

node | عقدة جزء في الساق النامي حيث تتصل الورقة

nondisjunction | عدم الانفصال خطأ في الانقسام
المنصف تفشل فيه الصبغيات المتماثلة في الانفصال
انفصالاً صحيحاً

nonrenewable resource | مورد غير متجدد مورد
لا يمكن إعادة تغذيته بالعملية الطبيعية في وقت مناسب

norepinephrine | نورإبينفرين هرمون تطلقه الغدد
الكظرية يزيد من سرعة القلب وضغط الدم ويعد الجسم
لنشاط بدني مكثف

notochord | حبل ظهري حبل داعم طويل يمر بجسم
الحبليات أسفل الحبل العصبي تماماً

nucleic acid | حمض نووي جزيئات كبيرة تحتوي على
الهيدروجين والأكسجين والنيتروجين والكربون والفسفور

nucleotide | نوكليوتيد وحدة فرعية تتكون منها
الأحماض النووية؛ وتتكون من 5- سكر كربوني
ومجموعة فوسفات وقاعدة نيتروجينية

nucleus | نواة مركز الذرة، والتي تحتوي على البروتونات
والنيترونات ؛ وفي الخلايا، بنية تحتوي على المادة
الوراثية للخلية في صورة حامض نووي وراثي

nutrient | مغذ مادة كيميائية يحتاجها الكائن الحي
للبقاء حياً

nymph | حوراء صورة غير ناضجة للحيوان تشبه هيئة
البلوغ، ولكنها تفتقد إلى الأعضاء الجنسية الوظيفية

O

observation | ملاحظة عملية ملاحظة الأحداث
والعمليات ووصفها بصورة حريصة ومنظمة

omnivore | قارت كائن حي يحصل على الطاقة بتناول
كل من النباتات والحيوانات

open circulatory system | جهاز دوري مفتوح
أحد أنواع الجهاز الدوري يتم فيه احتواء الدم احتواء
جزئياً فقط في نظام من الأوعية الدموية أثناء انتقاله في
جميع أنحاء الجسم

operant conditioning | اشتراط فعال نوع من
التعلم يتعلم فيه الحيوان أن يتصرف بصورة معينة من
خلال الممارسة المتكررة، ليتلقى مكافأة ويتجنب العقاب

operator | مشغل منطقة قصيرة للحامض النووي الوراثي،
ملامسة لمعزز المشغل بدائي النواة، يربط البروتينات
الكابحة المسئولة عن التحكم في معدل نسخ المشغل

operon | مشغل في بدائيات النواة، مجموعة من الجينات المتلامسة تشترك في مشغل ومعزز مشترك وتنسخ إلى حمض ريبي نووي رسول واحد

opposable thumb | إبهام مقابل أصبع إبهام يمكن من الإمساك بالأشياء واستخدام الأدوات

order | رتبة في التصنيف، مجموعة من العائلات التي تتصل اتصالاً لصيقاً

organ | عضو مجموعات من الأنسجة تعمل سوياً لأداء وظائف ترتبط ببعضها البعض ارتباطاً لصيقاً

organ system | جهاز عضوي مجموعة من الأعضاء تعمل سوياً لأداء وظيفة معينة

organelle | عضي بنية مخصصة تؤدي وظائف خلوية هامة في الخلية حقيقية النواة

osmosis | تناضح انتشار المياه خلال غشاء نافذ بصورة انتقائية

osmotic pressure | ضغط أزموزي الضغط الذي يجب أن يطبق لمنع الحركة الأزموزية خلال غشاء نافذ بصورة انتقائية

ossification | تعظم عملية تكوين العظام والذي يتم خلالها استبدال الغضروف بالعظم

osteoblast | بانية العظم الخلية العظمية التي تفرز رواسب معدنية تحل محل الغضروف في العظام النامية

osteoclast | ناقضة العظم خلية عظمية تحلل المعادن الموجودة في العظم

osteocyte | خلية عظمية خلية عظمية تساعد على إبقاء المعادن في النسيج العظمي والاستمرار في تقوية العظم النامي

ovary | مبيض في النباتات، البنية التي تحيط بالبذور وتحميها؛ في الحيوانات، عضو التناسل الأنثوي الأول ؛ ينتج البويضات

oviparous | بيوض نوع تنمو فيه الأجنة في البيض خارج جسم الأم

ovoviparous | بيوض ولود نوع تنمو فيه الأجنة داخل جسم الأم، ولكن تعتمد بالكلية على الكيس المحي لبيضاتها

ovulation | تبويض إطلاق البويضة الناضجة من المبيض إلى إحدى قناتي فالوب

ovule | بييضة بنية في أكواز البذور تنمو فيه النابتات المشيجية الأنثوية

ozone layer | طبقة الأوزون طبقة جوية يتركز فيها غاز الأوزون نسبياً؛ وتحمي الحياة على الأرض من الأشعة فوق البنفسجية الضارة من الشمس

pacemaker | منظم القلب مجموعة صغيرة من الألياف العضلية القلبية تحافظ على نظم ضخ القلب بإعداد معدل انقباض القلب؛ العقدة الجيبية الأذينية

paleontologist | عالم الدراسات القديمة العالم الذي يدرس الحفريات

palisade mesophyll | نسيج أوسط سياجي طبقة خلايا تحت البشرة العليا للورقة

parasitism | تطفل علاقة تكافلية يعيش فيها كائن حي على كائن حي آخر أو داخله ويصيبه بالأذى

parathyroid hormone (PTH) | هرمون جار درقي هرمون تفرزه الغدة الجار درقية تزيد من مستويات الكالسيوم في الدم

parenchyma | نسيج حشوي النوع الأساسي من النسيج الأرضي في النباتات ويحتوي على خلايا ذات جدران خلوية رقيقة وفجوات مركزية كبيرة

passive immunity | مناعة سلبية مناعة مؤقتة تنشأ كنتيجة للتعرض الطبيعي أو المتعمد لأحد المستضدات

pathogen | ممرض عامل مسبب للمرض

pedigree | شجرة النسب مخطط يظهر وجود أو غياب سمة ما طبقاً للعلاقات الموجودة في العائلة خلال العديد من الأجيال

pepsin | بيبسين إنزيم يحلل البروتينات إلى أجزاء عديدة البيبتيد أصغر

period | فترة قسم للوقت الجيولوجي يقسم داخله العصر تقسيماً فرعياً

peripheral nervous system | جهاز عصبي محيطي شبكة الأعصاب والخلايا الداعمة التي تحمل الإشارات إلى وخارج الجهاز العصبي المركزي

peristalsis | تمعج تقلصات العضلات الملساء توفر القوة التي تحرك الطعام خلال المريء إلى المعدة

permafrost | جليد سرمدي طبقة من التربة السفلى الجليدية الدائمة توجد في منطقة التندرا

petiole | سويقة ساق رفيعة تربط نصل الورقة بالساق

pH scale | مقياس جهد أيون الهيدروجين مقياس بقيم من صفر إلى 14، يستخدم لقياس تركيز أيونات الهيدروجين الموجب في المحلول. جهد أيون الهيدروجين من صفر إلى 7 يكون حمضياً، وجهد أيون الهيدروجين يساوي 7 يكون محايداً وجهد أيون الهيدروجين من 7 إلى 14 يكون قلوياً .

pharyngeal pouch | جيب بلعومي أحد زوجي بنيتين في منطقة الحلق في الفقاريات

pharynx | بلعوم قناة في مؤخرة الفم يعمل كممر لكل من الهواء والطعام؛ ويسمى أيضاً الحلق

phenotype | نمط ظاهري صفات فيزيائية للكائن الحي

phloem | لحاء نسيج وعائي ينقل المحاليل والغذاء والكربوهيدرات التي تنتج من البناء الضوئي عبر النبات

photic zone | منطقة ضوئية منطقة ضوء الشمس القريبة من سطح الماء

photoperiod | فترة التعرض للضوء استجابة النبات للطولين النسبيين للضوء والظلام

photosynthesis | بناء ضوئي العملية التي تستخدمها النباتات وذاتيات التغذية لالتقاط الطاقة الضوئية واستخدامها لتقوية التفاعلات الكيميائية التي تحول ثاني أكسيد الكربون والماء إلى هيدروجين وكربوهيدرات غنية بالطاقة مثل السكر والنشا

photosystem | نظام ضوئي مجموعة من الكلوروفيل والبروتينات توجد في الثيلاكويدات

phototropism | توجه ضوئي ميل النبات للنمو نحو مصدر الضوء

phylogeny | علم تطور السلالات دراسة العلاقات التطورية بين الكائنات الحية

phylum | شعبة في التصنيف، مجموعة من الأصناف شديدة الصلة

phytoplankton | عوالق نباتية طحالب ضوئية البناء توجد بالقرب من سطح المحيط

pigment | صبغ جزيئات تمتص الضوء تستخدم في النباتات مع الطاقة الشمسية

pioneer species | نوع رائد النوع الأول الذي يسكن في منطقة خلال الاستخلاف

pistil | متاع خباء مفرد أو مجموعة خباءات مندمجة؛ تحتوي على المبيض والقلم والميسم

pith | لب خلايا النسيج الحشوي داخل حلقة النسيج الوعائي في سيقان النباتات ثنائية الفلقة

pituitary gland | غدة نخامية غدة صغيرة توجد بالقرب من قاعدة الجمجمة تفرز هرمونات تنظم العديد من وظائف الجسم تنظيماً مباشراً وتتحكم في أفعال العديد من الغدد الصماء

placenta | مشيمة عضو متخصص في الثدييات المشيمية والذي يتم خلاله تبادل الغازات والمواد الغذائية والفضلات بين الأم وصغيرها النامي

plankton | عوالق كائنات حية ميكروسكوبية تعيش في البيئات المائية؛ وتشمل كل من العوالق النباتية والعوالق الحيوانية

plasma | بلازما بروتين الدم السائل ذو اللون الأصفر

plasmid | بلازميد قطعة صغيرة ودائرية من بروتين الحامض النووي الوراثي يقع في حشوة الكثير من البكتيريا

plasmodium | رغوي مرحلة التغذية الأميبية في دورة حياة العفن الغروي الرغوي

plate tectonics | الصفائح التكتونية عمليات جيولوجية، مثل الانجراف القاري، والبراكين، والزلازل والتي تنتج من حركة الطبقات

platelet | صفيحة دموية شظية خلوية يطلقها نخاع العظام وتساعد في تجلط الدم

pluripotent | متعدد القدرات خلايا قادرة على التطور إلى معظم أنواع خلايا الجسد ولكن ليس جميعها

point mutation | طفرة نقطية طفرة جينية يتغير فيها واحد من زوج القواعد في الحامض النووي الوراثي

pollen grain | حبوب اللقاح بنية تحتوي على جميع النابت المشيجي الذكري في النباتات البذرية

pollen tube | أنبوب اللقاح بنية في النبات تحتوي على نواتي نطفتين فرديتين

pollination | تلقيح نقل اللقاح من البنية التناسلية الذكرية للبنية التناسلية الأنثوية

pollutant | ملوث مادة ضارة يمكن أن تدخل إلى الكرة البيولوجية من خلال الأرض أو الجو أو الماء

polygenic trait | سمة متعددة الجينات سمة يتحكم فيها جينان أو أكثر

polymer | بوليمر جزيئات تتكون من العديد من المونيمرات؛ وتكون الجزيئات الكبيرة

polymerase chain reaction (PCR) | تفاعل سلسلة البوليميريز التقنية التي يستخدمها علماء الأحياء لصنع العديد من النسخ من جين معين

polypeptide | عديد البيبتيد سلسلة طويلة من الأحماض الأمينية التي تصنع البروتينات

polyploidy | تعدد الصيغ الصبغية الحالة التي يكون فيها للكائن الحي المزيد من مجموعات الصبغيات

population | سكان مجموع الأفراد من نفس النوع الذين يعيشون في نفس المنطقة

population density | كثافة سكانية عدد الأفراد لكل منطقة تمثل وحدة

predation | افتراس تفاعل يقوم فيه كائن حي (المفترس) بالإمساك بكائن حي آخر (الفريسة) والتغذي عليه

prehensile tail | ذيل ممسك ذيل طويل يمكن أن يلف بإحكام كاف حول فرع

pressure-flow hypothesis | افتراضية تدفق الضغط افتراضية تشرح طريقة انتقال عصارة اللحاء من خلال النبات من «مصدر» سكر إلى «حوض» سكر

primary growth | نمو أولي نموذج نمو يقع في قمم وبراعم النبات

primary producer | منتج أولي أول منتجين للمركبات الغنية بالطاقة والتي تستخدمها كائنات حية أخرى فيما بعد

primary succession | تعاقب أولي التعاقب الذي يظهر في منطقة لا يوجد فيها أثر لمجتمع سابق

principle of dominance | مبدأ السيادة استنتاج مندل الثاني والذي ينص على أن بعض الأليلات سائدة وبعضها متنح

prion | بريون الجسيمات البروتينية التي تسبب المرض

probability | احتمالية إمكانية وقوع حدث معين

product | منتج العناصر أو المركبات الناتجة من تفاعل كيميائي

prokaryote | بدائي النواة الكائن الحي وحيد الخلية الذي يفتقد إلى نواة

promoter | معزز منطقة معينة في الجين حيث يمكن لبوليميريز الحامض الريبي النووي أن ترتبط وتبدأ في التناسخ

prophage | طليعة ملتهم الجراثيم الحامض النووي الوراثي لملتهم الجراثيم الذي ينغرس في الحامض النووي الوراثي للمضيف البكتيري

prophase | طور أول أول وأطول طور في الانقسام الفتيلي حيث تتكثف المادة الوراثية داخل النواة وتصبح الصبغيات مرئية

prostaglandin | بروستاجلاندين أحماض دهنية معدلة تنتجها الكثير من الخلايا؛ وتؤثر عموماً في الخلايا والأنسجة القريبة منها فحسب

protein | بروتين جزيء كبير يحتوي على الكربون والهيدروجين والأكسجين والنيتروجين؛ يحتاجه الجسم للنمو والإصلاح

protostome | مسمي الفم حيوان يتكون فمه من فم الجسترولة

pseudocoelom | تجويف عام كاذب تجويف جسدي، ينتظم مع الأديم المتوسط انتظاماً جزئياً فقط

pseudopod | قدم كاذبة نتوء حشوي مؤقت تستخدمه بعض وحيدات الخلية في الحركة

puberty | بلوغ فترة نمو سريع ونضوج جنسي يؤدي خلالها الجهاز التناسلي وظيفته بالكامل

pulmonary circulation | دوران رئوي مسار للدوران بين القلب والرئتين

punctuated equilibrium | توازن مرقم نموذج تطور تنقطع فيه فترات طويلة من الاستقرار بفترات قصيرة من التغير الأسرع

Punnett square | مربع بانيت مخطط يمكن استخدامه للتنبؤ باتحادات النمط الجيني والنمط الظاهري للهجين الوراثي

pupa | شرنقة مرحلة في التحول الكامل تتطور فيه اليرقة إلى مرحلة البلوغ

pupil | بؤبؤ فتحة صغيرة في الحدقة تسمح بدخول الضوء إلى العين

R

radial symmetry | تناظر شعاعي خطة الجسم والتي يمكن فيها لأي أسطح تخيلية ترسم خلال مركز الجسم أن تقسمه إلى نصفين متساويين

radiometric dating | تأريخ بالقياس الإشعاعي طريقة لتحديد عمر عينة من كمية النظير المشع إلى النظير غير المشع لنفس العنصر في العينة

reabsorption | إعادة الامتصاص العملية التي ترجع فيها المياه والمواد الذائبة إلى الدم مرة أخرى

reactant | متفاعل العناصر أو المركبات التي تدخل في التفاعل الكيميائي

receptor | مستقبل على أو في الخلية، بروتين معين يتناسب شكله مع شكل رسول جزيئي مثل الهرمون

recombinant DNA | حامض نووي وراثي مركب حامض نووي وراثي منتج بتجميع حامض نووي وراثي من مصادر مختلفة

red blood cell | خلية الدم الحمراء خلية دموية تحتوي على الهيموجلوبين الذي يحمل الأكسجين

reflex | انعكاس استجابة سريعة وتلقائية لمثير

reflex arc | قوس انعكاسي المستقبل الحسي والخلية العصبية الحسية والمؤثر التي تشترك في الاستجابة السريعة للمنبه

relative dating | تأريخ نسبي طريقة لتحديد عمر الحفرية بمقارنة وضعها بوضع الحفريات في الطبقات الصخرية الأخرى

relative frequency | تردد نسبي عدد المرات التي يظهر فيها الأليل في مجموع الجينات مقارنة بعدد مرات ظهور الأليلات الأخرى لنفس الجين

releasing hormone | هرمون مطلق هرمون يطلقه الوطاء، تصنع الهرمونات المفرزة النخامية الأمامية

renewable resource | مورد متجددة مورد يمكن أن تنتجه أو تحل محله الوظائف الصحية للنظام البيئي

replication | نسخ عملية نسخ الحامض النووي الوراثي قبل انقسام الخلية

sapwood | خشب العصارة في الساق الخشبية، طبقة اللحاء الثانوي التي تحيط بالخشب القلبي؛ عادة ما تنشط في نقل السوائل

sarcomere | قصيم عضلي وحدة انقباض القلب؛ تتكون من خطي z والخيوط التي بينهما

scavenger | قمام حيوان يستهلك جثث الحيوانات الأخرى

science | علوم طريقة منظمة لجمع وتحليل الشواهد حول العالم الطبيعي

sclerenchyma | نسيج خشبي أحد أنواع النسيج الأرضي له جدران خلية سميكة وصلبة للغاية ويجعل النسيج الأرضي صلباً وقوياً

scrotum | صفن الكيس الخارجي الذي يستضيف الخصيتين

sebaceous gland | غدة دهنية غدة في الجلد تفرز الزهم (إفراز زيتي)

secondary growth | نمو ثانوي أحد أنواع النمو في ثنائيات الفلقة تزيد فيه السيقان في السمك

secondary succession | تعاقب ثانوي أحد أنواع التعاقب يظهر في منطقة مزقتها الاضطرابات تمزيقاً جزئياً فحسب

seed | بذرة جنين النبات ومزود غذائي يغطى في غطاء وقائي

seed coat | غطاء البذرة غطاء صلب يحيط بالجنين النباتي ويحميه ويحفظ محتويات البذرة من الجفاف

segregation | فصل فصل الأليلات خلال تكوين المشيج

selective breeding | تكاثر انتقائي طريقة للتكاثر تسمح فقط لتلك الكائنات الحية ذات الصفات المرغوب فيها لإنتاج الجيل التالي

selectively permeable | نافذ بانتقاء خاصية للأغشية البيولوجية تسمح لبعض المواد بأن تمر من خلالها بينما لا تستطيع غيرها من المواد أن تمر؛ ويسمى أيضاً بالغشاء شبه النافذ

semen | مني مجموع الحيوان المنوي والسائل المنوي

semicircular canal | قناة شبه دائرية إحدى هياكل ثلاثة في الأذن الداخلية تراقب موقف الجسم بالنسبة للجاذبية

seminiferous tubule | القناة المنوية واحد من مئات الأنابيب الصغيرة في كل خصية ينمو فيها الحيوان المنوي

sensory neuron | خلية عصبية حسية نوع من الخلايا العصبية التي تتلقى المعلومات من المستقبلات الحسية وتوصل الإشارات للجهاز العصبي المركزي

sex chromosome | صبغ جنسي أحد الصبغين اللذين يحددا جنس الفرد

reproductive isolation | عزل تناسلي فصل الأنواع أو السكان بحيث لا تتزاوج فيما بينها وتتطور إلى نوعين منفصلين

resource | مورد أي ضرورة من ضروريات الحياة، مثل الماء والمواد الغذائية والضوء والطعام والفضاء

response | استجابة رد فعل محدد لمنبه

resting potential | جهد الراحة شحنة كهربائية عبر غشاء الخلية للخلية العصبية للراحة

restriction enzyme | إنزيم الاقتطاع إنزيم يقطع الحامض النووي الوراثي في تتابع النيوكليوتيدات

retina | شبكية الطبقة الأعمق للعين؛ تحتوي على مستقبلات الضوء

retrovirus | فيروس قهقري فيروس الحمض النووي الريبوزي الذي يحتوي على الحمض النووي الريبوزي كمعلوماته الوراثية

ribonucleic acid (RNA) | حمض ريبي نووي (RNA) حمض نووي مفرد السلسلة يحتوي على ريبوز السكر

ribosomal RNA (rRNA) | حمض نووي ريبوزي ريباسي أحد أنواع الحمض النووي الريبوزي والذي يجتمع مع البروتينات لتشكيل الريبوسومات

ribosome | ريبوسوم عضيّ خلية يتكون من الحمض النووي الريبوزي والبروتينات ويوجد في جميع أنحاء الحشوة في الخلية؛ موضع تخليق البروتين

RNA interference (RNAi) | تداخل الحمض النووي الريبوزي إدخال حمض نووي ريبوزي مزدوج المعيار إلى الخلية لتثبيط تعبير اللجين

RNA polymerase | بوليميريز الحمض النووي الريبوزي إنزيم يربط السلسلة النامية لنيوكلوتيدات الحمض النووي الريبوزي معاً خلال عملية النسخ مستخدماً معيار الحامض النووي الوراثي كقالب معياري

rod | نبوت مستقبلة ضوئية في العينين ذات حساسية للضوء، ولكنها لا تستطيع تمييز الألوان

root cap | غطاء الجذر غطاء صلب لطرف الجذر تحمي المرستيمة

root hair | شعر الجذر شعيرات صغيرة في الجذر تحدث منطقة سطحية كبيرة تستطيع المياه والمعادن أن تدخل من خلالها

rumen | كرش غرفة المعدة في البقر والحيوانات ذات العلاقة تهضم فيها البكتريا المتعايشة السلولوز

sex-linked gene | جين مرتبط بالجنس جين يقع على الصبغ الجنسي

sexual reproduction | تكاثر جنسي أحد أنواع التكاثر تتحد فيها خلايا الأبوين لتكوين أول خلية للكائن الحي الجديد

sexually transmitted disease (STD) | مرض منقول جنسياً مرض ينتشر من شخص لشخص بالاتصال الجنسي

sieve tube element | عنصر الأنبوب المنخلي أنبوب مستمر خلال خلايا لحاء النبات، مرتبة نهاية لنهاية

single-gene trait | سمة أحادية الجين سمة يتحكم فيها جين واحد له أليلان اثنان

small intestine | الأمعاء الغليظة عضو هضمي يقع فيه معظم الهضم الكيميائي وامتصاص الطعام

smog | ضباب دخاني غشاوة ذات لون رمادي-بني تتكون من خلط المواد الكيميائية

society | مجتمع مجموعة من الحيوانات من نفس النوع ذات الصلة اللصيقة والتي تعمل سوياً لمصلحة الجماعة

solute | مذاب المادة التي تذوب في المحلول

solution | محلول نوع من الخليط تكون فيه جميع المكونات موزعة توزيعاً متساوياً

solvent | مذيب المادة المذيبة في المحلول

somatic nervous system | جهاز عصبي جسدي جزء من الجهاز العصبي المحيطي يحمل الإشارات من العضلات الهيكلية وإليها

speciation | تكون الأنواع تكون نوع جديد

species diversity | تنوع الأنواع عدد الأنواع المختلفة التي تكون منطقة معينة

spirillum (pl. spirilla) | حلزونية بدائية نواة على شكل حلزوني أو لولبي

spongy mesophyll | نسيج أوسط إسفنجي طبقة نسيج رخو توجد تحت النسيج الأوسط السياجي في الورقة

sporangium (pl. sporangia) | كيس بوغي كبسولة بوغية ينتج فيها الانقسام المنصف بويغات فردية

spore | بوغ في وحيدات الخلية وبدائيات النواة والفطريات، أي من مراحل دورة الحياة سميكة الجدار القادرة على البقاء في ظروف غير مفضلة ؛ في النباتات، خلية تناسلية فردية

sporophyte | نابت بوغي نبات منتج للبوغ؛ الطور الفردي متعدد الخلايا لدورة حياة النبات

stabilizing selection | انتقاء تثبيتي أحد صور الانتقاء الطبيعي التي يكون فيها للأفراد بالقرب من مركز منحنى التوزيع لياقة أعلى من الأفراد في أي من طرفي المنحنى

stamen | سداة الجزء الذكري للزهرة؛ تحتوي على المئبر والخيط

stem cell | خلية جذعية خلية غير متخصصة تستطيع أن تحدث نوعاً أو أكثر من الخلايا المتخصصة

stigma | ميسم جزء لزج في قمة القلم؛ متخصص في التقاط اللقاح

stimulus (pl. stimuli) | منبه إشارة يستجيب إليها الكائن الحي

stoma (pl. stomata) | ثغير فتحة صغيرة في بشرة النبات تسمح بانتشار ثاني أكسيد الكربون والماء والأكسجين من الورقة وإليها

stomach | معدة كيس عضلي كبير يواصل الهضم الميكانيكي والكيميائي للطعام

stroma | نير بروتين سائل في حبيبة الكلوروفيل؛ خارج الثايلاكويدات

substrate | ركيزة متفاعل لتفاعل يحفزه الإنزيم

suspension | مستعلق مزيج من الماء ومادة غير ذائبة

sustainable development | تنمية مستدامة استراتيجية لاستخدام الموارد الطبيعية دون استنزافها ولتوفير الاحتياجات البشرية دون إلحاق ضرر طويل المدى بالبيئة

symbiosis | تكافل علاقة يعيش فيها نوعان بالقرب من بعضهما البعض

synapse | نقطة الاشتباك العصبي النقطة التي يمكن عندها للخلية العصبية أن تنقل النبضة إلى خلية أخرى

systematics | علم التصنيف دراسة تنوع الحياة والعلاقات التطورية بين الكائنات الحية

systemic circulation | دوران مجموعي مسار دوران بين القلب وبقية الجسم

T

taiga | تيجة بيوم بشتاء طويل بارد وأشهر قليلة ذات جو دافئ؛ تسود فيها الخضرة الدائمة الصنوبرية؛ وتسمى أيضا بالغابة الشمالية

target cell | خلية مستهدفة خلية لها متلق لهرمون معين

taste bud | حليمة الذوق أعضاء الحس التي تكتشف المذاق

taxon (pl. taxa) | صنف مجموعة أو مستوى من التنظيم تصنف فيه الكائنات الحية

telomere | جزء طرفي الحامض النووي الوراثي المتكرر في نهاية الصبغ حقيقي النواة

telophase | طور نهائي طور الانقسام الفتيلي والذي فيه تبدأ الصبغيات الفردية المميزة في الانتشار داخل كتلة متشابكة من الكروماتين

temporal isolation | عزل زمني صورة للعزل التناسلي يتناسل فيه نوعان أو أكثر في أوقات مختلفة

tendon | وتر نسيج ضام صلب يصل العضلات الهيكلية بالعظام

territory | إقليم منطقة محددة يشغلها ويحميها حيوان أو مجموعة من الحيوانات

testis (pl. testes) | خصية عضو التناسل الذكري الأساسي؛ ينتج الحيوانات المنوية

tetrad | رباعية بنية تتكون من أربع شقات صبغية تتشكل أثناء الانقسام المنصف

tetrapod | رباعي الأرجل حيوان فقاري له أربعة أطراف

thalamus | مهاد هيكل المخ الذي يتلقى الرسائل من أعضاء الحس وينقل المعلومات إلى منطقة الدماغ المناسبة للمزيد من المعالجة

theory | نظرية تفسير مختبر جيداً يوحد مجموعة كبيرة من الملاحظات والفرضيات ويمكن العلماء من التبنؤ الدقيق بالمواقف الجديدة

thigmotropism | توجه باللمس استجابة النبات للمس

threshold | حد الحد الأدنى من المنبهات المطلوبة لإحداث نبضة

thylakoid | ثيلاكويد أغشية بنائية الضوء تشبه الكيس توجد في حبيبات الكلوروفيل

thyroxine | ثيروكسين هرمون تنتجه الغدة الدرقية، يزيد من المعدل الأيضي للخلايا في جميع أنحاء الجسم

tissue | نسيج مجموعة من الخلايا المتشابهة تؤدي وظيفة معينة

tolerance | تحمل قدرة الكائن الحي على البقاء والتكاثر في ظل الظروف التي تختلف عن ظروفه المثلى

totipotent | كلية الوسع خلايا قادرة على التطور إلى أي نوع من أنواع الخلايا الموجودة في الجسم (ويشمل ذلك الخلايا التي تكون الأغشية الظاهرة للجنين والمشيمة)

trachea | قصبة هوائية قناة تصل الحلق إلى الحنجرة؛ ويطلق عليه أيضاً اسم رغامى

tracheid | قصيبة خلية نباتية مجوفة في نسيج الخشب ذات جدران سميكة للخلية يقويها اللجنين

tracheophyte | تراشيوفايت نبات وعائي

trait | سمة صفة مميزة للفرد

transcription | نسخ تركيب جزيء الحمض النووي الريبوزي من قالب الحامض النووي الوراثي المعياري

transfer RNA (tRNA) | حمض نووي ريبوزي ناقل أحد أنواع الحمض النووي الريبوزي التي تنقل كل حمض أميني إلى الريبوسوم خلال تخليق البروتين

transformation | تحول عملية تغير أحد سلالات البكتيريا بجين أو جينات من سلالة بكتيرية أخرى

transgenic | محور جينياً مصطلح يستخدم للإشارة إلى كائن حي يحتوي على جينات من كائنات حية أخرى

translation | ترجمة عملية تحول تتابع قواعد الحمض النووي الريبي الرسول إلى تتابع للأحماض الأمينية لبروتين

transpiration | نتح فقدان النبات للمياه من خلال أوراقه

trochophore | حاملة الدائرة مرحلة يرقية حرة السباحة للرخويات المائية

trophic level | مرحلة غذائية كل خطوة في السلسلة الغذائية أو الشبكة الغذائية

tropism | توجه حركة النبات تجاه المنبه أو بعيداً عنه

tumor | ورم كتلة من الخلايا سريعة الانقسام يمكن أن تدمر النسيج المحيط

U

understory | طبقة تحتية طبقة في غابة مطرية توجد تحت الظلة وتتكون من الشجر والكرم القصير

ureter | حالب قناة تحمل البول من الكلية إلى المثانة البولية

urethra | إحليل قناة يترك البول من خلالها الجسد

urinary bladder | مثانة بولية عضو يشبه الكيس يخزن فيه البول قبل إخراجه

V

vaccination | تلقيح حقن ممرض ضعيف أو شبيه به ولكن أقل خطورة لإحداث مناعة

vaccine | لقاح إعداد كائنات ممرضة ضعيفة أو مقتولة لإحداث مناعة ضد المرض

vacuole | فجوة عضي خلوي يخزن المواد مثل الماء والأملاح والبروتينات والكربوهيدرات

valve | صمام مصراع للنسيج الضام يقع بين الأذين والبطين أو في الوريد، يمنع ارتجاع الدم

van der Waals forces | قوى فان دير فالس الجاذبية الطفيفة التي تنشأ بين منطقتين ذواتا شحنتين عكسيتين في الجزيئات القريبة

vas deferens | قناة دافقة قناة تحمل الحيوانات المنوية من البربخ إلى الإحليل

vascular bundle | حزمة وعائية تجمعات نسيج الخشب واللحاء في السيقان

W

weather | طقس الأحوال الجوية للغلاف الجوي، وتشمل درجة الحرارة والترسيب وعوامل أخرى

wetland | أرض مبتلة نظام بيئي يغطي فيه الماء التربة أو يكون موجوداً على السطح أو قريباً منه لما لا يقل عن جزء من العام

white blood cell | خلية الدم البيضاء أحد أنواع الخلايا الدموية تحمي ضد العدوى وتحارب الطفيليات وتهاجم البكتريا

woody plant | نبات خشبي أحد أنواع النباتات والتي تتكون في الأساس من الخلايا ولها جدران خلوية سميكة تدعم جسم النبات؛ وتشمل الأشجار والشجيرات والكرم

X

xylem | نسيج الخشب نسيج وعائي يحمل الماء من الجذور إلى أعلى لكل جزء من أجزاء النبات

Z

zoonosis (pl. zoonoses) | مرض حيواني مصدر مرض ينقله الحيوان إلى الإنسان

zooplankton | عوالق حيوانية حيوانات صغيرة طافية تمثل جزءً من العوالق

zygote | مشيج بويضة مخصبة

vascular cambium | قُلب وعائي مرستيمة تنتج أنسجة وعائية وتزيد من سمك السيقان

vascular cylinder | أسطوانة وعائية منطقة وسطى للجذر تشمل الأنسجة الوعائية – نسيج الخشب واللحاء

vascular tissue | نسيج وعائي نسيج مخصص في النباتات يحمل الماء والمواد الغذائية

vector | ناقل حيوان ينقل الكائن الممرض للإنسان

vegetative reproduction | تكاثر نباتي طريقة تكاثر غير جنسية في النباتات، تمكن النبات المفرد من إنتاج نسل مطابق له وراثياً

vein | وريد وعاء دموي يحمل الدم من الجسم إلى القلب مرة أخرى

ventricle | بطين الحجرة السفلية للقلب والتي تضخ الدم خارج القلب إلى باقي الجسم

vertebrate | فقاري حيوان له عمود فقري

vessel element | عنصر وعاء أحد أنواع نسيج الخشب والذي يشكل جزءً من أنبوب مستمر يمكن للماء أن ينتقل من خلالها

vestigial organs | أعضاء أثرية بنيات ذات حجم مصغر ولها وظيفة قليلة أو غير ذات وظيفة

villus (pl. villi) | زغبة نتوء يشبه الإصبع في الأمعاء الدقيقة تساعد على امتصاص الجزيئات المغذية

virus | فيروس جسيم يتكون من البروتينات والأحماض النووية وأحياناً الشحوم، يمكن أن تتضاعف عند إصابة خلايا حية فقط

vitamin | فيتامين جزيء عضوي يساعد على تنظيم عمليات الجسم

viviparous | ولود حيوانات تحمل صغاراً أحياء تغذى مباشرة من جسم الأم أثناء نموها

Brazilian Portuguese
Português Brasileiro

Miller & Levine
Biology Glossary

A

abiotic factor | fator abiótico fator físico ou não-vivo que dá forma a um ecossistema

abscisic acid | ácido abcísico fitohormônio que inibe a divisão da célula e, portanto, o crescimento

acetylcholine | acetilcolina neurotransmissor que produz um impulso numa célula muscular

acid | ácido composto que forma íons hidrogênicos (H^+) na solução; solução com pH inferior a 7

acid rain | chuva ácida chuva que contém ácidos nítrico e sulfúrico

actin | actina filamento delgado de proteína encontrado nos músculos

action potential | potencial de ação reversão de cargas através da membrana celular de um neurônio; conhecida também como um impulso nervoso

activation energy | energia de ativação energia necessária à obtenção da reação iniciada

active immunity | imunidade ativa imunidade que se desenvolve em decorrência de exposições naturais ou deliberadas a um antígeno

adaptation | adaptação característica hereditária que aumenta a capacidade do organismo de sobreviver e de se reproduzir num ambiente

adaptive radiation | radiação adaptativa processo pelo qual uma única espécie ou um pequeno grupo de espécies se transforma em diversas formas diferentes e vive de modos diferentes

adenosine triphosphate (ATP) | trifosfato de adenosina (ATP) composto usado pelas células para armazenar e liberar energia

adhesion | adesão uma força de atração entre diferentes tipos de moléculas

aerobic | aeróbico processo que requer oxigênio

age structure | estrutura etária número de machos e fêmeas de cada faixa etária numa população

aggression | agressão atitude ameaçadora usada por um animal para exercer domínio sobre outro animal

algal bloom | florescimento algáceo proliferação de algas e de outros produtores decorrente de uma grande entrada de um nutriente limitante

allele | alelo uma de uma série de formas diferentes de um gene

allergy | alergia reação exagerada do sistema imunológico a um antígeno

alternation of generations | alternação de gerações um ciclo de vida com duas fases alternativas—uma fase haplóide (N) e uma fase diplóide (2N)

alveolus (pl. alveoli) | alvéolo bolsas de ar minúsculas na extremidade de um brônquio nos pulmões que propicia a área de superfície onde ocorre a troca de gás

amino acid | aminoácido composto com um grupo amino numa extremidade e um grupo carboxilo na outra

amniotic egg | ovo amniótico ovo composto de casca e membranas, que cria um ambiente protegido em que o embrião pode se desenvolver fora d´água

amylase | amilase enzima da saliva responsável pela quebra das ligações químicas em moléculas de amido

anaerobic | anaeróbico processo que não requer oxigênio

anaphase | anáfase fase da mitose em que os cromossomos se separam e se deslocam em direção à extremidades opostas da célula

angiosperm | angiosperma grupo de plantas em que as sementes nascem numa camada de tecido que as protege; também conhecida como planta florescente

anther | antera estrutura da flor em que se produzem os grãos de pólen

antheridium (pl. antheridia) | anterídio estrutura reprodutora masculina em algumas plantas que produzem esperma

anthropoid | antropóide grupo primata formado por macacos, símios e humanos

antibiotic | antibiótico grupo de drogas usadas para bloquear o crescimento e a reprodução de patogenias bacterianas

antibody | anticorpo proteína que ataca antígenos diretamente ou produz proteínas de ligação do antígeno

anticodon | anticódon seqüência de três nucleotídeos do RNAt que complementa os três nucleotídeos de um códon do RNAm

antigen | antígeno toda substância capaz de iniciar uma reação imune

aphotic zone | zona afótica a camada escura dos oceanos, abaixo da zona fótica onde a luz do sol não penetra

apical dominance | dominância apical fenômeno em que quanto mais próximo esteja o botão do ápice do caule, mais seu crescimento é inibido

apical meristem | meristema apical grupo de células não especializadas que se divide para produzir um aumento no crescimento dos caules e das raízes

apoptosis | apoptose processo de morte celular programada

appendage | apêndice estrutura, como a da perna ou da antena, que se prolonga da parede do corpo

appendicular skeleton | esqueleto apendicular os ossos dos braços e das pernas em conjunto com os ossos da pélvis e da área dos ombros

aquaculture | aqüicultura criação de organismos aquáticos para consumo dos seres humanos

aquaporin | aquaporina proteína do canal aquático numa célula

Archaea | Arquea domínio composto de procariontes unicelulares com paredes celulares que não contêm peptidoglicano; corresponde ao reino da Arqueobactéria

archegonium (pl. archegonia) | arquegônio estrutura nas plantas que produz células-ovo

artery | artéria grande vaso sangüíneo que transporta o sangue do coração aos tecidos do corpo

artificial selection | seleção artificial cultivo seletivo de plantas e animais para promover a ocorrência de características desejáveis na progênie

asexual reproduction | reprodução assexual processo de reprodução envolvendo um único progenitor, resultando em prole geneticamente idêntica ao mesmo

asthma | asma disfunção respiratória crônica em que a passagem de ar se estreita, causando chiado, tosse e dificuldade de respirar

atherosclerosis | aterosclerose Enfermidade em que depósitos de gordura chamados de placas são construídos dentro das paredes arteriais e, eventualmente, causam o enrijecimento das artérias

atom | átomo a unidade básica da matéria

ATP synthase | síntese de ATP complexo de proteínas que cerca a membrana celular e permite a passagem de íons de hidrogênio (H^+) através dela

atrium (pl. atria) | átrio câmera superior do coração que recebe sangue do restante do corpo

autonomic nervous system | sistema nervoso autônomo parte do sistema nervoso periférico que regula as atividades involuntárias ou que não estejam sob o controle consciente, composto de subdivisões simpáticas e parassimpáticas

autosome | autossoma cromossomo que não é um cromossomo sexual; também conhecido como cromossomo autossomal

autotroph | autótrofo organismo capaz de capturar energia da luz solar ou de substâncias químicas, usando-a para produzir seu próprio alimento de compostos inorgânicos; também chamado de produtor

auxin | auxina substância regulatória produzida na extremidade de uma planta em crescimento que estimula o alongamento da célula e o crescimento de novas raízes

axial skeleton | esqueleto axial o esqueleto que apoia o eixo central do corpo; consiste da caveira, da coluna vertebral e da gaiola torácica

axon | axone fibra longa que transporta impulsos do corpo celular de um neurônio

B

bacillus (pl. bacilli) | Bacilo procarionte em forma de bastão

background extinction | extinção histórica extinção causada pelo processo lento e constante de seleção natural

Bacteria | Bactéria domínio de procariontes unicelulares com paredes celulares que contêm peptidoglicano; corresponde ao reino da eubacteria

bacteriophage | bacteriófago espécie de virus que infecta a bactéria

bark | casca de árvore os tecidos encontrados fora do câmbio vascular, incluindo o floema, o câmbio cortical e a cortiça

base | base um composto que produz íons hidróxidos (OH⁻) na solução; uma solução com pH superior a 7

base pairing | pareamento de bases princípio de que as ligações no DNA só podem formar-se entre a adenina e a timina e entre a guanina e a citosina

behavior | comportamento a forma como o organismo reage a mudanças em suas condições internas ou no ambiente externo

behavioral isolation | isolamento comportamental forma de isolamento reprodutivo em que duas populações desenvolvem diferenças em rituais de relacionamento ou outros comportamentos que os impedem de procriar

benthos | bentos organismos que vivem presos ou próximos ao fundo dos lagos, rios ou oceanos

bias | tendência preferência particular ou ponto de vista pessoal, não científico

bilateral symmetry | simetria bilateral plano do corpo em que uma única linha imaginária pode dividir o corpo em duas laterais, esquerda e direita, uma imagem refletindo a outra

binary fission | fissão binária tipo de reprodução assexuada em que um organismo replica seu DNA e se divide, produzindo duas células-filhas idênticas

binocular vision | visão binocular a capacidade de fundir imagens visuais dos dois olhos, proporcionando percepção de profundidade e uma visão tridimensional do mundo

binomial nomenclature | nomenclatura binomial sistema de classificação em que a cada espécie é atribuído um nome científico composto de duas partes

biodiversity | biodiversidade o total da variedade de organismos na biosfera; também chamada de diversidade biológica

biogeochemical cycle | Ciclo biogeoquímico Processo em que elementos, compostos químicos e outras formas de matéria são transferidos de um organismo para outro e de uma parte da biosfera para outra

biogeography | biogeografia O estudo da distribuição de organismos no passado e no presente

bioinformatics | bioinformática aplicação da matemática e da ciência da computação para armazenar, recuperar e analisar dados biológicos

biological magnification | magnificação biológica A concentração crescente de uma substância danosa nos organismos a níveis tróficos superiores em uma cadeia ou rede alimentar

biology | biologia O estudo científico da vida

biomass | biomassa O valor total do tecido vivo em um dado nível trófico

biome | bioma um grupo de ecossistemas que compartilham climas similares e organismos típicos

biosphere | biosfera parte da Terra em que existe vida terra, água e ar ou atmosfera

biotechnology | biotecnologia o processo de manipulação de organismos, células ou moléculas, para produzir produtos específicos

biotic factor | fator biótico qualquer parte viva do ambiente com a qual um organismo possa interagir

bipedal | bípede termo usado para referir-se à locomoção de bípedes

blade | lâmina parte delgada, achatada, da folha de uma planta

blastocyst | blastocisto estágio inicial de desenvolvimento em mamíferos que consiste de uma bola côncava de células

blastula | blástula Uma bola côncava de células que se desenvolve quando um zigoto passa por uma série de divisões celulares

bone marrow | medula óssea tecido mole encontrado nas cavidades ósseas

bottleneck effect | efeito gargalo mudança na freqüência de alelos que se segue à redução dramática no tamanho de uma população

Bowman's capsule | cápsula de Bowman estrutura em forma de taça que envolve o glomérulo; coleta resíduos filtrados do sangue

brain stem | tronco encefálico estrutura que conecta o cérebro à medula espinhal; inclui a medula oblonga e a ponte

bronchus (pl. bronchi) | brônquio um dos dois tubos grandes na cavidade peitoral que vai da traquéia ao pulmão

bryophyte | briófito grupo de plantas que possui órgãos reprodutores especializados, mas carece de tecido vascular; inclui musgo e seus correlatos

bud | broto estrutura da planta contendo o tecido do meristema apical que produz novos caules e folhas

buffer | corpo tampão composto que evita mudanças agudas, repentinas, no pH

C

calcitonin | calcitonina hormônio produzido pela tiróide que reduz os níveis de cálcio no sangue

Calorie | Caloria medida de energia calórica no alimento; equivalente a 1000 calorias

calorie | caloria a quantidade de energia necessária para elevar a temperatura de 1 grama de água em 1 grau centígrado

Calvin cycle | Ciclo Calvin as reações da fotossíntese, independentes da luz, em que a energia da ATP e da NADPH é usada para construir compostos altamente energéticos como o açúcar

cancer | câncer disfunção em que algumas células do corpo perdem a capacidade de controlar o crescimento

canopy | canópia cobertura densa formada pelas copas folhosas de árvores altas de florestas tropicais

capillary | vasos capilares menores vasos sangüíneos; transportam nutrientes e oxigênio para os tecidos e absorvem dióxido de carbono e resíduos

capillary action | ação capilar a tendência da água em elevar-se em um tubo delgado

capsid | capsídeo o revestimento da proteína que circunda um vírus

carbohydrate | carboidrato composto formado por átomos de carbono, hidrogênio e oxigênio; tipo de nutriente que é a maior fonte de energia do corpo

carnivore | carnívoro organismo que obtém energia alimentando-se de outros organismos

carpel | carpelo parte mais interna de uma flor que produz e abriga os gametófitos femininos

carrying capacity | capacidade de transportar o maior número de indivíduos de uma determinada espécie que um determinado ambiente pode suportar

cartilage | cartilagem tipo de tecido conectivo que suporta o corpo e é mais mole e mais flexível do que o osso

Casparian strip | tira Casparian tira à prova d'água que circunda as células endodermais da planta e está envolvida na passagem unidirecional de materiais no cilindro vascular das raízes das plantas

catalyst | catalisador substância que acelera o ritmo de uma reação química

cell | célula unidade básica de todas as formas de vida

cell body | corpo celular a maior parte de um neurônio típico, contém o núcleo e uma grande parte do citoplasma

cell cycle | ciclo celular série de ocorrências em que uma célula cresce, se prepara para a divisão e divide-se para formar duas células-filhas

cell division | divisão celular o processo pelo qual uma célula se divide em duas novas células-filhas

cell membrane | membrana celular barreira delgada, flexível, que circunda todas as células; regula o que entra e o que sai da célula

cell theory | teoria celular um conceito fundamental da biologia que enuncia que todas as coisas vivas compõem-se de células; que células são unidades básicas de estrutura e função em coisas vivas; e que novas células são produzidas a partir de células existentes

cell wall | parede celular camada forte, de apoio, que circunda a membrana celular em algumas células

cell-mediated immunity | imunidade intermediada pela célula a resposta imunológica que defende o corpo contra vírus, fungos e células cancerígenas anormais dentro das células vivas

cellular respiration | respiração celular o processo que libera energia através da quebra de glicose e de outras moléculas alimentares na presença de oxigênio

central nervous system | sistema nervoso central inclui o cérebro e a medula espinhal, processa informações, e cria uma resposta que é transmitida ao corpo

centriole | centríolo estrutura numa célula animal que ajuda a organizar a divisão celular

centromere | centrômero região de um cromossomo onde as duas cromátides irmãs se ligam

cephalization | cefalização a concentração de órgãos do sentido e de células nervosas na extremidade anterior de um animal

cerebellum | cerebelo a parte do cérebro que coordena os movimentos e controla o equilíbrio

cerebral cortex | córtex cerebral a camada externa do cérebro de um mamífero; centro do pensamento e de outros comportamentos complexos

cerebrum | cérebro a parte do cérebro responsável pelas atividades voluntárias do corpo; a região do cérebro responsável pelo "pensamento"

chemical digestion | digestão química o processo pelo qual as enzimas quebram o alimento em pequenas moléculas que o corpo pode usar

chemical reaction | reação química o processo que muda ou transforma um conjunto de elementos químicos em outro conjunto de elementos químicos

chemosynthesis | quimiossíntese o processo em que é usada energia química para produzir carboidratos

chitin | quitina carboidrato complexo que forma as paredes celulares dos fungos; também encontrado no exterior dos esqueletos de artrópodes

chlorophyll | clorofila principal pigmento das plantas e de outros organismos fotossintéticos

chloroplast | cloroplasto organela encontrada nas células de plantas e de alguns outros organismos, que captura a energia da luz solar e a transforma em energia química

chordate | cordado um animal que tem em pelo menos um estágio de sua vida: a corda nervosa dorsal côncava, uma notocorda, uma cauda que se estende além do ânus; e bolsas faríngeas

chromatid | cromátide uma das duas partes "irmãs", idênticas, de um cromossomo duplicado

chromatin | cromatina substância encontrada em cromossomos eucarióticos que consiste de DNA estreitamente espiralado em torno de histones

chromosome | cromossomo estrutura em forma de filamento dentro do núcleo que contém informações genéticas transmitidas de uma geração para a seguinte

chyme | quimo mistura de enzimas e alimentos digeridos parcialmente

cilium (pl. cilia) | cílio projeção curta semelhante a fios de cabelo que produz movimentos

circadian rhythm | ritmo circadiano ciclos comportamentais que ocorrem diariamente

clade | clado ramo evolutivo de um cladograma que inclui um único ancestral e todos os seus descendentes

cladogram | cladograma diagrama que ilustra padrões de características compartilhadas entre espécies

class | classe em classificação, um grupo de ordens estreitamente relacionadas

classical conditioning | condicionamento clássico tipo de aprendizagem que ocorre quando um animal faz uma conexão mental entre um estímulo e algum tipo de recompensa ou punição

climate | clima as condições médias ano-a-ano de temperatura e precipitação de uma área por um longo período

clone | clone membro de uma população de células geneticamente idênticas produzidas a partir de uma única célula

closed circulatory system | sistema circulatório fechado tipo de sistema circulatório em que o sangue circula totalmente nos vasos sangüíneos que se prolongam através do corpo

coccus (pl. cocci) | coco procariota esférico

cochlea | cóclea parte cheia de fluido do ouvido interno; contém células nervosas que detectam o som

codominance | co-dominância situação em que os fenótipos produzidos por ambos os alelos são inteiramente expressos

codon | códon grupo de bases trinucleotídeas em RNAm que especificam um determinado aminoácido a ser incorporado a uma proteína

coelom | celoma cavidade do corpo alinhada com a mesoderme

coevolution | co-evolução o processo pelo qual duas espécies evoluem em resposta a mudanças em cada uma delas com o passar do tempo

cohesion | coesão uma atração entre moléculas da mesma substância

collenchyma | colênquima nas plantas, um tipo de tecido de sustentação que tem paredes de células fortes e flexíveis; ajuda a apoiar as plantas maiores

commensalism | comensalismo um relacionamento simbiótico em que um organismo se beneficia e o outro nem é ajudado, nem danificado

communication | comunicação a passagem de informações de um organismo para outro

community | comunidade montagem de populações diferentes que vivem juntas numa área definida

companion cell | célula companheira nas plantas, célula floema que circunda elementos do tubo crivado

competitive exclusion principle | princípio de exclusão competitiva princípio que determina que duas espécies não podem ocupar o mesmo nicho no mesmo habitat ao mesmo tempo

compound | composto substância formada pela combinação química de dois ou mais elementos em proporções definidas

cone | cone no olho, um fotoreceptor que reage à luz de cores diferentes que produzem visão em cores

coniferous | coníferas termo usado para referir-se a árvores que produzem cones com sementes e possuem folhas delgadas em forma de agulhas

conjugation | conjugação processo em que a paramécia e alguns procariotas trocam informações genéticas

connective tissue | tecido conectivo tipo de tecido que proporciona suporte ao corpo e conecta suas partes

consumer | consumidor organismo que obtém energia e se alimenta de outros organismos; também chamado de heterótrofo

control group | grupo de controle grupo de um experimento que é exposto às mesmas condições do grupo experimental, exceto por algumas variáveis independentes ;

controlled experiment | experimento controlado um experimento em que apenas uma variável é trocada

convergent evolution | evolução convergente processo pelo qual organismos não relacionados desenvolvem similaridades de forma independente quando se adaptam a ambientes similares

cork cambium | câmbio cortical tecido meristemático que produz a camada exterior dos caules durante o crescimento secundário de uma planta

cornea | córnea camada dura e transparente do olho através da qual penetra a luz

corpus luteum | corpo lúteo o nome dado ao folículo após a ovulação devido a sua coloração amarela

cortex | córtex nas plantas, a região do tecido de sustentação dentro da raiz através da qual se movimentam a água e os minerais

corticosteroid | corticosteróide hormônio esteróide produzido pelo córtex adrenal

cotyledon | cotiledon primeira folha ou primeiro par de folhas produzido pelo embrião de uma planta que produz semente

courtship | corte tipo de comportamento em que um animal envia estímulos para atrair um membro do sexo oposto

covalent bond | ligação covalente tipo de ligação entre átomos em que os elétrons são compartilhados

crossing-over | sobrecruzamento processo em que cromossomos homólogos trocam parcelas de suas cromátides durante a meiose

cyclin | ciclina um componente de uma família de proteínas que regula o ciclo da célula nas células eucarióticas

cytokinesis | citoquinese A divisão do citoplasma para formar duas células-filhas separadas

cytokinin | citoquinina hormônio de planta produzido em raízes em crescimento e frutas e sementes em desenvolvimento

cytoplasm | citoplasma porção fluida da célula fora do núcleo

cytoskeleton | citosqueleto rede de filamentos de proteínas em uma célula eucariótica que dá à célula o seu formato e sua organização interna e auxiliam nos movimentos celulares

D

data | dados evidências; informações adquiridas através de observações

deciduous | decíduo termo usado para referir-se a um tipo de árvore que reveste suas folhas durante uma determinada estação específica todo ano

decomposer | decompositor organismo que distribui e obtém energia de matéria orgânica morta

deforestation | desmatamento a destruição de florestas

demographic transition | transição demográfica a troca numa população de altas taxas de nascimento e morte para baixas taxas de nascimento e morte

demography | demografia o estudo científico de populações humanas

dendrite | dendrite extensões do corpo da célula de um neurônio que transmitem impulsos do ambiente ou de outros neurônios para o corpo da célula

denitrification | desnitrificação processo pelo qual as bactérias do solo convertem nitratos em gás de nitrogênio

density-dependent limiting factor | fator limitante dependente de densidade fator limitante que depende da densidade populacional

density-independent limiting factor | fator limitante independente de densidade fator limitante que afeta todas as populações de forma similar, independentemente da densidade populacional

deoxyribonucleic acid (DNA) | ácido desoxirribonucleico (DNA) material genético que os organismos herdam dos genitores

dependent variable | variável dependente variável que é observada e que se altera em reação à variável independente; também chamada variável de resposta

derived character | característica derivada um traço que aparece em parcelas recentes de uma linhagem, mas não em seus membros mais antigos

dermis | derme camada da pele que se encontra embaixo da epiderme

desertification | desertificação menor produtividade da terra, causada por excesso de exploração do plantio, excesso de pastagem, secas sazonais e mudanças climáticas

detritivore | detritívoro organismo que se alimenta de restos de plantas e animais e de outros materiais inertes

deuterostome | deuterostômio grupo de animais em que o blastóporo se torna um anus e a boca é formada a partir de uma segunda abertura que se desenvolve

diaphragm | diafragma músculo largo e plano na parte inferior da cavidade torácica que auxilia a respiração

dicot | dicotiledônea angiosperma com dois cotilédones (folhas de semente) em seu ovário

differentiation | diferenciação processo durante o qual as células se especializam em estrutura e função

diffusion | difusão processo pelo qual as partículas tendem a se mover de uma área em que estão mais concentradas para uma área de menor concentração

digestive tract | trato digestivo um tubo que se inicia na boca e termina no anus

diploid | diplóide termo utilizado em referência a células contendo dois conjuntos de cromossomos homólogos

directional selection | seleção direcional forma de seleção natural em que os indivíduos em uma extremidade da curva de distribuição têm maior aptidão que indivíduos no meio ou na outra extremidade da curva

disruptive selection | seleção disruptiva quando indivíduos nas extremidades superior e inferior da curva têm maior aptidão que indivíduos próximos ao meio da curva

DNA fingerprinting | mapeamento de DNA ferramenta utilizada por biólogos que analisa a coleção de fragmentos de restrição de DNA exclusiva de um indivíduo para determinar se duas amostras de material genético são da mesma pessoa

DNA microarray | micromatriz de DNA slide de vidro ou chip de silicone com milhares de diferentes tipos de fragmentos de filamento único de DNA em uma grade. A micromatriz de DNA é utilizada para detectar e medir a expressão de milhares de genes ao mesmo tempo

DNA polymerase | polimerase DNA enzima principal envolvido na replicação de DNA

domain | domínio uma categoria taxonômica maior, mais inclusiva, que um reino

dopamine | dopamina neurotransmissor associado aos centros de prazer e recompensa do cérebro

dormancy | dormência período de tempo em que um embrião de uma planta está vivo, mas não está crescendo

double fertilization | fertilização dupla processo de fertilização em angiospermas em que o primeiro evento produz o zigoto e o segundo o endosperma dentro da semente

E

ecological footprint | mapeamento ecológico quantidade total de ecossistemas funcionais necessária para fornecer os recursos que uma população humana consome e para absorver os resíduos gerados por esta população

ecological hot spot | hot spot ecológico pequena área geográfica em que números significativos de habitats e espécies estão em perigo imediato de extinção

ecological pyramid | pirâmide ecológica ilustração das quantidades relativas de energia ou matéria contida em cada nível trófico de uma certa cadeia alimentar ou teia alimentar

ecological succession | sucessão ecológica série de alterações graduais que ocorrem em uma comunidade após um distúrbio

ecology | ecologia estudo científico das interações entre organismos e entre organismos e seu ambiente

ecosystem | ecossistema todos os organismos habitantes de um local, junto com seu ambiente inanimado

ecosystem diversity | diversidade de ecossistemas a variedade de habitats, comunidades e processos ecológicos na biosfera

ectoderm | ectoderme camada germinativa exterior; produz os órgãos do sentido e a camada exterior da pele

ectotherm | ectotermo animal cuja temperatura corporal é determinada pela temperatura do seu ambiente

electron | elétron partículas de carga negativa, localizadas no espaço ao redor do núcleo

electron transport chain | cadeia transportadora de elétron série de proteínas carregadoras de elétrons que transportam elétrons de alta energia durante reações geradoras de ATP

element | elemento uma substância pura, composta inteiramente de um tipo de átomo

embryo | embrião um estágio de desenvolvimento de um organismo multicelular

embryo sac | saco embrionário gametófito feminino dentro do óvulo de plantas florescentes

emerging disease | doença emergente doença que apareça pela primeira vez na população, ou uma doença antiga que subitamente se tornou mais difícil de controlar

emigration | emigração movimento de indivíduos para fora de uma área

endocrine gland | glândula endócrina glândula que libera secreções (hormônios) diretamente no sangue, que transporta as secreções para outras áreas do corpo

endoderm | endoderme 1 camada germinativa interior; desenvolve o revestimento interno do trato digestivo e a maior parte do sistema respiratório

endodermis | endoderme 2 em plantas, uma camada do tecido definitivo que envolve completamente o cilindro vascular

endoplasmic reticulum | reticulo endoplasmático sistema de membranas internas em células eucarióticas; local em que os componentes lipídicos da membrana celular são sintetizados

endoskeleton | endosqueleto esqueleto interno; sistema de suporte estrutural dentro do corpo de um animal

endosperm | endosperma tecido rico em nutrientes que alimenta a plântula enquanto esta cresce

endospore | endósporo estrutura produzida por procariotas em condições desfavoráveis; uma parede interna grossa envolvendo o DNA e uma porção do citoplasma

endosymbiotic theory | teoria endossimbiótica teoria propondo que as células eucarióticas se formaram a partir de uma relação simbiótica entre várias diferentes células procarióticas

endotherm | endotermo animal cuja temperatura corporal é regulada, pelo menos em parte, utilizando calor gerado dentro do seu corpo

enzyme | enzima catalisador de a proteína que acelera a velocidade de certas reações biológicas

epidermis | epiderme em plantas, camada única de células compondo o tecido dérmico ; em humanos, a camada exterior da pele

epididymis | epidídimo órgão no sistema reprodutivo masculino em que espermas maduros são armazenados

epinephrine | epinefrina hormônio liberado pelas glândulas supra-renais que aumenta o batimento cardíaco e pressão sanguínea e prepara o corpo para atividade física intensa; também chamado adrenalina

epithelial tissue | tecido epitelial tipo de tecido que reveste as superfícies interiores e exteriores do corpo

era | era uma divisão principal do geológico; geralmente dividida em dois ou mais períodos

esophagus | esôfago tubo conectando a boca ao estômago

estuary | estuário tipo de zona úmida formada quando um rio encontra o oceano

ethylene | etileno hormônio vegetal que estimula o amadurecimento das frutas

Eukarya | Eucariota domínio composto de todos os organismos que têm um núcleo; inclusive protistas, plantas, fungos e animais

eukaryote | eucarioto organismo cujas células contêm um núcleo

evolution | evolução alteração através do tempo; processo pelo qual os organismos modernos descenderam de organismos antigos

excretion | excreção processo pelo qual resíduos metabólicos são eliminados do corpo

exocrine gland | glândula exócrina glândula que libera secreções através de estruturas tubulares, chamadas dutos, diretamente em um órgão ou para fora do corpo

exon | éxon seqüência expressa de DNA; códigos para uma proteína

exoskeleton | exosqueleto esqueleto externo; cobertura externa resistente que protege e dá suporte ao corpo de muitos invertebrados

exponential growth | crescimento exponencial padrão de crescimento em que indivíduos de uma população se reproduzem a uma taxa constante

extinct | extinto termo utilizado em referência a uma espécie que deixou de existir e não tem nenhum membro vivo

extracellular digestion | digestão extracelular tipo de digestão em que o alimento é decomposto fora das células em um sistema digestivo e então absorvido

F

facilitated diffusion | difusão facilitada processo de difusão em que as moléculas passam pela membrana através de canais da membrana celular

family | família em sistemática, um grupo de gêneros semelhantes

fat | gordura lipídio; composta de ácidos graxos e glicerol; tipo de nutriente que protege os órgãos corporais, atua como isolante para o corpo e armazena energia

feedback inhibition | inibição por feedback processo em que um estímulo produz uma resposta que se opõe ao estímulo original; também chamado feedback negativo

fermentation | fermentação processo pelo qual as células liberam energia na ausência de oxigênio

fertilization | fertilização processo na reprodução sexual em que células reprodutivas masculina e feminina se unem para formar uma nova célula

fetus | feto nome dado a um embrião humano após oito semanas de desenvolvimento

fever | febre temperatura corporal elevada que ocorre em reação a uma infecção

filtration | filtração processo de passagem de um líquido ou gás através de um filtro para remover resíduos

fitness | aptidão quanto um organismo é capaz de sobreviver e se reproduzir em seu ambiente

flagellum (pl. flagella) | flagelo estrutura utilizada por protistas para se locomover; produz movimentos ondulares

food chain | cadeia alimentar série de etapas em um ecossistema pela qual organismos transferem energia ao comer e serem comidos

food vacuole | vacúolo alimentar pequena cavidade no citoplasma de protistas que armazena alimentos temporariamente

food web | teia alimentar uma rede de interações complexas formada pelas relações alimentares entre diversos organismos em um ecossistema

forensics | criminalística estudo científico das evidências da cena de um crime

fossil | fóssil restos preservados de organismos antigos

founder effect | efeito fundador alteração na freqüência de alelos como resultado da migração de um pequeno subgrupo de uma população

frameshift mutation | mutação por mudança da matriz de leitura mutação que desloca a "matriz de leitura" da mensagem genética pela inserção ou exclusão de nucleotídeos

fruit | fruta estrutura em angiospermas contendo um ou mais ovários maduros

fruiting body | corpo frutificante estrutura reprodutiva de um fungo que cresce a partir do micélio

G

gamete | gameta célula sexual

gametophyte | gametófito planta produtora de gameta; a fase haplóide multicelular do ciclo de vida das plantas

ganglion (pl. ganglia) | gânglio grupo de interneurônios

gastrovascular cavity | cavidade gastrovascular câmara digestiva com uma única abertura

gastrulation | gastrulação processo de migração celular resultante na formação das três camadas celulares — ectoderme, mesoderme e endoderme

gel electrophoresis | eletroforese em gel procedimento utilizado para separar e analisar fragmentos de DNA colocando uma mistura de fragmentos de DNA em uma extremidade de um gel poroso e aplicando uma voltagem elétrica ao gel

gene | gene seqüência do DNA que codifica uma proteína e, assim, determina um traço; fator passado dos genitores para a prole

gene expression | expressão genética processo pelo qual um gene produz seu produto e este produto realiza sua função

gene pool | pool genético todos os genes, inclusive todos os diferentes alelos para cada gene, presentes em uma população a qualquer momento

gene therapy | terapia genética processo de alteração de um gene para tratar uma doença ou distúrbio médico. Um gene ausente ou faltoso é substituído por um gene funcional normal

genetic code | código genético coleção de códons de mRNA, cada um pautando a incorporação de um aminoácido específico em uma proteína durante a síntese da proteína

genetic diversity | diversidade genética a quantia total de todas as diferentes formas de informações genéticas portadas por uma espécie em particular, ou por todos os organismos da Terra

genetic drift | deriva genética alteração aleatória na freqüência de alelos causada por uma serie de ocorrências fortuitas que fazem com que um alelo se torne mais ou menos comum em uma população

genetic equilibrium | equilíbrio genético situação em que as freqüências de alelos em uma população permanecem iguais

genetic marker | marcador genético alelos produtores de diferenças fenotípicas detectáveis, úteis na análise genética

genetics | genética estudo científico da hereditariedade

genome | genoma o conjunto completo de informações genéticas que um organismo porta em seu DNA

genomics | genômica estudo de genomas completos, inclusive dos genes e suas funções

genotype | genótipo composição genética de um organismo

genus | gênero um grupo de espécies estreitamente relacionadas; a primeira parte do nome científico na nomenclatura binomial

geographic isolation | isolamento geográfico forma de isolamento reprodutivo em que duas populações são separadas por barreiras geográficas, como rios, montanhas ou massas de água, levando à formação de duas subespécies distintas

geologic time scale | escala de tempo geológico linha do tempo utilizada para representar a história da Terra

germ theory of disease | teoria dos germes para doenças a idéia que doenças infecciosas são causadas por microorganismos

germination | germinação retomada do crescimento de embriões de plantas após o período de dormência

giberellin | giberelina hormônio de plantas que estimula o crescimento e pode causar aumentos dramáticos no tamanho

gill | brânquia estrutura especializada plumiforme para a troca de gases com água

global warming | aquecimento global aumento na média das temperaturas da Terra

glomerulus | glomérulo pequena rede de capilares alojada a extremidade superior dos nefrônios; onde ocorre a filtração do sangue

glycolysis | glicólise primeiro conjunto de reações na respiração celular, em que as moléculas de glicose dividida em duas moléculas de ácido pirúvico

Golgi apparatus | complexo de Golgi organela em células que modifica, classifica e acondiciona proteínas e outros materiais do retículo endoplasmático para seu armazenamento na célula ou liberação para fora da célula

gradualism | gradualismo evolução de uma espécie pelo acumulo gradual de pequenas alterações genéticas durante longos períodos de tempo

grafting | enxerto método de propagação utilizada plantas sem semente e variedades de plantas lenhosas que não podem ser propagadas a partir de estacas

gravitropism | gravitropismo reação de uma planta à força de gravidade

green revolution | revolução verde desenvolvimento de variações (estirpes) de colheita altamente produtivas e uso de técnicas agrícolas modernas para aumentar o rendimento das safras

greenhouse effect | efeito estufa processo pelo qual certos gases (dióxido de carbono, metano e vapor de água) prendem a energia da luz solar na atmosfera terrestre em forma de calor

growth factor | fator de crescimento um de um grupo de proteínas reguladoras externas que estimula o crescimento e divisão celular

guard cells | células-guardas células especializadas da epiderme das plantas que controlam a abertura e fechamento dos estômatos

gullet | citostoma reentrância em um dos lados de um ciliado permitindo a entrada de alimentos na célula

gymnosperm | gimnosperma grupo de plantas fanerogâmicas (com sementes) que portam suas sementes diretamente nas escamas de cones

H

habitat | habitat área onde um organismo vive, inclusive os fatores bióticos e abióticos que o afetam

habitat fragmentation | fragmentação de habitat a divisão de ecossistemas em pedaços

habituation | habituação tipo de aprendizado em que um animal diminui ou cessa suas reação a um estímulo repetitivo que nem recompensa nem pune o animal

hair follicle | folículo capilar bolsas tubulares de células epidérmicas que se estendem até a derme; células na base dos folículos capilares produzem cabelo

half life | meia-vida extensão de tempo necessária para que metade dos átomos radiativos em uma amostra se decomponha

haploid | haplóide termo utilizado em referência a uma célula com um conjunto único de genes

Hardy-Weinberg principle | princípio de Hardy-Weinberg princípio afirmando que as freqüências de alelos em uma população permanecem constantes exceto se um ou mais fatores causarem uma alteração nessas freqüências

Haversian canal | canal de Havers um de uma rede de tubos percorrendo osso compacto que contém vasos sanguíneos nervos

heart | coração órgão muscular oco que bombeia sangue por todo o corpo

heartwood | cerne em um tronco lenhoso, xilema mais antigo próximo ao centro do tronco que não conduz mais água

hemoglobin | hemoglobina proteína que contém ferro em glóbulos vermelhos, que se liga ao oxigênio e o transporta pelo corpo

herbaceous plant | planta herbácea tipo de planta com tronco liso e não; inclui dentes-de-leão, gérberas, petúnias e girassóis

herbivore | herbívoro organismo que obtém energia se alimentando de plantas

herbivory | herbivoria interação em que um animal (o herbívoro) se alimenta de produtores (como plantas),

heterotroph | heterotrófito organismo que obtém alimento pelo consumo de outros seres vivos; também chamado consumidor

heterozygous | heterozigoto tendo dois alelos diferentes para um gene específico

histamine | histamina composto químico liberado pelos mastócitos que aumenta o fluxo de sangue e fluidos para a área infectada durante uma reação inflamatória

homeobox gene | gene homeobox homeobox é uma seqüência de DNA de aproximadamente 130 pares básicos, encontrada em vários genes homeóticos que regulam o desenvolvimento. Genes contendo essa seqüência são denominados genes homeobox e codificam fatores de transcrição, proteínas que se vinculam ao DNA e regulam a expressão de outros genes

homeostasis | homeostase as condições químicas e físicas internas relativamente constantes que conservam os organismos

homeotic gene | gene homeótico classe de genes reguladores que determinam a identidade de regiões e partes do corpo em embriões de animais. Mutações nesses genes podem transformar uma parte do corpo em outra

hominine | hominino linhagem hominóide que resultou nos humanos

hominoid | hominóide grupo de antropóides que inclui os gibões, orangotangos, gorilas, chimpanzés e humanos

homologous | homólogo termo utilizado em referência a cromossomos em que um conjunto vem do genitor masculino e o outro do genitor feminino

homologous structures | estruturas homólogas estruturas semelhantes em espécies diferentes com ancestrais em comum

homozygous | homozigoto tendo dois alelos idênticos de um gene específico

hormone | hormônio composto químico produzido em uma parte de um organismo que afeta outra parte do mesmo organismo

Hox gene | gene Hox grupo de genes homeóticos aglomerados que determinam a identidade da cabeça aos pés das partes do corpo em animais. Todos os genes Hox contêm a seqüência de DNA homeobox

humoral immunity | imunidade humoral imunidade contra antígenos em fluidos corporais, como sangue e linfa

humus | húmus material formado pela decomposição de folhas e outras matérias orgânicas

hybrid | híbrido prole de cruzamentos entre genitores com diferentes traços

hybridization | hibridização técnica de criação que envolve o cruzamento de indivíduos dessemelhantes para unir os melhores traços de amos os organismos

hydrogen bond | ligação de hidrogênio a força de atração fraca entre um átomo de hidrogênio e outros átomos

hydrostatic skeleton | esqueleto hidrostático esqueleto composto de segmentos do corpo preenchidos com fluido funcionando com músculos para permitir que um animal se locomova

hypertonic | hipertônico na comparação de duas soluções, a solução com a maior concentração de solutos

hypha (pl. hyphae) | hifa um de vários filamentos longos e delgados que compõem o corpo de fungos

hypothalamus | hipotálamo estrutura do cérebro que age como central de controle para reconhecer a analisar fome, sede, fadiga, raiva e temperatura corporal

hypothesis | hipótese explicação possível para um conjunto de observações ou resposta possível a um questionamento científico

hypotonic | hipotônico na comparação de duas soluções, a solução com a menor concentração de solutos

I

immigration | imigração movimento de indivíduos para uma área ocupada por uma população existente

immune response | resposta do sistema imunológico a memória, o reconhecimento e a resposta específica do corpo a um ataque patogênico

implantation | implantação o processo pelo qual um blastocisto se prende à parede do útero

imprinting | impressão tipo de comportamento baseado em experiência remota/anterior; uma vez que isto ocorre, o comportamento não pode ser mudado

inbreeding | procriação consanguínea a procriação consanguínea continuada de indivíduos com características semelhantes para menter as características derivadas de um tipo de organismo

incomplete dominance | predominância incompleta situação em que um alelo não predomina inteiramente sobre outro alelo

independent assortment | seleção independente um dos princípios de Mendel segundo o qual genes para características diferentes podem separar-se de forma independente durante a formação dos gametas

independent variable | variável independente o fator em um experimento controlado que é alterado deliberadamente; também denominado variável manipulada

index fossil | fossil índice fóssil característico que costuma ser usado para comparer as idades relativas dos fósseis

infectious disease | doença infecciosa doença causada por microorganismo que desorganiza as funções normais do corpo

inference | inferência uma interpretação lógica com base em conhecimento e experiência anteriores

inflammatory response | resposta inflamatória reação de defesa não específica a dano ao tecido causado por lesão ou infecção

innate behavior | comportamento inato tipo de comportamento praticado de modo inteiramente funcional da primeira vez que ocorre, ainda que o animal não tenha tido experiência anterior com o estímulo ao qual reage; também denominado instinto

insight learning | aprendizado através de percepção interna tipo de comportamento em que um animal aplica algo que já aprendeu a uma situação nova, sem um período de tentativa e erro; também denominado raciocínio

interferon | interferon uma dentre um grupo de proteínas que ajuda as células a resistir à infecção viral

interneuron | interneurônio tipo de neurônio que processa as informações e pode retransmiti-las aos neurônios motores

interphase | interfase período do ciclo da célula entre as divisões celulares

intracellular digestion | digestão intracelular tipo de digestão em que o alimento é digerido dentro de célulcas especializadas que passam os nutrientes a outras células por difusão

intron | íntron sequência do DNA que não está envolvida na codificação de informações para uma proteína

invertebrate | invertebrado um animal que carece de uma espinha dorsal ou uma coluna vertebral

ion | íon um átomo que possui carga positiva ou negativa

ionic bond | ligação iônica ligação iônica formada de um ou mais elétrons que são transferidos de um átomo para outro

iris | íris a parte colorida de um olho

isotonic | isotônico quando a concentração de duas soluções é a mesma

isotope | isótopo uma das diversas formas de um único elemento, que contém o mesmo número de prótons mas diferentes números de nêutrons

J

joint | junta um local onde o osso se liga a outro osso

K

karyotype | cariótipo um micrógrafo do inteiro conjunto de cromossomos diplóide agrupado em pares e organizados em orde de tamanho decrescente

keratin | queratina proteína fibrosa reistente encontrada na pele

keystone species | espécie importante no ecossistema uma única espécie que, normalmente, não é abundante na comunidade, entretanto, exerce um forte controle na estrutura de uma comunidade

kidney | rim um órgão de excreção que separa os resíduos e o excesso de água do sangue

kin selection | seleção inclusiva teoria que enuncia que o auxiliar parentes pode melhorar a aptidão evolucionária de um indivíduo porque indivíduos aparentados compartilham uma grande proporção de genes

kingdom | reino o grupo maior e mais inclusivo na classificação

Koch's postulates | postulados de Koch conjunto de diretrizes desenvolvidas por Koch que auxiliam a identificar o microorganismo que causa uma doença específica

Krebs cycle | ciclo de Krebs segundo estágio da respiração celular no qual o ácido pirúvido é dissociado em dióxido de carbono em uma série de reações para extrair energia

L

language | linguagem sistema de comunicação que associa sons, símbolos e gestos de acordo com um conjunto de normas sobre seqüência e significado, tal como a gramática e a sintaxe

large intestine | intestino grosso órgão do sistema digestivo que retira a água do material não digerido que o atravessa; também denominado cólon

larva (pl. larvae) | larva o estágio imaturo de um organismo

larynx | laringe estrutura na garganta que contém as cordas vocais

learning | aprendizado mudanças no comportamento decorrentes de uma experiência

lens | cristalino estrutura ocular que focalize os raios luminosos na retina

lichen | líquen associação simbiótica entre um fungo e um organismo fotossintético

ligament | ligamento tecido conectivo rígido que segura os ossos em uma junta

light-dependent reactions | reações dependents da luz conjunto de reações em fotossíntese que usam a energia da luz para produzir ATP e NADPH

light-independent reactions | reações independents da luz conjunto de reações na fotossíntese que não requerem a luz; a energia da ATIP e da NADPH é usada para criar compostos energéticos tal com o açúcar; também denominado ciclo de Calvin

lignin | lignina substância em plantas vasculares que enrijece a parede das células

limiting factor | fator limitante um fator que leva o crescimento populacional a diminuir

limiting nutrient | nutriente limitante um único nutriente essencial que limita a produtividade em um ecossistema

lipid | lipídio macromolécula composta principalmente de átomos de carbono e hidrogênio; inclui gorduras, óleos e ceras

lipid bilayer | camada dupla de lipídio uma superfície de camada dupla flexível que compõe a membrana da célula, formando uma barreira entre a célula e seu ambiente

logistic growth | crescimento logístico padrão de crescimento em que o crescimento da população diminui e então pára após um período de crescimento exponencial

loop of Henle | loop de Henle uma seção do túbulo de nefron responsável por conservar a água e minimizar o volume de água filtrada

lung | pulmão órgão respiratório; local onde os gases são trocados entre o sangue e o ar inalado

lymph | linfa fluido que é filtrado para fora do sangue

lysogenic infection | infecção lisogênica tipo de infecção em que um vírus insere seu DNA no DANA da célula hospedeira e é replicado junto com o DNA da célula hospedeira

lysosome | lisossoma organela de célula que dissocia lipídios, carboidratos e proteínas em pequenas moléculas que podem ser usadas pelo resto da célula

lytic infection | infecção lítica um tipo de infecção pelo qual um vírus penetra em uma célula, se reproduz, e leva a célula a se romper

M

macroevolution | macroevolução alteração evolutiva em larga escala que ocorre durante longos períodos

Malpighian tubule | túbulo de Malpighi estrutura na maioria dos artrópodos terrestres que concentra o ácido úrico e o adiciona aos resíduos digestivos

mammary gland | glândula mamária glândula nas fêmeas dos mamíferos que produz leite para nutrir os filhotes

mass extinction | extinção em massa uma ocorrência durante a qual muitas espécies se tornam extintas durante um período relativamente curto

matrix | matriz o compartimento mais interno de uma mitocôndria

mechanical digestion | digestão mecânica a dissociação física de grandes parcelas de alimento em parcelas menores

meiosis | meiose um processo pelo qual o número de cromossomos por célula é dividido pela metade através da separação de cromossomos homólogos em uma célula diplóide

melanin | melanina pigmento marrom escuro na pele que auxilia a protegê-la através da absorção de raios ultravioleta

melanocyte | melanócito célula na pele que produz um pigmento marrom escuro denominado melanina

menstrual cycle | ciclo menstrual a seqüência regular de ocorrências em que um óvulo se desenvolve e é descartado do corpo

menstruation | menstruação o descarte de sangue e do óvulo não fertilizado do corpo

meristem | meristema regiòes de células não especializadas respon'saveis pelo crescimento contínuo durante o período de vida de uma planta

mesoderm | mesoderma folheto germinativo intermediário do qual derivam os músculos e uma boa parte dos sistemas circulatório, reprodutivo e excretor

mesophyll | mesofilo tecido fundamental especializado encontrado nas folhas que realize a maior parte de sua fotossíntese

messenger RNA (mRNA) | RNA mensageiro (mRNA) tipo de RNA que transmite cópias de instruções para que o resto da célula agrupe os aminoácidos em proteínas de DNA

metabolism | metabolismo a combinação de reações químicas através do qual um organismo associa ou dissocia materiais

metamorphosis | metamorfose o processo das mudanças que se verificam no aspecto e na forma da larva até se tornar um adulto

metaphase | metáfase fase da mitose em que os cromossomos se alinham no centro da célula

microclimate | microclima as condições ambientais em uma pequena área que diferem, consideravelmente, do clima da área adjacente

migration | migração comportamento sazonal que resulta no deslocamento de um ambiente para outro

mineral | mineral nutrientes inorgânicos que o corpo necessita, normalmente em pequenas doses

mitochondrion | mitocôndria organela da célula que converte a energia química armazenada no alimento em compostos mais convenientes para serem usados pela célula

mitosis | mitose parte da divisão da célula eucariótica durante a qual o núcleo da célula se divide

mixture | mistura um material composto de dois ou mais elementos ou compostos que se misturam fisicamente mas não se combinam quimicamente

molecular clock | relógio molecular método usado pelos pesquisadores que usa taxas de mutação no DNA para estimar o espaço de tempo durante o qual duas espécies tem se desenvolvido de modo independente

molecule | molécula menor unidade da maioria dos compostos que manifesta todas as propriedades daquele composto

molting | muda o processo de despojar-se de um exosqueleto e de desenvolver um novo

monocot | monocotiledônea angiosperma com uma folha seminal em seu ovário

monoculture | monocultura estratégia agrícola de plantar um único produto altamente produtivo, ano após ano

monomer | monômero pequena unidade química que forma um polímero

monophyletic group | grupo monofilético grupo que consiste de uma única espécie ancestral e de todos os seus descendentes, e exclui quaisquer organismos que não descendem daquele ancestral comum

monosaccharide | monossacarídeo molécula simples de açúcar

motor neuron | neurônio motor tipo de célula nervosa que transmite instruções de interneurônios para quaisquer das células musculares ou glandulares

multiple alleles | alelos múltiplas um gen que contém mais de dois alelos

multipotent | células progenitoras multipotentes células com potencial limitado de se desenvolverem em muitos tipos de células diferenciadas

muscle fiber | fibra muscular células longas e delgadas do músculo esquelético

muscle tissue | tecido muscular tipo de tecido que torna possível o movimento corporal

mutagen | mutagênico agentes ambientais químicos ou físicos que interagem com o DNA e podem causar uma mutação

mutation | mutação mudança no material genético de uma célula

mutualism | mutualismo uma relação simbiótica em que ambas as espécies se beneficiam da relação

mycelium (pl. mycelia) | micélio a rede densamente ramificada das hifas de um fungo

mycorrhiza (pl. mycorrhizae) | micorriza associação simbiótica de raízes de plantas e fungos

myelin sheath | invólucro de mielina membrana isolante que circunda o axônio em alguns neurônios

myocardium | miocárdio camada de músculo espessa e intermediária do coração

myofibril | miofibrila feixes de filamentos compactos encontrados nas fibras do músculo esquelético

myosin | miosina filamento espesso de proteína encontra nas células do músculo esquelético

N

NAD⁺ (nicotinamide adenine dinucleotide) | NAD⁺ (nicotinamida adenina dinucleótido) um transmissor de elétrons envolvido na glicólise

NADP⁺ (nicotinamide adenine dinucleotide phosphate) | NADP⁺ (nicotinamida adenina dinucleótido fosfato) uma molécula transmissora que transfere elétrons de alta energia da clorofila para outras moléculas

natural selection | seleção natural processo pelo qual os organismos mais adaptados ao seu ambiente sobrevivem e se reproduzem com maior sucesso; também denominado sobrevivência dos mais aptos

nephridium (pl. nephridia) | nefrídio estrutura excretora de um anelídeo que filtra o fluido corporal

nephron | nefrônio estrutura que filtra o sangue nos rins onde se filtram as impurezas e se recolhem os resíduos, e de onde o sangue purificado volta para a circulação

nervous tissue | tecido nervoso tipo de tecido que transmite os impulsos nervosos para o corpo

neuromuscular junction | junção neuromuscular o ponto de contato entre um neurônio motor e uma célula do músculo esquelético

neuron | neurônio célula nervosa; especializada em transmitir mensagens através do sistema nervoso

neurotransmitter | neurotransmissor substância química usada por um neurônio para transmitir um impulso atra'ves da sinapse com outra célula

neurulation | neurulação o primeiro passo no desenvolvimento do sistema nervoso

niche | nicho toda a variedade de condições físicas e biológicas em que vive um organismo e a forma como ele usa essas condições

nitrogen fixation | fixação de nitrogênio o processo de converter gás nitrogênio em compostos de nitrogênio que as plantas podem absorver e usar

node | nó parte de um talo em crescimento onde a folha está pendurada

nondisjunction | não-disjunção erro na meiose em que se verifica a falha na segregação adequada dos cromossomas homólogos

nonrenewable resource | fonte não renovável fonte que não pode ser reabastecida por um processo natural em um período razoável

norepinephrine | noraepinefrina hormônio liberado pelas glândulas adrenalinas que aceleram os batimentos cardíacos e a pressão sanguínea, preparando o corpo paa uma atividade física intensa

notochord | notocórdio uma longa estrutura de suporte em forma de vareta que atravessa o corpo dos cordados logo abaixo do cordão nervoso

nucleic acid | ácido nucleico macromoléculas que contém hidrogênio, oxigênio, nitrogênoi, carbono e fósforo

nucleotide | nucleotídeo subunidade que compõe o ácido nucléico; formada de um açúcar com 5 atómos de carbono, um grupamento fosfato e uma base nitrogenada

nucleus | núcleo o centro de um átomo, que contém os protons e os nêutrons ; nas células, a estrutura que contém seu manterial genético na forma de DNA

nutrient | nutriente substância química que um organismo necessita para preservar a vida

nymph | ninfa forma imatura de um animal que lembra a forma adulta, mas carece de órgãos sexuais funcionais

O

observation | observação o processo de observar e descrever ocorrências ou processos de forma meticulosa e organizada

omnivore | onívoro organismo que obtém energia alimentando-se de plantas e animais

open circulatory system | sistema circulatório aberto um tipo de sistema circulatório em nem todo o sangue que circula pelo corpo o faz dentro do sistema de vasos sanguíneos.

operant conditioning | condicionamento operante tipo de aprendizado em que um animal aprende a comportar-se de um certo modo através da prática repetitiva para receber recompensa ou evitar punição

operator | operador uma pequena região do DNA adjacente a um promotor de um operon procariótico, que liga as proteínas repressoras responsáveis por controlar a taxa de transcrição do operon

operon | operon nos procariontes, um grupo de genes adjacentes que compartilha um operador e um promoter comum e estão transcritos em um único mRNA

opposable thumb | polegar oponível um polegar que permite agarrar objetos e usar ferramentas

order | ordem na classificação, um grupo de famílias afins

organ | órgão grupos de tecidos que trabalham em conjunto para realizar funções afins

organ system | sistema orgânico um grupo de órgãos que trabalha em conjunto para realizar uma função específica

organelle | organela estrutura especializada que realiza funções celulares específicas em uma célula eucariótica

osmosis | osmose a difusão de água em uma membrana com permeabilidade seletiva

osmotic pressure | pressão osmótica a pressão que deve se aplicar para impedir o movimento osmótico através de uma membrana com permeabilidade seletiva

ossification | ossificação o processo de formação de ossos durante o qual a cartilagem é substituída pelo osso

osteoblast | osteoblasto célula óssea que segrega depósitos minerais que substituem a cartilagem nos ossos em desenvolvimento

osteoclast | osteoclasto célula óssea que degrada os minerais ósseos

osteocyte | osteócito célula óssea que ajuda a manter os minerais no tecido ósseo e continua a fortalecer o osso em crescimento

ovary | ovário nas plantas, a estrutura que envolve e protege as sementes ; nos animais, um órgão reprodutivo feminino fundamental; produz ovos/óvulos

oviparous | ovíparo espécie em que o embrião se desenvolve em ovos fora do corpo da progenitora

ovoviparous | ovovíparo espécie em que o embrião se desenvolve dentro do corpo da mãe, mas depende inteiramente do saco embrionário de seus óvulos

ovulation | ovulação a liberação de um óvulo maduro do ovário em uma das trompas de Falópio

ovule | óvulo estrutura em forma de cones femininos em que se desenvolvem os gametófitos femininos

ozone layer | camada de ozônio camada atmosférica em que o gás ozônico encontra-se relativamente concentrado; protege a vida na Terra de raios ultravioletas prejudiciais à luz do dia

P

pacemaker | marcapasso pequeno grupo de fibras musculares cardíacas que mantém o ritmo de bombeamento do coração, estabelecendo a freqüência de contrações cardíacas; o nó sinoatrial

paleontologist | paleontólogo cientista que estuda fósseis

palisade mesophyll | mesófilo em paliçada camada de células sob a epiderme superior de uma folha

parasitism | parasitismo uma relação simbiótica em que um organismo vive em ou dentro de outro organismo e o prejudica

parathyroid hormone (PTH) | hormônio da paratireóide (PTH) hormônio secretado pela glândula paratireóidea que aumenta os níveis de cálcio no sangue

parenchyma | parênquima principal tipo de tecido fundamental em plantas que contêm células com paredes delgadas de células e grandes vacúolos centrais

passive immunity | imunidade passiva imunidade temporária que se desenvolve em decorrência de exposição natural ou deliberada a um antígeno

pathogen | patógeno agente causador de doenças

pedigree | pedigree um mapa que mostra a presença ou ausência de um traço de acordo com as relações dentro de uma família ao longo de várias gerações

pepsin | pepsina uma enzima que desagrega proteínas em fragmentos polipeptídeos menores

period | período divisão de tempo geológico em que se subdividem as eras

peripheral nervous system | sistema nervoso periférico rede de nervos e células de suporte que transmite sinais para dentro e para fora do sistema nervoso

peristalsis | peristaltismo contrações de músculos lisos que, com sua força, impulsionam o alimento através do esôfago até o estômago

permafrost | permafrost camada de subsolo permanentemente gélido encontrado na tundra

petiole | pecíolo haste delgada que liga a lâmina de uma folha ao caule

pH scale | escala de pH uma escala com valores de 0 a 14, usada para medir a concentração de íons de H^+ em uma solução; um pH de 0 a 7 is ácido, um pH de 7 é neutro, e um pH de 7 a 14 é básico

pharyngeal pouch | bolsa faríngea um dos elementos em um par de estruturas na região da garganta de um cordado

pharynx | faringe tubo na parte posterior da boca que serve de passagem para o ar e para os alimentos; também denominado garganta

phenotype | fenótipo características físicas de um organismo

phloem | floema tecido vascular que transporta soluções de nutrientes e carbohidratos produzidos pela fotossíntese através da planta

photic zone | zona fótica região banhada pela luz próxima à superfície da água

photoperiod | fotoperíodo reação da planta a extensões relativas de luz e de obscuridade

photosynthesis | fotossíntese o processo usado pelas plantas e por outros autotróficos para captar a energia da luz e usá-la para acionar reações químicas que convertem dióxido de carbono e água em oxigênio e carboidratos ricos em energia como açúcares e amidos

photosystem | fotosistema aglomerado de clorofila e proteínas encontrado nos tilacóides

phototropism | fototropismo a tendência de uma planta de crescer na direção de uma fonte de luz

phylogeny | filogenia o estudo de relações evolutivas entre organismos

phylum | filo na classificação, um grupo de classes afins

phytoplankton | fitoplâncton algas fotosintéticas encontradas próximas à superfície dos oceanos

pigment | pigmento moléculas que absorvem a luz, usadas pelas plantas para coletar a energia solar

pioneer species | espécies pioneiras as primeiras espécies a popular uma área durante a sucessão

pistil | pistilo um único carpelo ou vários carpelos unidos; contém o ovário, o estilo e o estigma

pith | medula vegetal células de parênquima dentro do anel de tecido vascular em caules de dicotiledôneas

pituitary gland | glândula pituitária pequena glândula encontrada próxima à base do crânio que segrega hormônios que regulam diretamente funções corporais e controlem as ações de várias outras glândulas endócrinas

placenta | placenta órgão especializado em mamíferos placentários através do qual os gases respiratórios, os nutrientes e os resíduos são trocados entre a mãe e seu feto em gestação

plankton | plâncton organismos microscópicos que vivem em ambientes aquáticos; incluem o fitoplâncton e o zooplâncton

plasma | plasma parcela líquida do sangue, de cor de palha

plasmid | plasmídeo pequena parcela circular de DNA localizada no citoplasma de muitas bactérias

plasmodium | plasmódio o estágio alimentar de um amebóide no ciclo de vida de um mixomiceto plasmodial

plate tectonics | tectônica das placas processos geológicos, como desvio continental, vulcões e terremotos, que resultam no movimento das placas

platelet | plaqueta fragmento de célula liberado pela medula óssea que ajuda a coagular o sangue

pluripotent | células pluripotentes células capazes de se desenvolver na maioria de, mas não em todos os tipos de células do corpo

point mutation | ponto de mutação mutação do gene em que um único par de bases no DNA foi modificado

pollen grain | grão de pólen a estrutura que contém um gametófito masculino inteiro em plantas que têm sementes

pollen tube | tubo de pólen estrutura em uma planta que contém dois núcleos espermáticos haplóides

pollination | polinização a transferência do pólen da estrutura reprodutiva masculina para a estrutura reprodutiva feminina

pollutant | poluente material danoso que pode penetrar na biosfera pela terra, pelo ar ou pela água

polygenic trait | traço poligênico traço controlado por um ou mais gens

polymer | polímero moléculas compostas de muitos monômeros; compõem as macromoléculas

polymerase chain reaction (PCR) | reação em cadeia da polimerase (PCR) a técnica usada pelos biólogos para fazer muitas cópias de um gen em particular

polypeptide | polipeptídeo longa cadeia de aminoácidos que forma as proteínas

polyploidy | poliplóide condição na qual um organismo possui conjuntos adicionais de cromossomas

population | população grupo de indivíduos da mesma espécie que vive na mesma área

population density | densidade populacional o número de indivíduos por área unitária

predation | predação uma interação em que um organismo (o predador) capture e se alimenta de outro organismo (a presa)

prehensile tail | cauda preênsil longa cauda que pode se enroscar com firmeza envolta de um ramo de árvore

pressure-flow hypothesis | hipótese da pressão radicular hipótese que explica o método pelo qual a seiva do floema é transportada através da planta de uma "fonte" de açúcar para um "reservatório" de açúcar

primary growth | crescimento primário padrão de crescimento que ocorre nas extremidades e nos brotos de uma planta

primary producer | produtor primário os primeiros produtores de compostos ricos em energia que são utilizados posteriormente por outros organismos

primary succession | sucessão primária sucessão que ocorre na área em que não restam traços de uma comunidade anterior

principle of dominance | princípio da dominância Segunda conclusão de Mendel, que enuncia que alguns alelos são dominantes e outros são recessivos

prion | príon partículas de proteína que causam doença

probability | probabilidade a possibilidade de ocorrência de um determinado evento

product | produto os elementos ou compostos produzidos por uma reação química

prokaryote | procariota organismo unicelular que carece de um núcleo

promoter | promotor região específica de um gen onde a polimerase do RNA pode se ligar e iniciar a transcrição

prophage | prófago o DNA do bacteriófago que está inserido no DNA do hospedeiro da bactéria

prophase | profase a primeira e mais longa fase da mitose em que o material genético do núcleo se condensa e os cromossomos se tornam visíveis

prostaglandin | prostaglandina ácidos graxos modificados produzidos por uma ampla variedade de células; em geral, afetam apenas células e tecidos adjacentes

protein | proteína macromolécula que contem carbono, hidrogênio, oxigênio e nitrogênio, e que o corpo necessita para promover o crescimento e regeneração

protostome | protostômio um animal cuja boca se forma a partir do blastóporo

pseudocoelom | pseudoceloma cavidade do corpo alinhada, apenas em parte, com o mesoderma

pseudopod | pseudópode projeção citoplásmica temporária usada por alguns protistas para movimentar-se

puberty | puberdade um período de rápido crescimento e de maturação sexaul durante o qual o sistema reprodutor se torna plenamente funcional

pulmonary circulation | circulação pulmonar via circulatória entre o coração e os pulmões

punctuated equilibrium | punctuated equilibrium um padrão de evolução em que períodos longos estáveis são interrompidos por breve períodos

Punnett square | Quadrado de Punnett um diagrama que pode ser usado para predizer as combinações de genótipos e fenótipos de um cruzamento genético

pupa | pupa um estágio na metamorfose completa em que a larva se desenvolve em um adulto

pupil | pupila pequena abertura na íris que capta a luz no olho

R

radial symmetry | simetria radial plano corporal em que qualquer número de planos imaginários desenhados até o centro do corpo poderia dividi-lo em metades iguais

radiometric dating | datação radiométrica método empregado para determinar a idade de uma amostra a partir da comparação da quantidade de um isótopo radioativo ao isótopo não-radioativo do mesmo elemento da amostra

reabsorption | reabsorção processo através do qual água e substâncias dissolvidas retornam para o sangue

reactant | reagente elemento ou composto que desencadeia uma reação química

receptor | receptor em células, proteína específica que possui um determinado mensageiro molecular, como um hormônio, cuja forma corresponde à sua

recombinant DNA | DNA recombinante DNA produzido através da combinação do DNA de fontes distintas

red blood cell | hemácia célula sangüínea que contém hemoglobina e transporta oxigênio

reflex | reflexo resposta ou reação rápida, automática a um estímulo

reflex arc | arco reflexo sistema formado por um receptor sensorial, um neurônio sensorial, um neurônio motor e ensaio para que ocorra reação rápida a um estímulo

relative dating | datação relativa método para determinar a idade de um fóssil através da comparação da sua localização com a de fósseis de outras camadas de rocha

relative frequency | freqüência relativa número de ocorrências de um alelo em um pool genético comparado com o número de ocorrências de outros alelos do mesmo gene

releasing hormone | hormônio liberador hormônio produzido pelo hipotálamo que desencadeia a secreção de hormônios da glândula pituitária anterior

renewable resource | recurso renovável recurso que pode ser produzido ou substituído através das atividades de um ecossistema saudável

replication | replicação processo de cópia do DNA antes da divisão celular

reproductive isolation | isolamento reprodutivo separação de uma espécie ou população para impedir cruzamentos, levando ao desenvolvimento de duas espécies distintas

resource | recurso qualquer necessidade vital, como água, nutrientes, luz, alimento ou espaço

response | resposta reação específica a um estímulo

resting potential | potencial de repouso carga elétrica existente na membrana celular de um neurônio em repouso

restriction enzyme | enzima de restrição enzima que corta o DNA em uma seqüência de nucleotídeos

retina | retina camada interna do olho; contém fotorreceptores

retrovirus | retrovírus vírus de RNA em que o RNA é a carga genética

ribonucleic acid (RNA) | ácido ribonucléico ácido nucléico de cadeia simples contendo ribose de açúcar.

ribosomal RNA (rRNA) | RNA ribossômico (rRNA) tipo de RNA que se junta com proteínas para formar ribossomos

ribosome | ribossomo organelo celular composto por RNA e proteínas encontradas no citoplasma da célula; é onde ocorre a síntese de proteína

RNA interference (RNAi) | interferência por RNA (RNAi) inserção de RNA de dupla fita em uma célula para inibir a expressão do gene

RNA polymerase | RNA polimerase enzima que conecta a cadeia crescente de nucleotídeos de RNA durante a transcrição usando uma fita de DNA como modelo

rod | bastonete fotorreceptor dos olhos sensível à luz que não faz a distinção de cores

root cap | coifa cobertura resistente da ponta da raiz que protege o meristema

root hair | pêlos da raiz pêlos finos existentes na raiz que permitem a cobertura de uma grande área da superfície para otimizar a absorção de água e minerais

rumen | rúmen câmara situada no estômago de vacas e animais semelhantes onde bactérias simbióticas digerem a celulose

S

sapwood | alburno em troncos, é a camada de floema secundário situada em torno do cerne; geralmente, tem papel ativo no transporte de fluidos

sarcomere | sarcômero unidade de contração muscular; formada por duas linhas Z e os filamentos situados entre elas

scavenger | necrófago animal que consome as carcaças de outros animais

science | ciência maneira organizada de coleta e análise de dados sobre o mundo natural

sclerenchyma | esclerênquima tecido básico com paredes celulares rígidas e grossas, tornando o tecido básico firme e forte

scrotum | escroto saco externo que abriga os testículos

sebaceous gland | glândula sebácea glândula cutânea que secreta sebo (secreção oleosa)

secondary growth | crescimento secundário em dicotiledôneos, aumento da espessura do caule

secondary succession | sucessão secundária sucessão que ocorre em uma área parcialmente destruída por distúrbios

seed | semente embrião de uma planta e alimento encerrado em uma capa de proteção

seed coat | invólucro da semente tegumento, revestimento firme que envolve e protege o embrião da planta e evita que o conteúdo da semente seque

segregation | segregação separação de alelos durante a formação de gametas

selective breeding | cruzamento seletivo método de cruzamento através do qual apenas organismos com as características desejadas podem ser escolhidos para produzir a geração seguinte

selectively permeable | permeabilidade seletiva propriedade de membranas biológicas através da qual algumas substâncias podem passar enquanto outras não; também conhecidas como membranas semipermeáveis

semen | sêmen combinação de esperma e fluido seminal

semicircular canal | canal semicircular uma das três estruturas do ouvido interno que monitora a posição do corpo em relação à gravidade

seminiferous tubule | tubo seminífero um dentre as centenas de tubos de cada testículo onde o esperma se desenvolve

sensory neuron | neurônio sensorial tipo de célula nervosa que recebe informações de receptores sensoriais e envia sinais ao sistema nervoso central

sex chromosome | cromossomo sexual um dos dois cromossomos que determina o sexo de um indivíduo

sex-linked gene | gene sexual gene de um cromossomo sexual

sexual reproduction | reprodução sexuada tipo de reprodução em que células de dois pais se unem para formar a primeira célula de um novo organismo

sexually transmitted disease (STD) | doença sexualmente transmissível (DST) doença transmitida de um indivíduo a outro através do contato sexual

sieve tube element | elemento de tubo crivado tubo contínuo existente ao longo das células do floema das plantas, enfileiradas de uma extremidade a outra

single-gene trait | traço de gene único traço controlado por um gene com dois alelos

small intestine | intestino delgado órgão digestivo em que ocorre a maior parte do processo de digestão e absorção dos alimentos

smog | smog fumaça de coloração marrom acinzentada resultante de uma mistura de produtos químicos

society | sociedade grupo de animais intimamente relacionados da mesma espécie que trabalham em conjunto em benefício do grupo

solute | soluto substância dissolvida em uma solução

solution | solução tipo de mistura em que todos os componentes são distribuídos igualmente

solvent | solvente em uma solução, substância usada para dissolver

somatic nervous system | sistema nervoso somático parte do sistema nervoso periférico que transmite sinais de e para os músculos esqueletais

speciation | especiação formação de uma nova espécie

species diversity | diversidade de espécies número de espécies distintas que compõem uma determinada área

spirillum (pl. spirilla) | espirilo procariota de forma espiralada, como um saca-rolhas

spongy mesophyll | mesófilo esponjoso em uma folha, camada de tecido solto situada abaixo do mesófilo palissádico

sporangium (pl. sporangia) | esporângio cápsula de esporos em que esporos haplóides são produzidos através da meiose

spore | esporo em procariotas, protistas e fungos, qualquer variedade de estágios do ciclo de vida, de parede grossa, capaz de sobreviver em condições desfavoráveis; em plantas, célula reprodutiva haplóide

sporophyte | esporófito planta que produz esporos; fase diplóide multicelular do ciclo de vida de uma planta

stabilizing selection | seleção estabilizadora forma de seleção natural em que os indivíduos próximos ao centro de uma curva de distribuição são mais aptos do que indivíduos situados em uma das extremidades da curva

stamen | estame órgão masculino da flor; constituído pela antera e o filamento

stem cell | célula-tronco célula sem função específica que pode dar origem a um ou mais tipos de células específicas

stigma | estigma parte pegajosa encontrada no topo do pistilo para capturar pólen

stimulus (pl. stimuli) | estímulo sinal ao qual um organismo reage

stoma (pl. stomata) | estoma pequena abertura na epiderme da planta que permite a difusão de dióxido de carbono, água e oxigênio para dentro e para fora da folha

stomach | estômago grande saco muscular onde ocorre a digestão mecânica e química dos alimentos

stroma | estroma parte fluida do cloroplasto; parte externa dos tilacóides

substrate | substrato reagente em uma reação catalisada por enzimas

suspension | suspensão mistura de água e material não dissolvido

sustainable development | desenvolvimento sustentável estratégia para o uso de recursos naturais sem que sejam esgotados e para atender às necessidades do homem sem causar danos ambientais de longo prazo

symbiosis | simbiose relação mútua entre organismos de duas espécies distintas

synapse | sinapse ponto em que um neurônio pode transferir um impulso para outra célula

systematics | sistemática estudo da diversidade da vida e das relações evolutivas entre organismos

systemic circulation | circulação sistêmica caminho da circulação entre o coração e o resto do corpo

T

taiga | taiga bioma onde ocorrem longos invernos frios e poucos meses de clima quente; dominado por coníferas; também conhecido como floresta boreal

target cell | célula-alvo célula que possui um receptor para um determinado hormônio

taste bud | papila gustativa órgão sensorial do paladar

taxon (pl. taxa) | táxon grupo ou nível de organização para a classificação de organismos

telomere | telômero fileiras repetidas de DNA situadas na extremidade do cromossomo eucariótico

telophase | telófase fase mitótica em que cromossomos individuais distintos começam a se espalhar, formando uma rede de cromatina

temporal isolation | isolamento temporal forma de isolamento reprodutivo em que duas ou mais espécies se reproduzem em momentos distintos

tendon | tendão tecido firme de conexão que liga os músculos esqueletais aos ossos

territory | território área específica ocupada e protegida por um animal ou grupo de animais

testis (pl. testes) | testículo órgão reprodutivo masculino primário; produz esperma

tetrad | tétrade estrutura que contém quatro cromatídeos formada durante a meiose

tetrapod | tetrápodo vertebrado com quatro membros

thalamus | tálamo estrutura cerebral que recebe mensagens dos órgãos sensoriais e repassa as informações para a região pertinente do cérebro para dar continuidade ao processamento

theory | teoria explicação exaustivamente testada que unifica uma gama ampla de observações e hipóteses, permitindo que os cientistas façam afirmações precisas sobre novas situações

thigmotropism | tigmotropismo a reação de uma planta ao toque

threshold | limiar nível mínimo de estímulo necessário para causar um impulso

thylakoid | tilacóide membranas fotossintéticas em forma de saco encontradas em cloroplastos

thyroxine | tiroxina hormônio produzido pela glândula tireóide que aumenta a taxa metabólica de células no corpo

tissue | tecido grupo de células semelhantes que desempenham uma função específica

tolerance | tolerância capacidade de sobrevivência e reprodução de um organismo em circunstâncias que não sejam ideais

totipotent | totipotente células capazes de se transformar em qualquer tipo de célula do corpo, inclusive células que compõem as membranas extraembriônicas e a placenta

trachea | traquéia tubo que liga a faringe à laringe; também chamada de tubo de ar

tracheid | traqueíde célula vegetal perfurada do xilema com paredes celulares espessas reforçadas com lignina

tracheophyte | traqueófito planta vascular

trait | traço característica específica de um indivíduo

transcription | transcrição síntese de uma molécula de RNA a partir do modelo de DNA

transfer RNA (tRNA) | RNA transportador (tRNA) tipo de RNA que leva cada aminoácido a um ribossomo durante a síntese de proteína

transformation | transformação processo em que uma espécie de bactérias é alterada por um gene ou genes de outra espécie de bactérias

transgenic | transgênico refere-se a um organismo que contém genes de outros organismos

translation | tradução processo em que a seqüência de bases de mRNA é convertida na seqüência de aminoácidos de uma proteína

transpiration | transpiração perda de água de uma planta através das folhas

trochophore | trocóforo estágio larval de nado livre de um molusco aquático

trophic level | nível trófico cada etapa de uma cadeia ou teia alimentar

tropism | tropismo movimento de uma planta para perto ou longe de estímulos

tumor | tumor massa de células que se dividem rapidamente, podendo danificar o tecido à sua volta

U

understory | sub-bosque em florestas tropicais, camada situada sob a copa, formada por arbustos e plantas rasteiras

ureter | uréter tubo que leva urina de um rim à bexiga urinária

urethra | uretra tubo através do qual a urina sai do corpo

urinary bladder | bexiga urinária órgão em forma de saco onde a urina é armazenada antes de ser expelida

V

vaccination | vacinação injeção de um patógeno enfraquecido ou semelhante, porém menos perigoso, a fim de gerar imunidade

vaccine | vacina preparação de patógenos enfraquecidos ou mortos com o objetivo de gerar imunidade a uma doença

vacuole | vacúolo organelo celular que armazena matérias como água, sais, proteínas e carboidratos

valve | válvula aba de tecido conectivo situada entre um átrio e um ventrículo ou em uma veia para evitar o contrafluxo sangüíneo

van der Waals forces | forças de van der Waals pequena atração entre duas regiões de cargas opostas de moléculas próximas

vas deferens | duto deferente tubo que transporta o esperma do epidídimo à uretra

vascular bundle | feixe vascular aglomeração de tecido de xilema e floema em caules

vascular cambium | câmbio vascular meristema que produz tecidos vasculares, aumentando a espessura dos caules

vascular cylinder | cilindro vascular região central de uma raiz que inclui os tecidos vasculares – xilema e floema

vascular tissue | tecido vascular tecido especializado de vegetais que transporta água e nutrientes

vector | vetor animal que transporta um patógeno para um ser humano

vegetative reproduction | reprodução vegetativa método de reprodução assexuada em plantas que permite que uma única planta produza frutos geneticamente idênticos a ela

vein | veia vaso sangüíneo que leva sangue do corpo para o coração

ventricle | ventrículo câmara inferior do coração que bombeia o sangue do coração para o resto do corpo

vertebrate | vertebrado tipo de animal que possui espinha dorsal

vessel element | elemento de vaso tipo de célula do xilema que faz parte de um tubo contínuo através do qual a água passa

vestigial organs | órgãos vestigiais estruturas de tamanho reduzido que exercem uma função secundária ou nula

villus (pl. villi) | vilo projeção de forma semelhante a um dedo situada no intestino delgado que ajuda na absorção de moléculas de nutrientes

virus | vírus partícula formada por proteínas, ácidos nucléicos e ocasionalmente lipídeos que podem se reproduzir apenas através da infecção de células vivas

vitamin | vitamina molécula orgânica que ajuda a regular processos do corpo

viviparous | vivíparo animal que gera filhotes alimentados diretamente pelo corpo da mãe durante seu desenvolvimento

W

weather | clima condições da atmosfera dia após dia, incluindo temperatura, precipitação e outros fatores

wetland | zona úmida ecossistema onde a água cobre o solo ou está presente na superfície ou perto dela pelo menos durante parte do ano

white blood cell | leucócito tipo de célula sangüínea que protege contra infecções, combate parasitas e ataca bactérias

woody plant | planta madeireira tipo de planta formada basicamente de células de paredes espessas que sustentam o corpo da planta; inclui árvores, arbustos e plantas rasteiras

X

xylem | xilema tecido vascular que transporta água das raízes para o resto da planta

Z

zoonosis (pl. zoonoses) | zoonose doença transmitida de animais para seres humanos

zooplankton | zooplâncton pequenos animais que flutuam livremente e compõem o plâncton

zygote | zigoto ovo fertilizado

Simplified Chinese
简体中文

Miller & Levine
Biology Glossary

A

abiotic factor | 非生物因子 形成生态系统的物理或非生命因子

abscisic acid | 脱落酸 阻止细胞分裂，从而抑制生长的植物激素

acetylcholine | 乙酰胆碱 在肌肉细胞中产生冲动的神经递质

acid | 酸 能在溶液中析出氢离子（H⁺）的化合物；pH 值小于 7 的溶液

acid rain | 酸雨 含有氮、硫的降雨

actin | 肌动蛋白 肌肉中组成细肌丝的结构蛋白

action potential | 动作电位 神经细胞产生的可逆转的跨膜电位变化，又称神经冲动

activation energy | 活化能 启动一个反应所需的能量

active immunity | 自动免疫 机体受到自然或有目的的抗原刺激后所产生的免疫

adaptation | 适应性 可增加生物体在环境中存活和繁殖能力的可遗传性状

adaptive radiation | 适应辐射 单个物种或小群体在进化过程中为适应不同的生活方式而分化成多种类型的过程

adenosine triphosphate (ATP) | 三磷酸腺苷 (ATP) 细胞储存和释放能量的化合物

adhesion | 粘附力 不同分子之间的吸附作用

aerobic | 需氧 需要氧气的过程

age structure | 年龄结构 种群中各年龄组雄性和雌性的数量

aggression | 侵袭 某一动物试图统治另一动物的威胁性行为

algal bloom | 藻华 由于有限养分的大量输入而引起藻类和其它生物的数目激增

allele | 等位基因 同一基因座上的不同形式基因

allergy | 变态反应 免疫系统对抗原的过激反应

alternation of generations | 世代交替 一个生命周期中两种时期---单倍体（N）时期和双倍体（2N）时期---相互交替出现

alveolus (pl. alveoli) | 肺泡 位于肺细支气管终端的微小气囊，提供表面区域以进行气体交换

amino acid | 氨基酸 一端是氨基，另一端是羧基的化合物

amniotic egg | 羊膜卵 具有壳和膜的卵，能为胚胎提供保护性环境，使之脱离水中发育

amylase | 淀粉酶 存在于唾液中的一种酶，能水解淀粉中的化学键

anaerobic | 厌氧 不需要氧气的过程

anaphase | 后期 染色体分离并移向细胞两极的有丝分裂阶段

angiosperm | 被子植物 种子有果皮包被和保护的一类种子植物，又称开花植物

anther | 花药 产生花粉粒的一种花结构

antheridium (pl. antheridia) | 精子器 某些植物上产生精子的雄性生殖结构

anthropoid | 类人猿 由猴、猿和人类组成的灵长类动物

antibiotic | 抗生素 一类用于阻止病原菌生长繁殖的药物

antibody | 抗体 能直接攻击抗原或产生抗原结合蛋白的蛋白质

anticodon | 反密码子 tRNA 分子上的三联碱基，与 mRNA 上的三联碱基互补

antigen | 抗原 触发免疫反应的任何物质

aphotic zone | 无光带 海洋中透光带以下，阳光不能透过的黑暗层

apical dominance | 顶端优势 越接近茎的顶端的芽，其生长就越受到抑制的现象

apical meristem | 顶端分生组织 一群未特化的细胞，可分裂从而增加茎和根的长度

apoptosis | 凋亡 程序性细胞死亡

appendage | 附肢 由体壁延伸而来的结构，如腿或触角

appendicular skeleton | 附肢骨 位于手臂、大腿、骨盆以及肩膀部位的骨骼

aquaculture | 水产养殖 养殖水生有机物以供人类食用

aquaporin | 水通道蛋白 细胞中的水分子通道蛋白

Archaea | 古菌 由单细胞原核生物组成的一类生物域，细胞壁不含肽聚糖，与古细菌界相对应

archegonium (pl. archegonia) | 颈卵器 植物上能产生卵细胞的结构

artery | 动脉 能将血液从心脏输送到各机体组织的大血管

artificial selection | 人工选择 为促进子代的目的特性而对动植物进行选择性繁殖

asexual reproduction | 无性繁殖 由单亲代直接产生子代的一种繁殖方法，子代和亲代的遗传特性完全相同

asthma | 哮喘 慢性呼吸系统疾病，由于气道狭窄而导致喘息、咳嗽和呼吸困难

atherosclerosis | 动脉粥样硬化 由于脂质沉积而在动脉内壁形成斑块，最后导致动脉变硬的一种病理状态

atom | 原子 物质的基本单位

ATP synthase | ATP 合酶 允许氢离子 (H^+) 跨膜转运的蛋白簇

atrium (pl. atria) | 心房 位于心脏上部的空腔，可接受来自机体其它部位的血液

autonomic nervous system | 自主神经系统 可以不受意志支配而自主调控内脏活动的部分外周神经，包括交感神经和副交感神经

autosome | 常染色体 性染色体以外的其它染色体，又称体染色体

autotroph | 自养生物 能从太阳光或化学物质中摄取能量，并利用它从无机物中合成食物的生物体

auxin | 生长素 生长植物顶端产生的调节物质，可刺激细胞伸长和新根生长

axial skeleton | 中轴骨 支持机体中轴的骨骼，包括颅骨、脊柱和胸骨

axon | 轴突 神经元上的长突起，负责将神经冲动带离细胞体

B

bacillus (pl. bacilli) | 杆菌 杆状的原核生物

background extinction | 背景灭绝 由于自然选择而导致的缓慢而稳定的物种灭绝过程

Bacteria | 细菌 由单细胞原核生物组成的一类生物域，细胞壁含有肽聚糖，与真细菌界相对应

bacteriophage | 噬菌体 感染细菌的一类病毒

bark | 树皮 维管形成层以外的组织，包括韧皮、栓皮形成层和栓皮

base | 碱 能在溶液中形成氢氧离子 (OH^-) 的化合物；pH 值大于 7 的溶液

base pairing | 碱基配对 DNA 中的化学键只能形成于腺嘌呤和胸腺嘧啶，鸟嘌呤和包嘧啶之间的原则

behavior | 行为 生物对内部状态或外部环境的变化作出反应的方式

behavioral isolation | 行为隔离 两个种群在求偶仪式或其它阻碍繁殖的行为上发生分化，从而引起的一种生殖隔离形式

benthos | 底栖生物 居住在湖泊、溪流或海洋底部或附近的生物

bias | 偏见 一种人为而非科学的特定喜好或观点

bilateral symmetry | 两侧对称 可用一条中轴线将机体分成互为镜像的左右两部分的机体排列方式

binary fission | 二分裂 无性繁殖的一种类型，生物体复制 DNA 并一分为二，产生两个相同的子代细胞

binocular vision | 双眼视觉 融合来自两只眼睛的视觉形象，从而具有深度知觉和三维世界视觉的能力

binomial nomenclature | 双命名法 为每一个物种指定一个由两部分构成的科学名称的分类系统

biodiversity | 生物多样性 生物圈中的所有不同生物；又称生物学多样性

biogeochemical cycle | 生物地球化学循环 生态界中的各种元素、化学复合物及其它物质形式从一种生物转移到另一生物，从生物界的一部分转移到另一部分的过程

biogeography | 生物地理学 研究生物在时间和空间上的分布的一门学科

bioinformatics | 生物信息学 利用数学和计算机科学来储存、检索和分析生物学数据

biological magnification | 生物放大 在同一食物链或食物网中，营养级越高的生物，其体内的有害物质浓度越高

biology | 生物学 研究生命的一门科学

biomass | 生物量 特定营养级中生物组织的总量

biome | 生物群系 具有相似气候和典型生物的生态系统群

biosphere | 生物圈 地球上有生命存在的区域，包括陆地，水，空气或大气层

biotechnology | 生物技术 利用生物、细胞或分子来生产特定产品的工艺

biotic factor | 生物因子 在可能与生物体相互影响的环境中的任何有机体

bipedal | 两足动物 用两条腿运动的动物

blade | 叶片 植物叶子上薄而平的部分

blastocyst | 胚泡 哺乳动物的早期发育阶段，是一个由细胞组成的空心球

blastula | 囊胚 受精卵经过一系列细胞分裂而形成的一个由细胞组成的空心球

bone marrow | 骨髓 骨腔中的软组织

bottleneck effect | 瓶颈效应 由于种群规模急剧减小而导致等位基因频率的改变

Bowman's capsule | 鲍曼囊 包绕肾小球的杯状结构；收集来自血液的滤液

brain stem | 脑干 连接大脑和脊髓的结构，包括延髓和桥脑

bronchus (pl. bronchi) | 支气管 胸腔中从气管发出进入肺部的两大通气管道之一

bryophyte | 苔藓植物 具有特化生殖器官但体内无维管组织的一类植物，包括藓类及其亲缘植物

bud | 芽 植物上含有顶端分生组织，能产生新的茎叶的结构

buffer | 缓冲液 能防止 pH 值发生急剧、突然变化的化合物

C

calcitonin | 降钙素 甲状腺分泌的一种激素，能降低血钙水平

Calorie | 大卡 食物的热量单位，相当于 1000 小卡

calorie | 小卡 使 1 克水的温度升高 1 摄氏度所需的能量

Calvin cycle | 卡尔文循环 利用 ATP 和 NADPH 作为能源生成高能化合物（如，糖）的光合作用暗反应

cancer | 癌 部分机体细胞生长失控的一种病理状态

canopy | 林冠 高大雨林树木的顶部枝叶形成的浓密树盖

capillary | 毛细血管 最小的一类血管，能将营养物质和氧气带到组织中，同时吸收二氧化碳和废物

capillary action | 毛细管作用 液体在细管内趋于上升的现象

capsid | 衣壳 包绕病毒的一层蛋白质

carbohydrate | 碳水化合物 由碳、氢和氧原子组成的化合物，不仅是营养物质而且是机体的主要能量来源

carnivore | 食肉动物 以进食其它生物来摄取能量的生物

carpel | 心皮 花最里面的部分，能产生和保护雌配子

carrying capacity | 承载能力 特定环境所能容纳的某一物种的最大个体数

cartilage | 软骨 一种结缔组织，可为机体提供支撑，比骨骼更加柔软灵活

Casparian strip | 凯氏带 包绕植物内皮层细胞的防水带，与植物根部维管柱中的单向物质转运有关

catalyst | 催化剂 能加快化学反应速率的物质

cell | 细胞 所有生命形式的基本单位

cell body | 胞体 典型神经元的最大部分，包含细胞核和大量胞质

cell cycle | 细胞循环 细胞生长、准备分裂和分裂成两个子代细胞的一系列过程

cell division | 细胞分裂 细胞分裂成两个新的子代细胞的过程

cell membrane | 细胞膜 包绕整个细胞的薄而灵活的屏障，可控制物质出入细胞

cell theory | 细胞学说 生物学的基础概念，它提出所有生命体都由细胞构成，细胞是生命体结构和功能的基本单位，新细胞由原有细胞产生

cell wall | 细胞壁 在某些细胞上包绕细胞膜的坚固支持层

cell–mediated immunity | 细胞免疫 在机体中抵御病毒、真菌以及活细胞中异常癌细胞的一种免疫应答

cellular respiration | 细胞呼吸 在有氧条件下分解葡萄糖和其它食物大分子，从而释放能量的过程

central nervous system | 中枢神经系统 包括大脑和脊髓，负责处理传递给机体的信息并作出响应

centriole | 中心粒 动物细胞中的一个结构，能协助细胞分裂

centromere | 中心体 染色体上姐妹染色单体附着的区域

cephalization | 头部形成 感觉器官和神经细胞向动物身体前端集中的进化趋势

cerebellum | 小脑 脑的一部分，负责协调运动和控制平衡

cerebral cortex | 大脑皮层 哺乳动物的大脑外层，是思考和其它复杂活动的中心

cerebrum | 大脑 负责机体自主活动的脑结构

chemical digestion | 化学消化 利用酶将食物分解成可供机体使用的小分子物质的过程

chemical reaction | 化学反应 一组化学物质变成或转化成另一组化学物质的过程

chemosynthesis | 化学合成 利用化学能量来生成碳水化合物的过程

chitin | 几丁质 组成真菌细胞壁的复杂碳水化合物，亦见于节肢动物的外骨骼

chlorophyll | 叶绿素 植物和其它光合生物的主要色素

chloroplast | 叶绿体 植物和其它一些生物体的细胞器官，可从太阳光中摄取能量并将之转化成化学能

chordate | 脊索动物 个体发育过程中至少有一个阶段具有背神经管、脊索、肛后尾以及鳃裂的动物

chromatid | 染色单体 复制染色体中两条相同的"姐妹"单体之一

chromatin | 染色质 真核生物染色体中的物质，由螺旋状紧密包绕在组蛋白上的 DNA 组成

chromosome | 染色体 细胞核中的线状物质，含有可从亲代传递给子代的遗传信息

chyme | 食糜 由酶和部分消化的食物所组成的混合物

cilium (pl. cilia) | 纤毛 毛发状的短小凸出，具有产生运动的能力

circadian rhythm | 昼夜节律 生物体每天的生命行为周期

clade | 分支 进化树的进化分支，包括一个祖先及其所有后代

cladogram | 进化树 描述物种共同特征的示意图

class | 纲 生物学分类中一组具有较近亲缘关系的目的集合

classical conditioning | 经典条件反射 动物在刺激与某些奖励或惩罚之间建立起精神联系后所产生的一种学习类型

climate | 气候 一个地区长时间内温度和降水的年平均状态

clone | 克隆 由单个细胞繁殖形成，在遗传上完全相同的细胞群

closed circulatory system | 封闭循环系统 一种循环系统，血液完全在遍布整个机体的血管内循环

coccus (pl. cocci) | 球菌 球形的原核生物

cochlea | 耳蜗 内耳中充满液体的部分，含有可感觉声音的神经细胞

codominance | 共显性 两种等位基因完全表达时所产生的表型状态

codon | 密码子 mRNA 中的三联核苷酸碱基，可决定蛋白质分子中含有的特定氨基酸

coelom | 体腔 被中胚层所覆盖的空腔

coevolution | 共进化 两个物种长期相互适应对方变化而达到进化的过程

cohesion | 内聚力 相同物质的分子之间的吸附作用力

collenchyma | 厚角组织 植物的一种基本组织，具有牢固而灵活的细胞壁，有助于支撑更大的组织

commensalism | 偏利共生 一种共生关系，其中一种生物得益，另一种即不得益也不受害

communication | 通讯 信息由一个生物传递给另一生物

community | 群落 在一定区域内共同生活的不同种群的集合体

companion cell | 伴胞 植物中包绕筛管成分的韧皮细胞

competitive exclusion principle | 竞争排斥原理 生态位相同的两个物种不能于同一时间在相同生境中共存的原则

compound | 化合物 由两种或两种以上元素按一定比例通过化学反应形成的物质

cone | 锥体 眼睛中的一种感光器，能感受不同颜色的光，从而产生色彩视觉

coniferous | 针叶树 指能产生携带种子的球果并具有薄针形树叶的一种树

conjugation | 接合 草履虫和某些原核生物交换遗传信息的过程

connective tissue | 结缔组织 可以连接机体各部分并为之提供支持的组织类型

consumer | 消费者 依赖其它生物提供能量和食物的生物体，又称异养型生物

control group | 对照组 在试验中，除某项独立条件以外，受测条件与试验组完全相同的组

controlled experiment | 对照试验 仅改变一项条件的试验

convergent evolution | 趋同进化 不相关的生物体在相似环境中独立进化出相似性的过程

cork cambium | 木栓形成层 可于植物的次生生长期间生成外包被的分生组织

cornea | 角膜 眼睛的坚硬透明层，光可透过它进入眼睛

corpus luteum | 卵巢黄体 排卵后的黄色囊泡

cortex | 树皮 植物根内的基本组织部分，可运送水分和矿物质

corticosteroid | 皮质醇 由肾上腺皮质分泌的类固醇激素

cotyledon | 子叶 种子植物胚最先生成的一片或一对叶子

courtship | 求偶 动物发出刺激信号以吸引众多异性的行为

covalent bond | 共价键 相邻原子通过共用电子对而形成的化学键

crossing-over | 交换 减数分裂中同源染色体交换染色单体的过程

cyclin | 细胞周期蛋白 在真核细胞中调控细胞周期的一个蛋白家族

cytokinesis | 胞质分裂 细胞质分裂形成两个分离的子代细胞

cytokinin | 细胞分裂素 由生长的根、发育的果实以及种子产生的植物激素

cytoplasm | 细胞质 细胞中核以外的液体部分

cytoskeleton | 细胞骨架 真核细胞中的蛋白纤维网络结构，能维持细胞形态和内部结构，并参与细胞的移动

D

data | 数据 证据；由观察得来的信息

deciduous | 落叶树 在每年的特定季节都会落叶的树

decomposer | 分解者 可分解有机物并从中摄取能量的生物

deforestation | 滥伐 砍伐破坏森林

demographic transition | 人口转变 人口从高出生率和高死亡率向低出生率和低死亡率的转变

demography | 人口学 研究人类种群的一门科学

dendrite | 树突 神经元胞体的延伸，可将来自环境或其它神经元的神经冲动传递到胞体

denitrification | 脱氮作用 土壤菌将硝酸盐转化为氮气的过程

density-dependent limiting factor | 密度制约因素 依赖种群密度的制约因素

density-independent limiting factor | 非密度制约因素 对种群的影响与种群密度无关的制约因素

deoxyribonucleic acid (DNA) | 脱氧核糖核酸 (DNA) 生物体从亲本继承而来的遗传物质

dependent variable | 因变量 随自变量而变的可见变量，又称应变量

derived character | 衍生特征 在世系中新近出现的遗传特征，不见于年长成员

dermis | 真皮 表皮层以下的皮肤层

desertification | 荒漠化 由于过度耕种、过度放牧、季节性干旱以及气候变化所导致的耕地产量降低

detritivore | 食腐生物 以动植物残余物和其它已死亡物体为食的生物体

deuterostome | 后口动物 肛门由胚孔发展而来、口腔由第二开口发展而来的动物种群

diaphragm | 膈 位于胸腔底部，能帮助呼吸的大块水平肌肉

dicot | 双子叶植物 子房中有两个子叶的被子植物

differentiation | 分化 细胞向特定结构和功能发展的过程

diffusion | 扩散 微粒趋于自高浓度区向低浓度区移动的过程

digestive tract | 消化管道 始于口腔而终于肛门的管道

diploid | 二倍体 指包含有两套同源染色体的细胞

directional selection | 趋向性选择 自然选择的一种形式，位于分布曲线一端的个体相对位于曲线中部或另一端的个体具有更强的适应性

disruptive selection | 分裂性选择 位于曲线顶端和底端的个体相对接近曲线中部的个体具有更强的适应性

DNA fingerprinting | DNA 指纹 生物学家用来对个体独一无二的 DNA 限制片段集合进行分析的工具，可用来判别两个基因物质样本是否来自于同一个人

DNA microarray | DNA 芯片 携有数以千计以矩阵形式排列的不同类型单链 DNA 片段的玻璃片或硅芯片。DNA 芯片一次可检查和测量数以千计基因的表达序列

DNA polymerase | DNA 聚合酶 参与 DNA 复制的主要酶

domain | 域 比界更大、包罗范围更广的分类类别

dopamine | 多巴胺 与大脑的愉悦和奖励中心相关联的神经传递素

dormancy | 冬眠 植物胚芽保持存活但不生长的时期

double fertilization | 双授精 对被子植物进行授精的过程，第一次产生受精卵，第二次产生种子胚乳

E

ecological footprint | 生态足迹 提供一定人类种群所需的资源并吸收这些群体所产生的废物所需的功能性生态系统的总量

ecological hot spot | 生态热点 大量的自然环境和物种正濒临灭绝的小片地理区域

ecological pyramid | 生态金字塔 针对给定食物链或食物网中的各营养级所包含的相对能量或物质数量的图解

ecological succession | 生态演变 一个生物群落在干扰发生后出现的一系列渐变

ecology | 生态学 针对生物体之间及生物体与其环境之间相互作用的科学研究

ecosystem | 生态系统 生活在一定空间内的所有生物体及其非生命环境的统称

ecosystem diversity | 生态系统多样性 生物圈内的自然环境、群落和生态变化的多种多样

ectoderm | 外胚层 最外侧的胚层，将产生感觉器官、神经和外层皮肤

ectotherm | 冷血动物 体温由所处环境的温度决定的动物

electron | 电子 带负电的粒子，位于原子核周围的空间中

electron transport chain | 电子传递链 在ATP 生成反应中，负责传递高能电子的一系列电子携带蛋白

element | 元素 只包含一种类型原子的纯物质

embryo | 胚胎 多细胞生物体的一个发展阶段

embryo sac | 胚囊 位于开花植物胚珠内的雌性配子体

emerging disease | 新发传染病 首次在种群中出现的疾病或突然失去控制的已有疾病

emigration | 迁移 个体离开某一区域的活动

endocrine gland | 内分泌腺 直接向血液释放其分泌物（激素）的腺体，然后血液会将这些分泌物运送至身体的其他部位

endoderm | 内胚层 最内侧的胚层，将发展成消化系统和呼吸系统的大部

endodermis | 内皮 植物中完全包被维管柱的基本组织层

endoplasmic reticulum | 内质网 真核细胞内的内膜系统，可汇聚细胞膜中的液体成分

endoskeleton | 内骨骼 内部骨架，动物体内的结构性支撑系统

endosperm | 胚乳 在植物苗生长过程中为其提供丰富养料的组织

endospore | 芽胞 原核生物在不利情况下产生的结构；一层包裹 DNA 及部分细胞质的厚内壁

endosymbiotic theory | 内共生学说 该理论认为真核细胞是由多个不同原核细胞共生而成

endotherm | 恒温动物 可通过身体内部产生的热量来调节或部分调节体温的动物

enzyme | 酶 能加速特定生物反应速度的蛋白催化剂

epidermis | 表皮 对植物，构成真皮组织的单层细胞；对人类，外层皮肤

epididymis | 附睾 男性生殖系统的器官之一，精子在其中成熟和存储

epinephrine | 肾上腺素 肾上腺分泌的激素，能使心跳加快、血压升高，令身体为剧烈体力活动做好准备，又称为副肾素

epithelial tissue | 上皮组织 隔离机体内外表面的组织类型

era | 纪 地质年代的主要划分方式，通常由两个或更多时期组成

esophagus | 食道 连接口腔和胃的管道

estuary | 河口 因河流入海而形成的湿地类型

ethylene | 乙烯 刺激果实成熟的植物激素

Eukarya | 真核域 由所有拥有细胞核的生物体所组成的域，包括原生生物、植物、真菌和动物

eukaryote | 真核生物 细胞包含细胞核的生物体

evolution | 进化 生物随着时间流逝而不断发生的变化，现代生物由远古生物繁衍而来的过程

excretion | 排泄 新陈代谢的废物被排出体外的过程

exocrine gland | 外分泌腺 通过被称为输送管的管状结构直接向器官或体外释放其分泌物的腺体

exon | 外显子 DNA 的表达序列，含蛋白质编码

exoskeleton | 外骨骼 外部骨架；坚硬的外部包被，很多无脊椎动物都依靠它来保护和支撑身体

exponential growth | 指数增长 一种增长模式，种群内的个体都以固定速率进行繁殖

extinct | 灭绝 指某个物种已全部死亡，且不再有存活的成员

extracellular digestion | 细胞外消化 一种消化形式，食物在消化系统的细胞外被分解，然后被吸收

F

facilitated diffusion | 促进扩散 一种扩散过程，分子将通过细胞膜通道来透过细胞膜

family | 科 生物学分类中一组相似的种属

fat | 脂肪 油脂，由脂肪酸和甘油组成；一种可保护身体器官的营养成分，可为身体隔热和储存能量

feedback inhibition | 反馈抑制 刺激产生反应，而产生的反应又对原始刺激产生抑制的过程，又称为负反馈

fermentation | 发酵 细胞在缺氧的情况下释放能量的过程

fertilization | 授精 雄性生殖细胞和雌性生殖细胞共同形成新细胞的有性繁殖过程

fetus | 胎儿 已生长八个星期以上的人类胚胎

fever | 发烧 因感染反应而出现的体温上升

filtration | 过滤 令液体或气体通过过滤器以清除废物的过程

fitness | 适应性 生物体在其环境中生存和繁殖的状态好坏

flagellum (pl. flagella) | 鞭毛 原生生物用来移动的结构，能产生波动状的移动

food chain | 食物链 在生态系统中，生物体通过吃和被吃来传递能量的一系列步骤

food vacuole | 食物泡 原生生物用来暂存食物的细胞质内小洞

food web | 食物网 在生态系统中，由各种生物体之间的食物关系而形成的复杂相互作用网络

forensics | 法医学 调查犯罪证据的科学研究

fossil | 化石 远古生物体的留存部分

founder effect | 始祖效应 由于新亚群的融合而导致的等位基因频率的变化

frameshift mutation | 移码突变 由于核苷酸的插入或删除而导致遗传信息的"读码框"移位而导致的突变

fruit | 果实 被子植物中包含一个或多个已成熟卵巢的结构

fruiting body | 子实体 长自菌丝体的真菌的繁殖结构

G

gamete | 配子 性细胞

gametophyte | 配偶体 配子繁殖植物；植物生命周期中的多细胞单倍体阶段

ganglion (pl. ganglia) | 神经节 一组中间神经元

gastrovascular cavity | 肠腔 只有一个开口的消化室

gastrulation | 原肠胚形成 细胞融合并产生三个细胞层——外胚层、中胚层和内胚层的过程

gel electrophoresis | 凝胶电泳 通过在凝胶一端放置 DNA 片段的混合物并对凝胶施以一定电压来分离和分析 DNA 片段的方式

gene | 基因 决定蛋白编码及其特性的 DNA 序列；由父代传递于子代的因素

gene expression | 基因表达 基因产生出具有其功能的产物的过程

gene pool | 基因库 某一种群在任一时间点所呈现的全部基因，包括各基因的不同等位基因

gene therapy | 基因治疗 通过修改基因来治疗疾病或紊乱的方法。用正常工作的基因来代替缺失或有问题的基因

genetic code | 基因编码 mRNA 密码子的集合，其中每个密码都将决定蛋白质合成中某个特定的氨基酸将如何合并入蛋白质

genetic diversity | 基因多样性 由特定物种或地球上所有生物所携带的不同类型基因信息的总和

genetic drift | 基因漂移 因导致某种等位基因在种群中变得更常见或更不常见的一系列偶然事件而引起的等位基因频率的随机变化

genetic equilibrium | 遗传平衡 种群中的等位基因频率保持不变的情况

genetic marker | 遗传标记 能产生对基因分析非常有用的可监测表型差异的等位基因

genetics | 遗传学 研究生物遗传的一门科学

genome | 基因组 生物体在其 DNA 中携带的全部基因信息集合

genomics | 基因组学 研究整个基因组的科学，包括基因及其功能

genotype | 基因型 生物体的基因组成

genus | 属 紧密关联物种的集合；以双名法命名的学名的第一部分

geographic isolation | 地理隔离 一种生殖隔离形式，两个种群被地理界限所隔离，例如：河流、山脉、水体，从而导致两个独立亚种的形成

geologic time scale | 地质学时标 用来表示地球历史的时标

germ theory of disease | 细菌致病论 认为传染病是由微生物导致的理论

germination | 萌芽 植物胚芽在冬眠后重新恢复生长

giberellin | 赤霉素 植物激素，能刺激生长并可能导致植物大小的显著增长

gill | 腮 专门用于在水下进行气体交换的羽毛状结构

global warming | 全球暖化 地球上平均温度的增加

glomerulus | 肾小球 位于肾元上端的小型毛细血管网；也是进行血液过滤的位置

glycolysis | 醣酵解 细胞呼吸的初始阶段，一分子糖被分解成两分子丙酮酸

Golgi apparatus | 高尔基体 一种细胞器，主要功能是对自内质网合成的蛋白及其它物质进行加工、分类和包装，然后储存在细胞或分泌到细胞外

gradualism | 渐进 物种通过长时期地累积微小遗传变化而实现进化的过程

grafting | 嫁接 植物繁殖的一种方法，主要用于无种子植物和一些不能通过扦插进行繁殖的木本植物

gravitropism | 向地性 植物对重力的生长反应

green revolution | 绿色革命 培育高产的农作物品种，并使用现代农业技术来增加粮食作物的产量

greenhouse effect | 温室效应 由于某些气体（二氧化碳，甲烷以及水蒸汽）吸收地球大气层的太阳光能量而地球变暖的过程

growth factor | 生长因子 一种细胞外调节蛋白，可刺激细胞生长和分裂

guard cells | 保卫细胞 植物表皮的特化细胞，可控制气孔的开闭

gullet | 胞咽 纤毛虫类动物体表一侧的陷凹，允许食物进入细胞

gymnosperm | 裸子植物 种子植物的一个群，种子直接附着在球果的鳞片上

H

habitat | 栖息地 生物居住的区域，包括对其造成影响的生物因子和非生物因子

habitat fragmentation | 栖息地片段化 生态系统被分割成片状

habituation | 习惯化 一种学习类型，指动物对某一无害亦无益的反复刺激的反应削弱或消失

hair follicle | 毛囊 上皮细胞上的管状口袋，延伸至真皮。毛囊根部的细胞可生成毛发

half life | 半衰期 样本中的放射性元素有一半发生衰变所需的时间

haploid | 单倍体 指仅含有一套基因的细胞

Hardy–Weinberg principle | 哈迪–温伯格定律 在一个种群中，若没有外界因素影响，等位基因的频率将保持不变的原则

Haversian canal | 哈弗氏管 纵行于骨密质的管状构造之一，内含血管和神经

heart | 心脏 中空的肌肉器官，负责将血液泵入机体各部分

heartwood | 树心 木本茎中靠近茎中央的老年木质部分，不能再输送水分

hemoglobin | 血色素 血液红细胞中的含铁蛋白，可结合氧气并将其运输到机体各部分

herbaceous plant | 草本植物 具有柔软非木本茎的植物类别，包括蒲公英、百日草，矮牵牛，向日葵

herbivore | 食草动物 仅以植物为食来摄取能量的生物

herbivory | 食草作用 动物（食草动物）以生产者（例如植物）为食的相互作用

heterotroph | 异养生物 通过消耗其他有生命物体来获得食物的生物体，也称为消费者

heterozygous | 杂合 携带特定基因的两种不同等位基因的状态

histamine | 组胺 由肥大细胞分泌的化学物质，可在炎症反应期间增大流向感染区域的血液和体液量

homeobox gene | 同源异型盒基因 同源异型盒是由大约 130 个碱基对组成的 DNA 序列，常见于调节生长的多种同源异型基因。包含此序列的基因被称为同源异型基因，能编码转录因子、DNA 结合蛋白，并能调节其他基因的表达

homeostasis | 动态平衡 生物体保持的相对恒定的内部物理和化学环境

homeotic gene | 同源异型基因 调节基因的一类，能决定动物胚胎中机体部分和部位的表达。这些基因的突变可将身体的一部分转变成另一部分

hominine | 人亚科 人科下的亚科，包括人类

hominoid | 人科 类人猿的统称，包括长臂猿、猩猩、大猩猩、黑猩猩和人类

homologous | 同源的 指一套来自父系、一套来自母系的染色体

homologous structures | 同源结构 具有共同祖先的不同物种中存在的类似结构

homozygous | 纯合子 携带特定基因的两个相同等位基因的状态

hormone | 激素 由生物体的某一部分产生、能对同一生物体的其他部位产生影响的化学物质

Hox gene | 同源异型基因簇 一组成簇的同源异型基因，能决定动物从头到尾的全部部位表达。所有同源异型基因簇都包含同源异型基因序列

humoral immunity | 体液免疫 体液内能抵抗抗原的抗体，例如血液和淋巴液

humus | 腐殖质 由腐烂的树叶和其他有机质组成的物质

hybrid | 杂合体 由具有不同遗传特性的亲代杂交所产生的子代

hybridization | 杂交 不相同的个体之间进行交配，以产生兼具两类生物体最佳遗传特性的育种技术（15 rp）

hydrogen bond | 氢键 存在于氢原子及其他原子之间的弱吸引力

hydrostatic skeleton | 静水骨骼 由充满液体的机体段组成的骨骼，能与肌肉一起协作来令动物运动

hypertonic | 高渗溶液 在比较两种溶液时，溶质浓度更高的那一种溶液

hypha (pl. hyphae) | 菌丝 组成菌体的大量细长丝状物之一

hypothalamus | 视丘下部 作为控制中心，负责识别和分析饥饿、干渴、疲惫、愤怒和体温的脑结构

hypothesis | 假说 对一系列观测现象的可能解释或科学问题的可能答案

hypotonic | 低渗溶液 在比较两种溶液时，溶质浓度较低的那一种溶液

I

immigration | 迁入 个体向已有现有种群占领的区域移动的现象

immune response | 免疫应答 机体对病原体攻击的特定识别、应答和记忆

implantation | 着床 胚泡附着至子宫壁上的过程

imprinting | 胚教 基于早期体验的行为类型；一旦完成胚教，行为就不能再被改变

inbreeding | 同系繁殖 通过具有类似特性个体的持续性繁衍，来保持某种生物体的衍生特性

incomplete dominance | 不完全显性 一种等位基因未能完全压制另一种等位基因的现象

independent assortment | 自由组合 孟德尔遗传定律之一，具有不同遗传特性的基因可在配子形成期间独立分离

independent variable | 自变数 在对照试验中被有意调整的因素，又称操纵变量

index fossil | 标准化石 用来比较化石相对年代的特殊化石

infectious disease | 传染病 由可破坏正常机体功能的微生物所导致的疾病

inference | 推论 以之前的知识和经验为基础的逻辑推理

inflammatory response | 炎症反应 针对由伤害或感染引起的组织损伤的非特异性防御反应

innate behavior | 先天性行为 一种行为类型，指第一次进行就以全功能形式出现的行为，即使相应动物之前并无与该行为所针对的刺激相关的经验；又称本能

insight learning | 顿悟学习 一种行为类型，指动物在未经尝试和失败的情况下，将其已经学会的事物应用至一个全新的场景，又称推理

interferon | 干扰素 一种蛋白质，有助于细胞对抗病毒感染

interneuron | 中间神经元 一种神经元，能对信息进行处理并能将信息传递给运动神经元

interphase | 间期 细胞周期中处于两次细胞分裂之间的时期

intracellular digestion | 细胞内消化 食物在特化细胞内被消化，然后由这些细胞将营养通过扩散传递给其他细胞的消化方式

intron | 内含子 不编码蛋白的 DNA 序列

invertebrate | 无脊椎动物 不具有脊椎或脊柱的动物

ion | 离子 带正电或负电的原子

ionic bond | 共价键 因一个或多个电子从一个原子转移至另一个原子而形成的化学键

iris | 虹膜 眼睛中带颜色的部分

isotonic | 等压 两种溶液的浓度相同的情况

isotope | 同位素 同种元素的不同形式中的一种，包含相同数目的质子但中子数不同

J

joint | 关节 骨与骨相连的部位

K

karyotype | 核型 二倍体中的全部染色体，按其大小递减、成对排列而成的图像

keratin | 角蛋白 皮肤中坚硬的纤维蛋白

keystone species | 关键物种 在群落中数目通常不多但对群落结构具有重要影响的单个物种

kidney | 肾 从血液中分离废物和过量水的排泄器官

kin selection | 亲缘选择 认为由于存在亲缘关系的个体大部分基因均为相同，因而对亲缘个体进行帮助能提高个体进化适应性的理论

kingdom | 界 分类学中最大、最广泛的类别

Koch's postulates | 柯赫氏假设 由柯赫提出的一系列原则，旨在促进对引发特定疾病的微生物的识别

Krebs cycle | 三羧酸循环 细胞呼吸的第二阶段，丙酮酸经过一系列耗能反应最终被分解成二氧化碳

L

language | 语言 由符合一系列次序和意义规则（如语法和词法）的声音、符号和姿势组成的交流体系

large intestine | 大肠 消化系统器官，能吸收通过的未消化食物中的水，又称结肠

larva (pl. larvae) | 幼虫 生物体的未成熟阶段

larynx | 喉 咽喉中包含声带的结构

learning | 学习 因经验而导致的行为改变

lens | 晶状体 眼睛中的结构，能将光线聚焦至视网膜上

lichen | 地衣 真菌和光合生物的共生体

ligament | 韧带 关节处连接骨骼的坚韧结缔组织

light–dependent reactions | 光反应 光合作用的一系列反应，可利用太阳光的能量产生 ATP 和 NADPH

light–independent reactions | 暗反应 光合作用中的一系列反应，不需要光，能利用来自 ATP 和 NADPH 的能量生成高能化合物（如糖），亦称卡尔文循环

lignin | 木质素 维管植物中一种可维持细胞壁刚性的物质

limiting factor | 限制因素 引起种群增长减缓的因素

limiting nutrient | 限制性营养 对生态系统的生产力起限制作用的单一组分营养物质

lipid | 脂质 主要由碳氢原子组成的大分子物质，包括脂肪，油和蜡

lipid bilayer | 双脂质层 构成细胞膜，并且在细胞及其外环境之间形成屏障的灵活双层脂质结构

logistic growth | 对数增长 种群生长先经过指数生长期，然后是缓慢生长期，最后生长停滞的一种生长模式

loop of Henle | 亨利氏环 肾小管的一部分，负责保留水分和最小化滤液

lung | 肺 呼吸器官，是血液和吸入气之间进行气体交换的主要场所

lymph | 淋巴 从血液中滤出的液体

lysogenic infection | 溶原性感染 病毒感染的一种类型，病毒将其 DNA 整合到宿主细胞，并随宿主细胞的DNA 一起复制

lysosome | 溶酶体 一种细胞器，能将脂质、碳水化合物和蛋白质分解成可被细胞其它部位使用的小分子

lytic infection | 溶细胞性感染 病毒进入细胞，并进行自我复制，导致细胞裂解的一种感染类型

M

macroevolution | 宏观进化 发生在相当长的一段时间内的大规模进化改变

Malpighian tubule | 马尔皮基氏管 大多数陆栖节肢动物的排泄器官，能够浓缩尿酸，并将其添加到代谢废物中

mammary gland | 乳腺 雌性动物的腺器官，能够产生乳汁、营养幼子

mass extinction | 大灭绝 在一个相对短时期内，大量物种灭绝的事件

matrix | 基质 线粒体最内部的功能区隔

mechanical digestion | 机械性消化 将大块食物分解成更小部分的物理过程

meiosis | 减数分裂 在一个二倍体细胞中，由于同源染色体分离，导致细胞中的染色体数目减半的过程

melanin | 黑色素 皮肤中的黑褐色色素，能够吸收紫外线，从而对皮肤起保护作用

melanocyte | 黑色素细胞 皮肤中一种能产生黑褐色色素（黑色素）的细胞

menstrual cycle | 月经周期 卵细胞发育并从机体中释放出来的周期性事件

menstruation | 月经 从体内排出血液和未受精卵细胞的过程

meristem | 分生组织 植物中的未分化细胞区域，在其整个生命周期中具有持续生长能力

mesoderm | 中胚层 胚胎的中间胚层，可发育成肌肉以及大部分循环系统、生殖系统和排泄系统

mesophyll | 叶肉 植物叶子中已特化的基本组织，主要功能是进行光合作用

messenger RNA (mRNA) | 信使 RNA (mRNA) 一种 RNA，携带遗传信息，可指导将来自 DNA 的氨基酸装配成蛋白质，并运送到细胞的其它部位

metabolism | 新陈代谢 生物体通过一系列化学反应，合成或分解物质的过程

metamorphosis | 变态 幼虫经过一系列的外形变化，发展成成虫的过程

metaphase | 中期 有丝分裂中染色体排列在细胞中央的一个时期

microclimate | 小气候 与周边地区气候可能有很大差异的小范围区域内的环境条件

migration | 迁徙 动物从一环境迁到另一个环境的季节性行为

mineral | 无机物 机体所需的无机元素，通常量很少

mitochondrion | 线粒体 一种细胞器，能将储存在食物中的化学能转变成能被细胞更好利用的化合物

mitosis | 有丝分裂 真核生物的细胞分裂过程，细胞核裂解

mixture | 混合物 由两种或两种以上元素组成的物质，或物理上混合在一起但未发生化学结合的化合物

molecular clock | 分子钟 研究者利用 DNA 中的突变率来评价两个物种独立进化的时间长度的一种方式

molecule | 分子 大多数化合物的最小单位，具有该化合物的所有特性

molting | 蜕皮 脱去外骨骼并生成新外骨骼的过程

monocot | 单子叶植物 子房上只有一片子叶的被子植物

monoculture | 单一栽培 逐年种植单一高产农作物的农业战略

monomer | 单体 构成聚合物的小化学单位

monophyletic group | 单系类群 由一个祖先物种及其所有后代（不是由该共同祖先衍生而来的生物体除外）组成的生物群

monosaccharide | 单糖 简单的糖分子

motor neuron | 运动神经元 能将来自中间神经元的神经冲动传递给肌肉细胞或腺体的一类神经元(809)

multiple alleles | 复等位基因 拥有两种以上等位基因的基因

multipotent | 多能性细胞 分化成多种不同类型细胞的潜能有限的细胞

muscle fiber | 肌肉纤维 长丝状的骨骼肌细胞

muscle tissue | 肌肉组织 能令机体产生运动的一种组织类型

mutagen | 致变剂 环境中能与 DNA 相互作用并可能引起突变的化学或物理因素

mutation | 突变 细胞遗传物质的改变

mutualism | 互利共栖 两个物种都能从中受益的共栖关系

mycelium (pl. mycelia) | 菌丝体 由真菌的菌丝构成的致密网络

mycorrhiza (pl. mycorrhizae) | 菌根 植物根系与真菌的共生体

myelin sheath | 髓鞘 包绕在某些神经元的轴突外的绝缘膜

myocardium | 心肌 心脏中的厚实中央肌层

myofibril | 肌原纤维 存在于骨骼肌纤维中的紧密肌丝束

myosin | 肌球蛋白 粗肌丝的结构蛋白，存在于骨骼肌细胞中

N

NAD⁺ (nicotinamide adenine dinucleotide) | NAD⁺（烟酰胺腺嘌呤二核苷酸） 参与醣酵解的电子携带者

NADP⁺ (nicotinamide adenine dinucleotide phosphate) | NADP⁺（烟酰胺腺嘌呤二核苷酸磷酸） 能将高能电子从叶绿素传递给其他分子的携带者分子

natural selection | 自然选择 最适合所在环境的生物体才能得以最成功地生存和繁殖的过程；又称适者生存

nephridium (pl. nephridia) | 肾 环节动物的排泄结构，能过滤体液

nephron | 肾单位 肾脏内的血液过滤结构，能滤出杂质、收集废物并将血液送回到循环系统

nervous tissue | 神经组织 能在全身范围内传导神经冲动的一类组织

neuromuscular junction | 神经肌肉接头 运动神经元与骨骼肌细胞的结合点

neuron | 神经元 神经细胞；专门负责在整个神经系统中携带信息

neurotransmitter | 神经递质 在神经元通过突触将冲动传递给其他细胞的过程中起信息传递作用的化学物质

neurulation | 神经管形成 神经系统发育的第一步

niche | 生态位 生物体生活在其中的所有物理和生物条件，以及生物体利用这些条件的方式

nitrogen fixation | 固氮作用 将氮气转化成能被植物吸收和利用的氮化合物的过程

node | 节 生长茎上附着叶子的部位

nondisjunction | 不分离 减数分裂中，同源染色体未能正确分离

nonrenewable resource | 不可再生资源 无法在合理的时间内通过自然过程获得补充的资源

norepinephrine | 去甲肾上腺素 肾上腺分泌的激素，能使心跳加快、血压升高，令身体为剧烈体力活动做好准备

notochord | 脊索 贯穿脊索动物身体的支撑性长索，位于神经索之下

nucleic acid | 核酸 含有氢、氧、氮、碳和磷的大分子

nucleotide | 核苷酸 组成核酸的亚单位，由一个五碳糖、一个磷酸基和一个含氮碱基组成

nucleus | 核子/细胞核 原子的核心，由质子和中子组成；在细胞中，指含有细胞遗传物质（以 DNA 的形式）的结构

nutrient | 营养 生物体用来维持生命的化学物质

nymph | 幼虫 指动物已具有成熟的外型但缺乏有功能性器官的未成熟状态

O

observation | 观察 以仔细而有条不紊的方式注意和描述事件或过程的过程

omnivore | 杂食动物 既以植物又以动物为食来摄取能量的生物

open circulatory system | 开放式循环系统 当血液流经机体时，仅有部分血液存留在血管中的一种循环方式

operant conditioning | 操作性条件反射 一种学习类型，动物通过重复的练习来获得奖励或避免惩罚，从而学会以特定的方式来行动

operator | 操纵基因 原核细胞操纵子上一段与启动子相邻的 DNA 小片段，能与阻遏蛋白结合，控制操纵子的转录活性

operon | 操纵子 原核生物中具有相同操纵基因和启动子，并转录入成一条 mRNA 的一组相邻基因

opposable thumb | 对生拇指 能抓物和使用工具的拇指

order | 目 生物学分类中一组具有较近亲缘关系的科的集合

organ | 器官 能通过共同协作来执行一些紧密相关的功能的组织集合

organ system | 器官系统 能通过共同协作来执行特定功能的一组器官

organelle | 细胞器 在真核细胞中执行重要细胞功能的专门结构

osmosis | 渗透 指水通过选透性膜扩散

osmotic pressure | 渗透压 为防止通过选透膜的渗透性运动而必须施加的压力

ossification | 骨化 骨骼形成的过程，软骨将为骨骼所代替

osteoblast | 成骨细胞 能保持矿物质不流失的骨骼细胞，这些矿物质在骨骼的发育阶段将取代软骨

osteoclast | 破骨细胞 能分解骨矿物质的骨细胞

osteocyte | 骨细胞 有助于骨组织内矿物质的保持及持续巩固生长发育中骨骼的骨细胞

ovary | 子房/卵巢 在植物中，指包被和保护种子的结构；在动物中，是主要的女性生殖器官，能够产生卵子

oviparous | 卵生 胚胎在位于父母体外的卵子内进行发育的物种

ovoviparous | 卵胎生 胚胎在母体内发育但营养完全来自其卵子的卵黄囊的物种

ovulation | 排卵 将成熟的卵子自卵巢排入输卵管的过程

ovule | 胚珠 种实中形成雌配子的结构

ozone layer | 臭氧层 臭氧相对集中的大气层，可保护地球上的生命不被阳光中的紫外线所伤害

P

pacemaker | 起搏点 一小组心肌纤维，负责调控心脏收缩的频率，从而保持心脏供血的节奏；窦房（SA）结

paleontologist | 古生物学家 研究化石的科学家

palisade mesophyll | 栅栏组织 位于叶片上表皮之下的细胞层

parasitism | 寄生 一个生物体生活在另一生物体之上或之内并对之造成伤害的共生关系

parathyroid hormone (PTH) | 甲状旁腺素 (PTH) 由甲状旁腺分泌的激素，能提高血钙水平

parenchyma | 薄壁组织 植物基本组织的主要类型，所包含的细胞具有薄细胞壁和大中央液泡

passive immunity | 被动免疫 机体受到自然或有目的的抗原刺激后所产生的临时免疫

pathogen | 病原体 即致病因子

pedigree | 系谱 根据数代家族关系来显示某种遗传特征的出现或缺失的图解

pepsin | 胃蛋白酶 能将蛋白质分解成更小多肽段的酶

period | 期 地理年代的划分，可进一步划分为纪

peripheral nervous system | 外周神经系统 由神经和支持细胞共同构成的网络，负责将信号传入和传出中央神经系统

peristalsis | **蠕动** 平滑肌的收缩运动，可提供令食物通过食道并进入胃的动力

permafrost | **永冻层** 可见于冻土地带的永久性冻结土层

petiole | **叶柄** 连接叶与茎干的细茎

pH scale | **pH 范围** 从 0 到 14 的范围，用于测量溶液中 H^+ 离子的浓度；pH 值在 0 到 7 之间时为酸性，pH 值 7 为中性，pH 值在 7 到 14 之间时为碱性

pharyngeal pouch | **咽囊** 脊索动物在咽喉部位的一对组织之一

pharynx | **咽** 口腔背部的管道，是空气和食物的通道；又称咽喉

phenotype | **表现型** 生物体的物理特征

phloem | **韧皮部** 负责将营养液和由光合作用产生的碳水化合物运至植物各处的维管组织

photic zone | **透光层** 接近水体表面的受阳光照射的区域

photoperiod | **光周期** 植物对昼夜相对长度的反应

photosynthesis | **光合作用** 植物及其他自养生物利用光能来为将二氧化碳和水转变成氧气和富有能量的碳水化合物（如糖和淀粉）的化学反应提供能量的过程

photosystem | **光合体系** 类囊体中的叶绿素和蛋白质簇

phototropism | **向光性** 植物向光源生长的趋势

phylogeny | **系统发育学** 研究生物体间进化关系的学科

phylum | **门** 生物学分类中一组具有较近亲缘关系的纲的集合

phytoplankton | **浮游植物** 可见于海洋近表面的浮游藻类

pigment | **色素** 植物用来收集太阳能量的吸光分子

pioneer species | **先锋物种** 在演变过程中，首批进驻某一区域的物种

pistil | **雌蕊** 单个心皮或多个相互连接的心皮；其中包含有子房、花柱和柱头

pith | **木髓** 双子叶植物茎干的维管组织环内的软组织细胞

pituitary gland | **脑垂体** 颅骨底部附近的一个小腺体，其分泌的激素可直接调控多种机体功能，以及数种其它内分泌腺的活动

placenta | **胎盘** 有胎盘哺乳动物特有的器官，母体将通过该器官与正在发育的幼儿进行呼吸气体、营养和废物的交换

plankton | **浮游生物** 在水生环境下生活的微小生物，包括浮游植物和浮游动物

plasma | **血浆** 血液中的浅黄色液体部分

plasmid | **质粒** 存在于许多细菌细胞质中的微小环状 DNA

plasmodium | **原质团** 粘菌生命周期中由原生质组成的变形虫样营养体阶段

plate tectonics | **板块构造** 由于大陆漂移、火山爆发，地震等板块运动而导致的地质过程

platelet | **血小板** 骨髓释放的细胞成分，有助于凝血

pluripotent | **多能干细胞** 能够分化成大多数，但并不是全部机体细胞的细胞

point mutation | **点突变** DNA 中单个碱基发生改变的一种基因突变形式

pollen grain | **花粉粒** 种子植物中包含整个雄配子的结构

pollen tube | **花粉管** 植物中含有单倍体精核的结构

pollination | **授粉** 将花粉从雄性生殖结构传递给雌性生殖结构的过程

pollutant | **污染** 可通过土地、空气或水进入生物圈的有害物质

polygenic trait | **多基因特征** 由两个或两个以上基因控制的遗传特征

polymer | **聚合体** 由许多单体组成的分子，可构成大分子

polymerase chain reaction (PCR) | **聚合酶链反应 (PCR)** 生物学家用来扩增特定基因的一种技术

polypeptide | **多肽** 组成蛋白质的氨基酸长链

polyploidy | **多倍体** 具有额外染色体组的生物体状态

population | **种群** 生活在同一区域的相同物种的个体群

population density | **种群密度** 单位区域中的个体数量

predation | **捕食** 一个生物体（捕食者）捕捉并进食另一个生物体的过程（被捕食者）

prehensile tail | **卷尾** 能牢固缠绕在树枝上的长尾巴

pressure–flow hypothesis | **压力流动学说** 解释韧皮部液体同化糖在植物中从糖源头运送到糖储存区的学说

primary growth | **初生生长** 发生在植物顶端和根部的生长方式

primary producer | **初级生产者** 最先生成能量丰富的化合物，然后被其它生物利用的生产者

primary succession | **原生演替** 在未曾出现过群落痕迹的裸地上的生物演替过程

principle of dominance | 显性原则 孟德尔的第二个遗传规则，认为一些等位基因是显性的，而一些是隐性的

prion | 阮病毒 能引起疾病的蛋白颗粒

probability | 可能性 特定事件将发生的可能性

product | 产物 化学反应生成的元素或化合物

prokaryote | 原核生物 缺少细胞核的单细胞生物

promoter | 启动子 基因上的特定区域，能与 RNA 聚合酶结合并启动转录过程

prophage | 原噬菌体 整合入细菌宿主 DNA 中的噬菌体 DNA

prophase | 前期 有丝分裂中最初、最长的一段时期，这期间细胞核中的遗传物质浓缩，染色体清晰可见

prostaglandin | 前列腺素 由多种细胞产生的修饰性脂肪酸，通常只能影响邻近的细胞和组织

protein | 蛋白质 由碳、氢、氧、氮组成的大分子，是机体生长和修复的必需物质

protostome | 原口动物 口由胚孔发育而来的动物

pseudocoelom | 假体腔 只有部分被中胚层所覆盖的空腔

pseudopod | 伪足 细胞质临时向外突出的部分，是某些原生动物运动的方式

puberty | 青春期 快速生长和性成熟时期，该时期中生殖系统将成长从而具有完整功能

pulmonary circulation | 肺循环 位于心肺之间的一段循环路径

punctuated equilibrium | 间断平衡 长时间的稳定时期被变化加剧的短时期所打断的一种进化方式

Punnett square | 棋盘法 可以结合遗传交叉来预测基因型和表现型的遗传图解

pupa | 蛹 幼虫发育为成虫的完全变态阶段

pupil | 瞳孔 虹膜中的微小开口，允许光线进入眼睛

R

radial symmetry | 径向对称 机体的一种排列方式，从机体中心发出的所有虚构平面都能将机体分为对称的两部分

radiometric dating | 放射性年龄测定 根据样本中某一元素的放射性同位素含量与非放射性同位素含量的比例来测定样本年龄的一种方式

reabsorption | 重吸收 水和未溶解物质被重新吸收入血液的过程

reactant | 反应物 参加化学反应的元素或化合物

receptor | 受体 细胞表面或内部的特定蛋白，其形状与特定分子信使（如激素）可以很好地结合

recombinant DNA | 重组 DNA 不同来源的 DNA 重新结合所生成的新 DNA

red blood cell | 红细胞 含有能携氧的血红蛋白的血细胞

reflex | 反射作用 对于刺激的快速、自动反应

reflex arc | 反射弧 参与对刺激的快速反应的感受器、感觉神经元、运动神经元以及效应器

relative dating | 相对年代测定 通过比较化石在某一岩层与其它岩层中的分布来推测化石年龄的方式

relative frequency | 相对频率 某一等位基因在基因库中的出现次数与同一基因库中其它等位基因的出现次数的比率

releasing hormone | 释放激素 由下丘脑释放的激素，能促进垂体前叶分泌激素

renewable resource | 可再生能源 能够由健康的生态功能不断再生或替代的资源

replication | 复制 细胞分裂之前的 DNA 复制过程

reproductive isolation | 生殖隔离 对某个物种或种群进行隔离，令他们不再有机会交叉繁殖和发展成两个独立的物种

resource | 资源 生命的所有必需品，如水、营养、光、食物或空间

response | 应答 对刺激的特定反应

resting potential | 静息电位 跨静息神经元细胞膜的电位

restriction enzyme | 内切酶 能在某个核苷酸序列处对 DNA 进行切割的酶

retina | 视网膜 眼睛的最内层，包含有感光器

retrovirus | 逆转录病毒 含有 RNA 并以 RNA 为基因信息的 RNA 病毒

ribonucleic acid (RNA) | 核糖核酸 (RNA) 包含核糖的单股核酸

ribosomal RNA (rRNA) | 核糖体 RNA (rRNA) 一种 RNA，能与蛋白质结合生成核糖体

ribosome | 核糖体 由 RNA 和蛋白质组成的细胞器，存在于细胞的整个胞质中，是蛋白质合成的场所

RNA interference (RNAi) | RNA 干扰 (RNAi) 将双链 RNA 插入细胞从而抑制基因表达

RNA polymerase | RNA 聚合酶 在以 DNA 链为模板的转录过程中，负责将不断增长的 RNA 核苷酸链连接在一起的酶

rod | 杆状体 眼睛内的感光器，对光线敏感，但不能区分颜色

root cap | 根冠 根尖处的坚硬包被，负责保护分裂组织

root hair | 根毛 根上的细毛发，能产生大量能透过水和矿物质的表面

rumen | 瘤胃 牛及相关动物的胃室，共生细菌将在这里对纤维进行消化

S

sapwood | 边材 在木质茎中，包围在心材之外的第二层韧皮部，通常在液体的输送上具有重要作用

sarcomere | 肌节 肌肉收缩的单位，由两条 z 线及之间的肌丝组成

scavenger | 食腐动物 以其他动物的尸体为生的动物

science | 科学 有条理地对自然界的现象进行收集和分析的方法

sclerenchyma | 厚壁组织 具有极厚刚性细胞壁（能使该组织非常坚硬）的一种基本组织

scrotum | 阴囊 用于容纳睾丸的外部囊

sebaceous gland | 皮脂腺 皮肤内能分泌皮脂（油性分泌物）的腺体

secondary growth | 次生生长 双子叶植物的一种生长类型，茎干向更厚的方向生长

secondary succession | 次生演变 演变的一种类型，见于仅部分被干扰所摧毁的地区

seed | 种子 包被保护外壳的植物胚芽及营养供给

seed coat | 种皮 包被和保护植物胚芽的坚硬外壳，能保护种子的内容物不会干枯

segregation | 分离 等位基因在配子形成过程中相互分开

selective breeding | 选育 育种的一种方法，只允许具备预期特征的生物体繁殖下一代

selectively permeable | 选透膜 生物膜只允许某些物质通过而其他物质不能通过的性质；又称半透膜

semen | 精液 精子和精液的混合体

semicircular canal | 半规管 内耳的三大结构之一，能感知身体相对地球引力的位置

seminiferous tubule | 生精小管 产生精子的小管，每个睾丸都有数以百计这样的小管

sensory neuron | 感觉神经元 一种神经细胞，能接受来自感觉器官的信息并将信号传递给中枢神经系统

sex chromosome | 性染色体 能决定个体性别的两种染色体之一

sex-linked gene | 伴性基因 位于性染色体上的基因

sexual reproduction | 有性繁殖 一种繁殖类型，由来自父母的细胞共同组成新生物体的第一个细胞

sexually transmitted disease (STD) | 性传播疾病 (STD) 通过性接触在人与人之间传播的疾病

sieve tube element | 筛管分子 按端到端的方式贯穿植物韧皮部细胞的连续管道

single-gene trait | 单基因特征 由具有两个等位基因的基因控制的特征

small intestine | 小肠 消化器官，大部分的化学消化和食物吸收都将在该器官内完成

smog | 烟雾 由化学混合物形成的灰褐色雾霾

society | 社群 一群紧密相关的同种动物，它们共同协作，以令整个群体获益

solute | 溶质 溶解于溶液中的物质

solution | 溶液 所有组成成分均匀分布的一种混合物

solvent | 溶剂 溶液中负责溶解的物质

somatic nervous system | 躯体神经系统 外周神经系统的一部分，能将信号送入和传出骨骼肌

speciation | 物种形成 新物种的形成

species diversity | 物种多样性 特定区域内不同物种的数量

spirillum (pl. spirilla) | 螺菌 螺旋形的原核生物

spongy mesophyll | 海绵组织 疏松的组织层，存在于叶中的栅栏叶肉之下

sporangium (pl. sporangia) | 孢囊 孢子囊，在其中将以减数分裂的方式产生单倍体孢子

spore | 孢子 对原核生物、原生生物和真菌，指具有厚壁的、能在不利环境下存活的各类生命阶段之一；对植物，指单倍体生殖细胞

sporophyte | 孢子体 孢子繁殖植物；植物生命周期中的多细胞二倍体阶段

stabilizing selection | 稳定化选择 自然选择的一种形式，位于分布曲线中部的个体相对位于两端的个体具有更强的适应性

stamen | 雄蕊 花的雄性部分；包含花药和花丝

stem cell | 干细胞 能发展成一种或多种特化细胞的非特化细胞

stigma | 柱头 花柱顶端的黏性部分；专门用于捕捉花粉

stimulus (pl. stimuli) | 刺激 生物体将予以应答的信号

stoma (pl. stomata) | 气孔 植物表皮上的小开口，能允许二氧化碳、水和氧气向叶片内和叶片外扩散

stomach | 胃 能持续地对食物进行机械和化学消化的大肌肉囊

stroma | 基质 叶绿体的液体部分；位于类囊体的外侧

substrate | 底物 酶催化反应的反应物

suspension | 悬液 水和不可溶物的混合物

sustainable development | 可持续发展 使用自然资源来满足人类需求，但既不耗尽它们也不造成长期环境损害的战略

symbiosis | 共生 两个物种共同生活的关系

synapse | 突触 神经元通过其向其它细胞传递冲动的接触性位点

systematics | 分类学 研究生命多样性和生物体间进化关系的学科

systemic circulation | 体循环 位于心脏和机体其他部分之间的循环路径

T

taiga | 泰加林 具有长年严寒的冬天和数月温暖天气的生态区，主要覆盖有常青松树，又称针叶林

target cell | 靶细胞 具有针对特定激素的受体的细胞

taste bud | 味蕾 辨别味道的感觉器官

taxon (pl. taxa) | 分类单元 生物体分类的组织群落或等级

telomere | 端粒 真核生物染色体末端的 DNA 重复序列

telophase | 末期 有丝分裂的一个时期，清晰可见的独立染色体开始松散解聚，形成杂乱的染色质

temporal isolation | 时间隔离 生殖隔离的一种形式，指两个或多个物种具有不同的繁殖时间

tendon | 肌腱 将骨骼肌连接到骨骼上的坚韧结缔组织

territory | 领地 被某一个或一群动物占领并受其保护的特定区域

testis (pl. testes) | 睾丸 男性的主要生殖器官，能产生精子

tetrad | 四分体 减数分裂过程中形成的一种结构，具有四条染色单体

tetrapod | 四足动物 有四肢的脊椎动物

thalamus | 丘脑 接受来自感觉器官的信息并将其传递到大脑的正确部位以进行进一步处理的脑结构

theory | 理论 将大量的观察和假说总结起来，能让科学家对新形势作出精确预测，并经过反复检验的解释

thigmotropism | 向触性 植物对接触性刺激的一种反应

threshold | 阀值 产生冲动所需的最低刺激水平

thylakoid | 类囊体 叶绿体中的一种囊状光合膜

thyroxine | 甲状腺素 由甲状腺产生的一类激素，能增加整个机体的细胞代谢率

tissue | 组织 能执行特定功能的类似细胞群

tolerance | 耐受 生物体在非最佳条件的环境下存活和繁殖的能力

totipotent | 全能细胞 能够发育成机体中任何类型细胞的细胞（包括组成胚胎外膜和胎盘的细胞）

trachea | 气管 连接咽与喉的管道

tracheid | 管胞 木质部中的中空植物细胞，具有木质素化加厚的细胞壁

tracheophyte | 导管植物 即维管植物

trait | 特征 个体的典型特性

transcription | 转录 由 DNA 模板合成 RNA 分子的过程

transfer RNA (tRNA) | 转运 RNA (tRNA) 在蛋白质合成过程中，负责携带氨基酸至核糖体的一类 RNA

transformation | 转化 由于导入来自另一细菌的基因而使原来细菌发生改变的过程

transgenic | 转基因生物 指携带来自另一生物体的基因的生物

translation | 翻译 将 mRNA 的碱基序列变成编码蛋白质的氨基酸序列的过程

transpiration | 蒸腾 植物叶片上水分的丧失

trochophore | 担轮幼虫 水生软体动物的一种能自由游动的幼虫阶段

trophic level | 营养级 食物网中食物链上的每一个环节

tropism | 向性 植物面向或偏离刺激方向的运动

tumor | 肿瘤 一群快速分裂的细胞，能引起周围组织的损伤

U

understory | 林下叶层 热带雨林中位于冠层下的林层，由较矮小的乔木或蔓生植物组成

ureter | 输尿管 将尿液由肾脏输送到膀胱的管道

urethra | 尿道 将尿液排出体外的管道

urinary bladder | 膀胱 在尿液分泌之前储存尿液的囊状器官

V

vaccination | 接种 注射经过弱化、或相似但更为安全的病原体，以产生免疫的过程

vaccine | 疫苗 已弱化或已被杀死的病原体制品，可使机体产生针对某种疾病的免疫力

vacuole | 液泡 储存水、盐、蛋白质和碳水化合物的细胞器

valve | 瓣膜 位于心房和心室，或静脉之间的扁平结缔组织，能阻止血液回流

van der Waals forces | 范德华力 在相邻分子的电荷相反区域存在的一种弱吸引力

vas deferens | 输精管 将精子从附睾输送至尿道的管道

vascular bundle | 维管束 植物茎叶中由木质部和韧皮部组成的束状组织

vascular cambium | 形成层 能够产生维管组织、使根茎加粗的一种分生组织

vascular cylinder | 维管柱 植物根的中心区，包括维管组织——木质部和韧皮部

vascular tissue | 维管组织 植物中携带水分和营养的分化组织

vector | 媒介 把病原体传播给人类的动物

vegetative reproduction | 营养体繁殖 植物无性繁殖的一种方式，可使单株植物产生与之大体相同的后代

vein | 静脉 携带机体各部分的血流回到心脏的血管

ventricle | 心室 位于心脏下部的空腔，可将血液泵出心脏，输送到机体各部分

vertebrate | 脊椎动物 具有脊椎的动物

vessel element | 导管分子 木质部细胞的一种类型，可形成一条连续管道，允许水分子通过

vestigial organs | 发育不全器官 体积缩小、功能不全或丧失的一类结构

villus (pl. villi) | 绒毛 小肠内的指状突起，有助于营养物质的吸收

virus | 病毒 由蛋白和核酸（有时还有脂质）组成的粒子，只有感染生命细胞才能进行复制

vitamin | 维生素 有助于调节机体活动的有机物质

viviparous | 胎生 生育后代，且后代发育过程中所需的营养直接从母体获得的动物

W

weather | 天气 大气层每天的天气现象，包括气温、降水以及其它因素

wetland | 湿地 一年中至少有一段时间土壤上有水覆盖，或地表上（或附近）有积水的生态区

white blood cell | 白细胞 血细胞的一种类型，能防御感染、抵抗寄生虫、攻击细菌

woody plant | 木本植物 主要由能支撑植物体的厚壁细胞组成的一种植物，包括乔木、灌木及蔓生植物

X

xylem | 木质部 一种维管组织，负责将来自根部的水分向上运输至植物体各部分

Z

zoonosis (pl. zoonoses) | 动物传染病 由动物传播给人类的疾病

zooplankton | 浮游动物 作为浮游生物组成部分，能够自由漂浮的微小动物

zygote | 合子 即受精卵

Traditional Chinese 繁體中文

Miller & Levine
Biology Glossary

A

abiotic factor | 非生物因子 形成生態系統的物理或無生命因子

abscisic acid | 脫落酸 抑制細胞分裂乃至成長的植物荷爾蒙

acetylcholine | 乙醯膽鹼 使肌肉細胞產生衝動的一種神經傳導物質

acid | 酸 在溶液中形成氫離子的化合物；酸鹼值小於 7 的溶液

acid rain | 酸雨 含有硝酸與硫酸的雨

actin | 肌動蛋白質 肌肉中發現的蛋白質細肌絲

action potential | 動作電位 神經元細胞膜之間的電荷逆轉；亦稱為神經衝動

activation energy | 活化能 使反應開始所需要的能量

active immunity | 主動免疫 由於自然或故意暴露於抗原而產生的免疫

adaptation | 適應性 增加有機體在環境中生存與再製造能力的遺傳特徵

adaptive radiation | 適應輻射 單一物種或一小群物種演化成數種不同形式以不同方式生活的過程

adenosine triphosphate (ATP) | 三磷酸腺 (ATP) 細胞用來儲藏與釋放能量的化合物

adhesion | 附著力 不同種類的分子間的吸引力

aerobic | 需氧 需要氧氣的過程

age structure | 年齡構造 一個族群中每一個年齡的雄性與雌性的數目

aggression | 攻擊 一隻動物用來對另一隻動物取得優勢時的威脅性行為

algal bloom | 藻花 由於限制性營養素的大量輸入，而造成藻類與其他生產者的增加

allele | 對偶基因 基因的數個不同形式的其中一種

allergy | 過敏 免疫系統對抗原的一種過度反應

alternation of generations | 世代交替 一個生命週期有兩個輪流交替的階段 — 單倍體 (N) 階段與雙倍體 (2N) 階段

alveolus (pl. alveoli) | 肺泡 肺部支氣管末稍提供表面部位以產生氣體交換的細小氣囊

amino acid | 胺基酸 一端為胺基以及另一端為梭酸基的化合物

amniotic egg | 羊膜卵 由殼與膜組成的卵，形成一個保護的環境，使胚胎可以離開水中發展

amylase | 澱粉酵素 唾液中使澱粉中的化學鍵斷裂的酵素（酶）

anaerobic | 厭氧 不需要氧氣的過程

anaphase | 細胞分裂後期 染色體分開並移至細胞另一端的有絲分裂階段

angiosperm | 被子植物 在一層保護種子的組織內結種子的種子植物群；亦稱為顯花植物

anther | 花藥 製造花粉粒的花的構造

antheridium (pl. antheridia) | 藏精器 某些製造精子的植物的雄性生殖構造

anthropoid | 類人猿 由猴子、黑猩猩與人類組成的靈長類

antibiotic | 抗生素 用來阻礙細菌病原體生長與繁殖的藥群

antibody | 抗體 直接攻擊抗原或是製造抗原結合蛋白的蛋白質

anticodon | 反密碼子 一組在 tRNA 分子上與 mRNA 密碼子的三個鹼基互補的三個鹼基

antigen | 抗原 觸發免疫反應的任何物質

aphotic zone | 無光區 透光層以下陽光沒有穿透的海洋黑暗層

apical dominance | 頂芽優勢 花蕾愈靠近莖的尖部，其生長愈受到抑制的現象

apical meristem | 頂端分生組織 分裂以使莖部與根部增加長度的非特化細胞群

apoptosis | 細胞凋亡 程序性細胞死亡的過程

appendage | 附肢 從體壁延伸出來的構造，例如肢或觸角

appendicular skeleton | 附肢骨骼 沿著骨盆與肩膀部位骨頭的手臂與大腿骨頭

aquaculture | 水產養殖 養殖水生生物以供人類消耗使用

aquaporin | 水通道蛋白 細胞中的水通道蛋白質

Archaea | 古菌域 由細胞壁不含肽聚醣的單細胞原核生物所構成的域；對應於古細菌界

archegonium (pl. archegonia) | 藏卵器 製造卵細胞的植物構造

artery | 動脈 將血液從心臟輸送到身體組織的大血管

artificial selection | 人工選擇 植物與動物為促進所孕育的後代含有所希望的特徵的選擇性育種

asexual reproduction | 無性繁殖 涉及單親的繁殖過程，生出的下一代在基因上與上一代完全相同

asthma | 氣喘 氣道變窄造成發出氣喘聲、咳嗽與呼吸困難的慢性呼吸器官疾病

atherosclerosis | 動脈粥狀硬化 稱為硬化斑塊的脂肪沉積，慢慢堵塞動脈內壁而最終造成動脈硬化的情況

atom | 原子 物質的基本單位

ATP synthase | ATP 合成酶 橫蓋細胞膜並讓氫離子 (H⁺) 通過的蛋白質群集

atrium (pl. atria) | 心房 心臟接受身體各處流回的血液的上部腔室

autonomic nervous system | 自主神經系統 末梢神經系統的一部分，管制非自主或不受意識控制的活動；由交感與副交感分部所構成

autosome | 體染色體 非性染色體的染色體；亦稱為 autosomal chromosome（體染色體）

autotroph | 自養生物 能從陽光或化學物中捕捉能量並且加以利用，而從無機物中製造自己的食物的有機體；亦稱為生產者

auxin | 植物生長素 成長中植物的尖端所製造，以刺激細胞延伸因子與新根成長的調節性物質

axial skeleton | 中軸骨骼 支撐身體中軸的骨骼；由頭骨、脊柱與肋廓所組成

axon | 軸突 將神經元細胞體的衝動傳遞出去的長纖維

B

bacillus (pl. bacilli) | 桿菌 桿狀的原核生物

background extinction | 自然絕滅 緩慢與穩定的天擇過程所造成的絕滅

Bacteria | 細菌 有含肽聚醣細胞壁的單細胞原核生物域；對應於真細菌界

bacteriophage | 噬菌體 傳染細菌的病毒種類

bark | 外皮 維管束形成層外的組織，包括韌皮部、木栓形成層與木栓

base | 鹼基 溶液中製造氫氧離子 (OH⁻) 的化合物；酸鹼值大於 7 的溶液

base pairing | 鹼基配對 僅可於腺嘌呤與胸腺嘧啶之間以及鳥嘌呤與胞嘧啶之間形成 DNA 連結的原理

behavior | 行為 有機體對內部情況或外部環境變化的反應方式

behavioral isolation | 行為隔離 兩個族群在求偶儀式或其他行為中發展出差異以防止繁殖的生殖隔離形式

benthos | 底生生物 依附於湖泊、河流或海洋底部或是在附近的有機體

bias | 偏見 個人而非科學的特定偏好或觀點

bilateral symmetry | 兩側對稱 可以用一條假想線將身體分成左右相對的兩個鏡像的身體藍圖

binary fission | 二分裂 由有機體複製其 DNA 並分裂成兩半，製造出兩個完全相同的子細胞的一種無性繁殖

binocular vision | 雙眼視覺 合併雙眼視覺影像的能力，提供深度知覺與三度空間觀察

binomial nomenclature | 雙名法 每個物種被分派兩段式學名的分類系統

biodiversity | 生物多樣性 生物圈內有機體的所有種類；亦稱為 biological diversity（生物多樣性）

biogeochemical cycle | 生物地球化學週期 物質的元素、化學化合物與其他形式從一個有機體被傳送到另一個有機體以及從生物圈的一部分到另一部分的過程

biogeography | 生物地理學 對過去與目前有機體分佈的研究

bioinformatics | 生物資訊 數學與電腦資訊在儲存、檢索與分析生物資料方面的應用

biological magnification | 生物放大作用 食物鏈或食物網中較高階營養層的有機體中有害物質濃度的漸增

biology | 生物 生命的科學研究

biomass | 生物量 既有的營養層內活組織的總數量

biome | 生態群系 共享相似氣候與典型有機體的一群生態系統

biosphere | 生物圈 地球上存在生命的部分，包括陸地、水與空氣或大氣層

biotechnology | 生物科技 操縱有機體、細胞或分子以製造特定產物的過程

biotic factor | 生物因子 環境中有機體可能與之進行互動的任何有生命部分

bipedal | 兩足的 指以兩足移動

blade | 葉片 植物葉子薄而扁平的部分

blastocyst | 囊胚期 由細胞囊胚構成的哺乳動物早期發展階段

blastula | 囊胚 受精卵經過一系列的細胞分裂時所發展出的細胞空腔

bone marrow | 骨髓 骨腔中的軟組織

bottleneck effect | 瓶頸效應 族群規模的顯著降低後所產生的對偶基因頻率變化

Bowman's capsule | 包氏囊 包覆腎小球的杯狀構造；自血液中收集濾液

brain stem | 腦幹 連接腦與脊髓的構造；包括延髓和橋腦

bronchus (pl. bronchi) | 支氣管 胸腔內的兩條大管之一，連接氣管與肺部

bryophyte | 苔蘚植物門 有特殊生殖器官但是缺乏管狀組織的植物群；包括苔蘚類與其近親

bud | 花蕾 含有頂芽分生組織的植物構造，可以製造新的莖與葉

buffer | 緩衝物 防止酸鹼值突然劇烈變化的化合物

C

calcitonin | 抑鈣素 甲狀腺所產生的可降低血鈣濃度的荷爾蒙

Calorie | 大卡（千卡） 食物中的熱量測量單位；相當於 1000 卡路里

calorie | 卡路里 使 1 公克的水溫增加攝氏 1 度所需的能量

Calvin cycle | 卡爾文循環 光合作用的暗反應，其中來自 ATP 和 NADPH 的能量被用來形成諸如醣類的高能化合物

cancer | 癌症 身體的某些細胞失去控制生長能力的疾病

canopy | 冠層 雨林中高大而枝葉茂盛的樹梢所形成的緊密覆蓋

capillary | 微血管 最小的血管；將養分和氧氣輸送到身體組織並吸收二氧化碳和廢物

capillary action | 毛細作用 水在極細的管內向上爬升的傾向

capsid | 殼體 包覆住病毒的蛋白質殼衣

carbohydrate | 碳水化合物 由碳、氫和氧原子所構成的化合物；是做為身體能量的主要來源的一種養分

carnivore | 肉食者 藉由食用其他有機體而獲得能量的有機體

carpel | 心皮 製造與保護雌性配子體的花心最深處

carrying capacity | 容受力 一個特定環境所能支撐的某個特定物種的最大個體數量

cartilage | 軟骨 支撐身體並且比骨骼還要柔軟且更富有彈性的一種結締組織

Casparian strip | 卡氏帶 環繞植物內胚層細胞的防水帶，可將物質單向傳入植物根部維管柱

catalyst | 催化劑 一種能加速化學反應的物質

cell | 細胞 所有生命形式的基本單位

cell body | 細胞體 典型神經元最大的一部分，包含核子以及大多數細胞質

cell cycle | 細胞周期 細胞成長、準備分裂以及分裂後形成兩個子細胞的一連串活動

cell division | 細胞分裂 細胞分裂為兩個新的子細胞的過程

cell membrane | 細胞膜 環繞所有細胞的薄而有彈性的屏障；可調控進出細胞的物質

cell theory | 細胞學說 生物學的基本概念，說明所有生物都是由細胞所構成的；細胞是生物構造和功能的基本單位；而且新細胞是由現有細胞所產生的

cell wall | 細胞壁 某些細胞的細胞膜四周有一層強韌的支撐物

cell-mediated immunity | 細胞免疫 保護身體免受活細胞內的病毒、真菌和異常癌細胞侵害的免疫反應

cellular respiration | 細胞呼吸作用 在有氧氣的情況下分解葡萄糖及其他食物分子以釋放能量的過程

central nervous system | 中央神經系統 包括腦部和脊髓，會處理訊息並且產生反應以傳遞到身體

centriole | 中心粒 動物細胞內有助於組織細胞分裂的構造

centromere | 著絲點 染色體中兩個姊妹染色分體附著的部分

cephalization | 頭化現象 感覺器官和神經細胞集中在動物的前末端（頭部）

cerebellum | 小腦 腦部協調行動與控制平衡的部分

cerebral cortex | 大腦皮質 哺乳動物腦部的大腦外層；思考及其他複雜行為的中樞

cerebrum | 大腦 腦部負責身體自主性活動的部分；腦部的「思考」區域

chemical digestion | 化學消化 酶將食物分解成身體可以使用的小分子的過程

chemical reaction | 化學反應 將一組化學物變化或轉變為另一組化學物的過程

chemosynthesis | 化學合成 化學能量被用來產生碳水化合物的過程

chitin | 幾丁（甲殼素） 構成真菌細胞壁的複合碳水化合物；也存在於節肢動物的外骨骼

chlorophyll | 葉綠素 植物及其他光合有機體的主要色素

chloroplast | 葉綠體 存在於植物及其他某些有機體細胞內的胞器，能夠捕捉陽光的能量，然後轉換為化學能量

chordate | 脊索類動物 生命周期中至少一個階段具有下列特徵的一種動物：背脊中空的神經索、脊索、超過肛門部位的尾巴；和咽囊

chromatid | 染色分體 複製染色體兩個完全相同的「同胞」的其中一個

chromatin | 染色粒 存在於真核生物染色體內的物質，是由緊密地纏繞在組織蛋白四周的 DNA 構成

chromosome | 染色體 核子內包含從一代傳給下一代的遺傳資訊的線狀構造

chyme | 食糜 酵素及部分分解食物的混合物

cilium (pl. cilia) | 纖毛 產生動作的短毛般突出物

circadian rhythm | 晝夜節律 每天發生的行為周期

clade | 系群 包括單一祖先及其所有後代子孫的支序樹（親源圖）的一個進化分支

cladogram | 支序樹（親源圖） 描繪不同物種之間的共同特徵模式的一種圖表

class | 綱 在分類學上一組密切相關的目族

classical conditioning | 古典制約 當動物在刺激及某種獎勵或懲罰之間產生心理上的關聯的一種學習

climate | 氣候 一個區域經過一段很長的時間平均每年溫度條件及降雨量變化

clone | 複製 從單一細胞產生的遺傳特徵上完全相同的細胞族群成員

closed circulatory system | 閉鎖循環系統 一種循環系統，血液完全在延伸至全身各處的血管內循環

coccus (pl. cocci) | 球菌 球狀原核生物

cochlea | 耳蝸 內耳充滿液體的部分；包含察覺聲音的神經細胞

codominance | 共顯性 兩個對偶基因所產生的表現型完全顯現的情況

codon | 密碼子 mRNA 中指定要將某個特定的胺基酸併入蛋白質的三種苷酸鹼基群

coelom | 體腔 以中胚層為內襯的體內空腔

coevolution | 共同進化 兩個物種對應於彼此的改變而隨著時間進化的過程

cohesion | 內聚力 相同物質的分子之間的吸引力

collenchyma | 厚角組織 植物的一種基本組織，具有強韌而且富有彈性的細胞壁；有助於支撐較大植物

commensalism | 片利共生 一個有機體獲益，但是對另一方既無益又無害的一種共生性關係

communication | 通訊 訊息從一個有機體傳送給另一個有機體

community | 群落 共同居住在同一個區域內的不同族群的聚集

companion cell | 伴細胞 植物環繞篩管元素的韌皮部細胞

competitive exclusion principle | 競爭排斥原理 說明沒有兩種物種可以在同一時間，在相同的棲息地中佔有相同位置的原理

compound | 化合物 兩個或多個元素的定組成化合作用所形成的一種物質

cone | 錐細胞 眼睛的受光體，能對不同顏色的光做出反應以產生色彩視覺

coniferous | 針葉樹 指會結毬果而且葉細如針的樹木

conjugation | 接合（作用） 草履蟲和某些原核生物交換遺傳資訊的過程

connective tissue | 結締組織 為身體提供支撐並連接其各部分的一種組織

consumer | 消費者 依賴其他有機體供應能量和食物來源的有機體；亦稱為異營生物

control group | 對照組 實驗中除了一個獨立變量之外，暴露於與實驗組相同的條件之下的一個組

controlled experiment | 控制實驗 只改變一個變量的實驗

convergent evolution | 趨同進化 不相干的有機體在適應於類似的環境時，分別演化出相似特徵的過程

cork cambium | 木栓形成層 在植物次生長期間產生莖的外殼的分生組織

cornea | 角膜 眼睛讓光線由此射入的堅硬透明層

corpus luteum | 黃體 卵泡在排卵後由於呈現黃色而被如此命名

cortex | 皮層 植物根的內部基本組織部分，水和礦物質必須穿透它

corticosteroid | 皮質類固醇 腎上腺皮質所產生的類固醇荷爾蒙

cotyledon | 子葉 種子植物的胚芽所產生的第一片或第一對葉子

courtship | **求偶** 動物傳出刺激素以便吸引異性的一種行為

covalent bond | **共價鍵** 原子共用電子的一種連結型態

crossing-over | **互換** 同源染色體在減數分裂期間交換部分染色分體的過程

cyclin | **細胞周期蛋白** 調節真核細胞的細胞周期的一種蛋白質系列

cytokinesis | **細胞質分裂** 細胞質分裂以形成兩個不同的子細胞

cytokinin | **細胞分裂素** 為了助長根的生長以及發展果實和種籽所產生的植物荷爾蒙

cytoplasm | **細胞質** 細胞在核子之外含有液體的部分

cytoskeleton | **細胞骨架** 真核細胞內使細胞成形並構成內部組織並且與動作有關的蛋白絲網

D

data | **數據** 證據；由觀察搜集得來的資訊

deciduous | **落葉樹** 指每年在特定季節落葉的一種樹木

decomposer | **分解者** 分解死去的有機質並且從中獲取能量的有機體

deforestation | **濫伐森林** 森林的破壞

demographic transition | **人口轉型** 高出生率和高死亡率轉變為低出生率和低死亡率的人口變化

demography | **人口統計學** 有關人口的科學研究

dendrite | **樹突** 能從環境中或從其他神經元將衝動輸送到細胞體的神經元細胞體突出物

denitrification | **脫氮作用** 分解菌將硝酸鹽轉換成氮氣的過程

density-dependent limiting factor | **密度制約因素** 視人口密度而定的制約因素

density-independent limiting factor | **非密度制約因素** 無論人口密度如何而以類似方式影響所有人口的制約因素

deoxyribonucleic acid (DNA) | **去氧核糖核酸 (DNA)** 有機體從其親代承襲的遺傳物質

dependent variable | **因變量** 對獨立變量產生反應而改變的可見變量；亦稱為反應變量

derived character | **導出性狀** 出現在世系較近的部分，但是沒有出現在較遠的成員身上的一種特性

dermis | **真皮** 存在於表皮之下的皮層

desertification | **沙漠化** 過度耕作、過度放牧、季節性乾旱及氣候變化而導致土地生產力降低

detritivore | **食腐者** 以植物和動物屍體及其他無機物為食的有機體

deuterostome | **後口動物** 胚孔變成肛門，而出現的第二個開口形成口腔的動物群體

diaphragm | **橫膈膜** 胸腔底部幫助呼吸的一大塊扁肌

dicot | **雙子葉植物** 子房中具有兩片子葉的被子植物

differentiation | **分化** 細胞結構和功能變得專門化的過程

diffusion | **擴散** 粒子傾向於從一個較集中的區域移向一個較不集中的區域的過程

digestive tract | **消化道** 從口腔開始而在肛門結束的管道

diploid | **二倍體** 指包含兩組同源染色體的細胞

directional selection | **定向選擇** 一種形式的天擇，在分佈曲線一端的個體其適當性高於在曲線中間或另一端的個體

disruptive selection | **分裂選擇** 在曲線上端和下端的個體的適當性高於曲線中間的個體

DNA fingerprinting | **DNA 指紋分析** 生物學家用來分析一個人獨特的 DNA 限制片段集合的一種工具；用來決定兩個遺傳物質的樣本是否來自同一個人

DNA microarray | **DNA 微陣列** 載有安排在網格上的成千上萬種不同的單股 DNA 片段的玻璃玻片或矽晶片。DNA 微陣列技術可用來一次偵測與衡量成千上萬個基因的表現

DNA polymerase | **DNA 聚合酶** DNA 複製過程中的要素酶

domain | **域** 比界的涵蓋範圍更大的分類範疇

dopamine | **多巴胺** 與腦部的快感和酬償中樞有關的神經傳導物

dormancy | **休眠** 植物胚胎活著但是不生長的一段時期

double fertilization | **雙重受精** 被子植物中的受精過程，第一次受精產生合子，而第二次受精則產生種子中的胚乳

E

ecological footprint | **生態足跡** 提供族群所使用的資源以及吸收族群所產生的廢物所需的機能生態系統總數

ecological hot spot | **生態熱點** 其中有大量的棲息地和物種處於立即絕種危機的小塊地理區域

ecological pyramid | **生態金字塔** 特定的食物鏈或食物網中的每個營養層次內含的能量或物質的相對數量圖解

ecological succession | 生態演替 群落在混亂之後發生的一連串的逐漸變化

ecology | 生態學 有機體彼此之間以及有機體與其所在環境之間的互動的科學研究

ecosystem | 生態系統 共同生活在一個地方的所有有機體及其無生命環境

ecosystem diversity | 生態系多樣性 生物圈中的各種棲息地、群落和生態過程

ectoderm | 表皮層 最外層胚層；產生感覺器官、神經和皮膚外層

ectotherm | 外溫動物 體溫由其所在環境的溫度決定的動物

electron | 電子 帶負電粒子；位於環繞核子四周的空間中

electron transport chain | 電子傳遞鏈 在產生 ATP 反應的過程中往返移動高能電子的電子載體蛋白質系列

element | 元素 完全由一種原子所組成的純物質

embryo | 胚胎 多細胞有機體的發展階段

embryo sac | 胚囊 開花植物的胚珠內的雌性配子體

emerging disease | 新發疾病 首次發生於族群中的一種疾病，或是突然變得難以控制的一種舊有疾病

emigration | 遷出 人們從一個區域向外移出

endocrine gland | 內分泌腺 將分泌物（荷爾蒙）直接釋放到血液中，然後血液又將這些分泌物輸送到身體的其他部位的腺體

endoderm | 內胚層 最內層胚層；發展成為消化道和多半呼吸系統的內襯

endodermis | 內皮層 植物中完全圍繞維管柱的一層基本組織

endoplasmic reticulum | 內質網 存在於真核細胞的內膜組織；組合細胞膜血脂成分的地方

endoskeleton | 內骨骼 內部骨骼；在動物體內的結構支撐體系

endosperm | 胚乳 在籽苗生長時一面供給養分的富含食物的組織

endospore | 內生孢子 原核生物在不利條件下所產生的結構；圍繞 DNA 和一部分細胞質的厚內壁

endosymbiotic theory | 內共生理論 主張真核細胞是由數個不同的原核細胞之間的共生性關係所形成的理論

endotherm | 恆溫動物 至少體溫的一部分是利用其體內產生的熱來進行調節的一種動物

enzyme | 酶（酵素） 加速特定的生物反應的蛋白質催化劑

epidermis | 表皮 植物組成表皮組織的單層細胞；人類皮膚的外層

epididymis | 副睪 男性生殖系統中，精子在此器官中成熟並貯存

epinephrine | 腎上腺素 腎上腺所釋放的荷爾蒙，會使心率和血壓升高，讓身體準備進行劇烈的肢體活動；亦稱為 adrenaline（腎上腺素）

epithelial tissue | 上皮組織 排列在內部及外部身體表面的一種組織

era | 代 地質學時間的主要劃分；通常被分為兩或三個時期

esophagus | 食道 從口腔一直連接到胃部的管道

estuary | 河口 在河流與海洋交會處形成的一種濕地

ethylene | 乙烯 刺激果實成熟的植物荷爾蒙

Eukarya | 真核域 由具有核子的所有有機體所組成的生物範疇；包括原生生物、植物、真菌和動物

eukaryote | 真核生物 細胞內含有核子的有機體

evolution | 進化 隨時間變化；現代有機體從古代有機體轉變而來的過程

excretion | 排泄 新陳代謝廢物從體內排除的過程

exocrine gland | 外分泌腺 通過稱為導管的管狀結構將其分泌物直接釋放到器官或體外的腺體

exon | 外顯子 DNA 的表達序列；蛋白質編碼

exoskeleton | 外骨骼 外部骨骼；保護與支撐許多無脊椎動物的身體的堅韌外殼

exponential growth | 指數式成長 某族群的人口數以恆速繁殖的生長模式

extinct | 滅絕 指完全死絕並且沒有任何現存成員的物種

extracellular digestion | 胞外消化 食物在細胞外的消化系統中被分解然後被吸收的一種消化過程

F

facilitated diffusion | 促進擴散 分子經過細胞膜通道橫越細胞膜的擴散過程

family | 科 在分類學上一組相似的屬

fat | 脂肪 脂質；由脂肪酸和甘油組成；保護身體器官的一種養分，會隔絕身體並且貯存能量

feedback inhibition | 反饋抑制 刺激產生一種相對於原始刺激的反應的過程；也稱為負反饋

fermentation | 發酵作用 細胞在缺氧的情況下釋放能量的過程

fertilization | 受精現象 在有性生殖的過程中，雄性和雌性生殖細胞結合在一起形成新的細胞的過程

fetus | 胎兒 人類胚胎受孕後八週的稱法

fever | 發燒 體溫因對感染產生反應而上升

filtration | 過濾 液體或氣體通過過濾器以去除廢物的過程

fitness | 健康情況 有機體在其所在環境中生存與繁殖的情況如何

flagellum (pl. flagella) | 鞭毛 原生生物用來移動的構造；產生波浪狀的移動

food chain | 食物鏈 生態系統中有機體經由被食和進食轉換能量的一連串層級

food vacuole | 食泡 原生生物細胞質中暫時貯存食物的小洞

food web | 食物網 由生態系統中各種有機體之間的給食關係所形成的複雜互動網路

forensics | 鑑識 犯罪現場證據的科學研究

fossil | 化石 古代有機體被保存下來的軀殼

founder effect | 創始者效應 由於某族群的子群遷徙的結果，使得對偶基因頻率產生變化

frameshift mutation | 移碼突變 藉由插入或刪除核苷酸而轉移遺傳訊息的「讀碼區」的突變作用

fruit | 果實 被子植物中含有一個或多個成熟子房的構造

fruiting body | 子實體 真菌從菌絲長成的再生結構

G

gamete | 配子 性細胞

gametophyte | 配子體 產生配子的植物；植物生命週期的多細胞單倍期

ganglion (pl. ganglia) | 神經節 一組中間神經元

gastrovascular cavity | 臟管腔 只有一個開口的消化腔

gastrulation | 原腸形成 造成三個細胞層（外胚層、中胚層和內胚層）形成的細胞遷移過程

gel electrophoresis | 膠體電泳法 用來分離與分析 DNA 片段的程序，藉由在多孔膠的一端放置混合的 DNA 片段，並對多孔膠施加電壓

gene | 基因 為蛋白質編碼因此而決定一種特徵的 DNA 序列；父母遺傳給子女的因子

gene expression | 基因表現 基因產生其產物而產物執行其機能的過程

gene pool | 基因池 任一時間內存在於族群中的所有基因，包括每一種基因的所有不同的對偶基因

gene therapy | 基因療法 改變基因以治療疾病或失調不適的過程。利用正常運作的基因取代缺少或有缺陷的基因

genetic code | 遺傳密碼 mRNA 密碼子集合，每個集合在蛋白質合成期間指導特定的胺基酸併入蛋白質

genetic diversity | 遺傳多樣性 特定物種或是地球上所有生物所攜帶的基因資訊的所有不同形式的總和

genetic drift | 遺傳漂變 由於一系列的偶然事件，導致對偶基因在族群中變得更常見或較不常見，而造成對偶基因頻率的隨機變化

genetic equilibrium | 遺傳平衡 一個族群中的對偶基因頻率保持不變的情況

genetic marker | 遺傳標識 能產生有利於遺傳分析的可偵測表型差異的對偶基因

genetics | 遺傳學 遺傳的科學研究

genome | 基因組 有機體在其 DNA 中攜帶的一整組遺傳資訊

genomics | 基因體學 整個基因組的研究，包括基因和其機能

genotype | 基因型 有機體的遺傳組成

genus | 種 血緣十分接近的物種群；學名二名法的第一段名稱

geographic isolation | 地理隔離 生殖隔離的一種形式，兩種族群由於諸如河流、山岳或水域等地理障礙的分離而導致形成兩個不同的亞種

geologic time scale | 地質年代表 用來代表地球歷史的時間年表

germ theory of disease | 疾病細菌根源說 認為感染性疾病是由微生物所導致的觀念

germination | 萌芽 植物胚胎在休眠之後繼續恢復成長

giberellin | 赤霉素 刺激成長並且可能導致大小顯著增加的植物荷爾蒙

gill | 鰓 專司與水份交換氣體工作的羽狀結構

global warming | 全球暖化 地區平均溫度上升

glomerulus | 腎小球 被包覆在腎元上端由微血管構成的小型網路；血液在這裡進行過濾

glycolysis | 糖酵解 細胞呼吸的第一組反應，這時丙酮酸的一個葡萄糖分子被分為兩個分子

Golgi apparatus | 高基氏體 細胞內的胞器，能修飾、分類和包裝來自內質網的蛋白質和其他物質以貯存在細胞內或是在胞外釋放

gradualism | 漸進主義 物種在很長一段時間下來逐漸積累很小的基因改變而演化

grafting | 嫁接 用來繁殖無法利用扦插方式繁衍的隱花植物及各種木本植物的方法

gravitropism | 向地性 植物對地心引力產生的反應

green revolution | 綠色革命 高產量作物品種的開發以及利用現代農業技術增加食用作物產量

greenhouse effect | 溫室效應 特定的氣體（二氧化碳、甲烷和水蒸氣）將太陽能困在地球的大氣層中形成熱氣的過程

growth factor | 生長因素 刺激細胞的成長和分裂的其中一組外部調控蛋白

guard cells | 保衛細胞 植物表皮內控制氣孔開合的特化細胞

gullet | 齒室 纖毛蟲體側的鋸齒形缺口，可讓食物進入細胞

gymnosperm | 裸子植物 直接在毬果的鱗片上結種的種子植物群

H

habitat | 棲息地 有機體居住的區域以及影響該區域的有生命和無生命因素

habitat fragmentation | 棲息地破碎化 生態系統分為許多部分

habituation | 習慣化 一種學習，動物對所受到的既無益亦無害的重覆性刺激減少或停止反應

hair follicle | 毛囊 上皮細胞延伸入真皮中的管狀囊袋；在毛囊基部的細胞會產生毛髮

half life | 半衰期 樣本中半數放射性原子能量衰減所需的時間長度

haploid | 單倍體 指只含單組基因的細胞

Hardy-Weinberg principle | 哈溫定律 主張除非有一個或多個因素導致族群中的對偶基因頻率改變，否則頻率維持不變的原則

Haversian canal | 哈氏管 通過包含血管和神經的緻密骨的其中一個管道網

heart | 心臟 將血液打至全身各處的一個空心肌肉器官

heartwood | 木心 在木質莖當中，靠近莖的中心不再能傳導水份的較老的木質部

hemoglobin | 血紅蛋白 紅血球中與氧氣結合並輸送到身體去的含鐵蛋白質

herbaceous plant | 草本植物 莖部平滑而非木質的一種植物；包括蒲公英、菊花、牽牛花和向日葵等

herbivore | 食草動物 只靠食入植物來取得能量的有機體

herbivory | 食植行為 一種動物（食草動物）以生產者（例如植物）為食的互動關係

heterotroph | 異營 藉由消耗其他生物而取得食物的有機體；亦稱為消費者

heterozygous | 異型 一個特定的基因有兩個不同的對偶基因

histamine | 組織胺 巨細胞所釋放的化學物質，在炎性反應期間使流向受感染部位的血液和液體增加

homeobox gene | 同源序列基因 同源序列是由大約 130 個基質對所構成的 DNA 序列，存在於許多調節發展的同源異性基因。含此序列的基因被稱為同源序列基因，以及轉錄因子（附著在 DNA 上調節其他基因表現的蛋白質）編碼

homeostasis | 恆定 有機體體內所維持的相對恆定的物理和化學條件

homeotic gene | 同源異性基因 一類調節基因，決定動物胚胎內的身體部位及區域的區別。這些基因所產生的突變可能將身體部位轉型

hominine | 人科 最終演化為人類的類人世系

hominoid | 類人 包含長臂猿、猩猩、大猩猩、黑猩猩和人類在內的類人猿

homologous | 同種 指一組來自於雄性親代而另一組來自於雌性親代的染色體

homologous structures | 同源構造 共同血緣的不同物種之間類似的構造

homozygous | 同型 有特定基因兩個完全相同的對偶基因

hormone | 荷爾蒙 有機體中一部位所產生的會影響該有機體另一部位的化學物質

Hox gene | 同源區基因群 聚集在一起的一組同源異性基因，決定動物身體從頭部到尾巴的各個部位區別。所有同源區基因群都包含同源 DNA 序列

humoral immunity | 體液性免疫 抵抗如血液和淋巴等體液中的抗原的免疫性

humus | 腐植質 從腐爛的葉子和其他有機質所形成的物質

hybrid | 雜種 特徵不同的親代間雜交所生育的後代

hybridization | 雜交 使相異個體配種以結合雙方生物最佳遺傳性狀的配種技術

hydrogen bond | 氫鍵 氫原子和另一個原子之間的弱引力

hydrostatic skeleton | 液壓骨骼 動物身上由充滿液體的環節所構成的骨架，能與肌肉共同配合以助於移動

hypertonic | 高滲性 兩種溶液相比，溶質濃度較高的溶液

hypha (pl. hyphae) | 菌絲 構成真菌體的許多細長的肌絲

hypothalamus | 下視丘 做為辨別與分析飢餓、口渴、疲勞、憤怒和體溫等控制中樞的腦部結構

hypothesis | 假設 針對一連串觀察可能的解釋或針對科學問題可能的答案

hypotonic | 低滲性 兩種溶液相比，溶質濃度較低的溶液

I

immigration | 移民 人群移至另一個現有人口族群所佔據的地區

immune response | 免疫反應 身體對病原體攻擊的特定辨認、反應和記憶

implantation | 著床 囊胚附著在子宮壁的過程

imprinting | 銘記 根據早期經驗的行為類型；一旦發生銘記作用，行為就無法再改變

inbreeding | 同系繁殖 特徵相似的個體繼續交配以維持一種生物的衍生特性

incomplete dominance | 不完全顯性 一個對偶基因未完全控制另一個對偶基因的情況

independent assortment | 自由組合 孟德爾主張的基本原則之一，即不同遺傳性狀的基因在配子形成期間單獨分離的狀態

independent variable | 獨立變量 控制實驗中刻意改變的因素；也稱為操縱變量

index fossil | 標準化石 用來比較化石相對年齡的明顯不同的化石

infectious disease | 感染性疾病 微生物造成干擾身體正常機能的疾病

inference | 推論 根據先前的知識和經驗做出的邏輯解釋

inflammatory response | 炎症反應 對受傷或感染而造成的組織損傷的非特定防禦反應

innate behavior | 先天行為 雖然是第一次從事某種行為，但似乎完全合情合理，即使動物先前對其所反應的刺激從未有過經驗；也稱為直覺

insight learning | 頓悟行為 動物沒有經過嘗試和錯誤階段，便能將過去學到的東西應用在新情況的一種行為；也稱為推理

interferon | 干擾素 幫助細胞抵抗病毒感染的一種蛋白質

interneuron | 中間神經元 處理資訊並可能將訊息傳遞給運動神經元的一類神經元

interphase | 分裂期間 細胞分裂期間的細胞週期

intracellular digestion | 胞內消化 食物在特化細胞內消化的一種消化方式，藉由擴散將養分傳送給其他細胞

intron | 內含子 與蛋白質編碼不相干的 DNA 序列

invertebrate | 無脊椎動物 缺乏骨幹或脊柱的動物

ion | 離子 帶有正負電荷的原子

ionic bond | 離子鍵 一個或多個電子從一個原子傳送到另一個原子時形成的化學鍵

iris | 虹膜 眼睛的有色部分

isotonic | 等滲透 兩種溶液的濃度相等

isotope | 同位素 單一元素的許多形式之一，其中包含的質子數量相同但中子數量則不同

J

joint | 關節 一塊骨骼與另一塊骨骼相接之處

K

karyotype | 核型 配成一對的成組完整染色體二倍體顯微圖像，按體積由大到小排列

keratin | 角蛋白 存在於皮膚上堅硬的纖維狀蛋白質

keystone species | 關鍵物種 通常在群落中數量不多但是對群落的結構發揮很大控制力的單一物種

kidney | 腎臟 能從血液中離析廢物和多餘水份的排泄器官

kin selection | 親族選擇 說明協助親族可以改善一個人的演化適合度的一種理論，因為有親屬關係的人很大比例的遺傳基因都相同

kingdom | 界 分類學上最大而且涵蓋範圍最廣的分組

Koch's postulates | 柯霍氏法則 由柯霍氏發展出來的一套準則，有助於識別導致特定疾病的微生物

Krebs cycle | 克氏循環 細胞呼吸的第二階段，這時丙酮酸在一連串吸取能量的反應中被分解成二氧化碳

L

language | 語言 根據有關順序和意義的一組規則，例如文法和語法，將聲音、符號和姿勢結合在一起的溝通系統

large intestine | 大腸 消化系統內的器官，從通過其中未消化的物質去除水份；也稱為結腸

larva (pl. larvae) | 幼蟲 有機體的未成熟階段

larynx | 喉 喉嚨中含聲帶的構造

learning | 學習 由於經驗而造成行為上的改變

lens | 水晶體 眼睛內使光射線集中於視網膜上的構造

lichen | 地衣 真菌和光合生物間的共生群叢

ligament | 韌帶 使骨骼在關節內結合在一起的堅韌結締組織

light-dependent reactions | 光反應 光合作用中利用光線中的能量來產生 ATP 和 NADPH 的一組反應

light-independent reactions | 暗反應 光合作用中不需要光線的一組反應，來自 ATP 和 NADPH 的能量被用來形成諸如醣類的高能化合物；亦稱為卡爾文循環

lignin | 木質素 維管植物中使細胞壁挺直的物質

limiting factor | 制約因素 導致人口成長降低的因素

limiting nutrient | 限制營養素 限制生態系統生產力的一種重要養分

lipid | 脂質 大多由碳和氫原子構成的大分子；包含脂肪、油脂和蠟

lipid bilayer | 脂質雙層膜 構成細胞膜並且在細胞和其周圍組織間形成障礙的柔軟雙層薄膜

logistic growth | 邏輯型成長 人口的成長在一段指數型成長時期之後趨緩然後停止的成長模式

loop of Henle | 亨利氏環 腎元小管中負責保存水份並且儘可能減少過濾量的一部分

lung | 肺部 呼吸器官；氣體在血液和吸入的空氣間進行交換的地方

lymph | 淋巴 從血液中過濾出來的液體

lysogenic infection | 潛溶性感染 病毒將其 DNA 嵌入宿主細胞的 DNA，並與宿主細胞的 DNA 一起複製的一種感染

lysosome | 溶酶體 將脂質、碳水化合物和蛋白質分解為可供其餘細胞利用的小分子的細胞胞器

lytic infection | 溶解性感染 病毒進入細胞，自行複製，然後導致細胞崩解的一種感染

M

macroevolution | 巨演化 經過長時期所發生的大規模演進變化

Malpighian tubule | 馬氏管 大部分陸棲性節肢動物將尿酸濃縮後加入消化廢物中的構造

mammary gland | 乳腺 雌性哺乳動物製造乳汁以滋養幼兒的腺體

mass extinction | 大絕滅 很多物種在相當短的期間內絕跡的事件

matrix | 基質 粒線體最內部的空腔

mechanical digestion | 機械性消化 將大塊食物變成較小塊食物的物理性分解

meiosis | 減數分裂 每個細胞的染色體透過雙倍體細胞中同源染色體的分離分成兩半的過程

melanin | 黑色素 皮膚中藉由吸收紫外線幫助保護皮膚的暗棕色色素

melanocyte | 黑色素細胞 皮膚中製造稱為黑色素的暗棕色色素的細胞

menstrual cycle | 月經週期 卵子成熟而從身體排出的規律序列事件

menstruation | 月經 血液與未受精卵排出體外

meristem | 分生組織 負責在整個植物生命過程中持續成長的非特化細胞區

mesoderm | 中層 中間胎層；發展出肌肉與大部分的循環、生殖與排泄系統

mesophyll | 葉肉 葉子裡的特化基本組織；執行植物的大部分光合作用

messenger RNA (mRNA) | 傳訊物質 RNA (mRNA) 將胺基酸組成為蛋白質的指令樣本從 DNA 攜帶至細胞各部分的一種 RNA

metabolism | 新陳代謝 有機體組成或分解物質的化學反應組合

metamorphosis | 蛻變 幼體變成成體的形狀與形式的變化過程

metaphase | （細胞分裂）中期 染色體橫跨細胞中央排列的有絲分裂階段

microclimate | 小氣候 與周圍區域的氣候有顯著差別的小區域內的環境情況

migration | 遷移 造成從一個環境移動至另一個環境的季節性行為

mineral | 礦物 身體所需要（通常很少量）的無機營養素

mitochondrion | 粒線體 將儲存於食物中的化學能量轉化為使細胞更容易利用的化合物的細胞器官

mitosis | 有絲分裂 細胞核分裂中的真核細胞分裂階段

mixture | 混合物 由兩個或更多元素或化合物以物理性而非化學性組合在一起的物質

molecular clock | 分子時鐘 研究人員使用的方法，利用 DNA 突變率估算兩個物種已經獨立演化的時間長度

molecule | **分子** 大部分的化合物顯示其所有特質的最小單位

molting | **蛻殼** 蛻去外殼甲而長出新殼甲的過程

monocot | **單子葉植物** 子房中有含有一個子葉的被子植物

monoculture | **單作栽培** 年復一年種植單一、高產量作物的農業策略

monomer | **單體** 組成聚合物的小化學單位

monophyletic group | **單源群** 由單一祖先物種與其所有後代組成，但不包括並非其共同祖先的後代的任何有機體的群體

monosaccharide | **單醣類** 單醣分子

motor neuron | **運動神經元** 將指令自中間神經元攜帶至肌肉細胞或腺體的神經細胞種類

multiple alleles | **複數對偶基因** 有超過兩個對偶基因的基因

multipotent | **多能力細胞** 具有發展出很多種分化細胞的有限潛力的細胞

muscle fiber | **肌肉纖維** 細長的骨骼肌肉細胞

muscle tissue | **肌肉組織** 使身體可以運動的一種組織

mutagen | **誘導有機體突變的物質** 環境中與DNA 互相作用並可能造成突變的化學或物理媒介

mutation | **突變** 細胞遺傳物質的變化

mutualism | **互利共生** 兩個物種都從關係中獲利的共生關係

mycelium (pl. mycelia) | **菌絲體** 濃密聚集的真菌菌絲網

mycorrhiza (pl. mycorrhizae) | **菌根** 植物根與真菌的共生群叢

myelin sheath | **髓鞘** 某些神經元中的軸突周圍絕緣膜

myocardium | **心肌** 心臟的中間厚肌肉層

myofibril | **肌原纖維** 骨骼肌肉纖維內緊密包捆的肌絲束

myosin | **肌凝蛋白** 骨骼肌肉細胞內的蛋白質厚肌絲

N

NAD⁺ (nicotinamide adenine dinucleotide) | **NAD⁺（菸鹼胺腺呤雙核酸）** 涉及醣酵解的電子載體

NADP⁺ (nicotinamide adenine dinucleotide phosphate) | **NADP⁺（菸鹼胺腺呤雙核酸磷酸鹽）** 將高能量電子由葉綠素轉移至其他分子的載體分子

natural selection | **天擇** 最適應於環境的有機體最能成功生存與繁殖的過程；亦稱為適者生存

nephridium (pl. nephridia) | **腎管** 環節動物過濾體液的排泄構造

nephron | **腎單位** 腎臟內過濾雜質、收集廢物以及使淨化的血液回到循環中的濾血構造

nervous tissue | **神經組織** 在整個身體中傳遞神經衝動的一種組織

neuromuscular junction | **神經肌肉接點** 運動神經元與骨骼肌肉細胞之間的接觸點

neuron | **神經元** 神經細胞；專門攜帶訊息至整個神經系統

neurotransmitter | **神經傳導物質** 由神經元利用來將衝動經過一個神經突觸傳遞到另一個細胞的化學物質

neurulation | **神經形成** 神經系統發展的第一步

niche | **區位** 有機體生活在其中的物理與生物條件以及有機體利用這些條件的方式的完整範圍

nitrogen fixation | **固氮作用** 將氮氣轉為植物可吸收與利用的氮化合物的過程

node | **莖節** 葉子附著在成長中的莖部的部分

nondisjunction | **不分離現象** 同源染色體無法適當分開的減數分裂錯誤

nonrenewable resource | **不可再生資源** 無法在一段合理的時間內由自然過程再補充的資源

norepinephrine | **正腎上腺素** 由腎上腺所釋放，增加心率與血壓並使身體做好進行劇烈身體活動準備的荷爾蒙

notochord | **脊索** 通過脊索動物身體的長形支撐狀體，位於神經索正下方

nucleic acid | **核酸** 含有氫氣、氧氣、氮氣、碳與磷的巨分子

nucleotide | **核苷酸** 核酸組成的次單位；由 5 碳糖、磷酸根與含氮鹼基所組成

nucleus | **原子核** 原子的中心，含有質子與中子；含有 DNA 形式的細胞遺傳物質的構造

nutrient | **營養素** 有機體維續生命所需的化學物質

nymph | **若蟲** 動物的未成熟形式，與成體形式相仿但缺乏性器官的功能

O

observation | **觀察** 以謹慎有序的方式注意並描述活動或程序的過程

omnivore | **雜食動物** 藉由攝食植物和動物來取得能量的有機體

open circulatory system | 開放循環系統 當血液流經體內時,只有部分血液包含在血管系統中的一種循環系統

operant conditioning | 操作性反射條件 動物透過重複練習,學習如何表現特定的行為方式,以獲得獎勵或避免受罰的一種學習

operator | 操作子 短 DNA 區,與原核生物操縱元的啟動子相鄰,結合負責控制操縱元轉錄率的壓制劑蛋白

operon | 操縱元 原核生物中分享共同的操作子和啟動子並被轉錄為單一 mRNA 的一組鄰近基因

opposable thumb | 對向趾 可以抓東西和使用工具的拇指

order | 目 在分類學上一組密切相關的科

organ | 器官 共同執行密切相關的功能的組織群

organ system | 器官系統 共同執行特定功能的一組器官

organelle | 胞器 在真核細胞內執行重要細胞功能的專門構造

osmosis | 滲透作用 水份透過選擇性的滲透性薄膜而擴散

osmotic pressure | 滲透壓 為了防止沿著選擇性的滲透性薄膜滲透移動而必須施加的壓力

ossification | 骨化作用 軟骨被骨骼取代的骨骼形成過程

osteoblast | 造骨細胞 能分泌礦物質沉積而在骨骼發展過程中取代軟骨的骨骼細胞

osteoclast | 蝕骨細胞 能分解骨骼礦物質的骨骼細胞

osteocyte | 骨細胞 有助於維持骨組織內的礦物質並且繼續強化生長骨骼的骨骼細胞

ovary | 子房;卵巢 植物中圍繞與保護種籽的構造;雌性動物主要的生殖器官;會產生卵

oviparous | 卵生 胚胎在雙親體外的卵中發育的物種

ovoviparous | 卵胎生 胚胎在母體內發育,但養分完全取決於卵中的卵黃囊的物種

ovulation | 產卵;排卵 成熟的卵從卵巢釋放到其中一根輸卵管

ovule | 胚珠 種籽毬果內發展雌性配子體的構造

ozone layer | 臭氧層 大氣層中臭氧氣體相當密集的部分;能保護地球上的生物不受陽光中有害的紫外線照射

P

pacemaker | 起搏器 一小群心肌纖維,藉由設定心臟的收縮率來維持心臟的律動;竇房 (SA) 結

paleontologist | 古生物學者 研究化石的科學家

palisade mesophyll | 柵狀葉肉 葉子上表層之下的細胞層

parasitism | 寄生現象 一個有機體住在另一個有機體身上或體內並且對其造成傷害的共生關係

parathyroid hormone (PTH) | 副甲狀腺荷爾蒙 (PTH) 副甲狀腺所產生的可增加血液中鈣含量的荷爾蒙

parenchyma | 薄壁組織 植物基本組織的主要類型,內含具有薄細胞壁和大型中央液泡的細胞

passive immunity | 被動免疫 由於自然或刻意接觸抗原而發展出的臨時免疫性

pathogen | 病原體 造成疾病的介質

pedigree | 譜系 顯示根據一個家族幾代關係存在或缺乏遺傳性狀的圖表

pepsin | 胃蛋白 能將蛋白質分解為更小的多肽片段的一種酵素

period | 紀 進一步細分「代」的地質學時間劃分單位

peripheral nervous system | 周邊神經系統 傳遞訊號出入中央神經系統的神經和支持細胞網路

peristalsis | 蠕動 平滑肌收縮以提供讓食物經過食道來到胃部的作用力

permafrost | 永凍層 凍原上永久冰凍的下層土壤

petiole | 葉柄 將葉片與莖部相連的細柄

pH scale | pH 酸鹼值 介於 0 到 14 之間的數值量表,用來衡量溶液中 H^+ 離子濃度;0 到 7 的 pH 酸鹼值為酸性,7 的酸鹼值為中性,而 7 到 14 的酸鹼值為鹼性

pharyngeal pouch | 咽囊 脊索類動物喉部的一對構造之一

pharynx | 咽 口腔背部做為空氣和食物通道的管道;也稱為喉嚨

phenotype | 表現型 有機體的物理特徵

phloem | 韌皮部 在植物身上傳輸養分液和光合作用所產生的碳水化合物的血管組織

photic zone | 透光層 靠近水面的陽光區

photoperiod | 光週期 植物對明暗的相對時間長度的反應

photosynthesis | 光合作用 植物和其他自養生物用來捕捉光能的過程,可以提供化學反應所需的能量,將二氧化碳和水份轉換為氧氣以及如醣類和澱粉類等能量豐富的碳水化合物

photosystem | 光系統 存在於類囊體的葉綠素和蛋白質群集

phototropism | 向光性 植物朝向光源生長的傾向

phylogeny | 種系發生 有機體之間演化關係的研究

phylum | 門 在分類學上一組密切相關的綱

phytoplankton | 浮游植物 存在於海洋表面附近的光合成綠藻

pigment | 色素 植物用來收集太陽能的光吸收分子

pioneer species | 先驅物種 演替期間聚居於某個地區的第一個物種

pistil | 雌蕊 單一心皮或數個合生心皮；包含子房、花柱和柱頭

pith | 木髓 雙子葉莖維管組織的脈環內的薄壁組織細胞

pituitary gland | 腦下垂體 靠近顱骨基部的小型腺體，會分泌荷爾蒙以直接調節許多身體機能並控制其他幾種內分泌腺的行動

placenta | 胎盤 胎盤哺乳動物體內的專門器官，母體和發育中的下一代之間透過這個器官交換呼吸氣體、養分和廢物

plankton | 浮游生物 居住在水生環境中的顯微生物；包括浮游植物和浮游動物

plasma | 血漿 血液中的淡黃色液體部分

plasmid | 質體 位於許多細菌細胞質中的小型DNA 環塊

plasmodium | 變形體 胞質黏菌生命週期中的變形蟲攝食期

plate tectonics | 板塊構造學 由於板塊移動所造成的地質作用，例如大陸漂移、火山和地震

platelet | 血小板 骨髓所釋放的有助於血液凝結的細胞碎片

pluripotent | 複功能 能夠發展成大多數但非所有身體細胞類型的細胞

point mutation | 點突變 基因突變，其中 DNA 中的單鹼基已經被改變

pollen grain | 花粉粒 種子植物中包含整個雄性配子體的構造

pollen tube | 花粉管 植物中包含兩個單倍體精核的構造

pollination | 授粉 花粉從雄性再生結構至雌性再生結構的傳送過程

pollutant | 污染物 經由土地、空氣或水份進入生物圈的有害物質

polygenic trait | 多基因遺傳性狀 由兩個或多個基因所控制的遺傳性狀

polymer | 聚合體 由許多單聚物所構成的分子；組成大分子

polymerase chain reaction (PCR) | 聚合酶連鎖反應 (PCR) 生物學家用來製作特定基因的許多副本的方法

polypeptide | 多肽 製作蛋白質的氨基酸的長鏈

polyploidy | 多倍體 有機體多出幾對染色體的情況

population | 族群 居住在相同區域內相同物種的個體數

population density | 族群密度 每個單位面積的個體數

predation | 捕食行為 一種有機體（捕食者）捕食另一種有機體（被捕食者）的互動行為

prehensile tail | 抓握尾 可以緊緊地纏繞在樹枝上的長尾巴

pressure-flow hypothesis | 壓力流假說 解釋韌皮部汁液在植物中從糖「源頭」傳送到糖「儲存區」的方法的假設

primary growth | 初級生長 發生在植物梢頭和芽苗的生長模式

primary producer | 初級生產者 能量豐富的化合物的第一個生產者，該化合物稍後供其他有機體利用

primary succession | 初級演替 在一個沒有先前群落存在痕跡的區域中發生的演替

principle of dominance | 顯性原則 孟德爾的第二結論，說明某些對偶基因為顯性，而某些則為隱性

prion | 普林蛋白 導致疾病的蛋白質粒子

probability | 機率 特定事件將要發生的可能性

product | 產物 化學反應所產生的元素或化合物

prokaryote | 原核生物 缺乏細胞核的單細胞有機體

promoter | 啟動子 基因的特定區，RNA 聚合酶在此結合並開始轉錄

prophage | 原噬菌體 內嵌於細菌宿主的 DNA 中的噬菌體 DNA

prophase | 前期 有絲分裂的第一個也是最長的階段，此時細胞核內的遺傳物質凝結而且染色體變得可見

prostaglandin | 前列腺素 種類繁多的細胞所產生的改性脂肪酸；通常只影響附近的細胞和組織

protein | 蛋白質 包含碳、氫、氧和氮的大分子；為身體生長和修復所需

protostome | 原口動物 口部由胚孔所形成的一種動物

pseudocoelom | 假體腔 只有部分附有中胚層的一種體腔

pseudopod | 偽足 某些原生生物用來移動的細胞質臨時投射

puberty | 青春期 快速成長和性成熟期間，此時生殖系統可以完全發揮功能

pulmonary circulation | 肺循環 心臟和肺部之間的循環途徑

punctuated equilibrium | 中斷平衡 一段很長的穩定期被變化較快速的短暫時期打斷的演化模式

Punnett square | 龐氏表 可用來預測基因交配基因型和表現型組合的圖表

pupa | 蛹 幼蟲發展為成蟲，完成蛻變的階段

pupil | 瞳孔 虹膜上讓光線射入眼睛的小開口

R

radial symmetry | 輻射對稱 一種身體藍圖，可以畫出任何數目的想像平面切過身體中央，將身體分成等分的兩半

radiometric dating | 放射性年代測定法 利用樣本中同一元素從放射性同位素變成非放射性同位素的量而測定樣本年齡的方法

reabsorption | 再吸收 水與溶解的物質被帶回血液中的過程

reactant | 反應物 進入化學反應的元素或化合物

receptor | 接受器 一種細胞上或細胞內的特定蛋白質，其形狀吻合特定分子傳訊物質（例如荷爾蒙）

recombinant DNA | 重組 DNA 藉由結合不同來源的 DNA 而製造的 DNA

red blood cell | 紅血球 含有帶氧血紅素的血液細胞

reflex | 反射動作 對刺激所產生的快速、自動的反應

reflex arc | 反射弧 涉及對刺激產生快速反應的感覺接受器、感覺神經元、運動神經元與影響神經組織

relative dating | 相對日期測定法 藉由將一個化石位置與其他岩石層的化石位置進行比較而測定化石年齡的方法

relative frequency | 相對頻率 相較於相同基因發生其他對偶基因的次數，基因庫內發生對偶基因的次數

releasing hormone | 釋放激素 腦丘下部所製造使腦下垂體腺前葉分泌荷爾蒙的荷爾蒙

renewable resource | 可再生資源 可以被健康的生態系統功能製造或取代的資源

replication | 複製 細胞分裂前複製 DNA 的過程

reproductive isolation | 生殖隔離 物種或族群的分隔，使其不再異種交配而演化成兩個不同的物種

resource | 資源 任何生命的必需品，例如水、營養素、光、食物或空間

response | 反應 對刺激的特定回應

resting potential | 休止電位 橫跨休止神經元細胞膜的電荷

restriction enzyme | 限制酵素 減少核酸序列上 DNA 的酵素

retina | 視網膜 眼睛的最內層；含有受光體

retrovirus | 反轉錄病毒 含有 RNA 作為其基因資訊的 RNA 病毒

ribonucleic acid (RNA) | 核糖核酸 (RNA) 內含核糖的單股核酸

ribosomal RNA (rRNA) | 核糖體 RNA (rRNA) 與蛋白質結合形成核醣體的 RNA 種類

ribosome | 核醣體 在整個細胞內細胞質可找到的 RNA 與蛋白質所組成的細胞器官；蛋白質合成在此發生

RNA interference (RNAi) | RNA 干擾 (RNAi) 將雙股 RNA 引入細胞中以抑制基因表現

RNA polymerase | RNA 聚合酶 在轉錄過程中利用 DNA 股作為模板，將成長中的 RNA 核酸鏈連結在一起的酵素

rod | 桿細胞 眼睛內對光過敏但是無法區別顏色的光接受體

root cap | 根冠 根部尖端保護分生組織的堅韌覆蓋物

root hair | 根鬚 根部上的細鬚，可製造讓水與礦物質進入的大片表面區域

rumen | 瘤胃 牛與相關動物的胃腔，在裡面由共生細菌消化纖維素

S

sapwood | 邊材 木質莖中，圍繞心木的第二層韌皮部；通常活躍地運輸水份

sarcomere | 肌節 肌肉收縮單位；由兩條 Z 線和之間的肌絲所組成

scavenger | 食腐動物 以其他動物屍體為食的動物

science | 科學 收集並分析有關自然界證據的一種組織化的方式

sclerenchyma | 厚壁組織 具有極厚堅硬細胞壁使基本組織堅韌與強壯的基本組織種類

scrotum | 陰囊 包覆睪丸的外囊

sebaceous gland | 皮脂腺 分泌皮脂（油性分泌物）的皮膚腺體

secondary growth | 次生長 雙子葉植物莖部增加厚度的生長形態

secondary succession | 次級演替 一個區域中發生的只有部分被干擾毀滅的演替形態

seed | 種子 由保護覆蓋物所包覆的植物胚胎與食物供應

seed coat | 種皮 圍繞與保護植物胚胎並使種子的內容物避免乾枯的堅韌的覆蓋物

segregation | 隔離 配子形成過程中的對偶基因分離

selective breeding | 選擇性繁殖 製造只包含想要特徵的下一代的有機體繁殖方法

selectively permeable | 選擇性滲透 允許某些物質通過但不讓其他物質通過的生物膜特性；亦稱為半透膜

semen | 精液 精子與精子體液的組合

semicircular canal | 半規管 內耳的三個構造之一，監控身體相對於地心引力的位置

seminiferous tubule | 曲細精管 睪丸中精子在其中生長的數百個細管之一

sensory neuron | 感覺神經元 從感覺接受器接收資訊並將訊號傳遞至中央神經系統的神經細胞種類

sex chromosome | 性染色體 決定個人性別的兩個染色體之一

sex-linked gene | 性聯基因 位於性染色體的基因

sexual reproduction | 有性繁殖 從雙親的細胞結合成新的有機體第一個細胞的繁殖形態

sexually transmitted disease (STD) | 性傳播疾病 (STD) 藉由性行為從一個人傳染給另一個人的疾病

sieve tube element | 篩管元素 通過植物韌皮部細胞的連續管道，以末端對末端排列

single-gene trait | 單一基因特徵 由有兩個對偶基因的基因所控制的特徵

small intestine | 小腸 對食物進行大部分化學性消化與吸收的消化器官

smog | 煙霧 化學混合物所形成的灰棕色薄霧

society | 社會 一群為了團體的利益努力而合作的關係親密的同種動物

solute | 溶質 溶解於溶液中的物質

solution | 溶液 所有的組成物都平均分散的混合形態

solvent | 溶劑 溶液中的溶解物質

somatic nervous system | 軀體神經系統 攜帶訊號往返於骨骼肌肉之間的末梢神經系統部分

speciation | 物種形成 新物種的形成

species diversity | 物種多樣性 組成特定區域的不同物種的數目

spirillum (pl. spirilla) | 螺旋菌屬 螺旋狀或螺絲狀的原核生物

spongy mesophyll | 海綿葉肉組織 葉子的柵狀葉肉組織下方的疏鬆組織層

sporangium (pl. sporangia) | 孢子囊 單倍體孢子以減數分裂製造的孢子莢膜

spore | 孢子 在原核生物、單細胞生物與真菌中，能夠存活於不利情況下的任何厚壁生命週期階段；植物中的單倍體生殖細胞

sporophyte | 孢子體 製造孢子的植物；植物生命週期的多細胞雙倍體階段

stabilizing selection | 穩定選擇 天擇的形式，靠近分佈曲線中心的個體比曲線任一端的個體的適應力更強

stamen | 雄蕊 花的雄性部分；含有花藥與肌絲

stem cell | 幹細胞 一種可以長成一種或多種特化細胞的非特化細胞

stigma | 柱頭 花柱頂端的黏稠部分；專精於捕集花粉

stimulus (pl. stimuli) | 刺激 有機體對其回應的訊號

stoma (pl. stomata) | 氣孔 植物可以讓二氧化碳、水與氧氣向葉片內外擴散的表皮細小開口

stomach | 胃 繼續食物的機械性與化學性消化的大型肌肉囊

stroma | 漿質 葉綠素的液體部分；類囊體的外側

substrate | 基質 酵素催化反應的反應物

suspension | 懸浮液 水與非溶解物質的混合物

sustainable development | 永續發展 利用而不耗盡自然資源並且為人類提供所需而不造成長期環境傷害的策略

symbiosis | 共生 兩個物種緊密生活在一起的關係

synapse | 突觸 神經元可以將衝動轉移至另一個細胞的點

systematics | 系統論 生命多樣性與有機體之間演化關係的研究

systemic circulation | 體循環 心臟與身體其他部位之間的循環途徑

T

taiga | 寒帶針葉林 具有長而寒冷的冬天以及幾個月溫暖氣候的生態群系；以長綠針葉林為主；亦稱為北寒林

target cell | 目標細胞 有特定荷爾蒙接受器的細胞

taste bud | 味蕾 偵測味覺的感覺器官

taxon (pl. taxa) | 生物分類群 將有機體分類而成的組織群或組織層

telomere | 染色體末端端粒 真核染色體末端的重覆 DNA

telophase | 有絲分裂末期 不同的個別染色體開始向外擴散至染色質糾結的有絲分裂階段

temporal isolation | 繁殖季節隔離 兩個或多個物種在不同時間繁殖的生殖隔離形式

tendon | 筋腱 將骨骼肌肉連接至骨頭的強韌結締組織

territory | 地域 由一隻動物或一群動物所佔領並保護的特定區域

testis (pl. testes) | 睪丸 主要的雄性生殖器官；製造精子

tetrad | 四分體 減數分裂期間所形成含有四條染色分體的構造

tetrapod | 四足動物 有四肢的脊椎動物

thalamus | 視丘 接受來自感覺器官的訊息並將該訊息傳遞給大腦的適當區域做為將來處理之用的腦部構造

theory | 理論 經過完整測試的解釋，將範圍廣泛的觀察與假設統一化，並使科學家能對於新的情況進行正確的預測

thigmotropism | 向觸性 植物對接觸的反應

threshold | 臨界值 需要造成衝動的刺激最低值

thylakoid | 類囊體 葉綠體中的囊狀光合作用膜

thyroxine | 甲狀腺素 由甲狀腺製造的荷爾蒙，可增加身體各部位細胞的新陳代謝率

tissue | 組織 執行特定功能的相似細胞群

tolerance | 耐受性 有機體在不同於其最佳情況的環境下生存與繁殖的能力

totipotent | 全能性 能夠發展成身體內任何種類細胞的細胞（包括構成胚外膜與胎盤的細胞）

trachea | 氣管 連結咽與喉的管道；亦稱為windpipe（氣管）

tracheid | 管胞 具有厚細胞壁的木質部內中空植物細胞

tracheophyte | 導管植物 管狀植物

trait | 特性 個體的特定特徵

transcription | 基因轉錄 從 DNA 模板合成為RNA 分子

transfer RNA (tRNA) | 轉移 RNA (tRNA) 在蛋白質合成期間將每一個胺基酸輸送至核醣體的RNA 種類

transformation | 轉型 細菌由另外一種細菌品系的一個基因或多個基因所改變的過程

transgenic | 基因轉殖 指含有來自其他有機體基因的有機體

translation | 轉譯 mRNA 鹼基序列被轉為蛋白質胺基酸序列的過程

transpiration | 蒸散作用 植物透過葉片散失水份

trochophore | 擔輪幼蟲 水中軟體動物的自由游動型幼蟲階段

trophic level | 營養層 食物鏈或食物網的各個層級

tropism | 向性 植物朝向或遠離刺激的運動

tumor | 腫瘤 快速分裂而可能傷害周圍組織的細胞腫塊

U

understory | 地被層 雨林中樹木冠層下方由較矮的樹木與藤蔓所形成的植物層

ureter | 輸尿管 將尿液從腎臟輸送到膀胱的管道

urethra | 尿道 尿液藉以離開身體的管道

urinary bladder | 膀胱 貯藏尿液以供隨後排泄的囊狀器官

V

vaccination | 疫苗接種 為了產生免疫而以減弱或相似但較不危險的病原體進行的注射

vaccine | 疫苗 減弱或被殺死的病原體製劑，用來對疾病產生免疫

vacuole | 液泡 儲藏水、鹽、蛋白質與碳水化合物的細胞器官

valve | 瓣膜 位於心房與心室之間或是靜脈內的結締組織皮瓣，可防止血液倒流

van der Waals forces | 凡得瓦爾力 附近分子帶電性相反的區域之間所發展出的輕微吸引力

vas deferens | 輸精管 將精子從副睪輸送至尿道的管道

vascular bundle | 維管束 莖部的木質部與韌皮組織集束

vascular cambium | 維管形成層 製造管狀組織並增加莖部厚度的分生組織

vascular cylinder | 維管柱 根部的中央區域，包括管狀組織 -- 木質部與韌皮部

vascular tissue | 管狀組織 植物中輸送水份與營養素的特殊組織

vector | 病媒 將病原體傳給人類的動物

vegetative reproduction | 營養繁殖 植物無性繁殖的方法，使單一植物產生基因與本身完全相同的後代

vein | 靜脈 將血液從身體輸送回心臟的血管

ventricle | 心室 將血液從心臟抽打至身體其他部位的心臟下方腔室

vertebrate | 脊椎動物 有脊柱的動物

vessel element | 導管分子 一種形成連續管道的一部分讓水份通過的木質部細胞

vestigial organs | 退化器官 形狀變小以及幾乎或是完全沒有功能的構造

villus (pl. villi) | 絨毛 幫助營養分子吸收的小腸內指狀突出物

virus | 病毒 由蛋白質、核酸（有時亦含只能藉由感染的活細胞進行複製的脂質）所組成的粒子

vitamin | 維他命 有助於調節身體代謝的有機分子

viviparous | 胎生 胚胎成長時含在母體內而直接從母體吸收養分的動物

W

weather | 氣候 大氣層的每日條件，包括氣溫、降水量與其他因素

wetland | 濕地 一年中至少有某段期間水覆蓋土壤或是存在於或靠近地表的生態系統

white blood cell | 白血球 抵禦感染、對抗寄生蟲與攻擊細菌的一種血液細胞

woody plant | 木本植物 主要由具有厚細胞壁且可支撐植物身體的細胞所組成的植物種類；包括樹、灌木以及藤蔓

X

xylem | 木質部 將水份從根部往上輸送至植物各部位的管狀組織

Z

zoonosis (pl. zoonoses) | 人畜共通傳染病 從動物傳播給人類的疾病

zooplankton | 浮游動物 小型浮動式動物，屬於浮游生物的一部分

zygote | 受精卵 受精的卵子

Haitian Creole
Kreyòl Ayisyen

Biology Glossary

A

abiotic factor | faktè abyotik faktè fizik, oswa inanime ki fòme yon sistèm ekolojik

abscisic acid | asid absisik òmòn vejetal ki anpeche selil la divize, kidonk anpeche kwasans

acetylcholine | asetilkolin yon newotransmitè ki pwodwi yon enpilsyon nan yon selil miskilè

acid | asid yon konpoze ki libere iyon idwojèn (H⁺) an solisyon ; yon solisyon ki gen yon pH ki enferyè a 7

acid rain | lapli asid lapli ki genyen asid nitrik ak silfirik

actin | aktin filaman pwoteyin fen ou jwenn nan misk yo

action potential | potansyèl daksyon ranvèsman polarizasyon manbràn selilè yon newòn ; yo rele l tou yon enpilsyon nève

activation energy | enèji daktivasyon enèji ki nesesè pou pwodwi yon reyaksyon

active immunity | iminite aktif iminite ki vin devlope aprè yon ekspozisyon natirèl oswa delibere a yon antijèn

adaptation | adaptasyon yon karakteristik eredite ki ogmante kapasite yon òganis pou l siviv epi repwodwi nan yon anviwonman

adaptive radiation | radyasyon adaptiv pwosesis kote yon sèl espès oswa yon ti gwoup espès evolye nan plizyè diferan fòm ki viv nan diferan fason

adenosine triphosphate (ATP) | adenosin trifosfat (ATP) yon sibstans selil yo itilize pou estoke epi transpòte enèji

adhesion | adezyon yon fòs datraksyon ant diferan kalite molekil

aerobic | ayewobik pwosesis ki bezwen oksijèn

age structure | klasman selon laj kantite mal ak femèl nan chak laj nan yon popilasyon

aggression | agresyon konpòtman menasan yon bèt itilize pou l egzèse kontwòl sou yon lòt bèt

algal bloom | flè dlo yon ogmantasyon nan kantite plant ki leve nan dlo ak lòt pwodiktè akoz yon gwo kantite yon eleman nitritif ki limite

allele | alèl youn pami plizyè fòm diferan yon jèn

allergy | alèji yon reyaksyon egzajere sistèm iminitè a fè aprè yon kontak avèk yon antijèn

alternation of generations | altènans jenerasyon yon sik lavi ki gen de faz altènan— yon faz aployid (N) ak yon faz diployid (2N)

alveolus (pl. alveoli) | alveyòl ti sak ki plen lè ki nan pwent yon bwonkyòl nan poumon yo ki founi yon sifas pou echanj gaz ka fèt

amino acid | asid amine konpoze ki gen yon gwoup anime nan yon pwent epi yon gwoup kaboksilik nan lòt pwent la

amniotic egg | ze amnyotik yon ze ki gen yon kokiyaj ak manbràn ki kreye yon anviwonman pwoteje kote anbriyon an ka devlope andeyò dlo

amylase | amilaz yon anzim nan saliv la ki brize lyen chimik nan amidon

anaerobic | anayewobi pwosesis ki pa bezwen oksijèn

anaphase | anafaz faz mitoz la kote kwomozòm yo separe epi yo deplase al nan lòt bò selil la

angiosperm | anjyospèm gwoup plant a grenn ki pote grenn yo nan yon kouch tisi ki pwoteje grenn lan ; yo rele l tou plant a flè

anther | antè pati nan flè a ki pwodwi grenn polenn yo

antheridium (pl. antheridia) | anteridyòm estrikti repwodiktif maskilen nan kèk plant ki pwodwi espèm

anthropoid | antwopoyid gwoup primat ki genyen ladan l makak, senj ak moun

antibiotic | antibyotik yon gwoup medikaman yo itilize pou bloke kwasans ak repwodiksyon ajan patojèn bakteryen

antibody | antikò pwoteyin ki swa atake antijèn yo dirèkteman swa ki pwodwi pwoteyin lyezon antijèn

anticodon | antikodon gwoup twa nikleyotid ki sou yon molekil ARNt ki konplementè a kodon ki sou ARNm lan

antigen | antijèn tout sibstans ki deklannche yon repons iminitè

aphotic zone | zòn afotik kouch oseyan ki anba zòn afotik la kote limyè solèy la pa penetre

apical dominance | dominans apikal fenomèn kote pi pre boujon an ye pa rapò a pwent tij lan, se plis sa anpeche kwasans li

apical meristem | meristèm apikal gwoup selil non espesyalize ki divize pou yo ka pwodwi plis longè nan tij yo ak rasin yo

apoptosis | apoptoz pwosesis ki pwograme lanmò selil la

appendage | apenndis yon estrikti, tankou yon janm oswa antèn ki pwolonje apati de pawa kò a

appendicular skeleton | eskelèt apenndikilè zo bra ak janm yo ansanm ak zo ki nan zòn basen an ak zèpòl yo

aquaculture | Ua qoob loo hauv dej Kev yug tsiaj hauv dej coj los rau neeg noj

aquaporin | akwaporin pwoteyin ki pèmèt pasaj dlo nan yon selil

Archaea | Ache yon gwoup pwokaryòk iniselilè ki gen pawa selilè ki pa genyen peptidoglikàn ; koresponn a wayòm Achebakteri

archegonium (pl. archegonia) | achegòn estrikti nan plant ki pwodwi ovil

artery | atè gwo veso sangen ki kondwi san an sot nan kè a pou al nan tisi kò a

artificial selection | seleksyon atifisyèl elvaj seleksyon kèk plant ak bèt pou ankouraje pwopagasyon kèk karaktè dezirab nan desandans yo

asexual reproduction | repwodiksyon aseksye pwosesis repwodiksyon kote se yon sèl paran ki pwodwi yon desandans ki jenetikman idantik a paran an

asthma | opresyon maladi respiratwa kwonik kote vwa ayeryèn lan retresi, epi sa lakoz respirasyon siflan, tous ak difikilte pou respire

atherosclerosis | atewosklewoz yon kondisyon kote matyè gra ki rele plak akimile andedan pawa ateryèl yo epi evantyèlman sa koze atè yo vin rèd

atom | atòm eleman de baz matyè

ATP synthase | ATP sentaz yon gwoup pwoteyin ki lonje manbràn selilè a epi pèmèt iyon idwojèn (H⁺) pou pase ladan l

atrium (pl. atria) | atriyòm kavite siperyè kè a ki resevwa san ki sot nan rès kò a

autonomic nervous system | sistèm nève otonòm pati nan sistèm nève a ki responsab fonksyon otomatik yo, oswa ki pa sou kontwòl konsyan ; li konpoze de sistèm senpatik ak parasenpatik

autosome | otozòm kwomozòm aseksye ; yo rele l tou kwomozòn otozòm

autotroph | ototwòf òganis ki kapab kaptire enèji ki sot nan limyè solèy la oswa pwodwi chimik epi itilize l pou pwodwi pwòp manje l apati de konpoze inòganik ; yo rele l tou yon pwodiktè

auxin | oksin sibstans regilatè ki pwodwi nan pwent yon plant an kwasans ki estimile elongasyon selil la ak kwasans nouvo rasin

axial skeleton | eskelèt aksyal eskelèt ki sipòte aks santral kò a ; li konpoze de kràn lan, kolòn vètebral la ak kaj torasik la

axon | aksòn fib long ki kondwi enpilsyon nan direksyon opoze kò selilè yon newòn

B

bacillus (pl. bacilli) | basiy pwokaryòt an fòm batonè

background extinction | estèminasyon de fon estèminasyon seleksyon natirèl la pwovoke pa mwayen yon pwosesis ki lan epi estab

Bacteria | Bakteri òganis iniselilè, pwokaryòt kote pawa selilè yo genyen peptidoglikàn ; li koresponn a wayòm ebakteri

bacteriophage | bakteryofaj yon tip viris ki enfekte bakteri

bark | ekòs tisi ou jwenn padeyò kanbyòm lan ki genyen ladan l flèm oswa libè, felojèn ak lyèj

base | baz yon konpoze ki libere iyon idwoksil (OH⁻) an solisyon ; yon solisyon ki gen yon pH ki siperyè a 7

base pairing | apariman de baz prensip ki lye nan ADN ka fòme sèlman ant adenin ak timin epi ant gwanin ak sitosin

behavior | konpòtman fason yon òganis reyaji a chanjman nan kondisyon ekstèn li oswa nan anviwonman ekstèn li

behavioral isolation | izolman konpòtmantal
fòm izolman konpòtmantal kote de popilasyon
devlope diferans nan rit parad nipsyal oswa lòt
konpòtman ki anpeche yo repwodwi

benthos | benntos òganis ki viv nan fon oswa
apwoksimite fon lak, kou dlo oswa lanmè

bias | patipri yon preferans patikilye oswa
pwennvi ki pèsonèl, olye li syantifik

bilateral symmetry | simetri bilateral tip
simetri kote yon sèl plan ka travèse pou l koupe
òganis lan an bò goch ak bò dwat epi de mwatye
yo idantik

binary fission | fisyon binè tip repwodiksyon
aseksye kote yon òganis repwodwi ADN li epi
divize an mwatye, epi pwodwi de selil fi ki idantik

binocular vision | vizyon binokilè kapasite
pou fizyone imaj vizyèl toulè de zye yo, ki
founi pèsepsyon an pwofondè ak yon vizyon
tridimansyonèl lemonn

binomial nomenclature | nomanklati binominal
sistèm klasifikasyon kote yo asiyen chak espès
yon non syantifik ki gen de pati

biodiversity | byodivèsite total varyete òganis
ki nan byosfè a ; yo rele l tou divèsite byolojik

biogeochemical cycle | sik byojeyochimik
pwosesis kote eleman yo, konpoze chimik yo,
ak lòt fòm matyè pase de yon òganis a yon lòt
epi de yon pati byosfè a pou al nan yon lòt

biogeography | byojeyografi etid sou
distribisyon òganis nan pase ak prezan

bioinformatics | byo-enfòmatik aplikasyon
matematik ak enfòmatik pou estoke, rekipere
epi analize done byolojik

**biological magnification | anplifikasyon
byolojik** ogmantasyon konsantrasyon yon
sibstans toksik nan kèk òganis nan nivo twofik ki
pi wo nan yon chèn alimantè oswa rezo twofik

biology | byoloji etid syantifik èt vivan

biomass | byomas kantite total tisi vivan nan
yon kèlkonk nivo twofik

biome | byom yon gwoup sistèm ekolijik ki
pataje menm klima ak òganis tipik

biosphere | byosfè pati Latè kote lavi egziste epi
ki gen ladan l tè, dlo ak lè oswa atmosfè

biotechnology | byoteknoloji pwosesis kote yo
manipile òganis yo, selil yo oswa molekil yo pou
pwodwi kèk pwodwi esepsifik

biotic factor | faktè byotik tout pati vivan nan
anviwonman an kote yon òganis ka aji youn sou
lòt

bipedal | bipèd tèm yo itilize pou pale de
deplasman sou de pye

blade | lenb pati aplati, fen yon fèy nan yon plant

blastocyst | blastosis estaj nan kòmansman
devlopman mamifè yo ki konpoze de yon boul
selil ki vid

blastula | blastila Yon boul selil ki vid ki devlope
lè yon zigòt sibi yon seri divizyon selil

bone marrow | mwèl ose tisi mou ou jwenn
nan kavite zo yo

bottleneck effect | efè detrangleman Yon
chanjman nan frekans alèl la aprè yon rediksyon
konsiderab nan gwosè yon popilasyon

Bowman's capsule | kapsil Bowman fòmasyon
esferik ki antoure glomeril la ; li kolekte filtra ki
sot nan san an

brain stem | twon serebral estrikti ki konekte
sèvo a ak mwèl epinyè a ; li genyen ladan l bilb
rachidyen an ak pwotiberans anilè a

bronchus (pl. bronchi) | bwonch youn nan de
gwo tib nan kavite pwatrin lan ki soti nan trache
a epi ki ale nan poumon yo

bryophyte | briyofit gwoup plant ki gen ògàn
repwodiktif espesyalize men ki pa gen tisi
vaskilè ; gwoup sa a genyen ladan l mous yo ak
fanmi yo

bud | boujon estrikti plant ki genyen tisi meristèm
apikal ki ka pwodwi nouvo tij ak fèy

buffer | tanpon yon konpoze ki anpeche
chanjman bris, toudenkou nan pH

C

calcitonin | kalsitonin òmòn tiwoyid la pwodwi
ki redwi nivo kalsyòm nan san an

Calorie | Kalori mezi enèji kalorifik nan manje ;
ekivalan a 1000 kalori

calorie | kalori kantite enèji ki nesesè pou
ogmante tanperati 1 gram dlo pa 1 degre Sèlsiyis

Calvin cycle | sik Calvin reyaksyon fotosentèz k
ap dewoule san limyè kote yo itilize enèji ki sot
nan ATP ak NADPH pou bati konpoze ki fò an
enèji tankou sik

cancer | kansè twoub kote kèk nan selil nan kò a
pèdi kapasite pou kontwole kwasans

canopy | kouvè forestye kouvèti dans ki fòme
avèk fèy tèt pyebwa nan forè twopikal yo

capillary | kapilè veso sangen ki pi piti ; yo pote
eleman nitritif ak oksijèn nan tisi yo epi yo
absòbe dyoksid kabòn ak dechè

capillary action | aksyon kapilè tandans dlo
genyen pou l monte nan yon tib fen

capsid | kapsid kouch pwoteyin ki antoure yon viris

carbohydrate | idrat kabòn yon sibstans ki konpoze de atòm kabòn, idwojèn ak oksijèn ; tip eleman nitritif ki se pi gwo sous enèji pou kò a

carnivore | kanivò òganis ki jwenn enèji lè yo manje lòt òganis

carpel | kapèl pati ki pi pwofon nan yon flè ki pwodwi epi abrite ògàn femèl flè a

carrying capacity | kapasite chaj pi gwo kantite moun nan yon espès patikilye yon anviwònman an patikilye ka sipòte

cartilage | katilaj tip tisi konjonktif ki sipòte kò a epi ki pi mou epi pi flekib pase zo

Casparian strip | bann Casparian bann enpèmeyab ki antoure selil andodèmal plant lan epi li enplike nan pasaj a sans inik materyèl yo nan silenn vaskilè nan rasin plant yo

catalyst | katalizè yon sibstans ki akselere to yon reyaksyon chimik

cell | selil inite de baz ki nan tout bagay ki vivan

cell body | kò selilè pi gwo pati yon newòn tipik, ki genyen nwayo a ak pifò nan sitoplas lan

cell cycle | sik selilè yon seri etap kote yon selil grandi, li prepare pou l divize, epi li divize pou l fòme de selil fi

cell division | divizyon selilè pwosesis kote yon selil divize an de nouvo selil fi

cell membrane | manbràn plasmik baryè fen, fleksib ki antoure tout selil ; li kontwole sa ki rantre ak sa ki sòti nan selil la

cell theory | teyori selilè yon konsèp byoloji fondamantal ki deklare se selil ki konpoze tout èt vivan ; selil yo se inite de baz estrikti ak fonksyon nan èt vivan yo ; epi se selil ki la deja yo ki pwodwi nouvo selil yo

cell wall | pawa selilè kouch rezistan ki antoure manbràn plasmik la nan kèk selil

cell-mediated immunity | iminite a medyasyon selilè repons iminitè ki defann kò a kont kèk viris, chanpiyon ak selil kansè ki anòmal andedan selil vivan yo

cellular respiration | respirasyon selilè pwosesis ki libere enèji lè l dekonpoze glikoz ak lòt molekil alimantè yo an prezans oksijèn

central nervous system | sistèm nève santral li genyen ladan l sèvo a ak mwèl epinyè a, li trete enfòmasyon epi li kreye yon repons ki ale nan kò a

centriole | santriyòl estrikti nan yon selil animal ki ede òganize divizyon selilè a

centromere | santwomè pòsyon yon kwomozòm kote de kwomatid yo kole ansanm

cephalization | sefalizasyon konsantrasyon ògàn sans yo ak newòn yo nan ekstremite enteryè yon animal

cerebellum | sèvelè pati nan sèvo a ki koòdone mouvman epi kontwole ekilib

cerebral cortex | kòtèks serebral kouch eksteryè sèvo yon mamifè ; sant panse ak lòt konpòtman konplèks

cerebrum | sèvo pati nan sèvo a ki responsab pou aktivite volontè kò a ; pati nan sèvo a ki pèmèt ou "panse"

chemical digestion | dijesyon chimik pwosesis kote anzim yo dekonpoze manje pou fè l tounen ti molekil kò a ka itilize

chemical reaction | reyaksyon chimik pwosesis ki chanje, oswa transfòme, yon gwoup pwodwi chimik nan yon lòt gwoup pwodwi chimik

chemosynthesis | chimyosentèz pwosesis kote yo itilize enèji chimik pou pwodwi idrat kabòn

chitin | chitin sik konplèks ki konpoze pawa selilè chanpiyon ; ou jwenn li tou nan eskelèt eksteryè atwopòd yo

chlorophyll | klowofil pigman prensipal plant yo ak lòt òganis fotosentetik

chloroplast | klowoplas òganit ou jwenn nan selil plant yo ak kèk lòt òganis ki kaptire enèji nan limyè solèy la epi li konvèti l an enèji chimik

chordate | kòde yon animal ki genyen, pandan omwen yon etap nan lavi l ; yon chèn nève dòsal, yon kòd dòsal, yon ke ki depase anis lan; ak pòch farenje

chromatid | kwomatid youn nan de pati "sè" idantik yon kwomozòm double

chromatin | kwomatin sibstans ou jwenn nan kwomozòn ekaryotik ki konpoze de ADN ki anwoule byen fèm ozanviwon istòn yo

chromosome | kwomozòm estrikti an fòm fimalan ki nan nwayo a ki genyen enfòmasyon jenetik ki pase de yon jenerasyon a yon lòt

chyme | chim yon melanj anzim ak manje ki patyèlman dijere

cilium (pl. cilia) | sil pwojeksyon kout ki sanble ak cheve ki pwodwi mouvman

circadian rhythm | ritm sikadyen sik konpòtmantal ki fèt chak jou

clade | klad yon branch evolisyonè yon kladogram ki genyen yon sèl ansèt ak tout desandan l yo

cladogram | kladogram yon dyagram ki dekri modèl karakteristik komen pami kèk espès

class | klas nan klasman, yon gwoup òd ki aparante de prè

classical conditioning | kondisyònman klasik fòm aprantisaj ki fèt lè yon animal fè yon koneksyon mantal ant yon estimilan ak yon kèlkonk rekonpans oswa pinisyon

climate | klima mwayèn kondisyon tanperati ak presipitasyon tankou lapli ak nèj dane-an-ane nan yon zòn sou yon peryòd tan pwolonje

clone | klòn yon manm nan yon popilasyon selil ki jenetikman idantik ki pwodwi apati de yon sèl selil

closed circulatory system | sistèm sikilatwa fèm yon tip sistèm sikilatwa kote san an sikile antyèman nan veso sangen yo ki alonje atravè kò a

coccus (pl. cocci) | kòk pwokaryòk ki gen fòm awondi

cochlea | kokle pati entèn zòrèy la ki plen ak likid ; li genyen selil nève ki detekte son

codominance | kodominans sitiyasyon kote fenotip toulè de alèl yo pwodwi eksprime de fason konplè

codon | kodon gwoup twa baz nikleyotid nan ARNm ki presize yon asid amine an patikilye pou enkòpore nan yon pwoteyin

coelom | kolòm yon kavite kò a ki double avèk mezoblas

coevolution | ko-evolisyon pwosesis kote de espès evolye pou reponn a chanjman ki fèt nan youn lòt avèk letan

cohesion | kowezyon yon atraksyon ant molekil ki gen menm sibstans

collenchyma | kolenchim nan plant yo, se yon tip tisi nan tè a ki genyen pawa selilè ki rezistan, fleksib ; li ede sipòte plant ki pi gwo yo

commensalism | kòmansalis yon relasyon senbyotik kote yon òganis benefisye epi lòt la pa ni ede ni fè ditò

communication | kominikasyon pasaj enfòmasyon de yon òganis a yon lòt

community | kominote yon asanblaj popilasyon diferan ki abite ansanm nan yon zòn ki byen defini

companion cell | selil konpay nan plant yo, selil flèm ki antoure kèk eleman tib krible

competitive exclusion principle | prensip eksklizyon konpetitiv prensip ki deklare de espès paka okipe menm nich lan nan menm abita anmenmtan

compound | konpoze yon sibstan ki fòme avèk konbinezon de eleman oswa plis nan pwopòsyon presi

cone | kòn nan zye a, yon fotoreseptè ki reponn a limyè ki gen diferan koulè pou pwodwi vizyon an koulè

coniferous | konifè mo yo itilize pou pale de pyebwa ki pwodwi kòn ki pote grenn epi ki gen fèy fen ki gen fòm zegwi

conjugation | konjigezon pwosesis kote kèk paramesi ak kèk pwokaryòt echanje enfòmasyon jenetik

connective tissue | tisi konjonktif tip tisi ki bay sipò pou kò a epi ki konekte pati kò a

consumer | konsomatè òganis ki depann de lòt òganis pou l jwenn apwovizyònman enèji ak manje ; yo rele l tou etewotwòf

control group | gwoup temwen yon gwoup nan yon esè ki ekspoze a menm kondisyon avèk gwoup eksperimantal la eksepte pou yon faktè endepandan

controlled experiment | eksperyans kontwole yon eksperyans kote se sèlman yon faktè ki chanje

convergent evolution | evolisyon konvèjant pwosesis kote òganis ki pa aparante endepandamman devlope kèk similarite lè yo adapte a anviwònman similè

cork cambium | felojèn tisi meristèm ki pwodwi kouvèti eksteryè tij yo pandan kwasans segondè yon plant

cornea | kòne kouch transparan rezistan zye a kote limyè penetre

corpus luteum | kò jòn non yo bay yon folikil aprè ovilasyon an akoz li gen koulè jòn

cortex | kòtèks nan plant yo, zòn tisi ki nan tè a ki jis andedan rasin lan kote dlo ak mineral sikile

corticosteroid | kòtikoestewoyid òmòn estewoyid kòtèks sirenal la pwodwi

cotyledon | kotiledon premye fèy oswa premye pè fèy anbriyon yon plant ki pote grenn pwodwi

courtship | parad nipsyal tip konpòtman kote yon animal voye yon estimilan pou l ka atire yon manm nan sèks opoze a

covalent bond | lyezon kovalant tip lyezon ant atòm yo kote yo pataje elektwon yo

crossing-over | anjanbman yon pwosesis kote kwomozòm omològ yo fè echanj pòsyon nan kwomatid yo pandan mitoz

cyclin | siklin youn nan fanmi pwoteyin ki kontwole sik selilè nan ekaryotik yo

cytokinesis | sitosinèz divizyon sitoplas la pou fòme de selil fi separe

cytokinin | sitokinin òmòn vejetal rasin k ap grandi ak fwi k ap devlope ak grenn yo pwodwi

cytoplasm | sitoplas pòsyon likid selil la ki andeyò nwayo a

cytoskeleton | sitoeskelèt rezo filaman pwoteyin nan yon selil ekaryotik ki bay selil la fòm li ak òganizasyon entèn li epi li enplike nan mouvman

D

data | done prèv ; enfòmasyon yo ranmase apati obsèvasyon

deciduous | kadik mo yo itilize pou pale de yon tip pyebwa ki jete fèy li yo pandan yon sezon an patikilye chak ane

decomposer | dekonpozè òganis ki dekonpoze epi ki jwenn enèji apati de matyè òganik ki mouri

deforestation | deforestasyon destriksyon forè yo

demographic transition | tranzisyon demografik chanjman nan yon popilasyon de to nesans ak mòtalite ki wo a to nesans ak mòtalite ki ba

demography | demografi etid syantifik popilasyon imen

dendrite | dandrit ekstansyon kò selilè yon newòn ki pote enpilsyon ki sot nan anviwònman an oswa ki sot nan lòt newòn nan direksyon kò selilè a

denitrification | denitrifikasyon pwosesis kote bakteri nan tè a konvèti nitrat ann azòt

density-dependent limiting factor | faktè limitan ki depann de dansite faktè limitan ki depann de dansite popilasyon an

density-independent limiting factor | faktè limitan ki pa depann de dansite faktè limitan ki afekte tout popilasyon nan menm fason, san sa pa gen rapò ak dansite popilasyon an

deoxyribonucleic acid (DNA) | asid dezoksiribonikleyik (ADN) materyèl jenetik òganis yo erite de paran yo

dependent variable | varyab depandan varyab yo obsève epi ki chanje pou reponn a varyab endepandan ; yo rele l tou varyab reyaktif

derived character | karaktè derive yon trè karaktè ki parèt nan pati resan yon fanmi, men ou pa jwenn li nan manm ki pi aje yo

dermis | dèm kouch po ou jwenn anba epidèm lan

desertification | dezètifikasyon tè a pwodwi mwens akoz twòp kiltivasyon, twòp patiraj, sechrès sezonye, ak chanjman nan klima a

detritivore | detritivò òganis ki nouri de debri vejetal ak animal ansanm ak lòt matyè mò

deuterostome | detewostòm gwoup animal kote blatospò a vin tounen anis la, epi bouch la fòme apati de dezyèm ouvèti ki devlope a

diaphragm | dyafragm gwo misk aplati ki anba kavite pwatrin lan ki ede avèk respirasyon

dicot | dikotiledòn anjyospèm ki gen de fèy ki gen grenn nan ovè li

differentiation | diferansyasyon pwosesis kote selil yo vin espesyalize nan estrikti ak fonksyon

diffusion | difizyon pwosesis kote patikil yo gen tandans pou deplase sot nan yon zòn kote yo pi konsantre pou al nan yon zòn kote yo mwen konsantre

digestive tract | tib dijestif yon tib ki kòmanse nan bouch la epi ki fini nan anis lan

diploid | diploid mo yo itilize pou pale de yon selil ki genyen de seri kwomozòm omològ

directional selection | seleksyon direksyonèl yon fòm seleksyon natirèl lè endividi nan yon pwent koub distribisyon genyen plis fòm fizik pase endividi ki nan mitan oswa ki alafen koub la

disruptive selection | seleksyon pètibatè lè endividi yo ki nan de ekstremite koub la genyen plis fòm fizik pase endividi ki nan mitan koub la

DNA fingerprinting | idantifikasyon jenetik yon zouti byolojis yo itilize pou analize koleksyon fragman restriksyon ADN inik yon endividi ; yo itilize l pou detèmine si de echantiyon materyèl jenetik soti nan menm moun nan

DNA microarray | mikworezo ADN yon plak an vè oswa silisyòm ki transpòte dèmilye diferan kalite fragman ADN monokatenè ki aranje nan yon rezo. Yo itilize yon mikworezo ADN pou detekte epi mezire ekspresyon dèmilye jèn alafwa

DNA polymerase | ADN polimeraz anzim ki enplike nan repwodiksyon ADN

domain | domèn yon klasman taksinomik ki pi laj, pi enkliziv pase yon wayòm

dopamine | dopamin newotransmitè ki asosye avèk sant plezi ak rekonpans sèvo a

dormancy | dòmans yon peryòd tan kote anbriyon yon plant vivan men li pa p grandi

double fertilization | doub fegondasyon pwosesis fegondasyon nan anjyospèm yo kote premye evenman an pwodwi zigòt la epi dezyèm lan, andospèm lan andedan grenn lan

E

ecological footprint | anprent anviwònmantal
kantite total sistèm ekolojik k ap fonksyone ki
nesesè pou founi resous yon popilasyon imen
itilize, epi pou absòbe dechè popilasyon an
pwodwi

ecological hot spot | pwen cho ekolojik yon
ti zòn jeyografik kote yon kantite enpòtan abita
ak espès nan yon danje ekstèminasyon imedya

ecological pyramid | piramid ekolojik ilistrasyon
kantite relativ enèji oswa matyè ki genyen nan
chak nivo twofik nan yon kèlkonk chèn alimantè
oswa rezo twofik

ecological succession | siksesyon ekolojik
yon seri chanjman gradyèl ki rive nan yon
kominote aprè yon twoub

ecology | ekoloji etid syantifik entèaksyon ki
fèt pami òganis yo epi ant òganis yo ak
anviwonman yo

ecosystem | ekosistèm tout òganis k ap viv nan
yon kote, ansanm avèk anviwònman inanime yo

ecosystem diversity | divèsite ekolojik
varyete abita, kominote ak pwosesis ekolijik
nan byosfè a

ectoderm | ektodèm feyè eksteryè jèm lan ; li
pwodwi ògàn sans yo, nè yo, ak kouch eksteryè
po a

ectotherm | ektotèm yon animal kote se
tanperati nan anviwònman kote li ye a ki
detèmine tanperati kò li

electron | elektwon patikil ki gen yon chaj
elektrik negatif ; li sitiye nan espas ki antoure
nwayo a

electron transport chain | chèn respiratwa
yon seri pwoteyin manbranè ki transpòte
elektwon ki wo an enèji pandan reyaksyon ki
pwodwi ATP a

element | eleman yon sibstans ki pi ki konpoze
antyèman de yon tip atòm

embryo | anbriyon etap devlopman yon òganis
miltiselilè

embryo sac | sak anbriyonè gametofit femèl ki
nan ovil yon plant a flè

emerging disease | maladi emèjant yon
maladi ki parèt nan popilasyon an pou lapremyè
fwa, oswa yon ansyen maladi ki toudenkou vin
pi difisil pou kontwole

emigration | emigrasyon mouvman kote kèk
endividi ap kite yon zòn

endocrine gland | glann andokrin yon glann
ki libere sekresyon l yo (òmòn) dirèkteman nan
san an, epi san an transpòte sekresyon yo nan
lòt pati nan kò a

endoderm | andodèm feyè entèn jèm lan ; li
devlope an doubli nan tib dijestif la ak pifò
sistèm respiratwa a

endodermis | andodèm nan plant yo, yon kouch
selil ki konplètman antoure silenn vaskilè a

endoplasmic reticulum | retikilòm andoplasmik
sistèm manbranè entèn ou jwenn nan selil
ekaryotik yo ; plas kote konpozan lipid manbràn
plasmik yo asanble

endoskeleton | andoeskelèt eskelèt enteryè ;
sistèm sipò estriktiral andedan kò yon animal

endosperm | andospèm tisi ki rich an nitrisyon
ki nouri yon jèn plant pandan l ap grandi

endospore | andospò estrikti pwokaryòt yo
pwodwi nan kondisyon ki pa favorab ; yon pawa
enteryè epè ki antoure ADN lan ak yon pòsyon
sitoplas la

endosymbiotic theory | teyori andosenbyotik
teyori ki fè konnen selil ekaryotik yo fòme apati
de yon relasyon senbyotik ant plizyè diferan selil
pwokaryotik

endotherm | andotèm yon animal ki reglemante
pwòp tanperati kò li, omwen an pati, avèk chalè
ki soti andedan kò li

enzyme | anzim yon katalizè pwoteyin ki
akselere to reyaksyon byolojik espesifik

epidermis | epidèm nan plant yo, kouch selil
ki fòme tisi dèmik lan ; nan imen yo, kouch
eksteryè po a

epididymis | epididim ògàn nan sistèm
repwodiksyon gason an kote espèm lan vin
mi epi li estoke

epinephrine | epinefrin òmòn glann ki nan
ren yo sekrete ki ogmante frekans kadyak la ak
presyon ateryèl la epi li prepare kò a pou aktivite
fizik entans ; yo rele l tou adrenalin

epithelial tissue | tisi epitelyal kalite tisi ki
rekouvri sifas entèn ak ekstèn kò a

era | è jeyolojik inite premye òd tan jeyolojik ; li
divize souvan an de peryòd oswa plis

esophagus | ezofaj tib ki konekte bouch la ak
lestomak la

estuary | estiyè tip tè inonde kote yon rivyè
rankontre ak lanmè a

ethylene | etilèn òmòn vejetal ki estimile fwi
pou yo vin mi

Eukarya | Ekarya gwoup tout òganis ki genyen yon nwayo ; li genyen ladan l pwotis, plant, chanpiyon ak animal

eukaryote | ekaryòt òganis kote selil yo genyen yon nwayo

evolution | evolisyon chanjman ki fèt avèk le tan ; pwosesis kote òganis modèn yo te soti nan òganis ki te la anvan

excretion | eskresyon pwosesis kote dechè metabolik yo soti nan kò a

exocrine gland | glann ekzokrin yon glann ki libere sekresyon l yo atravè estrikti ki gen fòm tib ki rele kanal, dirèkteman nan yon ògàn oswa andeyò kò a

exon | egzon sekans ADN ; kòd pou yon pwoteyin

exoskeleton | egzoeskelèt eskelèt ekstèn ; kouvèti ekstèn rezistan ki pwoteje epi sipòte kò anpil envètebre

exponential growth | kwasans eksponansyèl modèl kwasans kote endividi nan yon popilasyon repwodwi a yon to ki konstan

extinct | dispari mo yo itilize pou pale de yon espès ki disparèt epi ki pa gen ankenn manm ki vivan

extracellular digestion | dijesyon ekstraselilè tip dijesyon kote manje a dekonpoze andeyò selil yo nan yon sistèm dijestif epi ki absòbe aprè

F

facilitated diffusion | difizyon fasilite pwosesis difizyon kote molekil yo pase atravè manbràn lan andedan kanal manbràn plasmik yo

family | fanmi nan klasman, yon gwoup jenerasyon ki similè

fat | grès lipid ; konpoze de asid gra ak glisewòl ; tip eleman nitritif ki pwoteje ògàn nan kò a, ki izole kò a epi ki estoke enèji

feedback inhibition | retwo-inibisyon pwosesis kote yon estimilan pwodwi yon reyaksyon ki opoze estimilan orijinal la ; yo rele l tou yon kont-reyaksyon

fermentation | fèmantasyon pwosesis kote selil yo libere enèji san oksijèn

fertilization | fegondasyon pwosesis nan repwodiksyon seksye kote selil repwodiksyon mal ak femèl rankontre pou fòme yon nouvo selil

fetus | fetis non yo bay yon anbriyon imen aprè uit semèn devlopman

fever | lafyèv ogmantasyon nan tanperati kò a pou reyaji a yon enfeksyon

filtration | filtrasyon pwosesis ki pèmèt likid oswa gaz pase atravè yon filt pou retire dechè

fitness | kapasite fizik kapasite yon òganis genyen pou l siviv epi repwodwi nan anviwònman li

flagellum (pl. flagella) | flajèl estrikti pwotis yo itilize pou mouvman ; li pwodwi mouvman nan yon fòm vag lanmè

food chain | chèn alimantè yon seri etap nan yon sistèm ekolojik kote òganis yo transfere enèji lè yo manje epi lè lòt manje yo

food vacuole | vakyòl dijestif ti kavite nan sitoplas yon pwotis ki tanporèman estoke manje

food web | rezo twofik yon rezo entèaksyon konplèks ki fòme pa relasyon alimantasyon pami diferan òganis nan yon sistèm ekolojik

forensics | kriminalistik etid syantifik sou prèv yo jwenn nan yon sèn krim

fossil | fosil vestij òganis ansyen yo prezève

founder effect | efè fondatè chanjman nan frekans alelik akoz migrasyon yon ti sou-gwoup yon popilasyon

frameshift mutation | mitasyon nan chanjman faz mitasyon ki chanje "faz lekti" mesaj jenetik la lè l ajoute oswa li pèdi yon nikleyotid

fruit | fwi estrikti nan anjyospèm yo ki genyen yon ovè oswa plis ki mi

fruiting body | aparèy esporifè estrikti repwodiktif yon chanpiyon ki grandi apati de miselyòm lan

G

gamete | gamèt selil seksyèl

gametophyte | gametofit plant ki pwodwi gamèt ; faz aployid miltiselilè nan sik lavi yon plant

ganglion (pl. ganglia) | gangliyon yon gwoup selil nève

gastrovascular cavity | kavite gastwo-vaskilè tib dijestif ki genyen yon sèl ouvèti

gastrulation | gastrilasyon pwosesis migrasyon selilè ki vin lakoz fòmasyon twa kouch selilè – ektodèm, mezodèm ak andodèm

gel electrophoresis | elektwoforèz an jèl pwosedi yo itilize pou separe epi analize fragman ADN lè yo mete yon melanj fragman ADN nan yon pwent yon jèl pore epi ou aplike yon tansyon elektrik nan jèl la

gene | jèn sekans ADN ki kode pou yon pwoteyin epi konsa li detèmine yon karakteristik ; yon faktè ki pase de yon paran a desandan yo

gene expression | ekspresyon jenetik pwosesis kote yon jèn fè pwodwi li epi pwodwi a akonpli fonksyon li

gene pool | fon jenetik komen tout jèn yo, ikonpri tout diferan alèl yo pou chak jèn, ki prezan nan yon popilasyon nan nenpòt peryòd tan

gene therapy | terapi jenetik pwosesis kote yo chanje yon jèn pou trete yon maladi medikal oswa yon twoub. Yon jèn ki absan oswa defektye ki ranplase pa yon jèn nòmal ki fonksyone byen

genetic code | kòd jenetik koleksyon kodon ARNm, chak ladan yo dirije enkòporasyon yon asid amine an patikilye nan yon pwoteyin pandan sentèz pwoteyin lan

genetic diversity | divèsite jenetik sòm total tout diferan fòm enfòmasyon jenetik yon espès an patikilye, oswa tout òganis pote

genetic drift | deriv jenetik chanjman o aza nan frekans alelik ki koze pa yon seri bagay ki rive pa chans ki koze yon alèl pou l vin plizoumwen komen nan yon popilasyon

genetic equilibrium | ekilib jenetik sitiyasyon kote frekans alelik yo nan yon popilasyon pa chanje

genetic marker | makè jenetik alèl ki pwodwi diferans fenotipik detektab ki itil nan analiz jenetik

genetics | jenetik etid syantifik sou eredite

genome | jenòm tout seri enfòmasyon jenetik yon òganis pote nan ADN li

genomics | jenomik etid jenòm konplè, ikonpri jèn yo ak fonksyon yo

genotype | jenotip estrikti jenetik yon òganis

genus | jan gwoup espès ki nan menm fanmi ; premye tèm non syantifik nan nonklamanti binominal

geographic isolation | izolman jeyografik fòm izolman repwodiktif kote de popilsyon separe avèk baryè jeyografik tankou rivyè, mòn oswa mas dlo, ki vin mennen nan fòmasyon de sou-espès separe

geologic time scale | echèl tan jeyolojik peryòd tan yo itilize pou reprezante istwa Latè

germ theory of disease | teyori mikwobyèn maladi lide ki fè konnen se mikwo-òganis ki lakoz maladi enfektye

germination | jèminasyon lè anbriyon plant lan reprann kwasans li aprè yon peryòd ralanti

giberellin | asid jiberelik òmòn vejetal ki estimile kwasans epi ki ka koze ogmantasyon dramatik nan gwosè

gill | branchi yon estrikti plime ki espesyalize pou echanj gaz avèk dlo

global warming | Lub ntiaj teb sov heev lawm Qhov uas ua rau tus koob ntsuas kev kub thiab kev txia hauv lub Ntiaj teb

glomerulus | glomeril ti rezo kapilè ki anbale nan pati siperyè nefwon an ; kote filtrasyon san an fèt

glycolysis | glikoliz premye seri reyaksyon nan respirasyon selilè kote yon molekil glikoz dekonpoze an de molekil asid pirivik

Golgi apparatus | aparèy Golgi ti ògàn nan selil yo ki modifye, triye epi anbale pwoteyin ak lòt materyèl ki sot nan retikilòm andoplasmik lan pou estokaj nan selil la oswa ki libere andeyò selil la

gradualism | pwogresivite evolisyon yon espès avèk akimilasyon pwogresif ti chanjman jenetik ki fèt sou yon long peryòd tan

grafting | grefaj yon metòd pwopagasyon yo itilize pou repwodui plant san grenn ak yon varyete plant liye ki paka repwodwi lè w koupe yo

gravitropism | gravitwopis reyaksyon yon plant fè ak fòs gravite

green revolution | revolisyon vèt devlopman kilti ki bay anpil rannman epi itilizasyon teknik agrikilti modèn pou ogmante pwodiksyon manje

greenhouse effect | efè desè pwosesis kote kèk gaz (dyoksid kabòn, metàn ak vapè dlo) trape enèji solèy la nan atmosfè Latè kòm chalè

growth factor | faktè kwasans youn nan gwoup ekstèn pwoteyin regilatè ki estimile kwasans ak divizyon selil yo

guard cells | selil mè selil espesyalize nan epidèm plant yo ki kontwole ouvèti ak fèmti estomat la

gullet | ezofaj yon ti twou nan yon bò yon silye ki pèmèt manje rantre nan selil la

gymnosperm | jimnospèm gwoup plant ki fè grenn epi ki pote grenn yo dirèkteman sou ekay kòn yo

H

habitat | abita zòn kote yon òganis abite ansanm avèk faktè byotik ak abyotik ki afekte li

habitat fragmentation | fragmantasyon abita divizyon sistèm ekolojik yo an plizyè pati

habituation | akoutimans tip aprantisaj kote yon animal redui oswa sispann reyaji a estimilan repetitif ki pa ni rekonpanse ni nwi animal la

hair follicle | folikil pile pòch selil epidèmik ki an fòm tib ki pwolonje nan dèm lan ; selil ki alabaz folikil pile yo ki pwodwi cheve

half life | demi-peryòd longè tan ki nesesè pou mwatye nan atòm radyoaktif ki nan yon echantiyon vin pouri

haploid | aployid mo yo itilize pou pale de yon selil ki genyen sèlman yon seri jèn

Hardy-Weinberg principle | prensip Hardy-Weinberg prensip ki deklare frekans alelik nan yon popilasyon rete konstan amwenske youn oswa plizyè faktè lakoz frekans sa yo chanje

Haversian canal | kanal Havers youn nan rezo tib ki travèse zo konpak ki genyen veso sangen ak nè yo

heart | kè yon ògàn miskilè kre ki ponpe san atravè tout kò a

heartwood | diramen (kè bwa) nan yon tij bwa, tisi liye ki toupre mitan tij la ki pa kondwi dlo ankò

hemoglobin | emoglobin pwoteyin ki genyen fè nan globil wouj yo ki lye oksijèn epi ki transpòte l nan kò a

herbaceous plant | plant èbase tip plant ki gen tij ki soup epi non-liye ; ladan yo genyen pisanlit, zinya, petinya ak flè solèy

herbivore | èbivò òganis ki jwenn enèji lè yo manje plant sèlman

herbivory | èbivoris yon entèaksyon kote yon animal (èbivò a) manje pwodiktè yo (tankou plant)

heterotroph | etewotwòf òganis ki jwenn manje lè yo manje lòt èt vivan ; yo rele yo tou yon konsomatè

heterozygous | etewozigòt ki gen de alèl diferan pou yon jèn an patikilye

histamine | istamin pwodwi chimik mastosit yo sekrete ki ogmante sikilasyon san ak likid nan zòn ki enfekte a pandan yon reyaksyon enflamatwa

homeobox gene | jèn bwat omeyotik Bwat omeyotik la se yon sekans ADN ki gen apeprè 130 pè baz, ou jwenn nan anpil jèn omeyotik ki reglemante devlopman. Jèn ki genyen sekans sa a rele jèn bwat omeyotik, ak kòd pou faktè transkipsyon, pwoteyin ki lye ak ADN epi ki reglemante ekspresyon lòt jèn yo

homeostasis | omeyostazi kondisyon entèn, fizik ak chimik ki relativman estab òganis yo mentni

homeotic gene | jèn omeyotik yon klas jèn regilatwa ki detèmine idantite pati kò a ak kèk zòn nan yon anbriyon animal. Mitasyon nan jèn sa yo ka transfòme yon pati kò a nan yon lòt

hominine | ominin desandans ominoyid ki te abouti a imen

hominoid | ominoyid gwoup antwopoyid ki genyen ladan l gibon, orangoutan, goril, chenpanze ak imen

homologous | omològ mo yo itilize pou pale de kwomozòm kote yon seri soti nan paran mal la epi yon seri soti nan paran femèl la

homologous structures | estrikti omològ estrikti ki similè nan diferan espès zansèt komen

homozygous | omozigòt ki gen de alèl idantik pou yon jèn espesifik

hormone | òmòn pwodwi chimik ki nan yon pati yon òganis ki afekte yon lòt pati menm òganis lan

Hox gene | jèn Hox yon gwoup jèn omeyotik ki gwoupe ansanm ki detèmine idantite tèt a ke pati nan kò animal yo. Tout jèn hox yo genyen sekans ADN bwat omeyotik la

humoral immunity | iminite imoral iminite kont antijèn nan likid kò a, tankou san ak sewòm san

humus | imis materyèl ki fòme apati de fèy k ap pouri ak lòt matyè òganik

hybrid | ibrid desandan kwazman ant paran yo ki gen diferan karakteristik

hybridization | ibridasyon teknik elvaj ki enplike kwazman endividi ki pa sanble pou rasanble meyè karakteristik nan toulè de òganis yo

hydrogen bond | lyezon idwojèn atraksyon fèb ant yon atòm idwojèn ak yon lòt atòm

hydrostatic skeleton | eskelèt idwostatik yon eskelèt ki konpoze ak segman kò a ki plen ak likid ki travay avèk misk yo pou pèmèt animal la deplase

hypertonic | ipètonik lè w ap konpare de solisyon, solisyon ki gen plis konsantrasyon sibstans ki an solisyon an

hypha (pl. hyphae) | ifa youn nan plizyè filaman long, mens ki konpoze kò yon chanpiyon

hypothalamus | ipotalamis estrikti sèvo a ki aji kòm yon sant kontwòl pou rekonèt epi analize grangou, swaf, fatig, kòlè, ak tanperati kò a

hypothesis | ipotèz eksplikasyon posib pou yon seri obsèvasyon oswa repons ki posib a yon kesyon syantifik

hypotonic | ipotonik lè w ap konpare de solisyon, solisyon ki gen mwens konsantrasyon sibstans ki an solisyon an

I

immigration | imigrasyon mouvman endividi nan yon zòn ki te deja genyen yon popilasyon

immune response | repons iminitè idantifikasyon ak repons espesifik kò a fè lè yon patojèn atake l

implantation | enplantasyon pwosesis kote blastosis la kole nan pawa iteris la

imprinting | enpreyasyon tip konpòtman ki baze sou eksperyans ki fèt bonè ; yon fwa enpreyasyon an fèt, konpòtman an paka chanje

inbreeding | andogami repwodiksyon kontinyèl endividi ki gen menm karakteristik pou ka mentni karakteristik derive yon kalite òganis

incomplete dominance | dominans enkonplè sitiyasyon kote yon alèl pa konplètman dominan sou yon lòt alèl

independent assortment | asòtiman endepandan youn nan prensip Mendel yo ki deklare jèn pou diferan karakteristik ka separe de fason endepandan pandan fòmasyon gamèt yo

independent variable | varyab endepandan faktè nan yon eksperyans kontwole ki delibereman chanje ; yo rele l tou varyab reglan

index fossil | fosil karakteristik fosil distenktif yo itilize pou konpare laj apwoksimatif fosil yo

infectious disease | maladi enfektye maladi ki koze pa mikwoòganis ki entèwonp fonksyon nòmal kò a

inference | enferans yon entèpretasyon lojik ki baze sou konesans ak eksperyans opreyalab

inflammatory response | reyaksyon enflamatwa reyaksyon defansif non-espesifik a domaj nan tisi a akoz yon blesi oswa yon enfeksyon

innate behavior | konpòtman ine tip konpòtman kote konpòtman an parèt nan fòm konplètman fonksyonèl lapremyè fwa li fèt menmsi animal la pa t gen ankenn eksperyans opreyalab avèk estimilan l ap reponn lan ; yo rele sa tou ensten

insight learning | aprantisaj pa entuisyon tip konpòtman kote yon animal aplike yon bagay li te deja aprann nan yon nouvo sitiyasyon, san yon peryòd esè ak erè ; yo rele l tou rezonnman

interferon | entèfewon youn nan gwoup pwoteyin ki ede selil yo reziste kont enfeksyon viral

interneuron | entènewòn tip newòn ki trete enfòmasyon epi ki ka retransmèt enfòmasyon an a newòn motè yo

interphase | entèfaz peryòd sik selilè a ant divizyon selilè yo

intracellular digestion | dijesyon entraselilè tip dijesyon kote manje a dijere andedan selil espesyalize ki pase eleman nitritif bay lòt selil pa difizyon

intron | entwon sekans ADN ki pa enplike nan kodaj pou yon pwoteyin

invertebrate | envètebre yon animal ki pa genyen yon epin dòsal, oswa yon kolòn vètebral

ion | iyon yon atòm ki genyen yon chaj pozitif oswa negatif

ionic bond | lyezon iyonik lyezon chimik ki fòme lè yon elektwon oswa plis transfere de yon atòm a yon lòt

iris | iris pati kolore je a

isotonic | izotonik lè konsantrasyon de solisyon se menm

isotope | izotòp youn nan plizyè fòm yon sèl eleman, ki genyen menm kantite pwoton men diferan kantite netwon

J

joint | jwenti kote yon zo atache avèk yon lòt zo

K

karyotype | karyotip yon mikwograf nan seri diplyoyid konplè kwomozòm yo ki gwoupe ansanm pa pè, ki aranje nan lòd dekwasan an gwosè

keratin | keratin pwoteyin fibre ki rezistan ou jwenn nan po a

keystone species | espès-kle yon sèl espès ki pa nòmalman abondan nan yon kominote men ki egzèse yon kokennchenn kontwòl sou estrikti yon kominote

kidney | ren yon ògàn eskresyon ki separe dechè ak eksè dlo nan san an

kin selection | seleksyon parante teyori ki deklare lè w ede fanmi w sa ka amelyore fòm fizik evolisyonè yon endividi paske endividi ki aparante pataje yon gwo pwopòsyon jèn yo

kingdom | wayòm gwoup ki pi gwo epi ki pi enklizif nan klasman

Koch's postulates | postila Koch yon seri direktiv Koch te devlope ki ede idantifye mikwoòganis ki koze yon maladi espesifik

Krebs cycle | sik Krebs dezyèm etap respirasyon selilè kote asid pirivik dekonpoze an dyoksid kabòn nan yon seri reyaksyon ki ekstrè enèji

L

language | langaj sistèm kominikasyon ki konbine son, senbòl ak jès selon yon seri règ konsènan sekans ak siyifikasyon, tankou gramè ak sentaks

large intestine | gwo trip ògàn nan sistèm dijestif la ki retire dlo nan materyèl ki pa dijere ki pase ladan l ; yo rele l tou kolon

larva (pl. larvae) | lav etap yon òganis ki pa mi

larynx | larenks estrikti nan gòj la ki genyen kòd vokal yo

learning | aprantisaj chanjman nan konpòtman akoz eksperyans

lens | lantiy estrikti nan je a ki fokalize reyon limyè sou retin lan

lichen | lichenn asosyasyon senbyotik ant yon chanpiyon ak yon òganis fotosentetik

ligament | ligaman tisi konjonktiv rezistan ki kenbe zo yo ansanm nan yon jwenti

light-dependent reactions | reyaksyon ki depann de limyè yon seri reyaksyon nan fotosentèz ki itilize enèji ki sot nan limyè pou pwodwi ATP ak NADPH

light-independent reactions | reyaksyon ki pa depann de limyè yon seri reyaksyon nan fotosentèz ki pa bezwen limyè ; yo itilize enèji ki sot nan ATP ak NADPH pou konstwi konpoze ki wo an enèji tankou sik ; yo rele sa tou sik Calvin

lignin | liyin sibstans nan plant vaskilè ki fè pawa selil yo rijid

limiting factor | faktè limitan yon faktè ki koze kwasans popilasyon an diminye

limiting nutrient | eleman nitritif limitan yon sèl eleman nitritif esansyèl ki limite pwodiktivite nan yon sistèm ekolojik

lipid | lipid makwomolekil ki fèt plis avèk kabòn ak atòm idwojèn ; li genyen ladan l grès, lwil ak lasi

lipid bilayer | lipid bikouch feyè fleksib a de kouch ki fòme manbràn plasmik la epi ki fòme yon baryè ant selil la ak anviwònman li

logistic growth | kwasans lojistik modèl kwasans kote kwasans yon popilasyon ralanti epi estope aprè yon peryòd kwasans eksponansyèl

loop of Henle | ans Henle yon seksyon nan tib nefwon an ki responsab pou konsève dlo epi minimize volim filtra a

lung | poumon ògàn respiratwa ; kote echanj gaz yo fèt ant san an ak lè ki rantre nan poumon an

lymph | lenf likid ki soti nan san an lè l filtre

lysogenic infection | enfeksyon lizojenik tip enfeksyon kote yon viris enplante ADN li nan ADN selil ot la epi li repwodwi ansanm avèk ADN selil ot la

lysosome | lizosòm ti ògàn nan yon selil ki dekonpoze lipid, idrat kabòn ak pwoteyin nan ti molekil rès selil la ka itilize

lytic infection | enfeksyon litik yon tip enfeksyon kote yon viris rantre nan yon selil, li fè kopi tèt li, epi li fè selil la eklate

M

macroevolution | makwoevolisyon chanjman evolisyonè a grann echèl ki fèt sou peryòd tan pwolonje

Malpighian tubule | tib Malpigi estrikti nan pifò atwopòd terès ki konsantre asid irik epi ajoute l nan dechè dijestif yo

mammary gland | glann mamè glann nan mamifè femèl ki pwodwi lèt pou nouri pitit yo

mass extinction | disparisyon an mas yon evenman kote anpil espès disparèt pandan yon peryòd tan ki relativman kout

matrix | matris konpatman nan mitokondri a ki pi pwofon

mechanical digestion | dijesyon mekanik dekonpozisyon fizik gwo moso manje an moso ki pi piti

meiosis | meyoz yon pwosesis kote kantite kwomozòm nan chak selil koupe an mwatye grasa separasyon kwomozòm omològ nan yon selil diployid

melanin | melanin pigman mawon fonse nan po a ki ede pwoteje po a lè l absòbe reyon iltravyolè yo

melanocyte | melanosit selil nan po a ki pwodwi yon pigman mawon fonse ki rele melanin

menstrual cycle | sik manstriyèl sekans regilye kote yon ze devlope epi kò a libere l

menstruation | manstriyasyon lè kò a dechaje san ak ze ki pa fegonde a

meristem | meristèm rejyon selil non-espesyalize ki responsab pou kwasans kontinyèl pandan tout lavi yon plant

mesoderm | mezodèm kouch lateral jèm lan ; li devlope an misk, ak pifò sistèm sikilatwa, repwodiktif ak ekskretwa

mesophyll | mezofil kouch selil espesyalize ki nan rasin lan ou jwenn nan fèy yo ; li fè pifò fotosentèz yon plant

messenger RNA (mRNA) | ARN mesaje (ARNm) tip ARN ki pote kopi enstriksyon yo pou asanblaj asid amine an pwoteyin ki sot nan ADN lan pou ale nan rès selil la

metabolism | metabolis konbinezon reyaksyon chimik kote yon òganis akimile oswa dekonpoze materyèl

metamorphosis | metamòfoz pwosesis chanj-man ki fèt nan nivo fòm yon lav pou l vin yon adilt

metaphase | metafaz faz mitoz kote kwomozòm yo aliyen nan mitan selil la

microclimate | mikwoklima kondisyon anviwònmantal andedan yon ti zòn ki diferan anpil de klima ki nan zòn anviwonan an

migration | migrasyon konpòtman sezonye ki vin lakoz mouvman de yon anviwònman a yon lòt

mineral | mineral eleman nitritif inòganik kò a bezwen, abityèlman nan ti kantite

mitochondrion | mitokondri ti ògàn nan yon selil ki konvèti enèji chimik ki estoke nan manje an konpoze ki pi pratik pou selil la itilize

mitosis | mitoz pati nan divizyon yon selil ekaryotik kote nwayo selil la divize

mixture | melanj yon materyèl ki konpoze avèk de eleman oswa konpoze oswa plis ki fizikman melanje ansanm men ki pa chimikman melanje

molecular clock | òlòj molekilè metòd chèchè yo itilize ki sèvi ak to mitasyon nan ADN pou estime peryòd tan de espès te evolye de fason endepandan

molecule | molekil pi piti inite nan pifò konpoze ki ekspoze tout pwopriyete konpoze sa a

molting | mi pwosesis ki jete yon egzoeskelèt epi yon lòt vin fòme

monocot | monokòt anjyospèm ki gen yon fèy ki gen grenn nan ovè li

monoculture | monokilti estrateji agrikilti kote yo plante yon sèl pwodwi ki bay anpil rannman ane aprè ane

monomer | monomè ti inite chimik ki konpoze yon polimè

monophyletic group | gwoup monofiletik gwoup ki genyen yon sèl espès ansestral ansanm avèk tout desandan l yo epi li eskli tout òganis ki pa soti nan ansèt komen sa a

monosaccharide | monosakarid molekil sik senp

motor neuron | newòn motè tip selil nève ki transpòte direksyon sot nan entènewòn yo swa nan selil miskilè yo swa nan glann yo

multiple alleles | alèl miltip yon jèn ki gen plis pase de alèl

multipotent | miltipotan selil ki gen potansyèl limite pou devlope an plizyè tip selil diferansye yo

muscle fiber | fib miskilè selil misk eskeletik li long epi mens

muscle tissue | tisi miskilè tip tisi ki rann mouvman kò a posib

mutagen | mitajèn ajan chimik oswa fizik nan anviwònman an ki entèaji ak ADN epi ki ka koze yon mitasyon

mutation | mitasyon chanjman nan materyèl jenetik yon selil

mutualism | mityalis yon relasyon senbyotik kote toulè de espès yo benefisye de relasyon an

mycelium (pl. mycelia) | miselyòm rezo ifa yon chanpiyon ki branche an mas

mycorrhiza (pl. mycorrhizae) | mikoriz asosyasyon senbyotik rasin plant yo ak chanpiyon

myelin sheath | anvlòp myelin manbràn izolan ki antoure aksòn nan kèk newòn

myocardium | myokad tinik miskilè kè a

myofibril | myofibril filaman kontraktil ki lye ansanm ou jwenn nan fib miskilè eskeletal la

myosin | myozin filaman pwoteyin epè ou jwenn nan selil misk eskeletik yo

N

NAD+ (nicotinamide adenine dinucleotide) | NAD+ (nikotinamid adenin dinikleyotid) yon elektwon ki aji kòm ajan transfè nan glikoz

NADP+ (nicotinamide adenine dinucleotide phosphate) | NADP+ (nikotinamid adenin dinikleyotid fosfat) yon molekil ki aji kòm ajan pou transfere elektwon ki wo an enèji sot nan klowofil pou ale nan lòt molekil yo

natural selection | seleksyon natirèl pwosesis kote òganis ki pi adapte a anviwònman yo siviv epi repwodwi avèk plis siksè ; yo rele sa tou sivivans pou sa ki pi apt la

nephridium (pl. nephridia) | nefridyòm estrikti eskretwa yon anelid ki filtre likid kò a

nephron | nefwon estrikti ki filtre san nan ren yo kote salte yo pase nan filtraj, dechè yo kolekte, epi san an ki fin pirifye retounen sikile nan kò a

nervous tissue | tisi nève tip tisi ki transmèt enpilsyon nève atravè kò a

neuromuscular junction | jonksyon newomiskilè pwen kontak ant yon newòn motè ak yon selil misk eskeletik

neuron | newòn selil nève ; espesyalize pou pote mesaj atravè sistèm nève a

neurotransmitter | newotransmitè pwodwi chimik yon newòn itilize pou l transmèt yon enpilsyon atravè yon sinaps nan yon lòt selil

neurulation | nerilasyon premye etap nan devlopman sistèm nève a

niche | nich kondisyon fizik ak byolojik kote yon òganis abite epi fason òganis lan itilize kondisyon sa yo

nitrogen fixation | fiksasyon azòt pwosesis kote yo konvèti azòt an konpoze azòt plant yo ka absòbe epi itilize

node | nodil pati yon tij k ap grandi kote yon fèy atache

nondisjunction | non-dijonksyon erè nan meyoz la kote kwomozòm omològ yo pa reyisi separe kòmsadwa

nonrenewable resource | resous non-renouvlab resous ki paka renouvle pa pwosesis natirèl nan yon kantite tan ki rezonab

norepinephrine | norepinefrin òmòn glann ki nan ren yo sekrete ki ogmante frekans kadyak la ak presyon ateryèl la epi li prepare kò a pou aktivite fizik entans

notochord | kòd dòsal yon batonè long ki travèse kò yon kòde ki jis anba chèn nève a

nucleic acid | asid nikleyik makwomolekil ki genyen idwojèn, oksijèn, azòt, kabòn ak fosfò

nucleotide | nikleyotid sou-inite ki konpoze asid nikleyik yo ; konpoze de 5 sik kabòn, yon gwoup fosfat, ak yon baz azote

nucleus | nwayo sant yon atòm, ki genyen pwoton ak netwon yo ; nan selil yo, estrikti ki genyen materyèl jenetik selil la nan fòm ADN

nutrient | eleman nitritif sibstans chimik yon òganis bezwen pou l soutni lavi

nymph | nenf fòm yon animal ki sanble ak fòm adilt la, men ki pa gen ògàn seksyèl ki fonksyone

O

observation | obsèvasyon pwosesis kote moun remake epi dekri kèk evenman nan yon fason ki pridan epi òdone

omnivore | omnivò òganis ki jwenn enèji lè yo manje plant ak animal

open circulatory system | sistèm sikilatwa ouvè yon tip sistèm sikilatwa kote san an sèlman kontni nan yon sistèm veso sangen pandan l ap sikile atravè kò a

operant conditioning | kondisyònman operan tip aprantisaj kote yon animal aprann pou l konpòte l nan yon sèten fason grasa pratik repete, pou l resevwa yon rekonpans oswa evite pinisyon

operator | operatè yon rejyon ADN ki kout, adjasan a pwomotè yon opewon pwokaryotik, ki lye pwoteyin represè ki responsab pou kontwole to transkripsyon opewon an

operon | opewon nan pwokaryòt yo, yon gwoup jèn adjasan ki pataje yon operatè ak yon pwomotè komen epi yo transkri nan yon sèl ARNm

opposable thumb | pous opozab yon pous ki pèmèt ou sezi objè epi itilize zouti

order | òd nan klasman, yon gwoup ki aparante de prè

organ | ògàn gwoup tisi ki travay ansanm pou akonpli fonksyon ki aparante de prè

organ system | sistèm òganik yon gwoup ògàn ki travay ansanm pou akonpli yon fonksyon espesifik

organelle | ti ògàn estrikti espesyalize ki akonpli fonksyon selilè enpòtan nan yon selil ekaryotik

osmosis | osmoz difizyon dlo atravè yon manbràn ki pèmeyab de fason selektif

osmotic pressure | presyon osmotik presyon ki dwe aplike pou anpeche mouvman osmotik atravè yon manbràn ki pèmeyab de fason selektif

ossification | osifikasyon pwosesis fòmasyon zo nan moman zo ap ranplase katilaj

osteoblast | osteyoblas selil ose ki sekrete depo mineral ki ranplase katilaj la nan zo k ap delvope yo

osteoclast | osteyoklas selil ose ki dekonpoze an mineral

osteocyte | osteyosit selil ose ki ede mentni mineral nan tisi ose a epi ki kontinye ranfòse zo a k ap grandi

ovary | ovè nan plant yo, estrikti ki antoure epi pwoteje grenn yo ; nan bèt yo, se prensipal ògàn repwodiktif femèl la ; li pwodwi ze yo

oviparous | ovipa espès kote anbriyon yo devlope andedan ze andeyò kò yon paran

ovoviparous | ovovipa espès kote anbriyon yo devlope andedan kò manman an, men li depann antyèman de sak vitelin ze yo

ovulation | ovilasyon liberasyon yon ze ki mi nan ovè a pou al nan youn nan twonp Falòp yo

ovule | ovil estrikti nan kòn ki pote grenn yo kote gametofit femèl la devlope

ozone layer | kouch ozòn kouch atmosferik kote gaz la relativman konsantre ; li pwoteje lavi sou Latè kont reyon iltravyolè danjre ki nan limyè solèy la

P

pacemaker | estimilatè kadyak ti gwoup fib miskilè kadyak ki mentni ritm ponpaj kè a lè l fikse to kontraksyon kè a ; ne sino-orikilè a (SA)

paleontologist | paleyontolojis syantis ki etidye fosil yo

palisade mesophyll | repli mezofil kouch selil ki anba epidèm siperyè yon fèy

parasitism | parazitis yon relasyon senbyotik kote yon òganis viv sou yon lòt òganis oswa andedan yon lòt òganis epi li fè l ditò

parathyroid hormone (PTH) | òmòn paratiwoyid (PTH) òmòn glann paratiwoyid la pwodwi ki ogmante nivo kalsyòm nan san an

parenchyma | paranchim tip prensipal kouch selil ki nan rasin plant yo kote selil yo genyen pawa selilè mens ak gwo vakyòl santral

passive immunity | iminite pasif iminite ki vin devlope tanporèman aprè yon ekspozisyon natirèl oswa delibere a yon antijèn

pathogen | patojèn ajan ki koze maladi

pedigree | ab jeneyalojik yon tablo ki montre prezans oswa absans yon karakteristik selon relasyon ki genyen nan yon fanmi atravè plizyè jenerasyon

pepsin | pepsin yon anzim ki dekonpoze pwoteyin an fragman polipeptid ki pi piti

period | peryòd divizyon peryòd jeyolojik kote yo sibdivize epòk yo

peripheral nervous system | sistèm nève periferik rezo nè ak selil soutyen yo ki pote siyal ale vini nan sistèm nève santral la

peristalsis | peristaltis kontraksyon misk lis yo ki founi fòs ki deplase manje atravè ezofaj la pou ale nan vant lan

permafrost | pèjelisòl yon kouch sousòl ki jele an pèmanans ou jwenn nan tounndra a

petiole | petyòl tij fen ki konekte lenb yon fèy a yon tij

pH scale | echèl pH yon echèl ki gen valè de 0 a 14, yo itilize pou mezire konsantrasyon iyon H^+ yo nan yon solisyon ; yon pH 0 a 7 se yon pH ki asidik, yon pH 7 se yon pH ki net, epi yon pH de 7 a 14 se yon pH de baz

pharyngeal pouch | pòch farenje youn nan yon pè estrikti nan zòn gòj yon kòde

pharynx | farenks tib ki pa dèyè bouch la ki sèvi kòm yon pasaj pou lè ak manje ; yo rele l tou gòj

phenotype | fenotip karakteristik fizik yon òganis

phloem | flèm tisi vaskilè ki transpòte solisyon sibstans nitritif ak idrat kabòn fotosentèz pwodwi nan plant lan

photic zone | zòn fotik zòn limyè solèy la touche ki touprè sifas dlo a

photoperiod | fotoperyòd yon reyaksyon plant lan fè a longè relatif jou ak nwit

photosynthesis | fotosentèz pwosesis plant yo ak lòt ototwòf itilize pou kaptire enèji limyè a epi itilize l pou alimante reyaksyon chimik ki konvèti dyoksid kabòn ak dlo an oksijèn ak idrat kabòn ki rich an enèji tankou sik ak anmidon

photosystem | fotosistèm gwoup klowofil ak pwoteyin ou jwenn nan tilakoyid yo

phototropism | fototwopis tandans yon plant genyen pou l grandi nan direksyon yon sous limyè

phylogeny | filojeni etid relasyon evolisyonè pami òganis yo

phylum | anbranchman nan klasman, yon gwoup klas ki aparante de prè

phytoplankton | fitoplankton alg fotosentetik ou jwenn touprè sifas oseyan an

pigment | pigman molekil ki absòbe limyè plant yo itilize pou rasanble enèji solèy la

pioneer species | espès pyonè premye espès pou peple yon zòn pandan yon siksesyon ekolojik

pistil | pistil youn oswa plizyè kapèl ki fizyone ansanm ; li genyen ovè a, estil ak estigmat

pith | mwèl selil paranchim andedan sèk tisi vaskilè nan tij dikotiledòn yo

pituitary gland | glann pititè ti glann ou jwenn touprè baz kràn lan ki sekrete òmòn ki dirèkteman reglemante anpil fonksyon nan kò a epi ki kontwole aksyon plizyè lòt glann andokrin

placenta | plasennta ògàn espesyalize nan mamifè yo kote gaz respiratwa, sibstans nitritif ak dechè echanje ant manman an ak pitit li k ap delvope a

plankton | plankton òganis mikwoskopik ki abite nan anviwonman akwatik ; sa enkli ni fitoplankton ni zooplankton

plasma | plasma pòsyon nan san an ki se yon likid ki gen koulè jonat

plasmid | plasmid moso ADN ki piti, an fòm sikilè ou jwenn nan sitoplas anpil bakteri

plasmodium | plasmòd etap alimantasyon amiboyid nan sik lavi yon limon

plate tectonics | plak tektonik pwosesis jeyolojik, tankou deriv kontinan yo, vòlkan yo, ak tranblemanntè, ki vin lakoz mouvman plak yo

platelet | plakèt fragman selilè mwèl epinyè a libere ki ede kowagile san an

pluripotent | selil pliripotant selil ki kapab devlope nan pifò tip selil nan kò a men pa tout

point mutation | mitasyon ponktyèl mitasyon jenetik kote yon sèl baz pè nan ADN te chanje

pollen grain | grenn polenn estrikti ki genyen tout gametofit mal nan plant ki pote grenn yo

pollen tube | tib polinik estrikti nan yon plant ki genyen de nwayo espèm aployid

pollination | polinizasyon transfè polenn ki sot nan estrikti repwodiktif mal la pou ale nan estrikti repwodiktif femèl la

pollutant | polyan materyèl danjre ki ka rantre nan byosfè a atravè tè, lè oswa dlo

polygenic trait | karakteristik polijenik karakteristik de oswa plizyè jèn kontwole

polymer | polimè molekil ki konpoze de plizyè monomè ; li konpoze makwomolekil yo

polymerase chain reaction (PCR) | anplifikasyon an chèn pa polimeraz (PCR) teknik byolojis yo itilize pou fè anpil kopi yon jèn an patikilye

polypeptide | polipeptid chèn asid amine ki long ki fè pwoteyin

polyploidy | poliployidi kondisyon kote yon òganis ki gen kèk seri kwomozòm siplemantè

population | popilasyon gwoup endividi ki nan menm espès ki abite nan menm zòn

population density | dansite popilasyon kantite endividi pa inite sifas

predation | predasyon yon entèaksyon kote yon òganis (predatè a) kaptire epi manje yon lòt òganis (viktim lan)

prehensile tail | ke preyansil ke long ki ka anwoule fèmeman sou yon branch

pressure-flow hypothesis | ipotèz dechajman sou presyon ipotèz ki eksplike metòd kote sèv flèm lan transpòte atravè plant lan apati de yon "sous" sik a yon "basen" sik

primary growth | kwasans primè modèl kwasans ki fèt nan pwent ak nan pous yon plant

primary producer | pwodiktè primè premye pwodiktè konpoze ki rich an enèji lòt òganis vin itilize pita

primary succession | siksesyon primè siksesyon ki fèt nan yon zòn kote pa gen ankenn tras te gen yon kominote ki te la avan

principle of dominance | prensip dominans dezyèm konklizyon Mendel, ki deklare gen kèk alèl ki dominan alòske gen kèk lòt ki resesif

prion | priyon patikil pwoteyin ki koze maladi

probability | pwobablite pwobablite kote yon evenman an patikilye pral rive

product | pwodwi eleman oswa konpoze yon reyaksyon chimik

prokaryote | pwokaryòt òganis iniselilè ki pa genyen yon nwayo

promoter | pwomotè zòn espesifik yon jèn kote ARN polimeraz lan ka lye epi inisye transkripsyon

prophage | pwofaj ADN yon bakteryofaj ki ankastre nan ADN bakteri ot la

prophase | pwofaz faz inisyal epi ki pi long mitoz la kote materyèl jenetik andedan nwayo a kondanse epi kwomozòm yo vin vizib

prostaglandin | pwostaglandin asid gra ki modifye yon gwo varyete selil pwodwi ; li jeneralman afekte sèlman selil ak tisi ki pwòch yo

protein | pwoteyin makwomolekil ki genyen kabòn, idwojèn, oksijèn ak azòt ; kò a bezwen l pou kwasans ak reparasyon

protostome | pwotostòm yon animal kote bouch li fòme apati de blastospò

pseudocoelom | sedokoyelòm yon kavite kò a, ki pasyèlman double avèk mezodèm sèlman

pseudopod | sedopòd pwojeksyon sitoplasmik tanporè kèk pwotis itilize pou fè mouvman

puberty | pibète yon peryòd kwasans rapid ak matirasyon seksyèl kote sistèm repwodiktif la vin konplètman fonksyonèl

pulmonary circulation | sikilasyon pilmonè vwa sikilasyon ant kè a ak poumon yo

punctuated equilibrium | ekilib ponktye yon modèl evolisyon kote kèk brèf peryòd chanjman ki pi rapid vin entèwonp peryòd estab ki long

Punnett square | kare Punnett yon dyagram yo ka itilize pou predi jenotip ak fenotip konbinezon yon kwazman jenetik

pupa | nenf yon etap nan metamòfoz konplè kote lav la devlope pou l vin tounen yon adilt

pupil | nwa je ti ouvèti nan iris la ki pèmèt limyè rantre nan je a

R

radial symmetry | simetri radyal plan transvèsal kote nenpòt kantite plan imajinè ki trase atravè mitan kò a ka divize l an de mwatye egal

radiometric dating | datasyon radyometrik yon metòd pou detèmine laj yon echantiyon apati de montan yon izotòp radyoaktif nan izotòp non-radyoaktif menm eleman nan yon echantiyon

reabsorption | reyabsòpsyon pwosesis kote dlo ak sibstans disou retounen nan san an

reactant | reyaktif eleman oswa konpoze ki rantre nan yon reyaksyon chimik

receptor | reseptè sou yon selil oswa nan yon selil, yon pwoteyin espesifik kote fòm li adapte a yon mesaje molekilè espesifik, tankou yon òmòn

recombinant DNA | ADN rekonbine ADN ki pwodwi lè w konbine ADN apati de diferan sous

red blood cell | globil wouj selil sangen ki nan emoglobin lan ki pote oksijèn

reflex | chua Chua ceev ceev, nws cia li chua nws xwb vim yog muaj tej yam kom nws chua lawm

reflex arc | ak reflèks reseptè sansoryèl, newòn sansoryèl, newòn motè, ak afektè ki enplike nan yon reyaksyon rapid a yon estimilan

relative dating | datasyon relativ metòd yo itilize pou detèmine laj yon fosil lè yo konpare plasman li avèk plasman fosil ki nan lòt kouch wòch

relative frequency | frekans relativ kantite fwa yon alèl fèt nan yon fon jenetik komen lè yo konpare l avèk kantite fwa lòt alèl yo fèt pou menm jèn yo

releasing hormone | faktè deklannchman òmòn ipotalamis la pwodwi, ki estimile sekresyon lob anteryè ipofiz lan

renewable resource | resous renouvlab resous fonksyon sistèm ekolojik ki an sante pwodwi oswa ranplase

replication | replikasyon pwosesis kote ADN lan kopye anvan selil la divize

reproductive isolation | izolman repwodiktif separasyon yon espès oswa popilasyon konsa yo pa kwaze ankò epi yo evolye an de espès separe

resource | resous tout nesesite lavi, tankou dlo, sibstans nitritif, limyè, manje oswa espas

response | reyaksyon yon reyaksyon espesifik a yon estimilan

resting potential | potansyèl repo chaj elektrik atravè manbràn plasmik yon newòn ki an repo

restriction enzyme | anzim restriksyon anzim ki koupe ADN lan nan yon sekans nikleyotid

retina | retin kouch ki pi entèn nan je a ; ki genyen fotoreseptè

retrovirus | retroviris viris ARN ki genyen ARN kòm enfòmasyon jenetik li

ribonucleic acid (RNA) | Lub laisbausnuskhlia Avxev (RNA) Yogib lub uas nws muaj ib-kab nuskhlias avxev (nucleic Acid) nyob ua ke nrog rau cov pem thaj (sugar ribose)

ribosomal RNA (rRNA) | ARN ribozomik (ARNr) tip ARN ki konbine avèk pwoteyin pou fòme ribozòm

ribosome | ribozòm ti ògàn selilè ki genyen ARN ak pwoteyin ou jwenn atravè sitoplas nan yon selil ; sit sentèz pwoteyin lan

RNA interference (RNAi) | entèferans ARN entwodiksyon doub bren ARN nan yon selil pou anpeche ekspresyon jèn yo

RNA polymerase | ARN polimeraz Yon anzim ki lye chèn nikleyotid ARN pandan transkripsyon lè l itilize yon bren ADN kòm yon modèl

rod | batonè fotoreseptè nan je a ki sansib a limyè, men ki paka distenge koulè

root cap | kwaf kouvèti rezistan pwent rasin lan ki pwoteje meristèm lan

root hair | pwal absòban ti pwal ki nan yon rasin ki pwodwi yon laj sifas kote dlo ak mineral ka penetre

rumen | rimen konpatiman lestomak nan bèf yo ak lòt riminan yo kote bakteri senbyotik dijere seliloz

S

sapwood | obye nan yon tij liyez, kouch flèm segondè a ki antoure bwa kè a ; li souvan aktif nan transpò likid

sarcomere | sakomè inite kontraksyon fib miskilè ; konpoze de de liy an z ak filaman yo ant yomenm

scavenger | chawonya bèt ki manje kadav lòt bèt

science | syans yon fason ki òganize pou ranmase epi analize prèv konsènan monn natirèl la

sclerenchyma | eskleranchim tip kouch selil ki nan rasin lan ki gen pawa selilè ki epè epi rijid ki fè selil nan rasin lan vin di epi rezistan

scrotum | eskwotòm yon sak ekstèn ki genyen testikil yo

sebaceous gland | glann sebase glann nan po a ki sekrete sebòm (sekresyon matyè gra)

secondary growth | kwasans segondè tip kwasans nan dikotiledòn yo kote tij yo vin pi epè

secondary succession | siksesyon segondè tip siksesyon ki fèt nan yon zòn ki te sèlman detwi pasyèlman akoz dislokasyon

seed | grenn yon anbriyon plant ak yon apò nitritif ki anbale nan yon kouvèti pwotektè

seed coat | tegiman kouvèti rezistan ki antoure epi pwoteje anbriyon plant lan epi ki anpeche sa ki nan grenn lan vin sèk

segregation | segregasyon separasyon alèl yo pandan fòmasyon gamèt la

selective breeding | elvaj selektif metòd elvaj ki pèmèt se sèlman òganis ki gen trè karakteristik dezirab ki pwodwi pwochen jenerasyon an

selectively permeable | pèmeyab de fason selektif pwopriyete manbràn byolojik ki pèmèt kèk sibstans pase ladan l alòske gen lòt ki paka pase ; yo rele l tou manbràn semipèmeyab

semen | espèm konbinezon espèm ak likid seminal

semicircular canal | kanal semi-sikilè youn nan twa estrikti nan zòrèy entèn lan ki kontwole pozisyon kò a pa rapò avèk gravite

seminiferous tubule | tib seminifè youn nan santèn tib nan chak testikil kote espèm lan devlope

sensory neuron | newòn sansoryèl tip selil nève ki resevwa enfòmasyon nan resètè sansoryèl yo epi voye siyal bay sistèm santral nève a

sex chromosome | kwomozòm seksyèl youn nan de kwomozòm ki detèmine sèks yon moun

sex-linked gene | jèn ki lye ak sèks yon jèn ki nan yon kwomozòm seksyèl

sexual reproduction | repwodiksyon seksyèl tip repwodiksyon kote selil ki sot nan de paran reyini pou fòme premye selil yon nouvo òganis

sexually transmitted disease (STD) | maladi seksyèlman transmisib (STD) maladi ki gaye de moun an moun pa kontak seksyèl

sieve tube element | eleman tib krible yon tib long ki travèse selil flèm plant lan, ki aranje de bout an bout

single-gene trait | karakteristik izole yon jèn yon karakteristik jèn ki gen de alèl kontwole

small intestine | ti trip ògàn dijestif kote pifò dijesyon chimik ak absòpsyon manje a fèt

smog | bwouya lafimen bwouya gri-mawon ki fòme avèk yon melanj pwodwi chimik

society | sosyete yon gwoup animal ki aparante ki nan menm espès k ap travay ansanm pou benefis gwoup la

solute | solite sibstans ki fonn nan yon solisyon

solution | solisyon yon tip melanj kote tout konpoze yo distribiye de fason egal

solvent | sòlvan sibstans k ap fonn nan yon solisyon

somatic nervous system | sistèm nève somatik pati nan sistèm nève periferik la ki pote siyal ale vini nan misk eskeletik la

speciation | espesyasyon fòmasyon yon nouvo espès

species diversity | divèsite espès yo kantite diferan espès ki konpoze yon zòn an patikilye

spirillum (pl. spirilla) | espirilòm pwokaryòt ki an fòm espiral oswa tir-bouchon

spongy mesophyll | mezofil esponjye kouch tisi lach ou jwenn anba repli mezofil nan yon fèy

sporangium (pl. sporangia) | esporanj kapsil spò kote meyoz pwodwi spò aployid yo

spore | spò nan pwokaryòt yo, pwotis yo, ak chanpiyon yo, nenpòt varyete etap sik lavi ki gen pawa epè ki kapab siviv nan kondisyon ki pa favorab ; nan plant yo se selil repwodiktif aployid la

sporophyte | spowofit plant ki pwodwi spò ; faz diployid miltiselilè nan sik lavi yon plant

stabilizing selection | seleksyon estabilizan fòm seleksyon natirèl kote endividi ki prè mitan yon koub distribisyon genyen plis fòm fizik pase endividi ki nan toulède pwent koub la

stamen | etamin pati mal nan yon flè ; li genyen antè a ak filaman

stem cell | selil souch yon selil non-diferansye ki ka pwodwi youn oswa plizyè tip selil diferansye

stigma | estigmat pati kolan ki nan tèt estil la ; espesyalize pou l kaptire polenn

stimulus (pl. stimuli) | estimilan yon siyal ki fè yon òganis reyaji

stoma (pl. stomata) | estomat ti ouvèti nan epidèm yon plant ki pèmèt dyoksid kabòn, dlo ak oksijèn difize anndan ak deyò fèy la

stomach | vant yon gwo sak miskilè ki kontinye dijesyon mekanik ak chimik manje a

stroma | estwoma pòsyon likid klowoplas la ; andeyò tilakoyid yo

substrate | sibstra reyaktif yon reyaksyon anzim katalize

suspension | sispansyon melanj dlo ak materyèl ki pa fonn

sustainable development | devlopman dirab yon estrateji pou itilize resous natirèl san w pa depafini yo epi pou founi nesesite pou lèzòm san w pa koze tò anviwònmantal ki dirab

symbiosis | senbyoz yon relasyon kote de espès viv pwòch ansanm

synapse | sinaps pwen kote yon newòn ka transfere yon enpilsyon nan yon lòt selil

systematics | sistematik etid divèsite lavi ak relasyon evolisyonè ant òganis yo

systemic circulation | sikilasyon sistemik vwa sikilasyon ant kè a ak rès kò a

T

taiga | tayiga byòm ki gen ivè ki long ak kèk mwa kote tanperati a cho ; li gen anpil plant konifè ; yo rele l tou forè boreyal

target cell | selil sib yon selil ki gen yon reseptè pou yon òmòn an patikilye

taste bud | papiy gistativ ògàn sans ki detekte gou

taxon (pl. taxa) | takson yon gwoup oswa nivo òganizasyon kote yo gwoupe òganis yo

telomere | telomè repetisyon ADN ki se eleman tèminal kwomozòm ekaryotik

telophase | telofaz faz mitoz kote kwomozòn endividyèl distenk kòmanse elaji nan yon kwomatin anbwouye

temporal isolation | izolman tanporal fòm izolman repwodiktif kote de espès oswa plis repwodwi nan diferan lè

tendon | tandon tisi konjonktif rezistan ki konekte misk eskeletal yo ak zo yo

territory | teritwa yon zòn espesifik yon animal oswa yon gwoup animal okipe epi pwoteje

testis (pl. testes) | testikil ògàn repwodiktif primè mal ; li pwodwi espèm

tetrad | tetrad estrikti ki genyen kat kwomatid ki fòme pandan meyoz

tetrapod | Noob neej Yam tsiaj 4 txais tes taw uas muaj txha nqaj qaum

thalamus | talamis estrikti sèvo a ki resevwa mesaj de ògàn sans yo epi transmèt enfòmasyon an bay zòn apwopriye nan sèvo a pou trete enfòmasyon sa yo

theory | teyori yon eksplikasyon ki byen teste ki inifye yon seri obsèvasyon ak ipotèz, epi li pèmèt syantis yo fè prediksyon ki egzat konsènan kèk nouvo sitiyasyon

thigmotropism | tigmotwopis reyaksyon yon plant fè lè yo touche l

threshold | sèy nivo minimòm yon estimilan ki nesesè pou koze yon enpilsyon

thylakoid | tilakoyid manbràn fotosentetik ki an fòm sak ou jwenn nan klowoplas yo

thyroxine | tiwoksin òmòn glann tiwoyid la pwodwi, ki ogmante to metabolik selil yo atravè kò a

tissue | tisi gwoup selil ki similè ki akonpli yon fonksyon an patikilye

tolerance | tolerans kapasite yon òganis genyen pou l siviv epi repwodwi nan sikonstans ki diferan de kondisyon maksimal yo

totipotent | totipotan selil ki ka devlope an nenpòt kalite selil ou jwenn nan kò a (ikonpri selil ki konpoze manbràn ekstra-anbriyonik yo ak plasennta a)

trachea | trache tib ki konekte farenks lan ak larenks lan ; yo rele l tou trache-atè

tracheid | tracheyid selil kre plant nan tisi liye a avèk pawa selilè ki epè ki ranfòse avèk liyin lan

tracheophyte | tracheyofit plant vaskilè

trait | karakteristik yon karakteristik espesifik yon endividi

transcription | transkripsyon sentèz yon molekil ARN apati yon modèl ADN

transfer RNA (tRNA) | ARN transfè (ARNt) tip ARN ki transpòte chak asid amine nan yon ribozòm pandan sentèz pwoteyin lan

transformation | transfòmasyon pwosesis kote yon jèn oswa plizyè jèn chanje yon souch bakteri de yon lòt souch bakteri

transgenic | transjenik tèm yo itilize pou pale de yon òganis ki genyen jèn ki sot nan lòt òganis

translation | tradiksyon pwosesis kote sekans baz yon ARNm konvèti an sekans asid amine yon pwoteyin

transpiration | transpirasyon lè yon plant pèdi dlo atravè fèy li yo

trochophore | twokofò yon molisk akwatik ki nan faz lav k ap naje

trophic level | nivo twofik chak etap nan yon chèn alimantè oswa rezo twofik

tropism | twopis mouvman yon plant fè nan direksyon oswa lwen yon estimilan

tumor | timè yon mas selil k ap divize rapidman ki ka domaje tisi ki antoure l yo

U

understory | vejetasyon sou-etaj kouch nan yon forè twopikal anba yon kanopi pyebwa ak viy ki pi kout fòme

ureter | tiyo ren yon tib ki pote pipi sot nan yon ren pou al nan vesi irinè a

urethra | irèt tib ki pèmèt pipi soti nan kò a

urinary bladder | vesi irinè ògàn ki gen fòm yon sak ki estoke pipi anvan l kite kò a

V

vaccination | vaksinasyon enjeksyon yon patojèn ki febli oswa ki similè, men ki mwen danjre pou ka pwodwi iminite

vaccine | vaksen yon preparasyon patojèn ki febli oswa patojèn yo touye epi yo itilize pou pwodwi iminite kont yon maladi

vacuole | vakyòl ti ògàn selilè ki estoke materyèl tankou dlo, sèl, pwoteyin ak idrat kabòn

valve | valv yon repli tisi konjonktif ki sitiye ant yon atriyòm ak yon vantrikil oswa nan yon ven, ki anpeche san an remonte nan direksyon opoze

van der Waals forces | fòs van der Waals fòs atraksyon fèb ki devlope ant molekil ki elektrikman chaje nan zòn opoze

vas deferens | kanal deferan kanal ki pote espèm lan sot nan epidim lan pou ale nan irèt la

vascular bundle | feso vaskilè gwoup tisi liye ak ti tisi vejetal nan tij yo

vascular cambium | kanbyòm vaskilè meristèm ki pwodwi tisi vaskilè epi ogmante epesè tij yo

vascular cylinder | silenn vaskilè rejyon santral yon rasin ki genyen ladan l tisi vaskilè yo – tisi liye a ak libè a

vascular tissue | tisi vaskilè tisi espesyalize nan plant yo ki pote dlo ak sibstans nitritif

vector | vektè yon animal ki transpòte yon patojèn bay yon imen

vegetative reproduction | repwodiksyon vejetativ metòd repwodiksyon aseksye nan plant yo, ki pèmèt yon sèl plant pwodwi desandans ki jenetikman idantik a limenm

vein | venn veso sangen ki pote san sot nan kò a pou retounen al nan kè a

ventricle | vantrikil kavite enferyè kè a ki ponpe san ki sot nan kè a pou al nan rès kò a

vertebrate | vètebre yon animal ki genyen yon kolòn vètebral

vessel element | eleman veso tip tisi liye ki se yon pati nan yon kanal kontinyèl kote dlo ka sikile

vestigial organs | ògàn vestijyo estrikti ki redwi nan gwosè yo epi yo gen yon fonksyon minim oswa yo pa gen akenn fonksyon nan kò a

villus (pl. villi) | vilozite pwojeksyon ki sanble ak yon dwèt nan ti trip la ki ede nan absòpsyon molekil nitritif

virus | viris yon patikil ki fèt ak pwoteyin, asid nikleyik epi pafwa ak lipid ki ka replike sèlman lè yo enfekte selil vivan yo

vitamin | vitamin molekil òganik ki ede reglemante pwosesis kò a

viviparous | vivipa animal kote tibebe fèt tou vivan nan vant manman l epi li nouri dirèkteman nan kò manman an pandan y ap devlope

W

weather | tan kondisyon atmosfè a ojoulejou, tankou tanperati, lapli oswa nèj ak lòt faktè

wetland | tè inonde yon sistèm ekolojik kote swa dlo kouvri tè a swa li prezan sou sifas tè a oswa touprè sifas tè a pandan omwen yon pati nan ane a

white blood cell | globil blan tip selil sangen ki pwoteje kont enfeksyon, konbat parazit epi atake bakteri

woody plant | vejetal liye tip plant ki fèt
prensipalman avèk selil ki gen pawa selilè epè ki
sipòte kò plant lan ; sa enkli pyebwa, ti pyebwa
ak viy

X

xylem | tisi liye tisi vaskilè ki pote dlo sot nan
rasin lan pou al nan tout pati plant lan

Z

zoonosis (pl. zoonoses) | zoonoz maladi
enfektye bèt ka transmèt a moun

zooplankton | zooplankton ti animal ki
deplase lib e libè ki fòme yon pati nan plankton

zygote | zigòt yon ze ki fegonde

Hmong
Hmoob

Miller & Levine
Biology Glossary

A

abiotic factor | av-bis-tiv fevtaw Lub cev, tsis muaj sia nyob, nws txawj hloov tej av, huab, cua, pob zeb thiab nroj tsuag

abscisic acid | avxiaxiv nab kauv Nroj tsuag li roj ntsha pab lawv cov "cell" sib faib sia, thiab pab lawv loj hlob

acetylcholine | Ev-tais-kau-lis Nws yog lub neurotransmitter uas ua kom lub Cell tej leeg txawj ntoj

acid | Nab kauv yogib yam hu ua hydrogen ions (H⁺) nyob ua kua; qhov kua muaj tus pH qis tshaj li 7

acid rain | Nag nab-kauv Nag uas muaj cov thaj Nitric thiab Sulfuric acids nyob nrog

actin | Ev-thee yogib plais tshais protein nyia nyia nriav pom hauv cov leeg

action potential | Evsees phaus-theeb-saus cov fais faib khiav mus khiav los ntawm qhov cell membrane hauv lub neuron; nws hu ua nerve impulse no

activation energy | Ev-tis-vev sees eb-naws-ntsis qhov zog uas yuav tsum muaj mas thiaj yuav pib muaj lub zog khiav mus lawm tom ntej

active immunity | ev-tiv is-mus-nis-tis kev tiv thaiv uas tshwm sim los los yog thaum muaj kab mob nkag

adaptation | Ev-dev-thev-sees cov noob muaj tus yam ntxwv pauv raw cheeb tsam kom lawv ciaj thiab muaj lawv tsis txawj tu noob

adaptive radiation | Ev-dev-tiv lav-dias-ev sees tus caj meem uas ib yam tsiaj los yog ib pab tsiaj hloov tsim tau noob coob loj hloob los kav ib cheeb tsam twg

adenosine triphosphate (ATP) | As-dis-naus- xees rhais-fauv-xas-fej (ATP) lub zog siab uas muaj peev xwm khaw thiab tsi tawm lub zog noob coj los siv

adhesion | Ev-hib-sees kev siv zog los ntawm cov mauleskhus ntawm ntau yam khoom sib txawv

aerobic | Ais-laus-biv tus caj meem uas yuav tau siv cua ov-xis-ntsees xwb xwb

age structure | Ej-xees-rav-tshaw Tus lej uas qhia hais tias txiv neej thiab poj niam ib pab twg muaj hnub nyug licas

aggression | As-qav-sees Tus yam ntxwv coj los ntawm ib tus tsiaj uas yog nws ua kom lwm tus paub hais tias nws yog tus xav khoom cov

algal bloom | es-nkaus-boo Yog qhov uas muaj cov (algae) thiab lwm yam ntau nyob hauv qhov uas ua cov khoom xa mus yug luv cev ntau

allele | Ev-liv-lis ib tug lej ntxawv nyob rau qe qhov chaw ntawm tus "gene."

allergy | Khaub txhuas kev tiv thaiv thaum lub cev txais taus tus kab mob lawm

alternation of generations | ib tiam quas ib tiam lub voj voog ntawm kev ciaj sia muaj ob theem (phases) xws li--a haploid (N) phase thiab diploid (2N)

alveolus (pl. alveoli) | as-ves-luv lub me nyuam hnab nyob ntawm bronchiole hauv lub ntsws uas yog qhov chaw rau cov cua sib hloov

amino acid | as-mib-naus As-xij cov khoom nyob tom kawm ntawm amino group thiab cov carboxyl group nyob rau ib tog

amniotic egg | luv qe as-nis-aus-tes lub qes uas muaj plaub los thaiv thiab muaj daim plaub nyias nyias los thaiv cia kom tus menyuam loj hlob yam tsis muaj dej

amylase | As-mis-lav Lub (enzyme) nyob cov aub ncaug uas yog zom cov khes-mis ntawm cov pem thaj

anaerobic | As-nes-luas-biv tus caj meem uas tsis tas siv cua ov-xis-ntsees (oxygen)

anaphase | As-nas-fej theem peb ntawm mis-thaus-xiv lub caij cov khlaus-mas-xoo sib cais thiab sib rub nyias mus rau nyias sab ntawm lub cev

angiosperm | Ees-ntsis-aus-xees-pees cov noob ntoo uas nws lub noob muaj plaub qhwv kom tiv thaiv tau lub noob cia; nws kuj hu ua ntoo tawg paj

anther | Ias-taw Qhov chaw hauv lub paj uas ntim cov zib uas yog qhov uas ua lub noob

antheridium (pl. antheridia) | Ias-tis-li-diam Yog txiv neej qhov khoom ua menyuam nyob rau tej yam nroj tsuag uas muaj tus kab menyuam

anthropoid | Ias-taus-pais cov tsiaj xws li liab, cuam thiab neeg

antibiotic | Tshuaj tua kab mob ib co tshuaj siv los thiav tsis pub kab mob loj thiab tsis pub kab mob xa menyuam ntxiv yog hu uas bacterial pathogens

antibody | Tshuaj tua kab mob cov plaus-tees uas ncaj nraim mus tua kab mob hu ua antigens los yog tsim ib co plaus-tees los tiv thaiv hu ua antigen-binding proteins

anticodon | Ess-tis-khaus-doos peb pawg nis-klis-aus-tiv uas yog los ntawm tRNA molecule uas yog pab tuav nrog rau peb yam mRNA khos-doos lub sij hawm txhais

antigen | Ees-thais-ntsees txhua yam plaus-tees uas ua rau lub cev txhais kev tiv thaiv kom ua hauj lwm

aphotic zone | Ees-fos-tiv Zoos Txheej dub dub hauv hiav txwv uas yog txheej uas duab tshaj ntuj must sis tseem li

apical dominance | Ees-pis-kaus Doos-mais-nias Nws yogib yam uas muaj nyob rau ntawm lub ntsis nroj es nws kawv zoo zoo, nws ua rau hlob zoo zoo heev

apical meristem | Ees-pis-kaus maw-lis-toom Yogib pab (cells) muaj hauj lwm txhwj xeeb thaum lawv sib faib ces ua rau nws ntev ntawm tus kav thiab cov cag

apoptosis | As-phas-taus-xis kev ua hauj lwm rau cov xias (cell) tuag lawm

appendage | As-phia-dej txua tawm, xws li ceg los yog tus as-tas-nas (antenna) los yog tej caj npab uas txuas lub cev

appendicular skeleton | As-phia-dis-kaus-lawm pob txha cov pob txha caj npab thiab kav ceg mus nrog rau lub ntsag thiab thaj tsam ntawm xwb pwg

aquaculture | Ua qoob loo hauv dej Kev yug tsiaj hauv dej coj los rau neeg noj

aquaporin | As-kua-paus-lis Nws yog kem dej nyob hauv lub (cell)

Archaea | Os-tshia ib pawg ntawm cov tsiaj uas muaj ib lub xia (cell), muaj lub prokaryotes uas muaj cell walls tsis muaj peptidoglycan nyob nrog; lawv yog cov tsiaj hauv lub kingdom Archeabacteria

archegonium (pl. archegonia) | Os-tshis-nnkaus-niam Lub khauj khaum nyob rau tej nroj tsuag uas yog ua cov qes (cells)

artery | Leeg Txoj hlab ntsha loj uas yog xa ntshav tawm ntawm lub plawv mus rau tej nqaij hauv lub cev

artificial selection | Kev xaiv Os-tis-fib-saum tus caj meem uas xaiv ib yam ntoo thiab tsiaj mus ua lwm yam ntoo los sis tsiaj uas tib neeg nyiam cov menyuam

asexual reproduction | Kev xeeb menyuam ib leeg kev tsim noob neej uas yog muaj tib tus niam ua tus caj meem yug menyuam tawm los muaj tus yam ntxwv zoo nkaus li nws xwb

asthma | hawb pob ib yam mob hawb pob uas yog cov hlab pa hauv lub ntsws txhaws es me me lawm, ua rau hawb pob, noo, thiab ua pa nyuaj

atherosclerosis | Ev-taw-laus-qia-liv Nws yog thaum uas muaj cov kiav roj hu ua (plaque) lo nyob rau hauv txoj hlab ntha sab hauv ua rau nws txhaw

atom | As-toom lub keeb ntawm txhua yam

ATP synthase | ATP xees-fej ATP yog ib plawg phaus-tees (proteins) ua kom lub (cell membrane) thiab tso cov ov-xis-ntsees ia-oo (hydrogen ions (H^+)) mus kom dhau

atrium (pl. atria) | Es-rhiam ib kem me me hauv lub plawv uas txais ntshav los thoob plaw ntawm lub cev los

autonomic nervous system | Lab npom pab xaj aus-taus-naus-miv nws yogi b qho ntawm qhov peripheral nervous system uas yog khoo txog cov hauj lwm uas nyias ua nyias, los yog ua mus lawm yam tsis nco qab khoo li; nws muaj qhov sympathetic thiab parasympathetic nyob ua ke nrog rau hauv

autosome | Aus-tau-xoos yog tus chromosome uas tsis yogib tug sex chromosome; nws muaj lub npe hu ua autosomal chromosome

autotroph | Aus-taus-rhauv yam no mas nws txawj muab cov duab tshav ntuj ntawm lub hnub los ua zog siv los yog cov khes-mis (chemicals) thiab siv los ua nws li zaub mov los ntawm tej yam tsis ciaj sia (inorganic compounds); nws muaj lub npe hu ua

auxin | Ov-xees yam no mas nws txawj siv lwm yam los ua kom tsob ntoo txib nws xias (cell elongation) hlob tuaj thiab hlav cav ntau ntxiv

axial skeleton | Cov txha avxias lub khoo loo uas pab txheem nruab nrab kom sawv tau nrog lub cev; nws muaj li pob txha tob haus, tej pob txha ntawm lub cev, thiav cov pob txha tav

axon | As-xoos ib txoj leeg ntev ntev uas cia rau fais faib tawm ntawm lub cev cov (cell body of a neuron) mus

B

bacillus (pl. bacilli) | Bav-xis-lus prokaryote no zoo li tus-pas

background extinction | dab neeg tuag tas los Kev tuag tu noob vim yog qeeb thiab yog kev xaiv los ntawm ib cheeb tsam nws nyob ntawd

Bacteria | kab mob Bev-taw-lias pab pawm muaj ib lub xia (cell) xwb los ciaj sia, prokaryotes muaj lub xias-vaus (cell walls) uas muaj cov peptidoglycan; lawv nyob rau pab tsiaj hu ua the kingdom eubacteria

bacteriophage | Bev-taw-lia-fej yam kab vais-lav (virus) raug cov kab mob bev-taw-lias (bacteria) lawm

bark | Tawv ntoo qhov no yog daim tawv uas nriav sab nraum cov leeg lawm sab nraud zoo li (phloem), (cork cambium), thiab (cork)

base | Lub qab yam no mas nws tsim tau cov ov-xis-ntsees ua kua "hydroxide ions (OH⁻)"; yam kua no mas muaj tus pH siab tshaj li 7

base pairing | Lub qab khub tus cai sib ntxuas ntawm DNA uas tsuas muaj nrog rau (adenine) nkaus xwb thiab (thymine) thiab nrog rau (guanine) thiab (cytosine) xwb

behavior | Yam ntxwv Kev uas tsiaj txhu ua raw kev hloov nyob rov sab hauv lawv lub cev los yog sab dhaum thaj chaw ua lawv nyob

behavioral isolation | Yam ntxwv nyob ib leeg nws yog kev tsim noob neej siv cais nyob rau ob pab pawg uas tsim muaj qhov sib txawv hais txog kev cai sib deev los yog lwm yam kev coj ntawm lawv ua rau ob pab tsiaj no tsis kam sib deev ua menyuam ua ke

benthos | Bes-toom Yog ib yam tsiaj ua nws lo rau los yog nyob rau hauv qab thu pas dej, tus dej ntws, los yog hauv hiav txwv

bias | Tsis ncaj Yogib qho ua tus neeg saib pom ntawd tsis pom qhov tseeb, uas tsis yog kev kawm tawm los

bilateral symmetry | Ob sab zoo ib yam nroj tsuag lub cev uas yog khij ib kab es muab faib ua ob lub cev xws li sab xis thiab sab lauj no ces pom nws zoo ib yam nkaus li nkawm yogi b lub cev nkaus xwb

binary fission | Bais-nes-lis dhau Yam tsiaj uas nws tsis sib deev cia li ua menyuam uas yog muab nws cov DNA faib ib nrab mus ua xwb, yeej mus ua tau ib khub (cells) menyuam ntxhais

binocular vision | qhov khoob xoo Qhov uas muaj peev xwm rub yam uas pom los ntawm ob lub qhov muag los ua ke, uas rau pom tseeb thiab pom muaj qhov xwm fab-xwm meem li lub ntiaj teb

binomial nomenclature | kev ua 2 tug lej nrog naus-mees-klhis-tshaws Nws yogib qho kev khaw tej tsiaj ua ke uas yog rau ob-lub npe rau ib tug lub npe

biodiversity | Bais-aus-dais-vaws-xib-tim Tas nro cov huab cua nyob rau saum ntuj nro peb; nws hu ua (biological diversity)

biogeochemical cycle | Voj vog bais-aus-khe-mis Yogib qhov ua cov khoom, cov khes-mis, thiab lwm yam khoom mus dhau ib tug tsiaj mus rau lwm uas yogib qho nyob hauv peb tej huab cua

biogeography | Bais-aus-ntsis-aus-nklas-fis kev kawm txog yam dhau los thiab tam sim no hais txog kev sib faib ciaj cim ntawm noob neej

bioinformatics | Bais-aus-ees-faus-mes-tiv Nws yogib qho siv los ua lej thiab siv hauv cov computer science los khaw, los nriav, thiab coj los xaiv txog (biological data)

biological magnification | Bais-aus-mes-nis-fis-khev-sees Thaum uas muaj cov tshuaj lwm yam uas ua tau rau neeg mob tau nyob saum tej huab cua es paug mus rau tej zaub mov thiab kev nriav noj

biology | Bais-aus-los-ntsis kev kawm txog noob neej txoj sia

biomass | Bais-aus-mev tas nro txhua yam ua cia li nqaij tawv nyob ua ke hauv ib qho (trophic level)

biome | Bais-aus-mes Nws yogib pab hauv lub (ecosystems) uas yog koom ib cov huab cua thiab ib co tsiaj txhu

biosphere | Bais-aus-xas-fias Nws yogib qhov hauv lub Ntiaj teb uas ciaj sia nyob saum npoo av, dej, thiab cov huab cua

biotechnology | Bais-aus-thev-nos-los-ntsis Yogib yam kev kawm tij los xaiv tsiaj, xaiv (cells), losyog xaiv (molecules), coj los ua ib yam tseem ceeb

biotic factor | Bais-aus-tiv fev-tawj Nws yog tej yam uas ciaj sia nyob hauv thaj tsam uas yog txhua yam tsiaj txhu siab tau ua ke

bipedal | Bais-phev-daum lo lus siv hais txog yam muaj ob-txhais taw mus kev

blade | Hniav nyias nyias, yog sab qaum nplooj ntoo

blastocyst | Blav-aus-xiv Nws yog thawj theem nyob hauv kev loj hlob los ntawm tej tsiaj txhu uas yog pib zoo li lub npas (cells) los

blastula | Blas-tub-la Zoo li lub npas (cells) khoob ntsuv thaum nws mus ua lub (zygote) nrog rau ntau yam kev cais hloov

bone marrow | Hlwb txha tus hlwb ntsha nyob hauv tus pob txha

bottleneck effect | Bov-daum-nev is-fev Kev hloov los ntawm cov (allele) kev siab qis lawv qab ntawm muaj kev hloov los ntawm cov pej xeem

Bowman's capsule | Bowman lub khev-xaum Lub zoo li lub khob uas yog (glomerulus); nws txoj hauj lwm yog sau ntshav los lim mus

brain stem | Txoj hlab hlwb Nws yog tus hlub nraub qaum uas txuas ntawm cov hlwv mus rau tus hlub nraub qaum; xws li (the medulla oblongata thiab the pons)

bronchus (pl. bronchi) | Hlab ntsws Yogib lub ntawm 2 lub raj cua loj loj uas tsuas ntawm caj dab mus rau hauv lub ntsws

bryophyte | Blais-aus-ti Yogib co nroj tsuag uas lawv muaj ib yam tshwj xeeb los ua menyuam tsuas yog lawv tsis muaj leeg xwb; xws li cov kab npauj thiab lawv cov txheeb ze

bud | Cos ntoo Nws los lub cos ntoo uas muaj cov ntsis mos mos nyob rau ntawm es hlav tau tus kav thiab daim nplooj

buffer | Bav-fawm yam uas tsis pub kom ntse, los cia li hloov kiag tus pH

C

calcitonin | Kas-xis-taus-nim yam kua faj siv (hormone) ua los ntawm lub og (thyroid) uas yog txo tsis pub muaj cov ntshav (calcium levels)

Calorie | Kas-laus-lis kev kuv los ntawm zaub mov li zog; nws luj li 1000 khas-las-lis (calories)

calorie | Kas-laus-lis Nws yog cov zog roj uas siv los uas kom lub cev txawj kub los sis txawj txias li (1 gram of water by 1 degree Celsius)

Calvin cycle | Voj voog Calvin Nws yog tus duab tshaj ntuj-coj los siv rau qhov (photosynthesis) zom ua zog ntawm ATP thiab NADPH thaum siv cov zog-ntau heev lawm xws li yog pem thaj

cancer | Khees-xaws Yog yam mob uas kho nyuaj nws tim rau qhov lub cev cov (cells) tsis khoom kev loj hlob li lawm

canopy | Kas-naus-pis ntxoov ntxoo muaj los ntawm nplooj ntoo roo hauv hav zoov loj loj

capillary | Kas-pis-las-lis Cov hlab ntsha me me; nws xa khoom noj thiab (oxygen) mus rau tej nqaij thiab lwm yam khoom

capillary action | Kas-pis-las-lis Ev-sees Qhov ua dej yuav nces nyob hauv lub rab nyias nyias

capsid | Kav-xij cov plhaus-tees (protein) uas qhwv tus kab vais-lav (virus)

carbohydrate | Khas-baus-hais-nres Yogib cov kua uas muaj (carbon, hydrogen, thiab oxygen atoms); nws yog yam khoom yug lub cev tseem ceeb rau lub cev heev

carnivore | Tsiaj noj nqaij noob nej muaj zog los ntawm kev noj lwm yam tsiaj txhu

carpel | Kas-pias Nws yog txheej nyob sab hauv kawg ntawm lub paj uas ua thiab thaiv qhov khoom poj niam (gametophytes) cia

carrying capacity | Peev xwm nqa Nws yog qhov uas ntau tshaj nyob rau ib pab tsiaj twg uas yog nyob rau ib thaj chaw twg es ciaj sia

cartilage | Pob txha mos Pob txha mos uas yog txuas rau nqaij thiab txheem lub cev thiab nw muaj thiab nkaus tau dua pob txha

Casparian strip | Kas-pis-xia Xees-riv Nws yogib qho ua ntub dej tsis thawm nyob qhwv daim tawv rau lub (endodermal cells) thiab nws txawj hloov los ib-txoj kev rau cov khoom dhaus cov leej raj hauv nroj tsuag li cag

catalyst | Kas-tas-lis yam khoom uas ua rau cov khes-mis (chemical reaction) siv tov ua hauj lwm ceev tuaj

cell | xes Lub hauv paus ntawm noob neej pib muaj txoj sia

cell body | Xes lub cev Nws yog qhov uas loj tshaj ntawm cov (neuron), nws ntim tau lub (nucleus) thiab ntau qhov (cytoplasm)

cell cycle | Xes li voj voog Nws yog ntau qhov ntawm lub (cell) li kev loj hlob, nws npaj sib cais, thiab siv mus ua ob lub (cells) menyuam ntxhais

cell division | Xes sib faib Nws yog qhov uas lub (cell) sib faib mus ua ob lub (cells) menyuam ntxhais division

cell membrane | Daim ntug xes Nyias nyiaj, nws muag muag qhwv cov cells; nws khoom saib yam twg nkag mus thiab yam twg tawm hauv lub cell los

cell theory | Lub tswv yim xes Nws yogib qho kev ntseeg hais tias txhua yam tsiaj ua ciaj siab mas yog cov (cells); cov (cells) yog thawj kauj ruam rau txoj sia thiab nws yog txoj hauj lwm rau ciaj sia; thiab cov (cells) los yeej yog ua los ntawm cov cells uas yeej nyob los lawm

cell wall | Ntug xes Yog qho khov khov, tiv thaiv qhwv lub (cell membrane) nyob rau ib co (cells)

cell-mediated immunity | Kev tiv thaiv xes Nws yog thaum uas lub cev qhov tiv thaiv kab mob pom tau hais tias muaj kab mob (viruses, fungi), thiab muaj cov cells tsis zoo nyob rau hauv cov cells

cellular respiration | Lub xes ua pa Nws qhov tso pa tawm mus luam cov pem thaj (glucose) los ua zog thiab lwm yam zaub mov cov (molecules) uas yog muaj nyob hauv oxygen

central nervous system | Lab npom pab xaj Qhov no mas muaj xws li cov paj hlwv thiab tus hlwv nraub qaum, uas yog cej luam txhua yam thiab xa xov mus qhia rau lub cev

centriole | Xeeb-rhis-saus Lub khauj khaum nyob rau hauv cov tsiaj lub (cell) uas yog pab npaj rau qhov uas cov (cell) sib faib

centromere | Xeeb-rhaus-mias Yogib qho nyob hauv (chromosome) uas yog2 tug viv ncaus (chromatids) txuas rau

cephalization | Xev-fas-li-za-sees Nws yog qhov uas muaj cov khoom uas hnov ntxiab thiab cov (nerve cells) nyob rau sav hauv ntawm tus tsiaj

cerebellum | Xes-le-be-loom Nws yog qhov nyob hauv lub paj hlwv uas khoom qhov txav mus los thiab thiab khoom kom sawv ntseg

cerebral cortex | Xeslesbaus kaus tem Nws yog txheej sab nraum ntawm lub (cerebrum) nyob hauv lub paj hlwb; qhov chaw uas xav thiab qhov chaw ua coj tus yam ntxwv txawv

cerebrum | Xesles nploos Nws yog qhov nyob hauv lub paj hlwb uas ua rau lub cev cia li nti; yog qhov chaw rau "xav" hauv lub paj hlwv

chemical digestion | Khes-mis Zom Nws yog qhov uas cov (enzymes) zom tej zaub mov kom cov (molecules) me me rau lub cev tau siv

chemical reaction | Khes-mis sib tov Nws yog qhov kev hloov, los yog kev pauv, muaj ib yam khes-mis hloov mus ua lwm yam khes-mis lawm

chemosynthesis | Khes-mis xeestesxis Nws yog qhov ua cov khes-mis siv lub zog los ua cov (carbohydrates)

chitin | Tshijteem Nws yog qhov txawv nyob hauv (carbohydrate) uas muaj cpv cell walls nyob hauv nceb; nws pom muaj nyob rau sab nraum lub khoo loo ntawm cov (arthropods)

chlorophyll | Khlaus lausfis Nws daim tawv ntoo thiab lwm yam nyob rau (photosynthetic organisms)

chloroplast | Khlaus lausplav Yam no mas pom muaj nyob rau nroj tsuag cov (cells) thiab lwm yam tsiaj uas siv duab tshaj ntuj los ua lub zog thiab hloov mus ua zog khes-mis

chordate | Khausdej Yam tsiaj uas muaj ib theem ntawm nws lub neej: lub nraub qaum, khoob ntsuv, li notochord, muaj tus ko tw ntej mus dhau lub qhov quav; thiab nws tseem muaj lub hnab (pharyngeal)

chromatid | Khaus mas thaij Nws yogib qho ntawm 2 tug "viv ncaus" zoo ib yam uas yog qhov kev tsim los ntawm lub (chromosome)

chromatin | khlaus mastees Nws yog khoom uas pom nyob hauv lub (eukaryotic chromosomes) uas muaj cov DNA sib kauv ceev ceev nyob rau hauv

chromosome | khlaus mausxoos Nws yog lub khauj khaum uas muaj theem tsawv nyob hauv lub (nucleus) uas yog ntim cov (genetic information) npaj xa mus rau tiam tshiab tom ntej

chyme | Tshees kev sib tov los ntawm cov (enzymes) thiab tej yam zaub mov uas zom-tas me ntsis lawm

cilium (pl. cilia) | Xibliam zoo li cov plaub luv luv tabsis txawj laim hauv lub cev

circadian rhythm | Lub suab xauskasdias tus yam ntxwv qub uas pheej tshwm sim los yuav luag txhua hnub

clade | khlaj Nws yog kev hloov hauv dab neeg los uas yog koom ib tug pog yawg thiab nws cov me nyuam

cladogram | Klavdaus klam Nws yog daim duab nraj los qhia txog cov tsiaj uas muaj tus yam txwv zoo sib xws

class | chav kev muab cai ua tej pab pawg, ib pab uas lawv yeej yog sib ze tshaj cov

classical conditioning | Lus tuav klasxivkaus Yog qhov kev kawm uas tshwm sim thaum tus tsiaj kawm tau hais tias qhov pib licas thiab qhov twg yog nws yuav tau rov qab los yog nws yuav raug ntaus xwb

climate | Huab cua Nws yog qhov kev kub los sis txias ib xyoos-rau-xyoo thiab tej chaw ua ntuj los nag tau ntej los lawm

clone | Khloos Qhov ua cia li muab ib tug tsiaj cov khoov hauv nws cov (cells) coj mus ua dua lwm tus produced from a single cell

closed circulatory system | kaw ntshav cias Nws yog qhov uas cov ntshav khiav nyob rau hauv cov leeg xa tawm mus thoov plaw rau lub cev

coccus (pl. cocci) | Khaus-kav lub qes qaum prokaryote

cochlea | kaus-qia Cov kua-ntim puv puv nyob hauv lub pob ntseg; nws muaj cov (nerve cells) uas mloog tau cov suab

codominance | Khausdausmisniam Nws yog thaum ua (phenotypes) ua tau 2 yam xws li (alleles) ua yog nyias tawm nyias li

codon | Khaus doos Ib pab ntawm 3 yam (nucleotide) uas nyob rau hauv mRNA uas qhia rau cov (amino acid) kom nws mus ua (protein)

coelom | Khaus esloos txheej tawm nqaij sab hauv lub cev

coevolution | Khaus evvausluvsees Nws yog thaum uas muaj 2 yam tsiaj nws hloov ua ke los ntev lawm ces nkawd sib txawv lawm xwb

cohesion | khaus hib sees kev sib nqus los ntawm cov mas-lej-kus (molecules) nyob nrog ib co kua ua ke

collenchyma | Khos leeskhaismas Nyob rau tej nroj tsuag, yam khoom no mas nws khov heev, nws muaj lub (cell walls) uas nkaus tau; pab txheem tus ntoo loj loj

commensalism | Khosmeesxalibxee Nws yogib qhov kev nyob taus ua ke los ntawm tej tsiaj thiab lwm uas tsis muaj qhov pab rau los yog tsis muaj qhov ua rau ploj tuag ib yam

communication | Hais lus kev cej luam los ntawm ib pab pawg mus rau lwm pab

community | Zej zog Nws yog qhov chaw uas txhua yam peb xeem los nyob ua ib pab ib pawg rau ib qho chaw

companion cell | Xes nyob ua ke Nyob rau tej nroj tsuag, lub (phloem cell) yog lub qhwv cov khoom tas nro

competitive exclusion principle | kev sib tw nyob ua ke Nws yog qhov kev ntseeg hais 2 yam tsiaj sib tw ua neej nyob rau ib qhov chaw rau tib lub sij hawm

compound | Koos paus Nws yog yam kua uas muaj ntau yam khes-mis los sib tov ua ke tshaj li 2 yam los yog ntau dua ntawm lawm

cone | Khoos Nyob hauv lub qhov muag, qhov chaw khaw cov duab tshaj ntuj uas muaj txawv xim coj los ua qhov pom cov xim ntawd

coniferous | Khoos nis faws lav Lo lus siv los qhia txog cov ntoo uas lmuaj lub noo-nyob rau hauv cov ntsiav thiab muaj daim nplooj ntev ntev li rab koob

conjugation | Khoos ntsaws nkev sees Yog qhov ua teb mus rau (paramecia) thiab lwm yam (prokaryotes) es sib paub cov (genetic information)

connective tissue | Leej nqais sib txuas Yog cov leej uas sib txuas los txheem lub cev thiab txhuas lwm qhov los ua ke

consumer | cov siv Yog yam tsiaj uas nws tos lawm yam tsiaj los ua nws lub zog thiab ua zaub mov noj; nws hu ua (heterotroph)

control group | Pab khoo Yogib pab nyob hauv qhov kev nriav kawm uas cia lawm ntsib tib cov teeb meem qhov uas txawv yog qhov uas tus kawm nriav es yog tus (independent variable) xwb

controlled experiment | Kev kawm uas muaj khoo kev tshawb sim kawm los ntawm qhov uas tsuas pub kom muaj ib mas thiaj li txawj hloov xwb

convergent evolution | Kev hloov los sib txhuam Nws yog qhov uas cov tsiaj tsis sib ze li los lawv tseem sib tw ua neej ua ke thaum qhov chaw nyob ntawm hloov

cork cambium | daim tawv tuab Nws yog daim tawv ntoo (meristematic tissue) uas yog qhov cov vov tus kav ntoo thaum tus ntoo ntawm tseem yuav loj hlov tuaj

cornea | Daim Ci Ci hauv qhov muag Nws yog txheej uas ci ci hauv lub qhov muag uas cia rau cov duab tshaj ntuj dhau mus

corpus luteum | Kauspav luvteem Lub npe no muab rau (follicle) thaum nws yug tawm los uas xim daj daj lawm

cortex | Hlwb qwb txws Nyob rau tej nroj tsuag, qhov no yog qhov nyob rau sab hauv tus cag sab rov hauv lawm uas yog dej thiab khoom yug lub cey dhau tau xwb

corticosteroid | Khaustibkostawlais vov kua faj siv (steroid hormone) yog tsim los ntaw (adrenal cortex) los

cotyledon | Khostaislisdoom Thawj daim nplooj los yog thawj ob daim nplooj tsim los ntawm lub nkaub qes (embryo)

courtship | Ke dib Hluas Nws yog qhov kev sib dib ntawm tej tsiaj ntxu uas yogh u kom lwm tus niam los sis tus txiv hnov ces los thawj

covalent bond | yyiaj pab kas Nws yog chaw sib txuas lso ntawm (atoms) uas cov (electrons) yog sawv daw siv tau

crossing-over | hla mus kom dau Nws yogib theem nyob hauv (homologous chromosomes) uas lawv sib paub cov khoom thaum nws tseem sib faiv hauv (meiosis)

cyclin | Xais qee Nws yogib tug ntawm tsev (proteins) uas khoom kom cov (eukaryotic cells) txawj hloov mus hloov los

cytokinesis | Xaistauskisnesxiv Yog qhov kev sib cais nyob hauv (cytoplasm) los ua 2 lub (cells) menyuam ntxhais

cytokinin | Xaistauskisnees Nws yog cov kua faj siv hauv tej nroj tsuag uas ua rau tus cag lhlob thiab loj mus tawg paj txi txiv thiab ua noob

cytoplasm | Xaistausplavxeem Nws yog cov kua nyob rau sab nraum ntawm lub (nucleus)

cytoskeleton | Xaistoskeleton Nws yog qhov sib chab sib chaw ntawm cov (protein filaments) nyob hauv lub (eukaryotic cell) uas yog khoom lub cell qhov nws zoo licas thiab nws cov khoom nyob sab hauv yog dabtsi thia nws yuav txav tau mus los licas

D

data | Qaub moo Pov thawj; cov qaub moo uas khaw tau los thaum ua tij zoo zov saib pom

deciduous | Disxaisdav lo lus no siv los hais txog cov ntoo uas zeeg nplooj rau ib lub caij nyob rau txhua txhua xyoo

decomposer | Rhuav yam kab no mas xwv kom tej khoom lwv thiab muab lwm yam tsiaj ua tuag lawm zom mus ua lub zog

deforestation | Ntov ntoo tas kev txov ntov tej xyoob ntoo

demographic transition | Tooj roob hauv pes hloov kev hloov ntawm pej xeem vim yog yug menyuam coob thiab cov pej xeem tuag tsawg nrog rau qhov yug thiab tuag

demography | Thaj tsam chaw kev kawm los tshawb nriav txog pej xeem

dendrite | Dees-laij kev ncau ib lub xia (cell body) tshiab los ntawm lub nus-los (neuron) uas yog cia rau fais fab khiav mus rau nws los yog khiav tawm mus rau lwm lub nus-los (neuron)rau lwm lub xia (cell body)dua

denitrification | Deesnisriskesees qhov uas cov kab bev-taw-lias (soil bacteria) hauv av muab cov thaj (nitrates) zom mus ua cov pa (nitrogen gas) nitrates

density-dependent limiting factor | coob npaum licas cov kev xaiv hais txog saib muaj pej xeem coob npaum licas

density-independent limiting factor | coob npaum li twg cov kev xaiv hais txog cov pej xeem uas zoo sib xws, tsis hais txog cov coob los tsawg npaum licas

deoxyribonucleic acid (DNA) | Ev-xiv (DNA) dis-auv-xaisbonuklia tas txhua yam uas tsiaj txhu no tau los ntawm niam thiab txiv los

dependent variable | tus txhais raw qhov uas soj ntsuam saib tus (independent variable) puas hloov thiab qhov kev los los ntawm tus (independent variable); nws hu ua (the responding variable) no thiab

derived character | tus yam ntxwv twv tus yeeb yam uas pom kiag ces paub hais tias ze li ntawm, tabsis tsis muaj nyob rau cov laus los li

dermis | Sab nraum txheej thib ob los yog hauv qab daim tawv

desertification | Ciaj suab puma ua rau av tsis zoo ua noj vim kev ua liaj teb, tus tsiaj ntau, muaj caij ntuj qhua heev, thiab huab cua hloov

detritivore | Dis-rhais-tib-vaus yam tsiaj uas noj nroj tsuag thiab tej tsiaj tuag li pob txha thiab lwm yam ua tuag lawm

deuterostome | Dus-taws-laus-xes-toos pab tsiaj hu ua (blastopore) xeeb txawm los thiab xub muaj qhov quav, thiab qhov ua ntej lwm yam mam muaj

diaphragm | Daim nplog plab daim leeg nqaij npog plab ntawm hauv siab uas pab rau ua pa yooj yim

dicot | dais-kauj qhov (angiosperm) muaj ob lub noob nyob lub qes (ovary)

differentiation | qhov txawv qhov uas cov xia (cells) los ua lub khauj khaum tshwj xeeb thiab ua hauj lwm

diffusion | tshau tawm qhov uas cov (particles) tsav mus kom ntau rau ib qho chaw tiam sis tseg ib qho chaw muaj me me xwb

digestive tract | plab nyuv lub uas pib pem lub qhov ncauj thiab mus xaus rau ntawm lub qhov quav

diploid | dais plois lo lus siv los hais txog lub xia (cell) ob yam hau-maus-zai-nkav kau-maum-xoo (homologous chromosomes)

directional selection | kev tig raw licas qhov kev xaiv uas thaum ib neeg nyob rau ib tog noj qab nyob zoo tshaj cov nyob hauv nruab nrab los yog cov nyob rau tom qhov kawg

disruptive selection | div-xas-tiv xes-lev-sees
qhov kev xaiv uas thaum uas cov nyob rau sab
saum thiab cov nyob rau qhov qis kawg noj qab
nyob zoo dua cov uas nyob rau hauv nruab nrab

DNA fingerprinting | DNA li kab tes yogib
qho kev siv los ntawm cov (biologists) kuaj saib
tus neeg ntawm cov DNA txawv cov licas; siv
los sim saib yam uas raug kuaj no puas yog los
ntawm ib tug neeg los

DNA microarray | DNA maivklaus asles yogib
ib daim iav lo yog ib daim txhais iav roj mab uas
yog muaj txog li 1000 tawm-cov DNA faib ua
tej kem tseg. Daim (DNA microarray) siv kuaj
thiab luj txog li 1000 tus (genes) ib zaug twg

DNA polymerase | DNA phausilismasias lus
tuam thawj (enzyme) muaj cov (DNA) txia
nyob hauv

domain | tus loj tus loj, muaj hwj chim rau nyob
hauv pab pawg ntawm

dopamine | daus-pas-mais Lub (neurotransmitter)
uas yog qhov uas koom nrog rau lub paj hlwv
teg dej num thiab lub chaw tau zoo ib yam

dormancy | Daus-mees-xis lub caij uas nroj
tsuag lub nkaub qes (embryo) tseem ciaj siab
tabsis nws tsis loj hlob li

double fertilization | qoo ob zaug qhov uas
cov sov xeeb thaum xub xub tsim tau lub nkaub
qes tus zej zeeg (zygote) thiab zaum thib ob, thaum
kuv kab txiv neej nkag rau lub noob kiag lawm

E

ecological footprint | keeb kwm hauv cov av
Tas nro cov (ecosystem) uas tseem ua hauj lwm
yuav tsum los yug rau noob neej, thiab nqus tej
yam khib nyiab uas noob neej tso tawm

ecological hot spot | av cov chaw kub Ib
qhov chaw me me uas muaj ib pab tsiaj nyob
hauv thiab pab tsiaj tab tom yuav ploj tuag tas
mus

ecological pyramid | av cov siab qis Nws nraj
txog cov zog sib ze los yog tej qhov qho nyob
rau hauv uas muaj cov (trophic) noj lwm yam
tsiaj los yog cov noj tsis tau nws lawm

ecological succession | av ploj tuag licas Ib
qhov kev hloov nyob rau ib thaj chaw uas kev
hloov mus puas tas rau ib thaj tsam ntawd

ecology | Kev ciaj sia Qhov kev kawm txog cov
tsiaj tej kev sib cog ua neej ua ke thiab tej tsiaj
ntawm nrog rau lawv tej chaw nyob

ecosystem | Lub npom eskausxivxabteem
Txhua yang tsiaj uas muaj nyob rau ib qho
chaw, tas nro tib si nrog rau lawv thaj chaw uas
lawv nyob tsis txawj hloov li

ecosystem diversity | Ntau yam hauv av Kev
hloov ntawm tej chaw nriav noj, chaw nyob,
thiab thaj chaw uas yog qhov pab rau tas nro
thaj tsham

ectoderm | Txheej tawv sab nraum Txheej
tawv sab nraum; yog qhov ua rau nws hnov, cov
txoov leeg, thiab daim tawm laus

ectotherm | Ev-taustees Yam tsiaj uas nws lub
cev ntawm qhov kub los sis txias yog qhov uas
tham chaw nws nyob ntawm xaiv rau nws

electron | Lub llevrhoos Nws yog cov uas muaj
qhov "-"; muaj nyob ze ncig lub (nucleus)

**electron transport chain | Txoj kab xa
Islevrhoos** Nws yogib co (electron) uas thauj
cov (proteins) khiav-ceev rawv cov (electrons)
thaum ATP-ua hauj lwm kiag lawm

element | Eslesmees Nws yogib yam khoom
nkaus xwb uas muaj ib cov (atom) xwb thiab

embryo | Eesnplais Qhov uas pib ntawm ib yam
tsiaj hu ua (multicellular organism)

embryo sac | Lub hnav Eesnplais Nws yog poj
niam qhov (gametophyte) uas nyob rau hauv
qhov tso cov paj tawm los

emerging disease | Kab mob tawm tshiab
Ib yam kab mob uas tshwm sim rau ib pab
neeg thawj thawj zaug, los yogib yam qub mob
uas cia li tawm kiag rov los es khoo nyuaj tshaj
lawm

emigration | Kev tsiv Kev uas ib co neeg tsiv
tawm ntawm ib thaj chaw mus

endocrine gland | lub qog Ees-dau-qee Nws
yog lub qhov hws uas tso cov (kua faj siv) tawm
mus rau hauv cov ntshav, uas yog xa cov kua no
mus yug rau lub cev

endoderm | Txheej tawv nyob sab hauv
Nws yog txheej tawv nyob hauv lub plab; nws
tsim muaj nyog hauv lub plab los sis tej nyuv
thiab mauj ntau nyob rau hauv cov leeg siv los
ua pa

endodermis | Txheej tawv vov Nyob rau tej
nroj tsuag, nws yog txheej tawv uas vov tas nro
cov leeg hauv tus ntoo lub cev

**endoplasmic reticulum | eesdausplavmiv
levtibkuloom** Daim npog plab uas yog nriav
pom nyob hauv (eukaryotic cells); yog qhov
chaw uas cov dej hauv lub (cell membrane) los
sib tov

endoskeleton | Eesdaussabkeslitoom Lub khauj khaum nyob sab hauv lub cev; nws yog yam txheem lub cev ntawm tus tsiaj

endosperm | Eesduasxabpees Yam nqaij uas muaj zaub-mov ntau ua noob rau koj loj sai

endospore | Eesdausxabpaus Lub khauj khaum ua yog lub (prokaryotes) tsim tsis tau li; nws muaj ib daim tawv nyias nyias xws li cov DNA thiab muaj ib co yog cov (cytoplasm)

endosymbiotic theory | kev cob qhia eesdausxisbai-aus-tiv Yam kev ntseeg hais tias lub (eukaryotic cells) tsim tawm vim yog muaj kev txheeb ze nrog rau ntau yam (prokaryotic cells)

endotherm | Eesdausteem Tug tsiaj uas nws lub cev ntawm txawj hloov qhov kub los sis txias, tsawg kawg ces yog me ntsis, siv cov hluav taw hauv nws lub cev tawm los

enzyme | Lub Ees-zais Yog cov plhau-tees kub (protein catalyst) uas yog ua kom tej yam ntawd lub cev ua hauj lwm ceev heev ntxiv

epidermis | Txheej tawv Nyob rau tej nroj tsuag, ib txheej tawv xwb los yeej yog cov (cells) tas lawm ; nyob rau tej neeg, txheej sab nraum yog daim tawv xwb

epididymis | Esphisdisdaismiv Yam khoom nyob hauv txiv neej qhov chaw mos uas yug cov kab menyuam kom loj thiab yog lawv qhov chaw nyob

epinephrine | Espisnisfee Kua faj siv tso tawm los ntawm lub (adrenal glands) ua rau kom lub plawv dhia ceev thiab cov ntsha nce thia npa kom lub cev npaj ua hauj lwm; nws hu ua (adrenaline) no

epithelial tissue | Nqaij Espithilia Tej nqaij uas nyob rov sab hauv thiab sab nraum daim tawv ntwm lub cev

era | Eslas Kev faib qhov loj kawg nyob hauv daim av; ntau zaus mas nws faib uas ob daim los yog ntau lub caij nyug los

esophagus | Txoj pas Lub raj ua txuas ntawm lub qhov ncauj rau hauv lub plab

estuary | Evtuaslis Qhov hav iav uas tus dej mus tshuam rau hiav txwv

ethylene | Evtaislees Cov kua faj siv hauv tej ntoo uas yog ua kom nws cov txiv siav

Eukarya | Yuskaya Pab tsiaj no lawv puav leej muaj lub (nucleus); xws li cov (protists), nroj tsuag, nceb, thiab lwm yam tsiaj

eukaryote | Uskayev Yam tsiaj ua nws lub (cells) muaj lub hu ua (nucleus) nyob hauv

evolution | Esvauslubsees Kev hloov los ntawm lub caij nyug; tej kev uas cov tsiaj txhu niaj hnub no yug los ntawm tej tsiaj txhu puag thaum ub los

excretion | Xa tawm Tej kev uas cov khib nyiab hauv lub cev rau xav tawm mus raw li cov qhov hws

exocrine gland | Qog Esxausqee Lub qhov hws uas tso nws cov khoom tawm raw cov raj hws uas yeej muaj tseg hauv lub khauj khaum lawm nws hu ua (ducts), nws txuas ncaj nraim rau cov plab plawv los yog tej qhaij tawv

exon | Esxos Kev coob qhia txog DNA; cov (codes) rau cov (protein)

exoskeleton | Pob txha Esxos Lub koo loo sab nraum; qhov uas tawv tshaj plaw vov cov rau sab hauv thiab txheem lub cev nrog rau cov pob tsha nraub qaum

exponential growth | Hlob sai Kev loj hlob los ntawm ib pab neeg uas yog tsis muaj qhov tu ncua los lawm ntev loo

extinct | tuag tu noob Los lus siv qhia txog yam tsiaj uas tuag tu noob lawm thiab tsis muaj ib tug ciaj li lawm

extracellular digestion | Kev zom zaub Evravkuslaw Tej yam uas zaub mov raug zom nyob sab nram lub (cells) hauv tej plab nyuv thiab raug ntxais mus

F

facilitated diffusion | pab daw mus Kev sib cais uas yog (molecules) khiav mus dhau daim tawv mus rau hauv lub (cell membrane) lawm

family | Tsev Kev muab caij ua tej tsev, ib pab ua muaj qhov zoo sib xws

fat | rog Npuas roj; nws yog cov (fatty acids) thiab cov (glycerol); nws yogib co khoom lov tiv thaiv cov plab plawv, nws tiv no, thiab nws txais tej khoom noj

feedback inhibition | lus rov hnov dua Tej kev uas ua rau nws hnov hais tias pib momb qhov twg tuaj; nws hu ua (negative feedback)

fermentation | tuag tshaib Tej kev uas cov (cells) tso lub zog tawm es tsis muaj (oxygen)

fertilization | Qoos Tej kev ua menyuam thaum tus poj niam thiab tus txiv cov kab qe los sib koom ua ib lub lawm xwb

fetus | Menyuam Lub npe muab rau tib neeg lub nkaug qes (embryo) xov xeeb lawv qab ntawm 8 lub lim piam

fever | Ua npaw Yog qhov uas kub rau lub cev thaum muaj ib qho voo nyob hauv lub cev

filtration | Lim tawm Tej kev uas dej los yog cua mus dhau lub lim dej lim cua es lim cov dej khib nyiab pov tseg

fitness | Haum Ib yam tsiaj muaj peev xwm ciaj tau zoo licas thiab lawv muaj menyuam nyob rau thaj chaw ntawm

flagellum (pl. flagella) | Fesntsibloom Lub khauj khaum siv rau cov (protists) mus los; ua menyuam nti li dej laim

food chain | sob zaub mov Nws yog kev noj zaub mov ua tej theem nyob hauv qhov (ecosystem) uas yog cov tsiaj siv zog noj zaub mov thiab lwm yam no lawv

food vacuole | zaub mov nqus Lub qhov me me nyob hauv (cytoplasm) uas yog khaw tej zaub mov tseg cia

food web | Khoom noj Nws yog tej yam txawv txawv los ntawm kev nriav noj nyob rau tej pab tsiaj hauv lawv qhov chaw ntawm lawv li (ecosystem) chaw nyob

forensics | Laj tham Yog kev kawm txog pov thawj rau hauv rooj ncauj lus

fossil | Pob txha Nws yog pob tsha rau tej tsiaj puag thaum ub lawm

founder effect | Nriav pom licas Kev hloov ntawm cov plaub ua rau muaj qhov siab qhov qis vim yog muaj kev txav ntawm tej pab neeg me me

frameshift mutation | Ruam vim hloov Kev hloov ua yog ruam "nyeem raw tus nplaim" uas yog cov (genetic message) nkag mus los yog hloov lub (nucleotide)

fruit | txiv ntoo Lub khauj khaum qhwv cov (angiosperms) uas muaj los yog ntau lub qe ua yeej qoo qoo lawm (matured ovaries)

fruiting body | Lubev txiv Kev ua menyuam ntawm tej nceb uas yog loj hlob los ntawm (mycelium)

G

gamete | Nkesmem Lub (cell) ua menyuam

gametophyte | Nkesmemtausfaij menyuam-ntoo ua los; qhov (multicellular haploid phase) yogib qho ntawm lawv lub neej

ganglion (pl. ganglia) | Nkaslias Yogib pab tsiaj muaj (interneurons)

gastrovascular cavity | /Plab nyuv khoob Nws cov plab nyuv tsuas muaj ib lub qhov xwb

gastrulation | plab nyuv li Yog qhov uas lub (cell) tsav vim yog nws tau txais 3 yam lus los ntawm—txheej tawm hauv (ectoderm), txheej nruab nrab (mesoderm), thiab txheej sab nraum (endoderm)

gel electrophoresis | Ntsias llevrausfauslisxix Yam ua siv los cais thiab xaiv cov DNA ua ke ua yog muab los sib tov DNA rau ib tom thaum nws khov lawm thiab muab cov fais fab ua kom khiav tau

gene | Keeb Cov DNA li qib los sis yog theem uas yog cov (codes) rau tus (protein) thiab mus xaiv nws yamt; qhov uas niam thiab txiv muab rau menyuam

gene expression | Keeb tshwm Yog qhov uas tus (gene) nws ua ib yam tawm los thiab yam uas nws ua tawm los ntawm muaj ib txoj hauj lwm ua

gene pool | keeb pawg Txhua tus (genes), xws tas nrog cov uas ua plaub nyob rau tej tus (gene), uas yog tshwm sim los ib zaum twg

gene therapy | Keeb kho Yog qhov uas hloov tus (gene) los kho tus kab mob los yog yam mob. Thaum tsis pom los yog tsis muaj (faulty gene) los hloov rau ib tug (gene) uas nws yeej tsis hauj lwm lawm

genetic code | Keeb cov lej Tas nro cov mRNA, ib tug twg ces yeej yog muaj ib co (amino acid) tshwj xeeb es mam mus ua (protein) rau thaum cov (protein) ho mus sib cais dua

genetic diversity | ntau yam keeb Tas nrog cov kev sib txawv ntawm cov (genetic information) uas yog muaj nyob hauv ib yam tsiaj xwb, los yog yam tsiaj nyob hauv lub Ntiaj teb no

genetic drift | Keeb txav Kev hloov uas tsis muaj tus twv tau ntawm tej plaub uas yog kev hloov ntawm cov plaub muaj ntau los yog tsawg nyob rau ib pab tsiaj twg

genetic equilibrium | keeb nyob nruab nrab Yog qhov uas tus plaub cia li txawj siab qis vim yogpab tsiaj ntawm nyob li qub

genetic marker | ua keeb Cov plaub muaj qhov ua pom tau hais tias cov (phenotypic) sib ntxawv hauv qhov (genetic analysis) lawm

genetics | keeb txheej Kev kawm txog saib noob neej yug mus yus los zoo licas

genome | Cov keeb Tas nrog cov (genetic infor-mation) uas ib tug tsiaj muaj nrog nws cov (DNA)

genomics | Ntsis-naus-miv Kev kawm txog cov (genomes), xws li (genes) thiab lawv tej hauj lwm uas lawv ua

genotype | Ntsis-naus-thaiv Yog qhov (genetic) hauv tus tsiaj tas nro

genus | ntsis nus Ib pab tsiaj uas yog sib ze tas tus; thawj thawj qhov uas raug tis cov (scientific name) npe rau pab tsiaj (binomial nomenclature) ntawm

geographic isolation | Nyob cais chaw Yogib qhov kev ua menyuam txawv uas 2 pab tsiaj zoo ib yam nyob rau ob qhov chaw sib txawv xws li muaj dej kem, muaj roob quas, los yog muaj pas dej thaiv, ua rau ob pab tsiaj no sib txawv nyias mus ua nyias ib pab lawm

geologic time scale | nrug sij hawm Lub sij hawm siv los qhia txog lub Ntiaj teb zaj lij xws

germ theory of disease | kev cob qhia txog kab mob Lub txwv yim uas hais tias kab mob mas yog muaj los ntawm cov (microorganisms) kab mob me me los

germination | kab mob Qhov uas nroj tsuag txawj loj hlob hauv lub nkaub tuaj raw li nws qhov uas nws muaj

giberellin | Nkivbawslelees Yog cov kua faj siv (plant hormone) hauv tej nroj tsuag uas yog ua rau koj lawv txawj loj thiab txawj hlob sai

gill | xiab Yogib lub khauj khaum uas tuaj tuaj plaub tshwj xeeb los hloov roj mus pauv dej

global warming | Lub ntiaj teb sov heev lawm Qhov uas ua rau tus koob ntsuas kev kub thiab kev txia hauv lub Ntiaj teb

glomerulus | Nklaus-maus-lus-lav Nws yogib qho kev sib tuav me me nyob saum qhov kawg ntawm (nephron); uas yog qhov chaw lim cov ntshav

glycolysis | Nklais-kaus-lis-xiv Thawj chov kev sib tov ua pa los ntawm lub cev uas yog maudj cov (molecule) uas yog pem thaj tawm mus ua 2 lub (molecules of pyruvic acid)

Golgi apparatus | Nkaus-ntsi Aspaslatav Nws yog lub (cells) ua txawj hloov, txawj xaiv, thiab txawj puab cov (proteins) thiab lwm yam khoom ua los ntawm lub (endoplasmic reticulum) los cia rau hauv lub (cell) los yog nyob rau sab nraum lub (cell) tseg

gradualism | hloov Kev hloov los ntawm ib yam tsiaj raw li lub caij nyug uas yog muaj kev hloov me me zuj zus raw li (genetic) hloov raw caij

grafting | txuas Nws yogib yam kev siv los tsim tej yam nroj tsuag los sis xyoob ntoo uas tsis muaj noob thiab nws kuv rau siv rau ntau yam ntoo uas tsis pub kom raug txiav pov tseg

gravitropism | Nklasvisrhausphia-sees Tej nroj tsuag qhov uas lawv sawv tsis pub vau raw li (gravity)

green revolution | Hloov mua ntsuab Tej kev tsim kom muaj cov qoob loo uas ua me tau ntau athinb siv tau cov khoom cog los sis tu tshiab tshiab tiam no los ua es kom tau qoob loon tau tshaj

greenhouse effect | Paj taw tshawb Yog qhov uas nws muaj ib co cua (carbon dioxide, methane, thiab water vapor) nws thaiv cov duab tshaj ntuj cia ib txheej ua ntej tus daub tshaj ntuj raug lub Ntiaj li kev kub los sis txias

growth factor | qhov loj hlob Yog ib pab (proteins) nyob rau sab nram uas yog ua rau kom loj thiab kom cov (cells) txawj sib faib sai

guard cells | xes zov Lub (cells) tshwj xeeb nyob dab nram daim tawv ntoo uas yog khoo qhov uas qhib thiab qos ntawm qhov (stomata)

gullet | Nkuslev Qhov caw pliav nyob rau ib sab ntawm nw uas yog cia rau cov zaub mov nkag mus hauv lub (cell)

gymnosperm | Ntsees-naus-xees-peem Ib co noob nroj tsuag uas muaj cov noob nyob rau hauv cov ntsiav txheej sab hauv

H

habitat | chaw nyob Thaj chaw ua tsiaj nyob xws li (biotic) thiab (abiotic factors) uas raug rau lawv

habitat fragmentation | vaj tsev khauv hlab tej kev pob ntawm lub (ecosystems) mus ua tej daim me me

habituation | chaw txoo Yam no mas kawm los xws lis tus tsiaj tsis kam los yog nres tsis pub kom nws tus kheej ua raw li qhov uas nws nyiam los yog yam ua yuav ua raug nws mob

hair follicle | plaub mos Lub hnab zoo li lub raj nyob rau lub (epidermal cells) uas nws xyab mus txog rau daim tawv (dermis); cov (cells) nyob rau hauv lub hauv paus uas nws tuaj plaub

half life | ib nrab Yogib nrab ntawm lub caij uas yuav siv rau (radioactive atoms) lwj mus txog ib nrab

haploid | Hav plais Lo lus siv rau lub (cell) uas tsuas nws ib khub (genes) xwb

Hardy-Weinberg principle | Yawg Hardy-Weinberg qhov cai Tus lav kas uas qhia hais tias cov plaub uas muaj qhov siab qis nyob rau ib cov neeg yuav nyob li ntawm mus tsuas ntshai muaj ib yam los yog ntau yam hloov ces pauv rau lawv xwb

Haversian canal | Lub raj Haversian Ib lub ntawm cov raj uas sib chab sib chaw hauv es khiav dhau cov pob txha uas muaj cov hlab ntsha thiab cov leeg nyob nrog

heart | plawv Yog lub plawv uas nws tswm ntshav kom khiav mus thoob rau lub cev

heartwood | plawv ntoo nws yog lub plawv ntoo, thooj ua laus dua nyob kiag rau hauv lub-plawv uas nws yeej tsis txais dej li lawm

hemoglobin | ntshav hau-muaj (protein) nyob rau hauv cov ntshav liab lub (cells) uas rau lub (oxygen) tsis pom thiab xa mus rau lub cev

herbaceous plant | Ntoo Herbaceous Yam nroj tsuag uas nws nplua nplua thiab tsis ua kav ntoo; xws li cov (dandelions, zinnias, petunias), thiab paj hnub hlis

herbivore | Tsiaj noj nqaij Yam tsiaj ua nws lub cev muaj zog los yog vim nws noj lwm yam nroj tsuag xwb

herbivory | Noj nqaij Nws yog qhov ua ib tug tsiaj ua vim (tus tsoak noj zaub) noj lwm yam khoom lawm (xws li noj ntoo),

heterotroph | Histawslausrhawv Yog yam tsiaj ua nws tej khoom noj yog nws noj cov tsiaj muaj sia los; nws hu ua (consumer)

heterozygous | Histawsluasnkauv Muaj 2 yam plaub (alleles) txawv nyob rau hauv ib tug (gene)

histamine | Hiv-tas-mee Cov khes-mis tso tawm los ntawm lub (mast cells) uas rau cov ntshav khiav ntau ntxiv thiab cov kua dej ntws mus rau chaw uas raug mob o o lawm

homeobox gene | Tus gene haus-mias-bov Qhov (homeobox) yog tus DNA cov theem uas nws muaj ze li 130 khub nyob hauv, nriav pom nyob rau ntau yam (homeotic genes) uas yog ua kom loj hlob. Cov (Genes) no muaj cov theem no muaj lub npe hu ua (homeobox genes), thiab tus (code) xaiv saib yuav ua licas, cov (proteins) thaiv tus DNA thiab ua rau koj nws yog qhov kev tshaj tawm ntawm lwm tus (genes)

homeostasis | Haus-mias-tas-xiv Nws ze nrog rau cov khoom nyob sab hauv thiab cov khes-mis uas ua rau yam tsiaj ntawm khaw tseg

homeotic gene | Haus-mias ntsis Nws yogib pab (genes) uas ua rau qhov xaiv saib lub cev ntawm yam twg thiab qhov twg thiaj pib hauv tus tsiaj lub nkaub tawm los. Kev hloov uas yog ruam los ntawm cov (genes) hloov tau ib qho hauv lub cev mus ua lwm qhov

hominine | Haus-mis-nai Yog qhov sib txuas ntawm leej tib neeg rov qab

hominoid | Haus-mis-nais Nws yogib pab (anthropoids) uas yog cov zoo li liab cuam lawv (gibbons, orangutans, gorillas, chimpanzees), thiab leej tib neeg ib yam

homologous | Haus-laus-nkauv Lo lus siv rau cov (chromosomes) uas yog los ntawm tus txiv los thiab nws muaj ib khub los ntawm tus niam los

homologous structures | haus-maus-nkauv Lub khauj khaum uas zoo ib yam nyob rau txhau yam tsiaj ua sib txawv vim lawv poj yawm

homozygous | Haus-zais-nkauv Yog qhov uas muaj 2 tug (alleles) zoo ib yam nyob hauv tus (gene)

hormone | Kua faj siv Yog cov khes-mis uas nyob rau ib qho ntawm tus tsiaj uas ua rau lwm yam ntawm tib tug tsiaj ntawm ib yam

Hox gene | Tus Hox ntsis Nws yogi b pab (homeotic genes) ua nyob ua ke xaiv ntawm tob hau mus txog tus ko tw kom qhia rau hais tias qhov twg yog yam twg ntawm tus tsiaj lub cev. Tas nrog cov (hox genes) muaj tus (homeobox DNA) nyob ua ntuv zus hauv

humoral immunity | Hus-maus-los zam Nws hloov los tiv thaiv cov kab mob nyob cov kua dej hauv lub cev, xws li yog ntshav thiab yog roj

humus | Husmas Yam no yog nplooj lwg lwj los ua thiab lwm yam tsiaj li

hybrid | txua los Tus menyuam uas yog niam thiab txiv sib txawv

hybridization | txuas tau Yog qhov kev ua menyuam los ntawm tib neeg muab lawm los sib tob ua ke ua kom tau menyuam los siv xwb

hydrogen bond | hais-dau-ntsi txuas tej kev sib txuas uas tsis muaj zog li los ntawm lub (hydrogen atom) thiab lwm lub (atom)

hydrostatic skeleton | Pob txha haisdautastiv Lub khoo loo ua yog ntim dej puv nkaus lub cev ua hauj lwm nrog rau cov leeg cia rau tus tsiaj txawj mus kev

hypertonic | Haispawsthawniv Thaum muab 2 yam kua coj los sib piv, yam kua ua nyeem tshaj yog cov ua hua ua (solutes)

hypha (pl. hyphae) | hais fam Ib yam ntawm cov kub ntev, nws tus yiag yiag muaj lub cev zoo li lub nceb

hypothalamus | Haispothalamav Lub khauj khaum rau lub paj hlwb uas khoom qhov nco qab thiab nco xaiv txog li tshaib plab, nqis dej, nkee nkee, chim chim, thiab lub cev kub los sis txias

hypothesis | kwv yees Kev twv txog li tej yam uas nws pom los lawm los yog kev teb raw li cov lus nug los ntawm cov txawj

hypotonic | Haispotausniv Thaum muab 2 yam kua coj los sib piv, yam kua uas tsis tshua nyeem yog cov hu ua (solutes)

I

immigration | Tsiv nkag qhov kev tsiv uas neeg khiav mus nyob rau qhov chaw yeej muaj neeg coob coob lawm

immune response | im-mus lesseespo lub cev nqaij li kev cim txhua yam, kev teb rov qab, thiab kev nco tseg hais tias muaj kab mob tuaj lawm

implantation | Cog qhov uas muaj qhov (blastocyst) txuas rau ntawm lub txoj nyuv menyuam

imprinting | Dim taw tus yam ntxwv ua yog zoo li tej nws yeej ua dhau los lawm; txij thaum qhov muaj (imprinting) no lawm, tus yam ntxwv hloov tsis tau lawm

inbreeding | Yuav cov ze qhov kev xaiv ua ua niam txiv yug menyuam kom muaj tus yam tcwj pwm zoo li qhov qub tas mus li ntawm ib pab pawg twg

incomplete dominance | tsis tas yog thaum uas muaj ib tug muaj lej txawv lawm ces nws yeej tas nro txhua pab nyob hauv li

independent assortment | tsis kav tas nro yogib ntawm (Mendel's principles) uas hais tias cov (genes) sib txawv mas lawv txawv sib cais nyob rau lub caij uas lawv pib sib faib ntawm

independent variable | variable/tus txhais tus caj meem no mas khoo tau kom nws hloov nyob rau thaum sim ua tas los lawm; nws hu ua (manipulated variable)

index fossil | maim pob txha Qhov uas qhia txog cov pob tshav qub qub los piv rau lawv cov tsiaj uas tseem ciaj no

infectious disease | yam mob kis tau Kab mob ua los ntawm cov (microorganism) uas rau lub cev ua tsis tau nws cov hauj lwm

inference | taw rau Kev txais tau vim yog nws muaj kev kawm paub ua ntej thiab sim dua los lawm

inflammatory response | o tuaj phim Nws tsis pom muab dab tsi los tiv thaiv vim raug mob lawm los yog pib voo tuaj lawm

innate behavior | yam ntxwv Tus yam ntxwv txawv uas muaj nyob rau tej yam tsiaj uas nws yog yeej nyob zoo thawj zaug nws yog ua tawm los ntawm tus tsiaj ua yeej tsis tau ua li no los dua li; nws hu ua (instinct)

insight learning | Yeej kawm tau Tus yam ntxwv txawv uas muaj nyob rau tej yam tsiaj uas nws twb yeej kawm tau yam no los ntev lawm, nws yeej ua tsis yuam kev li thiab tsis muaj txaum; nws hu ua (reasoning)

interferon | Ees-taws-fis-loo Ib pab (proteins) li kev pab cuam rau cov (cells) tiv thaiv tsis pub kom kis mob

interneuron | Ees-taws-nis-loo Yam (neuron) siv los cej luam thiab cheem cov khoom uas yuav khiav mus rau hauv lub (motor neurons)

interphase | Ees-taws-fej Nws yog lub caij hu ua (cell cycle) uas yog lub caij lawv siv faib

intracellular digestion | qhov chaw zom zaub Qhov chaw zom zaub mov uas yog tshwj xeeb rau cov (cells) pab xa cov khoom noj zoo mus rau lwm cov (cells) uas yog tshau mus

intron | tej theem Tej theem rau DNA uas yog koom tes nrog rau kev (coding for a protein)

invertebrate | txha nqaj qaum Cov tsiaj uas tsis muaj tus txha nqaj qaum, los yog hu ua) vertebral column)

ion | Ais-oom Lub (atom) ua muaj qhov "+" los yog "-" nyob nrog nws

ionic bond | aos-os-niv boo Khes-ms uas yog sib puab los ntawm ib los yog ntau tshaj tus (electrons) khiav ntawm ib lub (atom) mus rau lwm lub

iris | plaub muag Qhov ua muaj xim nyob hauv lub qhov muag

isotonic | Ais-xaus-thaus-niv Thaum muaj 2 yam kua nyeem ib yam nyob rau ib qhov chaw

isotope | Ais-xaus-thauv Nws yogib qho ntawm ntau ntau cov (element) nyob ua ke, uas yog muaj ib co lej (protons) zoo ib yam tabtsis nyias muaj nyiaj cov lej (neutrons) sib txawv

J

joint | txuas Qhov chaw uas ib tug pob txha txuas rau lwm tus pob txha

K

karyotype | Kaslisyauthaiv Nws yogi b qhov me me nyob hauv qhov (complete diploid set) hauv lub (chromosomes) ua ke ua tej khub, nws nyob chaw tus loj mus rau tus me

keratin | kaslastees Daim tawv (protein) uas tawv tshaj nyob rau daim tawv nqaij

keystone species | yam tsaij khisxabtoos
Yogib yam tsiaj xwb uas nws tsis kam tshais ntawm nws qhov chaw mus li vim nws khoo zoo zoo txog nws lub khauj khaum kawg

kidney | raum Lub raum uas yog cais khib nyiab thiab cov dej ntau ntau tawm hauv cov ntshav mus

kin selection | xaiv tus ze Qhov kev kawm qhia rau kom pab cov uas txheeb ze kom lawv qhov uas muaj nyob ntxiv mus muaj feem zoo yeeb vim cov no puav leej muaj ib co (genes) zoo sib xws

kingdom | Pab pawg Coob tshaj thiab muaj ntau yam nyob ua ke hauv qhov no

Koch's postulates | Koch pautulastes Nws yogib co kev cai tsim los ntawm Koch uas yog pab los xaiv cov (microorganism) mus ua pab vim yam mob uas lawv ua tshwm

Krebs cycle | Voj khlej Yog theem thib ob ntawm qhov (cellular respiration) uas muaj cov (pyruvic acid) zom ua me me mus ua cov (carbon dioxide) coj mus siv ua lub zog-hlawv lwm yam

L

language | lus Yog qhov kev sib tham es siv lub suab, khoom cim, thiab piav tes raw li ib co cai teev tseg kom muaj qib thiab muaj duas, xws li kev siv ntawv thiab sau ntawv

large intestine | Nyuv tw Txoj nyuv tws nyob hauv plab uas yog xa dej nrog rau cov khoom uas zom tsis tas tawm ntawm nws mus; nws hu ua (colon)

larva (pl. larvae) | ua kas Yog qib ua lub qes tseem tsis qoo

larynx | pob qa Lub khauj khaum hu ua pob qa uas yog qhov hais lus tawm

learning | kawm tau Kev hloov tus yam ntxwv yeeb vim yog muaj kev kawm

lens | iav Lub khauj khaum iav hauv lub qhov muab uas yog txais duab tshaj ntuj rau lub ntsiab muag (retina)

lichen | peeb Yog qhov cim ze rau cov nceb thiab yam (photosynthetic organism)

ligament | leeg txha Cov leeg tawv tawv uas txuas pob txha ua ke

light-dependent reactions | tus txais ci-raw Nws yog qhov kev txais duab tshaj ntuj (photosynthesis) los siv ua lub zog ATP thiab NADPH

light-independent reactions | tus txais ci-tsis-raw Nws yog qhov kev txais duab tshaj ntuj (photosynthesis) uas tsis siv duab tshaj ntuj; lub zog los ntawm ATP thiab NADPH siv los ua cov zog-log xws li pem thaj; nws hu ua (the Calvin cycle)

lignin | Laisnees Tej yam khoom nyob tus nroj tsua lub nrog cev nws ua cov (cell walls) tus ntug

limiting factor | feem cas kav Qhov uas ua rau cov pem xeem poob rov qab los rau qhov qis

limiting nutrient | cas kav zaub mov Muaj ib yam (nutrient) tseem ceeb thiab ua tsawg kawg nyob hauv qhov (ecosystem)

lipid | roj Roj (macromolecule) ua los ntawm cov (carbon) thiab (hydrogen atoms); xws li qhov rog, cov roj, thiab pluas roj

lipid bilayer | ob txheej roj Qhov ua nkaus tau muaj-ob txheej ua ke ua tau lub (cell membrane) thiab nws thaiv rau cov (cell) thiab thaj tsam uas muaj lawv ntawm

logistic growth | hlob raw kev cai Kev nce ntawm cov pej xeem uas qhia tau hais tias qeeb thiab nws cia li tsis muaj qhov nce tau ib lub caij lawm

loop of Henle | luv-os-his-le a section of the nephron tubule that is responsible for conserving water and minimizing the volume of the filtrate

lung | ntsw lub ntsws; qhov chaw ua pa los sib pauv ntawm cov ntshav thiab nqus cua mus ua pa

lymph | kua ntshav Cov kua ua lim cov ntshav

lysogenic infection | Mob Lysogenic Cov kab mob kis los ntawm tus kab (virus) ua nyob rau hauv DNA nyob hauv DNA yog tus txais thiab muab lawv yug dua nyob hauv lub (cell) DNA

lysosome | Laisxausxoos Lub (cell organelle) uas zom roj, (carbohydrates), thiab cov (proteins) kom mus ua tej lub me me es yug tas rau lub cev

lytic infection | mob lais-tiv Yam mob kis los ntawm cov kab (virus) nkag tau rau hauv lub (cell), nws yug nws tus kheej, thiab ua rau lub (cell) tawg

M

macroevolution | Kev hloov loj Ntau-dua ntawd lawm nws muaj kev hloov los ntev lawm

Malpighian tubule | Raj Maus-pis-ntsee Lub khauj khaum uas cov (terrestrial arthropods) muaj nyob nrog cov (uric acid) thiab nws ntxiv rau cov khib nyiab

mammary gland | qog meesmaslis Lub qog rau cov niam tsiaj uas muaj mis me los pub menyuam mos

mass extinction | kev ploj tuag coob Ib sij hawm ua ntau yam tsiaj tuag tas tu noob nro rau ib lub caij

matrix | kev ntsuas Qhov uas nyob sab hauv lub cev sav hauv uas yog lub (mitochondrion)

mechanical digestion | tim los zom Yogib yam uas zom zaub mov mus ua tej qhov me me

meiosis | me-aus-xis Yogib yam uas cov lej hauv lub (chromosomes) raug txiav ua ob sab vim yog sib cais los ntawm lub (homologous chromosomes) mus rau lub (diploid cell)

melanin | Meslasnis Daim tawv dub daj uas yog qhov tiv thaiv daim tawm rau cov (ultraviolet rays)

melanocyte | Meslasnosxaij Yog lub (cell) uas tsim los ntawm daim tawv dub daj hu ua (melanin)

menstrual cycle | Coj khaub ncaw Yog ib qho ua lub qes pib xeeb thiab npaj tawm hauv lub cev tawm mus

menstruation | Kev coj khaub ncaw Tso cov ntshav tawm thiab cov qes uas tsis tau xeeb zeej zeeg hauv lub cev

meristem | Melistees Qhov chaw ua cov (cells) tsis muaj hauj lwm tshwj xeeb rau lawv loj tuaj rau lawv lub neej

mesoderm | Txheej nruab nrab Txheej tawv nruab nrab; xeeb mus ua leeg, thiab mus cov leeg xa dej mus los, kev tsim ua menyuam, thiab kev tso khib nyiab tawm

mesophyll | Mevxausfais Cov leeg txhwj xeeb uas nriav pom nyob ntawm daim nplooj; nws ua txoj hauj lwm qus duab tshaj ntuj (photosynthesis) mus yug tsob ntoo

messenger RNA (mRNA) | Kev xa NNA Yog qhov RNA uas nqa ib qho keeb xwm mus ua cov (amino acids) nrog rau (proteins) los ntawm DNA xa mus rau tas nro cov (cell)

metabolism | Zom tas Txhua yam los sib tov ua ke ntawm khes-mis hauv yam tsiaj lub cev coj mus tsim ua lwm yam khoom

metamorphosis | Mevtasmausfovxis Yog qhov ua nws yam ntxwv thiab uas yog kas los txog rau tus laus

metaphase | Mevtasfe Yog theem thib ob nyob hauv (mitosis) uas yog cov (chromosomes) los ua kab sab hauv lub plawv

microclimate | Huab cua me Cov huab cua uas nyob rau ib qhov chaw ntawm thaj tsam me me txawv lwm qhov chaw nrog rau lwm cov huab cua

migration | tsiv Kev khloov los ntawm cwj pwm yeeb vim yog cov huab cua hloov lawm

mineral | khoom siv Cov thaj (nutrients) uas lub cev xav tau, ntau zaus mas me me xwb

mitochondrion | lub maistauskhoobnrias Lub (cell organelle) uas yog tig cov khes-mis mus ua zaub mov uas yog muab hloov mus uas lwm yam (cell)

mitosis | Maisthausxis Yogib qhov ntawm lub (eukaryotic cell) sib faib thaum nws lub (Cell nucleus) sib faib nws cov khoom

mixture | sib tov Nws yog 2 yam khoom los sib tov ua ke los yog ntau dua ntawm los yog cov khoom txhua yam los sib tov ua ke tabsis mas nws cov khes-mis tsis sib tov

molecular clock | /lub moos mauslekhuslas Yam uas tshawb kawm txog qhov kev hloov los ntawm DNA hais txog 2 yam tsiaj uas nws muaj nyob rau ib lub caij es nyias muaj nyiam yam

molecule | Lub mauslekhus Yogib yam me me uas nws yogib yam nyob hauv cov khoom

molting | ncuav tawm Yog qhov ua nws plis tawv (exoskeleton) thiab muaj daim tawv tshiab tuaj

monocot | Mausnauskhauj Yog cov paj ntoo lub qes (angiosperm) uas muaj lub noob nyob hauv nws lub (ovary)

monoculture | Mausnauskhabtshaw Yogib yam kev ua liaj ua teb cog ib yam khoom, yam khoom ua tau ntau nyob rau xyoo tom qab

monomer | Ib tus qho me me Ib qho khes-mis me me uas yog qhov (polymer)

monophyletic group | pab tsawg tsawg Ib pab tsiaj uas yog los ntawm ib tug pog yawg los thiab tas nro nws cov txheeb ze thiab tsis xam txog cov tsiaj uas kem sab nraud es tsis koom pog yawg

monosaccharide | pab me me Yogib lub pem thaj (molecule)

motor neuron | lub cav nus-las Yog qhov (nerve cell) uas nqa khoom los ntawm lub (interneurons) mus rau tom cov (muscle cells) lo yog cov qog

multiple alleles | cov plaub ntau ntau tus (gene) uas muaj ntau dua 2 tug (alleles)

multipotent | ntau ntau cov pa Lub (cells) uas yog muaj kev loj hlob me me xwb uas yog txawv rau txhua qhov nyob hauv cov (cells)

muscle fiber | cov sab nqaij Lub cev ntev nyob cov leeg lub (cells)

muscle tissue | leeg nqaij Qhov leeg uas ua rau nws nqaij nti tau lub cev mus los yooj yim

mutagen | Mutasntsees Khes-mis los yogi b yam dab tsi uas ua hauj lwm nrog rau cov DNA thiab ua rau muaj qhov ruam lawm

mutation | kev txia Kev hloov hauv cov noob (genetic material) nyob hauv lub (cell)

mutualism | pom zoo Tus kas maim qhia txog hais tias ob yam tsiaj ntawd puav leej yeej los ntawm qhov kev txheeb ze ntawm

mycelium (pl. mycelia) | mais-xeb-les Cov cag tuaj tuab tuab nyob rau ntawm cov zaub mus rau cov nceb muaj ceg rau hauv av

mycorrhiza (pl. mycorrhizae) | mais-khauslisxa Tus kas maim qhia txog zaub tej cag thiab nceb tej cag

myelin sheath | mais-is-li sej Daim tawv thaiv sab nraum lub (axon) nyob rau tej lub (neurons)

myocardium | Mais-aus-kaj-diam Qhov leeg tuab tuab nyob hauv lub plawv

myofibril | Mais-aus-fib-bla Yam puab-ceev ceev ua tawv uas yog pom nyob lub khauj khaum ntawm cov leeg

myosin | Yam tuab tuab Yam tuab tuab uas yog (protein) nriav pom nyob rau lub khauj khaum ntawm cov leeg

N

NAD⁺ (nicotinamide adenine dinucleotide) | Mais-yau-xees Lub (electron) uas nqa mus rau cov (glycolysis)

NADP⁺ (nicotinamide adenine dinucleotide phosphate) | NADP⁺ nws nqa Nws nqa lub (molecule) uas yog hloov qhov zog-siab mus rau cov (electrons) los ntawm qhov (chlorophyll) mus rau lwm lub (molecules)

natural selection | kev xaiv thamabxaj Yogib qho ua cov tsiaj nyob rau thaj chaw uas tsim nyob rau lawv ciaj sia thiab yeej noob lawm tom ntej; nws hu ua (survival of the fittest)

nephridium (pl. nephridia) | nes-fi-diam Lub khauj khaum uas yog lub lim cov kua dej hauv lub cev

nephron | Nesfoo Qhov lim-ntshav uas yog lub khauj khaum nyob hauv ob lub raum uas yog lim cov tsis huv tawm, khib nyiab raug khaw tseg, thiab cov ntshav raug xa rov mus yug lub cev dua

nervous tissue | lab npom leeg Yog yam nqaij uas xa xov rau thoob plaw lub cev

neuromuscular junction | qhov leej ntsib Yog qhov uas sib txuas ntawm lub (motor neuron) thiab cov (skeletal muscle cell)

neuron | Nes-loos Lub (nerve cell); txoj hauj lwm tshwj xeeb yog xa xov mus rau hauv (nervous system)

neurotransmitter | Nes-loos txais Khes-mis rau lub (neuron) siv los xa xov mus rau lub (synapse) ces mam xa mus rau lwm lub (cell)

neurulation | nes-loos chaw txais Thawj theem nyob hauv kev xov xeeb ntawm lub (nervous system)

niche | whov tshiab Yogib qho rau lub cev thiab txoj sia siv uas yog yam tsiaj ua ciaj siab thiab lawv li kev siv cov uas nyob ze lawv

nitrogen fixation | kho naisrhausntsees Yog qhov uas tig cov (nitrogen gas) cua mus cov (nitrogen compounds) ua lub kom tej nroj tsuag nqus tau thiab siv tau

node | pob nauv Yogib qho kev loj hlob los ntawm daim nplooj uas txuas rau tus ntoo

nondisjunction | Tsis muaj Qhov yuam kev nyob hauv qhov (meiosis) uas yog qhov (homologous chromosomes) tsis kam cais zoo

nonrenewable resource | tsis kho Kev pab uas tsis kam pab rau nws qhov uas nyias ua nyias tau raw li lub caij nyug

norepinephrine | Tsis ua Kua faj siv tso tawm los ntawm lub (adrenal glands) ua rau lub plawv dhia ceev ceev thiab cov ntshav siab thiab lub cev npaj rau qhov yuav tau ua hauj lwm nqav

notochord | Nos tos khoj Yog tus pas ntev ntev los txheem uas yog khiav thoob plawv lub cev mus txog kiag rau ntawm tus (nerve cord)

nucleic acid | nus khlis av-xij Qhov (macromolecules) uas muaj (hydrogen, oxygen, nitrogen, carbon, thiab phosphorus)

nucleotide | nus-khlia-thaj Yog qhov uas cov (nucleic acids) ua tawm los; nws muaj li 5-carbon sugar, ib tug phosphate, thiab ib co nitrogenous nyob ua kev hauv

nucleus | nuskhlia Yog lub plawv rau tus (atom), uas muaj (protons) thiab (neutrons) ; nyob rau hauv lub (cells), lub khauj khaum uas muaj lub (cell) nrog rau nws cov (genetic material) nyob hauv DNA

nutrient | khoom noj Yam khes-mis uas yam tsiaj yuav tsum muaj mas thiaj ciaj sia

nymph | nev Tus tsiaj ua tsis tau qoo tabsis nws twb zoo li niam thiab txiv lawm, tabsis mas nws tsis muaj qhov khoom ua menyuam uas ua hauj lwm

O

observation | Zov saib Qhov ua nco tau thiab qhia tau cov xwm txheej tseg, qhia tau muaj hnub nyug zias

omnivore | Oos-nis-vaus Yam tsiaj uas muaj zog los ntawm qhov nws noj ob yam xws li yog nroj tsuag thiab tsiaj txhu tib si

open circulatory system | system/qhov qhib Yog qhov chaw xa roj ntsha uas yeej muaj nyob hauv cov leeg ntshav es xa ntshav mus thoob ib ce

operant conditioning | kev siv Qhov kev kawm uas tus tsiaj kawm los ua tej li ua nws pheej rov ua tau vim yog nws xyaum los, ua tau zoo ces tau khoom noj los yog xam tsis pub raug ntau

operator | Tus siv a short DNA region, adjacent to the promoter of a prokaryotic operon, that binds repressor proteins responsible for controlling the rate of transcription of the operon

operon | siv tau Nyob hauv (prokaryotes), muaj ib pab (genes) nyob ntawm ib cag mas koom kev ua hauj lwm nrog nws thiab txawb nws thiab sau tau nws li mRNA

opposable thumb | tus ntiv xoo Tus ntiv tes xoo uas yog pab tuav tau khoom thiab siv tau khoom

order | xaj Yogib qho kev cais ua pab ua plawg, ib pab uas nws yeej zoo li yogib tsev lawm

organ | khiab nais Ib co nqaij uas ua hauj lwm ua kev los koom ua ib txoj hauj lwm zoo ib yam

organ system | plab nyuv Yogib co plab plawv ua koom ua hauj lwm ua ke los ua ib txoj hauj lwm nkaus xwb

organelle | khoom hauv plab Lub khauj khaum tshwj xeeb uas yog qhov tseem ceeb nyob rau hauv lub (eukaryotic cell)

osmosis | Os-xis-mauv-xiv Kev lim dej mus siv rau hauv lub lub plawv sab hauv

osmotic pressure | os-xis-maus-tiv Qhov uas yuav tsum siv xwb mas thiaj li yuav thaiv tau kom txhob txav dhau ntawm daim thaiv sab hauv lub cev

ossification | Os-xis-fis-khev-sees Yog qhov uas pob txha txawj hlav los ntawm cov pob txha mos los ua cov pob txha tawv

osteoblast | Os-xis-tia-blav Cov (bone cell) uas tso cov khoom tawm mus hloov cov pob txha mos kom nws dhau mus ua pob txha

osteoclast | Os-xis-tias-khev Lub (bone cell) uas zom cov khoom nyob hauv cov pob txha

osteocyte | os-xis-tiass-xaij Lub (bone cell) uas pab khaw cov khoom siv los yug tus pob txha thiab yug rau kom cov pob txha loj tuaj ces ho khov

ovary | lub zaus qe Nyob rau tej nroj tsuag, lub khauj khaum qhwv sab nraum thiab thaiv cov noob ; nyob rau tej tsiaj txhu, tus poj niam qhov chaw ua menyuam; yog ua qes

oviparous | osvispasliav Yam tsiaj uas lub (embryos) loj nyob rau lub qes thaum nws tawm ntawm tus niam lub cev los lawm

ovoviparous | Osvauvpaslu Yam tsiaj uas lub (embryos) loj nyob rau hauv tus niam lub cev, tabsis mas nws tsuas yog noj tib lub nkaub qes hauv rau qe nkaus xwb

ovulation | Tso zaus qe tawm Qhov uas tso cov qes ua yeej qoo lawm ntawm hauv lub (ovary) mus raw txoj (Fallopian tubes)

ovule | zaus qe Lub plaub rau cov ntsiav ua muaj lub noob nyob hauv uas yog loj nyob hauv poj niam qhov (gametophytes)

ozone layer | huab aus-zoo Yog txheej huab cua uas nws muaj cov cua (ozone gas) nyob ntau rau ntawm; nws txoj hauj lwm yog tiv thaiv yam ciaj sia nyob hauv lub Ntiaj teb kom tsis txhob rau cov (ultraviolet rays) los ntawm lub hnub heev

P

pacemaker | Lub phej mev kawm Ib pawg leeg me me nyob rau hauv lub plawv uas yog ua kom lub plawv dhia tsis paub xaus uas yog ua rau nws muaj qhov rub thiab nqus; qhov nyob yog "sinoatrial (SA) node"

paleontologist | Tus kawm txog pob txha Cov neeg kawm txog tej pob txha qub qub los lawm

palisade mesophyll | Paslisxav Mevxuasfais Ib txheej hauv lub (cells) nyob rau txheej hauv qab ntawm daim tawv hauv qab nplooj

parasitism | Cov cab haub plab Nws qhov ua ib tug tsiaj ua neej nyob rau hauv lwm tus tsiaj uas tseem ciaj ciaj lub cev los yog lwm yam tsiaj thiab ua tau rau nws tuag taus

parathyroid hormone (PTH) | kua faj siv hauv lub qog caj dab Yam kua faj siv ua tsim los ntawm lub (parathyroid gland) uas rau kom muaj cov (calcium) nyob rau haov cov ntshav

parenchyma | xov xes pasleeschimas Thawj daim tawv nyob rau tej ntoo nyob ntawm npoo av uas muaj cov (cell walls) thiab yog qhov loj rau (central vacuoles)

passive immunity | Phavxij eesmusnitis Yog ib qhov kev tiv thaiv ua tsim los siv raw li nws muaj xwb los yog thaum uas raug tau kab mob rau nws lawm

pathogen | kab mob Tus kab mob-txawj sib kis

pedigree | Daim ntawv Daim ntawv uas qhia txog tam sim no los yog tsis pom hais tias muaj kev sib ze qhov twg los rau tsev ntawm los tau ntau tiam lawm

pepsin | lub phejxee Lub (enzyme) uas zom cov (proteins) kom nws me me mus ua (polypeptide fragments)

period | caij nyug Kev faib raw caij nyug uas muaj lub caij lawv sib faib los lawm

peripheral nervous system | labnpom pawslifelau Cov leeg li kev sib chab sib chaw thiab txhawb cov (cells) ua xa moo mus thiab tawm hauv lub (central nervous system)

peristalsis | Pawslisxabtasxis Nws yog qhov uas muaj cov leeg nplua nplua ntau uas ua rau tej zaub mov txav tawm sai mus raw txoj hlab pas mus rau hauv lub plab

permafrost | Tawv nqaij Nws yogib tawv nqaij ua nkoog lawm es nriav pom nyob hauv (tundra)

petiole | tus ko Tus ko nyias nyias uas txuas daim nplooj rau tus kav ntoo

pH scale | kev ntsuas Yogib qhov kev ntsuas yam ua kua pib ntawm 0 txog 14, siv los ntsua saib tus H^+ ions muaj ntau npaum licas nyob hauv cov kua; tus pH uas yog li 0 txog 7 yog (acidic), tus pH uas yog li 7 yog nruab nrab (neutral), thiab tus pH txij li 7 txog 14 yog (basic)

pharyngeal pouch | lub pob qa Yogob lub khauj khaum khub nyob rau hauv lub pob qa

pharynx | Lub raj cua Lub raj cua nyob rau ntawm lub qhov ncauj sab nraum ub uas cua thiab zaub mov puav leej mus tau, nws hu ua qa (throat)

phenotype | Yam ntxwv Nws yog tus yam ntxwv rau ib yam tsiaj

phloem | Fis loos Nws yogi b txoj leeg nqaij ua yog chaw xa (nutrients) thiab (carbohydrates) uas tsim los ntawm (photosynthesis) nyob rau hauv tej nroj tsuag

photic zone | tus daub hnub Tus duab hnub nyob ze ntawm nplaim dej

photoperiod | Duab tshaj ntuj Tej nroj tsuag li kev tiv thaiv qhov uas tsis muaj duab tshaj ntuj thiab qhov tsaus ntuj nti

photosynthesis | kev zom faustausseesthexiv Qhov li hais yog siv los ntawm tej nroj tsuag thiab lwm yam (autotrophs) uas yog siv cov duab tshaj ntuj los ua zog thiab siv nws cov zog los ua khes-mis muab tig mus ua (carbon dioxide) thiab muab dej tig mus ua (oxygen) thiab qhov muaj zog-tshaj ntawm (carbohydrates) xws li cov pem thaj thiab kua pem thaj

photosystem | lab npom duab Ib pawg (chlorophyll) thiab (proteins) nriav pom nyob rau (thylakoids)

phototropism | Faustausrhaupibxee Yog qhov uas nroj tsuag no pheej loj hlob mus rau qhov ua muaj duab tshaj ntuj

phylogeny | faislaus ntsibnis Kev kawm txog noob neej li kev hloov nrog rau qhov lawv sib ze

phylum | faisloos Nyob hauv qhov kev cais pab cais pawg, nws yogib pab tsiaj uas siv ze heev

phytoplankton | fais-taus-plheejtoos Cov no yog cov ntxuab uas muaj nyob rau ntawm tej ntug hiav txwv

pigment | xim nqaij nqus-duab tshaj ntuj li (molecules) mus siv rau tej nroj tsuag ua lub zog

pioneer species | thawj yam Yog thawm pab tsiaj ua los nyob rau thaj chaw ntawm tau ntev los lawm

pistil | tus ko Ib tug (carpel) los yog ntau tus (carpels); nws muaj lub qe (ovary, style, thiab stigma)

pith | lub suab Lub (parenchyma cells) nyob rau hauv cov leeg sab hauv txuas rau (dicot stems)

pituitary gland | lub qog phibtusaislis Nws yogi b lub qog me me nriam pom nyob ze ntawm cov pob txha tob hau uas nyem kua faj siv tawm mus ua hauj lwm rau lub cev thiab nws tseem khoom ntau yam ntawm lub qog (endocrine glands)

placenta | txoj hlab ntaw Yogib yam khoom ua tshwj xeeb nyob rau tsiaj uas muaj txoj hlab ntaw rau lawv qhov ua pa, nutrients, thiab khib nyiab ntawm tus menyuam thiab uas rau tus menyuam loj hlob taus

plankton | Pheej toos Yogib yam tsiaj me me uas nyob rau tej qhov chaw muaj dej ; xws li 2 yam (phytoplankton thiab zooplankton)

plasma | ntshav Muaj xim-nqus dej nyob hauv law cov ntshav

plasmid | kua ntshav Tus hmob me me, nws kheej kheej nyob hauv DNA nriav pom nyob rau (cytoplasm) hauv cov kab mob (bacteria)

plasmodium | Cov ntshav Tej nriav noj nyob ze li ntawm cov (plasmodial)

plate tectonics | txha av Kev hloov nyob hauv tus txha av, xws li muaj av txav, roob tawg, thiab av qeeg, uas kev hloov los ntawm daim av

platelet | hlwb txha Lub (cell fragment) tso tawm hauv tus hlwb txha los pab rau cov ntshav

pluripotent | lub xes Lub (cells) muaj peev xwm mus ua txhua yam, tabsis nws ho ua tsis tau tas nro txhua yam (cell) nyob hauv lub cev

point mutation | tus gene txia Tus (gene) txia uas yogib khub nyob rau hauv DNA hloov lawm xwb

pollen grain | cov ntsiav phaus loos Lub plaub khauj khaum uas qhwv tas nro tus txiv cov (gametophyte) ua noob nyob rau tsob ntoo

pollen tube | /lub raj phaus loos Lub plaub khauj khaum ua ntim 2 tug (haploid sperm nuclei)

pollination | kev sib tov Qhov kev sib tov ua menyuam uas yog tus txiv cov noob nyob hauv lub plaub khauj khaum mus tov nrog rau tus niam li

pollutant | sib tov tas Yog cov khoom phem ua rau muaj mob mus nkag rau hauv tej huav cua tas ces ho los poob rau hauv av, saum cua, los yog hauv dej

polygenic trait | phauslisntesniv rhej Yog qhov ua khoo tau 2 los ntau tshaj ntawd tus (genes)

polymer | phaus lis mawm Lub (molecules) uas muaj ntau yam nyob hauv, nws mus ua tau lub (macromolecules)

polymerase chain reaction (PCR) | txoj saw phauslimaws Qhov no yog cov neeg kawm txog txoj sia kawm tau los siv cais tus (gene) zoo coj us siv ua lwm yam

polypeptide | Phauslispevthais Yog ib kab ntev ntev ntawm cov (amino acids) uas yog ua (proteins)

polyploidy | Phauslisplojdi Yog thaum uas ib yam tsiaj ntawm cia li muaj tshaj ib khub (chromosomes) lawm

population | pej xeem Nws yog ib pab neeg zoo ib yam nyob ib qho chaw twg

population density | pej xeem coob Nws yog tus lej rau ib tug neeg nyob rau ib qhov av twg

predation | noj nqaij Nws yog kev nyob ua ke los ntawm ib pab tsiaj uas mua (tus tsiaj noj nqaij) txhom thiab noj lwm yam tsiaj (tus tsiaj rau noj)

prehensile tail | tus ko tw Tus ko tw ua ntev coj los kauv tau ua ib pob tseg

pressure-flow hypothesis | lub yam ntxwv ntws Yogib qhov (hypothesis) coj los qhia rau qhov kev nriam kawm uas cov (phloem sap) rau xa mus thoob plaw tus ntoo los ntawm cov pem thaj "qhov ua muaj" cov pem thaj "tog tseg"

primary growth | kev hlob xub thawj Yog qhov kev loj hlob uas yog tawm saum lub ntis mus thiab tuaj tus kaus tas mam hlob mus lawm

primary producer | kev xub uas tus ua Thawj qhov chaw uas ua cov zog-siab tshaj nyob hauv cia rau tus tsiaj tau siv tom qab

primary succession | xub txhwm Kev ploj tuag uas yog muaj nyob rau ib thaj chaw ua rau ploj tag nrog tsis ib yam los ua poov rau niaj hnub no

principle of dominance | qhov uas yeej Yog Mendel qhov kev xaus, uas nws hais tias muaj ib co plaub (alleles) yeej tas txhua yam thiab muaj lwm yam mas tsis twv li

prion | Plis-oos Yog yam (protein) uas txawj ua mob tawm tuaj

probability | muaj ntsi khws Yog qhov twv hais ntshai yuav muaj yam ub yam no tawm tuaj

product | khoom tsim Tej yam khoom los yog tej cov kua dab tsi uas yog ua tau khes-mis sib tov tawm los

prokaryote | plauskasliyautiv Yog tus tsiaj uas muaj ib lub (cell) ces tsis muaj lub (nucleus)

promoter | tus txhawb Ib qhov chaw nyob tus (gene) uas muaj RNA polymerase thaiv thiab pib hloov mus

prophage | Plausfej Nws yog qhov nyob DNA uas ua rau cov kab mob txav tau los rau hauv DNA tau

prophase | phaufe Yog thawj theem nyob hauv qhov (mitosis) uas cov khoom nyob hauv lub (nucleus condenses) thiab lub (chromosomes) txwm tuaj rau pom

prostaglandin | lub phlaustaslasdis Yam no yog roj uas yog ua los ntau ntau ntawm cov (cells); ntau zaus mas nws tsuas raug rau cov (cells) thiab nqaij uas nyob ze ntawm xwb

protein | phlaus-tees Lub (macromolecule) no muaj cov (carbon, hydrogen, oxygen, thiab nitrogen); uas yuav tsum muaj nyob hauv lub cev mas thiaj loj thiab kho tau nyob hauv

protostome | Phlaustuastoom Tus tsiaj uas nws lub qhov ncauj ua lub (blastopore)

pseudocoelom | Xubdauskhausloom Qhov khoob hauv lub nrog cev, uas yog muaj ib nrab yog cov tawv nruab nrab

pseudopod | Xubdausphoj Yogib qho ua luv luv cia xwb (cytoplasmic projection) siv tau rau qhov uas nws txav tau

puberty | tiv me nyuam hluas Thaum tseem yuav loj hlob ntxiv thiab thaum uas yuav pib txawj sib deev vim yog lub cev ntawm muaj cov uas yuav ua menyuam tiav zuj zus lawm

pulmonary circulation | txoj leej ntsav Txoj leej los uas xa ntshav ntawm lub plawv mus rau hauv lub ntsw rov los

punctuated equilibrium | noob lilijxwm Yogib qho nyob hauv noob li lij xwm uas yog muaj tej yam los cuam tshuam lawm ces thiaj ua rau muaj kev hloov lawm xwb

Punnett square | Phusnes eeskuam Yog qhov (diagram) uas siv los twv txog cov (genotype) thiab cov (phenotype) ua kev nyob rau qhov (genetic) sib tov

pupa | puspas Yog theem uas cov pauj paim (metamorphosis) tiav kiag lawm yog ua tusk as mus txog rau thaum nws mus ua tus laus kiag

pupil | lub qhov hauv qhov muag Lub qhov hauv lub qhov muag uas yog tus zej zeeg muag tso duab tshaj ntuj mus rau hauv lub qhov muag

R

radial symmetry | qhov nraub nrab Qhov nraub nrab ntawm qhov phiam uas yog draj los kom muaj qhov nraub nrab yog hais tias muab faib mas tau ob qhov daim lo jib yam

radiometric dating | ntsuas lub caij nyug Yog qhov uas tsim los ntsuas lub hnub nyug ntawm yam khoom ua nriav tau uas muaj cov (radioactive isotope) los ntsuas coj uas tsis muaj xws li (nonradioactive isotope) los ntawm qhov khoom ntawm

reabsorption | yam txawj yaj Yog qho uas cia dej thiab yam uas txawj yaj nyob rau hauv cov ntshav

reactant | Lim tawm Yog yam khoom uas nws sib tov nrog rau cov khes-mis ua tau lwm yam tawm los

receptor | txais Nyob rau sab nraum los yog sab hauv lub (cell), muaj yam (protein) tshwj xeeb uas nws haum mus rau hauv lub (molecular messenger) uas tshwj xeeb, xws li yog (hormone)

recombinant DNA | cov DNA sib zwm DNA ua tau cov DNA ua ke los ntawm ntau yam khoom ua ke los

red blood cell | lub xes ntshav liab Cov (cell) hauv cov ntshav muaj (hemoglobin) ua xa cov (oxygen)

reflex | chua Chua ceev ceev, nws cia li chua nws xwb vim yog muaj tej yam kom nws chua lawm

reflex arc | qhov uas co Lub uas lav cov xov, xws li (sensory neuron, motor neuron, thiab affecter) uas cov uas ua kom muaj kev teb rov qab sais npaum li sai tau

relative dating | hnub sib ze Nws yogib yam kev tsim los ntsuas hnub nyug ntawm tej pob txha qub qub es muab piv rau lwm yam pob txh nyob ntawm tej pob zeb tib lub caij ntawm

relative frequency | qhov sib ze Tus lej uas cov plaub (allele) sim los nyob rau hauv cov (gene) yog muab los piv nrog rau lwm cov (alleles) ua ho muaj tus (gene) zoo ib yam li ntawm

releasing hormone | tso kua faj siv tawm Yam kua faj siv ua tsim cov (hypothalamus), uas yog cov cim sab hauv ntawm qhov uas nyem cov kua faj siv tawm los

renewable resource | yam hloov Yog yam uas ua tau tawm los los yog los hloov rau lub (ecosystem) uas tseem niaj hnub ua hauj lwm zoo

replication | Kev nthuas Qhov ua cov DNA rov qab luam nws tus kheej tawm los ua ntej cov (cell) sib faib

reproductive isolation | Kev cai tsim Tej uas tsiaj txhu txawj sib txawv los yog cov neeg uas sib txawv los sis ua rau kom lawv txhob sib deev ua tau me nyuam ua ke thiab nws ho muaj tawm li ob yam tsiaj tawm los

resource | Qhov qho Txhua yam uas tseem ceeb rau noob txoj sia, xws li dej, khoom yug txoj siab, duab tshav ntuj, zaub mov, los yog chaw nyob

response | Te rov Tej yam tshwj xeeb los ua rau kom hnov

resting potential | qhov chaw so Cov fais fab uas khiav ncig lub (cell membrane) nyob rau lub (neuron)

restriction enzyme | cov eeszais txwv Lub (enzyme) uas txiav DNA nyob qhov uas cov (nucleotides) sib txuas mus

retina | ntsiab muag Yog txheej sab hauv qab kawg rau lub qhov muag; nws muaj lub uas txais cov duab

retrovirus | Cov kab mov uas muaj RNA RNA yog cov kab uas muaj RNA yog nws li (genetic information)

ribonucleic acid (RNA) | Lub laisbausnuskhlia Avxev (RNA) Yogib lub uas nws muaj ib-kab nuskhlias avxev (nucleicAcid) nyob ua ke nrog rau cov pem thaj (sugar ribose)

ribosomal RNA (rRNA) | lais baus xaus maus Yog yam RNA uas nws muaj cov (proteins) nyob rau hauv lub (ribosomes)

ribosome | Laisbausxaus Lub (cell organelle) muaj cov RNA thiab cov (protein) uas nriav pom thoob plaw lub (cytoplasm) nyob hauv; nws yog qhov chaw luam cov (protein)

RNA interference (RNAi) | RNA txhuam Nws yog qhov tso tawm qhov two-qho kev xav txog RNA mus rau lub (cell) mus txog rau tus (gene) tib si

RNA polymerase | RNA phauslismawsiv Lub (enzyme) uas txuas ua tej kab kom loj mus txog rau cov RNA nucleotides nyob rau lub caij nws sau cov DNA ntawm los ua yam ntxwv tawm

rod | ya Qhov chaw txais tej duab nyob hauv lub qhov muag uas yog qhov pom duab tshaj ntuj ci, tabsis nws tsis pom xim li

root cap | ntsis cag Daim tawm ua qhwv tus cag ntoo pem qhov kawg kiag uas nws tiv thaiv cov (meristem)

root hair | cag plaub Cov cag ntoo me me uas nyob ze saum npoo av es txais dej thiab lwm yam khoom noj mus lub plawv ntoo

rumen | Txheej nyob huav lub plab Txheej nyob hauv lub plab nyuj thiab cov tsiaj uas ze nrog rau nyuj uas lawv siv cov kab (symbiotic bacteria) los zom lawv tej zaub

S

sapwood | kav ntoo Nyob rau tus kav ntoo, yog txheej thib ob uas qhwv lub plawv ntoo; uas yog qhov uas cov kua dej raug xa mus los

sarcomere | xaskhausmaw Ib qho leej ua txawj caw; nws muaj li 2 qho z-lines thiab cov filaments nyob kem lawv

scavenger | Tsiaj noj tsiaj tuag Yog yam tsiaj uas noj lwm yam tsiaj lub cev thaum lawv tuag lawm

science | kev kawm vithabnyaxaj Yog kev kawm vib thab nya xaj uas yog muaj kev nriav los ua ke thiab muab sij hawm los xav txog cov lav tham hauv lub ntiaj teb no

sclerenchyma | Xalileeschibmas Yog yam nqaij ua nws tuab thiab txhav heev nyob hauv lub (cell walls) es yog cov nqaij ua ruaj thiab khov heev

scrotum | plaub noob qes Nws yog lub hnav nyob sab nraum lub tsev sim

sebaceous gland | qog xesbaxisees Lub qog nyob hauv daim tawv nqaij uas tso cov roj "sebum" (ua kua roj tawm los)

secondary growth | kev hlob zaum ob Yog qhov kev loj hlob nyob rau ntoo uas tus kav txawj tuab thiab los tuaj

secondary succession | kev khom zoo zaum ob Nws kev ploj tuag zaum ob uas yog muaj los ntawm qhov uas muaj li ib nrab thiaj raug tuag xwb

seed | noob Yog lub noob txiv (embryo) thiab lub noob qoob loo uas muaj daim plaub vov nws zoo zoo

seed coat | phlaub noob Daim plaub nyob sab nraum thiab tiv thaiv tus ntoo lub (embryo) thiab pab khaw kom nws cov noob hauv qhuav qhuav

segregation | sib cais Qhov kev ntawm cov (alleles) nyob rau thaum lawv pib hloov los

selective breeding | xaiv ua menyuam Yog qhov kev tsim tsiaj txhu uas yog xaiv cov uas zoo cia thiab ua menyuam rau lwm tiam mus

selectively permeable | Kev xaiv tso Nws yogib qho nyob hauv kev kawm txog txoj sia uas yog cia rau tej yam dhau mus es muab ib co khuam cia; nws hu ua (semipermeable membrane)

semen | phev Cov phev uas muaj kab menyuam thiab nws muaj cov kua nrog

semicircular canal | Qhov xesmaisxawb-kuslaw Yog 3 lub plaub khauj khaum nyob rau hauv lub qhov ntsej uas yog saib xyuas txog qhov uas lub cev tiv thaiv lub zog (gravity)

seminiferous tubule | Raj xesmaisnisfesluv Nws ib lub ntawm ib puas tawm lub raj uas cov kab menyuam xeeb tawm los

sensory neuron | lub hnov Yog yam (nerve cell) uas tau txais cov lus cej luam los ntawm lub (sensory receptors) thiab hov xa cov lus ntawm mus rau hauv lub (central nervous system)

sex chromosome | khlausmausxoos Ib tug ntawm ob tug (chromosomes0 uas txiav txim saib tus neeg ntawm yuav yog poj niam los yog txiv neej

sex-linked gene | tus ntses txuas yog tus (gene) nyob hauv tus (chromosome) poj niam los yog txiv neej

sexual reproduction | kev ua niam txiv Yog qhov kev ua menyuam uas tus niam thiab tus txiv li (cells) los sib tov mas mam mus tau lub ib tus neeg tshiab lawm

sexually transmitted disease (STD) | kas cees Yog cov mob kas cee ua kis rau ib tug neeg dhau mus dual wm tus neeg vim yog kev sib deev xwb

sieve tube element | Khoom ua raj Yog lub raj sib txuas zws hauv tus ntoo lub (phloem cells), uas yog, nws yeej muaj hauv hauv paus mus txog lub ntsis

single-gene trait | tib tug ntses Tus yam ntxwv uas yog khoo los ntawm ib tug (gene) uas ho muaj 2 tug (alleles)

small intestine | nyuv me Cov nyuv mos uas yog cov khes-mis sib nqus mus ua zaub mov rau tus nroj tsuag

smog | pa taw Cov pa huab xim daj-li uas yog cov khes-mis sib ya saum tej

society | Xamkhum Ib pab tsiaj uas sib ze nyob rau ib pab ua hauj lwm ua ke kom zoo rau lawv tas pab

solute | lav Yog yam uas nws yaj hauv dej

solution | qhov yog Cov kua uas sib tov uas nws yog ntau yam ua ke sib tov sib npaug zos

solvent | sausveem Cov kua roj uas nws yaj ua kua lawm

somatic nervous system | cov xo los ntawm cov pob txha leeg Ib qho ntawm lub (peripheral nervous system) uas xa xov mus rau thiab coj xo los ntawm cov pob txha leeg los

speciation | tsiaj Qhov pib ntawm ib pab tsiaj tshiab tawm los

species diversity | muaj ntau yam tsiaj sib txawv Qhov uas muaj ntau yam tsiaj sib txawv nyob ua ke rau ib qhov chaw ua pab

spirillum (pl. spirilla) | nkaus Qhov nkaus ua voj vog los yog nkaus- zoo li lub haus hwj (prokaryote)

spongy mesophyll | Txheej plaub mos mos Txheej plaub mos mos nyob hauv daim qab nplooj (palisade mesophyll)

sporangium (pl. sporangia) | cipos es gees Lub qhov uas ua rau cov hmoov (haploid spores) tshwm los vim yog muaj qhov (meiosis)

spore | cipaus Nyob rau hauv (prokaryotes, protists, thiab fungi), nws muaj ib co tawv-tuab tuab ua voj vog uas nws muaj peev xwm ciaj taus nyob rau txhua yam huab cua ; nyob rau hauv nroj tsuag, yog lub (haploid reproductive cell)

sporophyte | ciphausfev Qhov chaw uas ua cov hmoov-ntoo; nyob hauv theem (multicellular diploid) hauv nroj tsuag lub neej

stabilizing selection | citinpaus liszees cilevsees Yog qhov kev noj nyob uas cov uas nyob rau hauv nruab nrab mas nws loj siab zoo dua cov uas nyob rau ob tog kawg tib si

stamen | citeesmees Qhov no yog paj ntoos tus qau; nws muaj zib thiab nws muaj (filament)

stem cell | citi xee Yog lub (cell) tshwj xeeb ua nws muaj tawm los ntawm that can give los yog 2 (cells) uas tshwj xeeb los

stigma | citimas Qhov no yog qhov uas npaum npaum; nws txoj hauj lwm tshwj xeeb yog ntes cov (pollen) xwb

stimulus (pl. stimuli) | kev xav xov Yog ib qho kev xav xov los ntawm tej tsiaj txhu

stoma (pl. stomata) | qhov me me Yog lub qhov me me ua tej nroj tsuag muaj es nws tso cai rau cov (carbon dioxide, dej, thiab oxygen) nkag mus thiab ntws tawm los ntawm daim nplooj

stomach | plab Lub plab uas yog ntim zaub mov thiab nws zom zaub mob

stroma | muaj kua Yog qhov uas muaj kua nyob hauv (chloroplast); nyob rau sab nraum lub (thylakoids)

substrate | sib tov Yogib qhov kev sib tov ntawm cov (enzyme-catalyzed)

suspension | res tseg tsis kam Qhov siv tov ntawm dej thiab lwm yam uas tsis kam yaj hauv dej

sustainable development | xad tees ed npaus Yogib qho kev sib cov qhov qho uas yus muaj yam tsis to leej twg li thiab ua rau tej neeg muaj kev tau zoo yam tsis rau lwm cov teeb meem rau lwm yam li

symbiosis | txheeb ze los ntawm 2 yam Kev txheeb ze los ntawm 2 yam tsiaj uas nyob sib ze

synapse | xa xov mus Yog qhov ntawm lub (neuron) xa xov mus qhia rau lwm lub (cell)

systematics | qhov kev kawm Yog qhov kev kawm ua teeb muaj paus xaus muaj ntsis nyob rau hauv noob neej nrog rau lawm li kev nyob ua ke nrog lwm yam

systemic circulation | qhov uas roj ntsha khiav hauv lub plawv mus Nws yog qhov uas roj ntsha khiav hauv lub plawv mus rau lub cev

T

taiga | tais gas Nws yog lub caij ntuj no no thiab ho muaj lub hli puav sov; nws yog ua los ntawm cov (coniferous evergreens); nws hu ua (boreal forest)

target cell | yog hom phiaj xes Lub (cell) ua txais cov kua faj siv los

taste bud | tsaj yoov Qhov uas ua rau paub hais tias nws yog qab los sis iab

taxon (pl. taxa) | tsiv tov Nws yogib pab lo yog ib txheej ntawm cov tsiaj ntxu ua muab los tso ua ke

telomere | tislo maws Nw yog qhov DNA nyob rau tog kawg ntawm lub (eukaryotic chromosome)

telophase | tislosfej Nws yogib theem ntaw (mitosis) ua yog sib faib cov (chromosomes) nyias mus nyias mus ua cov kaus (chromatin)

temporal isolation | teeb paus aus ais so lev sees Nws yogib qho kev ua menyuam txawv uas yog 2 los yog ntau tshaj ntawm yam tsiaj los ua ke nyob rau txawv sij hawm

tendon | teeb dees Nws yog cov leeg tawv tawv uas txuas pov txha rau nqaij mus rau pob txha

territory | chaw nyob thaiv Nws yogib qhov chaw nyob thiab thaiv los ntawm ib pab tsiaj twg tseg

testis (pl. testes) | tis tis Lub noob qes uas yog txiv neej li; nws ua cov kab menyuam

tetrad | tes rhej Lub plaub khauj khaum muaj 4 tus (chromatids) ua nyob rau thaum nws ua qhov (meiosis)

tetrapod | Noob neej Yam tsiaj 4 txais tes taw uas muaj txha nqaj qaum

thalamus | thaslas mas Qhov nyob hauv lub paj hlwv uas txais cov xov los ntawm tej plab plawv thiab xa cov xov ntawm mus rau qhov chaw uas tsim nyog kom xa mus ntxiv

theory | sim los Yogib uas yeej sim tau-zoo zoo los lawm uas qhia tau ntau yam uas saib no ces pom thiab sim los tau, thiab ua rau cov neeg kawm txog fab no twv tau raug kiag li qhov uas nws yuav tshwm sim los

thigmotropism | thismo rho ps zees Qhov kev txuas rau nroj tsuag uas yog tuav

threshold | lub qhov Qhov uas pib sawv tuaj mus es ua kom pib muaj qhov dhia

thylakoid | Thaislas kos Lub zoo li lub hnav (photosynthetic membranes) uas muaj nyob hauv lub (chloroplasts)

thyroxine | thais los xis Yog cov kua faj siv uas ua los ntawm lub qog caj dab (thyroid gland), uas yog pab rau qhov zom zaub mov kom ceev mus rau cov (cells) thoob plawv lub cev

tissue | txheej nqaij hauv qab tawv nqaij Yogib pab (cells) zoo ib yam tabsis nyias ua nyias ib txoj hauj lwm

tolerance | tolaws lees Yog qhov ua vim licas yam tsiaj ntawm thiaj ciaj thiab nws thiaj tseem muaj menyuam nyob rau thaj chaw uas txawv tshaj nws qhov lawm

totipotent | Totipau rhees Lub (cells) uas muaj peev xwv loj mus ua tau txhua yam (cell) uas muaj nyob hauv lub cev (xws li lub "cells" muaj nyob hauv (extraembryonic membranes thiab placenta)

trachea | rhe kis Txog hlab pas uas txuas ntaw lub pob qa mus hauv; nws hu ua (the windpipe)

tracheid | rhe khis Qhov no yog cov (cell) khoob khoob uas muaj nyob hauv (xylem) ua rau kom lub ntug tuab thiab khov

tracheophyte | leej leeg ntoo Yog cov leej leeg ntoo

trait | zoo kiag li Nws yog uas tus neeg ntawm zoo kiag licas

transcription | rhes krisees Qhov yog qhov cais tawm los ntawm lub (RNA molecule) hauv lub (DNA template) los

transfer RNA (tRNA) | hloov RNA Yog cov RNA uas nqa cov (amino acid) mus rau hauv lub (ribosome) nyob rau thaum lawv zom cov (protein)

transformation | hloov Yog qhov thaum uas ib yam kab mob (bacteria) cia li hloov nws tus (gene los yog cov genes) es mus ua dual wm yam kab mob (bacteria) lawm

transgenic | rhes gin nesdev Lo lus no siv los qhia hais tias yam tsiaj no mas muaj cov (genes) los ntawm lawm yam tsiaj los

translation | pes los yog tig Theem no yog theem ua tsis pom cov mRNA li lawm ces ntshai yog lawv muab tig mus ua cov (amino acids) hauv cov (protein) lawm

transpiration | ua dej lawm mus Qhov no yog qhov uas dej tawm hauv daim nplooj mus lawm

trochophore | rhoko- faws Tus kas uas nws-tau luam dej nyob rau hauv hav dej

trophic level | theem rhofis Yog ib theem ntawm zaub mov noj los yog kev nriav noj

tropism | rhopisze Kev txav ntawm tej nroj tsuag mua kom deb ntawm qhov ua chiv keeb

tumor | thubmawm Qhov kev sib faib ua ntau yam hauv cov (cells) uas yog ua rau puas tej yam nqaij nyob ze nws ntawm

U

understory | Txheej ntoo qis Txheej ntoo qis nyob hauv lub hav zoo loj uas roo tas lawm ces muaj cov ntoo qis thiab muaj hmab

ureter | Txoj nyuv tso zis Txoj nyuv tso zis los ntawm lub raum los tau hauv lub zais zis

urethra | Txoj nyuv zis Txoj nyuv zis ua tso zis tawm hauv lub cev mus

urinary bladder | zais zis Lub zais zis uas yog qhov chaw ntim zis tseg ua ntej tso tawm

V

vaccination | xav tshuaj zoo aw Kev txhaj tshuaj tuag aw los yog zoo li ntawm, tabsis nws ho tsis muaj teeb meem li cov kab mob uas tseem yuav los

vaccine | tshuaj xav zoo aw Cov tshuaj tuag aw uas yog tsim los tua cov kab mob sìv cov los tiv thaiv hauv lub cev ua ntej kab mob yuav tuaj

vacuole | vaskuas Lub (cell organelle) uas yog qhov chaw khaw cov dej, ntsev, (proteins), thiab (carbohydrates)

valve | leeg nqaij Nws yog qhov leeg nqaij nyob nraub nrab ntawm (atrium) thiab (ventricle), los yog cov leeg, cheem tsis pub kom cov zaub mov ntws rov qab

van der Waals forces | vad daws viad foj Yog cov duab ci uas tsim los qhov "+" & "-" nyob ze rau ntawm lub (molecules)

vas deferens | ves difaws yias Yog lub raj rau tus kab menyuam khiav los ntawm qhov (epididymis) mus rau ntwawm (urethra)

vascular bundle | ib pob vaskuslaws Yog ib pawg (xylem) thiab (phloem) nqaij yog nrog tus kav

vascular cambium | veskus- laws kausnpias Nws yog qhov uas ua cov leeg nqaij thiab ua rau kom tuab tuab zog tuaj nyob rau ntawm tus kav

vascular cylinder | veskuslaws tissus Qhov nraub nrab ntawm tus cag xam li cov leeg rau dej ntws--xylem thiab (phloem)

vascular tissue | veskuslaws tissus Qhov nqaij tshwj xeeb ntawm xyoob ntoo uas xa dej thiab xa (nutrients)

vector | vedtawm Yog tus tsiaj uas xa kab mob rau neeg

vegetative reproduction | vesgistestij liprodavsees Yog kev ua menyuam rau tej nroj tsuag uas tsis txawj sib ceev, uas yog tso cai rau ib tug nroj tsuag muaj taus menyuam uas yog zoo nkaus li nws niam

vein | leeg Txhoj leej ntshav uas xa ntshav mus rau lub cev rov los rau hauv lub plawv

ventricle | veb rhis kos Yog chav qis hauv lub plawv uas xa ntshav tawm mus rau lub cev nqaij

vertebrate | vaws tis npres Yam tsiaj uas muaj tus txha nqaj qaum

vessel element | vesso ilemees Yog yam (xylem cell) uas yog khoob li lub qhov raj rau dej ntws mus los

vestigial organs | vevstis gias os knees Lub plaub khauj khaum me thiab me me los yog tsis muaj hauj lwm tus dab tsi

villus (pl. villi) | vi las Nws yog cov zoo li ntiv tes nyob hauv cov nyuv mos uas yog nqus cov zaub mov li (nutrient molecules)

virus | Kab vais ras Yam ua tsim cov (proteins, nucleic acids, thiab lwm yam kua roj uas yog coj mus ua dua ntxiv tau yog rau tom cov (cells)

vitamin | tshuaj rhaub ntshav Cov tshuaj uas noj mus pab lub cev ua hauj lwm kom zoo

viviparous | vivi peb raus Yam tsiaj uas nws cia menyuam mos noj tus niam mis mus txog lub caij nws loj

W

weather | huab cua Tej huab cua ib hnub-dhau-hnub, xws li kev kub los sis txias, tsaus huab los nag, thiab lwm yam

wetland | hav iav Lub (ecosystem) hav iav uas muaj dej vov av los yog tas sim no los yog muaj dej nyob ze saum npoo av ib lub caij nyob rau ib xyoo twg

white blood cell | xev ntsav dawb Yog cov ntshav dawb uss tiv thaiv kab mob, hem cua nab, thiab noj cov (bacteria)

woody plant | ntoo tej tsob Ntoo ua yog muaj cov (cells) tuab tuab los thaiv daim tawv thiab txheem lub cev ntawv; xwv li ntoo, zaub nyuj, thiab hmab

X

xylem | Xais leem qhov nqaij uas xa dej nce mus thiab yam ua kua mus kom thoob lub nplawv ntoo

Z

zoonosis (pl. zoonoses) | zoo nos xes Yam kab mob uas hla tau ntawm tsiaj txhu mus rau neeg

zooplankton | zoo plhes thaus Yogib tus tsiaj uas nws-ntab hu ua (plankton)

zygote | zis nkaum yog thaum uas tus txiv cov kab mem nyuam thiab tus niam lub qe twb los siv tov tas lawm

Korean
한국어

Miller & Levine
Biology Glossary

A

abiotic factor | 비생물적 요소 생태계를
형성하는 물리적이거나 생명력이 없는 요소

abscisic acid | 아브시스산 세포 분열을
억제해서 생장을 시키는 식물 호르몬

acetylcholine | 아세틸콜린 근육 세포에서
자극을 유발시키는 신경 전달 물질

acid | 산 용액 내에서 수소 이온(H⁺)을 형성하는
화합물; pH가 7보다 낮은 용액

acid rain | 산성 비 질산과 황산을 함유하는 비

actin | 액틴 근육 내에 존재하는 가느다란
단백질 섬유 조직

action potential | 활동 전위 신경 단위 조직인
뉴런의 세포 막을 가로지르는 전하 역전
현상; 또는 신경 자극

activation energy | 활성화 에너지 어떤
반응이 일어나기 위해 필요한 에너지

active immunity | 능동 면역 자연적이거나 혹은
고의로 항원에 노출됨으로써 생기는 면역

adaptation | 적응 생명체가 어떤 환경에서
생존하고 번식하는 능력을 향상시키도록
하는 유전적 특성

adaptive radiation | 적응 방산 하나의 종 또는
하나의 종 집단이 여러 가지 다른 모습으로
살아갈 수 있도록 몇몇의 다른 형태로 진화해
가는 과정

**adenosine triphosphate (ATP) | 아데노신
3 인산(ATP)** 세포가 에너지를 저장하고
방출하는 데 쓰이는 화합물

adhesion | 부착 서로 다른 종류의 분자 사이에
작용하는 끌어당기는 힘

aerobic | 호기성의 산소를 필요로 하는 과정

age structure | 연령 구성 하나의 집단 안에서
나이가 같은 수컷과 암컷의 수

aggression | 공격성 어떤 동물이 다른 개체에
대해 우월성을 나타내기 위해 사용하는
위협적인 행동

algal bloom | 해조 개화 제한적 영양
물질의 대거 유입으로 인해 해조류나 다른
생산자들의 양이 증가되는 현상

allele | 대립 유전자 다양한 형태의 유전자
중 하나

allergy | 알레르기 어떤 항원에 대한 면역
체계의 과잉 반응

alternation of generations | 세대 교번 단수
(N)와 배수(2N)의 두 시기를 번갈아 가지는
생명 주기

alveolus (pl. alveoli) | 폐포 가스 교환이
일어나도록 표면적을 제공하는 폐의 세
기관지 끝에 위치하는 작은 공기 주머니(들)

amino acid | 아미노산 한쪽 끝에는 아미노기,
다른 한쪽에는 카르복실기를 가지는 화합물

amniotic egg | 양막이 있는 알 태아가 물
없이도 발육할 수 있도록 보호된 환경을
제공하는 껍데기와 막으로 이루어진 알

amylase | 아밀라제 전분 속에 들어있는 화학
결합을 깨뜨리는 침 속에 들어있는 효소

anaerobic | 혐기성의 산소를 필요로 하는 과정

anaphase | 핵분열 후기 염색체가 나누어져서 세포의 양쪽 끝으로 이동해가는 유사 분열 과정

angiosperm | 속씨 식물 씨를 보호하는 기관 내에 씨가 들어있는 종자 식물 군; 일명 화훼 식물

anther | 꽃밥 꽃가루를 생산하는 꽃의 기관

antheridium (pl. antheridia) | 장정기 (포자 생성기) 일부 포자를 생성하는 식물의 수술 생식 기관

anthropoid | 유인원 원숭이, 에이프, 인간으로 이루어진 영장류

antibiotic | 항생제 박테리아 병원균의 성장과 번식을 차단하는 약물군

antibody | 항체 직접 항원을 공격하거나 항원 결합 단백질을 생산하는 단백질

anticodon | 대응 코돈 mRNA코돈의 세 개의 염기에 상보적인 tRNA 분자에 들어 있는 세 개의 염기군

antigen | 항원 면역 반응을 일으키는 물질

aphotic zone | 무광층 바다에서 빛이 투과하는 투광층(photic zone)의 아래 부분으로 햇빛이 통과하지 않는 암흑 층

apical dominance | 정점 우성 꽃눈이 줄기의 끝에 가까이 있을수록 생장이 더욱 억제되는 현상

apical meristem | 정점 분열 분열되어 줄기와 뿌리의 길이가 커지게 하는 미분화 세포군

apoptosis | 자기사멸 계획된 세포 사멸 과정

appendage | 부속지 체벽으로부터 뻗어나간 다리나 안테나 같은 조직

appendicular skeleton | 충수 골격 어깨 부분에 이어지는 팔 뼈와 골반을 따라 이어지는 다리 뼈

aquaculture | 수산양식 인간이 소비하기 위해 수생 생물을 기르는 것

aquaporin | 아쿠아포린 세포 내에 있는 물이 통과하는 단백질

Archaea | 알카이아 단세포이고 펩티도글리칸이 들어있지 않은 세포벽을 가지는 원핵 생물로 이루어진 도메인; 고세균(Archeabacteria)에 해당

archegonium (pl. archegonia) | (이끼류의) 장란기 포자 세포를 생성하는 식물 기관

artery | 동맥 피를 심장으로부터 온몸 조직으로 보내는 커다란 혈관

artificial selection | 인위 선택 식물과 동물에서 원하는 형질의 자손이 생기도록 선택하여 교배

asexual reproduction | 무성 생식 하나의 모체에서 일어나 모체와 유전적으로 똑같은 자손이 생기게 되는 생식 과정

asthma | 천식 기도가 좁아지고, 쌔근거리고, 기침하고 숨쉬기가 어려운 만성 호흡기 질환

atherosclerosis | 동맥경화증 플라그라 불리는 지방 찌꺼기가 동맥 혈관 내에 쌓여서 결국은 동맥이 딱딱해지는 상태

atom | 원자 물질의 기본 단위

ATP synthase | ATP 신타제 세포벽을 일정 간격으로 벌려 수소 이온(H^+)을 통과시키는 일군의 단백질

atrium (pl. atria) | 심방 몸을 돈 피를 받는 심장의 위쪽 방

autonomic nervous system | 자율 신경계 불수의적이고 의식적인 통제가 되지 않는 몸의 활동을 조절하는 말초 신경계의 부분; 교감 신경계와 부교감 신경계로 되어 있음

autosome | 상(常) 염색체 성 염색체가 아닌 염색체; 상 염색체(autosomal chromosome)

autotroph | 자가 영양 생물 햇빛이나 화학 물질로부터 에너지를 포획할 수 있고, 무기 화합물로부터 자신의 식량을 생산하는 데 에너지를 사용하는 생물; 일명 생산자 (producer)

auxin | 옥신 세포 분열과 새로운 뿌리의 성장을 촉진하는 성장하는 식물의 말단에서 생성되는 조절 물질

axial skeleton | 중축 골격 신체에서 중심 축을 지지하는 골격; 두개골, 척추, 흉곽으로 이루어짐

axon | 축색 돌기 뉴런의 세포 체로부터의 자극을 전달하는 긴 섬유

B

bacillus (pl. bacilli) | 바실루스 막대 모양의 원핵 생물

background extinction | 배경 멸종 서서히 지속적으로 진행되는 자연 도태 과정으로 인한 멸종

Bacteria | 박테리아 단세포이고 펩티도글리칸이 들어있는 세포벽을 가지는 원핵 생물로 이루어진 도메인; 진정세균(eubacteria)에 해당

bacteriophage | 박테리오파아지 박테리아를 감염시키는 바이러스의 일종

bark | 나무 껍질 체관부, 형성층 그리고 코르크 피층을 포함하는 도관 형성층의 외부에서 발견되는 조직들

base | 염기 용액 내에서 수산화 이온(OH⁻)을 생성하는 화합물; pH가 7보다 높은 용액

base pairing | 염기쌍 배열 아데닌은 티민과 결합하고 구아닌은 시토신과 결합하는 DNA상에서의 염기 결합 법칙

behavior | 행동 생물이 내부 조건이나 외부 환경 변화에 반응하는 양식

behavioral isolation | 행동학적 격리 두 개의 집단이 서로 다른 구애 의식 또는 상호 교배를 방해하는 행동들을 발달시켜 생식적으로 상호 격리된 형태

benthos | 해저 저생 생물 호수, 시내 또는 바다의 바닥 또는 그 근처에 붙어서 살아가는 생물

bias | 선입견 과학적이라기보다는 개인적인 특별한 선호도 또는 관점

bilateral symmetry | 좌우 양측 대칭 하나의 가상 직선으로 몸을 좌우로 잘랐을 때 둘이 거울상으로 똑같은 몸체

binary fission | 이분열 생물이 자신의 DNA를 복제해서 반으로 나누어 두 개의 똑같은 딸 세포를 만드는 무성 생식의 형태

binocular vision | 쌍안 시력 깊은 지각 능력과 세상을 삼차원적으로 볼 수 있도록 두 개의 눈에서 보이는 상을 병합시키는 능력

binomial nomenclature | 이명법 각 종에 두 부분으로 이루어진 과학적 이름을 부여하는 분류 체계

biodiversity | 생물 다양성 생물권에 있는 모든 다양한 생명체를 의미하며 일명 생물학적 다양성

biogeochemical cycle | 생물지리화학적 주기 구성 요소, 화학적 화합물 그리고 다른 형태의 물질들이 하나의 생물에서 다른 생물로 그리고 하나의 생물권에서 다른 생물권으로 전달되는 과정

biogeography | 생물 지리학 과거 및 현재의 생물 분포에 대한 연구

bioinformatics | 생물 정보학 생물학적 데이터를 저장하고 불러오고 분석하는 데 수학과 컴퓨터 과학이 적용되는 학문

biological magnification | 생물학적 확대 먹이사슬 또는 먹이 그물에 있어 영양학적으로 고등 단계에 있는 생물의 유해 물질 농도가 증가하는 현상

biology | 생물학 생명에 관한 과학적 연구

biomass | 바이오메스 주어진 영양학적 기준에서 살아있는 조직의 총량

biome | 생물 군계 비슷한 기후와 전형적인 생물들을 공유하는 생태계의 한 집단

biosphere | 생물권 땅, 물, 공기 등의 주위 환경으로 이루어진 생명체가 살아가는 지구의 일부분

biotechnology | 생물 공학 생물, 세포 또는 분자가 특정 생산물을 생산할 수 있도록 조작하는 과정

biotic factor | 생물 요소 생물이 서로 상호 관계를 가지는 환경 중에서 생명력을 가지는 부분

bipedal | 두 발의 두 개의 발로 이동하는 것을 의미하는 용어

blade | 잎사귀 식물 잎의 얇고 평평한 부분

blastocyst | 배반포 속이 빈 공과 같은 상태의 세포로 이루어진 포유 동물의 초기 발생 단계

blastula | 포배 접합체가 일련의 세포 분열 단계를 거칠 때 발생되는 속이 빈 공과 같은 상태의 세포

bone marrow | 골수 뼈 강에서 발견되는 연한 조직

bottleneck effect | 병목 효과 대립 유전자 도수가 변화함에 따라 수반되는 개체군 크기의 현저한 감소 현상

Bowman's capsule | 보우만 주머니 사구체를 둘러싸는 컵을 닮은 구조; 혈액으로부터 여과된 액을 모음

brain stem | 뇌간 뇌와 척수를 연결하는 구조; 연수(medulla oblongata)와 뇌교(pons)를 포함함

bronchus (pl. bronchi) | 기관지 기관에서 폐까지에 이르는 흉강 내 두 개의 커다란 관 중 하나

bryophyte | 선태류 식물 분화된 생식 기관을 가지지만 도관 조직은 없는 식물군; 이끼류에 해당됨

bud | 꽃눈, 꽃봉우리 새로운 줄기와 잎을 생산하는 정점 분열 조직인 식물 조직

buffer | 완충제 가파르고 갑작스러운 pH의 변화를 방지하는 화합물

C

calcitonin | 칼시토닌 갑상선에서 분비되고 혈중 칼슘 수치를 감소시키는 호르몬

Calorie | 열량 음식물 내의 열에너지 측정치; 1000 칼로리(calories)에 해당됨

calorie | 칼로리 1g의 물을 1oC 올리는 데 필요한 에너지의 양

Calvin cycle | 칼빈 회로 광합성 과정 중 빛과 무관한 반응으로서 ATP와 NADPH 로부터 나오는 에너지가 당과 같은 고에너지 화합물을 생산하는 데 사용됨

cancer | 암 신체 세포의 일부가 성장을 조절하는 기능을 상실한 장애 상태

canopy | 천개 키가 큰 우림 지역 나무들의 위쪽 잎사귀들에 의해 덮여진 현상

capillary | 모세 혈관 가장 작은 혈관들; 영양소와 산소를 조직으로 운반해주고 이산화탄소와 노폐물을 흡수함

capillary action | 모세 혈관 작용 가는 관에서 물이 올라가는 현상

capsid | 캡시드 바이러스 주위를 둘러싸는 단백질

carbohydrate | 탄수화물 탄소, 수소 그리고 산소 원자로 이루어진 화합물; 몸에서 주 에너지원이 되는 영양소

carnivore | 육식 동물 다른 생물을 잡아 먹어서 에너지를 얻는 생물

carpel | 암술 잎 암술 배우체를 생산하고 보호하는 꽃의 가장 내부의 일부분

carrying capacity | (환경) 수용력 특정 환경에 수용이 가능한 특정 종의 최대한의 개체 수

cartilage | 연골 조직 몸을 지지하면서도 뼈보다는 연하고 유동적인 결합 조직의 한 형태

Casparian strip | 카스파리아 스트립 식물의 내배엽 세포를 둘러싸고 있고 물질을 식물 뿌리에 있는 관 다발 조직 한 쪽 방향으로만 통과시키는 방수 조직

catalyst | 촉매 화학 반응의 속도를 증가시키는 물질

cell | 세포 생명이 있는 모든 형태의 기본 단위

cell body | 세포체 핵과 많은 양의 세포질을 포함하는 전형적인 뉴런의 가장 큰 부분

cell cycle | 세포 주기 세포가 성장하고 분열을 준비하고 나누어져서 두 개의 딸 세포가 생기는 일련의 과정

cell division | 세포 분열 세포가 두 개의 새로운 딸 세포로 나뉘는 과정

cell membrane | 세포막 세포를 둘러싸는 얇으면서 유동성을 가지는 장벽; 세포에 들어가는 물질과 세포에서 빠져나올 물질을 조절함

cell theory | 세포설 세포는 살아있는 생명체의 구조와 기능을 가지는 기본 단위이고 기존의 세포들로부터 새로운 세포들이 생성된다고 하는 세포를 이루는 모든 생명체에 관한 생물학의 기본적인 개념

cell wall | 세포벽 일부 세포의 세포막 주위를 둘러싸는 강한 지지층

cell-mediated immunity | 세포 매개된 면역 살아있는 세포 내에서 바이러스, 곰팡이 그리고 비정상적인 암 세포 등에 대항해서 몸을 방어하는 면역 반응

cellular respiration | 세포 호흡 산소 존재 하에서 포도당과 다른 영양분자들을 분해시킴으로써 에너지를 방출하는 과정

central nervous system | 중추 신경계 뇌와 척수를 포함하면서 정보를 처리하고 몸으로 전달할 반응을 생성함

centriole | 중심체 세포 분열을 조직화하도록 도와주는 동물 세포 내 조직

centromere | 동원체, 중심립 두 개의 딸 염색 분체가 서로 붙어 있는 염색체의 일정 구역

cephalization | 두화 동물의 앞쪽 뇌(전두) 끝에 위치한 감각 기관과 신경 세포의 농도

cerebellum | 소뇌 몸의 움직임을 통합하고 균형 감각을 조절하는 뇌의 일부분

cerebral cortex | 대뇌 피질 포유 동물의 뇌에서 대뇌의 바깥 층으로 사고와 다른 복잡한 행동에 대한 중추

cerebrum | 대뇌 몸의 자발적인 활동을 담당하는 뇌의 일 부분으로서 뇌의 "사고" 영역에 해당됨

chemical digestion | 화학적 소화 효소들이 음식물을 몸이 사용할 수 있도록 작은 분자 상태로 분해하는 과정

chemical reaction | 화학 반응 임의의 화학 물질군이 다른 군의 화학 물질로 변화 또는 전환하는 과정

chemosynthesis | 화학 합성 탄수화물을 생산하는 데 화학 에너지가 사용되는 과정

chitin | 키틴 진균류의 세포벽을 이루는 복잡한 탄수화물의 일종으로 절지 동물과 바깥 골격에서 발견됨

chlorophyll | 엽록소 식물 또는 다른 광합성을 하는 생물에 존재하는 주요 색소

chloroplast | 엽록체 태양광으로부터 에너지를 얻어 화학 에너지로 바꾸는 기능을 하는 식물이나 다른 생물들의 세포에서 발견되는 세포 기관

chordate | 척색 동물 일생 동안 적어도 한 시기 동안은 등쪽에 속이 빈 신경 조직인 척색, 항문에서 뻗은 꼬리 그리고 인두 주머니를 가지는 기간을 가지는 동물

chromatid | 염색 분체 복제된 염색체에서 두 개의 똑같은 "형제" 염색체 중 하나

chromatin | 크로마틴 진핵 생물에서 발견되는 것으로 DNA가 히스톤의 주위를 단단하게 꼬아 감고 있는 형태의 물질

chromosome | 염색체 한 세대에서 다음 세대로 전달할 유전 정보를 담고 있는 세포 핵 내에 존재하는 실같이 가늘고 긴 조직

chyme | 유미즙 효소와 일부 소화된 음식의 혼합물

cilium (pl. cilia) | 섬모 운동 기능을 담당하는 짧은 털 같이 돌출된 모양의 것

circadian rhythm | 24시간 주기 리듬 매일 일어나는 행동의 주기

clade | 진화 파생도의 가지 한 조상과 그의 모든 자손을 나타내는 진화 파생도에서 한 개의 가지

cladogram | 진화 파생도 종 간에 발견되는 공통 특성의 패턴을 묘사하는 도표

class | (공통적 특징을 가지는) 종류 분류학상 가깝게 관련되는 집단군

classical conditioning | 고전적 조건 부여 어떤 동물이 자극과 그에 대한 보상 또는 체벌 간의 관계를 머리로 인지할 때 나타나는 학습의 형태

climate | 기후 오랜 시간대에 걸쳐 특정 지역에 매년 나타나는 온도와 강수량의 평균치

clone | 클론 하나의 세포로부터 생성된 유전적으로 동일한 세포 집단

closed circulatory system | 폐쇄 순환계 혈액이 몸 전체에 걸쳐 뻗어있는 혈관들을 통해 몸 전체를 돌아다니는 순환계 형태

coccus (pl. cocci) | 구균 구형의 원핵 생물

cochlea | 달팽이관 내이에 소리를 감지하는
신경 세포가 들어있고 액체가 차있는 부분

codominance | 공동 우성 두 대립 유전자에
의해 생기는 표현형들이 완전히 발현된 상태

codon | 코돈 단백질에 들어갈 특정
아미노산으로 바뀌게 되는 mRNA에 들어
있는 세 개의 뉴클레오타이드 염기들의 집단

coelom | 체강 중배엽과 함께 있는 몸의 구멍

coevolution | 공진화 두 개의 종이 시간에 걸쳐
각각 다른 변화에 대해 반응하여 진화하는
과정

cohesion | 결합력 같은 물질 내에서 분자들
사이에 작용하는 인력

collenchyma | 후각 조직 식물에서 자라는
식물을 지지하고 강하고 유연성이 있는 세포
벽을 가지는 기저 조직의 한 형태

commensalism | 공생 한 쪽은 이익을 보지만
다른 한 쪽은 이익 또는 해를 받지 않으면서
살아가는 공생 관계

communication | 상호 정보 전달 하나의
생물에서 다른 생물로의 정보 전달

community | 공동 사회 일정 지역 내에서 함께
살아가는 다른 개체군들의 집합체

companion cell | 반세포 식물에서 체 모양으로
된 도관 구성 요소를 둘러싸고 있는 체관부
세포

competitive exclusion principle | 경쟁적
배제의 법칙 두 개의 종이 동시대에 동일한
서식지에서 동일한 생태적 지위를 가질 수는
없다는 이론

compound | 화합물 두 개 혹은 그 이상의
성분들이 특정 비율로 화학 결합을 하여
생성되는 물질

cone | 추상체 눈에서 다른 색깔의 빛에 대해
반응함으로써 색깔을 구별할 수 있도록 하는
광 수용체

coniferous | 침엽수 씨앗이 든 열매를 맺고
바늘과 같은 모양의 가느다란 잎을 가지는
나무들을 총칭하는 용어

conjugation | 접합 짚신벌레나 다른 원핵생물들이
유전 정보를 교환하는 과정

connective tissue | 결합 조직 몸을 지탱하고
각 부분을 연결하는 기능을 하는 조직의 형태

consumer | 소비자 에너지와 영양분의 제공을
다른 생물에 의존하는 생물로서 일명 종속
영양 생물

control group | 대조군 한 개의 독립 변수를
제외하고 나머지는 실험군과 동일한 조건에
노출시키는 실험군

controlled experiment | 통제된 실험 오직
한 개의 변수만을 변화시키는 실험

convergent evolution | 수렴 진화 서로
독립적이고 관련성이 없는 생물들이 비슷한
환경에 적응해가면서 유사한 성질을
나타내며 진화해가는 과정

cork cambium | 코르크 형성층 식물의 2차
성장 기간 동안 줄기 바깥 부분을 감싸는
분열 조직

cornea | (눈의) 각막 빛이 들어가는 눈의
질기고 투명한 층

corpus luteum | 황체 배란이 일어난 후의
난포를 일컬으며 노란색을 띰

cortex | 피질 식물에서 물과 무기질이 이동하는
뿌리 속의 기저 조직 부분

corticosteroid | 코르티코스테로이드 부신
피질에서 분비되는 스테로이드 호르몬

cotyledon | 떡잎 종자 식물의 배아에서
자라나오는 한 개 또는 두 개의 최초의 잎

courtship | 구애 동물이 반대 성을 가진 동물을
유인하기 위해 보내는 자극적인 행동 형태

covalent bond | 공유 결합 원자 사이에 전자를
서로 공유하는 결합 형태

crossing-over | (염색체의) 교차 상동 염색체가
감수 분열을 하는 동안에 염색 분체의 일부를
서로 교환하는 과정

cyclin | 사이클린 진핵 생물에서 세포 주기를
조절하는 단백질 군의 하나

cytokinesis | 세포질 분열 세포질이 분열하여
두 개의 분리된 딸 세포를 형성하는 것

cytokinin | 사이토키닌 뿌리가 생장하고 열매와
씨를 맺는 동안 분비되는 식물 호르몬

cytoplasm | 세포질 세포에서 핵 바깥의 액체 부분

cytoskeleton | 세포 골격 진핵 세포에서 세포의 형태와 내부 조직을 유지하고 운동과 관련이 있는 단백질 섬유의 망상 조직

D

data | 데이터 증거; 관찰을 통해 수집된 정보

deciduous | 낙엽성의 일 년 중 특정 계절 동안 잎들이 떨어지는 나무 종류를 일컫는 용어

decomposer | 분해자 죽은 유기 물질을 분해하여 에너지를 얻는 생물

deforestation | 삼림 벌채 숲이 파괴되는 것

demographic transition | 인구학적 천이 인구 집단에서 높은 출생률과 사망률에서 낮은 출생률과 사망률로 변화되는 양상

demography | 인구 통계학 사람들 개체 집단에 대한 과학적인 연구

dendrite | 수지상 돌기 환경 또는 다른 뉴런으로부터의 자극을 세포체로 전달하는 기능을 담당하는 뉴런의 세포체에서 뻗어 나온 조직

denitrification | 탈 질소 작용 토양 박테리아가 질산염을 질산 가스로 전환시키는 과정

density-dependent limiting factor | 밀도 의존적 제한 인자 인구 밀도에 의존하는 제한 인자

density-independent limiting factor | 밀도 비의존적 제한 인자 인구 밀도와는 무관하면서 비슷한 방식으로 모든 개체에 영향을 주는 제한 인자

deoxyribonucleic acid (DNA) | 디옥시리보핵산 (DNA) 생물이 부모대로부터 물려 받는 유전자

dependent variable | 종속 변수 독립 변수에 대해 반응하고 변화하는 변수로 일명 반응 변수(responding variable)

derived character | 파생 특징 최근의 일부 혈통에서는 나타나지만 오래된 개체에서는 나타나지 않는 형질

dermis | 진피 외피 바로 아래의 피부층

desertification | 사막화 과도한 농경, 과도한 목초지의 사용, 계절적 가뭄 그리고 기후의 변화로 인해 토지의 생산성이 저하되는 현상

detritivore | 잔사식 생물/부식질 먹는 무리 식물이나 동물의 배설물 그리고 사체 등을 먹고 사는 생물

deuterostome | 신구(新口) 동물 원래의 입은 항문이 되고 발생 과정에서 두 번째로 열리는 구멍으로부터 입이 형성되는 동물 집단

diaphragm | 횡경막 흉강의 바닥쪽에 위치하고 호흡을 도와주는 크고 편평한 근육

dicot | 쌍떡잎 식물 수정란 안에 두 개의 종자 잎을 가지는 속씨 식물

differentiation | 분화 세포가 특정 구조와 기능을 가지도록 분화해가는 과정

diffusion | 확산 농도가 더 진한 구역에서 더 연한 구역으로 입자가 이동하는 과정

digestive tract | 소화관 입에서 시작해서 항문까지 연결된 관 조직

diploid | 배수의 두 쌍의 상동 염색체를 가지는 세포를 일컫는 용어

directional selection | 방향적 도태 분포 곡선의 한쪽 끝에 있는 개체가 분포 곡선의 중간이나 서로 다른 반대 끝에 있는 개체보다 더 잘 적응하는 자연 도태의 한 형태

disruptive selection | 파괴적 도태 곡선의 위쪽이나 아래쪽 끝에 있는 개체가 곡선의 중간에 있는 개체보다 더 잘 적응하는 현상

DNA fingerprinting | DNA 유전자 지문법 생물학자들이 사용하는 방법으로 개인 고유의 DNA 절단편들의 모음을 분석하고 두 시료에 들어 있는 유전자가 동일한 사람의 것인지 아닌지를 알아냄

DNA microarray | DNA 마이크로어레이 격자 위에 수 천 가지 다른 종류의 외가닥 DNA 조각들이 들어있는 유리 슬라이드나 실리콘 칩. DNA 마이크로어레이를 사용하면 한 번에 수 천 개의 유전자 발현을 감지하고 측정할 수 있다.

DNA polymerase | DNA 폴리머라제 DNA 복제에 관련된 주요 효소

domain | 도메인 분류학상 '계' 보다 더 크고 포괄적인 분류 범주

dopamine | 도파민 뇌의 압력과 보상 중추와 관련된 신경 전달 물질 중 하나

dormancy | 휴면기 식물 배아가 살아있기는 하나 자라지는 않는 기간

double fertilization | 중복 수정 접합자를 생성하고 종자 안에 내배엽이 존재하는 속씨식물의 수정 과정

E

ecological footprint | 생태적 발자취 사람이 사용하는 자원을 제공하고 여기서 생긴 노폐물을 다시 흡수하는 기능을 가지는 생태계의 총칭

ecological hot spot | 생태학적 온점 상당수의 서식지와 종들이 곧 멸종 위기에 처해 있는 조그만 지리학적 구역

ecological pyramid | 생태적 피라미드 주어진 먹이 사슬이나 먹이 그물 내에서 각각의 단계에 속해 있는 에너지나 물질의 상대적인 양을 나타낸 그림

ecological succession | 생태 천이 혼란기 이후에 집단 사회에서 점진적으로 발생하는 일련의 변화 과정

ecology | 생태학 생물체 간이나 생물과 환경 사이에 나타나는 상호 작용에 대한 과학적인 연구

ecosystem | 생태계 생명력이 없는 환경을 포함하여 어떤 한 장소에서 살아가는 모든 유기체

ecosystem diversity | 생태계 다양성 생물권내에 존재하는 서식지, 집단 그리고 생태학적 과정들의 다양성

ectoderm | 외배엽 지각 기관, 신경 그리고 피부의 바깥 층을 형성하게 되는 배아의 가장 바깥 쪽에 있는 층

ectotherm | 변온 동물 체온이 외부 환경의 온도에 의해 결정되는 동물

electron | 전자 공간에서 핵 주위를 둘러싸고 위치하는 음전하를 띠는 입자

electron transport chain | 전자 전달계 전자 전달 단백질들이 ATP를 생산하는 반응 도중에 고에너지 상태의 전자를 주고 받는 일련의 과정

element | 원소 하나의 원자로 이루어진 순수한 물질

embryo | 배아 다세포 생물의 발생 단계

embryo sac | 배낭 꽃이 피는 식물의 난세포에 들어있는 암술 배우체

emerging disease | 신흥 질병 개체 집단에서 처음으로 나타난 질병 또는 갑자기 통제하기가 힘들어진 오래된 질병

emigration | (타국으로의) 이주 다른 지역으로 개체가 이동함

endocrine gland | 내분비선 혈액으로 분비해 체내 다른 곳으로 운반되는 호르몬을 분비하는 선

endoderm | 내배엽 소화관이나 대부분의 호흡계로 발생하는 배아의 가장 안쪽에 있는 층

endodermis | 내피 식물에서 도관 조직을 완전히 감싸는 기저 조직층

endoplasmic reticulum | 세포질 망상 구조 세포막의 지질 성분들이 결집된 상태로 진핵 세포 내에 존재하는 막 구조 체계

endoskeleton | 내골격 동물 체내에서 구조를 지지하는 내부 골격 체계

endosperm | 배젖 자라면서 종자에 영양분을 공급하는 영양소가 풍부한 조직

endospore | 내생 포자 악조건에서 원핵 생물에 의해 생산되며 DNA와 세포질의 일부를 두꺼운 내부 벽이 둘러싸고 있는 형태

endosymbiotic theory | 내공생 학설 몇몇의 서로 다른 원핵 세포들 사이의 공생 관계를 통해 진핵 세포가 생겨났다는 학설

endotherm | 온혈 동물 체내에서 발생되는 에너지를 사용해서 체온이 어느 정도 조절되는 동물

enzyme | 효소 특정 생물학적 반응의 속도를 증가시키는 단백질 촉매

epidermis | 표피 식물에서는 피부 조직을 형성하는 세포층 중 하나. 사람에서는 피부의 제일 바깥 층

epididymis | 부고환 정자를 성숙시키고 보관하는 수컷의 생식기관

epinephrine | 에피네프린 심 박동수와 혈압을 올리고 신체가 강한 육체 활동을 할 수 있도록 작용하는 부신에서 분비되는 호르몬. 일명 아드레날린

epithelial tissue | 상피 세포 내부와 외부의 체 표면적을 형성하는 조직의 형태

era | 연대 둘 또는 그 이상의 시대로 나누어지는 지질학상 시간대의 주요 경계선

esophagus | 식도 입에서 위까지 연결되어 있는 관

estuary | 강 어귀 강이 대양을 만나는 곳에 형성되는 습지대의 일종

ethylene | 에틸렌 열매가 익도록 자극하는 식물 호르몬

Eukarya | 진핵계 원생 생물, 식물, 진균류 그리고 동물까지 포함하여 핵을 가지는 모든 유기체를 포함하는 도메인

eukaryote | 진핵 생물 세포에 핵을 가지는 생물

evolution | 진화 고대 생물들로부터 현대 생물들에 이르기까지 전해 내려오는 시간에 따른 변화

excretion | 배설 대사 노폐물을 체외로 배출시키는 과정

exocrine gland | 외분비선 도관이라고 하는 튜브같이 생긴 구조를 통해 기관으로 직접 또는 전신으로 호르몬을 분비하는 선

exon | 엑손 DNA의 발현 서열 즉 단백질을 만드는 코드 암호

exoskeleton | 외골격 많은 척추 동물을 보호하고 지지하는 질기면서 외부를 감싸는 외부 골격 체계

exponential growth | 기하급수적 성장 집단 내에서 개체수가 일정한 속도로 번식하는 성장 패턴

extinct | 멸종 어떤 종이 죽어서 없어지고 더 이상 살아있는 개체가 없는 상태를 일컫는 용어

extracellular digestion | 세포외 소화 음식물이 소화계의 세포 바깥 쪽에서 분해되고 다시 흡수되는 소화 형태

F

facilitated diffusion | 촉진 확산 분자가 세포막에 있는 통로를 통해서 막을 통과하는 확산 과정

family | 과 (생물학 분류) 분류학상 유사한 속들이 모인 집단

fat | 지방 몸의 기관을 보호하고 몸을 절연하며 에너지를 저장하는 영양소의 형태로서 지방산과 글리세롤을 포함하는 지질

feedback inhibition | 피드백 저해 자극에 의해 최초 자극에 대항하는 반응을 생성하는 과정으로 일명 음의 피드백이라고 함

fermentation | 발효 산소가 없는 조건에서 세포가 에너지를 방출하는 과정

fertilization | 수정 수컷과 암컷의 생식 세포가 합해져서 새로운 하나의 세포가 생기는 유성 생식 과정

fetus | 태아 발생한 지 9주 이상 지난 사람 배아를 일컬음

fever | 열 감염에 대한 반응으로 체온이 올라가는 현상

filtration | 여과 액체 혹은 기체의 여과를 통해 노폐물을 제거하는 과정

fitness | 적응도 하나의 유기체가 환경에서 얼마나 잘 생존하고 번식하는지에 대한 척도

flagellum (pl. flagella) | 편모 원생 생물이 파동 형태의 운동을 하는데 사용하는 기관

food chain | 먹이 사슬 생태계에서 생물이 먹고 먹히면서 에너지를 전달하는 일련의 단계

food vacuole | 식포 원생 생물의 세포질에 존재하고 일시적으로 식량을 저장하는 작은 체강

food web | 먹이 그물 생태계에서 여러 생물들 사이 먹이 관계에 의해 형성되는 복잡한 상호 관계를 나타내는 망상 조직

forensics | 과학 수사 범죄 장면의 증거에 대한 과학적 연구

fossil | 화석 고대 생물이 보존된 화석 유적

founder effect | 창시자 효과 개체군 내의 작은 단위 그룹이 이주한 결과로 나타나는 대립 유전자의 도수 변화

frameshift mutation | 프레임 쉬프트 돌연변이 뉴클레오타이드 한 개가 들어가거나 빠짐에 따라 유전 정보의 "해독 틀"이 바뀌게 되어 생긴 돌연 변이

fruit | 열매 한 개 혹은 그 이상의 성숙한 씨방을 가지는 속씨 식물의 구조

fruiting body | (균류의) 자실체 균류의 균사체로부터 자라난 생식 기관

G

gamete | 생식 세포 성(性) 세포

gametophyte | 배우체 생식 세포를 생산하는 식물에서 식물의 일대기 중 다세포의 단수 단계

ganglion (pl. ganglia) | 신경절 뉴런들 사이를 연결하는 중간 뉴런들

gastrovascular cavity | 소화 순환 강 입구가 하나이고 소화 기능을 하는 방

gastrulation | 장배 형성 세포 이동에 의해 세 개의 세포층(외배엽, 중배엽, 내배엽)이 형성되는 과정

gel electrophoresis | 겔 전기 영동법 구멍이 있는 겔 한쪽 끝에 DNA 단편을 놓고 겔에 전기 전압을 걸어서 DNA 단편을 분리하고 분석하는 방법

gene | 유전자 부모로부터 자손에게 전달되는 인자로서 코드화하여 단백질을 생산함에 따라 형질을 결정하게 되는 DNA 서열

gene expression | 유전자 발현 유전자가 생산물을 생산하고 그 생산물이 자기의 기능을 수행하게 되는 과정

gene pool | 유전자 풀 항상 개체 내에 동시에 존재하고 각 유전자에 대해 여러 가지의 다른 대립 유전자를 포함하는 모든 유전자들의 총칭

gene therapy | 유전자 치료 질병 혹은 장애 상태를 치료하기 위해 유전자를 변화시키는 것으로 결여되거나 잘못된 유전자를 정상적으로 작동하는 유전자로 대체하는 치료 방법

genetic code | 유전 암호 단백질을 합성하는 도중에 단백질로 특정 아미노산이 들어갈 수 있도록 지시하는 mRNA의 코돈 집합

genetic diversity | 유전 다양성 지구상의 특정 종 또는 모든 생물이 갖고 있는 여러 가지의 서로 다른 유전 정보들의 총합

genetic drift | 유전적 표류 일련의 기회 발생 과정 중에 개체군 내에서 대립 유전자가 어느 정도 공통적으로 존재하도록 하는 대립 유전자 도수의 무작위적 변화

genetic equilibrium | 유전 평형 개체군 내에서 대립 유전자의 도수가 동일하게 유지되는 상태

genetic marker | 유전자 표지 유전자 분석을 하는 데 유용할 수 있도록 감지가 가능한 표현형의 차이를 도출하는 대립 유전자

genetics | 유전학 형질 유전에 대한 과학적 연구

genome | 게놈 생물체가 DNA 안에 넣고 운반하는 유전 정보의 총체

genomics | 유전체학 유전자와 그들의 기능을 포함한 모든 게놈에 대한 연구

genotype | 유전자형 생명체의 유전적 성질

genus | 속 밀접한 관계를 가지는 종들의 집합. 이명법에 의한 명명 에서 과학적인 이름의 첫 부분에 해당

geographic isolation | 지리학적 격리 두 개의 개체군이 강, 산 또는 물 등의 지리적 장벽에 의해 헤어져 있을 경우 두 개의 서로 다른 아종을 생성하게 되는 생식적 격리의 형태

geologic time scale | 지질학상의 시간대 지구의 역사를 나타내는데 쓰이는 시간대

germ theory of disease | 질병의 매균설 감염성 질병은 미생물에 의해 발생한다는 생각

germination | 배태 휴면기 후에 오는 식물 배아 성장의 회복기

gibberellin | 지베렐린 성장을 자극해서 현저하게 크기가 커지게 하는 식물 호르몬

gill | 아가미 가스와 물의 교환이 일어나도록 분화된 깃털 모양의 조직

global warming | 지구 온난화 지구의 평균 기온 상승

glomerulus | 사구체 혈액의 여과가 일어나고 네프론의 위쪽 끝에 모세 혈관이 싸여 있는 작은 망상 조직

glycolysis | 해당과정 한 개의 포도당이 두 개의 피루빅 산으로 분해되는 과정으로 세포 호흡 단계에서 첫 번째 반응

Golgi apparatus | 골지체 세포 내에 저장하거나 세포 외부로 방출하기 위해 세포질 망상 구조에서 생성되는 단백질과 다른 물질들을 변형, 분리 및 포장하는 기능을 하는 세포 내 기관

gradualism | 점진주의 오랜 시간에 걸쳐 작은 유전적 변화들이 점진적으로 축척됨으로써 나타나는 종의 진화

grafting | 접목법 씨가 없는 식물들이나 절단에 의해 번식될 수 없는 다양한 수목들의 번식을 위해 사용되는 번식 방법

gravitropism | 중력지향성 중력에 대한 식물의 반응

green revolution | 녹색 혁명 높은 생산성을 나타내는 작물의 품종 개발과 식량 수확고를 증가시키기 위한 현대 농업 기술

greenhouse effect | 온실 효과 지구의 대기에서 이산화탄소, 메탄, 수증기 등의 가스들이 태양 에너지를 흡수하고 열은 내보내지 않는 현상

growth factor | 성장 인자 성장과 세포 분열을 자극하는 외부 조절 단백질들 중 하나

guard cells | 공변 세포 기공을 열고 닫기를 조절하고 식물 표피에 있는 분화된 세포

gullet | 걸렛 섬모의 한 쪽 면에 있는 톱니 모양의 구조로 음식물을 세포 안으로 들어가게 하는 기능을 가짐

gymnosperm | 겉씨 식물 씨가 솔방울의 비늘 위에 직접 붙어 있는 종자식물군

H

habitat | 서식지 자기에게 영향을 미치는 생명이 있거나 없는 인자들을 모두 포함해서 한 생물이 살아가는 구역

habitat fragmentation | 서식지 분열 생태계가 나뉘어져 분리되는 현상

habituation | 습관화 보상을 주지도 해를 끼치지도 않는 어떤 반복되는 자극들에 대해 동물이 이에 대한 반응을 감소 또는 중단하는 것을 학습하는 형태

hair follicle | 모낭 진피 속으로 뻗어 있는 튜브 같은 주머니 형태의 상피 세포로 모낭 기저에 있는 세포가 털을 생산함

half life | 반감기 시료 속에 들어있는 방사성 원소가 절반으로 감소하는데 걸리는 시간

haploid | (염색체가) 단수의 단지 한 쌍의 유전자를 가진 세포를 일컫는 용어

Hardy-Weinberg principle | 하디바인베르크의 법칙 한 개 또는 그 이상의 요인들에 의해 도수의 변화가 발생하지 않는다면 개체군 내에 존재하는 대립 유전자의 도수는 일정하게 유지된다는 법칙

Haversian canal | 하베르시 도관 혈관과 신경을 가진 조밀한 뼈 속에 들어있는 도관들의 망상 구조 중 하나

heart | 심장 몸 전체에 혈액을 펌프질하는 속이 빈 근육 기관

heartwood | 심재 나무의 목질부에서 더 이상 물을 전달하지 않는 줄기의 중심부에 가까운 오래된 물관

hemoglobin | 헤모글로빈 적혈구에 들어 있는 철을 함유한 단백질. 산소와 결합하여 온 몸으로 산소를 전달함

herbaceous plant | 초본 식물 민들레, 백일초, 페튜니아 그리고 해바라기 같이 줄기가 부드럽고 목질부가 아닌 식물

herbivore | 초식 동물 단지 식물을 먹어서 에너지를 얻는 생물

herbivory | 초식 관계 생산자(식물)와 이를 먹고 사는 동물(초식 동물)과의 상호 관계

heterotroph | 종속 영양 생물 다른 살아 있는 생명체를 먹음으로써 식량을 얻는 생물 즉 소비자

heterozygous | 이형 접합체 하나의 특정 유전자에 대해 두 개의 서로 다른 대립 유전자를 가지는 것

histamine | 히스타민 염증 반응이 일어나는 동안에 감염된 부위에서 혈액과 액체가 흘러 나오도록 작용하는 비만 세포에서 유리되는 화학 물질

homeobox gene | 호메오박스 유전자 호메오박스는 약130개 염기쌍을 가진 DNA 서열로서 발생을 조절하는 많은 호메오 유전자에서 발견됨. 이런 서열을 가지는 유전자가 호메오박스 유전자이며 전사 인자를 위한 암호와 DNA에 결합해서 다른 유전자들의 발현을 조절하는 단백질을 포함함

homeostasis | 항상성 생명체가 유지하는 상대적으로 일정한 내부의 물리 화학적 상태

homeotic gene | 호메오 유전자 동물 배아에서 몸의 각 부분의 정체성과 구역을 정하는 조절 유전자의 집합. 이 유전자들에서 일어나는 돌연변이는 몸의 어느 한 부분을 다른 것으로 변형시킬 수 있음

hominine | 인간과 흡사한 사람으로의 진화를 이끈 인간과 흡사한 특성의 계보

hominoid | 사람 비슷한 동물 긴팔 원숭이, 오랑우탄, 고릴라, 침팬지 그리고 사람을 포함하는 유인원 무리

homologous | 상동 부계로부터 한 쌍, 모계로부터 한 쌍씩을 전해 받은 염색체

homologous structures | 상동 기관 공통의 조상을 가진 서로 다른 종에서 발견되는 유사한 기관이나 조직

homozygous | 동질 접합체 특정 유전자에 대해 두 개의 동일한 대립 유전자를 가지는 것

hormone | 호르몬 생물의 어느 한 부분에서 생산되어 동일한 생물의 다른 부분에 어떤 영향을 주는 화학 물질

Hox gene | 혹스 유전자 동물의 머리에서 꼬리까지 몸 각 부분의 정체성을 결정하는 다발 형태로 함께 존재하는 호메오 유전자 군. 모든 혹스 유전자는 호메오박스 DNA 서열을 가짐

humoral immunity | 체액성 면역 혈액 또는 림프와 같은 체액에 존재하는 항원에 대한 면역

humus | 부식질 잎과 다른 유기 물질들이 부식하여 생기는 물질

hybrid | 잡종 다른 형질을 가진 부모들 사이에서 생긴 자손

hybridization | 이종 교배 두 생명체에서 가장 좋은 형질이 나오도록 서로 다른 개체를 교차시켜 교배하는 기술

hydrogen bond | 수소 결합 수소 원자와 다른 원자 사이에 발생하는 약한 인력

hydrostatic skeleton | 정수의 골격 동물이 이동할 수 있도록 하는 근육들과 함께 작동하는 체액으로 찬 몸의 부분들로 이루어진 골격

hypertonic | 고장액 두 용액을 비교할 때 용질의 농도가 더 높은 용액

hypha (pl. hyphae) | (균류의) 균사 균류의 몸체를 형성하는 길고 가느다란 많은 실들 중 하나

hypothalamus | 시상하부 배고픔, 갈증, 피로, 분노 그리고 체온 등을 인지하고 분석하는 통제 중추로서 작용하는 뇌의 구조

hypothesis | 가설 관찰 결과들에 대한 가능한 설명 또는 어떤 과학적 의문에 대한 가능한 답변들

hypotonic | 저장액 두 용액을 비교할 때 용질의 농도가 더 낮은 용액

I

immigration | (국내로의) 이주 개체 집단들이 이미 점령해서 살고 있는 지역으로 개체가 이동하는 것

immune response | 면역 반응 몸이 병원균의 공격에 대해 종 특이성을 보이며 인지하고 반응하고 기억하는 과정

implantation | 착상 배반포가 자궁의 벽에 달라 붙는 과정

imprinting | 각인 일단 각인 되면 행동이 변하지 않는, 즉 초기 경험에 근거한 행동 양식

inbreeding | 근친 교배 특정 생물에 전해 내려오는 특성을 유지하기 위해 비슷한 특성을 가지는 개체들을 계속해서 교배시키는 것

incomplete dominance | 불완전 우성 한 개의 대립 유전자가 다른 대립 유전자를 불완전하게 지배하는 현상

independent assortment | 독립 유전 배우자 생식을 하는 동안 에 서로 다른 형질을 나타내는 유전자들은 각각 독립적으로 분리할 수 있다고 하는 멘델의 법칙 중 하나

independent variable | 독립 변수 통제된 실험에서 고의적으로 변화되는 인자로 일명 조절 변수라고 함

index fossil | 지표 화석 화석의 상대적 연대를 비교하는데 사용되는 특유의 화석

infectious disease | 감염 질환 미생물에 의해 몸의 정상적인 기능이 붕괴되는 질환

inference | 추론 기존의 지식과 경험에 근거한 논리적 해석

inflammatory response | 염증 반응 상해나 감염에 의한 조직 손상에 대해 나타나는 불특정한 방어 반응

innate behavior | 타고난 행동 양식 동물이 이전에 반응한 경험이 없는 처음 받게 되는 자극에 대해서도 충분한 기능을 나타내는 행동 양식. 일명 본능

insight learning | 통찰 학습 동물이 이미 배운 무엇인가를 시행 착오 없이 새로운 상황에 적용시키는 행동 양식. 일명 추론

interferon | 인터페론 바이러스 감염에 저항하는 세포들을 도와주는 단백질 중 하나

interneuron | 중간 뉴런 정보를 처리하고 운동 뉴런에 정보를 전달해주는 뉴런의 형태

interphase | (세포 분열의) 간기 세포 분열이 일어나는 사이에 존재하는 세포 주기 기간

intracellular digestion | 세포내 소화 음식물이 특화된 세포 안에서 소화되고 영양소를 확산에 의해 다른 세포로 통과시키는 소화 형태

intron | 인트론 단백질을 위한 암호화와는 관련이 없는 DNA 서열

invertebrate | 무척추 동물 등뼈 혹은 척추가 없는 동물

ion | 이온 양 또는 음의 전하를 가지는 원자

ionic bond | 이온 결합 하나의 원자에서 다른 원자로 하나 이상의 전자가 전달되면서 생기는 화학 결합

iris | 홍채 눈에서 색깔이 있는 부분

isotonic | 등장의 두 용액의 농도가 같을 때

isotope | 동위원소 한 원소에서 양성자 수는 같고 중성자 수가 다른 여러 가지 형태 중 하나

J

joint | 관절 하나의 뼈가 다른 뼈에 붙는 부위

K

karyotype | 핵형 크기가 작아지는 순서대로 배열되어서 함께 쌍을 이루어 모여있는 염색체의 완전한 배수체 집합을 나타내는 현미경 사진

keratin | 케라틴 피부에서 발견되는 강인한 섬유질의 단백질

keystone species | 기본 종 집단 내에서 통상적으로 개체 수는 많지 않지만 집단의 구조에 대해 강한 통제를 발휘하는 하나의 종

kidney | 신장 노폐물을 과도한 물을 혈액으로부터 분리해 내는 배설 기관

kin selection | 종족 선택 가까운 개체들과는 유전자의 많은 부분을 공유하고 있으므로 가까운 일가를 돕는 것은 개인의 진화에 대한 적응력을 증진시킨다는 학설

kingdom | 왕국 분류학상 가장 크고
포괄적인 그룹

Koch's postulates | 고흐의 가설 특정 질병을
일으키는 미생물을 규명하는데 도움을 주는
고흐에 의해 개발된 지침서

Krebs cycle | 크렙스 회로 일련의 에너지 추출
과정을 거치면서 피루빅 산이 이산화 탄소로
분해 되기까지의 세포 호흡의 두 번째 단계

L

language | 언어 문법이나 구문법과 같이 배열
순서와 의미에 관한 일정한 규칙에 따라
소리, 기호 그리고 몸짓 등을 통합하는 의사
전달 수단

large intestine | 대장 소화되지 않은 물질이
통과하면서 물이 제거되는 소화기 기관으로
일명 결장이라고 함

larva (pl. larvae) | 유충 생명체의 미성숙 단계

larynx | 후두 성대를 포함하는 목구멍 내 구조

learning | 학습 경험에 따른 행동의 변화

lens | 렌즈 망막에 광선의 초점을 맞추도록
하는 눈의 구조

lichen | 이끼 균류와 광합성을 하는 생물과의
사이에서 공생 관계를 이루는 군집

ligament | 인대 관절에서 뼈를 함께 지탱하는
강한 결합 조직

light-dependent reactions | 빛 의존적 반응
빛으로부터 에너지를 사용하여 ATP와
NADPH를 생산하는 광합성 반응

**light-independent reactions | 빛 비의존적
반응** 빛을 필요로 하지 않고 ATP와
NADPH로부터 나오는 에너지를 당과 같은
고–에너지 화합물을 만드는데 사용하는
광합성 반응으로 일명 칼빈 회로라고 함

lignin | 리그닌 관다발 식물에서 세포벽을
딱딱하게 만드는 물질

limiting factor | 제한 요인 개체의 성장을
감소시키는 요인

limiting nutrient | 제한 영양소 생태계에서
생산성을 제한하는 하나의 필수 영양소

lipid | 지질 지방, 기름 그리고 왁스와 같이
대부분 탄소와 수소로 이루어진 거대분자

lipid bilayer | 지질 이중층 세포 막을 형성하고
세포와 주위 환경 사이에 장벽을 만드는
유동성을 가지는 이층 구조의 판

logistic growth | 논리적 성장 기하 급수적으로
성장하는 기간 후에 개체의 성장이
감소하거나 중단되는 성장 패턴

loop of Henle | 헨리 루프 물을 흡수해서
여과액의 부피를 최소로 하는 기능을 하는
네프론 세관의 한 부분

lung | 폐 혈액과 들이마신 공기 사이에서
가스가 교환되는 장소인 호흡기 기관

lymph | 림프 혈액의 외부로 여과되는 체액

lysogenic infection | 용원성 감염 바이러스가
자신의 DNA를 호스트 세포의 DNA에 끼워
넣어 호스트 세포의 DNA와 함께 복제가
일어나는 감염의 한 형태

lysosome | 리소좀 지질, 탄수화물 그리고
단백질을 세포의 나머지 부분에서 사용할 수
있도록 작은 분자로 분해시키는 세포 내 기관

lytic infection | 용해소의 감염 바이러스가
세포 내로 들어가서 자기 스스로 복제하여
세포가 터지도록 하는 감염의 한 형태

M

macroevolution | 대진화 오랜 기간에 걸쳐
일어나는 큰 규모의 진화론적 변화

Malpighian tubule | 말피 기관 요산을
농축시켜 그것을 소화 노폐물에 더하는
기능을 하는 기관으로 지구상에 존재하는
대부분의 절지 동물들에게 존재함

mammary gland | 유선 새끼를 키우기 위해
젖을 생산하는 암컷 포유류에 존재하는 선

mass extinction | 대량 멸종 상대적으로 짧은
기간 동안에 많은 종들이 멸종하는 사건

matrix | 세포간질 미토콘드리아의 맨 안쪽 부분

mechanical digestion | 기계적 소화 음식물의
큰 덩어리를 작은 조각으로 물리적으로
부수는 과정

meiosis | 감수분열 배수체 세포 안에서 상동 염색체의 분리를 통해 세포 한 개당 들어있는 염색체의 수가 반으로 감소하는 과정

melanin | 멜라닌 피부에 들어 있으면서 자외선을 흡수하여 피부를 보호하는 어두운 갈색 색소

melanocyte | 멜라노사이트 피부에 들어 있으면서 멜라닌이라고 불리는 어두운 갈색 색소를 생산하는 세포

menstrual cycle | 생리 주기 정기적으로 난자가 성숙하여 몸으로부터 분비되는 현상

menstruation | 생리 수정되지 않은 난자가 혈액과 함께 체외로 배출되는 현상

meristem | 분열조직 식물의 일대기를 통해 지속적인 성장을 담당하는 비 분화된 세포 영역

mesoderm | 중배엽 근육, 순환계, 생식계 및 배설계로 발달되는 중간 배아층

mesophyll | 잎살 식물 광합성의 대부분이 일어나는 잎에서 발견되는 분화된 기저 조직

messenger RNA (mRNA) | 전령 RNA DNA 로부터 단백질을 만드는 아미노산 집합체를 생산하기 위한 지령이 담긴 복제 정보를 세포의 다른 부분으로 운반하는 RNA의 형태

metabolism | 대사 생명체가 물질을 만들거나 분해하기 위해 일어나는 화학 반응들의 조합

metamorphosis | 변태 유충이 성체로 바뀌어 가기까지 형태가 변하는 과정

metaphase | (유사분열의) 중기 염색체가 세포내의 중간에 가로질러 정렬하는 유사 분열 단계

microclimate | 소 기후 주위 지역의 기후와는 확연히 다른 어떤 작은 지역 내의 환경 조건들

migration | 이주 계절에 따라 어떤 환경에서 다른 환경으로 옮겨가는 현상

mineral | 무기질 대부분 아주 소량으로 몸이 필요로 하는 무기 영양소

mitochondrion | 미토콘드리아 음식물 내에 저장된 화학 에너지를 다른 세포들이 사용하기에 더욱 편리한 화합물로 전환하는 기능을 담당하는 세포 내 기관

mitosis | 유사 분열/간접 핵분열 진핵 세포에서 일어나는 세포의 핵이 분열하는 세포 분열

mixture | 혼합물 물리적으로는 함께 섞이나 화학적으로는 결합하지 않는 둘 또는 그 이상의 원소 혹은 화합물들로 이루어진 물질

molecular clock | 분자 시계 두 개의 종이 각각 독립적으로 진화해 온 시간을 측정하기 위해 DNA에서 일어나는 돌연 변이 율을 이용하는 연구 기법

molecule | 분자 화합물이 가지는 모든 특징들을 가지는 화합물의 가장 작은 단위

molting | 탈피 외골격의 허물을 벗고 새로운 개체로 성장하는 과정

monocot | 단자엽 배아 안에 한 개의 떡잎을 가지는 속씨 식물

monoculture | 단종 재배 하나의 생산성이 우수한 작물을 해마다 번갈아 가며 키우는 농사 기법

monomer | 단량체 중합체를 형성하는 작은 화학 단위

monophyletic group | 단일 계통 집단 조상이 같지 않은 후손들은 배제하고 하나의 조상과 그의 모든 후손들로 이루어진 집단

monosaccharide | 단당류 단일의 설탕 분자

motor neuron | 운동 뉴런 인터뉴런으로부터 근육 세포나 선으로 자극을 전달하는 신경 세포

multiple alleles | 다수 대립 유전자 두 개 이상의 대립 유전자를 가지는 유전자

multipotent | 다분화성 여러 형태의 분화된 세포로 발전될 수 있는 한정된 능력을 가지는 세포

muscle fiber | 근육 섬유 길고 가느다란 골격 근육 세포들

muscle tissue | 근육 조직 몸의 움직임이 가능하도록 해주는 조직

mutagen | 돌연변이원 주위 환경에 존재하면서 DNA와 작용하여 돌연변이를 일으키는 물리 화학적 요인

mutation | 돌연변이 세포 내 유전 정보의 변화

mutualism | 상호 공조 양쪽 모두 이득을 얻는 공생 관계

mycelium (pl. mycelia) | 균사체 균류의 균사가 조밀하게 가지를 치면서 이룬 망상 구조

mycorrhiza (pl. mycorrhizae) | 균근 고등 식물 뿌리와 균류의 사이에서 공생 관계를 이루는 군집

myelin sheath | (신경세포의) 미엘린 초 어떤 뉴런들에서 관찰되는 축색 돌기을 둘러싸는 절연막

myocardium | 심근 심장의 두꺼운 중간 근육 층

myofibril | 근원섬유 골격 근육 섬유 조직에서 발견되는 빽빽하게 들어차 있는 섬유 다발

myosin | 미오신 골격근육 세포들에서 발견되는 두꺼운 섬유 단백질의 일종

N

NAD⁺ (nicotinamide adenine dinucleotide) | 니코틴 아미드 아데닌 디뉴클레오타이드 해당 과정에 관련하는 전자 운반체

NADP⁺ (nicotinamide adenine dinucleotide phosphate) | 니코틴 아미드 아데닌 디뉴클레오타이드 인산염 엽록소로부터 다른 분자로 고에너지 전자를 전달하는 운반 분자

natural selection | 자연 도태 환경에 가장 잘 맞는 생명체가 가장 성공적으로 생존하고 번식해 나가는 과정으로 적자생존을 의미함

nephridium (pl. nephridia) | 배설관 체액을 여과하는 환형 동물에서 볼 수 있는 배설 기관

nephron | 네프론 불순물을 여과해서 나오는 노폐물을 따로 모으고 정화된 혈액은 다시 순환계로 돌려 보내는 신장에 존재하는 혈액 여과 기관

nervous tissue | 신경 조직 신경 자극을 온 몸으로 전달하는 조직

neuromuscular junction | 신경근 접합부 운동 뉴런과 골격근 세포가 만나는 접점

neuron | 신경 단위, 뉴런 신경계를 통하여 정보를 운반하기 위해 특화된 신경 세포

neurotransmitter | 신경 전달 물질 시냅스 (synapse)를 통해 자극을 다른 세포로 전달하기 위해 뉴런이 사용하는 화학 물질

neurulation | 신경계화 신경계의 발달과정에서 첫 단계

niche | 생태적 지위 생명체가 그 속에서 살아가는 모든 범위의 물리적 생물학적 조건과 생명체가 그 조건들을 이용하는 방법

nitrogen fixation | 질소 고정 식물이 흡수해서 이용할 수 있도록 질소 가스를 질소 화합물로 전환하는 과정

node | 마디 성장하는 줄기에서 잎이 붙는 부분

nondisjunction | 상동 염색체의 비분리 상동 염색체가 적절하게 분리하는데 실패해서 생기는 감수 분열의 오류

nonrenewable resource | 재생 불가능한 자원 적당한 시간 안에 자연적으로 일어나는 과정에 의해 다시 재생될 수 없는 자원

norepinephrine | 노르에피네프린 심박동 수와 혈압을 증가시키고 몸이 강한 육체 활동을 할 수 있도록 작용하는 부신에서 분비되는 호르몬

notochord | 척색 신경 조직 바로 아래에 있으며 척사체를 통해 지나가는 긴 지주대

nucleic acid | 핵산 수소, 산소, 질소, 탄소 그리고 인을 포함하는 거대 분자

nucleotide | 뉴클레오타이드 5탄당, 인산기 그리고 질소 함유 염기로 이루어진 핵산이 들어있는 기본 단위

nucleus | 핵 양성자와 중성자가 들어있는 원자의 중심, 세포에서는 DNA의 형태로 세포 유전 물질이 들어있는 세포 내 구조

nutrient | 영양소 생명체가 생명을 유지하기 위해 필요로 하는 화학 물질

nymph | 애벌레 모습은 성체와 닮았지만 생식 기능을 하는 기관이 없는, 동물의 미성숙 형태

O

observation | 관찰 주의 깊고 체계적인
방법으로 어떤 사건이나 과정을 살펴보고
묘사하는 과정

omnivore | 잡식성 동물 식물과 동물 양쪽
모두를 먹고 에너지를 얻는 생물

open circulatory system | 개방 순환계 혈액의
일부만 온 몸을 돌아다니는 혈관 안에
들어있는 순환계

operant conditioning | 시행착오적 학습
동물이 보상은 받고 벌은 피하기 위해서
반복적인 연습을 통해 어떤 행동 양식을
배우게 되는 학습 방법

operator | 작동 유전자 원핵 생물의 오페론에
존재하는 프로모터 옆에 위치하고 억제
단백질에 결합하여 오페론의 전사 속도를
조절하는 기능을 하는 짧은 DNA 영역

operon | 오페론 원핵 생물에서 작동 유전자와
프로모터 인자를 함께 가지고 외가닥의
mRNA로 전사되는 하나의 유전자군

opposable thumb | 대항할 수 있는 엄지
물건을 잡고 기구를 사용할 줄 아는 엄지

order | (분류상의) 목 분류학상 서로 가까운
'과' 들의 집단

organ | 기관 서로 밀접하게 연관된 기능을
수행하기 위해 함께 작동하는 조직들의 집합

organ system | 기관계 특정 기능을 수행하기
위해 함께 작동하는 기관들의 집합

organelle | 세포기관 진핵 세포 내에서 중요한
세포 기능을 수행하도록 특수 분화된 구조

osmosis | 삼투 선택적 투과막을 통해 일어나는
물의 확산 운동

osmotic pressure | 삼투압 선택적 투과막을
가로 질러 삼투 이동이 일어나는 것을
방지하기 위해 적용되는 압력

ossification | 골화 작용 연골이 뼈에 의해
대체되는 뼈 생성 작용

osteoblast | 골아 세포 자라는 뼈 속에서
연골을 대체할 무기질 물질을 분비하는
뼈 세포

osteoclast | 파골 세포 뼈 무기질을 분해하는
뼈 세포

osteocyte | 골 세포 뼈 조직 속에서 무기질을
유지하고 계속해서 자라는 뼈를 강화하도록
도와주는 뼈 세포

ovary | (식물)씨방/(동물)난소 식물에서는
종자를 둘러싸고 보호하는 기관; 동물에서는
난자를 생산하는 암컷의 1차 생식기관

oviparous | 난생 배아가 모체 바깥의 알에서
발생하는 종

ovoviparous | 난태생 배아가 모체 안에서
발생하기는 하지만 알을 싸는 난황낭에
전적으로 의존해서 발생하는 종

ovulation | 배란 난소에서 나팔관으로 성숙된
난자가 유리되는 현상

ovule | 수정되지 않은 난자 암컷의 배우체가
발생하는 종자 추상체 조직

ozone layer | 오존층 지구 상의 생물을 태양의
해로운 자외선으로부터 보호하는 오존
가스가 상대적으로 농축된 대기층

P

pacemaker | 심장 박동 조절 장치 심장이
수축하는 속도를 정해주어 심장의 박동
리듬을 유지하는 심근 섬유의 작은 조직으로
일명 동방 결절(sinoatrial (SA) node)이라고 함

paleontologist | 화석학자 화석을 연구하는
과학자

palisade mesophyll | 울타리 잎살 잎의 위쪽
표피 아래에 있는 세포층

parasitism | 기생 생활 한 생명체가 다른
생명체의 위나 안에 들어가 살면서 해를
끼치는 공생 관계

**parathyroid hormone (PTH) | 부갑상선
호르몬 (PTH)** 혈액 중의 칼슘 농도를
증가시키는 작용을 하는 부갑상선에서
분비되는 호르몬

parenchyma | 실질 조직 세포벽 안에 세포를
가지고 중심에 커다란 액포를 가지는 식물
기저 조직의 주요 형태

passive immunity | 수동 면역 자연적으로나 고의적으로 항원에 노출되어서 생기는 일시적인 면역

pathogen | 병원체 질병을 일으키는 물질

pedigree | 가계 혈통 한 가계 내에서 몇 세대를 거치면서 그 관계에 따라 나타나기도 하고 안 나타나기도 하는 형질을 나타낸 그림

pepsin | 펩신 단백질을 작은 폴리펩타이드 조각으로 분해하는 효소

period | 시대 연대를 지질학적 시간에 따라 부차적으로 나눈 것

peripheral nervous system | 말초 신경계 중추신경계로 신호를 보내거나 중추신경계의 신호를 받는 역학을 하는 신경 망상 조직과 그 주변 세포들

peristalsis | 연동 운동 음식물을 식도를 통과해서 위로 보내는 힘을 제공하는 평활근의 수축 작용

permafrost | 영구 동토층 툰드라 지대에서 발견되는 영구적으로 얼어있는 심토 층

petiole | 잎 꼭지 잎사귀를 줄기에 연결시키는 가느다란 줄기

pH scale | pH 척도 용액 내 수소 농도를 측정한 0에서 14까지의 척도; pH가 1에서 7은 산성, pH 7은 중성 그리고 pH 7에서 14는 염기성

pharyngeal pouch | 인두 주머니 척색 동물의 목구멍에 있는 한 쌍의 기관

pharynx | 인두 공기와 음식물의 통로로 제공되는 입 뒤쪽에 있는 튜브처럼 생긴 기관으로 일명 목구멍이라 함.

phenotype | 표현형 생물의 신체적 특성

phloem | 체관부 식물에서 광합성에 의해 생산된 영양소와 탄수화물 용액을 운반하는 관 조직

photic zone | 투광층 물 표면 근처의 빛 투과 영역

photoperiod | 광주기 밝고 어두움의 상대적 길이에 따라 나타나는 식물의 반응

photosynthesis | 광합성 식물이나 다른 자가 영양 생물들이 빛 에너지를 포획하여 이산화탄소와 물을 산소와 고-에너지 탄수화물(당이나 전분)로 전환시키는 화학 반응에 사용하는 과정

photosystem | 광화학계 틸라코이드에서 발견되는 엽록소와 단백질의 묶음

phototropism | 굴광성 식물이 빛을 향해 자라는 성질

phylogeny | 계통 발생론 생명체 간의 진화 관계에 대한 연구

phylum | (분류상의) 문 분류학상 서로 가까운 '강' 들의 집단

phytoplankton | 식물성 플랑크톤 대양의 표면 가까이에서 발견되는 광합성 조류

pigment | 색소 식물이 태양 에너지를 모으는데 사용하는 빛 흡수 분자

pioneer species | 선구 종 세대가 내려가면서 어떤 지역에 거주하는 첫 번째 종들

pistil | 암술 씨방, 암술대 및 주두를 포함하고 한 개 또는 몇 개가 융합된 형태의 암술대

pith | 속 쌍 떡잎 식물의 줄기 안에 있는 관 조직의 원 안에 존재하는 실질 세포

pituitary gland | 뇌하수체 몸의 많은 기능을 직접 조절하거나 다른 내분비선의 기능을 통제하는 작용을 하는 호르몬들을 분비하는 두개골 아래쪽 근처에서 발견되는 작은 선

placenta | 태반 포유류에서 모체와 태아 사이에 호흡 가스, 영양소, 노폐물 등의 교환이 이루어지도록 특수 분화된 기관

plankton | 플랑크톤 물 속 환경에서 사는 현미경으로 관찰되는 미생물로 식물성 플랑크톤과 동물성 플랑크톤이 있음.

plasma | 혈장 혈액 중 담황색의 액체 부분

plasmid | 플라즈미드 많은 박테리아의 세포질에 존재하는 작고 원형인 DNA 조각

plasmodium | 변형체 변형균의 일생 주기에서 아메바처럼 먹이를 먹는 단계

plate tectonics | 지각 구조 판 지질학적 과정

platelet | 혈소판 골수에서 유리되는 혈액 응고를 도와주는 작용을 하는 세포 단편

pluripotent | 다 분화성의 모든 형태의 세포는 아니지만 대부분의 세포로 발생되는 능력을 가진 세포

point mutation | 점 돌연변이 DNA상에서 한 개의 염기 쌍이 변화 되어 생기는 유전자 돌연변이

pollen grain | 화분립 씨방 식물에서 모든 수술 배우자체를 가지는 기관

pollen tube | 화분관 식물에서 두 개의 단수 수술 핵을 가지는 기관

pollination | 수분 작용 수술 생식 기관으로부터 암술 생식 기관으로 꽃가루를 전달하는 작용

pollutant | 오염원 토양, 공기 또는 물을 통해 생물권으로 들어올 수 있는 해로운 물질

polygenic trait | 다원발생 형질 두 개 이상의 유전자에 의해 통제되는 형질

polymer | 중합체 많은 단량체들로 이루어진 분자 또는 고분자

polymerase chain reaction (PCR) | 폴리머라제 연쇄 반응 (PCR) 특정 유전자의 대량 복제를 위해 생물학자들이 이용하는 기술

polypeptide | 폴리펩타이드 단백질을 만드는 긴 아미노산 사슬

polyploidy | 배수성 생명체가 여분의 염색체를 가지는 조건

population | 개체군 동일한 지역에서 살아가는 동일한 종의 개체군

population density | 인구 밀도 단위 영역 당 인구의 수

predation | 포식 습성 생물(포식자)이 다른 생물(먹이)을 포획하고 먹는 상호 관계

prehensile tail | 물건 잡기 편리한 꼬리 나무 가지 주위를 충분히 단단하게 감을 수 있는 긴 꼬리

pressure-flow hypothesis | 압력-유동성 가설 만들어진 당 자원이 가라 앉을 때까지 체관부에서 액즙 상태로 식물을 통해 운반되는 것을 설명하는 가설

primary growth | 제1단계 성장 식물의 꼭대기나 새싹에서 일어나는 성장 패턴

primary producer | 제1차 생산자 추후 다른 생물에 의해 사용될 에너지가 풍부한 화합물의 1차 생산자

primary succession | 1차 천이 이전의 집단 사회의 흔적이 존재하지 않는 지역에서 일어나는 천이

principle of dominance | 우성 법칙 어떤 대립 유전자는 우성이고 다른 것은 열성이라는 멘델의 두 번째 법칙

prion | 프리온 질병을 일으키는 단백질 입자

probability | 가망성 어떤 사건이 발생할 가능성

product | 생산물 화학 반응에 의해 생산되는 원소 또는 화합물

prokaryote | 원핵 생물 핵이 없는 단세포 생물

promoter | 프로모터 RNA 폴리머라제가 결합해서 전사를 시작하는 유전자의 특정한 영역

prophage | 프로파아지 박테리아 호스트의 DNA에 들어 있는 박테리오파아지의 DNA

prophase | (유사 분열의) 전기 유전 정보가 핵 안으로 압축되고 염색체가 보이게 되는 체세포 분열에서 처음의 가장 긴 단계

prostaglandin | 프로스타글란딘 많은 세포에 의해 생산되고 근처의 세포나 조직에 영향을 미치는 변형된 지방산

protein | 단백질 탄소, 수소, 산소 그리고 질소를 포함하고 몸의 성장과 복구에 필요한 거대 분자

protostome | 선구 동물 입이 원구로부터 생성되는 동물

pseudocoelom | 위체강 일부가 중배엽과 연결된 체강

pseudopod | 위족 일부 원생 생물들이 운동을 하는데 사용하는 일시적 세포질의 변형 형태

puberty | 사춘기 성장이 빠르고 생식계가 완전한 기능을 하도록 성적으로 성숙하게 되는 시기

pulmonary circulation | 폐 순환 심장과 폐 사이에서 일어나는 순환

punctuated equilibrium | 깨진 평형 오랜
동안 안정적이던 시기가 더 빠른 변화를
보이는 짧은 시기에 의해 깨지는 진화 패턴

Punnett square | 푸네트 정방형 유전자의 교차
조합으로 유전자형과 표현형을 예측하는데
사용되는 도식

pupa | 번데기 유충이 성체로 발달하는
과정에서 완전한 변태가 일어나는 단계

pupil | 동공 빛이 눈으로 통과할 수 있도록 하는
홍채 내 작은 구멍

R

radial symmetry | 방사 대칭 몸체의 중심을
통과하는 가상의 선을 그었을 때 나뉜 두
쪽이 대칭적인 평면 몸체

radiometric dating | 방사성 연대 결정법
시료에 들어 있는 동일한 원소의 비방사성
동위원소에 대한 방사성 동위 원소의
양으로부터 시료의 시대를 결정하는 방법

reabsorption | 재흡수 물과 용해된 물질이
혈액으로 되돌아 가는 과정

reactant | 반응물, 화학 반응을 시작하는 원소
또는 화합물

receptor | 수용체 세포의 위나 안에 있으며 그
모양이 호르몬과 같은 특정 분자 전령에 꼭
맞는 특정 단백질

recombinant DNA | 재조합된 DNA 다른
자원으로부터 DNA를 합병함으로써
생산된 DNA

red blood cell | 적혈구 산소를 운반하는
헤모글로빈을 함유하는 혈액 세포

reflex | 반사 자극에 대한 신속하고
자동적인 반응

reflex arc | 반사궁 자극에 대한 빠른 반응을
일으키는 각 감각 수용체, 감각 뉴런, 운동
뉴런, 및 효과기.

relative dating | 상대적 연대 결정 화석이
있던 곳을 다른 암석층에 들어 있는 화석과
비교함으로써 화석의 시대를 결정하는 방법

relative frequency | 상대 돗수 동일한
유전자에서 발생하는 다른 대립 유전자들의
발생 횟수에 대한 유전자 풀에서 발생하는
특정 대립 유전자의 발생 횟수

releasing hormone | 유리 호르몬 뇌하수체
전엽이 호르몬을 분비하도록 하는
시상하부에서 생산되는 호르몬

renewable resource | 재생 가능한 자원
건강한 생태계의 기능에 의해 생산되고
재활용 가능한 자원

replication | 복제 세포 분열 이전에 DNA를
복사하는 과정

reproductive isolation | 생식적 격리 더 이상
이종 교배를 하여 두 개의 다른 종으로
진화가 일어나지 않도록 종이나 개체군이
분리됨

resource | 자원 물, 영양분, 빛, 음식 또는 공간
등 생명을 유지하기 위한 필수 요소

response | 반응 자극에 대한 특정 반응

resting potential | 휴식기 전위 휴식기 뉴런의
세포막을 사이에 두고 생기는 전기적 전하

restriction enzyme | 제한 효소 뉴클레오타이드
배열에서 DNA를 잘라내는 효소

retina | 망막 광수용기(시세포)가 들어 있는
눈의 가장 깊은 부분의 층

retrovirus | 레트로 바이러스 유전 정보를 RNA
에 갖고 있는 RNA 바이러스

ribonucleic acid (RNA) | 리보핵산 (RNA)
리보오스 당을 함유하는 단일 가닥의 핵산

ribosomal RNA (rRNA) | 리보솜 리보 핵산
단백질과 결합하여 리보솜을 만드는
RNA 형태

ribosome | 리보솜 세포 내 세포질에서
발견되고 단백질을 합성하는 장소로서
RNA와 단백질을 포함하는 세포 내 기관

RNA interference (RNAi) | 방해 리보 핵산
세포 내로 들어가서 유전자 발현을 저해하는
이중 나선 구조 RNA의 출현

RNA polymerase | 리보핵산 폴리머라제
주형으로 DNA 나선 구조를 이용하여 전사
과정이 일어나는 동안 RNA 뉴클레오타이드의
성장 사슬에 결합하는 효소

rod | 로드 빛에는 민감하고 색깔은 구별하지
못하는 눈에 있는 광수용기

root cap | 뿌리 덮개 분열 조직을 보호하는
뿌리 끝의 단단한 덮개

root hair | 뿌리 털 물과 무기질이 흡수되도록
큰 표면적을 제공하는 뿌리에 있는 작은 털

rumen | 반추위 소나 공생하는 박테리아가
섬유소를 소화하는 동물들의 위

S

sapwood | 백목질 목질부에서 심재를 둘러싸고
액체가 활발하게 운반되는 2차 체관부 층

sarcomere | 살코미어 두 개의 Z 구역과
그 사이의 필라멘트로 이루어진 근육
수축의 단위

scavenger | 청소 동물 다른 동물의 사체를
먹는 동물

science | 과학 자연계에 관하여 증거를 모으고
분석하는 조직적인 방법

sclerenchyma | 후막조직 기저 조직을 질기고
강하게 만드는 극단적으로 두껍고 단단한
세포벽을 가지는 기저 조직의 형태

scrotum | 음낭 고환이 들어 있는 외부
주머니 조직

sebaceous gland | 피지선 피지를 분비하는
피부에 있는 선

secondary growth | 제2차 성장 쌍떡잎
식물에서 줄기가 더 두꺼워지는 성장 형태

secondary succession | 2차 천이 혼동으로
인해 단지 일부가 파괴된 지역에서 볼 수
있는 천이의 형태

seed | 종자/씨앗 보호막에 싸인 식물 배아와
공급 영양분

seed coat | 씨앗 껍질 식물 배아를 둘러싸고
보호해서 씨앗의 내용물이 마르는 것을
방지하는 질긴 덮개

segregation | 격리 배우체가 생기는 동안 대립
유전자가 분리되는 현상

selective breeding | 선택 교배 단지 원하는
특징을 가지는 생물에 다음 세대를
생산하도록 허락하는 교배 방법

selectively permeable | 선택 투과성의 어떤
물질은 통과하고 어떤 물질은 통과하지
못하는 생물의 막 성질. 일명 반투성 막
(semipermeable membrane)이라고 함

semen | 정액 정자와 반 유동성 액체의 합

semicircular canal | 세반고리관 내이에
존재하고 중력에 대한 몸의 위치를 감지하는
세 개의 기관 중에서 하나

seminiferous tubule | 수정관 정자가 발육하는
정소 내에 존재하는 수천 개의 관 중 하나

sensory neuron | 2차 뉴런 지각 수용체로부터
정보를 받아서 중추 신경계로 신호를
전달하는 신경 세포의 형태

sex chromosome | 성(性) 염색체 개인의 성을
결정하는 두 개의 염색체중에서 하나

sex-linked gene | 성 관련 유전자 성 염색체에
존재하는 유전자

sexual reproduction | 유성 생식 양쪽
부모로부터 받은 세포가 하나로 합쳐져서
새로운 생물의 첫 세포를 만드는 생식 형태

**sexually transmitted disease (STD) | 성 매개
질병** 성 접촉을 통해 사람에서 사람으로
전달되는 질병

sieve tube element | 체 관상 요소 끝에서
끝까지 배열된 식물의 체관 세포를 통해
연속적으로 이어진 관

single-gene trait | 단일 유전 형질 두 개의
대립 유전자를 가지는 하나의 유전자에 의해
통제되는 형질

small intestine | 소장 대부분의 화학적 소화와
영양분 흡수가 일어나는 소화 기관

smog | 스모그 화학 물질의 혼합물에 의해
생기는 회갈색의 안개

society | 사회 집단의 이익을 위해 함께 일하는
같은 종으로 가장 가까운 동물들의 집단

solute | 용질 용액에 녹아 있는 물질

solution | 용액 모든 성분들이 고르게 분포된
혼합물의 형태

solvent | 용매 용액에서 녹이는 물질

somatic nervous system | 체 신경계 신호를 골격근으로 전달하거나 받는 말초 신경계의 일부분

speciation | 종 분화 새로운 종의 생성

species diversity | 종 다양성 특정 지역을 구성하는 서로 다른 종들의 수

spirillum (pl. spirilla) | 나선균 나선형 또는 나사 모양의 원핵 생물

spongy mesophyll | 해면질 잎살 잎에서 울타리 잎살 아래에 있는 느슨한 조직 층

sporangium (pl. sporangia) | 포자 주머니 감수 분열에 의해 생기는 단수성의 포자가 들어 있는 포자 주머니

spore | 포자 원핵 생물, 원생 생물, 균류의 경우 악조건에서 살아남을 수 있는 다양하고도 두꺼운 벽을 가지는 생명 주기, 식물의 경우 단수 생식 세포

sporophyte | 포자체 포자를 생산하는 식물의 일생 주기 중에서 다세포의 2배수체 단계

stabilizing selection | 안정 도태 분포 곡선의 중심 가까이에 있는 개체가 양 끝에 있는 개체에 비해 더 잘 적응하는 자연 도태의 한 형태

stamen | 수술 꽃밥과 꽃실을 가지는 꽃의 수술 부분

stem cell | 줄기 세포 하나 또는 그 이상의 분화된 세포 형태로 될 수 있는 미분화 세포

stigma | 주두 꽃가루를 포획하도록 특화된 암술대 맨 위에 끈끈한 부분

stimulus (pl. stimuli) | 자극 생물이 반응하는 신호

stoma (pl. stomata) | 기공 이산화탄소, 물 그리고 산소가 잎의 안과 밖으로 확산될 수 있도록 하는 식물의 표피에 난 작은 구멍

stomach | 위 음식물의 기계적 화학적 소화를 지속하는 커다란 근육 주머니

stroma | 엽록대 틸라코이드 바깥에 있는 엽록체의 액체 부분

substrate | 기질 효소에 의해 촉진되는 반응에서 반응물

suspension | 현탁액 물과 녹지 않는 물질의 혼합물

sustainable development | 환경친화적 개발 자연 자원을 고갈되지 않는 한도 내에서 사용하고 장기적 환경 훼손을 야기하지 않는 한도 내에서 사람에게 필요한 것을 제공하기 위한 전략

symbiosis | 공생 함께 가까이 살아가는 두 종 사이의 관계

synapse | 시냅스 뉴런이 자극을 다른 세포로 전달하는 위치

systematics | 계통 분류학 생명의 다양성과 생명체 간에 생기는 진화적 관계에 대한 연구

systemic circulation | 전신 순환 심장과 몸의 그 외 부분들 간의 순환 경로

T

taiga | 타이가 길고도 추운 겨울과 짧은 기간의 따뜻한 날씨를 보이고 침엽 상록수에 의해 지배되는 생물군계. 일명 아한대 숲

target cell | 목표 세포 특별한 호르몬을 위한 수용체를 가지는 세포

taste bud | 미뢰 맛을 느끼는 감각 기관

taxon (pl. taxa) | 분류군 생물이 분류되는 조직의 집단이나 기준

telomere | 말단 소립 진핵 생물의 염색체 끝에 존재하는 반복적인 DNA

telophase | (유사 분열의) 말기 뚜렷한 개개의 염색체가 얽힌 염색질로 뻗어나가기 시작하는 유사 분열의 한 단계

temporal isolation | 일시 격리 둘 또는 그 이상의 종들이 다른 시간에 생식하게 되는 생식적 격리의 한 형태

tendon | 힘줄 골격 근육과 뼈를 연결하는 강한 결합 조직

territory | 세력 범위 한 마리의 동물 또는 동물군에 의해 점령되고 보호되는 특정 지역

testis (pl. testes) | 정소, 고환 정자를 생산하는 1차 수컷 생식 기관

tetrad | 4분 염색체 감수 분열 동안 만들어지는 4개의 염색질을 포함하는 구조

tetrapod | 사지동물 수족이 넷인 척추동물

thalamus | 시상 지각 기관으로부터 정보를 받아서 이를 더 처리하기 위해 대뇌의 적당한 영역으로 정보를 전달하는 뇌의 구조

theory | 학설 광범위한 관찰과 가설을 하나로 통합하고 과학자들로 하여금 새로운 상황에 대한 정확한 예측을 하도록 하는 잘 검증된 설명

thigmotropism | 접촉 굴성 접촉에 대한 식물의 반응

threshold | 역치 욕구를 일으키는데 필요한 자극의 최소치

thylakoid | 틸라코이드 엽록체 안에서 발견되는 주머니 모양의 광합성 막

thyroxine | 티록신 전신에 걸쳐 세포의 대사 속도를 증가시키는 갑상선에서 분비되는 호르몬

tissue | 조직 특정 기능을 수행하는 유사한 세포들의 집단

tolerance | 내성 최적 환경과는 거리가 먼 환경에서 생존하고 번식하는 생물의 능력

totipotent | 분화 전능성의 몸에서 발견되는 어떠한 형태의 세포로도 발달할 수 있는 세포 (배체 외막과 태반을 이루는 세포를 포함함)

trachea | 기관 인두와 후두를 연결하는 관. 일명 기관

tracheid | 헛물관 물관부에 위치하고 리그닌에 의해 강화된 세포벽을 가진 속이 빈 식물 세포

tracheophyte | 관다발 식물 도관이 있는 식물

trait | 형질 개체가 가지는 명확한 특징

transcription | 전사 DNA 주형으로부터 RNA 분자가 합성되는 것

transfer RNA (tRNA) | 전이 RNA 단백질 합성이 일어나는 동안 리보솜까지 개개의 아미노산을 운반하는 아미노산의 형태

transformation | 형질 변환 한 종의 박테리아가 또 다른 박테리아 종으로부터 유전자를 받아 변화하는 과정

transgenic | 이식 유전자에 의한 어떤 생물이 다른 생물의 유전자를 가지게 되는 것을 의미하는 용어

translation | 해독 mRNAd에 들어 있는 염기 서열이 단백질의 아미노산 서열로 전환하는 과정

transpiration | 발한 잎을 통해 식물에서 물이 빠져나가는 현상

trochophore | 트로코포아 물에 사는 연체 동물의 자유로이 헤엄치는 유충 단계

trophic level | 영양 단계 먹이 사슬 또는 먹이 그물에서 각각의 단계

tropism | 굴성 식물이 어떤 자극을 향하거나 또는 피하게 되는 움직임

tumor | 종양 급격하게 분열하면서 주위 조직을 해치는 세포의 덩어리

U

understory | 아래층 천개 바로 아래에 작은 나무나 덩굴에 의해 생기는 열대우림층

ureter | 수뇨관 신장에서 방광까지 오줌을 운반하는 관

urethra | 요도 오줌을 체외로 배출하는 관

urinary bladder | 방광 배설되기 전에 오줌이 보관되는 주머니 같이 생긴 조직

V

vaccination | 예방 접종 약화되어 덜 위험한 병원균을 주사하여 면역이 생기도록 하는 것

vaccine | 백신 어떤 질병에 대해 면역이 생기도록 하는데 사용되는 약화되거나 죽은 병원균 제제

vacuole | 액포 물, 염, 단백질 그리고 탄수화물과 같은 물질을 저장하는 세포 내 기관

valve | 판막 심방과 심실의 사이에 있거나 정맥에 있으며 혈액이 역류하지 못하도록 하는 열렸다 닫혔다 하는 결합 조직

van der Waals forces | 반데르발스 힘 가까이 있는 분자에서 반대로 하전된 영역 사이에 발생하는 약한 인력

vas deferens | 정관 부고환에서 요도까지 이어진 정자를 운반하는 관

vascular bundle | 관다발 식물의 줄기부에 있는 물관과 체관을 합한 다발

vascular cambium | 도관 형성층 관 조직을 생성하고 줄기의 두께를 증가시키는 분열 조직

vascular cylinder | 도관 기둥 물관과 체관을 포함한 도관 조직으로 이루어진 뿌리의 중심 영역

vascular tissue | 도관 조직 식물에서 물과 영양분을 운반하도록 특화된 조직

vector | 벡터 사람에게 병원균을 전달하는 동물

vegetative reproduction | 식물 생식 하나의 식물이 자신과 유전적으로 똑같은 자손을 생산할 수 있는 식물에서 일어나는 무성생식 방법

vein | 정맥 몸 전체에서 심장으로 혈액을 운반하는 혈관

ventricle | 심실 심장으로부터 혈액을 펌프질해서 온 몸으로 내보내는 심장의 아래쪽에 있는 방

vertebrate | 척추 동물 등뼈를 가지는 동물

vessel element | 도관 요소 물이 이동할 수 있는 연속적인 관의 부분을 형성하는 물관 세포의 한 종류

vestigial organs | 퇴화 기관 크기가 작아져서 그 기능이 전혀 또는 거의 없는 조직

villus (pl. villi) | 융모 영양소 분자를 흡수하도록 도와주는 소장에 있는 손가락같이 돌출된 구조

virus | 바이러스 오로지 감염 세포에 의해서만 복제가 가능한 단백질, 핵산 때로는 지질로 이루어진 입자

vitamin | 비타민 몸에서 일어나는 과정을 조절하도록 도와주는 유기 분자

viviparous | 태생의 모체에서 직접 영양분을 공급받으면서 발육한 살아있는 새끼를 출산하는 동물

W

weather | 날씨 온도, 강수량 그리고 또 다른 인자들을 포함하는 일별 대기 조건

wetland | 습지대 년중 일부 기간 동안 물이 토양을 덮거나 표면이나 주변에 물이 존재하는 생태계

white blood cell | 백혈구 감염에 대항하고 기생충과 싸우며 박테리아를 공격하는 혈액 세포의 한 형태

woody plant | 목질 식물 수목, 관목 그리고 덩굴과 같이 주로 식물의 몸체를 지탱하는 두꺼운 세포벽을 가지는 세포로 이루어진 식물의 형태

X

xylem | 물관부 뿌리에서 위쪽 방향으로 식물의 모든 부분까지 물을 운반하는 관 조직

Z

zoonosis (pl. zoonoses) | 동물원성 감염증 동물로부터 사람에게 전해지는 질병

zooplankton | 동물성 플랑크톤 플랑크톤의 일부를 형성하며 몸이 작고 자유로이 떠 있는 동물

zygote | 접합체 수정된 알

Russian
Русский

Miller & Levine
Biology
Glossary

A

abiotic factor | абиотический фактор
физический фактор, т.е. фактор неживой
природы, который формирует экосистему

abscisic acid | абсцизовая кислота
растительный гормон, который ингибирует
деление клеток и, следовательно, рост

acetylcholine | ацетилхолин нейромедиатор,
который генерирует импульс в мышечной
клетке

acid | кислота соединение, которое образует
в растворе ионы водорода (H⁺); значение
pH раствора меньше 7

acid rain | кислотный дождь дождь,
содержащий азотные и серные кислоты

actin | актин белок, содержащийся в тонких
филаментах мышц

action potential | потенциал действия
обратимое распределение зарядов по разные
стороны клеточной мембраны нейрона;
другое название – нервный импульс

activation energy | энергия активации
энергия, которая необходима для
протекания реакции

active immunity | активный иммунитет
иммунитет, который развивается в
результате естественного или вызванного
намеренно воздействия антигена

adaptation | адаптация наследственная
особенность, которая усиливает
способность организмов к выживанию и
воспроизводству в окружающей среде

adaptive radiation | адаптивная радиация
процесс, в котором из одного вида или
небольшой группы видов развивается
несколько различных форм, эволюция
которых протекает в разных направлениях

**adenosine triphosphate (ATP) | аденозин-
трифосфат (АТФ)** соединение, используемое клетками для накопления и
выделения энергии

adhesion | адгезия сила сцепления между
различными видами молекул

aerobic | аэробный процесс, для протекания
которого необходим кислород

age structure | возрастная структура
количество мужчин и женщин каждого
возраста в популяции

aggression | агрессия угрожающее
поведение, используемое одним животным
для проявления превосходства над другим
животным

algal bloom | цветение воды массовое
развитие водорослей и других продуцентов,
явившееся результатом попадания в воду
большого количества лимитирующих
питательных веществ, без которых
рост замедляется

allele | аллель одна из возможных
структурных форм гена

allergy | аллергия чрезмерная реакция
иммунной системы на антиген

**alternation of generations | чередование
поколений** жизненный цикл, имеющий
две чередующиеся фазы – фаза гаплоида
(N) и фаза диплоида (2N)

alveolus (pl. alveoli) | альвеола крошечные
пузырьковидные образования на конце
бронхиолы в легких, обеспечивающие
площадь поверхности для протекания
газообмена

amino acid | аминокислота соединение с
аминогруппой на одном конце и карбок-
сильной группой на другом конце

amniotic egg | амниотическое яйцо яйцо, состоящее из оболочки и мембран, которые создают защитную среду для возможности развития эмбриона вне воды

amylase | амилаза фермент в слюне, который разрушает химические связи в крахмалах

anaerobic | анаэробный процесс, для протекания которого не требуется кислород

anaphase | анафаза фаза митоза, в которой хромосомы разделяются и перемещаются к противоположным концам клетки

angiosperm | покрытосеменное растение растение из группы семенных растений, семена которых находятся под слоем защитной ткани; другое название – цветковое растение

anther | пыльник часть тычинки цветка, в которой созревает пыльца

antheridium (pl. antheridia) | антеридий мужской репродуктивный орган некоторых растений, в котором образуется сперма

anthropoid | антропоид группа приматов, включающая обезьян, человекообразных обезьян и людей

antibiotic | антибиотик группа лекарств, используемая для подавления роста и размножения болезнетворных микроорганизмов

antibody | антитело белок, который либо сам атакует антигены, либо образует белки, связывающие антигены

anticodon | антикодон группа из трех оснований в молекуле тРНК, которые комплементарны трем основаниям кодона в мРНК

antigen | антиген любое вещество, которое вызывает иммунный отклик

aphotic zone | афотическая зона глубинный слой в океане ниже освещенной зоны, куда не проникает солнечный свет

apical dominance | доминирование верхушки явление, в котором чем ближе почка к верхушке стебля, тем сильнее замедляется ее рост

apical meristem | верхушечная меристема группа неспециализированных клеток, деление которых обеспечивает удлинение стеблей и корней

apoptosis | апоптоз процесс запрограммированной гибели клеток

appendage | отросток структура, такая как ножка или усик, которая выступает из стенок тела

appendicular skeleton | добавочный скелет кости рук и ног наряду с костями таза и области плеч

aquaculture | Аквакультура выращивание водных организмов для потребления человеком

aquaporin | аквапорин белок водных каналов в клетке

Archaea | архей особый домен, состоящий из одноклеточных, прокариот, у которых оболочки клеток не содержат пептидо-гликан; относится к царству архебактерий

archegonium (pl. archegonia) | архегоний орган в растениях, в котором образуются яйцеклетки

artery | артерия крупный кровеносный сосуд, по которому кровь поступает от сердца к тканям тела

artificial selection | искусственный отбор селективное размножение растений и животных, способствующее появлению желательных признаков в потомстве

asexual reproduction | бесполое размножение процесс размножения, включающий одного родителя и приводящий к потомству, которое генетически идентично родителю

asthma | астма хроническое заболевание дыхательных путей, при котором дыхательные пути сужаются, вызывая свистящее дыхание, кашель и удушье

atherosclerosis | атеросклероз состояние, при котором отложения жира, называемые бляшками, приводят к утолщению и уплотнению стенок артерий и потере эластичности

atom | атом наименьшая частица вещества

ATP synthase | АТФ-синтаза кластер белков, которые охватывают мембрану клетки и позволяют ионам водорода (H^+) проходить через нее

atrium (pl. atria) | предсердие верхняя камера сердца, в которую поступает кровь от остальной части тела

autonomic nervous system | автономная нервная система часть периферической нервной системы, которая регулирует непроизвольные функции, не поддающиеся сознательному контролю; подразделяется на симпатический и парасимпатический отделы

autosome | аутосома неполовая хромосома; другое название – аутосомная хромосома

autotroph | автотроф организм, который способен использовать энергию солнца или химических веществ для синтезирования пищи для себя из неорганических соединений; другое название – продуцент

auxin | ауксин регулирующее вещество, образующееся на верхушке растущего растения, которое стимулирует растяжение клеток и рост новых корней

axial skeleton | осевой скелет скелет, который поддерживает центральную ось тела; состоит из черепа, позвоночного столба и грудной клетки

axon | аксон длинное волокно, по которому от тела нервной клетки (нейрона) передаются нервные импульсы

B

bacillus (pl. bacilli) | бацилла прокариот в форме палочки

background extinction | фоновое вымирание Вымирание, являющееся следствием медленного и неуклонного процесса естественного отбора

Bacteria | бактерии домен одноклеточных, прокариот, у которых оболочки клеток содержат пептидогликан; относятся к царству эубактерий

bacteriophage | бактериофаг вид вируса, который инфицирует бактерии

bark | кора ткани, которые находятся поверх сосудистого камбия и включают флоэму (лубяную ткань), корковый камбий и вторичную кору

base | основание соединение, которое образует в растворе гидроксид-ионы (OH⁻); значение pH раствора больше 7

base pairing | спаривание оснований принцип, согласно которому связи в ДНК могут образовываться только между аденином и тимином и между гуанином и≈цитозином

behavior | поведение способ проявления реакций организма на изменения в его внутреннем состоянии или во внешней среде

behavioral isolation | поведенческая изоляция форма репродуктивной изоляции, в которой у двух популяций развивается разница в ритуалах ухаживания или в других отношениях, которая препятствует их скрещиванию

benthos | бентос организмы, обитающие на дне или вблизи дна озер, рек и океанов

bias | предвзятость особое предпочтение или точка зрения, которая является личной, а не научной

bilateral symmetry | билатеральная симметрия проекция тела, в которой одна воображаемая линия может поделить тело на левую и правую стороны, являющиеся зеркальными отображениями друг друга

binary fission | деление надвое тип бесполого размножения, в котором организм копирует свою ДНК и делится пополам, производя две идентичных дочерних клетки

binocular vision | бинокулярное зрение способность соединять изображения, увиденные каждым из двух глаз, обеспечивая восприятие глубины и трехмерное представление мира

binomial nomenclature | биноминальная номенклатура система классификации, в которой каждому виду назначается научное название из двух слов

biodiversity | биоразнообразие всё разнообразие организмов в биосфере; другое название – биологическое разнообразие

biogeochemical cycle | биогеохимический цикл процесс, в котором элементы, химические соединения и другие формы материи переходят из одного организма в другой и из одной части биосферы в другую

biogeography | биогеография исследование распределения организмов в прошлом и в настоящее время

bioinformatics | биоинформатика применение математики и информатики для сохранения, извлечения и анализа биологических данных

biological magnification | биологическое аккумулирование увеличение концентрации вредных веществ в организмах на более высоких трофических уровнях в цепи питания, или пищевой сети

biology | биология научное исследование жизни

biomass | биомасса общая масса живой ткани в пределах данного трофического уровня

biome | биом совокупность экосистем с одинаковым климатом и типичными организмами

biosphere | биосфера оболочка Земли, в пределах которой существует жизнь, включая сушу, воду и воздух или атмосферу

biotechnology | биотехнология процесс манипуляции с организмами, клетками или молекулами для получения особых продуктов

biotic factor | биотический фактор любая живая часть окружающей среды, с которой организм может взаимодействовать

bipedal | двуногий термин, который относится к передвижению на двух ногах

blade | листовая пластинка тонкая, плоская часть листа растения

blastocyst | бластоциста ранняя стадия развития у млекопитающих; представляет собой полый пузырек с клетками (зародышевый пузырь)

blastula | бластула зародышевый пузырь, который формируется, когда зигота претерпевает ряд делений клетки

bone marrow | костный мозг мягкая ткань, находящаяся в полостях костей

bottleneck effect | эффект "бутылочного горлышка" изменение частоты аллеля после резкого уменьшения размера популяции

Bowman's capsule | капсула Боумена чашевидная структура, в которой находится клубочек; здесь происходит фильтрация крови

brain stem | ствол мозга структура, которая соединяет мозг со спинным мозгом; включает продолговатый мозг и мост

bronchus (pl. bronchi) | бронх одно из двух больших ответвлений трахеи в грудной полости, идущих к легким

bryophyte | моховидные группа растений, которые имеют специальные органы размножения, но не имеют сосудистой ткани; сюда относятся мхи и близкие к ним формы

bud | почка часть растения, содержащая особую ткань – верхушечную меристему, которая может произвести новые стебли и листья

buffer | буфер состав, который предотвращает резкое, внезапное изменение pH

C

calcitonin | кальцитонин гормон, вырабатываемый щитовидной железой, который уменьшает уровень кальция в крови

Calorie | большая калория мера тепловой энергии в пище; эквивалентна 1000 калорий

calorie | калория количество энергии, необходимое для повышения температуры 1 грамма воды на 1 градус Цельсия

Calvin cycle | цикл Кальвина независимые от света реакции фотосинтеза, в которых энергия из АТФ и НАДНФ используется для образования богатых энергией соединений, например сахара

cancer | рак нарушение, при котором некоторые клетки тела теряют способность контроля роста

canopy | листовой полог плотный полог, образуемый лиственными верхушками деревьев высокого влажного леса

capillary | капилляр наименьший кровеносный сосуд; переносит питательные вещества и кислород к тканям и удаляет из тканей углекислый газ и продукты жизнедеятельности

capillary action | капиллярный эффект тенденция воды подниматься в тонкой трубке

capsid | капсид белковая оболочка, окружающая вирус

carbohydrate | углевод соединение, состоящее из атомов углерода, водорода и кислорода; тип питательных веществ, являющихся главным источником энергии для организма

carnivore | хищник организм, который получает энергию, поедая другие организмы

carpel | плодолистик самая внутренняя часть цветка, которая образует и защищает женские гаметофиты

carrying capacity | переносимый объем максимальный размер популяции организмов определенного вида, который может поддерживаться средой обитания

cartilage | хрящ тип соединительной ткани, которая является опорной тканью организма, но более мягкой и гибкой, чем кость

Casparian strip | поясок Каспари водоне-проницаемый участок, который опоясывает эндодермальные клетки растения и обеспечивает одностороннее направление транспортировки материалов в сосудистый цилиндр в корнях растения

catalyst | катализатор вещество, которое увеличивает скорость химической реакции

cell | клетка основная единица строения всех форм жизни

cell body | тело клетки наибольшая часть типичного нейрона, которая содержит ядро и много цитоплазмы

cell cycle | цикл клетки ряд событий, охваты-вающих рост клетки, подготовку к делению, а также ее деление с образованием двух дочерних клеток

cell division | деление клетки процесс, в котором клетка разделяется на две новых дочерних клетки

cell membrane | мембрана клетки тонкий, гибкий барьер, который окружает все клетки; регулирует состав материалов, проходящих в клетку и выходящих из нее

cell theory | клеточная теория фундамен-тальная концепция биологии, утверж-дающая, что все компоненты живой природы состоят из клеток, что клетки являются основными единицами строения и функций всего живого, и что новые клетки образуются из существующих клеток

cell wall | стенка клетки прочная оболочка вокруг мембраны в некоторых клетках

cell-mediated immunity | клеточный иммунитет иммунный отклик, который защищает организм от вирусов, грибков и патологических раковых клеток в живых клетках

cellular respiration | клеточное дыхание процесс, при котором выделяется энергия за счет расщепления глюкозы и других молекул пищи в присутствии кислорода

central nervous system | центральная нервная система включает головной и спинной мозг, обрабатывает информацию и производит отклик, который передается организму

centriole | центриоль структура в животной клетке, которая помогает организовать деление клеток

centromere | центромера участок хромосомы, где происходит соединение двух сестринских хроматид

cephalization | цефализация концентрация органов чувств и нервных клеток в головном отделе животного

cerebellum | мозжечок участок головного мозга, который координирует движения и управляет равновесием

cerebral cortex | кора головного мозга наружный слой головного мозга млекопитающих; центр мышления и других сложных форм поведения

cerebrum | головной мозг участок мозга, отвечающий за сознательные действия организма; "мыслительная" область мозга

chemical digestion | химическое перева-ривание пищи процесс, в котором ферменты расщепляют пищу на малые молекулы, которые организм может использовать

chemical reaction | химическая реакция процесс изменения или превращения одного набора химических веществ в другой набор химических веществ

chemosynthesis | хемосинтез процесс, в котором химическая энергия используется для образования углеводов

chitin | хитин сложный углевод, из которого построены стенки клеток грибков; также содержится во внешних скелетах членистоногих

chlorophyll | хлорофилл основной пигмент растений и других фотосинтезирующих организмов

chloroplast | хлоропласт органелла, содержащаяся в клетках растений и некоторых других организмов; она поглощает энергию солнечного света и преобразует ее в химическую энергию

chordate | хордовое животное животное, которое по крайней мере на одном этапе своей жизни имеет: дорсальный, полый нервный ствол, спинную струну (нотохорд), хвост, выходящий за пределы анального отверстия, и жаберные мешки

chromatid | хроматида одна из двух идентичных "сестринских" частей продублированной хромосомы

chromatin | хроматин вещество, содержащееся в эукариотических хромосомах, которое состоит из ДНК, плотно обвитой вокруг гистонов

chromosome | хромосома нитевидная структура в ядре, которая содержит генетическую информацию, передающуюся от одного поколения к следующему

chyme | химус смесь ферментов и частично переваренной пищи

cilium (pl. cilia) | ресничка короткий отросток, похожий на волос, который производит движения

circadian rhythm | циркадный ритм цикл ежедневных поведенческих процессов

clade | клад эволюционная ветвь кладограммы, которая включает одного предка и всех его потомков

cladogram | кладограмма диаграмма, показывающая общие характеристики среди видов

class | класс в классификации: группа тесно связанных родов

classical conditioning | классический условный рефлекс тип обучения, когда животное запоминает связь между раздражителем и некоторой наградой или наказанием

climate | климат средние ежегодные условия температуры и осадков в области в течение длительного периода времени

clone | клон член популяции генетически идентичных клеток, образовавшихся из одной клетки

closed circulatory system | закрытая кровеносная система тип кровеносной системы, в которой вся кровь циркулирует по кровеносным сосудам, проходящим по всему организму

coccus (pl. cocci) | кокк сферический прокариот

cochlea | улитка заполненная жидкостью часть внутреннего уха; содержит нервные клетки, которые воспринимают звук

codominance | кодоминантность ситуация, в которой полностью проявлены фенотипы, произведенные обоими аллелями

codon | кодон группа из трех нуклеотидных оснований в мРНК, которая определяет конкретную аминокислоту, которая будет включена в белок

coelom | целом полость тела, покрытая мезодермой

coevolution | коэволюция процесс, в котором два вида развиваются в ответ на изменения друг в друге с течением времени

cohesion | когезия сцепление между молекулами одного и того же вещества

collenchyma | колленхима в растениях: тип опорной ткани с прочными, гибкими стенками клеток; помогает поддерживать крупные растения

commensalism | комменсализм симбиотическое сосуществование, которое полезно для одного организма и безразлично для другого – не помогает и не вредит

communication | коммуникация передача информации от одного организма другому

community | сообщество совокупность различных популяций, обитающих в определенной области

companion cell | клетка-спутник в растениях: клетка флоэмы (лубяной ткани), окружающей элементы ситовидных трубок

competitive exclusion principle | принцип конкурентного исключения принцип, согласно которому никакие два вида не могут одновременно занимать одну и ту же нишу в одной и той же среде обитания

compound | соединение вещество, образованное химической комбинацией двух или более элементов в определенных пропорциях

cone | колбочка в глазу: фоторецептор, который реагирует на свет разного цвета, обеспечивая цветное зрение

coniferous | хвойный термин относится к деревьям, имеющим тонкие листья в виде иголок и плоды в виде семеносных шишек

conjugation | слияние процесс, при котором парамеции и некоторые прокариоты обмениваются генетической информацией

connective tissue | соединительная ткань тип ткани, которая является опорной для тела и соединяет его части

consumer | консумент организм-потребитель, который получает энергию и пищу из органических веществ, произведенных другими организмами; другое название – гетеротроф

control group | контрольная группа группа в эксперименте, для которой соблюдаются те же условия, как для экспериментальной группы, за исключением одной независимой переменной

controlled experiment | контролируемый эксперимент эксперимент, в котором изменяется только одна переменная

convergent evolution | конвергентная эволюция процесс, в котором при адаптации к подобным средам у неродственных организмов независимо формируются сходные признаки

cork cambium | пробковый камбий (или феллоген) – меристемная ткань, которая образует внешнее покрытие стеблей во время вторичного роста растения

cornea | роговица вязкий прозрачный слой глазного яблока, через который поступает свет

corpus luteum | желтое тело название, данное фолликулу после овуляции из-за его желтого цвета

cortex | кора в растениях: область покровной ткани прямо внутри корня, через которую поступают вода и минералы

corticosteroid | кортикостероид стероидный гормон, производимый корой надпочечников

cotyledon | семядоля первый лист или первая пара листьев, образуемых зародышем растения в семени

courtship | ухаживание тип поведения, когда животное посылает стимуляторы (раздражители) для привлечения животного противоположного пола

covalent bond | ковалентная связь тип связи между атомами, в которой они объединяют свои электроны

crossing-over | кроссинговер процесс, в котором гомологичные хромосомы обмениваются частью своих хроматид во время мейоза

cyclin | циклин одно из семейств белков, которое регулирует цикл клетки в эукариотических клетках

cytokinesis | цитокинез деление цитоплазмы для формирования двух отдельных дочерних клеток

cytokinin | цитокинин растительный гормон, производимый в растущих корнях и в развивающихся плодах и семенах

cytoplasm | цитоплазма жидкий компонент клетки снаружи ядра

cytoskeleton | цитоскелет трехмерная сетка из белковых нитей (филаментов) в эукариотической клетке, которая дает клетке ее форму и внутреннюю организацию и включается в движение клеток

D

data | Данные факты; информация, полученная путем наблюдений

deciduous | листопадные термин, относящийся к типу деревьев, которые каждый год сбрасывают листья в определенный сезон

decomposer | редуцент организм, который разлагает мертвые органические вещества и получает их энергию

deforestation | сведение лесов вырубка лесов

demographic transition | демографический сдвиг изменение в популяции от высокой рождаемости и смертности к низкой рождаемости и смертности

demography | демография научное исследование народонаселения

dendrite | дендрит отросток тела клетки нейрона, который передает импульсы от среды или от других нейронов в тело клетки

denitrification | денитрификация процесс, в котором бактерии почвы превращают нитраты в газообразный азот

density-dependent limiting factor | лимитирующий фактор, зависящий от плотности лимитирующий фактор, который зависит от плотности популяции

density-independent limiting factor | лимитирующий фактор, не зависящий от плотности лимитирующий фактор, который одинаково влияет на все популяции, независимо от плотности популяции

**deoxyribonucleic acid (DNA) | дезоксири-
бонуклеиновая кислота (ДНК)** вещество
с генетической информацией, которое
организмы наследуют от своих родителей

**dependent variable | зависимая
переменная** переменная, которая
отслеживается и которая изменяется в
соответствии с независимой переменной;
другое название – отвечающая переменная

derived character | производный признак
признак, который появляется у недавних
потомков, но отсутствует у более ранних
членов потомства

dermis | дерма слой кожи, располагающийся
под эпидермисом

desertification | опустынивание снижение
плодородия земли, вызванное чрезмерно
интенсивным земледелием, выбиванием
пастбищ, сезонными засухами и изменением
климата

detritivore | детритофаг организм, который
питается останками животных и растений и
другими неживыми веществами

deuterostome | вторичноротые группа
животных, у которых бластопор преобра-
зуется в заднепроходное отверстие, а
ротовое отверстие образуется заново

diaphragm | диафрагма большая плоская
мышца внизу грудной полости, которая
участвует в дыхании

dicot | двудольные покрытосеменные
растения с двумя семядолями в зародыше

differentiation | дифференциация процесс,
в котором клетки становятся специфичными
по структуре и функциям

diffusion | диффузия процесс, в котором
частицы имеют тенденцию перемещаться из
области, в которой их концентрация больше,
в область с меньшей концентрацией

digestive tract | пищеварительный тракт
канал, который начинается во рту и оканчи-
вается в заднем проходе

diploid | диплоид термин, обычно
относящийся к клетке, которая содержит
два набора гомологичных хромосом

**directional selection | направленный
отбор** форма естественного отбора, когда
особи на одном конце кривой распределения
имеют более высокую приспособляемость,
чем особи в середине или на другом конце
кривой

disruptive selection | дизруптивный отбор
форма естественного отбора, когда особи на
верхнем и нижнем концах кривой распределения имеют более высокую приспособляемость, чем особи в средней части кривой

DNA fingerprinting | ДНК-генотипоскопия
средство, используемое биологами, которые
анализируют уникальный набор фрагментов
рестрикции ДНК; используется, чтобы
определить, принадлежат ли два образца
генетического материала одному и тому же
человеку

DNA microarray | ДНК - микрочипы
предметное стекло или силиконовая
пластинка, которые содержат пробы тысяч
различных видов фрагментов одноцепо-
чечной ДНК, организованных в сетку.
ДНК-микрочипы используются для
одновременного определения и измерения
экспрессии тысяч генов

DNA polymerase | ДНК-полимераза
основной фермент, участвующий в
репликации ДНК

domain | домен более крупная и разноо-
бразная классификационная категория,
чем царство

dopamine | допамин нейромедиатор,
который связан с центрами удовольствия и
награды в мозге

dormancy | покой период времени, когда
зародыш растения жив, но не растет

**double fertilization | двойное оплодот-
ворение** процесс оплодотворения в
покрытосеменных растениях, в которых в
первом событии в семени образуется зигота,
а во втором – эндосперм

E

ecological footprint | экологический след
общий размер функционирующей экосистемы,
необходимой и для обеспечения ресурсов,
которые использует население, и для
поглощения отходов, производимых
населением

**ecological hot spot | экологическая
"горячая точка"** небольшая географи-
ческая область, в которой значительная
часть населения, а также растительных и
животных видов находится под непосред-
ственной угрозой вымирания

ecological pyramid | экологическая пирамида иллюстрация относительного количества энергии или материи, содержащегося в пределах каждого трофического уровня в цепи питания, или пищевой сети

ecological succession | экологическая сукцессия ряд постепенных изменений, которые происходят в сообществе после нарушения равновесия

ecology | экология научное исследование взаимодействий между организмами, а также между организмами и их средой обитания

ecosystem | экосистема все организмы, которые обитают в определенном месте, наряду с их неживой средой

ecosystem diversity | экосистемное многообразие разнообразие сред обитания, сообществ и экологических процессов в биосфере

ectoderm | эктодерма наружный слой зародыша; из него образуются органы чувств, нервы и наружный слой кожи

ectotherm | эктотермные (холоднокровные) животные, температура тела которых определяется температурой их среды обитания

electron | электрон отрицательно заряженная частица, расположенная в пространстве вокруг ядра атома

electron transport chain | цепь переноса электронов ряд белков-переносчиков электронов, которые переносят электроны с высокой энергией во время реакций с образованием АТФ

element | элемент чистое вещество, которое целиком состоит из одного типа атомов

embryo | эмбрион (или зародыш) – стадия развития многоклеточного организма

embryo sac | зародышевый мешок женский гаметофит в яйцеклетке цветкового растения

emerging disease | развивающаяся болезнь болезнь, которая появляется в популяции впервые, или старая болезнь, которую внезапно становится трудно контролировать

emigration | эмиграция переселение людей из области проживания

endocrine gland | эндокринная железа железа, выделяющая свои секреты (гормоны) непосредственно в кровь, которая переносит их в другие области организма

endoderm | эндодерма внутренний зачаток эмбриона; в дальнейшем из него образуется слизистая оболочка пищеварительного тракта и органов дыхания

endodermis | эндодерма в растениях: слой покровной ткани, которая полностью охватывает сосудистый цилиндр

endoplasmic reticulum | эндоплазмати-ческий ретикулум внутренняя система мембран в эукариотических клетках; место, где происходит сбор липидных компонентов мембран клетки

endoskeleton | эндоскелет внутренний скелет; опорная структура в теле животного

endosperm | эндосперм питательная ткань, которая питает проросток, пока он растет

endospore | эндоспора структура, образуемая прокариотами в неблаго-приятных условиях; толстая внутренняя стенка, которая защищает ДНК и часть цитоплазмы

endosymbiotic theory | Теория эндосимбиоза теория, согласно которой эукариотические клетки образовались в результате симбио-тического сосуществования нескольких разных прокариотических клеток

endotherm | эндотермные (теплокровные) животные, температура тела которых регулируется, по крайней мере, частично, за счет теплоты, выделяемой внутри их тела

enzyme | фермент белковый катализатор, который ускоряет определенные биологи-ческие реакции

epidermis | эпидермис у растений: один слой клеток, образующий покровную ткань ; у людей: наружный слой кожи

epididymis | эпидидимис орган в мужской репродуктивной системе, в котором вызревает и хранится сперма

epinephrine | эпинефрин гормон, выделяемый надпочечниками, который увеличивает частоту сердечных сокращений и артериальное давление и подготавливает тело к интенсивной физической активности; другое название – адреналин

epithelial tissue | эпителиальная ткань тип ткани, которая покрывает внутренние и внешние поверхности организма

era | эра большой промежуток геологического времени; обычно делится на два или более периодов

esophagus | пищевод канал, соединяющий рот и желудок

estuary | эстуарий (дельта, устье) – заболоченная территория, образуемая в месте впадения реки в океан

ethylene | этилен вещество, стимулирующее созревание плодов; может синтезироваться самими растениями

Eukarya | эукарии домен, охватывающий все организмы, у которых есть ядро; включает протисты, растения, грибы и животных

eukaryote | эукариот организм, клетки которого содержат ядро

evolution | эволюция изменение с течением времени; процесс, согласно которому современные организмы развились из древних организмов

excretion | экскреция процесс выведения из организма отходов жизнедеятельности

exocrine gland | экзокринная железа железа, выделяющая свои секреты через трубчатые структуры, называемые протоками, непосредственно в орган или из тела

exon | экзон выраженная последовательность ДНК; коды для белка

exoskeleton | экзоскелет внешний скелет; жесткий внешний покров, который защищает и поддерживает тела многих беспозвоночных

exponential growth | экспоненциальный рост тип роста, при котором люди в популяции воспроизводятся с постоянной скоростью

extinct | исчезнувшие термин, относящийся к видам, которые вымерли и уже не существуют в природе

extracellular digestion | внеклеточное переваривание пищи тип пищеварения, в котором пища расщепляется вне клеток в пищеварительной системе, а затем абсорбируется

F

facilitated diffusion | облегченная диффузия процесс диффузии, в котором молекулы проходят через мембрану по мембранным каналам клетки

family | семейство в классификации: группа сходных родов

fat | жир (липид) – состоит из жирных кислот и глицерина; тип питательного вещества, которое защищает органы тела, изолирует тело и сохраняет энергию

feedback inhibition | ингибирование по типу обратной связи (ингибирование конечным продуктом) – процесс, в котором раздражитель вызывает реакцию, которая противодействует исходному раздражителю; другое название – отрицательная обратная связь

fermentation | ферментация процесс высвобождения энергии клетками при отсутствии кислорода

fertilization | оплодотворение процесс в половом размножении, в котором мужская и женская репродуктивные клетки сливаются с образованием новой клетки

fetus | плод название человеческого эмбриона после восьми недель развития

fever | лихорадка (жар) – повышение температуры тела в ответ на инфекцию

filtration | фильтрация процесс прохождения жидкости или газа через фильтр для удаления отходов

fitness | приспособляемость относительная способность организма выживать и размножаться в его среде обитания

flagellum (pl. flagella) | жгутик (ресничка) – структура, используемая протистами; производит волнообразное движение

food chain | цепь питания (пищевая цепь) – последовательность шагов в экосистеме, в которой организмы передают энергию, когда поедают пищу и сами поедаются другими организмами

food vacuole | пищеварительная вакуоль малая полость в цитоплазме протиста, в которой временно хранится пища

food web | пищевая сеть совокупность сложных взаимодействий, которые формируются отношениями, связанными с питанием, среди различных организмов в экосистеме

forensics | криминалистика наука, которая исследует закономерности, связанные с совершенным преступлением

fossil | окаменелость (ископаемое) – сохранившиеся останки древних организмов

founder effect | эффект основателя изменение частоты аллеля в результате переселения малой подгруппы популяции

frameshift mutation | мутация со сдвигом рамки считывания мутация, которая смещает "рамку считывания" генетической информации за счет вставки или удаления нуклеотида

fruit | плод структура в покрытосеменных растениях, которая содержит один или несколько зрелых яичников

fruiting body | плодоносящее тело репродуктивная структура гриба, которая вырастает из мицелия

G

gamete | гамета половая клетка

gametophyte | гаметофит растение, образующее гаметы; многоклеточная гаплоидная фаза жизненного цикла растения

ganglion (pl. ganglia) | ганглион (узел) – группа интернейронов

gastrovascular cavity | гастроваскулярная полость пищеварительная камера с одним отверстием

gastrulation | гаструляция процесс миграции клеток, приводящий к формированию трех слоев клеток: эктодерма, мезодерма и эндодерма

gel electrophoresis | гель-электрофорез процедура, используемая для отделения и анализа фрагментов ДНК, когда смесь фрагментов ДНК помещается в одном конце пористого геля, а затем к гелю подается электрическое напряжение

gene | ген последовательность ДНК, в которой закодирован белок и которая, следовательно, определяет признак; фактор, который передается от родителя к потомству

gene expression | экспрессия гена процесс, в котором ген производит свой продукт, а этот продукт выполняет свою функцию

gene pool | генный пул (генофонд) – все гены, включая все разные аллели для каждого гена, которые присутствуют в популяции в любой конкретный момент

gene therapy | генотерапия процесс изменения гена для излечения болезни или исправления нарушения. Отсутствующий или дефектный ген заменяется нормально действующим геном

genetic code | генетический код последовательность кодонов мРНК, каждый из которых служит сигналом для встраивания определенной аминокислоты в белок во время синтеза белка

genetic diversity | генетическое многообразие вся совокупность всех разнообразных форм генетической информации, переносимой определенным видом или всеми организмами на Земле

genetic drift | генетический дрейф случайное изменение частоты аллеля, вызванное рядом случайных событий, которые приводят к более высокому или более низкому распространению аллеля в популяции

genetic equilibrium | генетическое равновесие ситуация, при которой частоты аллелей в популяции остаются неизменными

genetic marker | генетический маркер аллели, которые производят поддающиеся обнаружению фенотипические модификации, полезные в генетическом анализе

genetics | генетика наука о наследственности

genome | геном весь набор генетической информации, которую хранит организм в его ДНК

genomics | геномика исследование целых геномов, включая гены и их функции

genotype | генотип совокупность всех наследственных свойств организма

genus | род группа родственных видов; первая часть научного названия в биноминальной номенклатуре

geographic isolation | географическая изоляция форма репродуктивной изоляции, в которой две группы отделены географическими барьерами, такими как реки, горы или водоемы, что приводит к формированию двух отдельных подвидов

geologic time scale | шкала геологического времени хронологическая шкала, отражающая историю Земли

germ theory of disease | микробная теория болезней идея о том, что инфекционные болезни вызваны микроорганизмами

germination | прорастание возобновление роста зародыша растения после состояния покоя

giberellin | гиббереллин растительный гормон, который стимулирует рост и может привести к значительному увеличению размера

gill | жабра перистая структура, предназначенная для обмена газами с водой

global warming | глобальное потепление увеличение средней температуры на Земле

glomerulus | клубочек сеть кровеносных капилляров в верхней части капсулы нефрона, где происходит фильтрация крови

glycolysis | гликолиз первый набор реакций в клеточном дыхании, в котором молекула глюкозы расщепляется на две молекулы пировиноградной кислоты

Golgi apparatus | аппарат Гольджи органелла в клетках, предназначенная для модификации, сортировки и упаковки белков и других материалов из эндоплазматического ретикулума для хранения в клетке или вывода за пределы клетки

gradualism | градуализм эволюция видов путем постепенного накопления малых генетических изменений за длительные периоды времени

grafting | пересадка метод размножения бессеменных растений и разновидностей древесных растений, которые не могут размножаться черенками

gravitropism | гравитропизм реакция растения на земное притяжение (силу тяжести)

green revolution | зеленая революция развитие высокоурожайных сортов и использование современных методов и агротехники для повышения урожайности продовольственных культур

greenhouse effect | парниковый эффект процесс, в котором определенные газы в земной атмосфере (углекислый газ, метан и водяной пар) улавливают энергию солнечного света в виде тепла

growth factor | фактор роста одна из групп внешних регуляторных белков, которые стимулируют рост и деление клеток

guard cells | защитные клетки специализированные клетки в эпидермисе растений, которые управляют открытием и закрытием устьиц

gullet | ротовое отверстие открытая щель на одной стороне инфузории, через которую пища поступает в клетку

gymnosperm | голосеменные группа семенных растений, у которых семена находятся непосредственно на чешуйках их шишек

H

habitat | местообитание область, где живет организм, отвечающая биотическим и абиотическим требованиям этого организма

habitat fragmentation | фрагментация мест обитания разделение экосистем на части

habituation | привыкание тип обучения, в котором происходит ослабление или прекращение реакции животного при многократном повторении раздражителя, который и не подкрепляется наградой, и не вредит животному

hair follicle | волосяной фолликул трубкообразные карманы эпидермальных клеток, которые распространяются в дерму; из клеток нижней части волосяных фолликулов формируются волосы

half life | период полураспада отрезок времени, необходимый для распада половины радиоактивных атомов в образце

haploid | гаплоид термин, обычно относящийся к клетке, которая содержит один набор генов

Hardy-Weinberg principle | закон Харди-Вайнберга принцип, согласно которому частоты аллелей в популяции остаются постоянными, пока один или несколько факторов не приведут к изменению этих частот

Haversian canal | Гаверсов канал одна из сетей трубок, проходящих через компактную кость; содержит кровеносные сосуды и нервы

heart | сердце полый мышечный орган, обеспечивающий ток крови по всему организму

heartwood | сердцевина в древесном стебле: самая старшая ксилема около центра стебля, которая больше не проводит воду

hemoglobin | гемоглобин железосодержащий белок в эритроцитах, который связывает кислород и транспортирует его по организму

herbaceous plant | травянистое растение тип растения, имеющего гладкие и недревесные стебли; включает одуванчики, циннии, петунии и подсолнечники

herbivore | травоядные организмы, которые получают энергию, поедая только растения

herbivory | растительноядность пример отношений, в которых одно животное (травоядное) питается продуцентами (например, растениями)

heterotroph | гетеротроф организм, который получает пищу, поедая другие живые существа; другое название – потребитель (консумент)

heterozygous | гетерозиготный имеющий два разных аллеля для определенного гена

histamine | гистамин химическое вещество, выделяемое тучными клетками, которое увеличивает поток крови и жидкостей к зараженной области во время воспалительной реакции

homeobox gene | гомеобокс-содержащий ген гомеобокс – последовательность ДНК, состоящая приблизительно из 130 пар азотистых оснований; содержится во многих гомеотических генах, которые регулируют развитие. Гены, содержащие эту последовательность, называются гомеобокс-содержащими генами. Они кодируют факторы транскрипции, белки, которые присоединяются к ДНК и регулируют экспрессию других генов

homeostasis | гомеостаз способность организмов сохранять относительное постоянство внутренних физических и химических условий

homeotic gene | гомеотический ген класс регуляторных генов, которые определяют идентичность частей организма и областей в эмбрионе животных. Мутации в этих генах обусловливают трансформацию одного органа в другой

hominine | гоминин родословная гоминида, ведущая к человеку

hominoid | гоминид группа антропоидов, которая включает гиббонов, орангутанов, горилл, шимпанзе и людей

homologous | гомологичные термин, обычно относящийся к хромосомам, у которых один набор получен от предка мужского пола, а другой набор – от предка женского пола

homologous structures | гомологичные структуры структуры, которые подобны в различных видах с общим происхождением

homozygous | гомозиготный имеющий два идентичных аллеля для определенного гена

hormone | гормон химическое вещество, образующееся в одной части организма и действующее на другую часть того же организма

Hox gene | hox-гены (гомеобокс-содержащие гены) – группа гомеотических генов, собранных вместе, которые определяют идентичность каждой части тела у животных, от головы до хвоста. Все hox-гены содержат гомеобокс-последовательность ДНК

humoral immunity | гуморальный иммунитет иммунитет к антигенам в жидкостях организма, таких как кровь и лимфа

humus | гумус материал, образуемый из гниющих листьев и других органических веществ

hybrid | гибрид потомство от скрещивания родителей с разными признаками

hybridization | гибридизация метод размножения, включающий скрещивание несхожих особей для получения потомства с лучшими признаками обоих организмов

hydrogen bond | водородная связь слабая связь между атомом водорода и другим атомом

hydrostatic skeleton | гидростатический скелет скелет, состоящий из заполненных жидкостью сегментов тела, которые наряду с мышцами обеспечивают способность животного двигаться

hypertonic | гипертонический при сравнении двух растворов: раствор с большей концентрацией растворенных веществ

hypha (pl. hyphae) | гифа одна из многих длинных, тонких нитей, из которых состоит мицелий (грибница)

hypothalamus | гипоталамус структура мозга, действующая как центр управления для распознавания и анализа чувств голода, жажды, усталости, гнева и температуры тела

hypothesis | гипотеза возможное объяснение ряда наблюдений или возможный ответ на научный вопрос

hypotonic | гипотонический при сравнении двух растворов: раствор с меньшей концентрацией растворенных веществ

I

immigration | иммиграция переселение отдельных представителей популяции в область, занятую существующей популяцией

immune response | иммунный отклик распознавание, реакция и память о воздействии микроорганизмов, являющиеся специфическими для организма

implantation | имплантация процесс, в котором бластоциста прикрепляется к стенке матки

imprinting | импринтинг (запечатление) – тип поведения, основанный на ранее приобретенном опыте; после того как произойдет импринтинг, поведение не может быть изменено

inbreeding | инбридинг (близкородственное скрещивание) – продолжительное скрещивание особей со сходными признаками для сохранения выведенных признаков вида организмов

incomplete dominance | неполное доминирование ситуация, в которой один аллель не полностью доминирует над другим аллелем

independent assortment | независимое распределение один из принципов Менделя, согласно которому гены для разных признаков могут независимо распределяться во время формирования гамет

independent variable | независимая переменная фактор в контролируемом эксперименте, который намеренно изменяется; другое название – управляемая переменная

index fossil | руководящая окаменелость характерная окаменелость, которая служит для определения относительного возраста других окаменелостей

infectious disease | инфекционная болезнь болезнь, вызванная микроорганизмом, который нарушает нормальные функции организма

inference | вывод логическое умозаключение, основанное на накопленных знаниях и опыте

inflammatory response | воспалительная реакция неспецифическая защитная реакция на повреждение тканей, вызванная травмой или инфекцией

innate behavior | врожденное поведение тип поведения, которое проявляется в полнофункциональной форме, даже если у животного не было никакого предшествующего опыта с раздражителями, вызывающими это поведение; другое название – инстинкт

insight learning | обучение по типу инсайта тип поведения, в котором животное применяет уже имеющийся навык в новой ситуации без предварительных проб и ошибок; другое название – рассуждение (мышление)

interferon | интерферон одна из групп белков, помогающих клеткам сопротивляться вирусной инфекции

interneuron | интернейрон (промежуточный нейрон) – тип нейрона, который обрабатывает информацию и может передавать информацию мотонейронам

interphase | интерфаза (промежуточная фаза) – период цикла между двумя последовательными делениями клетки

intracellular digestion | внутриклеточное переваривание пищи тип пищеварения, в котором пища переваривается в специализированных клетках, которые передают питательные вещества к другим клеткам путем диффузии

intron | интрон последовательность ДНК, которая не участвует в кодировании белка

invertebrate | беспозвоночные животные, не имеющие позвоночника или позвоночного столба

ion | ион атом, имеющий положительный или отрицательный заряд

ionic bond | ионная связь химическая связь, образуемая, когда один или несколько электронов переходят от одного атома к другому

iris | радужная оболочка (ирис) – окрашенная часть глаза

isotonic | изотонический когда концентрации двух растворов одинаковы

isotope | изотоп одна из нескольких форм элемента, которые содержат одинаковое число протонов, но разное число нейтронов

J

joint | сустав участок, в котором одна кость соединяется с другой костью

K

karyotype | кариотип микрофотография полного диплоидного набора хромосом, сгруппированных парами и расположенных в порядке уменьшения размера

keratin | кератин жесткий фибриллярный белок наружного слоя кожи

keystone species | основополагающий вид отдельный вид, который обычно не изобилует в сообществе, но оказывает сильное влияние на структуру сообщества

kidney | почка орган выделительной системы, который удаляет из крови продукты жизнедеятельности и избыточную воду

kin selection | семейный отбор теория, согласно которой помощь родственным формам может повысить эволюционную приспособляемость особей, так как родственные особи имеют много общих генов

kingdom | царство самая большая и наиболее многообразная группа в классификации

Koch's postulates | постулаты Коха набор руководящих принципов, разработанных Кохом, которые помогают идентифицировать микроорганизм, вызывающий определенную болезнь

Krebs cycle | цикл Кребса вторая стадия клеточного дыхания, в которой пировиноградная кислота расщепляется до углекислого газа в серии реакций извлечения энергии

L

language | язык система общения, в которой звуки, символы и жесты комбинируются по определенным правилам чередования и значения, таким как грамматика и синтаксис

large intestine | задняя кишка орган в пищеварительной системе, в котором вода удаляется из проходящего по нему непереваренного материала; другое название – толстая кишка

larva (pl. larvae) | личинка одна из ранних стадий развития некоторых организмов

larynx | гортань структура в горле, которая содержит голосовые связки

learning | обучение изменения в поведении в результате приобретенного опыта

lens | хрусталик структура в глазу, которая фокусирует лучи света на сетчатке

lichen | лишайник симбиоз между грибом и фотосинтезирующим организмом

ligament | связка прочная соединительная ткань, которая скрепляет кости в суставе

light-dependent reactions | светозависимые реакции ряд реакций в фотосинтезе, которые используют энергию света для образования АТФ и НАДНФ

light-independent reactions | светонезависимые реакции набор реакций в фотосинтезе, которые не требуют света; энергия АТФ и НАДНФ используется для получения богатых энергией соединений, таких как сахар; другое название – цикл Кальвина

lignin | лигнин вещество в сосудистых растениях, которое придает прочность оболочкам клеток

limiting factor | лимитирующий фактор фактор, который уменьшает прирост популяции

limiting nutrient | лимитирующее питательное вещество одно существенное питательное вещество, нехватка которого ограничивает продуктивность экосистемы

lipid | липид макромолекула, состоящая главным образом из атомов углерода и водорода; включает жиры, масла и воски

lipid bilayer | липидный бислой гибкий двойной слой молекул, который образует мембрану клетки и служит барьером между клеткой и окружающей средой

logistic growth | логистический рост модель роста, в которой рост популяции замедляется, а затем прекращается после периода экспоненциального роста

loop of Henle | петля Генле часть почечного канальца, которая отвечает за сохранение воды и уменьшение объема фильтрата

lung | легкое орган дыхательной системы; место, где происходит газообмен между кровью и вдыхаемым воздухом

lymph | лимфа жидкость, которая фильтруется из крови

lysogenic infection | лизогенная инфекция тип инфекции, в котором вирус внедряет свою ДНК в ДНК клетки-хозяина, и происходит репликация внедренной ДНК наряду с ДНК клетки-хозяина

lysosome | лизосома органелла клетки, расщепляющая липиды, углеводы и белки на малые молекулы, которые могут использоваться остальной частью клетки

lytic infection | литическая инфекция тип инфекции, при которой вирус внедряется в клетку, копирует сам себя и вызывает разрыв клетки

M

macroevolution | макроэволюция крупномасштабное эволюционное изменение, которое происходит за продолжительные периоды времени

Malpighian tubule | мальпигиев сосуд орган у большинства земных членистоногих, который концентрирует мочевую кислоту и добавляет ее к продуктам пищеварения

mammary gland | молочная железа железа у женских особей млекопитающих, которая вырабатывает молоко для кормления детенышей

mass extinction | массовое вымирание событие, во время которого многие виды вымирают за сравнительно короткий промежуток времени

matrix | матрикс самый внутренний отдел митохондриона

mechanical digestion | механическое переваривание пищи механическое расщепление больших комков пищи на более мелкие части

meiosis | мейоз (редукционное деление) – процесс, в котором число хромосом в клетке уменьшается вдвое за счет разделения гомологичных хромосом в диплоидной клетке

melanin | меланин темно-коричневый пигмент кожи, который помогает защитить кожу, поглощая ультрафиолетовые лучи

melanocyte | меланоцит клетка в коже, которая вырабатывает темно-коричневый пигмент, меланин

menstrual cycle | менструальный цикл регулярная последовательность событий, в которых яйцеклетка развивается и выделяется из организма

menstruation | менструация выделение крови и неоплодотворенной яйцеклетки из организма

meristem | меристема области неспециализированных клеток, ответственных за продолжение роста на всем протяжении жизни растения

mesoderm | мезодерма средний слой эмбриона; развивается в мышцы и большую часть кровеносной, репродуктивной и выделительной систем

mesophyll | мезофилл специализированная покровная ткань, содержащаяся в листьях; выполняет большую часть процессов фотосинтеза растения

messenger RNA (mRNA) | матричная РНК (мРНК) тип РНК, которая переносит копии инструкций для сборки аминокислот в белки из ДНК в остальную часть клетки

metabolism | метаболизм комбинация химических реакций, посредством которых организм образует или расщепляет материалы

metamorphosis | метаморфоз процесс изменения формы и превращения личинки во взрослую особь

metaphase | метафаза фаза митоза, во время которой хромосомы сосредотачиваются в центре клетки

microclimate | микроклимат климатические условия в пределах малой области, которые значительно отличаются от климата окружающих областей

migration | миграция сезонное поведение, заключающееся в перемещении из одной среды в другую

mineral | минеральные неорганические питательные вещества, обычно необходимые организму в малых количествах

mitochondrion | митохондрион органелла клетки, которая преобразует химическую энергию, сохраненную в пище, в соединения, которые более удобны для усвоения клеткой

mitosis | митоз этап деления эукариотической клетки, во время которого разделяется ядро клетки

mixture | смесь материал, состоящий из двух или более элементов или соединений, которые смешиваются физически, но не связаны химически

molecular clock | молекулярные часы метод исследования, использующий частоты мутаций в ДНК для оценки периода времени, в течение которого два вида развивались независимо

molecule | молекула наименьшая частица большинства соединений, которая сохраняет все свойства данного соединения

molting | линька процесс сбрасывания наружной оболочки (экзоскелета) и роста новой

monocot | однодольные покрытосеменные растения с одной семядолей в зародыше

monoculture | монокультура сельскохозяйственная стратегия выращивания одной высокоурожайной культуры год за годом

monomer | мономер наименьшая структурная единица полимера

monophyletic group | монофилетическая группа группа организмов, которая состоит из одного потомственного вида и всех его потомков, и не включает никаких организмов, которые не происходят от общего предка данной группы

monosaccharide | моносахарид молекула простого сахара

motor neuron | мотонейрон тип нервной клетки, которая передает сигналы от интернейронов к мышечным клеткам или железам

multiple alleles | серия аллелей ген, имеющий более двух аллелей

multipotent | многофункциональные клетки с ограниченным потенциалом для развития во многие типы дифференцированных клеток

muscle fiber | мышечное волокно клетки длинных тонких скелетных мышц

muscle tissue | мышечная ткань тип ткани, которая обеспечивает возможность движений тела

mutagen | мутаген химические или физические агенты в окружающей среде, которые взаимодействуют с ДНК и могут вызвать мутацию

mutation | мутация изменение в генетическом материале клетки

mutualism | мутуализм симбиотическое сосуществование, которое полезно для обоих взаимодействующих видов

mycelium (pl. mycelia) | мицелий сеть многочисленных ответвлений (гиф) гриба

mycorrhiza (pl. mycorrhizae) | микориза симбиотическая ассоциация корней растений и грибов

myelin sheath | миелиновая оболочка изолирующая мембрана, окружающая аксон в некоторых нейронах

myocardium | миокард плотный средний мышечный слой сердца

myofibril | миофибрилла плотно упакованная структура волокон в скелетной мышце

myosin | миозин плотные волокна белка, содержащиеся в клетках скелетных мышц

N

NAD⁺ (nicotinamide adenine dinucleotide) | НАД⁺ (никотинамидадениндинуклеотид) переносчик электронов, участвующий в гликолизе

NADP⁺ (nicotinamide adenine dinucleotide phosphate) | НАДФ⁺ (никотинамидадениндинуклеотидфосфат) молекула-переносчик, по которой передаются богатые энергией электроны от хлорофилла к другим молекулам

natural selection | естественный отбор процесс, в ходе которого выживают и успешно размножаются те организмы, которые наиболее приспособлены к данной окружающей среде; другое название – выживание наиболее приспособленных

nephridium (pl. nephridia) | нефридий выделительная структура кольчатого червя, которая фильтрует жидкость организма

nephron | нефрон структура фильтрации крови в почках, с помощью которой отфильтровываются примеси и отделяются продукты жизнедеятельности, а очищенная кровь возвращается в систему кровообращения

nervous tissue | нервная ткань тип ткани, передающей нервные импульсы по всему организму

neuromuscular junction | нервно-мышечное соединение точка контакта между мотонейроном и клеткой скелетной мышцы

neuron | нейрон нервная клетка, специализи-рованная для передачи сигналов по нервной системе

neurotransmitter | нейромедиатор химикат, используемый нейроном для передачи импульсов через синапс к другой клетке

neurulation | нейруляция первый шаг в развитии нервной системы

niche | ниша полный диапазон физических и биологических условий, в которых живет организм, и способ, которым организм использует эти условия

nitrogen fixation | фиксация азота процесс превращения газообразного азота в азотсо-держащие соединения, которые могут абсорбироваться и усваиваться растениями

node | узел участок крепления листа на растущем стебле

nondisjunction | нерасхождение ошибка в мейозе, при которой гомологичные хромосомы не разделяются должным образом

nonrenewable resource | невозобнов-ляемый ресурс ресурс, который не может восполниться естественным образом в разумный интервал времени

norepinephrine | норэпинефрин (адреналин) – гормон, выделяемый надпочечниками, который увеличивает частоту сердечных сокращений и артери-альное давление и подготавливает тело к интенсивной физической активности

notochord | хорда (спинная струна) – длинный опорный стержень в теле хордового животного, находящийся сразу под нервным стволом

nucleic acid | нуклеиновая кислота макромолекулы, содержащие водород, кислород, азот, углерод и фосфор

nucleotide | нуклеотид структурная единица, из которой построены нуклеиновые кислоты; состоит из 5-углеродного сахара, фосфатной группы, и азотистого основания

nucleus | ядро центральная часть атома, которая содержит протоны и нейтроны; в клетках: структура, содержащая генети-ческий материал клетки в форме ДНК

nutrient | питательное вещество химическое вещество, необходимое организму для поддержания жизни

nymph | нимфа стадия развития животного, которая напоминает взрослую форму, но не имеет функциональных половых органов

O

observation | наблюдение процесс тщательного отслеживания и точного описания событий или процессов

omnivore | всеядные организмы, которые получают энергию, поедая и растения, и животных

open circulatory system | открытая кровеносная система тип кровеносной системы, в которой только часть крови содержится в кровеносных сосудах при циркуляции по организму

operant conditioning | оперантное обучение тип обучения, при котором животное путем многократных повторений учится вести себя определенным образом, чтобы получить награду или избежать наказания

operator | оператор короткий участок ДНК, смежный промотору прокариотического оперона, который связывает репрессорные белки, ответственные за регулирование скорости транскрипции оперона

operon | оперон в прокариотах: группа смежных генов, использующих общий оператор и промотор и транслирующихся в одну мРНК

opposable thumb | отстоящий большой палец большой палец, который позволяет захватывать предметы и использовать инструменты

order | род в классификации: группа тесно связанных семейств

organ | орган группы тканей, предназна-ченных для совместного выполнения близко связанных функций

organ system | система органов группа органов, работающих вместе для выполнения определенной функции

organelle | органелла специализированная структура, которая выполняет важные клеточные функции в эукариотической клетке

osmosis | осмос диффузия воды через селективно-проницаемую мембрану

osmotic pressure | осмотическое давление давление, которое должно быть приложено, чтобы предотвратить осмотическое движение через селективно-проницаемую мембрану

ossification | окостенение процесс формирования костей, во время которого хрящ заменяется костью

osteoblast | остеобласт костная клетка, которая продуцирует минеральные отложения, заменяющие хрящ в формирующихся костях

osteoclast | остеокласт костная клетка, которая расщепляет костные минералы

osteocyte | остеоцит костная клетка, которая поддерживает подачу минералов в костную ткань и продолжает упрочнять формирующуюся кость

ovary | яичник в растениях: завязь – структура, которая окружает и защищает семена ; у животных: яичник – первичный женский репродуктивный орган; образует яйцеклетки

oviparous | яйцекладущие виды, у которых эмбрионы развиваются в яйцах вне родительского организма

ovoviparous | яйцеживородящие виды, у которых эмбрионы развиваются в пределах организма матери, но полностью зависят от желточного мешка их яиц

ovulation | овуляция выход зрелой яйцеклетки из яичника в одну из фаллопиевых труб

ovule | семязачаток структура в семеносных шишках, в которой развиваются женские гаметофиты

ozone layer | озоновый слой атмосферный слой, в котором относительно сконцентрирован озон; защищает жизнь на Земле от вредных ультрафиолетовых лучей в солнечном свете

P

pacemaker | ритмоводитель малая группа волокон сердечной мышцы, которая поддерживает насосный ритм сердца, устанавливая частоту сердечных сокращений; синусовый (SA) узел

paleontologist | палеонтолог ученый, который изучает окаменелости

palisade mesophyll | палисадный мезофилл слой клеток под верхним эпидермисом листа

parasitism | паразитизм симбиотическое сосуществование, при котором один организм живет на другом или внутри другого и вредит ему

parathyroid hormone (PTH) | паратгормон (ПТГ) гормон, вырабатываемый паращитовидной железой, который повышает уровень кальция в крови

parenchyma | паренхима основной тип покровной ткани в растениях; содержит клетки с тонкими оболочками и большими центральными вакуолями

passive immunity | пассивный иммунитет временный иммунитет, который развивается в результате естественного или вызванного намеренно воздействия антигена

pathogen | патоген возбудитель болезни

pedigree | генеалогическая схема диаграмма, показывающая наличие или отсутствие признака в зависимости от родственных связей в пределах семейства на протяжении нескольких поколений

pepsin | пепсин фермент, расщепляющий белки на более мелкие полипептидные фрагменты

period | период отрезок геологического времени в пределах эры

peripheral nervous system | периферическая нервная система сеть нервов и поддерживающих клеток, по которой происходит обмен сигналами между центральной нервной системой и организмом

peristalsis | перистальтика сокращения гладких мышц, которые способствуют продвижению пищи по пищеводу к желудку

permafrost | вечная мерзлота слой постоянно промерзшей почвы в приполярной тундре

petiole | черешок тонкая ножка, которая соединяет пластину листа со стеблем

pH scale | шкала pH шкала с делениями от 0 до 14, используемая для измерения концентрации ионов H^+ в растворе; от 0 до 7 – кислые растворы, 7 – нейтральный раствор и от 7 до 14 – щелочной раствор

pharyngeal pouch | фарингеальный мешочек одна из парных структур в области горла хордового организма

pharynx | глотка трубка в конце ротовой полости, которая служит проходом и для воздуха, и для пищи; другое название – горло

phenotype | фенотип совокупность всех физических свойств организма

phloem | флоэма (лубяная ткань) – сосудистая ткань, которая транспортирует по растению растворы питательных веществ и углеводов, полученных путем фотосинтеза

photic zone | фотическая зона область проникновения солнечного света вблизи поверхности воды

photoperiod | фотопериод (световой день) – отклик растения на относительную продолжительность светлого и темного времени суток

photosynthesis | фотосинтез процесс, используемый растениями и другими автотрофами для поглощения энергии света и ее использования для химических реакций превращения углекислого газа и воды в богатые кислородом и энергией углеводы, такие как сахар и крахмалы

photosystem | фотосистема кластер из хлорофилла и белков, находящийся в тилакоидах

phototropism | фототропизм тенденция растения тянуться в направлении источника света

phylogeny | филогенез исследование эволюционных зависимостей среди организмов

phylum | тип в классификации: группа тесно связанных классов

phytoplankton | фитопланктон фотосинтезирующие морские водоросли, растущие вблизи поверхности океана

pigment | пигмент светопоглощающие молекулы, используемые растениями для поглощения энергии солнца

pioneer species | пионерный вид первые виды, заселяющие область во время сукцессии

pistil | пестик один плодолистик или несколько сросшихся плодолистиков; содержит завязь, пестик и рыльце

pith | сердцевина клетки паренхимы в кольце сосудистой ткани в стеблях двудольных растений

pituitary gland | гипофиз малая железа вблизи основания черепа, вырабатывающие гормоны, которые непосредственно регулируют многие функции организма и управляют действиями некоторых других эндокринных желез

placenta | плацента специализированный орган у плацентарных млекопитающих, через который происходит обмен дыхательными газами, питательными веществами и продуктами жизнедеятельности между матерью и развивающимся плодом

plankton | планктон микроскопические организмы, которые живут в водных средах; включает как фитопланктон, так и зоопланктон

plasma | плазма жидкая часть крови соломенно-желтого цвета

plasmid | плазмиды небольшие кольцевые молекулы ДНК, находящиеся в цитоплазме многих бактерий

plasmodium | плазмодий амебоидная стадия питания в жизненном цикле слизевиков

plate tectonics | тектоника плит геологические процессы, такие как дрейф континентов, вулканы и землетрясения, возникающие в результате сдвигов плит

platelet | тромбоцит фрагмент клетки, выделяемый костным мозгом; способствует свертыванию крови

pluripotent | плюрипотентные клетки, которые способны к превращению в большую часть, но не во все типы клеток организма

point mutation | точечная мутация генная мутация, вызванная изменением одной пары азотистых оснований в ДНК

pollen grain | пыльцевое зерно структура, которая содержит весь мужской гаметофит в семенных растениях

pollen tube | пыльцевая трубка структура, которая содержит два гаплоидных ядра спермия

pollination | опыление перенос пыльцы от мужской репродуктивной структуры к женской репродуктивной структуре

pollutant | загрязнитель вредный материал, который может попасть в биосферу через почву, воздух или воду

polygenic trait | полигенный признак признак, контролируемый двумя или несколькими генами

polymer | полимер молекулы, состоящие из множества мономеров; образует макромолекулы

polymerase chain reaction (PCR) | полимеразная цепная реакция (ПЦР) метод, используемый биологами для получения множества копий определенного гена

polypeptide | полипептид длинная цепь аминокислот, образующих белки

polyploidy | полиплоидия условие, при котором у организма возникают избыточные наборы хромосом

population | популяция группа особей одинаковых видов, обитающих в одной области

population density | плотность популяции число особей на единице площади

predation | хищничество взаимодействие, в котором один организм (хищник) захватывает и поедает другой организм (жертву)

prehensile tail | цепкий хвост длинный хвост, который может достаточно крепко обматываться вокруг ветки

pressure-flow hypothesis | гипотеза противопотока гипотеза, которая объясняет способ транспортировки сока флоэмы по растению от "источника" сахара к "сливу" сахара

primary growth | первичный рост модель роста, наблюдаемая на верхушках и отростках растения

primary producer | первичный продуцент первые продуценты богатых энергией соединений, которые затем используются другими организмами

primary succession | первичная сукцессия сукцессия, происходящая в области, в которой нет следов предшествующих сообществ

principle of dominance | принцип доминирования второй принцип Менделя, согласно которому одни аллели являются доминантными, а другие рецессивными

prion | прион белковые частицы, вызывающие болезнь

probability | вероятность вероятность того, что определенное событие произойдет

product | продукт элементы или соединения, образующиеся путем химической реакции

prokaryote | прокариот одноклеточный организм, не имеющий ядра

promoter | промотор определенный участок гена, где РНК-полимераза может присоединиться и начать считывание кода

prophage | профаг ДНК бактериофага, которая встроена в ДНК бактериальной клетки-хозяина

prophase | профаза первая и самая длинная фаза митоза, в которой генетический материал ядра конденсируется и хромосомы становятся видимыми

prostaglandin | простагландин модифицированные жирные кислоты, вырабатываемые широким диапазоном клеток; обычно действует только на соседние клетки и ткани

protein | белок макромолекула, которая содержит углерод, водород, кислород и азот; необходим организму для роста и восстановления

protostome | первичноротые животные, у которых ротовое отверстие образуется из бластопора

pseudocoelom | псевдоцелом полость тела, только частично покрытая мезодермой

pseudopod | псевдоподия временная цитоплазматическая проекция, используемая некоторыми протистами для движения

puberty | половая зрелость период быстрого роста и полового созревания, во время которого репродуктивная система становится полностью функциональной

pulmonary circulation | малый круг кровообращения система кровообращения между сердцем и легкими

punctuated equilibrium | прерывистое равновесие модель эволюции, в которой длительные устойчивые периоды прерываются краткими периодами более быстрого изменения

Punnett square | решетка Пеннетта диаграмма, которая может использоваться для предсказания комбинаций генотипа и фенотипа для генетического скрещивания

pupa | куколка стадия в полном метаморфозе, в которой личинка развивается во взрослый организм

pupil | зрачок малое отверстие в радужной оболочке, через которое свет проходит в глаз

R

radial symmetry | радиальная симметрия проекция тела, в которой любая воображаемая плоскость, проходящая через центр тела, разделит его на равные половины

radiometric dating | радиометрическое датирование метод определения возраста образца по соотношению количеств радиоактивного и нерадиоактивного изотопа одного и того же элемента в образце

reabsorption | реабсорбция процесс, посредством которого вода и растворенные вещества поступают обратно в кровь

reactant | реагент элементы или соединения, вступающие в химическую реакцию

receptor | рецептор на клетке или внутри клетки: определенный белок, к форме которого подходит форма молекулярного посредника, такого как гормон

recombinant DNA | рекомбинантная ДНК ДНК, полученная объединением ДНК из разных источников

red blood cell | красная кровяная клетка (эритроцит) – клетка крови, содержащая гемоглобин, которая переносит кислород

reflex | рефлекс быстрый, автоматический ответ на раздражение

reflex arc | рефлекторная дуга сенсорный рецептор, сенсорный нейрон, мотонейрон и эффекторный нейрон, которые включаются в быстрый отклик на раздражитель

relative dating | относительное датирование метод определения возраста окаменелости, путем сравнения ее размещения с размещением окаменелостей в других пластах породы

relative frequency | относительная частота число наблюдений аллеля в генном пуле по сравнению с числом наблюдений других аллелей этого гена

releasing hormone | высвобождающий гормон гормон, вырабатываемый гипоталамусом, который стимулирует переднюю долю гипофиза к выделению гормонов

renewable resource | возобновляемый ресурс ресурс, который может быть произведен или заменен функциями благополучной экосистемы

replication | репликация процесс копирования ДНК перед делением клетки

reproductive isolation | репродуктивная изоляция разделение вида или популяции таким образом, чтобы не было возможности их перекрестного скрещивания, а развивались два отдельных вида

resource | ресурс любая потребность для жизни, такая как вода, питательные вещества, свет, пища или пространство

response | отклик специфическая реакция на раздражитель

resting potential | потенциал покоя электрический заряд покоящейся клетки (нейрона) между ее внутренним содержимым и внеклеточной средой, разделенным мембраной

restriction enzyme | ограничивающий фермент фермент, который рассекает ДНК на специфические последовательности нуклеотидов

retina | сетчатка самый внутренний слой глаза; содержит зрительные рецепторы

retrovirus | ретровирус РНК-содержащий вирус, в котором РНК служит для хранения его генетической информации

ribonucleic acid (RNA) | рибонуклеиновая кислота (РНК) одноцепочечная нуклеиновая кислота, содержащая рибозу

ribosomal RNA (rRNA) | рибосомальная РНК (рРНК) тип РНК, которая соединяется с белками для образования рибосомы

ribosome | рибосома органелла клетки, состоящая из РНК и белка, находящихся в цитоплазме клетки; место протекания белкового синтеза

RNA interference (RNAi) | РНК-интерференция (РНКi) введение двухспиральной РНК в клетку, чтобы ингибировать генную экспрессию

RNA polymerase | РНК-полимераза Фермент, который связывает растущую цепь нуклеотидов РНК во время транскрипции, используя цепь ДНК в качестве матрицы

rod | палочка зрительный рецептор в глазах, который чувствителен к свету, но не различает цвета

root cap | корневой чехлик жесткое покрытие конца корня, которое защищает меристему

root hair | корневой волосок тонкие волоски на корне, обеспечивающие большую площадь поверхности для поступления воды и минералов

rumen | рубец камера желудка у коров и родственных животных, в которой симбиотические бактерии переваривают целлюлозу

S

sapwood | заболонь в древесном стебле: слой вторичной флоэмы вокруг ядра древесины; обычно участвует в передаче жидкости

sarcomere | саркомер структурный элемент сокращения мышцы; состоит из двух z-линий и филаментов между ними

scavenger | падальщик животное, питающееся останками других животных

science | наука систематизированный способ сбора и анализа данных о естественном мире

sclerenchyma | склеренхима тип покровной ткани с чрезвычайно плотными и твердыми оболочками клеток, которые делают покровную ткань жесткой и прочной

scrotum | мошонка внешний мешочек, в котором находятся яички

sebaceous gland | сальная железа железа в коже, которая выделяет сало (салоотделение)

secondary growth | вторичный рост тип роста у двудольных растений, при котором стебли увеличиваются по толщине

secondary succession | вторичная сукцессия тип сукцессии, встречающийся в области, которая только частично пострадала от неблагоприятных явлений

seed | семя зародыш растения и питательная среда, заключенные в защитную оболочку

seed coat | семенная оболочка жесткое покрытие, которое окружает и защищает зародыш растения и предотвращает высыхание содержимого

segregation | разъединение разделение аллелей во время формирования гаметы

selective breeding | селективное скрещивание метод скрещивания, при котором производить потомство следующего поколения позволяется только организмам с желательными признаками

selectively permeable | селективно проницаемые способность биологических мембран пропускать одни вещества и не пропускать другие; другое название – полупроницаемая мембрана

semen | сперма комбинация спермы и семенной жидкости

semicircular canal | полукружный канал одна из трех структур во внутреннем ухе, которые контролируют положение тела с учетом силы притяжения

seminiferous tubule | семявыносящая трубочка одна из сотен трубочек в каждом яичке, в которых формируется сперма

sensory neuron | сенсорный нейрон тип нервной клетки, которая получает информацию от сенсорных рецепторов и передает сигналы центральной нервной системе

sex chromosome | половая хромосома одна из двух хромосом, определяющих пол человека

sex-linked gene | ген, сцепленный с полом ген, находящийся в половой хромосоме

sexual reproduction | половое размножение тип размножения, в котором клетки от двух родителей объединяются и образуют первую клетку нового организма

sexually transmitted disease (STD) | болезнь, передающаяся половым путем болезнь, которая передается от человека к человеку при половых контактах

sieve tube element | элемент ситовидной трубки непрерывная трубка из клеток флоэмы растения, которые выстраиваются по всей длине

single-gene trait | моногенный признак признак, контролируемый одним геном, имеющим два аллеля

small intestine | тонкая кишка пищеварительный орган, в котором происходит основное химическое переваривание и поглощение пищи

smog | смог серо-коричневая дымка, образованная смесью химических веществ

society | сообщество группа родственных животных одного вида, которые совместно действуют на пользу группы

solute | растворенное вещество вещество, которое растворено в растворе

solution | раствор тип смеси, в которой все компоненты равномерно распределены

solvent | растворитель вещество, в котором растворяются другие компоненты раствора

somatic nervous system | соматическая нервная система часть периферической нервной системы, которая передает и получает сигналы от скелетных мышц

speciation | видообразование формирование нового вида

species diversity | многообразие видов совокупность разных видов, населяющих определенную область

spirillum (pl. spirilla) | спирилла спиральный прокариот или прокариот в форме изогнутой палочки

spongy mesophyll | зубчатый мезофилл слой рыхлой ткани ниже палисадного мезофилла в листе

sporangium (pl. sporangia) | спорангий капсула спор, в которой в процессе мейоза образуются гаплоидные споры

spore | спора у прокариотов, протистов и грибов: стадии жизненного цикла любого из разнообразных толстостенных, способных к выживанию в неблагоприятных условиях; у растений: гаплоидная репродуктивная клетка

sporophyte | спорофит растение, образующее споры; диплоидная многоклеточная фаза в жизненном цикле растения

stabilizing selection | стабилизирующий отбор форма естественного отбора, в которой особи вблизи центра кривой распределения имеют более высокую приспособляемость, чем особи на обоих концах кривой

stamen | тычинка мужская часть цветка; состоит из пыльника и тычиночной нити

stem cell | стволовая клетка неспециа-лизированная клетка, которая может превратиться в один или несколько типов специализированных клеток

stigma | рыльце липкая часть верхушки пестика; предназначена для улавливания пыльцы

stimulus (pl. stimuli) | раздражитель сигнал, на который реагирует организм

stoma (pl. stomata) | устьице небольшое отверстие в эпидермисе растения, через которое происходит диффузия углекислого газа, воды и кислорода в лист и из листа

stomach | желудок большой мышечный мешок, в котором продолжается механи-ческое и химическое переваривание пищи

stroma | строма жидкая часть хлоропласта; за пределами тилакоидов

substrate | субстрат реагент в реакции, катализируемой ферментом

suspension | суспензия смесь воды и нерастворимого вещества

sustainable development | устойчивое развитие стратегия использования природных ресурсов, не исчерпывая их, и обеспечения потребностей людей, не принося продолжительного вреда окружающей среде

symbiosis | симбиоз близкое сосуще-ствование двух видов

synapse | синапс зона контакта, в которой нейрон может передать импульс другой клетке

systematics | систематика исследование многообразия форм жизни и эволюционных взаимосвязей между организмами

systemic circulation | большой круг кровоо-бращения система кровообращения между сердцем и остальной частью организма

T

taiga | тайга биом с длинными холодными зимами и коротким периодом теплой погоды; доминирование хвойных вечнозеленых растений; другое название – бореальный лес

target cell | клетка-мишень клетка, имеющая рецептор для определенного гормона

taste bud | вкусовой сосочек чувстви-тельный орган, который определяет вкус

taxon (pl. taxa) | таксон группа или уровень организации в классификации организмов

telomere | теломера повторяющаяся ДНК на концевом участке эукариотической хромосомы

telophase | телофаза фаза митоза, в которой различные индивидуальные хромосомы начинают распространяться в структуру хроматина

temporal isolation | изоляция во времени форма репродуктивной изоляции, в которой два или более видов воспроизводятся в разное время

tendon | сухожилие плотная соединительная ткань, которая скрепляет скелетные мышцы с костями

territory | территория определенная область, занятая и защищаемая животным или группой животных

testis (pl. testes) | яички первичный мужской репродуктивный орган; вырабатывает сперму

tetrad | тетрада структура, содержащая четыре хроматиды, которая формируется во время мейоза

tetrapod | Четвероногое позвоночное животное с четырьмя конечностями

thalamus | таламус структура головного мозга, которая получает сигналы от органов чувств и передает информацию в соответствующую область головного мозга для дальнейшей обработки

theory | теория надежно проверенное объяснение, которое объединяет широкий круг наблюдений и гипотез и позволяет ученым делать точные предсказания относительно новых ситуаций

thigmotropism | тигмотропизм реакция растения на соприкосновение с твердым телом

threshold | порог минимальный уровень раздражителя, необходимый для вызова импульса

thylakoid | тилакоид фотосинтетические мембраны в форме мешочков, находящиеся в хлоропластах

thyroxine | тироксин гормон, вырабатываемый щитовидной железой, который увеличивает уровень метаболизма клеток во всем организме

tissue | ткань группа подобных клеток, выполняющих определенную функцию

tolerance | выносливость способность организма к выживанию и воспроизведению при обстоятельствах, которые отличаются от оптимальных условий его жизни

totipotent | тотипотентные клетки, которые способны превращаться в любой тип клеток, имеющихся в организме (включая клетки внезародышевой оболочки и плаценты)

trachea | трахея трубка, соединяющая глотку с гортанью; другое название – дыхательное горло

tracheid | трахеида полая растительная клетка в ксилеме; имеет толстые стенки, укрепленные лигнином

tracheophyte | трахеофит сосудистое растение

trait | признак специфическая характеристика особи

transcription | транскрипция синтез молекулы РНК на матрице ДНК

transfer RNA (tRNA) | транспортная РНК (tРНК) тип РНК, которая транспортирует аминокислоты к рибосоме во время белкового синтеза

transformation | трансформация процесс, в котором штамм бактерий изменяется геном или генами от другого штамма бактерий

transgenic | трансгенный термин, обычно относящийся к организму, который содержит гены от других организмов

translation | трансляция процесс, в котором последовательность оснований мРНК преобразуется в последовательность аминокислот белка

transpiration | транспирация потеря воды растением через его листья

trochophore | трохофора стадия свободно плавающей личинки в жизни водного моллюска

trophic level | трофический уровень каждый шаг в цепи питания или пищевой сети

tropism | тропизм движение растения в направлении раздражителя или от раздражителя

tumor | опухоль масса быстро делящихся клеток, которые могут повредить окружающую ткань

U

understory | подлесок находящийся под листовым пологом слой во влажном лесу, образуемый более низкими деревьями и лианами

ureter | мочеточник трубка, по которой проходит моча из почки в мочевой пузырь

urethra | уретра (мочеиспускательный канал) – трубка, по которой моча выводится из организма

urinary bladder | мочевой пузырь орган в форме мешка, в котором накапливается моча перед выведением из организма

V

vaccination | вакцинация инъекция ослабленного или подобного, но менее опасного, инфекционного агента для выработки иммунитета

vaccine | вакцина препарат на основе ослабленных или инактивированных инфекционных агентов, предназначенный для выработки иммунитета к заболеванию

vacuole | вакуоль органелла клетки, в которой хранятся такие вещества, как вода, соли, белки и углеводы

valve | клапан лоскут соединительной ткани, расположенный между предсердием и желудочком, или в вене; предотвращает обратный поток крови

van der Waals forces | ван-дер-ваальсовские силы слабое притяжение, возникающее между противоположно заряженными областями соседних молекул

vas deferens | семявыносящий проток сосуда трубка, по которой проходит сперма от эпидидимиса к уретре

vascular bundle | сосудистый пучок кластеры ксилемы и ткани флоэмы в стеблях

vascular cambium | сосудистый камбий меристема, которая формирует сосудистые ткани и увеличивает толщину стеблей

vascular cylinder | сосудистый цилиндр центральная область корня, которая содержит сосудистые ткани – ксилему и флоэму

vascular tissue | сосудистая ткань специализированная ткань в растениях, которая переносит воду и питательные вещества

vector | вектор (переносчик инфекции) – животное, которое передает инфекционный агент человеку

vegetative reproduction | вегетативное размножение способ бесполого размножения у растений, который позволяет одному растению производить потомство, идентичное родительскому растению

vein | вена кровеносный сосуд, возвращающий кровь от органов к сердцу

ventricle | желудочек нижняя камера сердца, из которой кровь подается к остальной части тела

vertebrate | позвоночные животные, у которых есть позвоночник

vessel element | элемент сосуда тип клеток ксилемы, которые образуют непрерывную трубку, по которой может проходить вода

vestigial organs | рудименты структуры, которые уменьшены в размере и либо выполняют незначительные функции, либо не выполняют никаких функций

villus (pl. villi) | ворсинки пальцевидные отростки в тонкой кишке, которые участвуют в поглощении молекул питательных веществ

virus | вирус частица, состоящая из белков, нуклеиновых кислот и иногда липидов; может копироваться только путем заражения живых клеток

vitamin | витамин органическая молекула, которая помогает отрегулировать процессы организма

viviparous | живородящие животные, вынашивающие живых детенышей, которые при внутриутробном развитии получают питание непосредственно из организма матери

W

weather | погода ежедневные атмосферные условия, включая температуру, осадки и другие факторы

wetland | заболоченная территория экосистема, в которой вода либо покрывает почву, либо находится близко к поверхности, по крайней мере, часть года

white blood cell | белая кровяная клетка (лейкоцит) – тип клеток крови, которые противодействуют инфекции, паразитам и атакуют бактерии

woody plant | древесное растение тип растений, состоящих главным образом из толстостенных клеток, которые поддерживают тело растения, включает деревья, кусты и лианы

X

xylem | ксилема сосудистая ткань,
переносящая воду от корней вверх
к каждой части растения

Z

zoonosis (pl. zoonoses) | зооноз болезнь,
передающаяся от животного человеку

zooplankton | зоопланктон мелкие свободно
плавающие животные, которые являются
частью планктона

zygote | зигота оплодотворенное яйцо

Spanish
Español

Miller & Levine
Biology
Glossary

A

abiotic factor | factor abiótico factor físico, o inanimado, que da forma a un ecosistema

abscisic acid | ácido abscísico hormona vegetal que inhibe la división celular y, por ende, el crecimiento

acetylcholine | acetilcolina neurotransmisor que produce un impulso en una célula muscular

acid | ácido compuesto que en una solución produce iones hidrógeno (H^+); una solución con un pH inferior a 7

acid rain | lluvia ácida lluvia que contiene ácido nítrico y ácido sulfúrico

actin | actina microfilamento de proteína que se halla en los músculos

action potential | potencial de acción inversión de las cargas a través de la membrana de una neurona; también llamado impulso nervioso

activation energy | energía de activación energía necesaria para que comience una reacción

active immunity | inmunidad activa inmunidad que se desarrolla a consecuencia de la exposición natural o deliberada a un antígeno

adaptation | adaptación característica heredable que aumenta la capacidad de un organismo de sobrevivir y reproducirse en un medio ambiente

adaptive radiation | radiación adaptativa proceso mediante el cual una sola especie o un grupo pequeño de especies evoluciona y da lugar a diferentes seres que viven de diversas maneras

adenosine triphosphate (ATP) | trifosfato de adenosina (ATP) compuesto utilizado por las células para almacenar y liberar energía

adhesion | adhesión fuerza de atracción entre diferentes tipos de moléculas

aerobic | aeróbico proceso que requiere oxígeno

age structure | estructura etaria número de machos y de hembras de cada edad en una población

aggression | agresión comportamiento amenazador que emplea un animal para ejercer control sobre otro animal

algal bloom | florecimiento de algas aumento de la cantidad de algas y otros productores debido a una gran entrada de un nutriente limitante

allele | alelo cada una de las diversas formas de un gen

allergy | alergia reacción exagerada del sistema inmune ante un antígeno

alternation of generations | alternancia de generaciones ciclo vital con dos fases que se alternan, una fase haploide (N) y una fase diploide (2N)

alveolus (pl. alveoli): | alvéolos pequeños sacos, ubicados en las terminaciones de los bronquiolos pulmonares, que proporcionan una superficie en la que tiene lugar el intercambio gaseoso

amino acid | aminoácido compuesto que contiene un grupo amino en un extremo y un grupo carboxilo en el otro extremo

amniotic egg | huevo amniota huevo formado por una cáscara y membranas que crea un ambiente protegido en el cual el embrión puede desarrollarse en un medio seco

amylase | amilasa enzima de la saliva que fragmenta los enlaces químicos de los almidones

anaerobic | anaeróbico proceso que no requiere oxígeno

anaphase | anafase fase de la mitosis en la cual los cromosomas se separan y se desplazan hacia los extremos opuestos de la célula

angiosperm | angiospermas grupo de plantas con semillas, que están protegidas con una capa de tejido. Se conocen también como plantas que florecen.

anther | antera estructura de la flor en la cual se generan los granos de polen

antheridium (pl. antheridia) | anteridio en algunas plantas, estructura reproductora masculina que produce esperma (anterozoides)

anthropoid | antropoide grupo de primates constituido por monos, simios y humanos

antibiotic | antibiótico grupo de drogas utilizadas para bloquear el desarrollo y la reproducción de organismos patógenos bacterianos

antibody | anticuerpo proteína que ataca directamente a los antígenos o produce proteínas que se unen a los antígenos

anticodon | anticodón grupo de tres bases en una molécula de ARN de transferencia que son complementarias a las tres bases de un codón de ARN mensajero

antigen | antígeno cualquier sustancia que provoca una respuesta inmune

aphotic zone | zona afótica sección oscura de los océanos donde no penetra la luz solar, situada debajo de la zona fótica

apical dominance | dominancia apical fenómeno por el cual cuanto más cerca de la punta del tallo está un brote, más se inhibe su crecimiento

apical meristem | meristemo apical grupo de células no especializadas que se dividen para producir un aumento en la longitud de tallos y raíces

apoptosis | apoptosis proceso de muerte celular programada

appendage | apéndice estructura, como una pierna o una antena, que se proyecta desde la superficie corporal

appendicular skeleton | esqueleto apendicular los huesos de los brazos y de las piernas junto con los huesos de la pelvis y del área de los hombros

aquaculture | acuicultura cría de organismos acuáticos para el consumo humano

aquaporin | acuaporina proteína que canaliza el agua en una célula

Archaea | Arqueas dominio formado por procariotas unicelulares cuyas paredes celulares no contienen peptidoglicano; corresponden al reino de las Arqueabacterias

archegonium (pl. archegonia) | arquegonio estructura de las plantas que produce óvulos

artery | arteria vaso sanguíneo grande que transporta la sangre desde el corazón a los tejidos del cuerpo

artificial selection | selección artificial cría selectiva de plantas y animales para fomentar la ocurrencia de rasgos deseados en la progenie

asexual reproduction | reproducción asexual proceso de reproducción que involucra a un único progenitor y da por resultado descendencia genéticamente idéntica a ese progenitor

asthma | asma enfermedad respiratoria crónica en la cual las vías respiratorias se estrechan, provocando jadeos, tos y dificultad para respirar

atherosclerosis | arteriosclerosis o ateroesclerosis enfermedad en la cual se acumulan depósitos de grasa llamados placas en el interior de las paredes arteriales que, con el tiempo, causan un endurecimiento de las arterias

atom | átomo unidad básica de la materia

ATP synthase | ATP sintasa complejo de proteínas unidas a la membrana celular que permiten el paso de los iones de hidrógeno (H^+) a través de ella

atrium (pl. atria) | aurícula cavidad superior del corazón que recibe sangre del resto del cuerpo

autonomic nervous system | sistema nervioso autónomo parte del sistema nervioso periférico que regula las actividades involuntarias, o que son independientes de la conciencia; está compuesto por las subdivisiones simpática y parasimpática

autosome | autosoma cromosoma que no es un cromosoma sexual; también llamado cromosoma autosómico

autotroph | autótrofo organismo capaz de atrapar la energía de la luz solar o de las sustancias químicas y utilizarla para producir su propio alimento a partir de compuestos inorgánicos; también llamado productor

auxin | auxina sustancia reguladora producida en la punta de una planta en crecimiento que estimula el alargamiento celular y el crecimiento de raíces nuevas

axial skeleton | esqueleto axial esqueleto que sostiene al eje central del cuerpo; consiste en el cráneo, la columna vertebral y la caja torácica

axon | axón fibra larga que lleva los impulsos desde el cuerpo celular de una neurona

B

bacillus (pl. bacilli) | bacilo procariota con forma de bastón

background extinction | extinción de fondo extinción causada por un proceso lento y continuo de selección natural

Bacteria | Bacteria pertenece al dominio de los unicelulares procariota cuyas paredes celulares contienen peptidoglicano; corresponde al reino de las Eubacterias

bacteriophage | bacteriófago clase de virus que infecta a las bacterias

bark | corteza tejidos que se hallan fuera del cámbium vascular, incluidos el floema, el cámbium suberoso y el corcho

base | base compuesto que en una solución produce iones hidróxido (OH⁻); una solución con un pH superior a 7

base pairing | apareamiento de bases principio que establece que los enlaces en el ADN sólo pueden formarse entre adenina y timina y entre guanina y citocina

behavior | comportamiento manera en que un organismo reacciona a los cambios que ocurren en su condición interna o en el medio ambiente externo

behavioral isolation | aislamiento conductual forma de aislamiento reproductivo en la cual dos poblaciones desarrollan diferencias en sus rituales de cortejo o en otros comportamientos que evitan que se apareen

benthos | bentos organismos que viven adheridos al fondo, o cerca del fondo, de lagos, arroyos u océanos

bias | parcialidad preferencia especial o punto de vista que es personal en lugar de ser científico

bilateral symmetry | simetría bilateral diseño corporal en el cual una línea imaginaria divide al cuerpo en dos lados, izquierdo y derecho, que son imágenes reflejas una del otra

binary fission | fisión binaria tipo de reproducción asexual en la cual un organismo replica su ADN, se divide por la mitad y produce dos células hijas idénticas

binocular vision | visión binocular capacidad de fusionar las imágenes visuales provenientes de ambos ojos, lo cual proporciona una percepción profunda y una visión tridimensional del mundo

binomial nomenclature | nomenclatura binaria sistema de clasificación en el cual a cada especie se le asigna un nombre científico que consta de dos partes

biodiversity | biodiversidad totalidad de los distintos organismos que se hallan en la biósfera; también denominada diversidad biológica

biogeochemical cycle | ciclo biogeoquímico proceso en el cual los elementos, los compuestos químicos y otras formas de materia pasan de un organismo a otro y de una parte de la biósfera a otra

biogeography | biogeografía estudio de la distribución pasada y presente de los organismos

bioinformatics | bioinformática aplicación de las matemáticas y de la informática para almacenar, recuperar y analizar información biológica

biological magnification | bioacumulación concentración creciente de sustancias perjudiciales en los organismos de los niveles tróficos más elevados de una cadena o red alimentaria

biology | biología estudio científico de la vida

biomass | biomasa cantidad total de tejido vivo dentro de un nivel trófico dado

biome | bioma un grupo de ecosistemas que comparten climas similares y organismos típicos

biosphere | biósfera parte de la Tierra en la cual existe vida, y que incluye el suelo, el agua y el aire o atmósfera

biotechnology | biotecnología proceso de manipular organismos, células o moléculas con el fin de obtener productos específicos

biotic factor | factor biótico cualquier parte viva del medio ambiente con la cual un organismo podría interaccionar

bipedal | bípedo término utilizado para referirse a la locomoción sobre dos pies

blade | lámina foliar o limbo parte delgada y plana de la hoja de una planta

blastocyst | blastocisto etapa temprana del desarrollo de los mamíferos que consiste en una bola hueca formada por una capa de células

blastula | blástula esfera hueca de células que se desarrolla cuando un cigoto atraviesa una serie de divisiones celulares

bone marrow | médula ósea tejido blando que se halla en las cavidades de los huesos

bottleneck effect | efecto cuello de botella un cambio en la frecuencia alélica que resulta cuando el tamaño de una población reduce drásticamente

Bowman's capsule | cápsula de Bowman estructura en forma de taza que encierra al glomérulo; recoge los filtrados provenientes de la sangre

brain stem | tronco cerebral estructura que conecta al cerebro con la médula espinal; incluye el bulbo raquídeo y el puente de Varolio

bronchus (pl. bronchi) | bronquio cada uno de los dos conductos largos ubicados en la cavidad torácica que parten desde la tráquea y llegan a los pulmones

bryophyte | briofitas grupo de plantas que tienen órganos reproductores especializados pero carecen de tejido vascular; incluyen a los musgos y sus congéneres

bud | yema o gema estructura de las plantas que contiene tejido del meristemo apical y puede producir nuevos tallos y hojas

buffer | solución amortiguadora compuesto que evita cambios bruscos y repentinos en el pH

C

calcitonin | calcitonina hormona producida por la tiroides que reduce los niveles de calcio en la sangre

Calorie | Caloría medida de la energía térmica de los alimentos, equivalente a 1000 calorías

calorie | caloría cantidad de energía necesaria para elevar la temperatura de 1 gramo de agua en 1 grado Celsius

Calvin cycle | ciclo de Calvin reacciones de la fotosíntesis independientes de la luz en las cuales se utiliza la energía del ATP y del NADPH para elaborar compuestos con alto contenido energético, como el azúcar

cancer | cáncer enfermedad en la cual algunas de las células del cuerpo pierden la capacidad de controlar su crecimiento

canopy | dosel forestal cubierta densa formada por las copas de los árboles altos del bosque tropical

capillary | capilar más pequeño de los vaso sanguíneo más pequeño; lleva nutrientes y oxígeno a los tejidos y absorbe dióxido de carbono y productos de desecho

capillary action | capilaridad tendencia del agua a ascender en un tubo delgado

capsid | cápsida cobertura de proteínas que rodea a un virus

carbohydrate | hidrato de carbono compuesto formado por átomos de carbono, hidrógeno y oxígeno; tipo de nutriente que es la fuente principal de energía para el cuerpo

carnivore | carnívoro organismo que obtiene energía al comer otros animales

carpel | carpelo parte interna de una flor que produce y alberga los gametofitos femeninos

carrying capacity | capacidad de carga mayor cantidad de individuos de una especie en particular que un medio ambiente específico puede mantener

cartilage | cartílago tipo de tejido conectivo que sostiene al cuerpo y es más blando y flexible que el hueso

Casparian strip | banda de Caspary banda impermeable que rodea a las células endodérmicas de las plantas y participa en el transporte unidireccional de las sustancias hacia el interior del cilindro vascular de las raíces de las plantas

catalyst | catalizador sustancia que acelera la velocidad de una reacción química

cell | célula unidad básica de todas las formas de vida

cell body | cuerpo celular parte más grande de una neurona típica; que contiene el núcleo y gran parte del citoplasma

cell cycle | ciclo celular serie de sucesos en los cuales una célula crece, se prepara para dividirse y se divide para formar dos células hijas

cell division | división celular proceso por el cual una célula se divide en dos células hijas nuevas

cell membrane | membrana celular barrera flexible y delgada que rodea a todas las células; regula lo que entra y sale de la célula

cell theory | teoría celular concepto fundamental de la Biología que establece que todos los seres vivos están compuestos por células; que las células son las unidades básicas estructurales y funcionales de los seres vivos; y que las células nuevas se producen a partir de células existentes

cell wall | pared celular capa resistente que sirve de sostén y está situada alrededor de la membrana celular de algunas células

cell-mediated immunity | inmunidad celular respuesta inmune que desde las células defiende al cuerpo contra virus, hongos y células anormales cancerígenas

cellular respiration | respiración celular proceso que libera energía al descomponer la glucosa y otras moléculas de los alimentos en presencia de oxígeno

central nervous system | sistema nervioso central incluye el cerebro y la médula espinal; procesa información y genera una respuesta que es enviada al cuerpo

centriole | centríolo estructura de una célula animal que contribuye a organizar la división celular

centromere | centrómero región de un cromosoma donde se unen las dos cromátidas hermanas

cephalization | cefalización concentración de órganos sensoriales y células nerviosas en el extremo anterior de un animal

cerebellum | cerebelo parte del encéfalo que coordina el movimiento y controla el equilibrio

cerebral cortex | corteza cerebral capa externa del cerebro de un mamífero; centro del raciocinio y otros comportamientos complejos

cerebrum | cerebro parte del encéfalo responsable de las actividades voluntarias del cuerpo; región "pensante" del encéfalo

chemical digestion | digestión química proceso por el cual las enzimas descomponen los alimentos en moléculas pequeñas que el cuerpo puede utilizar

chemical reaction | reacción química proceso que cambia, o transforma, un grupo de sustancias químicas en otro grupo de sustancias químicas

chemosynthesis | quimiosíntesis proceso en el cual la energía química se utiliza para producir hidratos de carbono

chitin | quitina hidrato de carbono complejo que forma las paredes celulares de los hongos; también se halla en los esqueletos externos de los artrópodos

chlorophyll | clorofila pigmento fundamental de las plantas y de otros organismos fotosintéticos

chloroplast | cloroplasto orgánulo de las células de las plantas y de otros organismos que captura la energía de la luz solar y la convierte en energía química

chordate | cordado animal que, al menos durante una etapa de su vida, tiene un cordón nervioso hueco y dorsal, un notocordio, una cola que se prolonga más allá del ano y bolsas faríngeas

chromatid | cromátida una de las dos partes "hermanas" idénticas de un cromosoma duplicado

chromatin | cromatina sustancia que se halla en los cromosomas eucarióticos y que consiste en ADN enrollado apretadamente alrededor de las histonas

chromosome | cromosoma estructura filiforme situada dentro del núcleo que contiene la información genética que se transmite de una generación a la siguiente

chyme | quimo mezcla de enzimas y alimentos parcialmente digeridos

cilium (pl. cilia) | cilio pequeña prolongación parecida a un pelo que produce movimiento

circadian rhythm | ritmo circadiano ciclos conductuales que ocurren diariamente

clade | clado rama evolutiva de un cladograma que incluye a un único ancestro y a todos sus descendientes

cladogram | cladograma diagrama que representa patrones de características compartidas entre especies

class | clase en la clasificación, un grupo de varios órdenes relacionados estrechamente

classical conditioning | condicionamiento clásico tipo de aprendizaje que ocurre cuando un animal realiza una conexión mental entre un estímulo y algún tipo de recompensa o castigo

climate | clima promedio anual de las condiciones de temperatura y precipitación en un área durante un largo período de tiempo

clone | clon miembro de una población de células genéticamente idénticas producidas a partir de una célula única

closed circulatory system | sistema circulatorio cerrado tipo de sistema circulatorio en el cual la sangre circula completamente dentro de los vasos sanguíneos que se extienden por todo el cuerpo

coccus (pl. cocci) | coco procariota de forma esférica

cochlea | cóclea parte del oído interno llena de fluidos; contiene las células nerviosas que detectan el sonido

codominance | codominancia situación en la cual los fenotipos producidos por ambos alelos están expresados completamente

codon | codón grupo de tres bases de nucleótidos en el RNA mensajero que especifican la incorporación de un aminoácido en particular en una proteína

coelom | celoma cavidad corporal revestida de mesodermo

coevolution | coevolución proceso por el cual dos especies evolucionan en respuesta a cambios mutuos en el transcurso del tiempo

cohesion | cohesión atracción entre moléculas de la misma sustancia

collenchyma | colénquima en las plantas, tipo de tejido fundamental que tiene paredes celulares fuertes y flexibles; contribuye a sostener las plantas más grandes

commensalism | comensalismo relación simbiótica en la cual un organismo se beneficia y el otro ni se beneficia ni sufre daño

communication | comunicación traspaso de información desde un organismo a otro

community | comunidad conjunto de varias poblaciones que viven juntas en un área definida

companion cell | célula anexa en las plantas, célula del floema que rodea a los vasos cribosos

competitive exclusion principle | principio de exclusión competitiva principio que afirma que dos especies no pueden ocupar el mismo nicho en el mismo hábitat al mismo tiempo

compound | compuesto sustancia formada por la combinación química de dos o más elementos en proporciones definidas

cone | cono en el ojo, receptor de luz que responde a la luz de diferentes colores, produciendo la visión a color

coniferous | coníferas término utilizado para referirse a los árboles que producen conos portadores de semillas y que tienen hojas delgadas con forma de aguja

conjugation | conjugación proceso mediante el cual los paramecios y algunos procariotas intercambian información genética

connective tissue | tejido conectivo tipo de tejido que proporciona sostén al cuerpo y conecta sus partes

consumer | consumidor organismo que depende de otros organismos para obtener su energía y su provisión de alimentos; también llamado heterótrofo

control group | grupo de control en un experimento, grupo que está expuesto a las mismas condiciones que el grupo experimental, excepto por una variable independiente

controlled experiment | experimento controlado experimento en el cual sólo se cambia una variable

convergent evolution | evolución convergente proceso mediante el cual organismos no relacionados evolucionan independientemente hacia caracteres similares cuando se adaptan a ambientes parecidos

cork cambium | cámbium suberoso tejido del meristemo que produce la cubierta exterior de los tallos durante el crecimiento secundario de una planta

cornea | córnea membrana dura y transparente del ojo a través de la cual entra la luz

corpus luteum | cuerpo lúteo nombre dado a un folículo después de la ovulación debido a su color amarillo

cortex | corteza radicular en las plantas, región de tejido fundamental situada en el interior de la raíz a través de la cual pasan el agua y los minerales

corticosteroid | corticosteroide o corticoide hormona esteroídica producida por la corteza de las glándulas adrenales

cotyledon | cotiledón primera hoja o primer par de hojas producidas por el embrión de una planta fanerógama

courtship | cortejo tipo de comportamiento en el cual un animal emite estímulos para atraer a un miembro del sexo opuesto

covalent bond | enlace covalente tipo de enlace entre átomos en el cual se comparten los electrones

crossing-over | entrecruzamiento proceso por el cual los cromosomas homólogos intercambian partes de sus cromátidas durante la meiosis

cyclin | ciclina un componente de la familia de proteínas que regulan el ciclo celular de las células eucariotas

cytokinesis | citocinesis división del citoplasma para formar dos células hijas separadas

cytokinin | citoquinina hormona vegetal que se genera en las raíces en crecimiento y en los frutos y semillas en desarrollo

cytoplasm | citoplasma parte fluida de la célula externa al núcleo

cytoskeleton | citoesqueleto en una célula eucariota, red de filamentos proteínicos que otorga a la célula su forma y su organización interna y participa en el movimiento

D

data | datos evidencia; información reunida a partir de observaciones

deciduous | caduco término utilizado para referirse a un tipo de árbol que pierde sus hojas cada año durante una estación en particular

decomposer | descomponedor organismo que descompone y obtiene energía de la materia orgánica muerta

deforestation | deforestación destrucción de los bosques

demographic transition | transición demográfica cambio de una población desde índices de nacimiento y mortalidad altos a índices de nacimiento y mortalidad bajos

demography | demografía estudio científico de las poblaciones humanas

dendrite | dendrita prolongación del cuerpo celular de una neurona que transporta impulsos desde el medio ambiente o desde otras neuronas hacia el cuerpo celular

denitrification | desnitrificación proceso por el cual las bacterias del suelo convierten los nitratos en gas nitrógeno

density-dependent limiting factor | factor limitante dependiente de la densidad factor limitante que depende de la densidad de la población

density-independent limiting factor | factor limitante independiente de la densidad factor limitante que afecta a todas las poblaciones de manera similar, sin importar la densidad de la población

deoxyribonucleic acid (DNA) | ácido desoxirribonucleico (ADN) material genético que organismos heredan de sus padres

dependent variable | variable dependiente variable que está siendo observada y cambia en respuesta a la variable independiente; también llamada variable de respuesta

derived character | carácter derivado rasgo que aparece en los descendientes recientes de un linaje, pero no en sus miembros más viejos

dermis | dermis capa de la piel situada debajo de la epidermis

desertification | desertificación disminución de la productividad de la tierra debido al cultivo y al pastoreo excesivo, a la sequía estacional y al cambio climático

detritivore | detritívoro organismo que se alimenta de restos animales y vegetales y demás materia orgánica muerta

deuterostome | deuteróstomos grupo de animales en los cuales el blastoporo se convierte en ano y la boca se forma a partir del desarrollo de una segunda abertura

diaphragm | diafragma músculo plano y grande ubicado en la parte inferior de la cavidad torácica que participa en la respiración

dicot | dicotiledónea angiosperma con dos cotiledones (hojas embrionarias) en su ovario

differentiation | diferenciación proceso en el cual las células se especializan en estructura y función

diffusion | difusión proceso por el cual las partículas tienden a desplazarse desde un área donde están más concentradas hacia un área donde están menos concentradas

digestive tract | tracto digestivo tubo que comienza en la boca y termina en el ano

diploid | diploide término utilizado para referirse a una célula que contiene dos series de cromosomas homólogos

directional selection | selección direccional forma de selección natural en la cual los individuos que se hallan en un extremo de la curva de distribución poseen una mayor capacidad de adaptación que los individuos que se hallan en el centro o en el otro extremo de la curva

disruptive selection | selección disruptiva forma de selección natural en la cual los individuos que se hallan en los extremos superior e inferior de la curva poseen una mayor capacidad de adaptación que los individuos que se hallan cerca del centro de la curva

DNA fingerprinting | prueba de ADN herramienta utilizada por los biólogos mediante la cual se analiza el conjunto de los fragmentos de restricción de ADN exclusivo de cada individuo; utilizada para determinar si dos muestras de material genético pertenecen a la misma persona; también llamada huella genética o análisis de ADN

DNA microarray | chip de ADN superficie de vidrio o chip de silicona que contiene miles de diferentes tipos de fragmentos de ADN de una sola cadena dispuestos en una cuadrícula. Un chip de ADN se utiliza para detectar y medir la expresión de miles de genes a la vez

DNA polymerase | ADN polimerasa enzima fundamental involucrada en la replicación del ADN

domain | dominio categoría taxonómica más amplia e inclusiva que un reino

dopamine | dopamina neurotransmisor que está asociado con los centros de placer y de recompensa del cerebro

dormancy | latencia período de tiempo durante el cual un embrión vegetal está vivo pero no crece

double fertilization | doble fertilización proceso de fecundación de las angiospermas en el cual se produce, en el primer suceso el cigoto y en el segundo, el endospermo dentro de la semilla

E

ecological footprint | huella ecológica cantidad total de ecosistema en funcionamiento necesaria para proporcionar los recursos que utiliza una población humana y para absorber los residuos que genera esa población

ecological hot spot | zona de conflicto ecológico área geográfica pequeña donde cantidades importantes de hábitats y especies se hallan en peligro de extinción inmediato

ecological pyramid | pirámide ecológica ilustración de las cantidades relativas de energía o materia contenidas dentro de cada nivel trófico en una cadena o red alimenticia dada

ecological succession | sucesión ecológica serie de cambios graduales que ocurren en una comunidad después de una alteración

ecology | ecología estudio científico de las interacciones entre organismos y entre los organismos y su medio ambiente

ecosystem | ecosistema todos los organismos que viven en un lugar, junto con su medio ambiente inanimado

ecosystem diversity | diversidad de ecosistemas variedad de hábitats, comunidades y procesos ecológicos que existen en la biósfera

ectoderm | ectodermo capa embrionaria más externa; desarrolla órganos sensoriales, nervios y la capa exterior de la piel

ectotherm | animal de sangre fría animal cuya temperatura corporal está determinada por la temperatura de su medio ambiente

electron | electrón partícula con carga negativa; ubicada en el espacio que rodea al núcleo

electron transport chain | cadena de transporte de electrones serie de proteínas transportadoras que llevan electrones de alta energía, durante las reacciones generadoras de ATP

element | elemento sustancia pura que consiste íntegramente en un tipo de átomo

embryo | embrión una de las etapas de desarrollo de un organismo multicelular

embryo sac | saco embrionario gametofito femenino dentro del óvulo de una planta que produce flores

emerging disease | enfermedad emergente enfermedad que aparece en una población por primera vez o una enfermedad antigua que de pronto se vuelve más difícil de controlar

emigration | emigración desplazamiento de individuos fuera de un área

endocrine gland | glándula endocrina glándula que vierte sus secreciones (hormonas) directamente en la sangre, para ser transportadas a otras áreas del cuerpo

endoderm | endodermo capa embrionaria más interna, a partir de la cual se desarrollan los revestimientos del tracto digestivo y gran parte del sistema respiratorio

endodermis | endodermis en las plantas, un capa de tejido fundamental que envuelve completamente al cilindro vascular

endoplasmic reticulum | retículo endoplasmático sistema de membranas internas de las células eucariotas; lugar donde se reúnen los componentes lipídicos de la membrana celular

endoskeleton | endoesqueleto esqueleto interno; sistema estructural de sostén dentro del cuerpo de un animal

endosperm | endospermo tejido nutritivo que alimenta a una plántula a medida que crece

endospore | endospora estructura producida por los procariotas en condiciones desfavorables; una gruesa pared interna que encierra al ADN y a una parte del citoplasma

endosymbiotic theory | teoría endosimbiótica teoría que propone que las células eucariotas se formaron a partir de una relación simbiótica entre varias células procariotas distintas

endotherm | endotermo animal cuya temperatura corporal se regula, al menos en parte, utilizando el calor generado dentro de su cuerpo

enzyme | enzima proteína catalizadora que acelera la velocidad de reacciones biológicas específicas

epidermis | epidermis en las plantas, única capa de células que forma el tejido dérmico; en los seres humanos, la capa exterior de la piel

epididymis | epidídimo órgano del sistema reproductor masculino en el cual el esperma madura y se almacena

epinephrine | epinefrina hormona liberada por las glándulas adrenales que aumenta la frecuencia cardíaca y la presión sanguínea y prepara al cuerpo para una actividad física intensa; también llamada adrenalina

epithelial tissue | tejido epitelial tipo de tejido que reviste el interior y el exterior de las superficies del cuerpo

era | era división principal del tiempo geológico; usualmente dividida en dos o más períodos

esophagus | esófago tubo que conecta la boca con el estómago

estuary | estuario tipo de humedal que se forma donde un río se encuentra con el océano

ethylene | etileno hormona vegetal que estimula la maduración de los frutos

Eukarya | Eukarya (eucariontes) dominio compuesto por todos los organismos que tienen un núcleo; incluye a los protistas, las plantas, los hongos y los animales

eukaryote | eucariota organismo cuyas células contienen un núcleo

evolution | evolución cambio en el transcurso del tiempo; el proceso por el cual los organismos actuales se derivaron de los organismos antiguos

excretion | excreción proceso por el cual se eliminan del cuerpo los residuos metabólicos

exocrine gland | glándula exocrina glándula que vierte sus secreciones directamente a un órgano o al exterior del cuerpo a través de estructuras tubulares denominadas conductos

exon | exón secuencia expresada de ADN; codifica una porción específica de una proteína

exoskeleton | exoesqueleto esqueleto externo; cubierta externa dura que protege y sostiene el cuerpo de muchos invertebrados

exponential growth | crecimiento exponencial patrón de crecimiento en el cual los individuos de una población se reproducen a una tasa constante

extinct | extinto término utilizado para referirse a una especie que ha desaparecido y de la que ninguno de sus miembros está vivo

extracellular digestion | digestión extracelular tipo de digestión en la cual el alimento es degradado fuera de las células dentro de un sistema digestivo y luego se absorbe

F

facilitated diffusion | difusión facilitada proceso de difusión en el cual las moléculas atraviesan la membrana a través de los canales de la membrana celular

family | familia en la clasificación, grupo de géneros similares

fat | grasa lípido; compuesto de ácidos grasos y glicerina; tipo de nutriente que protege a los órganos del cuerpo, actua como aislante térmico y almacena energía

feedback inhibition | inhibición de la retroalimentación proceso en el cual un estímulo produce una respuesta que se opone al estímulo original; también llamada retroalimentación negativa

fermentation | fermentación proceso por el cual las células liberan energía en ausencia de oxígeno

fertilization | fecundación proceso de la reproducción sexual en el cual las células reproductoras masculinas y femeninas se unen para formar una célula nueva

fetus | feto un embrión humano después de ocho semanas de desarrollo

fever | fiebre temperatura corporal elevada que se produce como respuesta a una infección

filtration | filtración proceso de hacer pasar un líquido o un gas a través de un filtro para quitar los residuos

fitness | aptitud capacidad de un organismo para sobrevivir y reproducirse en su medio ambiente

flagellum (pl. flagella) | flagelo estructura utilizada por los protistas para desplazarse; produce un desplazamiento con un movimiento semejante al de una onda

food chain | cadena alimenticia serie de pasos en un ecosistema, en que los organismos transfieren energía al alimentarse y al servir de alimento

food vacuole | vacuola alimenticia pequeña cavidad situada en el citoplasma de los protistas que almacena alimentos por algún tiempo

food web | red alimenticia red de interacciones complejas constituida por las relaciones alimenticias entre los varios organismos de un ecosistema

forensics | ciencias forenses estudio científico de las pruebas en la escena del crimen

fossil | fósil restos conservados de organismos antiguos

founder effect | efecto fundador cambio en las frecuencias alélicas como consecuencia de la migración de un subgrupo pequeño de una población

frameshift mutation | mutación de corrimiento de estructura mutación que cambia el "marco de lectura" del mensaje genético insertando o eliminando un nucleótido

fruit | fruto estructura de las Angiospermas que contiene uno o más ovarios maduros

fruiting body | cuerpo fructífero estructura reproductora de los hongos que se desarrolla a partir del micelio

G

gamete | gameto célula sexual

gametophyte | gametofito planta que produce gametos; fase haploide multicelular del ciclo vital de una planta

ganglion (pl. ganglia) | ganglio nervioso grupo de interneuronas

gastrovascular cavity | cavidad gastrovascular cámara digestiva con una sola apertura

gastrulation | gastrulación proceso de migración celular que da por resultado la formación de las tres capas celulares—el ectodermo, el mesodermo y el endodermo

gel electrophoresis | electroforesis en gel procedimiento utilizado para separar y analizar fragmentos de ADN colocando una mezcla de fragmentos de ADN en un extremo de un gel poroso y aplicando al gel un voltaje eléctrico

gene | gen secuencia de ADN que contiene el código de una proteína y por lo tanto determina un rasgo; factor que se transmite de un progenitor a su descendencia

gene expression | expresión génica proceso por el cual un gen produce su producto y el producto lleva a cabo su función

gene pool | caudal de genes todos los genes, incluidos todos los alelos diferentes para cada gen, que están presentes en una población en un momento dado

gene therapy | terapia genética o génica proceso en el cual se cambia un gen para tratar una enfermedad o una afección médica. Se reemplaza un gen ausente o defectuoso con un gen de funcionamiento normal.

genetic code | código genético conjunto de codones del ARN mensajero, cada uno de los cuales dirige la incorporación de un aminoácido en particular a una proteína durante la síntesis proteica

genetic diversity | diversidad genética suma de todas las distintas formas de información genética portadas por una especie en particular, o por todos los organismos de la Tierra

genetic drift | tendencia genética alteración al azar de la frecuencia alélica causada por una serie de acontecimientos aleatorios que hacen que un alelo se vuelva más o menos común en una población

genetic equilibrium | equilibrio genético situación en la cual las frecuencias alélicas de una población se mantienen iguales

genetic marker | marcador genético alelos que producen diferencias fenotípicas detectables, útiles en el análisis genético

genetics | genética estudio científico de la herencia

genome | genoma todo el conjunto de información genética que un organismo transporta en su ADN

genomics | genómica estudio integral de los genomas, incluyendo los genes y sus funciones

genotype | genotipo composición genética de un organismo

genus | género grupo de especies relacionadas estrechamente; la primera parte del nombre científico en la nomenclatura binaria

geographic isolation | aislamiento geográfico forma de aislamiento reproductivo en el cual dos poblaciones están separadas por barreras geográficas como ríos, montañas o masas de agua, dando lugar a la formación de dos subespecies distintas

geologic time scale | escala de tiempo geológico línea cronológica utilizada para representar la historia de la Tierra

germ theory of disease | teoría microbiana de la enfermedad idea de que las enfermedades infecciosas son causadas por microorganismos

germination | germinación reanudación del crecimiento del embrión de la planta después de la latencia

giberellin | giberelina hormona de las plantas que estimula el crecimiento y puede causar aumentos significativos de tamaño

gill | branquia estructura tegumentaria especializada en el intercambio de los gases con el agua

global warming | calentamiento global aumento del promedio de temperatura en la tierra

glomerulus | glomérulo pequeña red de capilares encerrados en el extremo superior del nefrón; donde tiene lugar la filtración de la sangre

glycolysis | glicólisis primer conjunto de reacciones en la respiración celular, en las cuales una molécula de glucosa se descompone en dos moléculas de ácido pirúvico

Golgi apparatus | aparato de Golgi orgánulo de las células que modifica, clasifica y agrupa las proteínas y otras sustancias provenientes del retículo endoplasmático para almacenarlas en la célula o enviarlas fuera de la célula

gradualism | gradualismo evolución de una especie por la acumulación gradual de pequeños cambios genéticos ocurridos en el transcurso de largos períodos de tiempo

grafting | injerto método de propagación utilizado para reproducir plantas sin semillas y algunas variedades de plantas leñosas que no pueden propagarse a partir de esquejes

gravitropism | geotropismo respuesta de una planta a la fuerza de la gravedad

green revolution | revolución verde el desarrollo de variedades de cultivos altamente productivos y el uso de técnicas agrícolas modernas para aumentar el rendimiento de los cultivos

greenhouse effect | efecto invernadero proceso mediante el cual ciertos gases (dióxido de carbono, metano y vapor de agua) atrapan la energía de la luz solar en la atmósfera terrestre en forma de calor

growth factor | factor de crecimiento una de las proteínas del grupo de proteínas reguladoras externas que estimulan el crecimiento y la división de las células

guard cell | células de guarda (o células oclusivas) células especializadas de la epidermis vegetal que controlan la apertura y el cierre de los estomas

gullet | citofaringe hendidura a un costado de un ciliado que permite que los alimentos entren a la célula

gymnosperm | Gimnospermas grupo de plantas fanerógamas que tienen sus semillas directamente sobre las escamas de los conos

H

habitat | hábitat área donde vive un organismo, incluidos los factores bióticos y abióticos que lo afectan

habitat fragmentation | fragmentación del hábitat la ruptura, o separación en partes, de los ecosistemas

habituation | habituación tipo de aprendizaje en el cual un animal disminuye o cancela su respuesta ante un estímulo repetido que no recompensa ni castiga al animal

hair follicle | folículo piloso sacos tubulares de las células epidérmicas que se prolongan hacia el interior de la dermis; las células situadas en la base de los folículos pilosos, producen pelo

half life | vida media período de tiempo requerido para que se desintegre la mitad de los átomos radiactivos de una muestra

haploid | haploide tipo de célula que posee un solo juego de cromosomas

Hardy-Weinberg principle | principio de Hardy-Weinberg el principio que afirma que las frecuencias alélicas de una población permanecen constantes a menos que uno o más factores ocasionen que esas frecuencias cambien

Haversian canal | conducto de Havers uno de los tubos de una red que recorre longitudinalmente el hueso compacto y contiene vasos sanguíneos y nervios

heart | corazón órgano muscular hueco que bombea la sangre a todo el cuerpo

heartwood | duramen en un tallo leñoso, el xilema más viejo situado cerca del centro del tallo que ya no conduce agua

hemoglobin | hemoglobina proteína de los glóbulos rojos que contiene hierro, fija el oxígeno y lo transporta al organismo

herbaceous plant | planta herbácea tipo de planta que tiene tallos blandos y no leñosos; incluye dientes de león, cinias, petunias y girasoles

herbivore | herbívoro organismo que obtiene energía alimentándose solo de plantas

herbivory | herbivorismo interacción en la cual un animal (el herbívoro) se alimenta de productores (como las plantas)

heterotroph | heterótrofo organismo que obtiene su alimento consumiendo otros seres vivos; también llamado consumidor

heterozygous | heterocigota que tiene dos alelos diferentes para un gen dado

histamine | histamina sustancia química liberada por los mastocitos que aumenta el flujo de la sangre y los fluidos hacia el área infectada durante una respuesta inflamatoria

homeobox gene | gen homeobox el homeobox es una secuencia de ADN de aproximadamente 130 pares de bases, presente en muchos genes homeóticos que regulan el desarrollo. Los genes que contienen esta secuencia se denominan genes homeobox y codifican los factores de transcripción, las proteínas que se adhieren al ADN y regulan la expresión de otros genes

homeostasis | homeostasis las condiciones internas, químicas y físicas, que los organismos mantienen relativamente constantes

homeotic gene | gen homeótico tipo de genes reguladores que determinan la identidad de las partes y regiones del cuerpo en un embrión animal. Las mutaciones de estos genes pueden transformar una parte del cuerpo en otra

hominine | homínino linaje hominoide que dio lugar a los seres humanos

hominoid | homínido grupo de antropoides que incluye a los gibones, orangutanes, gorilas, chimpacés y seres humanos

homologous | homólogos término utilizado para referirse a los cromosomas en los que un juego proviene del progenitor masculino y un juego proviene del progenitor femenino

homologous structures | estructuras homólogas estructuras que son similares en distintas especies que tienen un ancestro común

homozygous | homocigota que tiene dos alelos idénticos para un gen dado

hormone | hormona sustancia química producida en una parte de un organismo que afecta a otra parte del mismo organismo

Hox gene | gen Hox grupo de genes homeóticos agrupados en un conjunto que determinan la identidad posicional de las partes del cuerpo de los animales. Todos los genes Hox contienen la secuencia de ADN homeobox

humoral immunity | inmunidad humoral inmunidad contra los antígenos presentes en los fluidos corporales, como la sangre y la linfa

humus | humus material formado a partir de hojas en descomposición y otros materiales orgánicos

hybrid | híbrido descendencia del cruce entre progenitores que tienen rasgos diferentes

hybridization | hibridación técnica de cría que consiste en cruzar individuos diferentes para reunir los mejores rasgos de ambos organismos

hydrogen bond | enlace de hidrógeno atracción débil entre un átomo de hidrógeno y otro átomo

hydrostatic skeleton | esqueleto hidrostático esqueleto constituido por segmentos corporales llenos de fluido que trabajan con los músculos para permitir el movimiento del animal

hypertonic | hipertónica al comparar dos soluciones, la solución que tiene la mayor concentración de solutos

hypha (pl. hyphae) | hifa uno de muchos filamentos largos y delgados que componen el cuerpo de un hongo

hypothalamus | hipotálamo estructura del cerebro que funciona como un centro de control para el reconocimiento y el análisis del hambre, la sed, la fatiga, el enojo y la temperatura corporal

hypothesis | hipótesis explicación posible para un conjunto de observaciones o respuesta posible a una pregunta científica

hypotonic | hipotónica al comparar dos soluciones, la solución que tiene la menor concentración de solutos

I

immigration | inmigración desplazamiento de individuos a un área ocupada por una población ya existente

immune response | respuesta inmune reconocimiento, respuesta y memoria específicos que tiene el cuerpo respecto al ataque de un organismo patógeno

implantation | implantación proceso en el cual la blástula se adhiere a la pared del útero

imprinting | impronta tipo de comportamiento basado en las primeras experiencias; una vez que ocurre la impronta, el comportamiento no puede cambiarse

inbreeding | endogamia la cría continua de individuos con características semejantes para mantener las características derivadas de un tipo de organismo

incomplete dominance | dominancia incompleta situación en la cual un alelo no es completamente dominante sobre otro alelo

independent assortment | distribución independiente uno de los principios de Mendel que establece que los genes para rasgos diferentes pueden segregarse independientemente durante la formación de los gametos

independent variable | variable independiente en un experimento controlado, el factor que se modifica a propósito; también llamada variable manipulada

index fossil | fósil guía fósil distintivo usado para comparar las edades relativas de los fósiles

infectious disease | enfermedad infecciosa enfermedad causada por un microorganismo que altera las funciones normales del cuerpo

inference | inferencia interpretación lógica basada en la experiencia y en conocimientos previos

inflammatory response | respuesta inflamatoria reacción defensiva no específica al daño causado a los tejidos por una herida o una infección

innate behavior | comportamiento innato tipo de comportamiento en el cual la conducta aparece en forma completamente funcional la primera vez que se lleva a cabo, aunque el animal no tenga ninguna experiencia previa con los estímulos a los que responde; también llamado instinto

insight learning | aprendizaje por discernimiento tipo de comportamiento en el cual un animal aplica algo que ya ha aprendido a una situación nueva, sin un período de ensayo y error; también llamado razonamiento

interferon | interferón un tipo de proteína que ayuda a las células a combatir las infecciones virales

interneuron | interneurona tipo de neurona que procesa información y la puede transmitir para estimular las neuronas

interphase | interfase período del ciclo celular entre las divisiones celulares

intracellular digestion | digestión intracelular tipo de digestión en la cual los alimentos se digieren dentro de células especializadas que pasan los nutrientes a otras células mediante difusión

intron | intrón secuencia de ADN que no participa en la codificación de una proteína

invertebrate | invertebrado animal que carece de columna vertebral

ion | ion átomo que tiene una carga positiva o negativa

ionic bond | enlace iónico enlace químico que se forma cuando uno o más electrones se transfieren de un átomo a otro

iris | iris parte coloreada del ojo

isotonic | isotónica cuando la concentración de dos soluciones es la misma

isotope | isótopo cada una de las diferentes formas de un único elemento, que contiene la misma cantidad de protones pero cantidades distintas de neutrones

J

joint | articulación sitio donde un hueso se une a otro hueso

K

karyotype | cariotipo micrografía de la totalidad del conjunto diploide de cromosomas agrupados en pares, ordenados por tamaño decreciente

keratin | queratina proteína fibrosa y resistente que se halla en la piel

keystone species | especie clave especie que habitualmente no es abundante en una comunidad y sin embargo ejerce un fuerte control sobre la estructura de esa comunidad

kidney | riñón órgano excretor que separa los residuos y el exceso de agua de la sangre

kin selection | selección de parentesco teoría que enuncia que ayudar a los congéneres puede mejorar la aptitud evolutiva de un individuo porque los individuos emparentados comparten una gran parte de sus genes

kingdom | reino en la clasificación, el grupo mayor y más inclusivo

Koch's postulates | postulados de Koch conjunto de pautas desarrolladas por Koch que ayudan a identificar al microorganismo que causa una enfermedad específica

Krebs cycle | ciclo de Krebs segunda fase de la respiración celular en la cual el ácido pirúvico se descompone en dióxido de carbono en una serie de reacciones que liberan energía

L

language | lenguaje sistema de comunicación que combina sonidos, símbolos y gestos según un conjunto de reglas sobre la secuencia y el significado, como la gramática y la sintaxis

large intestine | intestino grueso órgano del sistema digestivo que extrae el agua del material no digerido que pasa por él; también llamado colon

larva (pl. larvae) | larva etapa inmadura de un organismo

larynx | laringe órgano situado en la garganta que contiene las cuerdas vocales

learning | aprendizaje cambios en el comportamiento a consecuencia de la experiencia

lens | cristalino estructura del ojo que enfoca los rayos luminosos en la retina

lichen | liquen asociación simbiótica entre un hongo y un organismo fotosintético

ligament | ligamento tejido conectivo resistente que mantiene unidos a los huesos en una articulación

light-dependent reactions | reacciones dependientes de la luz en la fotosíntesis, conjunto de reacciones que emplean la energía proveniente de la luz para producir ATP y NADPH

light-independent reactions | reacciones independientes de la luz en la fotosíntesis, conjunto de reacciones que no necesitan luz; la energía proveniente del ATP y del NADPH se emplea para construir compuestos con gran contenido energético, como el azúcar; también llamado ciclo de Calvin

lignin | lignina sustancia de las plantas vasculares que hace rígidas a las paredes celulares

limiting factor | factor limitante un factor que hace disminuir el crecimiento de la población

limiting nutrient | nutriente limitante un solo nutriente esencial que limita la productividad de un ecosistema

lipid | lípido macromolécula compuesta principalmente por átomos de carbono e hidrógeno; incluye las grasas, los aceites y las ceras

lipid bilayer | bicapa lipídica lámina flexible de dos capas que constituye la membrana celular y forma una barrera entre la célula y su entorno

logistic growth | crecimiento logístico patrón de crecimiento en el cual el desarrollo de una población se reduce y luego se detiene después de un período de crecimiento exponencial

loop of Henle | asa de Henle una sección del túbulo de nefrón responsable de conservar el agua y minimizar el volumen del material filtrado

lung | pulmón órgano respiratorio; lugar donde se intercambian los gases entre la sangre y el aire inhalado

lymph | linfa fluido procedente de la sangre

lysogenic infection | infección lisogénica tipo de infección en la cual un virus inserta su ADN en el ADN de la célula huésped y se replica junto con el ADN de dicha célula huésped

lysosome | lisosoma orgánulo celular que descompone los lípidos, los hidratos de carbono y las proteínas en moléculas pequeñas que pueden ser utilizadas por el resto de la célula

lytic infection | infección lítica tipo de infección en la cual un virus penetra una célula, hace copias de sí mismo y provoca la ruptura o muerte celular

M

macroevolution | macroevolución cambio evolutivo a gran escala que tiene lugar en el transcurso de largos períodos de tiempo

Malpighian tubule | túbulo de Malpighi estructura de la mayoría de los artrópodos terrestres que concentra el ácido úrico y lo incorpora a los residuos digestivos

mammary gland | glándula mamaria glándula de las hembras de los mamíferos que produce leche para alimentar a las crías

mass extinction | extinción masiva suceso durante el cual se extinguen muchas especies durante un período de tiempo relativamente corto

matrix | matriz compartimento más interno de la mitocondria

mechanical digestion | digestión mecánica descomposición física de grandes pedazos de comida en pedazos más pequeños

meiosis | meiosis proceso por el cual el número de cromosomas por célula se reduce a la mitad mediante la separación de los cromosomas homólogos de una célula diploide

melanin | melanina pigmento marrón oscuro de la piel que contribuye a protegerla al absorber los rayos ultravioletas

melanocyte | melanocito célula de la piel que produce un pigmento marrón oscuro llamado melanina

menstrual cycle | ciclo menstrual secuencia regular de sucesos en la cual un huevo se desarrolla y se elimina del cuerpo

menstruation | menstruación descarga de sangre y del huevo no fertilizado del cuerpo

meristem | meristemos regiones de células no especializadas responsables del crecimiento continuo de una planta durante su vida

mesoderm | mesodermo capa embrionaria media; se desarrolla para dar lugar a los músculos y gran parte de los sistemas circulatorio, reproductor y excretor

mesophyll | mesófilo tejido fundamental especializado que se halla en las hojas; realiza la mayor parte de la fotosíntesis de una planta

messenger RNA (mRNA) | ARN mensajero tipo de ARN que transporta copias de las instrucciones para el ensamblaje de los aminoácidos en proteínas, desde el ADN al resto de la célula

metabolism | metabolismo la combinación de reacciones químicas a través de las cuales un organismo acumula o desintegra materiales

metamorphosis | metamorfosis proceso de cambios en la estructura y forma de una larva hasta que se convierte en adulto

metaphase | metafase fase de la mitosis en la cual los cromosomas se alinean a través del centro de la célula

microclimate | microclima condiciones medioambientales de un área pequeña que difieren significativamente del clima del área circundante

migration | migración comportamiento estacional que da por resultado el desplazamiento desde un medio ambiente a otro

mineral | mineral nutriente inorgánico que el cuerpo necesita, usualmente en pequeñas cantidades

mitochondrion | mitocondria orgánulo celular que convierte la energía química almacenada en los alimentos en compuestos más apropiados para que la célula los use

mitosis | mitosis fase de la división de las células eucariotas durante la cual se divide el núcleo celular

mixture | mezcla material compuesto por dos o más elementos o compuestos que están mezclados físicamente pero no están combinados químicamente

molecular clock | reloj molecular método de investigación que emplea las tasas de mutación del ADN para estimar el lapso de tiempo en que dos especies han evolucionado independientemente

molecule | molécula la unidad más pequeña de la mayoría de los compuestos que exhibe todas las propiedades de ese compuesto

molting | muda proceso de desprendimiento de un exoesqueleto y el crecimiento de uno nuevo

monocot | monocotiledónea angiosperma con un cotiledón (hoja embrionaria) en su ovario

monoculture | monocultivo estrategia agrícola que consiste en plantar año tras año un único cultivo altamente productivo

monomer | monómero pequeña unidad química que forma un polímero

monophyletic group | grupo monofilético grupo que consiste en una especie con un único ancestro y todos sus descendientes y excluye a todos los organismos que no descienden de ese ancestro común

monosaccharide | monosacárido molécula de azúcar simple

motor neuron | neurona motora tipo de célula nerviosa que lleva las instrucciones provenientes de las interneuronas a las células musculares o las glándulas

multiple alleles | alelos múltiples un gen que tiene más de dos alelos

multipotent | multipotentes células con potencial limitado para generar muchos tipos de células diferenciadas

muscle fiber | fibra muscular células largas y delgadas de los músculos esqueléticos

muscle tissue | tejido muscular tipo de tejido que hace posibles los movimientos del cuerpo

mutagen | mutágeno agentes físicos o químicos del medioambiente que interaccionan con el ADN y pueden causar una mutación

mutation | mutación cambio en el material genético de una célula

mutualism | mutualismo relación simbiótica en la cual ambas especies se benefician

mycelium (pl. mycelia) | micelio la red de filamentos muy ramificados de las hifas de un hongo

mycorrhiza (pl. mycorrhizae) | micorriza asociación simbiótica entre las raíces de las plantas y los hongos

myelin sheath | vaina de mielina membrana aislante que rodea al axón de algunas neuronas

myocardium | miocardio capa media, gruesa y musculosa del corazón

myofibril | miofibrilla manojos de filamentos muy apretados que se hallan dentro de las fibras de los músculos esqueléticos

myosin | miosina filamento grueso de proteína que se halla en las células de los músculos esqueléticos

N

NAD⁺ (nicotinamide adenine dinucleotide) | NAD⁺ (dinucleótido de nicotinamida adenina) transportador de electrones que participa en la glucólisis

NADP⁺ (nicotinamide adenine dinucleotide phosphate) | NADP⁺ (fosfato de dinucleótido de nicotinamida adenina): molécula transportadora de electrones que transfiere electrones de alta energía desde la clorofila a otras moléculas

natural selection | selección natural proceso por el cual los organismos más adaptados a su medioambiente sobreviven y se reproducen más exitosamente; también llamada supervivencia del más apto

nephridium (pl. nephridia) | nefridio estructura excretora de los anélidos que filtra el fluido corporal

nephron | nefrón estructura filtradora de la sangre en los riñones, en la cual se filtran las impurezas, se recogen los desechos y la sangre purificada se devuelve a la circulación

nervous tissue | tejido nervioso tipo de tejido que transmite los impulsos nerviosos por el cuerpo

neuromuscular junction | unión neuromuscular el punto de contacto entre una neurona motora y una célula de un músculo esquelético

neuron | neurona célula nerviosa; especializada en conducir mensajes a través del sistema nervioso

neurotransmitter | neurotransmisor sustancia química utilizada por una neurona para transmitir un impulso a otra célula a través de una sinapsis

neurulation | neurulación primer paso en el desarrollo del sistema nervioso

niche | nicho toda la variedad de condiciones biológicas y físicas en las que vive un organismo y la manera en la que dicho organismo utiliza esas condiciones

nitrogen fixation | fijación de nitrógeno el proceso por el cual el gas nitrógeno se convierte en los compuestos nitrogenados que las plantas pueden absorber y utilizar

node | nudo parte de un tallo en crecimiento donde está adherida una hoja

nondisjunction | no disyunción error que ocurre durante la meiosis, en el que cromosomas homólogos no logran separarse adecuadamente

nonrenewable resource | recurso no renovable recurso que no se puede reponer mediante un proceso natural dentro de un período de tiempo razonable

norepinephrine | norepinefrina o noradrenalina hormona liberada por las glándulas adrenales que aumenta la frecuencia cardíaca y la presión sanguínea y prepara al cuerpo para realizar actividad física intensa

notochord | notocordio extenso bastón de apoyo que se extiende a lo largo del cuerpo de los cordados, justo por debajo del cordón nervioso

nucleic acid | ácido nucleico macromoléculas que contienen hidrógeno, oxígeno, nitrógeno, carbono y fósforo

nucleotide | nucleótido subunidad que constituye los ácidos nucleicos; compuesta de un azúcar de 5 carbonos, un grupo fosfato y una base nitrogenada

nucleus | núcleo el centro de un átomo, contiene los protones y los neutrones; en las células, la estructura que contiene el material genético de la célula en forma de ADN

nutrient | nutriente sustancia química que un organismo necesita para continuar con vida

nymph | ninfa forma inmadura de un animal que se parece a la forma adulta, pero carece de órganos sexuales funcionales

O

observation | observación el método de percibir y describir sucesos o procesos de manera atenta y ordenada

omnivore | omnívoro organismo que obtiene energía alimentándose de plantas y animales

open circulatory system | sistema circulatorio abierto tipo de sistema circulatorio en el cual la sangre, cuando fluye por el cuerpo, está solo parcialmente contenida dentro de un sistema de vasos sanguíneos

operant conditioning | acondicionamiento operante tipo de aprendizaje en el cual un animal aprende a comportarse de cierta manera mediante una práctica repetida, para recibir una recompensa o evitar un castigo

operator | operador pequeña región de ADN, adyacente al promotor del operón de una procariota, que une las proteínas represoras responsables de controlar la tasa de transcripción del operón

operon | operón en las procariotas, grupo de genes adyacentes que comparten un operador y un promotor en común y que son transcritas a un solo ARN mensajero

opposable thumb | pulgar oponible o prensible un pulgar que permite aferrar objetos y utilizar herramientas

order | orden en la clasificación, un grupo de familias relacionadas estrechamente

organ | órgano grupo de tejidos que trabajan juntos para realizar funciones estrechamente relacionadas

organ system | sistema de órganos grupo de órganos que trabajan juntos para realizar una función específica

organelle | orgánulo estructura especializada que realiza funciones celulares importantes dentro de una célula eucariota

osmosis | ósmosis la difusión de agua a través de una membrana de permeabilidad selectiva

osmotic pressure | presión osmótica la presión que debe aplicarse para evitar el movimiento osmótico a través de una membrana de permeabilidad selectiva

ossification | osificación el proceso de formación de hueso durante el cual el cartílago es reemplazado por hueso

osteoblast | osteoblasto célula ósea que secreta depósitos minerales que reemplazan al cartílago de los huesos en desarrollo

osteoclast | osteoclasto célula ósea que degrada los minerales óseos

osteocyte | osteocito célula ósea que ayuda a conservar los minerales en el tejido óseo y continúa fortaleciendo al hueso en crecimiento

ovary | ovario en las plantas, la estructura que rodea a las semillas y las protege; órgano reproductor femenino fundamental en los animales; produce huevos

oviparous | ovíparo especie animal en la cual los embriones se desarrollan en huevos fuera del cuerpo del progenitor

ovoviparous | ovovíparo especie animal en la cual los embriones se desarrollan dentro del cuerpo de la madre, pero dependen completamente del saco vitelino de sus huevos

ovulation | ovulación liberación de un huevo maduro desde el ovario a una de las trompas de Falopio

ovule | óvulo estructura de las semillas coníferas donde se desarrollan los gametos femeninos

ozone layer | capa de ozono capa atmosférica en la cual el gas ozono se encuentra relativamente concentrado; protege a los seres vivos de la Tierra de los perjudiciales rayos ultravioletas de la luz solar

P

pacemaker | marcapasos grupo pequeño de fibras musculares cardíacas que mantiene el ritmo de bombeo del corazón estableciendo la frecuencia a la que se contrae el corazón; el nodo sinusal

paleontologist | paleontólogo científico que estudia los fósiles

palisade mesophyll | mesófilo en empalizada capa de células situada bajo la epidermis superior de una hoja

parasitism | parasitismo relación simbiótica en la cual un organismo vive sobre otro organismo o en su interior y lo perjudica

parathyroid hormone (PTH) | hormona de la paratiroides hormona producida por la glándula paratiroides que aumenta los niveles de calcio en la sangre

parenchyma | parénquima tipo principal de tejido fundamental de las plantas que contiene células con paredes celulares delgadas y vacuolas centrales grandes

passive immunity | inmunidad pasiva inmunidad transitoria que se desarrolla a consecuencia de una exposición natural o deliberada a un antígeno

pathogen | patógeno agente que causa una enfermedad

pedigree | árbol genealógico diagrama que muestra la presencia o ausencia de un rasgo de acuerdo con las relaciones intrafamiliares a través de varias generaciones

pepsin | pepsina enzima que descompone las proteínas en fragmentos de polipéptidos más pequeños

period | período división del tiempo geológico en la que se subdividen las eras

peripheral nervous system | sistema nervioso periférico red de nervios y células de apoyo que transporta señales hacia y desde el sistema nervioso central

peristalsis | peristalsis contracciones de los músculos lisos que proporcionan la fuerza que hace avanzar los alimentos a través del esófago hacia el estómago

permafrost | permacongelamiento capa de subsuelo congelado en forma permanente que se halla en la tundra

petiole | pecíolo pedúnculo delgado que une la lámina de una hoja con un tallo

pH scale | escala del pH escala con valores de 0 a 14, utilizada para medir la concentración de iones H^+ en una solución; un pH de 0 a 7 es ácido, un pH de 7 es neutro y un pH de 7 a 14 es básico

pharyngeal pouch | bolsa faríngea cada una de las dos estructuras situadas en la región de la garganta de los cordados

pharynx | faringe tubo situado a continuación de la boca que sirve de conducto para que pasen el aire y los alimentos; también llamada garganta

phenotype | fenotipo características físicas de un organismo

phloem | floema tejido vascular que transporta por toda la planta las soluciones de nutrientes e hidratos de carbono producidos en la fotosíntesis

photic zone | zona fótica región cerca de la superficie del mar en la que penetra la luz solar

photoperiod | fotoperíodo la respuesta de una planta a los tiempos relativos de luz y oscuridad

photosynthesis | fotosíntesis proceso empleado por las plantas y otros organismos autótrofos para atrapar la energía luminosa y utilizarla para impulsar reacciones químicas que convierten el dióxido de carbono y el agua en oxígeno e hidratos de carbono de gran contenido energético, como azúcares y almidones

photosystem | fotosistema conjunto de clorofila y proteínas que se hallan en los tilacoides

phototropism | fototropismo la tendencia de una planta a crecer hacia una fuente de luz

phylogeny | filogenia estudio de las relaciones evolutivas entre los organismos

phylum (pl. phyla) | filo en la clasificación, un grupo de clases estrechamente relacionadas

phytoplankton | fitoplancton algas fotosintéticas que se hallan cerca de la superficie del océano

pigment | pigmento moléculas que absorben la luz, empleadas por las plantas para recolectar la energía solar

pioneer species | especies pioneras las primeras especies en poblar un área durante la sucesión ecológica

pistil | pistilo un único carpelo o varios carpelos unidos; contiene el ovario, el estilo y el estigma

pith | médula en los tallos de las dicotiledóneas, las células parenquimatosas ubicadas en el interior del anillo de tejido vascular

pituitary gland | glándula pituitaria pequeña glándula situada cerca de la base del cráneo que secreta hormonas que regulan directamente muchas funciones corporales y controla las acciones de varias otras glándulas endocrinas

placenta | placenta órgano especializado de los mamíferos placentarios a través del cual se intercambian los gases respiratorios, los nutrientes y los residuos entre la madre y su cría en desarrollo

plankton | plancton organismos microscópicos que viven en medios ambientes acuáticos; incluye el fitoplancton y el zooplancton

plasma | plasma parte líquida de la sangre de color amarillento

plasmid | plásmido pequeña porción circular de ADN ubicada en el citoplasma de muchas bacterias

plasmodium | plasmodio etapa de alimentación ameboide del ciclo vital de los mohos mucilaginosos

plate tectonics | tectónica de placas procesos geológicos, como la deriva continental, los volcanes y los terremotos, que son consecuencia de los movimientos de las placas

platelet | plaqueta fragmento celular liberado por la médula espinal que interviene en la coagulación de la sangre

pluripotent | pluripotentes células capaces de convertirse en la mayoría de células del cuerpo, pero no en todas

point mutation | mutación puntual mutación genética en la cual se ha modificado un único par de bases en el ADN

pollen grain | grano de polen la estructura que contiene a todo el gametofito masculino en las plantas fanerógamas

pollen tube | tubo polínico en una planta, estructura que contiene dos núcleos espermáticos haploides

pollination | polinización transferencia de polen desde la estructura reproductora masculina hacia la estructura reproductora femenina

pollutant | contaminante material nocivo que puede ingresar en la biósfera a través de la tierra, el aire o el agua

polygenic trait | rasgo poligénico rasgo controlado por dos o más genes

polymer | polímero molécula compuesta por muchos monómeros; forma macromoléculas

polymerase chain reaction (PCR) | reacción en cadena de la polímerasa (PCR) técnica usada por los biólogos para hacer muchas copias de un gen específico

polypeptide | polipéptido cadena larga de aminoácidos que constituye las proteínas

polyploidy | poliploidía condición en la cual un organismo tiene grupos adicionales de cromosomas

population | población grupo de individuos de la misma especie que viven en la misma área

population density | densidad de población número de individuos que viven por unidad de superficie

predation | depredación interacción en la cual un organismo (el predador) captura y come a otro organismo (la presa)

prehensile tail | cola prensil cola larga que puede enrollarse apretadamente alrededor de una rama

pressure-flow hypothesis | teoría de flujo por presión teoría que explica el método por el cual la savia del floema recorre la planta desde una "fuente" de azúcar hacia un "vertedero" de azúcar

primary growth | crecimiento primario patrón de crecimiento que tiene lugar en las puntas y en los brotes de una planta

primary producer | productor primario los primeros productores de compuestos ricos en energía que luego son utilizados por otros organismos

primary succession | sucesión primaria sucesión que ocurre en un área en la cual no hay rastros de la presencia de una comunidad anterior

principle of dominance | principio de dominancia segunda conclusión de Mendel, que establece que algunos alelos son dominantes y otros son recesivos

prion | prión partículas de proteína que causan enfermedades

probability | probabilidad la posibilidad de que ocurra un suceso dado

product | producto elemento o compuesto producido por una reacción química

prokaryote | procariota organismo unicelular que carece de núcleo

promoter | promotor región específica de un gen en donde la ARN polimerasa puede unirse e iniciar la transcripción

prophage | profago ADN del bacteriófago que está alojado en el interior del ADN del huésped bacteriano

prophase | profase primera y más prolongada fase de la mitosis, en la cual el material genético dentro del interior del núcleo se condensa y los cromosomas se hacen visibles

prostaglandin | prostaglandina ácidos grasos modificados que son producidos por una amplia gama de células; generalmente afectan solo a las células y tejidos cercanos

protein | proteína macromolécula que contiene carbono, hidrógeno, oxígeno y nitrógeno; necesaria para el crecimiento y reparación del cuerpo

protostome | protóstomo animal cuya boca se desarrolla a partir del blastoporo

pseudocoelom | pseudoceloma o falso celoma cavidad corporal que está revestida sólo parcialmente con mesodermo

pseudopod | seudópodo prolongación citoplasmática transitoria utilizada por algunos protistas para moverse

puberty | pubertad período de crecimiento rápido y de maduración sexual durante el cual el sistema reproductor se vuelve completamente funcional

pulmonary circulation | circulación pulmonar recorrido de la circulación entre el corazón y los pulmones

punctuated equilibrium | equilibrio interrumpido patrón de evolución en el cual los largos períodos de estabilidad se ven interrumpidos por breves períodos de cambio más rápido

Punnett square | cuadro de Punnett un diagrama que puede utilizarse para predecir las combinaciones de genotipos y fenotipos en un cruce genético

pupa | pupa etapa de la metamorfosis completa en la cual la larva se convierte en un adulto

pupil | pupila pequeña abertura en el iris que deja pasar la luz al ojo

R

radial symmetry | simetría radial diseño corporal en el cual cualquier número de ejes imaginarios dibujados a través del centro del cuerpo lo dividirá en mitades iguales

radiometric dating | datación radiométrica método para determinar la edad de una muestra a partir de la cantidad de isótopo radioactivo en relación a la de isótopo no radiactivo del mismo elemento en dicha muestra

reabsorption | reabsorción proceso por el cual el agua y las sustancias disueltas regresan a la sangre

reactant | reactante elemento o compuesto que participa en una reacción química

receptor | receptor proteína específica que puede encontrarse en la membrana celular o dentro de la célula, cuya forma se corresponde con la de un mensajero molecular específico, por ejemplo una hormona

recombinant DNA | ADN recombinante ADN producido por la combinación de ADN de orígenes diferentes

red blood cell | glóbulo rojo célula sanguínea que contiene hemoglobina y transporta oxígeno

reflex | reflejo respuesta rápida y automática a un estimulo

reflex arc | arco reflejo el receptor sensorial, la neurona sensorial, la neurona motora y el efector que participan en una respuesta rápida a un estímulo

relative dating | datación relativa método para determinar la edad de un fósil comparando su ubicación con la de los fósiles hallados en otras capas de roca

relative frequency | frecuencia relativa número de veces que aparece un alelo en un caudal genético, compararado con la cantidad de veces que aparecen otros alelos en ese mismo gen

releasing hormone | hormona liberadora hormona producida por el hipotálamo que hace que la glándula pituitaria anterior secrete hormonas

renewable resource | recurso renovable recurso que se puede producir o reemplazar mediante el funcionamiento saludable del ecosistema

replication | replicación proceso de copia de ADN previo a la división celular

reproductive isolation | aislamiento reproductor separación de una especie o de una población de tal manera que ya no pueden aparearse y evolucionan hasta formar dos especies separadas

resource | recurso todo lo necesario para la vida, como agua, nutrientes, luz, alimento o espacio

response | respuesta reacción específica a un estímulo

resting potential | potencial de reposo carga eléctrica que pasa a través de la membrana celular de una neurona en reposo

restriction enzyme | enzima restrictiva enzima que corta el ADN en una secuencia de nucleótidos

retina | retina membrana más interna del ojo; contiene receptores susceptibles a la luz

retrovirus | retrovirus ARN viral cuya información genética está contenida en el ARN

ribonucleic acid (RNA) | ácido ribonucleico (ARN) hebra única de ácido nucleico que contiene el azúcar ribose

ribosomal RNA (rRNA) | ARN ribosomal tipo de ARN que se combina con proteínas para formar los ribosomas

ribosome | ribosoma orgánulo celular formado por ARN y proteína que se halla en el citoplasma de una célula; lugar donde se sintetizan las proteínas

RNA interference (RNAi) | ARN de interferencia introducción de un ARN de doble hebra en una célula para inhibir la expresión de genes específicos

RNA polymerase | ARN polimerasa enzima que enlaza los nucleótidos de la cadena de ARN en crecimiento durante la transcripción, usando una secuencia de ADN como patrón o molde

rod | bastoncillo receptor ubicado en los ojos que es susceptible a la luz, pero que no puedé distinguir el color

root cap | cofia cubierta dura de la punta de las raíces que protege al meristemo

root hair | pelo radicular pelos pequeños sobre una raíz que producen una superficie extensa a través de la cual pueden entrar el agua y los minerales

rumen | panza cavidad del estómago de las vacas y otros rumiantes en la cual las bacterias simbióticas digieren la celulosa

S

sapwood | albura en un tallo leñoso, la capa de floema secundario que rodea al duramen; participa usualmente en el transporte de fluidos

sarcomere | sarcómero unidad de contracción muscular; compuesto por dos líneas "z" y los filamentos que hay entre ellas

scavenger | carroñero animal que consume los cadáveres de otros animales

science | ciencia manera organizada de reunir y analizar la información sobre el mundo natural

sclerenchyma | esclerénquima tipo de tejido fundamental con células extremadamente rígidas y gruesas que lo hacen fuerte y resistente

scrotum | escroto bolsa externa que contiene a los testículos

sebaceous gland | glándula sebácea glándula de la piel que secreta sebo (secreción oleosa)

secondary growth | crecimiento secundario tipo de crecimiento de las dicotiledóneas en el cual los tallos aumentan su grosor

secondary succession | sucesión secundaria tipo de sucesión que ocurre en un área destruida sólo parcialmente por alteraciones

seed | semilla embrión vegetal y fuente de alimento encerrada en una cubierta protectora

seed coat | envoltura de la semilla cubierta dura que rodea y protege al embrión de la planta y evita que el contenido de la semilla se seque

segregation | segregación separación de los alelos durante la formación de gametos

selective breeding | reproducción selectiva o selección artificial método de reproducción que solo permite la producción de una nueva generación a aquellos organismos con características deseadas

selectively permeable | permeabilidad selectiva propiedad de las membranas biológicas que permite que algunas sustancias pasen a través de ellas mientras que otras no pueden hacerlo; también llamada membrana semipermeable

semen | semen combinación de esperma y de fluido seminal

semicircular canal | canal semicircular una de las tres estructuras ubicadas en el oído interno que controlan la posición del cuerpo en relación con la fuerza de la gravedad

seminiferous tubule | túbulo seminífero uno de los cientos de túbulos situados en cada testículo, en los cuales se produce el esperma

sensory neuron | neurona sensorial tipo de célula nerviosa que recibe información de los receptores sensoriales y transmite señales al sistema nervioso central

sex chromosome | cromosoma sexual uno de los pares de cromosomas que determina el sexo de un individuo

sex-linked gene | gen ligado al sexo gen situado en un cromosoma sexual

sexual reproduction | reproducción sexual tipo de reproducción en la cual las células de dos progenitores se unen para formar la primera célula de un nuevo organismo

sexually transmitted disease (STD) | enfermedad de transmisión sexual (ETS) enfermedad que se transmite de una persona a otra por contacto sexual

sieve tube element | tubo crivoso tubo continuo que atraviesa las células del floema vegetal, que están puestas una junto a otra

single-gene trait | rasgo de un único gen (monogénico) rasgo controlado por un gen que tiene dos alelos

small intestine | intestino delgado órgano digestivo en el cual tiene lugar la mayor parte de la digestión química y la absorción de los alimentos

smog | esmog neblina marrón grisácea formada por una mezcla de compuestos químicos

society | sociedad grupo de animales de la misma especie, estrechamente relacionados, que trabajan juntos para el beneficio del grupo

solute | soluto sustancia que está disuelta en una solución

solution | solución tipo de mezcla en la cual todos los compuestos están distribuidos de forma homogénea

solvent | disolvente sustancia que disuelve una solución

somatic nervous system | sistema nervioso somático parte del sistema nervioso periférico que conduce señales hacia y desde los músculos esqueléticos

speciation | especiación formación de una nueva especie

species diversity | diversidad de especies número de especies diferentes que forman un área determinada

spirillum (pl. spirilla) | espirilo procariota con forma helicoidal o espiral

spongy mesophyll | mesófilo esponjoso capa de tejido suelto situado debajo del mesófilo en empalizada de una hoja

sporangium (pl. sporangia) | esporangio cápsula en la cual se producen las esporas haploides mediante meiosis

spore | espora en los procariotas, los protistas y los hongos, cada una de las células que, en un momento de su ciclo de vida, produce una membrana gruesa y resistente capaz de sobrevivir en condiciones desfavorables

sporophyte | esporofito planta productora de esporas; la fase diploide multicelular del ciclo vital de una planta

stabilizing selection | selección estabilizadora forma de selección natural en la cual los individuos situados cerca del centro de una curva de distribución tienen mayor aptitud que los individuos que se hallan en cualquiera de los extremos de la curva

stamen | estambre parte masculina de una flor; contiene la antera y el filamento

stem cell | célula troncal célula no especializada que puede originar uno o más tipos de células especializadas

stigma | estigma parte pegajosa situada en la parte superior del estilo; especializado en atrapar el polen

stimulus (pl. stimuli) | estímulo señal a la cual responde un organismo

stoma (pl. stomata) | estoma pequeña abertura en la epidermis de una planta que permite que el dióxido de carbono, el agua y el oxígeno entren y salgan de la hoja

stomach | estómago gran bolsa muscular que continúa la digestión mecánica y química de los alimentos

stroma | estroma parte fluida del cloroplasto; en el exterior de los tilacoides

substrate | sustrato reactante de una reacción catalizada por enzimas

suspension | suspensión mezcla de agua y material no disuelto

sustainable development | desarrollo sostenible estrategia para utilizar los recursos naturales sin agotarlos y para satisfacer las necesidades humanas sin causar daños ambientales a largo plazo

symbiosis | simbiosis relación en la cual dos especies viven en estrecha asociación

synapse | sinapsis punto en el cual una neurona puede transferir un impulso a otra célula

systematics | sistemática estudio de la diversidad de la vida y de las relaciones evolutivas entre los organismos

systemic circulation | circulación sistémica recorrido de la circulación entre el corazón y el resto del cuerpo

T

taiga | taiga bioma con inviernos largos y fríos y pocos meses de tiempo cálido; dominado por coníferas de hojas perennes; también llamada bosque boreal

target cell | célula diana o célula blanco célula que posee un receptor para una hormona determinada

taste bud | papila gustativa órgano sensorial que percibe los sabores

taxon (pl. taxa) | taxón grupo o nivel de organización en que se clasifican los organismos

telomere | telómero ADN repetitivo situado en el extremo de un cromosoma eucariota

telophase | telofase fase de la mitosis en la cual los distintos cromosomas individuales comienzan a separarse y a formar hebras de cromatina

temporal isolation | aislamiento temporal forma de aislamiento reproductivo en la cual dos o más especies se reproducen en épocas diferentes

tendon | tendón tejido conectivo resistente que une los músculos esqueléticos a los huesos

territory | territorio área específica ocupada y protegida por un animal o un grupo de animales

testis (pl. testes) | testículo órgano reproductor masculino fundamental; produce esperma

tetrad | tétrada estructura con cuatro cromátidas que se forma durante la meiosis

tetrapod | tetrápode vertebrado con quatro membros

thalamus | tálamo estructura cerebral que recibe mensajes de los órganos sensoriales y transmite la información a la región adecuada del cerebro para su procesamiento ulterior

theory | teoría explicación basada en pruebas que unifica una amplia gama de observaciones e hipótesis; permite que los científicos hagan predicciones exactas ante situaciones nuevas

thigmotropism | tigmotropismo respuesta de una planta al tacto

threshold | umbral nivel mínimo que debe tener un estímulo para causar un impulso

thylakoid | tilacoide membranas fotosintéticas con forma de bolsa situadas en los cloroplastos

thyroxine | tiroxina hormona producida por la glándula tiroides que aumenta el metabolismo de las células de todo el cuerpo

tissue | tejido grupo de células similares que realizan una función en particular

tolerance | tolerancia capacidad de un organismo de sobrevivir y reproducirse en circunstancias que difieren de sus condiciones óptimas

totipotent | totipotentes células capaces de convertirse en cualquier tipo de célula del cuerpo (incluidas las células que forman las membranas situadas fuera del embrión y la placenta)

trachea | tráquea tubo que conecta a la faringe con la laringe

tracheid | traqueida célula vegetal ahuecada del xilema con paredes celulares gruesas, fortalecida por la lignina

tracheophyte | traqueófita planta vascular

trait | rasgo característica específica de un individuo

transcription | transcripción síntesis de una molécula de ARN a partir de una secuencia de ADN

transfer RNA (tRNA) | ARN de transferencia tipo de ARN que transporta a cada aminoácido hasta un ribosoma durante la síntesis de proteínas

transformation | transformación proceso en el cual una cepa de bacterias es transformada por uno o más genes provenientes de otra cepa de bacterias

transgenic | transgénico término utilizado para referirse a un organismo que contiene genes provenientes de otros organismos

translation | traducción (genética) proceso por el cual la secuencia de bases de un ARN mensajero se convierte en la secuencia de aminoácidos de una proteína

transpiration | transpiración pérdida del agua de una planta a través de sus hojas

trochophore | trocófora estado larvario de un molusco acuático durante el cual puede nadar libremente

trophic level | nivel trófico cada paso en una cadena o red alimenticia

tropism | tropismo movimiento de una planta hacia los estímulos o en dirección opuesta a ellos

tumor | tumor masa de células que se dividen rápidamente y pueden dañar al tejido circundante

U

understory | sotobosque en un bosque tropical, la capa de vegetación que se halla bajo el dosel forestal, formada por árboles más bajos y enredaderas

ureter | uréter conducto que transporta la orina del riñón a la vejiga urinaria

urethra | uretra conducto por donde la orina sale del cuerpo

urinary bladder | vejiga urinaria órgano en forma de bolsa en el cual se almacena la orina antes de ser excretada

V

vaccination | vacunación inyección de un patógeno debilitado o similar al original, pero menos peligroso, para producir inmunidad

vaccine | vacuna preparación hecha con organismos patógenos debilitados o muertos que se utiliza para producir inmunidad a una enfermedad

vacuole | vacuola orgánulo celular que almacena sustancias como agua, sales, proteínas e hidratos de carbono

valve | válvula pliegue de tejido conectivo ubicado entre una aurícula y un ventrículo, o en una vena, que impide el retroceso de la sangre

van der Waals force | fuerzas de van der Waals atracción leve que se desarrolla entre las regiones con cargas opuestas de moléculas cercanas

vas deferens | conducto deferente tubo que transporta el esperma desde el epidídimo a la uretra

vascular bundle | hacecillo vascular manojo de tejidos del xilema y del floema en los tallos

vascular cambium | cámbium vascular meristemo que produce tejidos vasculares y aumenta el grosor de los tallos

vascular cylinder | cilindro vascular región central de una raíz que incluye a los tejidos vasculares xilema y floema

vascular tissue | tejido vascular tejido especializado de las plantas que transporta agua y nutrientes

vector | vector animal que transmite un patógeno a un ser humano

vegetative reproduction | reproducción vegetativa método de reproducción asexual de las plantas que permite que una única planta produzca descendencia genéticamente idéntica a sí misma

vein | vena vaso sanguíneo que transporta la sangre del cuerpo de regreso al corazón

ventricle | ventrículo cavidad inferior del corazón que bombea la sangre fuera del corazón hacia el resto del cuerpo

vertebrate | vertebrado animal que posee columna vertebral

vessel element | elemento vascular (o vaso) tipo de célula del xilema que forma parte de un tubo continuo a través del cual el agua puede desplazarse

vestigial organs | órgano vestigial estructura que está reducida en tamaño y tiene poca o ninguna función

villus (pl. villi) | vellosidad proyección en forma de dedo en el intestino delgado que contribuye a la absorción de las moléculas nutrientes

virus | virus partícula compuesta por proteínas, ácidos nucleicos y, a veces, lípidos, que puede replicarse sólo infectando células vivas

vitamin | vitamina molécula orgánica que ayuda a regular los procesos corporales

viviparous | vivíparo animal que da a luz crías vivas que se nutren directamente dentro del cuerpo de la madre mientras se desarrollan

W

weather | tiempo condiciones diarias de la atmósfera, entre las que se incluyen la temperatura, la precipitación y otros factores

wetland | humedal ecosistema en el cual el agua cubre el suelo o está presente en la superficie durante al menos una parte del año

white blood cell | glóbulo blanco tipo de célula sanguínea que protege de las infecciones, combate a los parásitos y ataca a las bacterias

woody plant | planta leñosa tipo de planta constituida fundamentalmente por células con paredes celulares gruesas que sostienen el cuerpo de la planta; en este tipo se incluyen los árboles, arbustos y vides

X

xylem | xilema tejido vascular que transporta el agua hacia arriba, desde las raíces a cada parte de una planta

Z

zoonosis (pl. zoonoses) | zoonosis enfermedad transmitida por un animal a un ser humano

zooplankton | zooplancton pequeños animales que flotan libremente y forman parte del plancton

zygote | cigoto huevo fertilizado

Vietnamese
Tiếng Việt

Miller & Levine

Biology Glossary

A

abiotic factor | nhân tố vô sinh một yếu tố vật chất, không có sự sống, đóng vai trò trong việc định hình một hệ sinh thái

abscisic acid | axít abscisic một hoóc môn trong cây ức chế việc phân chia tế bào, nhờ đó hạn chế sự tăng trưởng của cây

acetylcholine | acetylcholine một chất dẫn truyền thần kinh tạo ra xung điện trong tế bào cơ

acid | axít một hợp chất tạo ra ion hiđrô (H⁺) khi được hòa tan trong dung dịch; một dung dịch có độ pH thấp hơn 7

acid rain | mưa axít nước mưa chứa axít nitric và axít sunfuric

actin | actin một protein hình sợi mỏng có trong cơ

action potential | thế động tác sự thay đổi điện thế xảy ra ngang qua màng tế bào thần kinh; còn được gọi là xung điện thần kinh

activation energy | năng lượng hoạt hóa năng lượng cần thiết để kích hoạt một phản ứng

active immunity | miễn dịch chủ động trạng thái miễn dịch phát triển được khi cơ thể tiếp xúc một cách tự nhiên hay cố ý với một kháng nguyên

adaptation | đặc điểm thích ứng một đặc tính di truyền tăng thêm khả năng một sinh vật có thể sống sót và sinh sản được trong một môi trường nhất định

adaptive radiation | phát tán thích nghi là quá trình một loài vật hay nhóm nhỏ loài vật tiến hóa thành các chủng loại mới có những cách sống khác nhau

adenosine triphosphate (ATP) | adenosine triphosphate (ATP) một hợp chất được tế bào sử dụng để tích trữ và giải phóng năng lượng

adhesion | sự kết dính lực hút giữa các loại phân tử khác nhau

aerobic | ưa khí bất cứ tiến trình nào cần oxy

age structure | cơ cấu tuổi tác số lượng nam và nữ ở mọi lứa tuổi trong một quần thể

aggression | tính hiếu chiến hành vi đe dọa mà một động vật sử dụng để tỏ ra có ưu thế đối với một động vật khác

algal bloom | bùng nổ rong tảo tình trạng tảo và các sinh vật sản xuất khác phát triển tăng vọt khi một chất dinh dưỡng thường bị hạn chế lại đổ vào môi trường với số lượng nhiều

allele | alen một trong nhiều dạng khác nhau của một gen

allergy | dị ứng khi hệ miễn dịch phản ứng quá thái với một kháng nguyên

alternation of generations | sự giao thế thế hệ chu kỳ sống có hai giai đoạn luân phiên nhau--giai đoạn đơn bội (N) và giai đoạn lưỡng bội (2N)

alveolus (số nhiều: alveoli) | phế nang các túi khí nhỏ xíu nằm ở phần cuối tiểu phế quản trong phổi; việc trao đổi khí xảy ra xuyên qua diện tích bề mặt của các túi này

amino acid | axít amin một hợp chất có nhóm amin ở một đầu và nhóm cacboxyl ở đầu kia

amniotic egg | trứng có màng ối loại trứng có vỏ và màng bọc ngoài tạo nên một môi trường an toàn để phôi thai có thể phát triển không cần nằm trong nước

amylase | amilaza enzym được tìm thấy trong nước bọt có tác dụng phân giải các liên kết hóa học trong tinh bột

anaerobic | kỵ khí bất cứ tiến trình nào không cần oxy

anaphase | kỳ sau một giai đoạn trong quá trình nguyên phân, trong đó các nhiễm sắc thể tách nhau và chuyển về hai cực của tế bào

angiosperm | thực vật hạt kín nhóm thực vật hình thành hạt trong vòng một lớp mô bảo vệ; còn được gọi là thực vật có hoa

anther | bao phấn cấu trúc trong hoa là nơi sản xuất hạt phấn

antheridium (số nhiều: antheridia) | túi đực cơ quan sinh dục đực trong một số loại cây có chức năng sản xuất tinh trùng

anthropoid | vượn người nhóm động vật linh trưởng bao gồm khỉ có đuôi và không đuôi và người

antibiotic | kháng sinh nhóm thuốc được dùng để ngăn chặn sự tăng trưởng và sinh sản của các loại vi khuẩn gây bệnh

antibody | kháng thể một chất protein có tác dụng hoặc trực tiếp tấn công kháng nguyên hoặc sản xuất protein khác bám vào kháng nguyên

anticodon | bộ ba đối mã nhóm ba bazơ trên phân tử tRNA ứng với ba bazơ trong bộ ba mã hóa của mRNA

antigen | kháng nguyên bất cứ chất nào kích thích phản ứng miễn dịch

aphotic zone | tầng thiếu sáng trong đại dương, đây là tầng tối nằm dưới tầng sáng nơi ánh sáng không lọt vào được

apical dominance | ưu thế ngọn hiện tượng trong đó chồi cây càng gần ngọn cây thì sự tăng trưởng càng bị ức chế

apical meristem | mô phân sinh ngọn nhóm các tế bào chưa chuyên hóa phân chia để tạo thêm chiều dài cho rễ và thân của cây

apoptosis | cơ chế gây chết tế bào quá trình tế bào chết theo chương trình

appendage | phần phụ một cấu trúc thí dụ như chân hay râu chìa ra từ cơ thể

appendicular skeleton | xương chi xương chân tay cộng với xương chậu và vùng bả vai

aquaculture | nghề nuôi trồng thủy sản việc nuôi các loại sinh vật sống trong nước để ăn

aquaporin | kênh protein vận chuyển nước kênh protein vận chuyển nước trong tế bào

Archaea | Cổ Khuẩn lĩnh giới bao gồm các sinh vật nhân sơ đơn bào có thành không chứa peptidoglycan; tương ứng với giới Vi Khuẩn Cổ

archegonium (số nhiều: archegonia) | túi chứa noãn cấu trúc trong thực vật có chức năng sản xuất tế bào trứng

artery | động mạch mạch máu lớn chở máu từ tim đến các mô cơ thể

artificial selection | chọn lọc nhân tạo việc gây giống chọn lọc ở thực vật và động vật sao cho thế hệ con có được các đặc điểm mong muốn

asexual reproduction | sinh sản vô tính quá trình sinh sản chỉ có một cá thể "cha mẹ" sinh ra con giống hệt về mặt gen với cá thể đó

asthma | suyễn bệnh hô hấp mãn tính do các ống khí bị hẹp đi dẫn đến các triệu chứng thở khò khè, ho, và khó thở

atherosclerosis | xơ vữa động mạch tình trạng mỡ đóng thành mảng được gọi là mảng vữa bên trong thành động mạch và từ từ khiến cho động mạch cứng đi

atom | nguyên tử đơn vị cơ bản nhất của vật chất

ATP synthase | enzym tổng hợp ATP một chùm các protein nằm xuyên qua màng tế bào và cho phép ion hyđrô (H^+) di chuyển qua màng

atrium (số nhiều: atria) | tâm nhĩ buồng trên của tim, là nơi nhận máu từ khắp cơ thể trở về tim

autonomic nervous system | hệ thần kinh tự trị một phần của hệ thần kinh ngoại biên điều khiển các hoạt động không tự chủ, tức là không ý thức được; được cấu tạo bởi hai hệ phụ là hệ thần kinh giao cảm và hệ thần kinh phó giao cảm

autosome | thể thường nhiễm sắc nhiễm sắc thể không phải là loại quy định giới tính; còn được gọi là thể nhiễm sắc điển hình

autotroph | sinh vật tự dưỡng một sinh vật có thể hấp thụ năng lượng từ ánh nắng hay hóa chất để dùng vào việc tự sản xuất thức ăn cho mình từ các hợp chất vô cơ; còn được gọi là sinh vật sản xuất

auxin | auxin chất điều hòa được sản xuất ở ngọn cây đang tăng trưởng có tác dụng kích thích tế bào dài ra và phát triển rễ cây

axial skeleton | bộ xương trục phần bộ xương nâng đỡ trục giữa của cơ thể; bao gồm hộp sọ, cột sống, và xương sườn

axon | sợi trục sợi dài chở xung điện đi từ thân tế bào thần kinh

B

bacillus (số nhiều: bacilli) | trực khuẩn một loại sinh vật nhân sơ có hình que

background extinction | tuyệt chủng do bối cảnh hiện tượng tuyệt chủng gây ra bởi tiến trình từ từ là sự chọn lọc tự nhiên

Bacteria | Vi khuẩn lĩnh giới bao gồm các sinh vật nhân sơ đơn bào có thành chứa peptidoglycan; tương ứng với giới vi khuẩn thật sự

bacteriophage | thể thực khuẩn một loại vi rút gây nhiễm ở vi khuẩn

bark | vỏ cây các mô bên ngoài tượng tầng libe gỗ, bao gồm libe, tượng tầng sube nhu bì, và sube

base | chất kiềm một hợp chất cho ra ion hyđrô (OH⁻) khi hòa tan trong dung dịch; một dung dịch có độ pH nhiều hơn 7

base pairing | hiện tượng ghép đôi bazơ theo nguyên tắc này, các liên kết trong DNA chỉ có thể hình thành giữa adenine và thymine và giữa guanine và cytosine

behavior | hành vi cách thức một sinh vật phản ứng với những thay đổi bên trong cơ thể hay ở môi trường bên ngoài

behavioral isolation | sự cách ly do tập tính một dạng cách ly sinh sản trong đó hai quần thể phát triển các tập tính khác nhau bao gồm tập tính hôn phối, do đó không thể sinh sản với nhau

benthos | sinh vật đáy các sinh vật sống bám vào hay gần đáy hồ, sông hay đại dương

bias | thiên kiến một khuynh hướng hay quan điểm cá nhân, không mang tính chất khoa học

bilateral symmetry | tính đối xứng hai bên hình dạng cơ thể có thể được chia đôi bằng một đường thẳng tưởng tượng thành bên phải và bên trái và là những hình ảnh phản chiếu với nhau

binary fission | phân đôi dạng sinh sản vô tính trong đó một sinh vật nhân bản DNA của mình và chia mình thành hai tế bào con giống hệt nhau

binocular vision | thị giác hai mắt khả năng kết hợp hình ảnh có được từ cả hai con mắt, tạo hình ảnh ba chiều, có chiều sâu về thế giới bên ngoài

binomial nomenclature | hệ danh pháp tên kép hệ thống phân loại theo đó mỗi loài được chỉ định một tên khoa học gồm hai phần

biodiversity | sự đa dạng sinh học tổng thể tất cả các sinh vật đa dạng trong sinh quyển; còn được gọi là biological diversity

biogeochemical cycle | chu trình địa hóa sinh vật học quá trình trong đó các nguyên tố, hợp chất hóa học và các dạng vật chất khác được truyền từ một sinh vật sang sinh vật khác và từ nơi này đến nơi khác ở sinh quyển

biogeography | địa lý sinh vật học môn nghiên cứu sự phân phối các sinh vật hiện nay và trong quá khứ

bioinformatics | tin sinh học môn áp dụng toán học và tin học vào việc tích trữ, truy lục và phân tích dữ kiện sinh học

biological magnification | sự lan truyền sinh học việc một chất có hại truyền từ các sinh vật ở bậc thấp hơn lên các sinh vật ở bậc cao hơn của chuỗi thức ăn, càng lên cao thì càng cô đặc hơn

biology | sinh học môn khoa học nghiên cứu về sự sống

biomass | sinh khối tổng số lượng mô sống ở một bậc dinh dưỡng nhất định

biome | quần xã sinh vật một tập hợp các hệ sinh thái có chung khí hậu và các sinh vật điển hình giống nhau

biosphere | sinh quyển phần Trái Đất có sự sống, bao gồm đất, nước, và khí hay khí quyển

biotechnology | công nghệ sinh học việc sử dụng các sinh vật, tế bào hay phân tử để sản xuất ra những sản phẩm cụ thể

biotic factor | nhân tố hữu sinh bất cứ phần nào của môi trường có sự sống và có thể tương tác với một sinh vật

bipedal | đi bằng hai chân từ được dùng để chỉ hiện tượng đi lại bằng hai chân

blade | phiến (lá) phần dẹp, mỏng của lá cây

blastocyst | túi phôi giai đoạn đầu trong tiến trình thai nghén của động vật có vú, lúc này phôi thai chỉ là một tập hợp tế bào hình quả cầu rỗng

blastula | phôi nang một tập hợp tế bào hình cầu rỗng phát triển được khi một hợp tử được phân chia nhiều lần

bone marrow | tủy xương mô mềm ở hốc bên trong xương

bottleneck effect | hiệu ứng cổ chai việc tần số alen thay đổi sau khi một quần thể bị giảm đáng kể

Bowman's capsule | nang Bowman cơ cấu có hình giống như một cái cốc bao bọc cầu thận; thu thập các chất lọc ra từ máu

brain stem | thân não cơ cấu nối giữa bộ não và tủy sống; bao gồm hành não và cầu não

bronchus (số nhiều: bronchi) | phế quản một trong hai ống lớn trong lồng ngực dẫn từ khí quản vào phổi

bryophyte | rêu nhóm thực vật có cơ quan sinh sản chuyên dụng nhưng không có mô mạch; bao gồm rêu và các loài cùng họ với rêu

bud | chồi cơ cấu thực vật chứa mô phân sinh ngọn và có thể sinh ra thân và lá mới

buffer | chất đệm một hợp chất ngăn cản việc độ pH đột ngột thay đổi đáng kể

C

calcitonin | canxitoni hoóc môn được sản xuất trong tuyến giáp trạng, có tác dụng giảm mức canxi trong máu

Calorie | Calo đơn vị dùng để đo nhiệt lượng trong thực phẩm; tương đương với 1000 calo

calorie | calo số năng lượng cần thiết để tăng nhiệt độ của 1 gram nước lên 1 độ Celsius

Calvin cycle | chu trình Calvin các phản ứng không cần ánh sáng trong tiến trình quang hợp dùng năng lượng từ ATP và NADPH để tổng hợp các hợp chất giầu năng lượng thí dụ như đường

cancer | ung thư một tình trạng rối loạn xảy ra khi một số tế bào trong cơ thể mất khả năng tự kiểm soát sự tăng trưởng của mình

canopy | tán cây lớp bao phủ dày đặc được tạo thành bởi vô số lá ở đỉnh cây trong rừng mưa nhiệt đới

capillary | mao mạch mạch máu nhỏ nhất; cung cấp chất dinh dưỡng và oxy đến các mô trong cơ thể và hấp thụ cacbon điôxit và các chất thải khác

capillary action | tác dụng mao dẫn khuynh hướng di chuyển lên trên của nước trong một ống nhỏ

capsid | capsit vỏ protein bao bọc một virút

carbohydrate | hiđrat cacbon hợp chất được cấu tạo từ nguyên tử cacbon, hyđrô, và oxy; một chất dinh dưỡng là nguồn năng lượng chính cho cơ thể

carnivore | loài ăn thịt các sinh vật kiếm năng lượng bằng cách ăn thịt các sinh vật khác

carpel | lá noãn phần ở tận trong cùng bông hoa có chức năng sản sinh và bảo vệ thể giao tử cái

carrying capacity | sức chứa số lượng tối đa các cá thể của một loài cụ thể mà một môi trường có thể chứa được

cartilage | sụn loại mô liên kết mềm dẻo hơn xương, có chức năng nâng đỡ cơ thể

Casparian strip | Đai Caspari đai không thấm nước nằm xung quanh các tế bào nội bì thực vật đóng vai trò trong việc đưa các chất theo một chiều vào trụ mạch ở rễ cây

catalyst | chất xúc tác chất tăng tốc độ của một phản ứng hóa học

cell | tế bào đơn vị căn bản của tất cả các hình thức sự sống

cell body | thân tế bào bộ phận lớn nhất của một tế bào thần kinh thông thường, chứa nhân và phần lớn tế bào chất

cell cycle | chu kỳ tế bào một chuỗi sự kiện trong đó một tế bào tăng trưởng, chuẩn bị phân chia, và chia ra thành hai tế bào con

cell division | phân bào quá trình trong đó một tế bào phân chia thành hai tế bào con mới

cell membrane | màng tế bào màng mỏng, dẻo bao bọc tất cả các tế bào; có chức năng kiểm soát các chất ra vào tế bào

cell theory | học thuyết tế bào một khái niệm cơ bản trong sinh học nói rằng tất cả các sinh vật được cấu thành bởi tế bào; rằng tế bào là đơn vị căn bản tạo ra các cấu trúc và chức năng trong tất cả sinh vật; và rằng các tế bào mới được sinh ra từ tế bào hiện có

cell wall | vách tế bào trong một số tế bào, đây là lớp dai nằm ngoài, hỗ trợ cho màng tế bào

cell-mediated immunity | miễn dịch qua trung gian tế bào phản ứng miễn dịch bảo vệ cơ thể khỏi bị tấn công bởi virút, nấm và tế bào ung thư bất thường có trong các tế bào sống

cellular respiration | hô hấp tế bào tiến trình giải phóng năng lượng bằng cách phân giải glucoza và các phân tử thực phẩm khác trong môi trường có oxy

central nervous system | hệ thần kinh trung ương bao gồm bộ não và tủy sống; hệ thống này xử lý thông tin và tạo ra phản ứng để truyền đến các bộ phận cơ thể

centriole | trung thể một cấu trúc trong tế bào động vật giúp tổ chức việc phân chia tế bào

centromere | tâm động phần trên nhiễm sắc thể nơi hai nhiễm sắc tử chị em dính vào

cephalization | sự hình thành đầu quá trình dồn các bộ phận giác quan và tế bào thần kinh về phía trước của một động vật

cerebellum | tiểu não phần não phối hợp các động tác và kiểm soát việc giữ thăng bằng

cerebral cortex | vỏ não lớp ngoài của não động vật; trung tâm sinh phát sự tư duy và các hành vi phức tạp khác

cerebrum | đại não phần của não có chức năng quản lý các hoạt động tự chủ của cơ thể; phần não "biết suy nghĩ"

chemical digestion | tiêu hóa hóa học quá trình trong đó các enzym phân giải thực phẩm thành những phân tử nhỏ cho cơ thể dễ sử dụng

chemical reaction | phản ứng hóa học tiến trình thay đổi hay biến đổi một tập hợp hóa chất thành tập hợp hóa chất khác

chemosynthesis | hóa tổng hợp quá trình trong đó năng lượng hóa học được sử dụng để sản xuất hiđrat cacbon

chitin | kitin một chất hiđrat cacbon phức hợp cấu thành vách tế bào trong nấm; cũng được tìm thấy trong bộ xương ngoài của các động vật có chân đốt

chlorophyll | chất diệp lục sắc tố chính trong thực vật và các sinh vật khác sống nhờ sự quang hợp

chloroplast | hạt diệp lục bào quan trong tế bào thực vật và một số sinh vật khác có thể hấp thụ năng lượng từ ánh sáng mặt trời để biến thành năng lượng hóa học

chordate | động vật có dây sống một động vật mà, trong ít nhất một giai đoạn đời, đã có: một dây sống rỗng phía sau lưng, một dây nguyên sống, một cái đuôi kéo dài qua hậu môn; và một số túi hầu

chromatid | nhiễm sắc tử một trong hai phần "chị em" giống hệt nhau của một nhiễm sắc thể đã được nhân bản

chromatin | chất nhiễm sắc chất được tìm thấy trong nhiễm sắc thể của tế bào có nhân chuẩn, được cấu tạo bởi DNA cuốn chặt vào các histon

chromosome | nhiễm sắc thể cấu trúc hình sợi trong nhân tế bào chứa thông tin gen được di truyền từ thế hệ này sang thế hệ sau

chyme | dưỡng trấp hỗn hợp chứa các enzym với thực phẩm được tiêu hóa một phần

cilium (số nhiều: cilia) | tiêm mao bộ phận dạng sợi ngắn chĩa ra từ tế bào và giúp nó di chuyển

circadian rhythm | nhịp ngày đêm các chu kỳ hành vi xảy ra hàng ngày

clade | đơn vị huyết thống đơn tố một nhánh tiến hóa trong biểu đồ phân nhánh huyết thống thể hiện một tổ tiên và tất cả các hậu thế của nó

cladogram | biểu đồ phân nhánh huyết thống một biểu đồ thể hiện các đặc điểm chung của các loài khác nhau

class | lớp trong hệ thống phân loại, lớp là một tập hợp các bộ có họ gần nhau

classical conditioning | điều kiện hóa cổ điển một phương pháp huấn luyện thú vật liên tưởng một tác nhân kích thích với một phần thưởng hay hình phạt

climate | khí hậu tình trạng nhiệt độ và lượng mưa tuyết trung bình ở một vùng nhất định từ năm nay qua năm khác, qua một thời gian dài

clone | dòng vô tính một cá thể trong quần thể các tế bào có gen giống hệt nhau được sản sinh từ một tế bào mẹ

closed circulatory system | hệ tuần hoàn khép kín một loại hệ tuần hoàn trong đó việc tuần hoàn máu được thực hiện hoàn toàn trong các mạch máu chạy khắp cơ thể

coccus (số nhiều: cocci) | cầu khuẩn một loại sinh vật nhân sơ có hình cầu

cochlea | ốc tai bộ phận đầy nước ở tai trong; chứa các tế bào thần kinh cảm nhận được âm thanh

codominance | tính đồng trội tình trạng kiểu hình của cả hai alen đều được biểu hiện đầy đủ

codon | bộ ba mã hóa nhóm ba bazơ nucleotit trong mRNA có chức năng xác định một axít amin cụ thể để kết hợp thành protein

coelom | khoang cơ thể một khoang rỗng trong cơ thể có lớp trung bì

coevolution | đồng tiến hóa quá trình trong đó hai loài cùng tiến hóa để thích ứng với những thay đổi ở loài kia qua một thời gian dài

cohesion | sự kết dính lực hút giữa các phân tử có cùng bản chất

collenchyma | mô dày trong thực vật, đây là loại mô nền có vách tế bào dai và dẻo; mô này giúp nâng đỡ các loại cây lớn hơn

commensalism | hiện tượng hội sinh một quan hệ cộng sinh có lợi cho một bên còn bên kia không được hưởng lợi nhưng cũng không bị hại

communication | sự truyền thông tin việc truyền thông tin từ một sinh vật đến sinh vật khác

community | quần xã một tập hợp các quần thể khác nhau cùng sống trong một vùng cụ thể

companion cell | tế bào kèm trong thực vật, đây là các tế bào libe bao vây các thành viên ống sàng

competitive exclusion principle | nguyên lý loại trừ cạnh tranh nguyên tắc cho rằng không thể có hai loài khác nhau cùng một lúc chiếm cùng một ổ sinh thái trong một môi trường sống

compound | hợp chất một chất được tạo ra khi kết hợp hai hoặc nhiều hơn nguyên tố theo tỷ lệ nhất định bằng phương pháp hóa học

cone | tế bào thần kinh hình nón trong mắt, đây là các tế bào cảm quang phản ứng với những màu ánh sáng khác nhau và cho phép chúng ta nhìn thấy màu sắc

coniferous | có quả nón từ được dùng để chỉ các loại cây sinh ra hạt trong quả nón và có lá mỏng hình kim

conjugation | sự tiếp hợp quá trình trao đổi thông tin di truyền được sử dụng bởi trùng đế giày và một số sinh vật nhân sơ

connective tissue | mô liên kết loại mô nâng đỡ cơ thể và liên kết các bộ phận với nhau

consumer | sinh vật tiêu thụ một sinh vật kiếm năng lượng và thực phẩm nhờ vào các sinh vật khác; còn được gọi là sinh vật dị dưỡng

control group | nhóm đối chứng trong cuộc thí nghiệm, nhóm này có cùng các điều kiện giống như nhóm thí nghiệm, ngoại trừ một biến độc lập

controlled experiment | cuộc thí nghiệm có đối chứng một cuộc thí nghiệm chỉ thay đổi một biến độc lập

convergent evolution | sự tiến hóa đồng quy quá trình trong đó các sinh vật không có họ với nhau lại tiến hóa độc lập những đặc điểm giống nhau do thích ứng với các môi trường tương tự

cork cambium | tượng tầng sube nhu bì mô phân sinh ngọn tạo ra vỏ ngoài của thân cây trong giai đoạn sinh trưởng thứ cấp

cornea | giác mạc lớp dai, trong phủ mắt và cho ánh sáng lọt vào

corpus luteum | thể vàng nang buồng trứng được gọi bằng tên này sau khi rụng trứng vì nó trở màu vàng

cortex | vùng vỏ trong thực vật, đây là vùng mô nền nằm ngay bên trong rễ cho phép nước và khoáng chất di chuyển đến khắp cây

corticosteroid | corticosteroid một hoóc môn dạng steroid được sản xuất ở vỏ thượng thận

cotyledon | lá mầm cái lá hay đôi lá đầu tiên được mọc ra từ phôi thai của một cây có hạt

courtship | tập tính hôn phối một loại hành vi đặc thù của động vật nhằm phát ra tín hiệu để thu hút bạn khác giới

covalent bond | mối liên kết cộng hóa trị kiểu liên kết giữa các nguyên tử khi có chung những cặp điện tử

crossing-over | trao đổi chéo quá trình hai nhiễm sắc thể tương đồng trao đổi các đoạn nhiễm sắc tử trong quá trình giảm phân

cyclin | cyclin một trong các protein cùng họ có chức năng điều hòa chu kỳ tế bào trong các tế bào nhân chuẩn

cytokinesis | sự phân chia tế bào chất việc phân chia tế bào chất để tạo thành hai tế bào con riêng biệt

cytokinin | cytokinin một hoóc môn thực vật được sản xuất ở rễ, trái và hạt trong giai đoạn phát triển

cytoplasm | tế bào chất, bào tương phần lỏng của tế bào nằm ngoài nhân

cytoskeleton | bộ xương tế bào mạng lưới các sợi protein trong tế bào nhân chuẩn tạo hình dạng và cấu trúc bên trong của tế bào cũng như giúp tế bào di chuyển

D

data | dữ liệu chứng cớ; thông tin thu thập được từ việc quan sát

deciduous | có lá rụng từ dùng để chỉ loại cây rụng lá theo mùa hàng năm

decomposer | sinh vật phân hủy một sinh vật kiếm năng lượng từ việc phân hủy chất hữu cơ đã chết

deforestation | phá rừng việc phá hủy rừng

demographic transition | sự chuyển tiếp nhân khẩu học khi một quần thể chuyển từ trạng thái có tỷ lệ sinh tử cao đến trạng thái có tỷ lệ sinh tử thấp

demography | nhân khẩu học môn khoa học nghiên cứu các nhóm dân số

dendrite | sợi nhánh các bộ phận chĩa ra từ thân tế bào thần kinh và chuyên chở xung điện từ môi trường xung quanh hay từ các tế bào thần kinh khác đến thân tế bào của nó

denitrification | khử nitơ quá trình chuyển hóa nitrat thành khí nitơ được thực hiện bởi các loại vi khuẩn đất

density-dependent limiting factor | nhân tố hạn chế phụ thuộc mật độ một nhân tố hạn chế phụ thuộc vào mật độ dân số

density-independent limiting factor | nhân tố hạn chế không phụ thuộc mật độ một nhân tố hạn chế tác động giống nhau lên tất cả các quần thể bất kể mật độ dân số nhiều hay ít

deoxyribonucleic acid (DNA) | axít deoxyribonucleic (ADN) chất di truyền mà mỗi sinh vật thừa hưởng từ cha mẹ mình

dependent variable | biến phụ thuộc biến thay đổi phụ thuộc vào một biến độc lập; đây chính là điều được quan sát trong một cuộc thí nghiệm; còn được gọi là biến đáp ứng

derived character | đặc điểm dẫn xuất một đặc điểm xuất hiện trong các thế hệ gần đây của một dòng giống nhưng không có ở các thế hệ trước

dermis | bì lớp da nằm dưới lớp thượng bì

desertification | sa mạc hóa việc năng suất của đất giảm đi do trồng trọt, chăn thả quá mức, hạn hán theo mùa, và khí hậu thay đổi

detritivore | loài ăn chất thải sinh vật ăn xác thực vật, động vật hoặc các thứ khác đã chết

deuterostome | động vật có miệng thứ sinh trong nhóm động vật này, lỗ phôi trở thành hậu môn và miệng được hình thành từ một lỗ thứ hai phát triển sau

diaphragm | cơ hoành cơ to, dẹp nằm ở đáy lồng ngực và giúp trong việc thở

dicot | song tử diệp cây hạt kín có hai lá mầm trong hạt

differentiation | sự phân hóa quá trình trong đó các tế bào được chuyên hóa về cấu trúc và chức năng

diffusion | sự khuếch tán quá trình trong đó các hạt có khuynh hướng di chuyển từ vùng có mật độ cao hơn đến vùng có mật độ thấp hơn

digestive tract | đường tiêu hóa một đường ống bắt đầu ở miệng và kết thúc ở hậu môn

diploid | thể lưỡng bội từ được dùng để chỉ một tế bào có hai bộ nhiễm sắc thể tương đồng

directional selection | sự chọn lọc có định hướng hình thức chọn lọc tự nhiên xảy ra khi các cá thể nằm ở một đầu của đường cong phân phối có khả năng thích ứng tốt hơn so với các cá thể nằm ở phần giữa hay đầu kia của đường cong

disruptive selection | sự chọn lọc đứt quãng tình trạng các cá thể ở đầu trên và đầu dưới của đường cong phân phối có khả năng thích ứng tốt hơn so với các cá thể nằm ở phần giữa đường cong

DNA fingerprinting | in dấu ADN một phương pháp được các nhà sinh học sử dụng để phân tích tập hợp các đoạn ADN giới hạn độc đáo của một cá nhân; phương pháp này nhằm xác định xem hai mẫu chất di truyền có phải có từ cùng một người hay không

DNA microarray | microarray ADN một tấm thủy tinh hay chip silic được gắn hàng ngàn đoạn ADN sợi đơn thuộc nhiều loại khác nhau, được xếp thành đường kẻ ô. Microarray ADN được dùng để phát hiện và đo lường sự biểu hiện của hàng ngàn gen vào cùng một lúc

DNA polymerase | ADN polymerase enzym chính trong quá trình nhân bản ADN

domain | lĩnh giới trong hệ thống phân loại, một cấp lớn hơn, bao gồm nhiều loài hơn so với cấp giới

dopamine | dopamine một chất dẫn truyền thần kinh có liên hệ đến các trung tâm khoái lạc và khen thưởng ở não bộ

dormancy | trạng thái ngủ thời kỳ một phôi thực vật đang sống nhưng không tăng trưởng

double fertilization | sự thụ phấn kép quá trình thụ phấn trong cây hạt kín, trước hết sinh ra hợp tử và sau đó sinh ra nội nhũ bên trong hạt

E

ecological footprint | dấu chân sinh thái tổng lượng hệ sinh thái lành mạnh cần thiết để cung cấp cả các tài nguyên được sử dụng bởi một quần thể con người cũng như tiêu thụ các chất thải từ quần thể đó

ecological hot spot | điểm nóng sinh thái một vùng địa lý nhỏ nơi một số đáng kể những môi trường sống và loài sinh vật đang gặp nguy cơ cao có thể bị tuyệt chủng

ecological pyramid | hình tháp sinh thái hình minh họa tổng số năng lượng hay vật chất tương đối có ở mỗi bậc dinh dưỡng trong một chuỗi hay mạng lưới thức ăn nhất định

ecological succession | diễn thế sinh thái một chuỗi các biến đổi tuần tự xảy ra trong một quần thể sau khi bị xáo trộn

ecology | sinh thái học môn khoa học nghiên cứu về cách những sinh vật tương tác với nhau và với môi trường xung quanh

ecosystem | hệ sinh thái tất cả các sinh vật sống trong một nơi cùng với các yếu tố không sống trong môi trường xung quanh

ecosystem diversity | sự đa dạng hệ sinh thái các môi trường sống, quần xã và quá trình sinh thái khác nhau trong sinh quyển

ectoderm | ngoại phôi bì lớp tế bào phôi ngoài cùng; lớp này phát triển thành các bộ phận giác quan, dây thần kinh, và lớp da ngoài

ectotherm | động vật ngoại nhiệt động vật mà nhiệt độ thân thể thay đổi theo nhiệt độ môi trường

electron | điện tử một hạt có điện tích âm quay xung quanh hạt nhân

electron transport chain | chuỗi dẫn truyền điện tử một chuỗi các protein dẫn truyền điện tử chuyên chở điện tử năng lượng cao trong các phản ứng tạo ATP

element | nguyên tố một nguyên chất được cấu tạo bởi chỉ một loại nguyên tử

embryo | phôi một giai đoạn trong quá trình phát triển của các sinh vật đa bào

embryo sac | túi phôi thể giao tử cái có trong noãn của các loại cây có hoa

emerging disease | bệnh mới nổi một căn bệnh xuất phát lần đầu tiên ở một quần thể, hoặc một bệnh đã có từ lâu nhưng đột nhiên trở thành khó kiểm soát

emigration | sự xuất cư việc các cá thể di chuyển ra khỏi một vùng

endocrine gland | tuyến nội tiết tuyến/hạch tiết ra các chất (hoóc môn) trực tiếp vào dòng máu để được chở đến những bộ phận cơ thể khác

endoderm | nội phôi bì lớp tế bào phôi trong cùng; lớp này phát triển thành đường tiêu hóa và phần lớn hệ hô hấp

endodermis | nội bì trong thực vật, đây là tầng mô nền bao bọc toàn bộ ống mạch

endoplasmic reticulum | mạng lưới nội chất hệ thống màng nằm trong các tế bào nhân chuẩn; nơi sản xuất các thành phần lipit dùng để tạo thành màng tế bào

endoskeleton | bộ xương trong bộ xương bên trong cơ thể; đây là hệ thống nâng đỡ cấu trúc cơ thể động vật

endosperm | nội nhũ mô giàu dinh dưỡng là thức ăn cho cây mới nảy mầm giúp cho nó trưởng thành

endospore | nội bào tử các sinh vật nhân sơ sinh ra cấu trúc này khi gặp điều kiện không thuận lợi; cấu trúc này bao gồm một vách dày bên trong bao bọc ADN và một phần tế bào chất của sinh vật đó

endosymbiotic theory | thuyết nội cộng sinh học thuyết cho rằng các tế bào nhân chuẩn đã tiến hóa từ quan hệ cộng sinh giữa nhiều loại tế bào nhân sơ

endotherm | động vật nội nhiệt một động vật có thể tự điều hòa nhiệt độ thân thể, ít nhất một phần, bằng cách dùng nhiệt của chính cơ thể mình

enzyme | enzym một chất xúc tác bằng protein có tác dụng tăng tốc độ của các phản ứng sinh học cụ thể

epidermis | biểu bì trong thực vật, đây là lớp mỏng, có chiều dầy bằng một tế bào, tạo thành mô bì ; ở người, đây là lớp ngoài cùng của da

epididymis | mào tinh hoàn bộ phận thuộc hệ sinh sản của nam giới, là nơi phát triển và tích trữ tinh trùng

epinephrine | hoóc môn vỏ thượng thận hoóc môn được tiết ra từ tuyến thượng thận có tác dụng tăng nhịp tim và huyết áp để chuẩn bị cho cơ thể bắt đầu hoạt động mạnh; còn được gọi là adrenaline

epithelial tissue | mô biểu bì loại mô phủ kín các bề mặt trong và ngoài cơ thể

era | nguyên đại một đơn vị phân chia các niên đại địa chất; thường được chia nhỏ thành hai hoặc nhiều kỷ

esophagus | thực quản ống dẫn nối miệng với bao tử

estuary | cửa sông vùng đất ngập nước hình thành ở nơi sông chảy vào biển

ethylene | etylen hoóc môn thực vật kích thích quá trình trái cây chín

Eukarya | Nhân Chuẩn lĩnh giới bao gồm tất cả các sinh vật có tế bào chứa nhân; bao gồm sinh vật đơn bào, thực vật, nấm và động vật

eukaryote | sinh vật nhân chuẩn các sinh vật có tế bào chứa nhân

evolution | quá trình tiến hóa sự biến đổi qua thời gian; tất cả các sinh vật hiện thời đã phát triển từ các sinh vật cổ theo quá trình này

excretion | sự bài tiết quá trình loại các chất thải từ việc chuyển hóa ra khỏi cơ thể

exocrine gland | tuyến ngoại tiết tuyến/hạch tiết ra các chất trực tiếp vào một bộ phận hay ra ngoài cơ thể thông qua các cấu trúc hình ống gọi là ống bài tiết

exon | exon một trình tự ADN đã được biểu hiện; đơn vị mã tổng hợp một protein cụ thể

exoskeleton | bộ xương ngoài bộ xương nằm bên ngoài cơ thể; vỏ dai bên ngoài có chức năng bảo vệ và nâng đỡ cơ thể của nhiều động vật không xương sống

exponential growth | tăng trưởng theo hàm mũ là trạng thái tăng trưởng trong đó các cá thể thuộc một quần thể sinh sản theo một tỷ lệ không thay đổi

extinct | tuyệt chủng từ dùng để chỉ một loài đã chết hết, không còn một cá thể nào sống

extracellular digestion | sự tiêu hóa ngoài tế bào một cơ chế tiêu hóa, trong đó thức ăn được phân giải trong hệ tiêu hóa nằm bên ngoài các tế bào và sau đó được hấp thụ vào tế bào

F

facilitated diffusion | sự khuếch tán có trợ lực quá trình khuếch tán trong đó các phân tử di chuyển qua màng tế bào thông qua các kênh trong màng

family | họ trong hệ thống phân loại, họ là một nhóm các chi gần giống nhau

fat | mỡ chất lipit; được cấu thành bởi axít béo và glyxerin; là một loại chất dinh dưỡng có tác dụng bảo vệ các cơ quan nội tạng, giữ nhiệt cho cơ thể, và tích trữ năng lượng

feedback inhibition | ức chế phản hồi quá trình trong đó một tác nhân kích thích gây ra phản ứng chống lại chính sự kích thích đó; còn được gọi là phản hồi âm

fermentation | lên men quá trình giải phóng năng lượng của các tế bào trong môi trường không có oxy

fertilization | thụ tinh trong quá trình sinh sản hữu tính, đây là lúc hai tế bào sinh sản đực và cái kết hợp với nhau để tạo thành một tế bào mới

fetus | bào thai tên gọi cho phôi thai người sau khi được phát triển tám tuần

fever | sốt thân nhiệt tăng lên do cơ thể phản ứng với sự nhiễm trùng

filtration | lọc quá trình đưa một chất lỏng hay khí qua một bộ lọc để loại chất thải

fitness | khả năng thích nghi khả năng sống sót và sinh sản của một sinh vật trong môi trường của mình

flagellum (số nhiều: flagella) | lông roi cấu trúc trong các sinh vật đơn bào có chức năng di chuyển; chúng di động nhịp nhàng như làn sóng

food chain | chuỗi thức ăn chuỗi nhiều bậc trong một hệ sinh thái theo đó các sinh vật truyền năng lượng cho nhau bằng cách ăn sinh vật khác hay bị sinh vật khác ăn mình

food vacuole | không bào tiêu hóa hốc nhỏ trong tế bào chất của sinh vật đơn bào có chức năng tạm trữ thức ăn

food web | mạng lưới thức ăn mạng lưới các tương tác phức tạp được tạo ra từ các quan hệ thức ăn giữa mọi sinh vật trong một hệ sinh thái

forensics | pháp y môn khoa học nghiên cứu các dấu vết để lại ở hiện trường xảy ra vụ án

fossil | hóa thạch vết tích được bảo tồn của các sinh vật cổ

founder effect | hiệu ứng sáng lập việc tần số alen trong một quần thể thay đổi do một nhóm phụ nhỏ di cư đến chỗ khác

frameshift mutation | đột biến dịch khung đột biến làm lệch đi "khung đọc" thông tin di truyền bằng cách thêm vào hay xóa đi một nucleotit

fruit | trái cây cấu trúc trong các loại cây hạt kín chứa một hay nhiều bầu noãn đã trưởng thành

fruiting body | thể quả bộ phận sinh sản của nấm, mọc ra từ hệ sợi nấm

G

gamete | giao tử tế bào sinh dục

gametophyte | thể giao tử loại thực vật có giao tử; giai đoạn đơn bội, đa bào trong chu trình sống của thực vật

ganglion (số nhiều: ganglia) | hạch một tập hợp các tế bào thần kinh trung gian

gastrovascular cavity | xoang vị buồng tiêu hóa có một cửa duy nhất

gastrulation | sự hình thành phôi vị quá trình di chuyển tế bào dẫn đến việc hình thành ba lớp tế bào—ngoại bì, trung bì và nội bì

gel electrophoresis | điện di trên gel quy trình dùng để tách ra và phân tích các đoạn ADN bằng cách đặt một tập hợp các đoạn ADN ở đầu bản gel có nhiều lỗ rồi tạo điện trường trên gel

gene | gen một chuỗi ADN có vùng mã hướng dẫn quá trình tổng hợp một protein đặc thù, bằng cách đó quyết định một đặc điểm; một yếu tố được di truyền từ cha mẹ xuống con cái

gene expression | sự biểu hiện của gen quá trình trong đó một gen sinh ra sản phẩm và sản phẩm đó thực hiện chức năng của nó

gene pool | vốn gen tất cả các gen, bao gồm tất cả các alen khác nhau của từng gen, có trong một quần thể vào một thời điểm nhất định

gene therapy | liệu pháp gen thủ thuật biến đổi gen để chữa trị một căn bệnh hay tình trạng rối loạn y khoa Trong thủ thuật này, gen bị thiếu hay có lỗi được thay thế bằng gen bình thường có khả năng hoạt động tốt

genetic code | mã di truyền tập hợp các bộ ba mã hóa của mRNA, mỗi bộ ba hướng dẫn việc kết hợp một axít amin cụ thể thành một protein trong quá trình tổng hợp protein

genetic diversity | sự đa dạng di truyền tổng thể tất cả các hình thức thông tin di truyền khác nhau được mang trong một loài cụ thể hay bởi tất cả các sinh vật trên Trái Đất

genetic drift | sự lạc dòng di truyền việc tần số alen thay đổi một cách ngẫu nhiên do một loạt các sự kiện tình cờ khiến cho alen đó xuất hiện nhiều hay ít hơn trong một quần thể

genetic equilibrium | sự cân bằng di truyền trạng thái các tần số alen trong một quần thể không thay đổi

genetic marker | dấu chuẩn di truyền các alen tạo ra những kiểu hình khác nhau, có thể dò tìm được, thường được dùng trong việc phân tích gen

genetics | di truyền học môn khoa học nghiên cứu sự di truyền

genome | bộ gen toàn bộ thông tin di truyền mà một sinh vật mang trong ADN của mình

genomics | bộ gen học môn nghiên cứu các bộ gen đầy đủ, bao gồm các gen và chức năng của chúng

genotype | kiểu gen các loại gen tạo thành một sinh vật

genus | chi nhóm bao gồm các loài có họ gần nhau; phần đầu của tên khoa học trong hệ danh pháp tên kép

geographic isolation | sự cách ly địa lý một hình thức cách ly sinh sản, theo đó hai quần thể bị cách ly bởi các vật cản địa lý như sông, núi, hay vùng nước và do đó tiến hóa thành hai loài phụ riêng biệt

geologic time scale | hệ thống niên đại địa chất trục thời gian được sử dụng để thể hiện lịch sử Trái Đất

germ theory of disease | lý thuyết về vi trùng và bệnh tật khái niệm rằng các bệnh truyền nhiễm là do vi sinh vật gây ra

germination | nảy mầm việc phôi thực vật bắt đầu phát triển lại sau một thời gian trong trạng thái ngủ

giberellin | giberellin hoóc môn thực vật kích thích sự tăng trưởng, có thể giúp cây tăng trưởng mạnh mẽ

gill | mang cấu trúc hình răng lược có chức năng chuyên biệt là trao đổi khí và nước

global warming | sự hâm nóng địa cầu hiện tượng nhiệt độ trung bình tăng lên trên khắp Trái Đất

glomerulus | cầu thận mạng lưới các mao mạch nhỏ nằm ở đầu trên của ống sinh niệu; là nơi diễn ra việc lọc máu

glycolysis | đường phân chuỗi phản ứng đầu tiên trong quá trình hô hấp tế bào, trong đó một phân tử glucoza được phân giải thành hai phân tử axít pyruvic

Golgi apparatus | thể Golgi bào quan có chức năng biến đổi, phân loại và đóng gói các protein và chất khác có từ mạng lưới nội chất để tích trữ trong tế bào hay giải phóng ra ngoài

gradualism | thuyết tiệm tiến quá trình tiến hóa một loài mới qua những thay đổi nhỏ, từ từ tích lũy trong gen qua một thời gian dài

grafting | kỹ thuật ghép phương pháp nhân giống được dùng đối với thực vật không có hạt và các loại cây gỗ không thể nhân giống bằng phương pháp giâm cành

gravitropism | địa hướng động phản ứng của cây đối với trọng lực

green revolution | cuộc cách mạng xanh phong trào phát triển các giống cây trồng có sản lượng cao và sử dụng các kỹ thuật nông nghiệp hiện đại nhằm tăng cao sản lượng hoa màu thu hoạch được

greenhouse effect | hiệu ứng nhà kính quá trình trong đó một số loại khí (cacbon điôxit, mêtan và hơi nước) giữ lại năng lượng từ ánh sáng mặt trời và tăng nhiệt độ trong bầu khí quyển của Trái Đất

growth factor | yếu tố tăng trưởng một trong nhóm các protein điều hòa bên ngoài có tác dụng kích thích tế bào tăng trưởng và phân chia

guard cells | tế bào bảo vệ các tế bào chuyên hóa trong biểu bì thực vật có chức năng mở đóng lỗ khí

gullet | họng chỗ lõm ở một tế bào có tiêm mao cho phép thức ăn vào bên trong

gymnosperm | thực vật hạt trần nhóm các cây sinh hạt trực tiếp trên vảy quả nón

H

habitat | môi trường sống vùng sống của một sinh vật, bao gồm các nhân tố hữu sinh và vô sinh có ảnh hưởng đến sinh vật đó

habitat fragmentation | phân tán môi trường sống việc chia các hệ sinh thái thành những phần nhỏ hơn

habituation | tạo thành tập tính cách đổi tập tính, theo đó một động vật được tiếp xúc nhiều lần với một tác nhân kích thích không mang lại sự vui thú nhưng cũng không gây hại cho nó và nhờ đó phản ứng ít hơn hay không còn phản ứng gì hết đối với tác nhân đó

hair follicle | nang lông/tóc các lỗ dạng ống ở lớp bì chứa tế bào biểu bì; các tế bào nằm ở đáy nang sinh ra lông/tóc

half life | thời gian bán hủy khoảng thời gian cần thiết để phân hủy hết một phân nửa nguyên tử phóng xạ trong một mẫu

haploid | thể đơn bội từ dùng để chỉ các tế bào chỉ chứa một bộ gen

Hardy-Weinberg principle | nguyên lý Hardy-Weinberg nguyên lý cho rằng tần số alen trong một quần thể không thay đổi trừ phi có một hay nhiều yếu tố khiến tần số phải thay đổi

Haversian canal | ống Havers một trong nhiều ống chứa mạch máu và dây thần kinh tạo thành mạng lưới trong mô xương đặc

heart | tim một bộ phận rỗng, mạnh có chức năng bơm máu đến khắp cơ thể

heartwood | ruột gỗ trong thân cây gỗ, đây là phần mô mộc già hơn nằm gần trung tâm thân và không còn có khả năng dẫn nước

hemoglobin | huyết cầu tố protein chứa sắt trong hồng cầu có chức năng bám vào oxy và chở oxy đến khắp cơ thể

herbaceous plant | thực vật thân cỏ loại thực vật có thân trơn, không chứa gỗ; bao gồm cây bồ công anh, cúc zinnia, dã yên thảo và hướng dương

herbivore | loài ăn thực vật các sinh vật kiếm năng lượng bằng cách chỉ ăn thực vật

herbivory | sự tiêu thụ thực vật một sự tương tác trong đó một động vật (thuộc loài ăn thực vật) ăn các sinh vật sản xuất (thí dụ như cây cỏ)

heterotroph | sinh vật dị dưỡng các sinh vật kiếm thức ăn từ việc ăn những sinh vật khác; còn được gọi là sinh vật tiêu thụ

heterozygous | dị hợp tử hiện tượng có hai alen khác nhau trong một gen cụ thể

histamine | histamin hóa chất được phóng thích bởi tế bào mast kích thích việc tăng lưu lượng máu và các chất lỏng đến vùng bị nhiễm trùng; điều này được gọi là phản ứng viêm

homeobox gene | gen homeobox homeobox là một trình tự ADN gồm khoảng 130 cặp bazơ có trong nhiều gen homeotic có chức năng điều hòa sự phát triển. Các gen có trình tự này được gọi là gen homeobox và mã hóa yếu tố phiên mã, là loại protein kết dính với ADN và điều hòa sự biểu hiện của các gen khác

homeostasis | tính nội cân bằng trạng thái tương đối ổn định về mặt vật lý và hóa học mà các sinh vật duy trì được bên trong cơ thể mình

homeotic gene | gen homeotic một nhóm gen điều hòa có chức năng xác định các bộ phận và vùng cơ thể trong phôi động vật. Nếu loại gen này bị đột biến thì co thể biến một bộ phận cơ thể thành bộ phận cơ thể khác

hominine | hominine nhóm phân loại bao gồm các loài họ người; loài người hiện đại đã tiến hóa từ nhóm này

hominoid | họ người nhóm vượn người bao gồm vượn, đười ươi, khỉ đột, tinh tinh, và người

homologous | tương đồng từ dùng để miêu tả các nhiễm sắc thể thành cặp, trong đó một bộ nhiễm sắc thể có từ cha và bộ kia có từ mẹ

homologous structures | các cấu trúc tương đồng các cấu trúc tương tự nhau trong những loài có cùng tổ tiên

homozygous | đồng hợp tử hiện tượng có hai alen giống nhau ở một gen cụ thể

hormone | hoóc môn hóa chất được tạo ra ở một bộ phận trong cơ thể sinh vật và tác động đến bộ phận khác trong cùng sinh vật đó

Hox gene | gen Hox một chùm gen homeotic có chức năng xác định các bộ phận cơ thể trong động vật từ đầu đến đuôi. Tất cả các gen hox đều chứa trình tự ADN homeobox

humoral immunity | miễn dịch dịch thể tính miễn nhiễm đối với kháng nguyên trong các loại dịch cơ thể như máu và bạch huyết

humus | đất mùn chất được tạo ra từ quá trình phân hủy lá và các chất hữu cơ khác

hybrid | vật lai từ dùng để chỉ con của hai cha mẹ có những đặc điểm khác nhau

hybridization | lai giống phương pháp gây giống trong đó hai cá thể có những đặc điểm khác nhau được giao phối với nhau nhằm tạo ra thế hệ con mang những đặc điểm có lợi của cả hai cha mẹ

hydrogen bond | liên kết hyđrô lực hút yếu giữa một nguyên tử hyđrô và nguyên tử khác

hydrostatic skeleton | bộ xương thủy tĩnh bộ xương được cấu thành bởi các đoạn cơ thể chứa nước; các đoạn này phối hợp với cơ để cho phép động vật di chuyển được

hypertonic | ưu trương khi so sánh hai dung dịch khác nhau, dung dịch nào có nồng độ chất tan nhiều hơn thì gọi là ưu trương

hypha (số nhiều: hyphae) | sợi nấm một trong nhiều sợi mỏng, dài cấu thành thể nấm

hypothalamus | vùng dưới đồi cấu trúc trong não có chức năng kiểm soát việc nhận ra và phân tích các cảm giác đói, khát, mệt, giận, và thân nhiệt

hypothesis | giả thuyết một cách giải thích có lý về một tập hợp các hiện tượng quan sát được, hoặc một câu trả lời đối với một câu hỏi khoa học

hypotonic | nhược trương khi so sánh hai dung dịch khác nhau, dung dịch nào có nồng độ chất tan ít hơn thì gọi là nhược trương

I

immigration | sự nhập cư việc các cá thể di chuyển vào một vùng có sẵn những sinh vật cư trú ở đó

immune response | phản ứng miễn dịch việc cơ thể nhận ra, đáp ứng, và nhớ lại các mầm bệnh đã tấn công mình

implantation | bám phôi quá trình trong đó túi phôi cấy vào thành tử cung

imprinting | quá trình hòa đồng với đồng loại các hành vi học được từ những trải nghiệm hồi trẻ thơ; một khi đã hòa đồng, những hành vi này không thể thay đổi được

inbreeding | giao phối cận huyết việc tiếp tục cho hai cá thể có những đặc điểm giống nhau giao phối với nhau nhằm có thế hệ con duy trì được các đặc điểm dẫn xuất của sinh vật đó

incomplete dominance | tính trội không hoàn toàn tình trạng một alen không trội hẳn một alen khác

independent assortment | phân ly độc lập một trong những định luật của Menđen cho rằng các gen mã cho những đặc điểm khác nhau có thể phân ly một cách độc lập trong quá trình sinh giao tử

independent variable | biến độc lập trong cuộc thí nghiệm có đối chiếu, đây là biến được cố ý thay đổi; còn được gọi là biến điều khiển

index fossil | hóa thạch định tầng hóa thạch dễ phân biệt được dùng để so sánh tuổi của các hóa thạch đối với nhau

infectious disease | bệnh truyền nhiễm bệnh gây ra bởi các vi sinh vật gây rối ở các chức năng cơ thể bình thường

inference | suy luận một cách giải thích hợp lôgic căn cứ vào các kiến thức và kinh nghiệm có từ trước

inflammatory response | phản ứng viêm một phản ứng không đặc hiệu khi mô bị tổn thương do chấn thương hay nhiễm trùng

innate behavior | hành vi bẩm sinh loại hành vi được thể hiện một cách hoàn chỉnh ngay từ đầu; động vật biết cách phản ứng cho dù chưa hề trải nghiệm tác nhân kích thích phản ứng đó; còn được gọi là bản năng

insight learning | học từ khả năng suy ra cách học tập tính mới, theo đó một động vật giải quyết những vấn đề mới bằng cách áp dụng những gì vốn biết thay vì thử đại nhiều cách khác nhau để xác định cách nào đúng hay sai; còn được gọi là suy luận

interferon | interferon một trong các nhóm protein giúp tế bào chống lại sự nhiễm virút

interneuron | tế bào thần kinh trung gian loại tế bào thần kinh có chức năng xử lý thông tin và có thể truyền thông tin đến tế bào thần kinh vận động

interphase | kỳ trung gian giai đoạn trong chu kỳ tế bào giữa những lần phân bào

intracellular digestion | tiêu hóa nội bào dạng tiêu hóa trong đó thức ăn được tiêu hóa bên trong các tế bào chuyên hóa, sau đó chất dinh dưỡng được truyền cho các tế bào khác qua sự khuếch tán

intron | intron trình tự ADN không liên quan đến việc mã hóa các protein

invertebrate | động vật không xương sống các động vật không có xương sống hay cột sống

ion | ion nguyên tử có điện tích dương hay âm

ionic bond | liên kết ion liên kết hóa học được tạo thành khi một hay nhiều electron được truyền từ nguyên tử này đến nguyên tử khác

iris | mống mắt phần màu của mắt

isotonic | đẳng trương trình trạng hai dung dịch có nồng độ như nhau

isotope | chất đồng vị một trong vài dạng khác nhau của cùng một nguyên tố, trong dạng này số proton như nhau nhưng số neutron thì khác nhau

J

joint | khớp nơi một xương được gắn vào xương khác

K

karyotype | kiểu nhân ảnh soi bằng kính hiển vi cho thấy đầy đủ một bộ nhiễm sắc thể lưỡng bội xếp thành cặp và theo thứ tự từ lớn đến nhỏ

keratin | chất sừng protein dai, chứa nhiều sợi có trong da

keystone species | loài chủ chốt một loài có tác động kiểm soát mạnh lên cơ cấu của một quần thể cho dù số lượng loài này không đông

kidney | thận bộ phận bài tiết có chức năng lọc chất thải và nước dư ra khỏi máu

kin selection | chọn lọc họ hàng lý thuyết cho rằng việc giúp cho những người có quan hệ họ hàng với mình có thể tăng cao khả năng truyền gen của mình đến thế hệ sau trong quá trình tiến hóa, vì những người họ hàng thường có chung nhiều gen giống nhau

kingdom | giới trong hệ thống phân loại, đây là nhóm lớn nhất, bao gồm nhiều loài nhất

Koch's postulates | định đề Koch các nguyên tắc hướng dẫn do Koch đặt ra để giúp nhận diện vi sinh vật nào đã gây ra một bệnh cụ thể

Krebs cycle | chu trình Kreb giai đoạn thứ hai trong quá trình hô hấp tế bào, trong đó axít pyruvic được phân giải thành cacbon điôxít trong một loạt các phản ứng lấy năng lượng

L

language | ngôn ngữ hệ thống trao đổi thông tin kết hợp các âm thanh, ký hiệu, và cử chỉ theo những quy tắc về trình tự và ý nghĩa thí dụ như ngữ pháp và cú pháp

large intestine | ruột già bộ phận trong hệ tiêu hóa rút nước từ các chất chưa tiêu hóa được chuyển qua nó; còn được gọi là đại tràng

larva (số nhiều: larvae) | ấu trùng giai đoạn non của một sinh vật

larynx | thanh quản cấu trúc ở họng chứa dây thanh âm

learning | học tập việc thay đổi hành vi do các trải nghiệm

lens | thủy tinh thể cấu trúc trong mắt có chức năng hội tụ các tia ánh sáng vào võng mạc

lichen | lichen quan hệ cộng sinh giữa một loài nấm và một sinh vật quang hợp

ligament | dây chẳng mô liên kết dai có chức năng định vị xương trong khớp

light-dependent reactions | phản ứng cần ánh sáng một loạt phản ứng trong quá trình quang hợp sử dụng năng lượng có từ ánh sáng để tạo ra ATP và NADPH

light-independent reactions | phản ứng không cần ánh sáng một loạt phản ứng trong quá trình quang hợp không cần ánh sáng; năng lượng từ ATP và NADPH được sử dụng để tạo ra các hợp chất năng lượng cao như đường; còn được gọi là chu trình Calvin

lignin | linhin chất có trong cây có mạch giúp vách tế bào được cứng chắc

limiting factor | nhân tố giới hạn một yếu tố khiến cho dân số giảm đi

limiting nutrient | chất dinh dưỡng giới hạn một chất dinh dưỡng cốt yếu giới hạn sự sinh sản trong một hệ sinh thái

lipid | lipit đại phân tử được cấu thành chủ yếu bởi nguyên tử cacbon và hyđrô; bao gồm các chất mỡ, dầu, và sáp

lipid bilayer | cấu trúc hai lớp lipit màng dẻo có hai lớp cấu thành màng tế bào và là màng chắn giữa tế bào và môi trường xung quanh

logistic growth | sự tăng trưởng theo đường cong logistic là trạng thái tăng trưởng trong đó một quần thể phát triển chậm lại rồi dừng hẳn sau một thời kỳ phát triển theo hàm mũ

loop of Henle | quai Henle một phần của ống sinh niệu có chức năng hấp thụ lại nước để giảm thiểu khối lượng chất lọc

lung | phổi bộ phận hô hấp; nơi trao đổi khí giữa máu và khí hít vào

lymph | bạch huyết chất lỏng được lọc ra từ máu

lysogenic infection | tiềm tan virút dạng nhiễm trùng trong đó virút tiêm ADN của mình vào ADN của tế bào vật chủ để được nhân bản theo ADN của tế bào vật chủ

lysosome | lizozim bào quan có chức năng phân giải lipit, hiđrat cacbon và protein thành các phân tử nhỏ để tế bào có thể tiêu thụ được

lytic infection | pha tan virút dạng nhiễm trùng trong đó virút nhập tế bào và tự nhân bản khiến tế bào bị vỡ tung ra

M

macroevolution | tiến hóa vĩ mô các thay đổi tiến hóa lớn xảy ra qua khoảng thời gian rất dài

Malpighian tubule | ống Malpighi cấu trúc trong đa số các động vật có chân đốt và sống trên cạn, có chức năng làm axít urê cô đặc lại và trộn nó với chất thải từ hệ tiêu hóa để bài tiết ra khỏi cơ thể

mammary gland | tuyến vú tuyến có trong động vật cái có vú, có chức năng sinh sữa cho con bú

mass extinction | sự tuyệt chủng hàng loạt việc nhiều loài bị tuyệt chủng trong khoảng thời gian tương đối ngắn

matrix | chất nền khoang trong cùng của ty thể

mechanical digestion | tiêu hóa cơ học việc nghiền nát các miếng thức ăn to thành những miếng nhỏ hơn

meiosis | giảm phân quá trình trong đó số nhiễm sắc thể trong mỗi tế bào được giảm phân nửa qua việc tách ra các nhiễm sắc thể tương đồng trong tế bào lưỡng bội

melanin | hắc tố sắc tố màu nâu đậm có trong da, giúp bảo vệ da bằng cách hấp thu tia cực tím

melanocyte | tế bào sắc tố tế bào trong da tạo ra sắc tố màu nâu đậm được gọi là hắc tố

menstrual cycle | chu kỳ kinh nguyệt trình tự phát triển và rụng trứng xảy ra thường kỳ

menstruation | kỳ hành kinh việc xuất huyết và loại bỏ trứng không thụ tinh ra khỏi cơ thể

meristem | mô phân sinh những vùng tế bào không chuyên hóa có chức năng giúp cây tiếp tục tăng trưởng trong suốt đời

mesoderm | trung phôi bì lớp tế bào phôi ở giữa; có thể phát triển thành cơ và phần lớn hệ tuần hoàn, hệ sinh sản và hệ bài tiết

mesophyll | thịt lá mô nền chuyên hóa có trong lá; mô này thực hiện phần lớn quá trình quang hợp cho cây

messenger RNA (mRNA) | ARN thông tin (mRNA) loại ARN mang bản sao hướng dẫn về cách ghép axít amin thành protein từ ADN đến các phần khác trong tế bào

metabolism | sự chuyển hóa sự kết hợp các phản ứng hóa học nhờ đó một sinh vật có thể tạo dựng hay phân giải các chất trong cơ thể

metamorphosis | biến thái quá trình đổi hình dạng từ ấu trùng thành sinh vật trưởng thành

metaphase | kỳ giữa giai đoạn trong quá trình nguyên phân trong đó các nhiễm sắc thể xếp thành hàng ngang qua trung tâm tế bào

microclimate | vi khí hậu các điều kiện môi trường đặc thù trong một vung nhỏ khác đáng kể so với khí hậu của những vùng xung quanh

migration | sự di cư hành vi di chuyển từ một môi trường sang môi trường khác theo mùa,

mineral | khoáng chất các chất dinh dưỡng vô cơ cần thiết cho cơ thể, thường là với số lượng ít

mitochondrion | ty thể bào quan chuyển đổi năng lượng hóa học có trong thức ăn thành các hợp chất mà tế bào có thể tiêu thụ dễ dàng hơn

mitosis | nguyên phân một phần của quá trình phân chia tế bào nhân chuẩn, trong đó nhân tế bào chia thành hai

mixture | hỗn hợp chất được cấu thành bởi hai hoặc nhiều nguyên tố hay hợp chất được trộn với nhau nhưng không được kết hợp bằng liên kết hóa học

molecular clock | đồng hồ tiến hóa phương pháp do các nhà nghiên cứu sử dụng căn cứ vào tỷ lệ đột biến trong ADN để ước lượng xem hai loài đã tiến hóa độc lập trong bao lâu

molecule | phân tử trong phần lớn các hợp chất, đây là đơn vị nhỏ nhất vẫn giữ được tất cả tính chất của hợp chất đó

molting | lột da/vỏ quá trình lột ra da/vỏ cứng ngoài cũ và mọc bộ mới

monocot | đơn tử diệp cây hạt kín có một lá mầm trong hạt

monoculture | độc canh chiến lược trồng trọt theo kiểu hàng năm chỉ trồng một vụ có sản lượng rất cao

monomer | chất đơn phân một đơn vị hóa học nhỏ kết hợp để tạo thành chất trùng hợp

monophyletic group | nhóm đơn ngành nhóm bao gồm một loài tổ tiên và tất cả các hậu thế của nó, và không bao gồm bất cứ sinh vật nào không phải là hậu thế của tổ tiên chung đó

monosaccharide | monosacarit phân tử đường đơn giản

motor neuron | tế bào thần kinh vận động loại tế bào thần kinh mang thông tin hướng dẫn từ tế bào thần kinh trung gian đến tế bào cơ hay tuyến hạch

multiple alleles | đa alen một gen có nhiều hơn hai alen

multipotent | đa năng loại tế bào có tiềm năng hạn chế để phát triển thành nhiều loại tế bào khác biệt

muscle fiber | sợi cơ tế bào thon, dài ở cơ xương

muscle tissue | mô cơ loại mô cho phép cơ thể chuyển động được

mutagen | tác nhân gây đột biến hóa chất hay tác nhân vật lý trong môi trường tương tác với ADN và có thể gây đột biến

mutation | đột biến một thay đổi trong chất di truyền của tế bào

mutualism | sự hỗ sinh quan hệ cộng sinh mang lợi ích cho cả hai bên

mycelium (số nhiều: mycelia) | hệ sợi mạng lưới chằng chịt gồm nhiều sợi nấm

mycorrhiza (số nhiều: mycorrhizae) | rễ nấm quan hệ cộng sinh giữa rễ thực vật và nấm

myelin sheath | bao myelin màng bảo vệ bao bọc sợi trục trong một số dây thần kinh

myocardium | cơ tim lớp cơ tim dày được kẹp giữa hai lớp màng

myofibril | tơ cơ các bó sợi nhỏ ép chặt có trong sợi cơ xương

myosin | sợi myosin sợi protein dày có trong tế bào cơ xương

N

NAD⁺ (nicotinamide adenine dinucleotide) | NAD⁺ (nicotinamide adenine dinucleotide) một electron truyền tải tham gia vào quá trình đường phân

NADP⁺ (nicotinamide adenine dinucleotide phosphate) | NADP⁺ (nicotinamide adenine dinucleotide phosphate) một loại phân tử truyền tải mang electron năng lượng cao từ chất diệp lục đến các phân tử khác

natural selection | chọn lọc tự nhiên quá trình trong đó những sinh vật nào có khả năng thích ứng tốt nhất với môi trường sống sót và sinh sản nhiều nhất; còn được gọi là "mạnh được, yếu thua"

nephridium (số nhiều: nephridia) | đơn thận bộ phận bài tiết trong loài giun đốt có chức năng lọc sạch các dịch cơ thể

nephron | ống sinh niệu cấu trúc lọc máu trong thận có chức năng lọc ra và thu thập chất thải để máu sạch có thể trở lại dòng tuần hoàn

nervous tissue | mô thần kinh loại mô truyền xung điện thần kinh đến khắp cơ thể

neuromuscular junction | khớp thần kinh-cơ điểm tiếp xúc giữa một dây thần kinh vận động và tế bào cơ xương

neuron | tế bào thần kinh tế bào thần kinh; được chuyên hóa để truyền tải thông tin trong suốt hệ thần kinh

neurotransmitter | chất dẫn truyền thần kinh hóa chất do các tế bào thần kinh sử dụng để truyền xung điện qua khớp thần kinh đến tế bào khác

neurulation | sự hình thành ống thần kinh bước đầu trong quá trình phát triển hệ thần kinh

niche | ổ sinh thái toàn bộ các điều kiện vật lý và sinh học trong môi trường sống của một sinh vật và cách sinh vật sử dụng những điều kiện đó

nitrogen fixation | cố định đạm quá trình biến đổi khi nitơ thành các hợp chất nitơ cho thực vật dễ hấp thu và tiêu thụ

node | mấu, mắt nơi lá mọc ra trên cuống cây đang phát triển

nondisjunction | hiện tượng không phân ly lỗi trong quá trình giảm phân trong đó các nhiễm sắc thể tương đồng không tách ra đúng cách

nonrenewable resource | tài nguyên không thể tái tạo được nguồn tài nguyên không thể phục hồi được qua các tiến trình tự nhiên trong khoảng thời gian hợp lý

norepinephrine | norepinephrin hoóc môn được tiết ra từ tuyến thượng thận có tác dụng tăng nhịp tim và huyết áp để chuẩn bị cho cơ thể bắt đầu hoạt động mạnh

notochord | dây nguyên sống ở động vật có dây sống, đây là trụ đỡ dài chạy dọc cơ thể ngay dưới dây thần kinh

nucleic acid | axít nucleic đại phân tử chứa hyđrô, oxy, nitơ, cácbon và phốtpho

nucleotide | nucleotit đơn vị phụ cấu tạo nên axít nucleic; nucleotit được tạo thành bởi đường 5 cacbon, một nhóm phốtpho, và bazơ nitric

nucleus | nhân trung tâm của nguyên tử, chứa các proton và neutron ; đối với tế bào, nhân là cấu trúc chứa chất di truyền dưới dạng ADN

nutrient | chất dinh dưỡng hóa chất mà tất cả các sinh vật đều cần để duy trì sự sống

nymph | thiếu trùng giai đoạn non của một số loài sinh vật có hình thái giống với giai đoạn trưởng thành nhưng bộ phận sinh dục chưa hoạt động được

O

observation | sự quan sát việc để ý đến và miêu tả các sự kiện hay tiến trình một cách kỹ càng, mạch lạc

omnivore | loài ăn tạp các sinh vật kiếm năng lượng bằng cách ăn cả thực vật và động vật

open circulatory system | hệ tuần hoàn hở một loại hệ tuần hoàn trong đó việc tuần hoàn máu chỉ được thực hiện một phần trong các mạch máu chạy khắp cơ thể

operant conditioning | điều kiện hóa thao tác, một phương pháp huấn luyện trong đó thú vật đổi tập tính để nhận phần thưởng hay tránh hình phạt trong những buổi tập đi tập lại

operator | gen điều khiển ở sinh vật nhân sơ, đây là một vùng ADN ngắn gần gen khởi động của operon và kết dính các protein ức chế có chức năng kiểm soát tốc độ phiên mã của operon

operon | operon ở sinh vật nhân sơ, đây là một nhóm các gen kế liền có chung một gen điều khiển và gen khởi động và được phiên mã thành một mRNA

opposable thumb | ngón tay cái đối diện với các ngón còn lại ngón cái kiểu này giúp ta cầm lấy đồ vật và sử dụng dụng cụ

order | bộ trong hệ thống phân loại, bộ là một tập hợp các họ gần nhau

organ | cơ quan tập hợp các loại mô hoạt động phối hợp với nhau để thực hiện các chức năng có liên hệ chặt chẽ

organ system | hệ cơ quan một nhóm các cơ quan hoạt động phối hợp với nhau để thực hiện một chức năng cụ thể

organelle | bào quan cấu trúc chuyên hóa thực hiện các chức năng quan trọng trong tế bào nhân chuẩn

osmosis | sự thẩm thấu hiện tượng nước khuếch tán qua một màng thấm chọn lọc

osmotic pressure | áp lực thẩm thấu áp lực cần thiết để ngăn chặn việc nước thẩm thấu qua màng thấm chọn lọc

ossification | sự hóa xương quá trình tạo xương trong đó sụn được thay thế bằng xương

osteoblast | tế bào tạo xương tế bào xương tiết ra lớp tích khoáng chất từ từ thay thế sụn trong xương đang phát triển

osteoclast | tế bào hủy xương tế bào xương phân hủy các khoáng chất trong xương

osteocyte | tế bào xương tế bào giúp giữ lại khoáng chất trong mô xương và củng cố xương đang phát triển

ovary | buồng trứng, bầu noãn ở thực vật, đây là cấu trúc bao bọc và bảo vệ hạt ; ở động vật cái/phụ nữ, đây là bộ phận sinh dục chính; có chức năng sinh ra trứng

oviparous | noãn sinh ở loài noãn sinh, phôi phát triển trong quả trứng bên ngoài cơ thể mẹ

ovoviparous | noãn thai sinh ở loài noãn thai sinh, phôi phát triển ở trứng trong bụng mẹ nhưng lấy dinh dưỡng hoàn toàn từ túi noãn hoàng của trứng

ovulation | rụng trứng việc giải phóng trứng trưởng thành từ buồng trứng vào sống dẫn trứng

ovule | noãn cấu trúc trong quả nón, là nơi sinh trưởng thể giao tử cái

ozone layer | tầng ôzôn tầng lớp trong bầu khí quyển là nơi có nông độ khí ôzôn tương đối cao; tầng này bảo vệ sự sống trong Trái Đất khỏi bị phơi nhiễm tia cực tím có hại trong ánh nắng mặt trời

P

pacemaker | trung tâm tạo nhịp nhóm nhỏ các sợi cơ tim duy trì nhịp bơm tim bằng cách quy định tốc độ co bóp tim; còn được gọi la nút xoang nhĩ

paleontologist | nhà cổ sinh vật học nhà khoa học nghiên cứu hóa thạch

palisade mesophyll | mô giậu lớp tế bào nằm dưới biểu bì trên của lá

parasitism | hiện tượng ký sinh quan hệ cộng sinh trong đó một sinh vật sống bám vào hay ở trong sinh vật khác và gây hại cho sinh vật đó

parathyroid hormone (PTH) | hoóc môn tuyến cận giáp hoóc môn được tạo ra bởi tuyến cận giáp có tác dụng tăng mức canxi trong máu

parenchyma | nhu mô loại mô nền chính trong thực vật, mô này chứa tế bào có vách mỏng và không bào lớn ở trung tâm

passive immunity | miễn dịch thụ động trạng thái miễn dịch tạm thời phát triển được khi cơ thể tiếp xúc một cách tự nhiên hay cố ý với một kháng nguyên

pathogen | mầm bệnh tác nhân gây ra bệnh

pedigree | phả hệ biểu đồ cho thấy sự tồn tại hay biến mất của một đặc điểm theo các quan hệ trong gia đình qua nhiều thế hệ

pepsin | pepsin enzym phân giải protein thành các mảnh polipeptit nhỏ hơn

period | kỳ trong hệ thống niên đại địa chất, đại được chia thành đơn vị phụ này

peripheral nervous system | hệ thống thần kinh ngoại biên mạng lưới các dây thần kinh và tế bào hỗ trợ truyền tải các tín hiệu ra vào hệ thần kinh trung ương

peristalsis | nhu động hiện tượng co bóp ở các cơ trơn gây áp lực chuyển thức ăn qua thực quản vào bao tử

permafrost | tầng đất đóng băng vĩnh cửu tầng đất cái bị đóng băng vĩnh cửu ở vùng lãnh nguyên

petiole | cuống lá cọng mỏng nối phiến lá với thân cây

pH scale | thang pH thang giá trị từ 0 đến 14 được dùng để đo nồng độ ion H^+ trong dung dịch; độ pH từ 0 đến 7 là axít, độ pH 7 là trung hòa, và độ pH từ 7 đến 14 là kiềm (bazơ)

pharyngeal pouch | túi hầu một trong hai cấu trúc trong vùng họng của các động vật có dây sống

pharynx | hầu ống nằm phía sau miệng, là đường ra vào cho khí và thức ăn; còn được gọi là họng

phenotype | kiểu hình các đặc điểm vật lý của một sinh vật

phloem | libe mô mạch dẫn truyền đến khắp cây các dung dịch chứa dưỡng chất và hiđrat cacbon được sản xuất bởi quá trình quang hợp

photic zone | tầng sáng vùng gần mặt nước đầy ánh sáng mặt trời

photoperiod | chu kỳ sáng phản ứng của thực vật với độ dài của các khoảng thời gian sáng và tối

photosynthesis | sự quang hợp quá trình được sử dụng bởi thực vật và các sinh vật tự dưỡng khác để hấp thu năng lượng ánh sáng rồi dùng năng lượng này để tiến hành các phản ứng hóa học biến đổi cacbon điôxít và nước thành oxy và các hiđrat cacbon giàu năng lượng như đường và tinh bột

photosystem | hệ thống quang hóa chùm chất điệp lục và protein có trong các túi tilacôit

phototropism | quang hướng động khuynh hướng của cây là phát triển theo hướng ánh sáng

phylogeny | cây phát sinh chủng loại môn nghiên cứu các quan hệ tiến hóa giữa những sinh vật khác nhau

phylum | ngành trong hệ thống phân loại, ngành là một tập hợp các lớp có họ gần nhau

phytoplankton | thực vật phù du loại tảo quang hợp sống ở biển gần mặt nước

pigment | sắc tố các phân tử hấp thụ ánh sáng được sử dụng bởi các loại thực vật trong việc thu thập năng lượng từ mặt trời

pioneer species | loài tiên phong loài đầu tiên đến định cư ở một vùng trong quá trình diễn thế

pistil | nhụy một lá noãn hay vài lá noãn kết nối với nhau; chứa bầu noãn, vòi và đầu nhụy

pith | ruột cây, lõi xốp các tế bào nhu mô bên trong vòng mô mạch ở thân cây song tử diệp

pituitary gland | tuyến yên tuyến nhỏ ở gần đáy hộp sọ tiết ra các hoóc môn trực tiếp điều tiết nhiều chức năng cơ thể và kiểm soát hoạt động của một số tuyến nội tiết khác

placenta | nhau cơ quan chuyên hóa trong các động vật có vú; các khí hô hấp, chất dinh dưỡng và chất thải được trao đổi giữa mẹ và thai nhi trong bụng thông qua cơ quan này

plankton | phù du các vi sinh vật sống trong môi trường nước; bao gồm thực vật phù du và động vật phù du

plasma | huyết tương phần máu dạng lỏng, có màu vàng nhạt

plasmid | plasmit miếng ADN nhỏ, hình tròn có trong tế bào chất của nhiều vi khuẩn

plasmodium | thể nhầy giai đoạn dinh dưỡng dạng amip trong chu trình sống của nấm nhầy hợp bào

plate tectonics | kiến tạo địa tầng các tiến trình địa chất như trôi dạt lục địa, núi lửa và động đất gây ra bởi sự di chuyển của các mảng kiến tạo

platelet | tiểu cầu mảnh tế bào được tủy xương phóng thích để giúp đông cục máu

pluripotent | tế bào vạn năng các tế bào có khả năng phát triển thành phần lớn nhưng không phải tất cả các loại tế bào trong cơ thể

point mutation | đột biến điểm một đột biến gen, trong đó duy nhất một cặp bazơ ADN bị thay đổi

pollen grain | hạt phấn trong các loại cây có hạt, đây là cấu trúc chứa toàn bộ thể giao tử đực

pollen tube | ống phấn ở thực vật, cấu trúc này chứa hai nhân tinh trùng đơn bội

pollination | thụ phấn việc truyền phấn từ cấu trúc sinh sản đực sang cấu trúc sinh sản cái

pollutant | chất ô nhiễm chất độc hại có thể xâm nhập sinh quyển qua đất, không khí, hay nước

polygenic trait | tính trạng đa gen đặc điểm được chi phối bởi hai hoặc nhiều gen

polymer | chất trùng hợp các phân tử được cấu thành bởi nhiều đơn phân; chất trùng hợp kết hợp thành đại phân tử

polymerase chain reaction (PCR) | phản ứng chuỗi trùng hợp phương pháp được các nhà sinh học sử dụng để nhân một gen cụ thể thành nhiều bản

polypeptide | polipeptit chuỗi axít amin dài kết hợp thành protein

polyploidy | tính đa bội là tình trạng một sinh vật có bộ nhiễm sắc thể dự thừa

population | dân số/quần thể số cá thể cùng loài sống trong cùng một vùng

population density | mật độ dân số/quần thể số cá thể ở mỗi đơn vị diện tích

predation | động vật ăn mồi một sự tương tác trong đó một sinh vật (thú ăn mồi) bắt và ăn thịt một sinh vật khác (con mồi)

prehensile tail | đuôi có thể cầm nắm được đuôi dài có thể cuốn chặt vào một cành cây

pressure-flow hypothesis | giả thuyết về dòng áp lực giả thuyết giải thích cách nhựa trong libe được dẫn truyền qua cây từ nguồn đường đến nơi tiêu thụ đường

primary growth | sự sinh trưởng sơ cấp sự tăng trưởng xảy ra ở ngọn và chồi cây

primary producer | sinh vật sản xuất sơ cấp sinh vật ban đầu sản xuất các hợp chất giầu năng lượng mà sau này các sinh vật khác tiêu thụ

primary succession | diễn thế nguyên sinh quá trình diễn thế xảy ra ở một vùng hoàn toàn hoang vắng, không có bất cứ vết tích nào cho thấy một quần thể đã sống ở đó trước kia

principle of dominance | quy luật trội lặn kết luận thứ hai của Menđen cho rằng một số alen có tính trội và số khác có tính lặn

prion | prion các hạt protein có thể gây bệnh

probability | xác suất khả năng một sự kiện cụ thể sẽ xảy ra

product | sản phẩm các nguyên tố hay hợp chất được tạo ra bởi một phản ứng hóa học

prokaryote | sinh vật nhân sơ sinh vật đơn bào không có nhân

promoter | vùng khởi động một vùng cụ thể ở gen, nơi RNA polymerase có thể kết dính và bắt đầu quy trình phiên mã

prophage | thể tiền thực khuẩn ADN của một thực khuẩn được tiêm vào ADN của vi khuẩn vật chủ

prophase | kỳ trước giai đoạn đầu, dài nhất của quá trình nguyên phân trong đó chất di truyền bên trong nhân hóa đặc và nhiễm sắc thể xuất hiện

prostaglandin | prostaglandin axít béo biến đổi được tạo ra bởi nhiều loại tế bào khác nhau; thường chỉ ảnh hưởng đến các tế bào và mô gần kề

protein | protein đại phân tử chứa cacbon, hyđrô, oxy và nitơ; cần thiết cho việc tăng trưởng và chữa lành cơ thể

protostome | động vật miệng nguyên sinh trong nhóm động vật này, lỗ phôi trở thành miệng

pseudocoelom | khoang giả một khoang rỗng trong cơ thể chỉ được lót trung bì một phần

pseudopod | chân giả trong một số loài sinh vật đơn bào, đây là một bộ phận tạm thời mọc ra từ tế bào chất để giúp trong việc di chuyển

puberty | tuổi dạy thì một giai đoạn tăng trưởng nhanh khi bộ phận sinh dục được trưởng thành và các chức năng của hệ sinh sản bắt đầu thực hiện được đầy đủ

pulmonary circulation | tuần hoàn phổi đường tuần hoàn giữa tim và phổi

punctuated equilibrium | giả thuyết cân bằng gián đoạn một mô hình tiến hóa trong đó những thời kỳ ổn định lâu dài thỉnh thoảng bị gián đoạn bởi những thời kỳ ngắn có nhiều thay đổi nhanh hơn

Punnett square | bảng Punnett biểu đồ có thể sử dụng để tiên đoán các kết hợp kiểu gen và kiểu hình có được từ việc liên kết hai gen với nhau

pupa | nhộng một giai đoạn trong quá trình biến thái hoàn toàn trong đó ấu trùng trưởng thành

pupil | đồng tử lỗ nhỏ ở mống mắt cho phép ánh sáng lọt vào mắt

R

radial symmetry | tính đối xứng xuyên tâm hình dạng cơ thể có thể được chia đôi bởi một mặt phẳng tưởng tượng chạy xuyên qua trung tâm theo bất cứ góc độ nào và cơ thể vẫn được cắt thành hai phần giống hệt nhau

radiometric dating | xác định niên đại bằng phương pháp đo phóng xạ phương pháp xác định tuổi của một mẫu bằng cách so sánh số lượng đồng vị phóng xạ và đồng vị không phóng xạ trong cùng một nguyên tố lấy được từ mẫu

reabsorption | sự tái hấp thụ quá trình trong đó nước và các chất đã được hòa tan được hấp thụ lại vào máu

reactant | chất phản ứng các nguyên tố hay hợp chất góp phần vào một phản ứng hóa học

receptor | thụ thể một protein đặc hiệu trên hay trong tế bào có hình dạng khớp với một phân tử truyền tải cụ thể thí dụ như một hoóc môn

recombinant DNA | ADN tái tổ hợp ADN được tạo ra bằng cách kết hợp ADN từ nhiều nguồn khác nhau

red blood cell | hồng cầu tế bào máu chứa huyết cầu tố và có chức năng truyền tải oxy

reflex | phản xạ việc tự động phản ứng nhanh với một tác nhân kích thích

reflex arc | cung phản xạ cơ quan thụ cảm, tế bào thần kinh cảm giác, tế bào thần kinh vận động, và cơ quan đáp ứng, là các thành phần tham gia vào việc cơ thể phản ứng nhau với một tác nhân kích thích

relative dating | xác định niên đại bằng phương pháp đối chiếu phương pháp xác định tuổi của một hóa thạch bằng cách đối chiếu vị trí của nó với hóa thạch ở các tầng đá khác

relative frequency | tần số tương đối số lần một alen xuất hiện trong một vốn gen so với số lần xuất hiện của các alen khác của cùng gen đó

releasing hormone | hoóc môn giải phóng kích tố hoóc môn được tạo ra bởi vùng dưới đồi có tác dụng kích thích thùy trước của tuyến yên bắt đầu sản xuất hoóc môn

renewable resource | tài nguyên có thể tái tạo được nguồn tài nguyên được tạo ra hay thay thế một cách tự nhiên trong các hệ sinh thái lành mạnh

replication | nhân bản quá trình sao lại ADN trước khi bắt đầu phân chia tế bào

reproductive isolation | cách ly sinh sản hiện tượng hai loài hay quần thể bị cách ly, không thể sinh sản lẫn nhau nên tiến hóa thành hai loài riêng biệt

resource | tài nguyên bất cứ thứ nào cần thiết cho sự sống, thí dụ như nước, dưỡng chất, ánh sáng, thức ăn, hay không gian

response | đáp ứng một phản ứng đặc hiệu đối với một tác nhân kích thích

resting potential | điện thế nghỉ điện tích bên ngoài và bên trong màng của một tế bào thần kinh không bị kích thích

restriction enzyme | enzym giới hạn enzym cắt ADN tại một trình tự nucleotit

retina | võng mạc lớp trong cùng của mắt; là nơi chứa các tế bào cảm quang

retrovirus | retrovirus virút ARN chứa thông tin di truyền trong ARN

ribonucleic acid (RNA) | axít ribonucleic (ARN) loại axít nucleic dạng mạch đơn chứa đường ribose

ribosomal RNA (rRNA) | ARN ribosome loại ARN kết hợp với protein để tạo ra ribosom

ribosome | ribô thể bào quan ở tế bào chất được cấu tạo bởi ARN và protein; là nơi diễn ra việc tổng hợp protein

RNA interference (RNAi) | cơ chế can thiệp ARN việc tiêm ARN sợi đôi vào tế bào để ức chế sự biểu hiện của gen

RNA polymerase | ARN polymerase một enzym sử dụng sợi ADN làm mẫu và liên kết chuỗi nucleotit ARN càng lúc càng dài trong quá trình phiên mã

rod | tế bào thần kinh hình que tế bào cảm quang trong mắt có thể cảm thụ ánh sáng nhưng không phân biệt được màu sắc

root cap | chóp rễ lớp dai bọc đầu rễ và bảo vệ mô phân sinh

root hair | lông hút các sợi lông nhỏ ở rễ tạo diện tích rộng để hút nước và khoáng chất vào cây

rumen | dạ cỏ túi dạ dày ở bò và các động vật cùng họ chứa một loại vi khuẩn cộng sinh tiêu hóa xenluloza

S

sapwood | dác gỗ trong thân cây gỗ, đây là lớp libe thứ cấp xung quanh phần ruột; thường có vai trò dẫn truyền nước

sarcomere | tâm cơ đơn vị co cơ; được cấu thành bởi hai vạch z và các tơ nối giữa

scavenger | loài ăn xác thối động vật ăn xác của các thú khác

science | khoa học phương pháp thu thập và phân tích dữ liệu về thế giới tự nhiên một cách có tổ chức

sclerenchyma | mô cứng loại mô nền có vách tế bào cực dày và cứng giúp cho mô nền dai và bền

scrotum | bìu dái bao bên ngoài có chức năng chứa tinh hoàn

sebaceous gland | tuyến bã nhờn tuyến trong da có chức năng tiết ra bã nhờn (dịch nhờn)

secondary growth | sự sinh trưởng thứ cấp trong cây song tử diệp, đây là việc thân cây phát triển về độ dày

secondary succession | diễn thế thứ sinh quá trình diễn thế xảy ra ở một vùng chỉ bị phá một phần bởi các sự kiện xáo động

seed | hạt một phôi thực vật cùng với lượng thực phẩm được chứa trong một lớp vỏ bảo vệ

seed coat | vỏ hạt lớp dai bao bọc và bảo vệ phôi thực vật và giúp các chất bên trong hạt không bị khô héo

segregation | phân ly việc các alen tách ra khỏi nhau trong quá trình tạo giao tử

selective breeding | gây giống chọn lọc phương pháp gây giống trong đó chỉ những sinh vật nào có các tính trạng mong muốn được phép sinh ra thế hệ sau

selectively permeable | tính thấm chọn lọc tính chất của các màng sinh học cho phép một số chất thấm qua nhưng những chất khác thì không; còn được gọi là màng bán thấm

semen | tinh dịch hỗn hợp được cấu thành bởi tinh trùng và dung dịch tinh dịch

semicircular canal | ống bán khuyên một trong ba cấu trúc ở tai trong có chức năng theo dõi vị trí cơ thể đối với hướng trọng lực

seminiferous tubule | ống sinh tinh một trong hàng trăm ống nhỏ có trong mỗi tinh hoàn, là nơi tinh trùng được sinh ra

sensory neuron | tế bào thần kinh cảm giác loại tế bào thần kinh nhận thông tin từ các cơ quan thụ cảm và truyền tín hiệu đến hệ thần kinh trung ương

sex chromosome | nhiễm sắc thể giới tính một trong hai nhiễm sắc thể quyết định giới tính của một cá thể

sex-linked gene | gen liên hệ với giới tính một gen trên nhiễm sắc thể giới tính

sexual reproduction | sinh sản hữu tính quá trình sinh sản trong đó hai tế bào từ hai sinh vật cha mẹ kết hợp với nhau thành tế bào đầu tiên của sinh vật con

sexually transmitted disease (STD) | bệnh lây qua đường tình dục (STD) bệnh lây truyền từ người này sang người khác qua quan hệ sinh dục

sieve tube element | yếu tố rây các tế bào libe được xếp nối đầu nhau để thành một ống liền trong thực vật

single-gene trait | tính trạng đơn gen đặc điểm được chi phối bởi một gen có hai alen

small intestine | ruột non cơ quan tiêu hóa phần lớn thức ăn qua việc tiêu hóa hóa học và hấp thụ

smog | sương khói sương màu nâu xám được cấu thành bởi nhiều hóa chất khác nhau

society | xã hội, quần xã một nhóm các động vật cùng loài hay người có quan hệ họ hàng gần cùng hợp tác với nhau để mang lại lợi ích cho cả nhóm

solute | chất tan chất được hòa tan trong một dung dịch

solution | dung dịch chất hỗn hợp trong đó tất cả các thành phần được phân phối đều đặn

solvent | dung môi chất làm hòa tan chất khác trong một dung dịch

somatic nervous system | hệ thần kinh bản thể một phần của hệ thần kinh ngoại biên mang tín hiệu từ và đến cơ xương

speciation | sự hình thành loài việc một loài mới được hình thành

species diversity | sự đa dạng loài số loài khác nhau sống ở một vùng nhất định

spirillum (số nhiều: spirilla) | xoắn khuẩn sinh vật nhân sơ có hình xoắn ốc

spongy mesophyll | mô khuyết lớp mô xốp nằm dưới mô giậu trong lá

sporangium (số nhiều: sporangia) | túi bào tử nang đựng bào tử, là nơi các bào tử đơn bội được tạo ra bởi quá trình giảm phân

spore | bào tử ở sinh vật nhân sơ, sinh vật đơn bào và nấm, đây là giai đoạn trong chu trình sống có thể diễn ra dưới nhiều hình thức khác nhau nhưng luôn có việc tạo vách dày giúp sống qua các điều kiện không thuận lợi ; ở thực vật, đây là tế bào sinh sản đơn bội

sporophyte | thể bào tử loại thực vật sinh bào tử; giai đoạn đa bào lưỡng bội trong chu trình sống của thực vật

stabilizing selection | sự chọn lọc ổn định hình thức chọn lọc tự nhiên xảy ra khi các cá thể nằm gần phần giữa đường cong phân phối có khả năng thích ứng tốt hơn so với các cá thể nằm ở hai đầu của đường cong

stamen | nhị hoa bộ phận sinh dục đực của hoa; chứa bao phấn và chỉ

stem cell | tế bào gốc một tế bào chưa chuyên hóa có thể phát triển thành một hay nhiều loại tế bào chuyên hóa khác nhau

stigma | đầu nhụy bộ phận ở đầu vòi nhụy có mặt dính; chuyên thu thập phấn

stimulus (số nhiều: stimuli) | tác nhân kích thích một tín hiệu khiến cho một sinh vật phản ứng lại

stoma (số nhiều: stomata) | lỗ khí lỗ nhỏ ở biểu bì thực vật cho phép cacbon điôxit, nước và oxy khuếch tán ra vào lá

stomach | bao tử túi lớn, mạnh giúp trong việc tiêu hóa cơ học và hóa học các loại thức ăn

stroma | thể nền phần lỏng của hạt diệp lục; nằm ngoài các túi tilacôit

substrate | chất nền chất phản ứng trong một phản ứng do enzym xúc tác

suspension | huyền phù một hỗn hợp bao gồm nước và một chất khác chưa được hòa tan

sustainable development | sự phát triển bền vững một chiến lược sử dụng các nguồn tài nguyên sao cho không bị cạn kiệt và đáp ứng các nhu cầu của con người mà không gây hại lâu dài cho môi trường

symbiosis | hiện tượng cộng sinh một quan hệ giữa hai loài sống gần nhau

synapse | khớp thần kinh nơi một tế bào thần kinh có thể truyền xung động đến tế bào khác

systematics | phân loại học môn nghiên cứu tính đa dạng của sự sống và mối quan hệ tiến hóa giữa các sinh vật

systemic circulation | hệ đại tuần hoàn đường tuần hoàn giữa tim và các bộ phận cơ thể khác

T

taiga | taiga một quần xã sinh vật có mùa đông dài và lạnh, quanh năm chỉ có vài tháng được ấm; thực vật chính là cây thường xanh có quả nón; còn được gọi là rừng phương bắc

target cell | tế bào đích tế bào có thụ thể ứng với một hoóc môn cụ thể

taste bud | nụ vị giác cơ quan cảm nhận được vị giác

taxon (số nhiều: taxa) | đơn vị phân loại một nhóm hay cấp tổ chức dùng để phân loại các sinh vật

telomere | đoạn cuối nhiễm sắc thể phần ADN lặp đi lặp lại ở phần cuối nhiễm sắc thể của tế bào nhân chuẩn

telophase | kỳ cuối giai đoạn trong quá trình nguyên phân trong đó các nhiễm sắc thể riêng biệt, có hình dạng rõ ràng bắt đầu dãn xoắn và hợp thành chất nhiễm sắc

temporal isolation | bị cách ly vì thời gian một hình thức cách ly sinh sản, theo đó hai hoặc nhiều loài sinh sản vào hai thời gian khác nhau

tendon | gân mô liên kết dai có chức năng liên kết cơ xương với xương

territory | lãnh thổ/lãnh địa một vùng cụ thể do một động vật hay nhóm động vật cư trú và bảo vệ

testis (số nhiều: testes) | tinh hoàn cơ quan sinh dục chính của nam giới; sản xuất tinh trùng

tetrad | tứ tử cấu trúc chứa bốn nhiễm sắc tử được hình thành trong quá trình giảm phân

tetrapod | động vật bốn chân động vật có xương sống và bốn chi

thalamus | đồi não cấu trúc ở não có chức năng tiếp nhận tín hiệu từ các cơ quan cảm giác và truyền thông tin đó đến vùng thích hợp ở đại não để được xử lý tiếp

theory | lý thuyết một mô hình đã qua nhiều cuộc thí nghiệm thông nhất hóa nhiều hiện tượng và giả thuyết khác nhau vào một khuôn khổ chung và cho phép những nhà khoa học tiên đoán chính xác các hiện tượng mới

thigmotropism | tính hướng tiếp xúc phản ứng của cây đối với sự tiếp xúc

threshold | ngưỡng mức kích thích tối thiểu cần thiết để gây xung điện

thylakoid | túi tilacôit các màng dạng túi trong hạt diệp lục và là nơi diễn ra quá trình quang hợp

thyroxine | tyroxin hoóc môn được sản xuất bởi tuyến giáp trạng có tác dụng tăng tốc độ chuyển hóa ở các tế bào trong khắp cơ thể

tissue | mô một nhóm tế bào cùng loại hợp tác cùng nhau để thực hiện một chức năng cụ thể

tolerance | khả năng chịu đựng khả năng sống sót và sinh sản của một sinh vật trong các điều kiện không thuận lợi

totipotent | tế bào toàn năng các tế bào có khả năng phát triển thành bất cứ loại tế bào nào trong cơ thể (bao gồm tế bào cấu thành màng ngoài phôi và nhau)

trachea | khí quản ống nối hầu với thanh quản còn được gọi là ống thở

tracheid | quản bào ở thực vật, đây là một loại tế bào rỗng, có vách dày được củng cố bởi linhin được tìm thấy trong chất gỗ

tracheophyte | thực vật có mạch ống các loại thực vật có mạch

trait | tính trạng một đặc điểm cụ thể của một cá thể

transcription | phiên mã việc tổng hợp một phân tử ARN trên khuôn ADN

transfer RNA (tRNA) | ARN vận chuyển loại ARN chuyên chở từng axít amin đến một thể ribô trong quá trình tổng hợp protein

transformation | sự biến dạng quá trình trong đó một dòng vi khuẩn bị thay đổi bởi một hay nhiều gen từ dòng vi khuẩn khác

transgenic | chuyển gen từ dùng để chỉ một sinh vật chứa gen có từ các sinh vật khác

translation | dịch mã quá trình trong đó chuỗi bazơ của một ARN thông tin được chuyển thành chuỗi axít amin của một protein

transpiration | sự thoát hơi nước hiện tượng các thực vật bị mất nước qua lá

trochophore | ấu trùng bánh xe giai đoạn ấu trùng của một số loại động vật thân mềm sống trong nước, trong giai đoạn này ấu trùng có thể bơi tự do

trophic level | bậc dinh dưỡng một bậc trong chuỗi hay mạng lưới thức ăn

tropism | tính hướng kích thích khuynh hướng của cây là hướng theo một sự kích thích

tumor | khối u một khối tế bào phân chia nhanh và có thể gây hại cho mô xung quanh

U

understory | cây tầng dưới trong rừng mưa nhiệt đới, đây là tầng nằm dưới tán cây, gồm nhiều cây thấp và dây leo

ureter | niệu quản ống dẫn nước tiểu từ thận đến bàng quang

urethra | niệu đạo ống dẫn nước tiểu từ bàng quang ra ngoài

urinary bladder | bàng quang cơ quan dạng túi có chức năng trữ nước tiểu trong khi chờ bài tiết ra ngoài

V

vaccination | chích ngừa gây miễn dịch bằng cách chích mầm bệnh đã bị làm yếu đi hay mầm bệnh giống với nhưng đỡ hơn mầm bệnh nguy hiểm

vaccine | thuốc ngừa thuốc chứa mầm bệnh đã chết hay bị làm yếu đi được sử dụng để gây miễn dịch đối với một căn bệnh

vacuole | không bào bào quan có chức năng tích trữ các chất như nước, muối, protein, và hiđrat cacbon

valve | van nắp bằng mô liên kết nằm giữa tâm nhĩ và tâm thất hoặc nằm bên trong mạch máu và giúp chặn máu không chảy ngược lại

van der Waals forces | lực van der Waals lực hút nhẹ giữa hai vùng có điện tích ngược nhau ở những phân tử gần nhau

vas deferens | ống dẫn tinh ống chuyên chở tinh trùng từ mào tinh hoàn đến niệu đạo

vascular bundle | bó mạch các chùm mô gỗ và libe trong thân cây

vascular cambium | tượng tầng libe gỗ vùng mô phân sinh tạo ra mô mạch và kích thích tăng trưởng đường kính của thân cây

vascular cylinder | trụ mạch phần trong cùng của rễ, bao gồm hai loại mô mạch là chất gỗ và libe

vascular tissue | mô mạch ở thực vật, đây là mô chuyên hóa dẫn truyền nước và dưỡng chất

vector | vật truyền nhiễm một thú vật truyền mầm bệnh đến con người

vegetative reproduction | sinh sản sinh dưỡng phương pháp sinh sản vô tính ở thực vật cho phép một cây duy nhất có thể sinh ra thế hệ con mang gen giống hệt của mẹ

vein | tĩnh mạch mạch máu chở máu từ các bộ phận cơ thể trở lại tim

ventricle | tâm thất buồng tim dưới có chức năng bơm máu ra khỏi tim đến các bộ phận cơ thể

vertebrate | động vật có xương sống các động vật có xương sống

vessel element | yếu tố mạch loại tế bào gỗ nối đầu nhau để hình thành ống liền có chức năng dẫn nước

vestigial organs | cơ quan tiêu giảm các cấu trúc bị teo nhỏ và mất một phần hay toàn bộ chức năng

villus (số nhiều: villi) | lông nhung những miếng mô trông giống ngón tay nhô ra từ vách ruột non và hỗ trợ việc hấp thụ các phân tử dưỡng chất

virus | virút một hạt được cấu tạo bởi protein, axít nucleic, và đôi khi chất lipit có cách nhân bản duy nhất là xâm nhập các tế bào sống

vitamin | sinh tố một phân tử hữu cơ giúp điều tiết các tiến trình cơ thể

viviparous | loài thai sinh các động vật sinh ra con sống và nuôi con trực tiếp bằng sữa mẹ

W

weather | thời tiết tình trạng khí quyển hàng ngày, bao gồm nhiệt độ, mưa tuyết và những yếu tố khác

wetland | vùng đất ngập nước một hệ sinh thái hoặc bị ngập nước hoặc có nước trên hay ngay dưới mặt đất trong ít nhất một thời kỳ của mỗi năm

white blood cell | bạch cầu loại tế bào máu bảo vệ cơ thể chống lại nhiễm trùng, vật ký sinh, và tấn công vi khuẩn

woody plant | thực vật có gỗ loại cây được cấu thành chủ yếu bởi các tế bào có vách dày giúp nâng đỡ thân cây; bao gồm cây, cây bụi, và dây leo

X

xylem | chất gỗ mô mạch dẫn nước từ rễ lên đến tất cả các bộ phận của cây

Z

zoonosis (số nhiều: zoonoses) | bệnh từ thú sang người một căn bệnh lây truyền từ thú vật sang người

zooplankton | động vật phù du các động vật nhỏ nổi tự do trong nước, là một phần cấu thành phù du

zygote | hợp tử một quả trứng đã được thụ tinh